CW00516383

Investment Advice Diploma

Securities

Edition 12, October 2021

This workbook relates to syllabus
version 12.1 and will cover examinations from
31 December 2021 to 30 December 2022

APPROVED WORKBOOK

Welcome to the Chartered Institute for Securities & Investment's Securities study material.

This workbook has been written to prepare you for the Chartered Institute for Securities & Investment's Securities examination.

Published by:
Chartered Institute for Securities & Investment
© Chartered Institute for Securities & Investment 2021
20 Fenchurch Street
London
EC3M 3BY
Tel: +44 20 7645 0600
Fax: +44 20 7645 0601

Email: customersupport@cisi.org
www.cisi.org/qualifications

Author:
Kevin Petley, Chartered FCSI

Reviewers:
JB Beckett, Chartered MCSI
Kim Holding, Chartered MCSI

This is an educational workbook only and the Chartered Institute for Securities & Investment accepts no responsibility for persons undertaking trading or investments in whatever form.

While every effort has been made to ensure its accuracy, no responsibility for loss occasioned to any person acting or refraining from action as a result of any material in this publication can be accepted by the publisher or authors.

A learning map, which contains the full syllabus, appears at the end of this workbook. The syllabus can also be viewed on cisi.org and is also available by contacting the Customer Support Centre on +44 20 7645 0777. Please note that the examination is based upon the syllabus. Candidates are reminded to check the Candidate Update area details (cisi.org/candidateupdate) on a regular basis for updates as a result of industry change(s) that could affect their examination. Please note that, as part of exam security, hand-held calculators are not allowed in CISI exam venues. Candidates must use the onscreen calculator for all CISI CBT exams in all languages in the UK and internationally.

The questions contained in this workbook are designed as an aid to revision of different areas of the syllabus and to help you consolidate your learning chapter by chapter.

Workbook version: 12.1 (October 2021)

Learning and Professional Development with the CISI

The Chartered Institute for Securities & Investment is the leading professional body for those who work in, or aspire to work in, the investment sector, and we are passionately committed to enhancing knowledge, skills and integrity – the three pillars of professionalism at the heart of our Chartered body.

CISI examinations are used extensively by firms to meet the requirements of government regulators. Besides the regulators in the UK, where the CISI head office is based, CISI examinations are recognised by a wide range of governments and their regulators, from Singapore to Dubai and the US. Around 50,000 examinations are taken each year, and it is compulsory for candidates to use CISI workbooks to prepare for CISI examinations so that they have the best chance of success. Our workbooks are normally revised every year by experts who themselves work in the industry and also by our Accredited Training Partners, who offer training and elearning to help prepare candidates for the examinations. Information for candidates is also posted on a special area of our website: cisi.org/candidateupdate.

This workbook not only provides a thorough preparation for the examination it refers to, it is also a valuable desktop reference for practitioners, and studying from it counts towards your Continuing Professional Development (CPD). Mock examination papers, for most of our titles, will be made available on our website, as an additional revision tool.

CISI examination candidates are automatically registered, without additional charge, as student members for one year (should they not be members of the CISI already), and this enables you to use a vast range of online resources, including CISI TV, free of any additional charge. The CISI has more than 40,000 members, and nearly half of them have already completed relevant qualifications and transferred to a core membership grade.

Completing a higher level examination enables you to progress even more quickly towards personal Chartered status, the pinnacle of professionalism in the CISI. You will find more information about the next steps for this at the end of this workbook.

Securities Analysis

The advisor is and provide apparances of the divisors later quarters.

It is estimated that this workbook will require approximately 140 hours of study time.

What next?

See the back of this book for details of CISI membership.

Need more support to pass your exam?

See our section on Accredited Training Providers.

Want to leave feedback?

Please email your comments to learningresources@cisi.org

Before you open Chapter 1

It's free

We love a book! ...but don't forget you have been sent a link to an ebook, which gives you a range of tools to help you study for this qualification

Depending on the individual subject being studied and your device, your ebook may include features such as:

Watch video clips related to your syllabus

Read aloud function*

Adjustable text size allows you to read comfortably on any device*

Pop-up definitions

Highlight, bookmark and make annotations digitally*

Images, tables and animated graphs

Links to relevant websites

End of chapter questions and interactive multiple choice questions

* These features are device dependent. Please consult your manufacturers guidelines for compatibility

Chapter One
Cash, Money Markets and the Foreign Exchange (FX) Market

This syllabus area will provide approximately 7 of the 80 examination questions

1.   Cash Instruments and Markets

1.1   Cash Deposit Accounts

Learning Objective

1.1.1   Be able to analyse the main investment characteristics, behaviours and risks of cash deposit accounts: deposit-taking institutions and credit risk assessment; term, notice, liquidity and access; fixed and variable rates of interest; inflation; statutory protection; foreign currency deposits; structured deposits

1.1.1   Characteristics of Cash Deposit Accounts

Cash deposits generally comprise bank, building society and National Savings products, all of which are targeted at retail investors, though companies and financial institutions also make short-term cash deposits with banks.

The main characteristics of cash deposits are:

*   The return simply comprises interest income with no potential for capital growth.
*   The amount invested is repaid in full at the end of the investment term.

1.1.2   Deposit-Taking Institutions

Deposit-taking institutions that accept and manage deposits and make loans in the UK are primarily banks (often known as retail or high street banks), building societies, credit unions, trust companies, mortgage loan companies and money market mutual funds. Some 'digital only' or 'virtual' challenger banks also offer interest-bearing accounts.

In the UK, an authorised deposit-taking institution is a deposit-taker within the meaning of Section 31 of the Financial Services and Markets Act (FSMA) 2000.

1.1.3   Term, Notice, Liquidity and Access

There are various different ways of making a deposit and they can vary in relation to the term of the deposit, the period of notice which is required to withdraw the deposit and hence the liquidity of the deposit and one's access to it. The term reflects the amount of time for which the lender commits the cash to the deposit-taking institution. As a general rule of thumb, the longer the lender is willing to grant the deposit without seeking withdrawal, the higher the rate of interest which will be paid.

Under some arrangements the depositor may be required to give notice of intent to withdraw, and, if the withdrawal takes place prior to a pre-agreed term with the deposit-taker, a penalty for early withdrawal or **redemption** may be applied.

Liquidity, in this context, is essentially the speed and ease with which the deposit instrument can be converted into cash.

1.1.4   Fixed and Variable Rates of Interest

The interest rate applied to the deposit is usually:

- a flat rate or an effective rate (an effective rate, also known as an annual equivalent rate (AER), is when interest is compounded more frequently than once a year)
- fixed or variable
- paid gross of tax, and
- dependent upon its term and/or notice required by the depositor – fixed-term deposits are usually subject to penalties if an early withdrawal is made.

Fixed-term deposits can also be made in the interbank market. The interbank market originally served the short-term deposit and borrowing needs of the commercial banks, but it has since been tapped by institutional investors and large corporates with short-term cash surpluses or borrowing needs in excess of £0.5 million. The term of deposits made on the interbank market can range from overnight to one year, with deposit rates being paid on a simple basis at the London Interbank Bid Rate (LIBID) and short-term borrowing being charged at the London Interbank Offered Rate (LIBOR). LIBOR is scheduled to be replaced with a substitute benchmark – Sterling Overnight Index Average (SONIA) for sterling by 2022.

The **Bank of England (BoE)** and the **Financial Conduct Authority (FCA)** are working with market participants to catalyse a transition to the Secured Overnight Financing Rate (SOFR) by June 30 2023.

1.1.5   Certificates of Deposit (CDs)

Certificates of deposit (CDs) are negotiable **bearer securities** issued by commercial banks in exchange for fixed-term deposits, with a fixed-term and a fixed-rate of interest, set marginally below that for an equivalent bank time deposit. The holder can either retain the CD until **maturity**, or realise the security in the money market whenever access to the money is required. CDs can be issued with terms of up to five years.

As they are a **fixed-interest security**, the price will fluctuate with the competitiveness of the interest rate compared to the prevailing **yields** (see chapter 2, section 1.3).

1.1.6   Cash Individual Savings Accounts (ISAs)

An individual savings account (ISA) is a tax-free wrapper in which money can be held to protect it from income and capital gains tax (CGT). Anyone who is aged 16 or over, and resident in the UK for tax purposes, can invest in a cash ISA. However, accounts must be opened in a single name only. See chapter 8, section 3.3.4 for the current limits.

1.1.7   Money Market Funds

These are managed funds that invest in short-term, low-risk credit securities. They aim to achieve maximum returns while minimising credit, market and liquidity risks. They typically invest in assets such as government securities, short-term bonds, **commercial paper (CP)**, repurchase agreements or even other money market funds.

1.1.8 Inflation

Inflation is a measure of the rate of change in the general level of prices in an economy. While more commonly in economic history there has been a trend towards increasing prices, there have been times, including periods during 2020, when the general level of prices has declined, which is known as deflation.

Increasing prices lead to erosion in the purchasing power of money, especially for those whose incomes are fixed or rise at a slower pace than the rate of the price increases. Controlling inflation is a prime focus of economic policy and, in the specific case of savings in the form of cash deposits, the presence of inflation must be factored into the real rate of return after allowing for inflation. If the inflation rate exceeds the nominal interest rate, the real interest rate is actually negative.

Real interest rates are calculated as follows:

$$\text{Real interest rate} = ([1 + \text{Nominal interest rate}] / [1 + \text{Inflation rate}]) - 1$$

So, the real return takes into account the inflation rate.

The best known measure of inflation in the UK is the **retail prices index (RPI)**. Originally launched in 1947, this measures the rate at which the prices of a representative basket of goods and services purchased by the average UK household change over the course of a month. The **consumer prices index (CPI)** is also used. See also chapter 2, section 1.4.1.

1.1.9 Statutory Protection

All retail cash deposits placed with licensed deposit-taking institutions in the UK are covered by the FCA's Financial Services Compensation Scheme (FSCS). The maximum level of compensation is £85,000 for single-name bank accounts, and £170,000 for joint accounts. The £85,000 figure represents the sterling equivalent of €100,000, as required by the recast Deposit Guarantee Schemes Directive.

The FSCS will provide a £1 million protection limit for temporary high balances, for a maximum of 12 months, held with an individual's bank, building society or credit union if it fails.

1.1.10 Foreign Currency Deposits

If cash is deposited in a foreign currency account, depositors should also consider the following:

- The costs of currency conversion and the potential **exchange rate** risks if sterling deposits cannot be accepted.
- The creditworthiness of the banking system and the chosen deposit-taking institution, whether a depositors' protection scheme exists and whether there is any statutory protection.
- The tax treatment of interest applied to the deposit.
- Whether the deposit will be subject to any exchange controls that may restrict access to the money and its ultimate repatriation.

1.1.11 Structured Deposits

Structured cash deposits are offered by banks, building societies and National Savings & Investments (NS&I). The rate of return is generally based on the performance of a stock market index or other benchmark. If the market falls, there is generally no return at all but the amount of capital invested is protected as per any other savings account. These products can be sold as ISAs or as growth plans or bonds.

When the investor buys a structured deposit, they agree to tie up their money for a set time – often five or six years – in return for a lump sum at maturity. Unlike many other investment products, structured deposits guarantee that the initial investment will be returned at maturity, irrespective of how the benchmark performs.

Structured deposits are also sometimes referred to as guaranteed equity bonds (GEBS).

The variable return is also usually dependent on a cap which limits the amount of the return, or a participation rate that specifies that only some of the investment can participate in the potential gains.

Example 1

A two-year structured deposit of £100,000 is entered into with a 10% cap.

The benchmark index has risen by 30% at maturity.

The income is based on 10% or £10,000.

Example 2

A two-year structured deposit of £100,000 is entered into with a participation rate of 50%.

The benchmark index has risen by 30% at maturity.

The income is based on 50% of the deposit that earns the index growth (or £50,000 at 30%) which is £15,000.

It should be understood that while these products offer stock market exposure with a guarantee that investors receive their initial investment, irrespective of how the index performs, the income will generally be lower than direct stock market investment, for example, through an ISA tracker fund.

If a structured deposit is made, for example, through a bank or insurance company and that bank or insurance company buys some complex underlying investments from one or more other companies, there is a risk that if any of the other companies fail, the structured deposit could fail to return the invested amount or provide the promised return.

1.2   Treasury Bills

Learning Objective

1.1.2   Be able to analyse the main investment characteristics, behaviours and risks of Treasury bills: purpose and method of issue; minimum denomination; normal life; zero coupon and redemption at par; market access, trading and settlement

UK Treasury bills, or T-bills as they are commonly known, are short-term loan instruments, guaranteed by the UK government, with a maturity date of less than one year at issue. Generally, they are issued with either one month (28 days), three months (91 days) or six months (182 days) to redemption, with the three-month T-bill the most common. There are also 12-month bills (up to 364 days), although to date no 12-month tenders have been held. They pay no **coupon**, and consequently are issued at a discount to their **nominal value**, the discount representing the return available to the investor.

The UK Debt Management Office (DMO) is the agency that issues and services the UK government's borrowing. Sterling Treasury bills form an important constituent in the DMO's Exchequer cash management operations and an intrinsic component in the UK government's stock of marketable debt instruments, alongside gilts. Since they are guaranteed by the government, Treasury bills provide a very secure investment for **market** participants with short-term investment horizons. The return on a Treasury bill is wholly dependent upon the price paid, and the way to calculate the effective yield can be seen in section 1.2.3.

Unlike gilts, which the DMO uses for long-term public financing needs, Treasury bills are used as a monetary policy instrument to absorb excess liquidity in the money markets, so as to maintain short-term money market rates, or the price of money, as close as possible to base rate. These activities are sometimes referred to as open market operations and are similar to those practised by the Federal Reserve system in the US.

In essence, Treasury bills do not pay coupons but are redeemed at par.

1.2.1   Treasury Bill Issuance

Since April 1998, the issuance of Treasury bills has been handled by the DMO on behalf of HM Treasury. The DMO took over debt issuance from the BoE following the transfer of responsibility for setting interest rates from HM Treasury to the Bank in May 1997.

UK Treasury bills are issued at weekly **auctions**, known as tenders, held by the DMO at the end of the week (usually a Friday). These tenders are open to bids from a group of eligible bidders which include all of the major banks. The bids are tendered competitively. Only those bidding at a high enough price will be allocated any Treasury bills, and they will pay the price that they bid. The bids must be for a minimum of £500,000 nominal of the Treasury bills, and above this level bids must be made in multiples of £50,000. In subsequent trading, the minimum denomination of Treasury bills is £25,000.

Treasury bills require settlement on the following business day. Members of the public wishing to purchase Treasury bills at the tenders must do so through one of the Treasury bill primary participants.

1.2.2 Primary Participants

Treasury bill primary participants are banks that have agreed to bid at Treasury bill tenders on behalf of investors. They are registered financial institutions that are regulated by the FCA and the **Prudential Regulation Authority (PRA)** and are subject to their rules and guidance in their activities. These firms also provide **secondary market** dealing levels for Treasury bills.

A list of banks that act as Treasury bill primary participants can be found in chapter 2, section 4.1.4.

1.2.3 Calculating Yields on Treasury Bills

The principal measures used to calculate the effective yield on Treasury bills are as follows:

$$\text{Discount rate} = \frac{100 - \text{Discounted value}}{100 \times \text{Days}/365}$$

The yield of a Treasury bill can be derived by using the following formula:

$$\text{Yield} = \frac{100 - \text{Discounted value}}{\text{Discounted value} \times \text{Days}/365}$$

As an example consider the yield of a Treasury bill issued at 98 for 91 days:

$$\text{Interest rate or yield} = \frac{100 - 98}{98 \times 91/365} = 0.0819 \text{ or } 8.19\%$$

1.2.4 General Collateral Sale and Repurchase Agreements (GC Repo)

One of the cornerstones for determining the prevailing rates in the money markets, which act as a guideline to the yields which should be available from the DMO Treasury bill auctions, is the GC repo rate, which is explained below.

Gilt sale and repurchase (gilt repo) transactions involve the temporary exchange of cash and gilts between two parties. They are a means of short-term borrowing using gilts as collateral. The lender of funds holds gilts as collateral, so is protected in the event of default by the borrower. General collateral (GC) repo rates refer to the rates for repurchase agreements in which any gilt may be used as collateral. Hence, GC repo rates should in principle be close to true risk-free rates.

Repo contracts are actively traded for maturities out to one year. The rates prevailing on these contracts are very similar to conventional gilts of comparable maturity.

1.2.5 Market Access and Current Pricing and Yield for Treasury Bills

The reference prices for UK Treasury bills are published by the DMO at the end of each business day. They are based on a money market yield-to-maturity calculation priced around prevailing GC repo rates, as explained above, adjusted by a **spread** reflecting recent Treasury bill tender results and, if applicable, any specific supply and demand factors.

These reference prices provide indicative mid-prices for the purpose of valuation of collateral transfers and are not intended to represent market prices at which the securities can be traded.

It is important to note that, in determining the yield on Treasury bills in the UK, the day count convention is Actual/365. Most other markets use the convention of Actual/360.

1.3 Commercial Paper

Learning Objective

1.1.3   Be able to analyse the main investment characteristics, behaviours and risks of commercial paper: purpose and method of issue; maturity; discounted security; unsecured and secured; asset-backed; credit rating; market access, trading and settlement

1.3.1 Commercial Paper (CP)

Commercial paper (CP) is unsecured short-term promissory notes issued primarily by corporations, although there are also municipal (local) and sovereign issuers. It represents the largest segment of the money market. The vast majority is issued as discount instruments in bearer form. In the US, terms rarely exceed 270 days, since this exempts the paper from registration under the Securities Act of 1933. Outside the US, the term for CP can be as long as one year, but it is typical in all territories for the term to be between one and three months.

Yields are quoted on a discount basis. Virtually all countries use the Actual/360 convention, except the UK, which uses the Actual/365 convention. CP is the corporate equivalent of a Treasury bill. Large companies issue CP to assist in the management of their liquidity. Rather than borrowing directly from banks, these large entities run CP programmes that are placed with institutional investors.

The various companies' CP is differentiated by credit ratings – when the large credit rating agencies assess the stability of the issuer.

1.3.2 Asset-Backed Commercial Paper (ABCP)

Although the standard vanilla form of CP is unsecured, there are asset-backed versions as well. An asset-backed commercial paper (ABCP) is a short-term investment vehicle with a maturity that is typically between 90 and 180 days. The security itself will be issued by a bank or other financial institution, and the notes are backed by physical assets such as trade receivables or commercial property or even credit card receivables.

Finance companies will typically provide consumers with home loans, unsecured personal loans and retail automobile loans. These receivables are then used by the finance company as collateral for raising money in the CP market. Some finance companies are wholly owned subsidiaries of industrial firms that provide financing for purchases of the parent firm's products.

1.3.3 CP Issuance

CP issuance and marketability tends to be deeper and more prevalent in the US than in Europe and, in recent times since the banking crisis of 2008, the market has been somewhat subdued. It was not until the 1980s that CP was first issued outside the US, reflecting a global trend towards disintermediation of banks.

Historically, the market for CP first developed in the US during the 19th century. The fractured, localised banking industry was ill-equipped to meet the liquidity needs of emerging industrial corporations. If a business was unable to secure loans from local banks, it might raise the funds by issuing promissory notes in New York or Boston. Very likely, the purchaser would be a bank in one of those financial centres, so CP was a vehicle for raising short-term funds out-of-state in the absence of cross-state banking.

In the 20th century, consumer finance companies turned to CP to finance their lending to purchasers of automobiles, appliances and other consumer products. General Motors Acceptance Corporation (GMAC) was a pioneer in such issuances. Today, finance companies issue a significant proportion of CP.

There are two methods of issuing CP. Larger issuers, especially finance companies, have the market presence to issue their paper directly to investors, including buy-and-hold investors such as money market funds. Their paper is called direct paper. Direct issuers of CP usually are financial companies that have frequent and sizeable borrowing needs and find it more economical to sell paper without the use of an intermediary.

Alternatively, issuers can sell the paper to a dealer, who then sells the paper in the market, in which case the paper is called dealer paper. The dealer market for CP involves large securities firms and subsidiaries of bank holding companies.

Unlike bonds or other forms of long-term indebtedness, a CP issuance is not all brought to market at once. Instead, an issuer will maintain an ongoing CP programme. It advertises the rates at which it is willing to issue paper for various terms, so buyers can purchase the paper whenever they have funds to invest.

1.3.4 Secondary Market

There is an inactive secondary market for CP, but dealers will make a market in paper they issue. Direct issuers will generally honour requests to repay CP early. Some do so at principal plus accrued interest; others credit interest based on the rate the investor would have received if they had purchased the paper with a term equal to their actual holding period.

1.3.5   Credit Rating of CP

CP entails credit risk, and programmes are rated by the major rating agencies. Because CP is a rolling form of debt, with new issues generally funding the retirement of old issues, the main risk is that the issuer will not be able to issue new CP. This is called 'rollover risk'.

Issuers of CP may obtain credit enhancements for their programmes. These may include instruments such as a letter of credit or a third-party guarantee or insurance contract provided by another financial institution.

The table below summarises the credit ratings assigned to commercial paper by Moody's, Standard & Poor's (S&P) and Fitch Ratings inc.

CP Credit Ratings			
	Moody's	S&P's	Fitch
Superior	P1	A1+ or A1	F1+ or F1
Satisfactory	P2	A2	F2
Adequate	P3	A3	F3
Speculative	NP	B or C	F4
Defaulted	NP	D	F5

CP will offer yields above the equivalent rates available from Treasury bills. This is due both to their credit risk and the fact that interest from Treasury bills may have tax advantages. For example, in the US, interest on Treasury bills is not taxed at the state and local level. In the US, the Federal Reserve reports the previous day's average rates on CP for several maturities and types of issuers. These CP rates are a standard index used as a basis in various interest rate swaps and other **derivatives**.

CP Following the Financial Crisis of 2007–08

During Q4 2008, the CP and asset-backed paper sectors of the money markets became effectively frozen as there was no liquidity in the marketplace. Banks were unwilling to accept any collateral other than government paper, because of fears as to the solvency of the issuers of CP. The BoE, as lender of last resort, had to intermediate in the money market and accept a wider variety of collateral – such as CP – than it had previously been willing to accept, as security for providing short-term liquidity to the commercial banks and other institutions which required cash and liquidity for their ongoing operations.

1.4 Repurchase Agreements or Repos

Learning Objective

1.1.4 Be able to analyse the main investment characteristics, behaviours and risks of repurchase agreements: purpose; sale and repurchase at agreed price, rate and date; tri-party repos; documentation

---

The term **repo** stands for a sale and repurchase agreement, and is similar to a secured loan.

One party agrees to sell securities, for example gilts, to the other and receives collateral of, say, cash to secure the loan. At the same time the parties agree to repurchase the same or equivalent securities at a specific price in the future. At that point, the securities are returned by the borrower and the lender returns the collateral. The cost of this secured finance is given by the difference between the sale and repurchase price of these bonds and is known as the repo rate.

A reverse repo is simply the same repurchase agreement from the buyer's viewpoint, not the seller's. Hence, the seller executing the transaction would describe it as a repo, while the buyer in the same transaction would describe it a reverse repo. So repo and reverse repo are exactly the same kind of transaction, just described from opposite viewpoints.

The purpose of the repo market as implemented by **central banks**, such as the BoE and the European Central Bank (ECB), is to provide or remove liquidity from the money markets.

If the central bank wishes to increase the money supply, it will enter into repo agreements as the reverse repo participant, with other money market institutions such as banks being the repo participant. As the reverse repo participant, the central bank will provide cash for the collateral provided under the repo.

In contrast, if the central bank wishes to drain liquidity from the money markets, then it will use repo transactions. This time the central bank will be the repo participant, initially selling instruments and, therefore, withdrawing cash from the system.

1.4.1 Tri-Party Repos

In the case of a tri-party repo, a custodian bank or clearing organisation acts as an intermediary between the two parties to the repurchase or repo agreement outlined above.

The tri-party agent is responsible for the administration of the transaction including collateral allocation, the marking to market, and, when required, the substitution of collateral. The lender and the borrower of cash both enter into tri-party transactions in order to avoid the administrative burden of the simpler form of bilateral repos. Moreover, there is an added element of security in a tri-party repo because the collateral is being held by an agent and the counterparty risk is reduced.

1.4.2   Repos and Monetary Policy

The BoE is a principal participant in the repo market and will accept qualifying collateral – Treasury bills, for example – as part of a repurchase agreement. In fact, the widely reported base rate is the repo rate currently in effect with the BoE and other financial institutions in the money markets, and it is the rate which is fixed by the **Monetary Policy Committee (MPC)** of the BoE at its regular meetings.

It is worth observing that a consequence of the liquidity crisis, which arose in 2007–08, is that central banks in general, especially the Federal Reserve in the US and the BoE in the UK, have relaxed the requirements on the quality of the collateral which is acceptable under a repo agreement with the central bank. Commercial banks were permitted to use many kinds of asset-backed securities, which had previously been considered to be below the acceptable standards in terms of credit risk and quality, in their repo agreements with central banks. This was one method used by central banks and policymakers to provide greater financial liquidity during the banking crisis.

1.4.3   Repo Market Illustration

The following diagram illustrates the principal characteristics of a repo agreement.

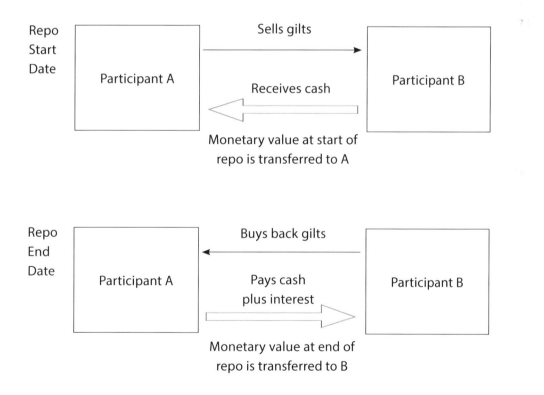

Diagrammatically, both parts of the repo transaction are agreed between the participants at the outset: Participant A has entered into a repo transaction; Participant B has entered into a reverse repo agreement. The amount of cash paid over by Participant B at the start of the repo will be less than the amount paid over to Participant B at the end of the repo period. The difference between the two amounts, expressed as a percentage, is the effective interest rate on the repo transaction. It is usually referred to as the repo rate.

The cash transaction results in transfer of money to the borrower in exchange for legal transfer of the security to the lender, while the promise to repurchase – known as a **forward** contract – ensures repayment of the loan to the lender and return of the collateral of the borrower. The difference between the price which is laid out in the forward contract committing the borrower to repurchase is known as the forward price. The difference between it and the spot price provides, in similar fashion to the discounting mechanism, the implicit rate of interest on the loan, and the settlement date stipulated in the forward contract is the maturity date of the loan.

The obvious benefit to Participant A in the above example is that A is able to raise finance against the security of the gilts that it holds – potentially a relatively cheap source of short-term finance. If Participant B is considered a conventional bank simply providing finance, then the benefit of using the repo is the security gained by holding the gilts. However, Participant B may be a gilt-edged market maker (GEMM) that has sold gilts that it does not hold. The repo transaction enables the GEMM to access the gilts that it requires to meet its settlement obligations. In this way, gilt repos facilitate the smooth running of the secondary market in gilts.

The smooth running of the gilts market is further assisted by the DMO's standing repo facility. This enables any GEMM or other DMO counterparty to enter into a reverse repo arrangement with the DMO, perhaps to cover a **short position** in gilts. They must first sign the relevant documentation provided by the DMO and then are able to request any amount of a gilt above £5 million nominal. This facility is for next-day settlement, and the facility can be rolled forwards for up to two weeks. The DMO does charge a slightly higher than normal repo rate for firms accessing the standing repo facility. Although the gilt market has been used as an example, it should be noted that the use of repos is an important liquidity provider for debt markets as a whole.

1.4.4 Risks of a Repo

From the point of view of the lender, a repo is a simple loan transaction. They lend their surplus cash in return for interest, and have the support of collateral by the holding of the bond during the life of the contract. However, as with any collateralised loan, there are three types of primary risk.

- **Legal risk** – the agreement that is made is a legal document and as such there are potential legal issues which could arise as in the case of any contractual claim, although the likelihood of this when standardised documentation is used is minimal.
- **Counterparty/credit risk** – there is a creditworthiness risk as in all dealings with counterparties. However, this risk is minimised in the repo transaction by the passing of collateral and, in this sense, the lender then faces the second element of risk.
- **Market and collateral risk** – this risk arises from the fact that the **underlying** assets provided as collateral may deteriorate to such an extent that, should the counterparty fail on the repayment date, then the lender will be left with insufficient collateral compared to the amount of the loan. To cover this third risk element, repo arrangements allow for margin calls to be made against the borrower in the form of initial margin and variation margin.

Initial and Variation Margin

The initial margin or haircut will be taken as a reduction in the amount of money lent against the bond. As a result, the amount lent will seldom be 100% of the value of the bond. The scale of this initial haircut will be influenced by such factors as the quality of the collateral, the quality of the counterparty and the term of the repo.

Variation margin will allow for the collateral to be marked-to-market throughout the term of the repo. This may be on a daily basis or it may be at specific dates throughout the term. Many agreements will specify a frequency of marking-to-market and, within this, a minimum level of variation necessary to initiate the margin call. As a result, when the collateral falls in value by only a small amount, no additional margin is required to be put up, reducing the transaction costs.

The availability of variation margin obviously reduces the level of market risk that exists on repo transactions. While there is still counterparty risk, the variation margin should ensure that the collateral more than repays the principal of the loan.

Case Study: Repo 105

In 2001, a new accounting standard in the US, Statement of Financial Accounting Standards (SFAS) 140, offered an opportunity to change the terms of the repo market in favour of banks. In the past, these deals were booked as only temporary, because of the short-term nature of the funding, so the assets did not actually leave the banks' balance sheets. However, the relaxing of the rules went far enough that some have questioned whether the use of a particular provision known as Repo 105 can be used to mislead market participants as to the fairness of a company's financial position when it uses a repo procedure in a certain manner.

In 2008, just before Lehman Brothers filed for bankruptcy, it transferred $50.38 billion in a Repo 105 arrangement, reducing its leverage from 13.9% to 12.1%.

Anton Valukas of Jenner & Block, who was appointed as examiner by the judge handling Lehman's bankruptcy, said:

> 'Unable to find a United States law firm that would provide it with an opinion letter permitting the the true sale accounting treatment under US law, Lehman conducted its Repo 105 programme under the aegis of an opinion letter to the Linklaters law firm in London'.

A 2,200-page report, authored by Valukas, into the collapse of Lehman reveals that the firm used balance sheet manipulation in the form of the accounting practice known as Repo 105 without telling investors or regulators, which had the effect of making the business appear healthier than it actually was. Lehman initially had sought legal clearance from an American law firm to permit Repo 105 transactions but was denied. It then sought advice from Linklaters in London, which said that the deals were possible under English law.

In the run-up to a reporting period, Lehman would enter an arrangement to sell and then repurchase financial assets. Normally, such deals are accounted as transactions, but by adding a cash element Lehman was able to call them sales. The bank's balance sheet, therefore, could be pumped up with cash from the sale and would also reduce its borrowings. At the beginning of a new quarter, Lehman would borrow more money and repurchase the assets to put them back on its balance sheet.

The assets were transferred through Lehman's London operations so that the Repo 105 deals could be conducted under English law. Under Repo 105, banks could book the transactions as sales because banks had to take a bigger loss on the value of the assets in return for the loan. While the terms might have been less favourable on the face of it, the benefit was considerable. Banks hold capital against their assets to cover possible losses from loans. Removing some of those loans from the balance sheet boosted the amount of capital banks held against their remaining assets, making them appear financially stronger than if the loans were still on the balance sheet.

2. Foreign Exchange (FX) Instruments and Markets

2.1 Overview

Learning Objective

1.2.1 Understand the role, structure and main characteristics of the foreign exchange market: OTC market; quotes, spreads and exchange rate information; market participants and access to markets; volume, volatility and liquidity; risk mitigation: rollovers and stop losses; regulatory/supervisory environment

The foreign exchange market (or forex or FX) is the collective way of describing all the transactions in which national currencies are exchanged for others, anywhere in the world. The **forex** market is an example of a decentralised market, in that it is distributed throughout the world from different trading terminals and there are no central trading exchanges as in the trading of stocks at the **London Stock Exchange (LSE)** or the New York Stock Exchange (NYSE).

The FX market is purely an over-the-counter (OTC) market, conducted electronically through platforms including those referred to as electronic communications networks (ECNs). It bears a strong resemblance to the decentralised OTC dealer networks which exist for the trading of most bonds and derivatives. However, the forex market is dominated by the banks and there are no formal **market makers** as such but rather banks which act as dealers. Also, unlike a typical domestic OTC market which is organised around the opening hours of the domestic stock exchange, the forex market, being decentralised and truly global, trades 24 hours a day, five days a week, closing effectively after the conclusion of trading in North America on a Friday and reopening with the onset of trading in Asia on Monday.

2.1.1 Quotes, Spreads and Exchange Rate Information

All foreign exchange quotations involve specifying an exchange rate/relationship between two currencies. As a general rule of thumb, exchange rates around the world are often quoted against the US dollar. However a great amount of trading takes place between currencies which do not include the US dollar. Technically speaking, a cross rate is any foreign currency rate that does not include the US dollar. For example, the Great Britain pound/Japanese yen (GBP/JPY) is a cross rate.

A currency pair is the quotation of the relative value of a currency unit against the unit of another currency in the FX market. The currency that is used as the reference is called the **base currency** or transaction currency, and the currency that is quoted in relation to it is called the counter currency or quote currency.

Currency pairs are written by concatenating currency codes, which are formalised in ISO 4217, of the base currency and the counter currency, separating them with a slash character. Often the slash character is omitted. A widely traded currency pair is the relation of the euro against the US dollar, designated as EUR/USD. The quotation EUR/USD 1.2500 means that one euro is exchanged for 1.2500 US dollars.

The most traded currency pairs in the world are called the majors. They involve the euro (EUR), US dollar (USD), Japanese yen (JPY), pound sterling (GBP), Australian dollar (AUD), New Zealand dollar (NZD), Canadian dollar (CAD) and Swiss franc (CHF).

In everyday foreign exchange market trading and news reporting, the currency pairs are often referred to by nicknames. These are often reminiscent of national or geographic connotations. The GBP/USD pairing is known by traders as cable, which has its origins from the time when a communications cable under the Atlantic Ocean synchronised the GBP/USD quote between the London and New York markets. The following nicknames are also common: fiber for EUR/USD, chunnel for EUR/GBP, loonie for USD/CAD, aussie for AUD/USD, geppie for GBP/JPY, and kiwi for the New Zealand NZD/USD pairings.

Currencies are traded in fixed contract sizes, specifically called lot sizes, or multiples thereof. The standard lot size is 100,000 units of the base currency. Retail brokerage firms also offer 10,000 units or mini-lots.

Leverage is widely employed in forex trading and it is not uncommon for brokerage accounts to offer leverage of up to 200:1, which can be quite dangerous for the retail investor considering the volatility of many currency pairs.

Both spot and forward rates are quoted by dealers in the form of a buying rate (the bid) and a selling rate (the offer). The officially quoted rate is a spot price. In a trading market, however, currencies are offered for sale at an offering price, the ask price. Traders looking to buy a position seek to do so at their bid price, which is always lower or equal to the asking price. This price differential is known as the spread. For example, if the quotation of EUR/USD is 1.1207/1.1209, then the spread is USD 0.0002, or 2 pips. In general, markets with high liquidity exhibit smaller spreads than less frequently traded markets.

The spread offered to a retail customer with an account at a brokerage firm, rather than a large international forex market maker, is larger and varies between brokerages. Brokerages typically increase the spread they receive from their market providers, as compensation for their service to the end customer, rather than charge a transaction fee. A *bureau de change* which is used for some retail foreign exchange transactions will usually have extremely wide spreads and using a high street bank to convert currencies is not recommended, as the spreads/commissions can be quite exorbitant in comparison to the rates available to a professional. There are FX dealers who will provide much better rates to retail customers who need foreign currency for large international purchases/transactions.

2.1.2 Main Characteristics of the FX Market

FX is by far the largest type of capital market in the world, in terms of cash value traded, and includes trading between large banks, central banks, currency speculators, multinational corporations, hedge funds, governments and other institutions.

The Bank for International Settlements (BIS) provides the most useful information on the size and turnover of the global forex market. It has conducted a triennial survey every three years since April 1989, with the most recent having been conducted in April 2019, with the results published in September 2019. The results of the latest survey can be found on the BIS's website (bis.org).

It can be seen from these surveys that London continues to be the dominant centre for FX transactions and the substantial increase in FX trading since 2007 owes much to the increasing importance of the speculative and trading activity of other institutions, in addition to the large banks which continue to be the main participants.

2.1.3 Volatility, Volume and Liquidity

The volume of transactions is quite staggering, with an estimated $8.21 trillion in nominal amounts traded daily. Just as with derivatives, the nominal amount traded is somewhat misleading, since the speculative activity in forex is focused on the amount that is traded at the margin. In other words, if one places an order to sell $1 million to purchase £600,000 but only holds the position for a few hours (or minutes) there is a sense in which the nominal amounts are not really exchanged, but, just as in the case of a **swap** or contract for difference (CFD), it is the marginal difference which is really being traded or is at risk.

Nonetheless, the FX market is extremely liquid and, in the case of major currency pairs such as the EUR/USD, there is great depth to trading within the interbank market. Some other currency pairs, involving more exotic or less traded currencies such as the Hungarian forint, will obviously be far less liquid, with much wider spreads between the bid and the ask than for EUR/USD or GBP/USD.

FX markets can be extremely volatile at times, especially when the markets in other asset classes are acting in an erratic manner.

The most volatile periods for forex trading are often seen in conjunction with the release of key economic data. The US Labour Department issues its monthly employment data, more commonly known as the Non-Farm Payroll (NFP) report, on the first Friday of each month at 08:30 Eastern time, and this can often be a major mover of foreign exchange rates.

Other economic events which can strongly impact the FX market are releases of inflation data, **gross domestic product (GDP)** data and retail sales data from major government organisations such as the Office for National Statistics (ONS) in the UK, and Eurostat, which provides economic data for the EU. Also important to the sudden movements of exchange rates are the results of auctions of government securities and any changes in short-term rates announced by central banks.

2.1.4   Risk Mitigation: Rollovers

The spot rate is the current market price, also called the benchmark price. Spot transactions do not require immediate settlement, or payment on the spot. The settlement date, or value date, is the second business day after the deal date (or trade date) on which the transaction is agreed to by the two traders. The two-day period provides time to confirm the agreement and arrange the clearing and necessary debiting and crediting of bank accounts in various international locations.

Rollover is the process of extending the settlement date of an open position in forex. In most currency trades, a trader is required to take delivery of the currency two days after the transaction date. However, by rolling over the position – simultaneously closing the existing position at the daily close rate and re-entering at the new opening rate the next trading day – the trader artificially extends the settlement period by one day.

Often referred to as tomorrow next, rollover is useful in FX because many traders have no intention of taking delivery of the currency they buy. Rather, they want to profit from changes in the exchange rates. Since every forex trade is transacted by borrowing one country's currency to buy another, receiving and paying interest is a regular occurrence. At the close of every trading day, a trader who took a **long position** in a high-yielding currency relative to the currency that they borrowed will receive an amount of interest in their account. Conversely, a trader will need to pay interest if the currency they borrow has a higher interest rate relative to the currency that they purchase.

2.1.5   Risk Mitigation: Stop Losses

In trading foreign exchange, or any instrument for that matter, if one is using proper risk management techniques, it is customary to establish what is called a stop loss for the position taken. This will provide a safety mechanism so that, if the trade turns adversely against the trader, the position will be exited at a pre-determined level.

As an example, let us suppose that an investor has a bullish view on sterling versus the US dollar. The investor purchases a lot at the spot rate of $1.33 with an expectation that the rate will move to $1.34 in a short time frame. However, if sterling suddenly starts to drop against the US dollar, perhaps following some unexpected poor economic news in the UK, then a stop loss level set at $1.32 will get the investor out of the trade with a loss of only one cent. If there was no stop loss in place and sterling dropped precipitously, given the leverage levels used in forex trading, it is easy to lose large sums of money quickly.

There is one important proviso regarding stop losses, however. Even if one sets a stop loss level at $1.38, as in the example provided, there is no guarantee that the trade will actually be executed at this level. Depending on the type of order placed and the access that the investor has, if sterling were to drop quickly in a relatively illiquid market environment, an order might be filled at, say, $1.3760 after the stop loss level was triggered. This problem with risk management of trading positions is not confined to the forex market but can be seen across most asset classes including trading in equities, stock index futures and commodities.

2.1.6 The Regulatory Environment

In view of the global reach of the forex market, the regulations covering it, such as they are, will tend to be regulations relating to the manner in which brokerages operate in different jurisdictions.

The following is a list of some of the regulatory bodies that have regulatory authority and powers within various jurisdictions.

The Financial Conduct Authority (FCA)

The FCA is an independent non-governmental body, which replaced the Financial Services Authority (FSA) in April 2013. It has statutory powers provided by the Financial Services and Markets Act 2000. The FCA regulates the financial services sector in the UK. It has regulation-making, investigatory and enforcement powers. The FCA is obliged to have regard to the principles of good regulation.

The Prudential Regulation Authority (PRA)

The PRA was formed under the Financial Services Act (2012) and is part of the BoE. It is also one of the successors to the FSA. Its responsibility is the prudential regulation and supervision of banks, building societies, insurance companies and larger financial investment firms. The PRA's main objectives are to promote the financial safety of these firms and (mainly for insurance companies) to contribute to ensuring adequate protection for consumers/policy holders.

The National Futures Association (NFA)

The NFA is a self-regulatory organisation for the US futures industry; its purpose is to safeguard market integrity and protect investors in US derivatives, particularly forex derivatives, by implementing regulations. Membership of the NFA is mandatory for any futures or forex broker operating in the US. It is an independent regulatory body, with no ties to any specific marketplace.

The Commodity Futures Trading Commission (CFTC)

Created by Congress, the CFTC was formed in 1974 as an independent agency with the mandate to issue forex regulations for financial markets in the US. Its regulations encourage competitiveness and efficiency in the US forex markets and protect market participants against any abusive forex trading practices.

Various National Authorities

Each country has its own national body for regulating its financial service industry. These are the bodies that decide on forex regulations, which should ensure that dealers/brokers are obliged to operate in accordance with that country's forex trading regulations.

2.2 Spot FX Prices

Learning Objective

1.2.2 Understand the determinants of spot foreign exchange prices: currency demand – transactional and speculative; economic variables; cross-border trading of financial assets; interest rates; free, pegged and managed rates

2.2.1 Currency Demand

The users of the FX market fall into two broad camps:

- **Transactional** – settling accounts for international trade.
- **Speculative** – including arbitrageurs and financial engineers using derivatives.

2.2.2 International Trade

FX transactions are partly driven by international trade. Trade can be in either goods or services. Using the wider definition of trade, to include financial services and financial instruments such as bonds, helps to explain the bulk of the transactional component to the movements in exchange rates.

From a traditional product perspective, if for example a Japanese company sells goods to a US customer, they might invoice the transaction in US dollars. These dollars will need to be exchanged for Japanese yen by the Japanese company and this will require an FX transaction. The Japanese company may not be expecting to receive the dollars for a month after submission of the invoice. This gives them two choices:

- they can wait until they receive the dollars and then execute a spot transaction, or
- they can enter into a forward transaction to sell the dollars for yen in a month's time. This will provide them with certainty as to the number of yen they will receive and assist in their budgeting efforts.

In this section, the discussion will be confined to the spot market. Spot FX dealings are those which occur with immediate effect where the transaction is settled with reference to the actual or real-time pricing of foreign currencies in the highly liquid FX market.

2.2.3 Speculation in the FX Market

Speculative transactions are another major factor which account for FX transactions. If an investor thinks that the US dollar is likely to weaken against the euro, they will buy the euro from the proceeds of selling dollars in either the spot or forward market and will profit if they are correct.

Other ways in which the FX market provides speculative opportunities are in relation to very small **arbitrage** opportunities related to interest rate differentials between two or more countries. Other speculative activities in FX are related to complex derivative products and swaps created through financial engineering. Although they will be more focused on the forward market in FX, they will impact the spot market.

2.2.4 The Spot FX Market

In the spot market, the base currency is usually the US dollar. However, when sterling is quoted against the US dollar, sterling is the base currency and the US dollar is the quoted currency. So, £1 is quoted in terms of its value in dollars rather than $1 being quoted in terms of its value in pounds.

Speculators and traders in currencies can participate in the forex market by opening accounts with brokers who will enable them to do one or more of the following:

- trade in the spot market with or without leverage
- trade in the futures markets for currencies which are listed on some futures exchanges, eg, the Chicago Mercantile Exchange (CME)
- trade via a derivative such as an exchange-traded fund or via a spread betting instrument.

The convention in the spot market is for the exchange rate to be quoted as a mid-rate and then a bid-offer spread around this mid-rate. The mid-rate is the mid-point between the bid and **offer prices**.

2.2.5 Economic Variables and Global Capital Flows

When looking at the fundamental factors which help to determine exchange rates, the demand and supply considerations which arise through international trade and to some extent speculation will be much influenced by macroeconomic factors within both the world economy and the economies of the two countries for which a particular exchange rate is being determined. The key factors are as follows.

World Demand and Global GDP

During recessions and periods of slow economic growth, there will be less international trade, as was the experience in 2009 in the aftermath of the 2007–08 banking crisis. This will tend to affect all countries and, thus, not greatly influence any specific currency.

Safe-Haven Currencies

During times of economic and financial stress, the US dollar, Swiss franc and Japanese yen have proven to be the most sought-after currencies. It is also fair to say that the so-called commodity currencies, such as the Australian and Canadian dollar, will tend to fall in value against the US dollar, especially as the demand for commodities falls and as these currencies are seen as less safe.

Debt/GDP Ratios

Global capital flows for the purchase of government debt are increasingly affecting global exchange rates. Those countries or currency unions, in the case of the eurozone, where the public debt/GDP is relatively high will, on the whole, attract less capital for their respective bond markets and the currencies will underperform those countries with lower debt/GDP ratios. This is more complex than it appears, as a country like the UK which has a high debt/GDP ratio also has a separate currency which it can manage internally, whereas a country like Germany which has a lower debt/GDP ratio is part of the eurozone and has seen the value of its currency – the euro – fall more with respect to the dollar as a result of the high debt/GDP ratios of its other eurozone partners.

Interest Rates and the Carry Trade

One of the principal driving factors for speculative capital flows is to exploit interest rate differentials between countries. This has given rise to what is called the forex carry trade. In essence, large institutional investors such as hedge funds will borrow funds in a currency where there is a relatively low borrowing rate, eg, the yen, and will invest those funds, after converting to another currency such as Australian dollars, where there is a higher rate of interest available for short-term deposits. The spread between the borrowing cost and the interest-earning rates motivates the trades, but this will also affect the cross rates.

Economic Growth and Outlook

Capital flows are a primary determinant of exchange rates, decisions made by investors regarding the attractiveness of investments in international equities and fixed-income investments. If an individual economy reveals positive economic fundamentals, such as a relatively high rate of annual GDP growth, low inflation and stable monetary policy, this will prove more attractive to foreign investors than those economies which are stagnating and where there is a much more uncertain economic outlook.

Capital Account Flows

There are considerable imbalances in the global trade of goods and services, with many nations running large deficits on their visible trade accounts (ie, the trade in products) and having to export more invisibles (eg, financial services) while attracting capital flows from the large surplus nations. The trading relationship between China and the US provides a good illustration of this. In 2016, their trade deficit between was $347 billion, with similar amounts having been seen for several years. In order to finance these persistent deficits, the US has had to export a huge supply of US Treasury securities to the Chinese central bank (the People's Bank of China (PBOC)), and these appear on the capital account of the balance of payments between China and the US. Although China has been reducing its exposure to US Treasuries of late, according to some estimates, the PBOC owns over $1 trillion of US government bonds and agency securities, ie, government-sponsored enterprise (GSE) obligations.

2.2.6 Determination of Exchange Rates

Free Floating

The FX system which has emerged, for much of the global economy, has some elements of management of rates by central banks and governments, but is largely a system which is described as free floating.

- Pure free float is when no government intervention takes place and only market force rates determine exchange rates.
- The present-day system is largely based upon the activities of the large banks and other institutions which are conducting transactions between themselves in the forex market.
- The central banks can issue policy statements and from time to time may intervene directly into the market to buy or sell their currency or another currency from their reserves.
- Central banks will attempt to guide the markets with respect to determining factors such as interest rates, trade policies and other capital market incentives.

In contrast to (more or less) freely floating exchange rates, there are alternative models which have been used historically and which could conceivably reappear in the future.

Managed Floating

- If market forces are interspersed with intervention by government via central banks, the term used is managed floating.
- To keep a currency within specified bands, interest rates can be manipulated to induce foreigners to either buy or sell the currency.
- Exchange controls can be applied – ranging from direct controls on the flow of currency to withholding taxes and export controls.
- Retaliation and administration costs/losses from speculation are big costs involved in interventionism.

Fixed Exchange Rates (Pegged)

The post-1945 era saw a period of rigid fixed exchange rates in which no floating was permitted. There was a rigid regulation of market forces to ensure that currencies were pegged. This was less arduous in that era, as there was so much less free movement of capital around the globe than there is today.

- Under this fixed rate regime all central banks cooperated to achieve fixed rates.
- Sometimes, if market forces become too misaligned countries are forced into devaluations or revaluations.
- Sterling was devalued on 19 September 1949, as the pound/dollar rate was reduced by 30%, from US$4.03 to US$2.80.
- In the mid-1960s the pound came under renewed pressure, since the exchange rate against the dollar was considered too high. In the summer of 1966, with the value of the pound falling in the currency markets, exchange controls were tightened by the Wilson government.
- Among the measures, tourists were banned from taking more than £50 out of the country, until the restriction was lifted in 1970.
- The pound was eventually devalued by 14.3% to US$2.41 in November 1967.
- Since then the currency has floated with respect to the US dollar.

Consequences of Floating Exchange Rates

- Free floating allows for natural adjustments to disequilibrium in the balance of payments.
- Market forces eventually become so overwhelming that governments cannot control the exchange rate.
- Having to maintain a fixed rate of exchange gets in the way of other government objectives.
- Raising interest rates to protect a fixed rate of exchange may be unhelpful from other monetary and fiscal perspectives – as it was in the UK in September 1992.

The Euro

In a referendum in June 2016, the UK voted to leave the EU (Brexit). Article 50 is part of European law, provided for in the 2009 Treaty of Lisbon which made provision for any country that wishes to exit the EU. On 28 March 2017, the UK Prime Minister signed a letter invoking Article 50 which was submitted on 29 March 2017 to the EU. The UK officially left the EU in January 2020 and since then most EU Regulations impacting financial services have been carried over into UK law.

An issue for the UK in relation to its FX rate policy is the status of sterling with regard to the trading currency of what have been its most important trading partners in the eurozone – the euro.

- The euro is the official currency of many of the EU member states known as the 'eurozone'.
- The euro is the single currency for more than 300 million people in Europe.
- Including areas using currencies pegged to the euro, the euro affects more than 480 million people.
- The euro was introduced to world financial markets as an accounting currency in 1999 and launched as physical coins and banknotes in 2002. All EU member states are eligible to join if they comply with certain monetary requirements, and eventual use of the euro is mandatory for all new EU members.
- Among EU countries that are not using the euro are Denmark and Sweden
- The euro is managed and administered by the Frankfurt-based ECB and the European System of Central Banks (ESCB) (composed of the central banks of its member states).
- As an independent central bank, the ECB has sole authority to set monetary policy. The ESCB participates in the printing, minting and distribution of notes and coins in all member states, and also the operation of the eurozone payment systems.

Reserve Currencies

- The euro is widely perceived to be one of two, or perhaps three, major global reserve currencies, making inroads on the widely used US dollar, which has historically been used by commercial and central banks worldwide as a stable reserve on which to ensure their liquidity and facilitate international transactions.
- A currency is attractive for foreign transactions when it demonstrates a proven track record of stability, a well-developed financial market to dispose of the currency in, and proven acceptability to others. While the euro has made substantial progress towards achieving these features, there are a few challenges that undermine the ascension of the euro as a major reserve currency.
- The Chinese renminbi (RMB), also referred to as the Yuan (CNY), is one of the world's reserve currencies and was pegged to the US dollar until 2005. Since 2012, RMB has been allowed to float but within a narrow margin set by a basket of global currencies.

2.3   Forward Exchange Rates

Learning Objective

1.2.3   Be able to calculate forward foreign exchange rates by adding or subtracting forward adjustments; interest rate parity

1.2.4   Be able to analyse how foreign exchange contracts can be used to buy or sell currency relating to overseas investments or to hedge non-domestic currency exposure: spot contracts; forward contracts; currency futures; currency options; non-deliverable forwards

2.3.1   Quoting Forward Exchange Rates

When considering a quotation for a currency pair, it is important to distinguish between the base currency and the quote currency. Interpreting an FX quote should follow two simple rules: the currency first quoted is the base currency and this is followed by the quote currency; the second rule is that the value of the base currency is always equal to one. For example, if the spot FX quote is for USD/CAD and the rate quoted is 1.3085 (on the bid), this shows that one can sell one US dollar to purchase 1.3085 Canadian dollars in the spot market.

Many FX pairs are quoted with the US dollar as the base currency, but there are three important exceptions which are for sterling (GBP), the Australian dollar (AUD), and for the euro (EUR), when it is customary for these three currencies to be the base currency in each quotation and the US dollar is the quote currency.

For example, in the case of GBP/USD, the base currency is GBP or sterling and the quote currency is the US dollar.

One further convention to note is that it is customary in the FX market to specify a quotation to four decimal places (in most cases with the exception of quotations which involve the Japanese yen) and the smallest unit to four decimal places is referred to as a pip or point. For example, the difference between a spot quotation of £1 = $1.3160 and £1 = $1.3220 is 60 pips.

A simple rule is that all exchange rates in the forex market are expressed using the following:

$$\text{Base currency/quote currency} = \text{Bid/ask}$$

Example

A spot quotation for GBP/USD of £1 = $1.3220/24 shows the bid/offer spread (with a four pip spread between the bid/offer). The bid is the price at which one can sell the base currency and the offer is the price at which one can buy the base currency. So, a US dollar-based investor (the quote currency in this instance) will need to pay $1.3224 (the offer price) to purchase £1, and will receive $1.3220 (the bid price) if selling £1 in exchange for dollars.

2.3.2 Interest Rate Parity

The concept of interest rate parity in determining the exchange rate between currencies arises from one of the cornerstone ideas in financial theory, which is that of rational pricing and the notion of arbitrage.

Rational pricing is the assumption in financial economics that asset prices will reflect the arbitrage-free price of the asset as any deviation from this price will be arbitraged away.

Arbitrage is the practice of taking advantage of a pricing anomaly between securities that are trading in two (or possibly more) markets. One market can be the physical or underlying market; the other can often be a derivative market.

When a mismatch or anomaly can be exploited (ie, after transaction costs, storage costs, transport costs and dividends), the arbitrageur locks in a risk-free profit. In general terms, arbitrage ensures that the law of one price will prevail. Interest rate parity results from recognising a possible arbitrage condition and arbitraging it away.

Consider the returns from borrowing in one currency, exchanging that currency for another currency and investing in interest-bearing instruments of the second currency, while simultaneously purchasing futures contracts to convert the currency back at the end of the investment period. Under the assumption of arbitrage, the returns available should be equal to the returns from purchasing and holding similar interest-bearing instruments of the first currency.

If the returns are different, investors could theoretically arbitrage and make risk-free returns. Interest rate parity says that the spot and future prices for currency trades incorporate any interest rate differentials between the two currencies.

A forward exchange contract is an agreement between two parties to either buy or sell foreign currency at a fixed exchange rate for settlement at a future date. The **forward exchange rate** is the exchange rate set today even though the transaction will not settle until some agreed point in the future, such as in three months' time.

The relationship between the spot exchange rate and forward exchange rate for two currencies is simply given by the differential between their respective nominal interest rates over the term being considered. The relationship is purely mathematical and has nothing to do with market expectations.

The idea behind this relationship is embodied in the principle of interest rate parity and is expressed as follows:

$$\text{Forward rate for GBP/USD} = \text{£ Spot rate} \times \left[\frac{(1 + \text{US \$ Short-term interest rate})}{(1 + \text{UK £ Short-term interest rate})} \right]$$

Example

The GBP/USD spot exchange rate = 1.3220. If the three-month interest rate for the UK is 4.88% and for the US, 3.20%, what will the three-month forward exchange rate be?

As the three-month interest rates are quoted on a per annum basis, they must be divided by four to obtain the rate of interest that will be payable (%) over three months (it could also be calculated according to the more complex market convention of using actual days or 30/360 days for each month. See chapter 2, section 6.6.3 for day count conventions):

Sterling: 4.88%/4 = 1.22%
Dollar: 3.20%/4 = 0.8%

Applying the interest rate parity formula:

$$\text{Forward rate for GBP/USD} = \$1.3220 \times \left[\frac{(1 + 0.008)}{(1 + 0.012)} \right] = \$1.3165$$

The forward exchange rate in the above example of $1.3165 is lower than the spot exchange rate of $1.3220. That is, in three months' time, £1 will buy $1.3165, or $0.0055 fewer dollars than is available at the spot rate (ie, the difference is 55 pips). If this relationship did not exist, then an arbitrage opportunity would arise between the spot and forward rates.

It is important to realise that the forward rate calculated under the notion of arbitrage and interest rate parity is not a forecast of what the rate of exchange will actually be in three months. The actual rate will vary according to all of the factors which influence exchange rates in the forex market. The three-month forward rate in this example is simply a mathematically derived rate resulting from the interest rate differentials prevailing between the two currencies being exchanged.

2.4   Currency Contracts: Spot, Forward and Future

Foreign currency risk can be reduced, though not completely eliminated, by employing the following **hedging** instruments or strategies:

* spot contracts
* forward contracts
* foreign currency options
* foreign currency futures, and
* currency swaps.

2.4.1   FX Transactions

In conducting FX transactions, there are several ways to proceed depending on the purpose of the transaction. The purposes include the purchase of a foreign asset by an investor, the settlement of an international trade in merchandise or services, the need to hedge an investment or the need to lock in a particular exchange rate for a future purchase at a price which is known and can be specified today.

2.4.2   Spot Contracts

If one requires immediacy in the transaction the most appropriate form of transaction will involve entering into a spot contract. The term spot is used in a number of markets as well as the FX market and refers to the current price of an asset which can normally be obtained in real time. In the interbank forex market, which trades 24 hours a day, it is always possible to find the exact pricing on a foreign exchange by regarding the prices prevailing at the time of inquiry. Other markets where spot prices are used are in the commodities area, where, for example, the spot price of gold is determined at a fixing each day in London. Crude oil is also often quoted on a spot basis.

A typical euro/US dollar (EUR/USD) spot quote might look something like this:

EUR/USD spot rate = 1.1360/1.1365

Conventionally, the quote might be simplified as simply 60/65, since FX traders are more focused on the pip values at the end of the quote rather than the big figure values, which are less likely to be changing so rapidly during daily trading.

The bid is the price at which one can sell the base currency and the offer is the price at which one can buy the base currency. So, in the example just cited, a dollar-based investor (the quote currency in this instance) needs to pay $1.1365 (the offer price) to purchase one euro, and will receive $1.1360 (the bid price) if selling one euro in exchange for US dollars. The difference between the buyer's and seller's rates is generally referred to as the bid-offer spread. It enables the bank offering the deals to make money.

Entering into a spot contract can be done with a bank and there may be **commissions** and transfer charges involved. Settlement will normally be executed within a maximum of 48 hours, at which time the foreign currency funds are available. Speculators in the forex market will often use spot prices for trading purposes, and in the very active interbank market the bid/ask spreads may be tighter than those shown in the above example.

2.4.3 Forward Contracts

The forward market is almost exactly the same as the spot market, except that currency deals are agreed for a future date, but at a rate of exchange fixed now. These rates of exchange are not directly quoted. Instead, quotes on the forward market state how much must be added to, or subtracted from, the present spot rate.

For example, the three-month GBP/USD quote might be:

spot $1.3055–$1.3145

three-month forward $1.00–0.97c pm

pm stands for premium. It is used when the dollar is going to be more expensive relative to sterling in the future. It is deducted from the quoted spot rate in order to arrive at the forward rate. £1 will buy fewer dollars in three months' time and, if you have dollars in three months' time, the bank will sell you more sterling per dollar than they will now. The premium is quoted in cents, unlike the spot rate, which is quoted in dollars. So, 1.00 pm is a premium of 1 cent or 0.01 dollars (100 pips), and 0.97 pm is a premium of 0.97 cents or 0.0097 dollars (97 pips).

The three-month forward quote is, therefore: $1.2955–$1.3048.

Alternatively the three-month forward rate may exhibit a discount, rather than a premium, for example:

spot $1.3055–$1.3145

three-month forward   0.79–0.82c dis

'dis' stands for discount. The discount is used when the dollar is going to be cheaper relative to sterling in the future. It needs to be added to the quoted spot rate to arrive at the forward rate. £1 will buy more dollars in three months' time and, if you have dollars in three months' time, the bank will sell you less sterling per dollar than they will now. The three-month forward quote is therefore:

three-month forward $1.3134–$1.3227

The logic is that the forward rate will always exhibit a wider spread than the spot rate.

A variant of the forward contract is a **non-deliverable forward (NDF)**. As the name suggests, the contract does not result in the exchange of notional currencies. It is usually a short-term forward contract where the counterparties agree to take the opposite sides of a currency trade, at a set notional amount and exchange rate. At maturity, the profit/loss is calculated by taking the difference between the contracted exchange rate and the spot rate.

It is estimated that more than 60% of NDFs are traded for speculation purposes with the main base currencies being the US dollar or euro.

2.4.4   Currency Futures Contracts

The interbank market has grown enormously since the abandonment of the fixed exchange rate regime in the early 1970s. The major FX players are the multinational banks, and the OTC market in forex dealing is the largest capital market by far in operation on a daily basis, with trillions of dollars in nominal terms traded each day.

Most of the transactions which take place will be within the interbank market and will employ either spot contracts, forward contracts or swap arrangements. There are, however, futures contracts, which can also be used in FX, and these can be useful in relation to hedging.

A **futures** contract is an exchange-traded transaction where a standardised asset – such as 100 barrels of West Texas Intermediate crude oil, a stipulated monetary value of a stock index such as the S&P 500, or a stipulated amount of a foreign currency – is traded for delivery at a pre-determined date in the future at a price which is established at the time at which the futures trade takes place. The buyer of the futures contract agrees to take delivery, or, as is much more common, make a cash settlement for the item traded at a future date, whereas the seller of the contract agrees to deliver the item traded, or again, as is much more common, to make a cash settlement which covers the difference between the spot price prevailing for that item in the marketplace at the time of the delivery versus the price agreed at the time at which the parties entered the futures contract.

Currency futures were first created at the Chicago Mercantile Exchange (CME) in 1972, less than one year after the system of fixed exchange rates was abandoned along with the gold standard. The International Monetary Market (IMM), a division of the CME, was launched and trading began in seven currency futures in May 1972. Other futures exchanges that trade currency futures are NYSE Liffe, the Tokyo Financial Exchange and the **Intercontinental Exchange (ICE)**.

As with other futures and **options**, the conventional maturity dates are the IMM dates, namely the third Wednesday in March, June, September and December.

Futures contracts can be used to hedge against FX risk. If an investor will receive a payment denominated in a foreign currency on some future date, that investor can lock in the current exchange rate by entering into an offsetting currency futures position that expires on the date that the payment should be received.

Example

A US-based investor expects to receive €1,000,000 on 1 December. The current exchange rate implied by the futures is $1.2/€. One can lock in this exchange rate by selling €1,000,000 worth of futures contracts expiring on 1 December. By doing so, the investor has guaranteed an exchange rate of $1.2/€ regardless of exchange rate fluctuations in the meantime.

Currency futures can also be used to speculate as the following example shows.

Example

A speculator buys ten September CME Euro FX Futures, at $1.2713/€. At the end of the day, the futures close at $1.2784/€. The change in price is $0.0071/€. As each contract is equivalent to €125,000, and the speculator has ten contracts, their profit is $8,875. Being an exchange-traded contract the settlement takes place immediately.

One of the drawbacks of the above examples is that the timing and the amounts of futures contracts, as they are standardised, do not provide for the kind of customisation which many investors and merchants require when wanting to engage in a foreign currency transaction.

2.4.5   Currency Swaps (Foreign Exchange Swap, Forex Swap, or FX Swap)

A short-term currency swap is a contract that commits two parties to exchange pre-agreed foreign currency amounts now and to re-exchange them back at a given future date (the maturity date).

One currency is defined as the primary currency, and most deals are structured so that the nominal value of the primary currency exchanged on the two dates is equal. The other currency is the secondary currency, and the nominal value of this exchanged on the two dates is a function of the spot rate and the swap market forward rate.

The terms 'buyer' and 'seller' relate to these swap arrangements from the point of view of the primary currency cash flows at inception. The buyer is the person who, at inception, purchases the primary currency (selling the secondary currency). The seller is the individual who, at inception, sells the primary currency (buying the secondary currency).

From a diagrammatic perspective, the following example shows a simple short-term currency swap involving sterling and the US dollar. The buyer is the purchaser of the primary currency, which is the US dollar in this instance, and the seller is the seller of the dollars and the purchaser of the agreed amounts of sterling.

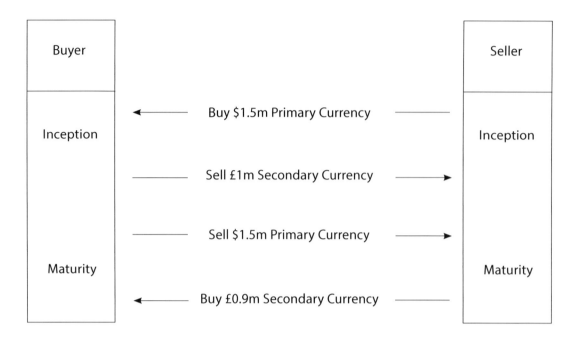

2.4.6   Synthetic Agreement for Forward Exchange (SAFE)

A SAFE is a variation on the short-term currency swap, in which there is no actual exchange of principal at inception or at maturity, the arrangement being a CFD based on notional cash sums. In this case, large notional sums may be referenced in the swap agreement but the resulting cash flow may be relatively small, especially if there has been only a slight variation between the rates at the time of inception and at the time of maturity.

When the two parties agree to execute a SAFE, they agree the exchange rates at which the notional deals will be executed at inception and maturity. At maturity, one party pays to the other the difference in the value of the secondary currency between the rate originally contracted and the rate actually prevailing. In essence this is exactly how a CFD for any asset purchase works, including equity CFDs.

2.4.7   Currency Options Contracts

A currency option is a form of contract which confers the right but not the obligation for the purchaser of the option to buy or sell a currency at a pre-agreed exchange rate on a specified date which is established at the time when the contract is agreed. The execution of the contract results in a forex option trade.

Most of the FX option volume is traded OTC and is lightly regulated, but a fraction is traded on exchanges like the International Securities Exchange (ISE), the Philadelphia Stock Exchange (PHLX), or the CME for options on futures contracts.

Example

It is conventional for forex quotes to be made to four decimal places. For example, even if the rate of exchange between sterling and the dollar was exactly £1 = $2 the convention is that the mid-rate (ie, the mid-point between the bid and the ask) should be quoted as £1:$2.0000.

A GBP/USD FX option might be specified by a contract giving the owner the right, but not the obligation, to sell £1,000,000 and buy $2,000,000 in three months' time. In this case the pre-agreed exchange rate, or strike price, is 2.0000 USD per GBP (or 0.5000 GBP per USD) and the notionals are £1,000,000 and $2,000,000.

This type of contract is both a call on dollars and a put on sterling, and is often called a GBP/USD put by market participants, as it is a put on the exchange rate; it could equally be called a USD/GBP call, but market convention is quote GBP/USD (USD per GBP).

Let us assume that the rate is 1.9000 or lower than 2.0000 in three months' time, meaning that the dollar is stronger than the rate stipulated in the option (and the pound is weaker). The option will be exercised, allowing the owner to sell GBP at 2.0000 and immediately buy it back in the spot market at 1.9000.

The result of this exercise of the option is that a profit of (2.0000 GBP/USD−1.9000 GBP/USD) x 1,000,000 GBP = 100,000 USD can be made in the process. From a sterling perspective, this will amount to $100,000/1.9000 = 52,631.58 GBP.

End of Chapter Questions

Think of an answer to each question and refer to the appropriate section for confirmation.

1. What are the age and residency requirements in order to invest in a cash individual savings account (ISA)?
    Answer reference: Section 1.1.6

2. Provide a simple formula which illustrates how to determine the real interest rate available as a return from holding a security.
    Answer reference: Section 1.1.8

3. What is the current level of protection provided to depositors at UK-licensed, deposit-taking institutions and where is this level stipulated?
    Answer reference: Section 1.1.9

4. What is the key characteristic and purpose of a gilt repo?
    Answer reference: Sections 1.2.4 and 1.4

5. What does the term 'cross rate' in the foreign exchange market, when used in its precise sense, mean?
    Answer reference: Section 2.1.1

6. Explain what is meant by rolling over a position in the foreign exchange (FX) market.
    Answer reference: Section 2.1.4

7. Explain what is meant by the term 'managed floating' in relation to exchange rates and give an example of when that mechanism has been used.
    Answer reference: Section 2.2.6

8. If the sterling/US dollar spot exchange rate is $1.3500, and the three-month interest rate for the UK is 1.35% and for the US, 0.65%, what will the three-month forward exchange rate be?
    Answer reference: Section 2.3.2

9. If the three-month rate of interest is lower in the eurozone than in the US, would the EUR/USD forward rate be higher or lower than the spot rate?
    Answer reference: Section 2.3.2

10. If the spot rate for sterling against the US dollar is $1.3420–$1.3426, and a three-month discount of 0.57c–0.63c is quoted, then what would be the quotation for the three-month forward exchange?
    Answer reference: Section 2.4.3

Chapter Two
Fixed-Income Securities

This syllabus area will provide approximately 20 of the 80 examination questions

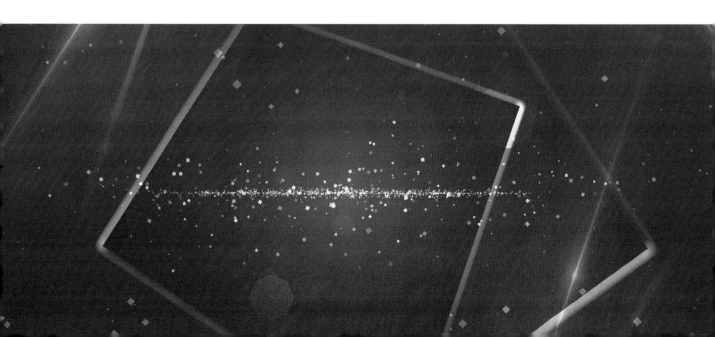

1. Fixed-Income Securities

1.1 Characteristics of Fixed-Income Securities

Learning Objective

2.1.1 Understand the main characteristics of fixed-income securities: short-, medium- and long-dated; dual-dated; floating rate; zero coupon; use of ratings; credit enhancements

2.1.2 Understand the main risks of fixed-income securities: the impact of ratings; the concept of risk-free; currency, credit and inflation risks

Fixed-income securities (or bonds) are effectively loans with the features of most of this type of instrument being as follows:

- **Maturity date** – fixed-income securities are usually established for an agreed period of time and the issuer will repay (redeem) the loan at maturity.
- **Interest** – fixed-income securities will usually pay a fixed or variable rate of interest to the bondholders on set dates (often half yearly or quarterly) for the period of the loan.

These features are consistent among most bonds, whether the issuers are governments, municipal authorities, other public bodies or corporates.

1.1.1 Short-, Medium- and Long-Dated Bonds

In many bond markets, the instruments are subdivided or categorised based on the period of time that remains until the bond matures:

A typical classification is as follows:

- **Short** – less than seven years to redemption.
- **Medium** – between seven and 15 years to redemption.
- **Long** – over 15 years to redemption.

However, the ranges in some countries can be different. For example, in the US, government bonds are classed as short-term (one to five years), medium-term (six to 12 years) and long-term (greater than 12 years).

Dual-Dated Gilts

Some fixed-interest securities have two specified redemption dates and the issuer can choose to repay the bond at any point between the two dates. The maturity classification applied to dual-dated gilts is short-, medium- or long-dated, depending upon the time remaining to the later of the two dates.

Example

5% DEF plc 2023–27 corporate bond enables the issuer to choose to redeem the bond at the earliest in 2023 and at any time up to the later date of 2027. What would make the issuer redeem early or late?

The answer may depend upon the interest rates at the time. If, in 2023, the interest rate that the issuer has to pay to provide the funds for redemption is only 4%, then it will redeem at the earliest point – saving 1% pa. In contrast, if the interest rate is greater than 5%, the issuer would not redeem, potentially, until it was forced to in 2027.

1.1.2 Fixed- or Floating-Rate Bonds

With many bonds, such as government bonds, the periodic coupon payment is usually a fixed amount which is established at the time of issue.

Government-sponsored entities, such as the Federal National Mortgage Association (Fannie Mae) in the US, have been issuers of floating rate bonds, where the coupon rate varies. The rate is adjusted in line with published, market interest rates. The published interest rates that are normally used are based on the **LIBOR**. LIBOR is the average rate at which banks in London offer loans to other banks. LIBOR was previously published by the British Bankers' Association (BBA) using quotes provided by a panel of banks.

In 2013, however, following a LIBOR-fixing scandal that came to prominence in 2012–13 when several banks received large fines, individual traders were put on trial, and a criminal investigation into LIBOR manipulation was carried out by the UK Serious Fraud Office, with NYSE Euronext being awarded the contract by the FCA to take over and reform the running of LIBOR. From early 2014, LIBOR was calculated by an entity owned by NYSE Euronext, but following the takeover of NYSE Euronext by the Intercontinental Exchange (ICE), the entity is now called ICE Benchmark Administration ltd and is overseen by the FCA.

Immediately after 31 December 2021, the sterling, euro, Swiss franc and Japanese yen settings, and the one-week and two-month US dollar settings will cease to be provided and will be replaced by alternative benchmark rates. Immediately after 30 June 2023, the remaining US dollar settings will cease to be provided.

Sterling LIBOR will be replaced by the Sterling Overnight Index Average (SONIA) and US dollar LIBOR replaced by the Secured Overnight Financing Rate (SOFR).

Floating rate notes (FRNs) typically add a margin to the LIBOR rate, measured in basis points (bps), with each basis point representing one hundredth of 1%. A corporate issuer may offer floating rate bonds to investors at three-month sterling LIBOR plus 75 basis points. If LIBOR is at 4%, the coupon paid will be 4.75%, with the additional 75 basis points compensating the investor for the higher risk of payment default.

1.1.3 Zero Coupon Bonds (ZCBs)

A zero coupon bond (ZCB) is, as the name suggests, a bond which has a single repayment amount, which is received at the end of the term without any interim coupon payments. Its yield is calculated through assessing the rate of return between the eventual payment and the discounted amount which is paid for the bond at the time of issue or purchase.

1.1.4 Credit Ratings

Bondholders face the risk that the issuer of the bond may default on its obligation to pay interest and/or the principal amount upon maturity. The risk of default is referred to as credit risk and can be assessed in terms of the probability that an issuer will default on some, or all, of its payment obligations, resulting in a loss to the bondholder. There are several independent credit rating agencies that assess and report on this degree of likelihood. Three companies in particular are heavily relied on and their ratings therefore affect the price of the bonds (see also section 6.2.2 of this chapter).

The three main credit rating agencies that provide these ratings, independent of one another, are Moody's, Standard & Poor's (S&P) and Fitch Ratings. Bond issues subject to credit ratings can be divided into two distinct categories: those accorded an investment grade rating and those categorised as non-investment grade, speculative or junk bonds. Investment grade issues offer the greatest safety and liquidity.

The three rating agencies use similar methods to rate issuers and individual bond issues. They assess whether the cash flow generated by the borrower will comfortably service and, ultimately, repay the debt. The table below provides an abridged version of the credit ratings available from the three agencies.

Risk	Moody's	S&P	Fitch Ratings
Investment Grade	Aaa to Baa3	AAA to BBB–	AAA to BBB–
Speculative Grade	Ba1 to B3	BB+ to B–	BB+ to B–
High Likelihood of Bankruptcy	Caa to Ca	CCC to C	CCC to C
Bankrupt or in Default	C	D	D

Credit enhancement is often a key part of the securitisation transaction when issuing securities that are backed by assets, such as loans (see also section 6.2.5 of this chapter).

1.1.5 Credit Rating Agencies

Many governments have the highest credit ratings of those issued by the big three global credit rating agencies. The highest rating for both S&P and Fitch Ratings is AAA, while the highest rating for Moody's is Aaa.

In recent years, the UK, Norwegian and German governments, among others, have enjoyed the highest credit rating available from these agencies. However, in June 2016, after the result of the EU Referendum, the UK had its credit rating outlook cut to negative by Moody's who stated that the result would herald '*a prolonged period of uncertainty*'. Moody's was the first ratings agency to take concrete action after the Brexit vote. While traditionally the UK often enjoyed a AAA status, at the time of writing (June 2021), the UK rating stood at AA with S&P (with a stable outlook) AA- with Fitch (with a negative outlook), and Aa3 with Moody's (also with a stable outlook). The cutting of a credit rating makes it more expensive for governments to raise money with their sovereign bond issues, as it will require higher coupon payments to attract investors who perceive more risk in a lower-rated government bond.

1.1.6 Risk Free

Government bonds have historically been described as risk free, since the assumption is made that governments do not default on their debt. While this has been largely true, there have been academic studies by Harvard professor Stephen Rogoff which illustrate that many governments have either defaulted or partially defaulted on their obligations.

In recent times, with concerns about the possible default of the government debt of eurozone countries, the issue has been raised that there is a difference between sovereign borrowers that can pay back debt by simply issuing more of their own currency, and those which cannot. The US and UK are able to print more sterling and dollars in order to service their debts, whereas eurozone countries are not in that position: they cannot print more euros as that role is restricted to the European Central Bank (ECB).

Printing more currency to service debts is only done in extreme circumstances, and it may have unwanted consequences, such as provoking a currency crisis, but from a theoretical point of view the facility of printing more money provides a slightly unorthodox reassurance that most government debt is risk-free.

1.1.7 Index-Linked Bonds

Index-linked bonds (such as **index-linked gilts** and US Treasury Inflation-Protected Securities (TIPS)) differ from conventional bonds in that the coupon payments and the principal are adjusted in line with a published index of price inflation. This means that both the coupons and the principal on redemption paid by these bonds are adjusted to take account of inflation since the bond's issue. Assuming inflation is positive, the nominal amount outstanding of an index-linked bond is less than the redemption value that the government will pay on maturity.

Because these bonds are uplifted by increases in the relevant price index, they are effectively inflation-proof. In times of inflation, they will increase in price and preserve the purchasing power of the investment. In a period of zero inflation, index-linked bonds will pay the coupon rate with no uplift and simply pay back the nominal value at maturity.

The UK offers a number of index-linked gilts, as do a number of other governments including the US, France, Germany and Japan.

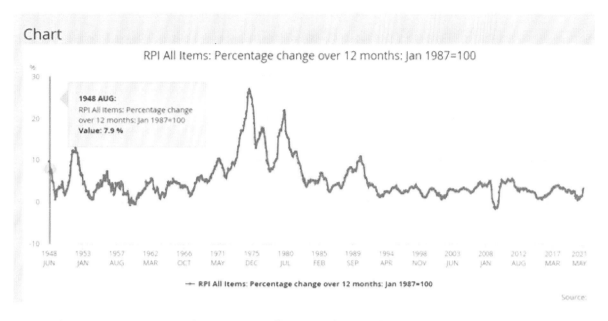

Chart

RPI All Items: Percentage change over 12 months: Jan 1987=100

1948 AUG:
RPI All Items: Percentage change
over 12 months: Jan 1987=100
Value: 7.9 %

—•— RPI All Items: Percentage change over 12 months: Jan 1987=100

Source:

Source: https://www.ons.gov.uk/economy/inflationandpriceindices/timeseries/czbh/mm23

1.2 Characteristics of Government Bonds

Learning Objective

2.2.1 Understand the main investment characteristics, behaviours and risks of government debt (for example, USA, Germany, Japan and the UK)

1.2.1 Governments Bonds

Government bonds are dominant in the bond markets, with most modern governments running a budget deficit leading to the large-scale issuance of bonds. Sometimes, the secondary market is run on stock exchanges (as in Germany and the UK) and sometimes outside stock exchanges (as in the US). Like any type of bond, government bonds have the exposure to risk.

Credit risk is the risk of a default of the issuer. Some regard them as near risk-free as a government has various ways in which to raise money to continue to pay interest and make repayment at maturity. However, historically, government defaults have been known, eg, Russia in 1998 and Argentina numerous times since 2001.

For holders of a bond denominated in a currency of a different country, currency risk presents itself as there is a risk that the value of the currency repaid will be less than the investors' own currency. Most bonds, apart from those that are index-linked, also carry inflation risk which is the risk that the value of the funds paid as interest or at maturity will decline in real terms over time.

US

In the US, the Treasury issues government bonds known as Treasury bills and Treasury notes. There are also TIPS. The management of government debt is the responsibility of the Bureau of the Fiscal Service.

US Treasury securities are extremely liquid and all trade on the secondary market. The US Treasury ten-year note is widely quoted and acts as a benchmark when evaluating the performance of US government stocks.

Germany

The German Federal Government issues bonds called *Bunds* (from *Bundesanleihen*). Maturities generally range from two to 30 years. Index-linked German government bonds have been added recently to bond market offerings.

German bonds are considered a benchmark in Europe and of being of the highest quality despite the introduction of the euro. They are auctioned in the **primary market** and traded in the secondary market on various German exchanges.

Japan

Japanese Government Bonds (JGBs) are issued by the Ministry of Finance in Japan and play a huge role in the financial securities market in Japan. They are the most popular market for government bond dealers across Asia and its ten-year bond is one of the most price-tracked across the globe.

JGBs are issued with a range of two to 40 years, with the ten-year bond usually providing a benchmark to establish the level of demand for other JGBs, such as 20- and 30-year bonds. Japan is regularly regarded as a stable bond issuer with JGBs regularly used as a safer haven in times of turbulence. The secondary bond market is split between trading on the stock exchange and transactions that are made over-the-counter (OTC). OTC is the dominant trading method. However, two-year, five-year, ten-year, 20-year, 30-year and 40-year fixed-rate JGBs are listed on the stock exchanges in Tokyo and Nagoya.

UK

Bonds issued, serviced and managed by the UK's Debt Management Office (DMO) on behalf of the UK Treasury are known as gilts. Like other bonds, UK gilts are issued with a given nominal value that will be repaid at the bond's redemption date and a coupon rate representing the percentage of the nominal value that will be paid to the holder of the bond each year. Obviously, different gilts have different redemption dates and the coupon is payable at different points of the year (generally at semi-annual intervals). Older issues are named Treasury or exchequer stocks while newer issues are known as Treasury gilts. Those that are index linked are known as index-linked gilts.

Typically, UK gilts have maturities stretching much further into the future than other European government bonds, which has influenced the development of pension and life insurance markets in the respective countries.

Example

Gilts are denoted by their coupon rate and their redemption date, for example 6% Treasury Stock 2028. The coupon indicates the cash payment per £100 nominal value that the holder will receive each year. This payment is made in two equal semi-annual payments on fixed dates, six months apart. An investor holding £1,000 nominal of 6% Treasury Stock 2028 will receive two coupon payments each year of £30 each, on 7 June and 7 December, until the repayment of the £1,000 on 7 December 2028.

1.2.2   Term of Government Debt

Government debt, such as UK gilts, can be divided into three broad classes:

*   short-, medium- and long-dated
*   dual dated
*   undated (the last remaining undated bonds in the UK gilt category were redeemed on 5 July 2015. This concluded a process first initiated by the Chancellor of the Exchequer in October 2014 against the backdrop of prevailing historically low long gilt yields).

1.2.3   Separate Trading of Registered Interest and Principal (STRIP)

Some of the UK gilt issuance can be stripped into individual cash flows, ie, the periodic coupon payments as well as the eventual repayment of the principal. All of these cash flows can be traded separately as zero coupon gilts or gilt strips.

As an example, a ten-year gilt can be stripped to make 21 separate securities: 20 strips based on the coupons, which are entitled to just one of the half-yearly interest payments; and one strip entitled to the redemption payment at the end of the ten years.

As each ZCB is purchased at a discount to this redemption value, the entire return is in the form of a capital gain. A STRIP can be used both as a portfolio management tool and as a personal financial planning tool. The redemption proceeds from these bonds, each with their own unique redemption date, can be used to coincide with specific future liabilities or known future payments.

1.3   Interest Rates and Government Bond Prices

Learning Objective

2.2.2   Understand the relationship between interest rates and bond prices: yield (flat yield and yield to maturity); interest payable; accrued interest (clean and dirty prices); effect of changes in interest rates

Because many bonds usually have semi-annual coupons (eg, as with gilts), the semi-annual cash flows should be discounted at the semi-annual rate. The market convention for gilts is to quote the annual yield by simply doubling the semi-annual figure.

Bonds, most of which have definite schedules of cash flow values with precise timings as to when they will be paid out, are ideally suited to the application of discounted cash flow (DCF) evaluation techniques.

1.3.1 Discounted Cash Flow (DCF)

The formula for a DCF evaluation is as follows:

$$PV = \frac{C_1}{(1+r/cf)^1} + \frac{C_2}{(1+r/cf)^2} + \frac{C_3}{(1+r/cf)^3} + ... + \frac{F}{(1+r/cf)^n}$$

where:

PV = present value of the bond
C = coupon amount paid on the bond
cf = frequency of the coupon payment on an annual basis, eg, semi-annual payments equal 2
r = assumed discount rate (compounded in accordance with the frequency of payments of the coupon and compounding)
F = face value or redemption amount of the bond
n = the number of time periods until the bond matures

The formula adds together the present value of all of the coupon payments, discounted in accordance with the annual rate of interest (compounded at the frequency rate), and the redemption amount is also discounted in similar fashion.

1.3.2 DCF and Gross Redemption Yield (GRY)

To state it quite simply, a yield of a bond is a measure of percentage return (the return versus the cost of the bond). The **gross redemption yield (GRY)** or yield to maturity (YTM) represents the total return from a bond, after considering the price paid, all of the coupon payments and the repayment of the principal. Unlike flat yield, which is a rather simplistic measure, the GRY is the benchmark used in the markets for measuring the so-called yield of a bond. Calculating the GRY is best understood by referencing the discounted cash flow method outlined in section 1.3.1.

The following table shows a hypothetical UK government bond which has a maturity of five years with the first coupon payment of 2.5% (ie, half of the quoted annual coupon rate) being paid in August 2019, and continuing until February 2024 when the bond will be redeemed at its face value. The tabular layout uses the DCF approach to illustrate the exact nature of the cash flows. For simplification the GRY is assumed to be the same as the nominal yield resulting in a value/current price that would be at par.

Bond Pricing – Discounted Cash Flow Evaluation			
Bond Price	£100.00	Gross Redemption Yield – GRY	5.00%
Face Value	£100.00	Coupon Frequency	2
Coupon Rate	5.00%		
Life in Years	5		
Period	Date	Cash Flow	PV Cash Flows (excluding purchase amount)
	Calendar Date when Cash Flow is Paid	Nominal Cash Flow	Discounted Cash Flow = Nominal Cash Flow/ [(1+YTM/Coupon Frequency)^Period]
0		−£100.00	
1	15 August 2019	£2.50	£2.44
2	15 February 2020	£2.50	£2.38
3	15 August 2020	£2.50	£2.32
4	15 February 2021	£2.50	£2.26
5	15 August 2021	£2.50	£2.21
6	15 February 2022	£2.50	£2.16
7	15 August 2022	£2.50	£2.10
8	15 February 2023	£2.50	£2.05
9	15 August 2023	£2.50	£2.00
10	15 February 2024	£2.50	£1.95
10	15 February 2024	£100.00	£78.12
Total		£25.00	£100.00
Sum of Present Values of Coupon Payments		£21.88	
Discounted Value (ie, PV) of Face Value		£78.12	
Total Sums Received at Present Value		£100.00	

The manner in which the table is laid out shows the initial outlay of £100 at time 0 followed by the ten semi-annual payments of £2.50 and the redemption amount being paid at period ten, ie, after five years. What is useful about this manner of presentation is that the present value of all coupon payments can be seen in isolation from the present value of the redemption value.

The nominal value of the coupon payment is, as expected, £25, ie, five years times £5; and with a 5% discount factor the present value of the coupon payments is £21.88; and the present value of the redemption amount when received five years hence is £78.12.

As one would expect, exactly the same result can be obtained by evaluating the price of the bond using an annuity discount factor with the appropriate values shown in the table. The advantage of using this approach is that there is less need to calculate all of the separate cash flow amounts but rather the present values of all the coupons can be calculated in one step followed by the calculation of the present values of the redemption amount.

Estimating Current Bond Price	Annual GRY	5.00%	Desired Yield	5.00%
Semi-Annual Cash Flows	Cash Flow in £	Discount Factor	Discount Factor at Desired Yield	Present Value
10	£2.50	$[1/0.025] \times [1-(1/1.025^{10})] = 8.75$	8.75	£21.88
10	£100.00	$[1/1.025^{10}] = 0.78$	0.78	£78.12
			Bond Price	£100.00

The next diagram will provide a useful insight into what can happen to bonds of long duration during periods of inflation when, as interest rates rise, investors will demand a much higher GRY and this could be considerably higher than the nominal interest rate paid out by the bond through its coupons.

Estimating Current Bond Price	Annual GRY	5.00%	Desired Yield	10.00%
Semi-Annual Cash Flows	Cash Flow in £	Discount Factor	Discount Factor at Desired Yield	Present Value
20	£2.50	$[1/0.05] \times [1-(1/1.050^{20})] = 12.46$	12.46	£31.16
20	£100.00	$[1/1.050^{20}] = 0.38$	0.38	£37.69
			Bond Price	£68.85

The above bond would exemplify a 5% gilt with ten years' maturity issued with a 5% nominal yield but where the GRY or desired yield to maturity has risen to 10% and the bond's price in the secondary market would have to fall to £68.85.

The value of a bond has two elements: the underlying capital value of the bond itself (the clean price which is quoted) and the coupon that it is accruing over time (accrued interest). Each coupon is distributed as income to people who are registered as at the ex-div date (which for gilts is normally seven business days prior to payment date).

The **dirty price** calculated above using DCF is the price that is paid for a bond, which combines these two elements. Consequently, ignoring all other factors that might affect the price, a dirty price will rise gradually as the coupon builds up, and then fall back as the stock is either marked ex-div or pays the dividend.

The dirty price of a bond will decrease on the days coupons are paid, resulting in a saw-tooth pattern for the bond value. This is because there will be one less future cash flow (ie, the coupon payment just received) at that point.

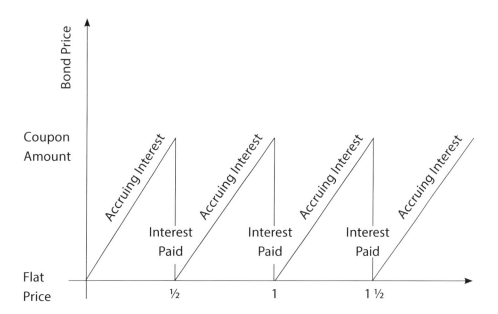

To separate out the effect of the coupon payments, the accrued interest between coupon dates is subtracted from the value determined by the dirty price to arrive at the **clean price**.

The clean price more closely reflects changes in value due to issuer risk and changes in the structure of interest rates. Its graph is smoother than that of the dirty price. Use of the clean price also serves to differentiate interest income (based on the coupon rate) from trading profit and loss.

It is market practice to quote bonds on a clean-price basis. When a bond settles, the accrued interest is added to the value based on the clean price to reflect the full market value.

Historically, investors, rather than claiming the coupon, could sell the bond at the high price just prior to the payment of the coupon, and this gain was free of tax. This process was known as bond washing. In 1986, the UK moved to a system of clean pricing that separates the two elements. Under clean pricing, whenever an investor purchases a bond, they pay the quoted price (the clean price), which represents the capital value of the underlying bond with an allowance made for the interest element, allowing the two elements (income and gain) to be taxed separately.

1.3.3   Cum Interest Bargains

A purchase made before the ex-div date is referred to as a cum div bargain. In this situation, the buyer of the bond will be the holder on the next ex-interest date and will therefore receive the full coupon for the period. The seller, however, has held the bond for part of this period and is therefore entitled to a part of that coupon. To account for this, the purchaser of the bond must compensate the seller for the coupon which they have earned.

The purchaser will therefore pay the clean price plus the interest from the last payment date up to the purchase date. On the next payment date, the holder will receive the whole of the interest for the six months. However, on a net basis, they will only have received the interest for the period of ownership.

The formula used by the DMO in the gilts market is as follows.

$$\text{Dirty price} = \text{Clean price} + \text{Period's coupons} \times \frac{\text{Days}}{\text{Days in period}}$$

where:

Days = number of days from the day after the last coupon payment date up to, and including, the settlement day

Days in period = number of days from the last coupon payment date up to and including the calendar day before the next coupon

Example

For a particular gilt, the coupons are paid on 1 April and 1 October of each year. On 10 July, an investor buys £10,000 nominal of Treasury 8% @ 101.50 for settlement on 11 July. The following are the steps required in the calculations of the clean and dirty pricing.

April	From last coupon (inclusive)	29	30
May		31	31
June		30	30
July	To settlement date (inclusive)	11	31
August			31
September			30
	Totals	101	183

Clean Price	£10,000 @ 101.50	£10,150.00
Accrued Interest	(£10,000 x 4%) x 101/183	£220.77
Dirty Price		£10,370.77

1.3.4 Summary of Influences on Bond Prices

The previous scenarios illustrate two key features of bond pricing:

- There is an inverse relationship between bond prices and interest rates, ie, as market interest rates rise, or specifically the required yield from investors rises, so the present or market value of a bond will fall (and vice versa).
- When the coupon rate on the bond is equal to the prevailing interest rate (or desired yield), the bond will be valued at par, as illustrated above when interest rates are at 5%.

These two features are vital for understanding the way in which bond pricing works, and students should familiarise themselves with the reasoning behind them.

In most cases, the income (coupon) from a bond remains the same throughout its life. However, during the life of the bond, there are many factors, especially inflation and the changes in the interest rate environment, that can make it more or less attractive to investors. These factors lead to the alteration in price of bonds.

The inverse relationship means that if investors see interest rates rising, the prices of bonds will fall. The reason for this can be seen if we appreciate that investors will require a particular level of return, depending upon rates of interest generally. If interest rates rise, investors' required rate of return rises. This means that they will be prepared to pay less for a particular bond with a fixed coupon rate than they were prepared to pay previously. If interest rates generally fall, investors will be prepared to pay more for a fixed-rate bond than previously, and bond prices will tend to rise.

Investors will generally require a higher return if the expected rate of inflation rises. Therefore, prices of fixed-rate bonds will tend to fall with rising expectations of inflation. However, index-linked bonds have a return that is linked to the inflation rate, with the result that the price of index-linked stock will tend to rise when higher inflation is expected.

1.4 Index-Linked Debt

Learning Objective

2.2.3 Understand the main investment characteristics, behaviours and risks of index-linked debt: retail prices and consumer prices indices as measures of inflation; process of index linking; indexing effects on price, interest and redemption; return during a period of zero inflation; harmonised price index

1.4.1 The Retail Prices Index (RPI) and Consumer Prices Index (CPI)

The retail prices index (RPI) has historically been the main inflation index used in the UK. The RPI is calculated by looking at the prices of a basket of more than 700 goods and services. The prices are then weighted to reflect the average household's consumption patterns, so those important items on which more money is spent get a higher weighting than peripheral items.

The index itself is based on movements in prices since a particular base period. Markets concentrate on inflation indices as they are a good indicator of the level of inflation and, consequently, government reaction to it. They also signal the need for potential increases in the yield paid on bonds in order to compensate for the erosion of real returns.

Two more refined measures were introduced in the 1990s.

*   **RPIX** – excludes the impact of mortgages.
*   **RPIY** – excludes mortgages and indirect charges (VAT and local authority taxes).

Historically, the RPIX was used by the government in specifying its inflation target at a level of 2.5%. In December 2003, the Chancellor of the Exchequer changed the UK inflation target to a new base, the **Harmonised Index of Consumer Prices (HICP)** which, in the UK, has subsequently been renamed the consumer prices index (CPI). The level of the new CPI inflation target for the BoE's Monetary Policy Committee was set at 2% from 10 December 2003. HICPs were originally developed in the EU to assess whether prospective members of the European Monetary Union (EMU) would pass the required inflation-convergence criterion; they then graduated to acting as the measure of inflation used by the ECB to assess price stability in the eurozone area.

Like the RPI, the CPI is calculated each month by taking a sample of goods and services that a typical household might buy, including food, heating, household goods and travel. There are significant differences, however, between the CPI and the RPI. The CPI excludes a number of items that are included in the RPI, mainly related to housing. These include council tax and a range of owner-occupier housing costs such as mortgage interest payments, house depreciation, buildings insurance and estate agency fees. The CPI covers all private households, whereas the RPI excludes the top 4% by income and pensioner households who derive at least three-quarters of their income from state benefits. The CPI also includes residents of student hostels and foreign visitors to the UK. It also covers some items that are not in the RPI, such as **unit trust** and stockbrokers' fees, university accommodation fees and foreign students' university tuition fees.

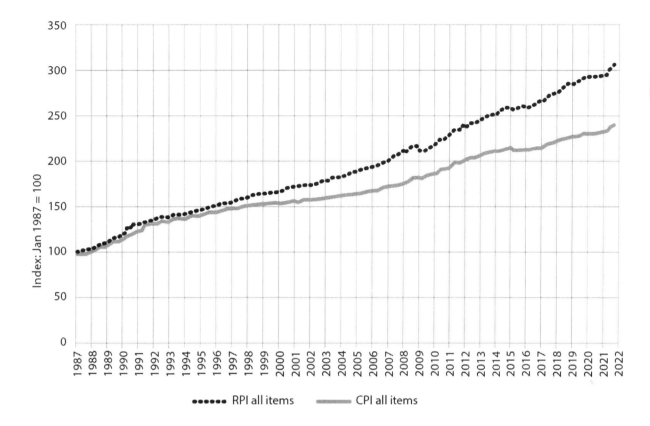

●●●●●● RPI all items   ━━━ CPI all items

Source: https://www.inflationarypressure.com/

Although, in most cases, the same underlying price data is used to calculate the two indices, there are some specific differences in price measurement. The two indices are also calculated differently. The CPI uses the geometric mean to combine prices within each expenditure category, whereas the RPI uses arithmetic means. The different techniques used to combine individual prices in the two indices tend to reduce CPI inflation relative to RPIX; this is known as the formula effect. When the Chancellor announced the changeover in target measure, the annual rate of RPIX exceeded the CPI by more than 1%.

In November 2020, the UK Government announced that index-linked gilts, from 2030, will no longer be linked to the RPI rather to the newer CPI that also includes housing costs, known as the CPIH. The CPIH is regarded as the UK's leading measure of inflation and is the same as the CPI except that it includes owner occupiers' housing (OOH) costs.

1.4.2 Index-Linked Issues

With an index-linked gilt (ILG), all cash returns – both interest payments and redemption proceeds – vary with inflation following the issue reference date. Index-linked gilts use the RPI to calculate the inflation, as the following illustration shows.

Example

A 5% semi-annual ILG which was issued several years previously has just paid a coupon. The RPI at the issue reference date stood at 100. The RPI at the reference date for the coupon just paid stood at 150. To determine the proper pricing of this ILG at the time of the last payment, it is necessary to undertake a more detailed examination of the cash flows and appropriate discounting factors to apply.

If the RPI was still at 100, ie, there had been no inflation, the coupon and redemption proceeds would be as follows:

- The coupon value will be £2.50 (£100 × 5% × ½).
- The redemption proceeds will be £100.00.

However, the current RPI value of 150 shows there has been 50% inflation since issue and, therefore, the coupon amount and the redemption amounts will have to be adjusted.

- The adjusted coupon value will be £2.50 x 150/100 = £3.75.
- The adjusted redemption amount will be £100 x 150/100 = £150.

So, for all ILGs, there needs to be a reference date for measuring the RPI value which is to be used. That reference date was historically eight months prior to the related cash flow, but for issues since June 2005 this was reduced to three months. For more recently issued ILGs, the appropriate values are as follows:

- The issue reference date is three months prior to issue.
- The reference date for any coupon is three months prior to its payment date.
- The reference date for the redemption proceeds is three months prior to redemption.

As the base index figure is the one three months prior to the issue date, and the final reference rate is the index value three months prior to redemption, the holder is compensated for inflation for the three months prior to the issue, but exposed to inflation for the last three months. It is, therefore, true to say that holders are not guaranteed a real rate of return in any period, owing to the time lag involved.

Example

The following table considers a 5% ILG issued several years ago which is redeemable in 2½ years. The RPI for the issue reference date was 100, and the RPI for the last coupon (just paid) was 150. Inflation has recently been running at 3% every six months and is expected to continue at this level. Bondholders require a return of 5% every six months.

The task is to calculate the price of the gilt in the secondary market at present.

RPI at Issue	100	Original Semi-Annual Coupon	Future Semi-Annual Coupon	Current Inflation Rate	Desired Yield
Current RPI	150	£2.50	2.5 x 150/100 = £3.75	3%	10.00%
Semi-Annual Cash Flows	Inflation Adjusted	Cash Flow in £	Discount Factor	Discount Factor at Desired Yield	Present Value
1	£3.75 x 1.03^1	£3.86	$[1/1.05]^1$	0.95	£3.68
2	£3.75 x 1.03^2	£3.98	$[1/1.05]^2$	0.91	£3.61
3	£3.75 x 1.03^3	£4.10	$[1/1.05]^3$	0.86	£3.54
4	£3.75 x 1.03^4	£4.22	$[1/1.05]^4$	0.82	£3.47
5	£153.75 x 1.03^5	£178.24	$[1/1.05]^5$	0.78	£139.65
				Bond Price	£153.95

The coupon will need to be adjusted from its issue value of £2.50 to £3.75 to reflect the change in the RPI from 100 to 150. Using similar reasoning, the redemption amount of the bond will also have to be adjusted to £150 – and this is shown in the left-hand column of the table where the final payment will need to be the adjusted coupon of £3.75 + adjusted redemption value of £150, ie, the final payment will need to be £153.75.

The second column shows how these new base amounts as of the evaluation task have themselves to be adjusted in nominal terms by uplifting them each six months by the level of inflation expected. So each value has to be raised by 1.03 on a compounding basis.

Having performed that task, we can then apply the standard discounting factor to these nominal cash flows by discounting on a compounding basis at 5% per semi-annual period.

An alternative approach is to discount the real (pre-inflation) flows at real rates.

The required nominal return every six months is 5%, though 2% of this will be satisfied by appreciation in the cash flow values due to inflation. The real required return is provided by the Fisher relationship:

$$(1+r) \quad = \quad (1+i)(1+R)$$

where:

r = the monetary or nominal rate (5%)
i = inflation rate (3%)
R = real rate of return

Therefore:

$$1.05 = 1.03(1 + R)$$
$$1 + R = 1.019$$
$$R = 0.019 \text{ (or 1.9\%)}$$

RPI at Issue	100	Original Semi-Annual Coupon	Current Inflation Rate	Future Semi-Annual Coupon
Current RPI	150	£2.50	3%	2.5 x 150/100 = £3.75
Desired Semi-Annual Coupon		5.00%	Discount Factor	1.94%
Semi-Annual Cash Flows	Cash Flow in £	Discount Factor	Discount Factor at Desired Yield	Present Value
5	£3.75	$[1/0.019] \times [1-(1/1.019)^5]$ = 4.73	4.73	£17.71
5	£150.00	$[1/1.019^5] = 0.91$	0.91	£136.25
			Bond Price	£153.95

1.4.3 Summary of Index-Linked Debt

Ignoring the minor impact of the time lag, because index-linked bonds are uplifted by increases in the relevant price index, they are effectively inflation-proof. In times of inflation, they will increase in price and preserve the purchasing power of the investment.

In a period of zero inflation, index-linked bonds will pay the coupon rate with no uplift and simply pay back the nominal value at maturity.

1.5   Other Governmental and Authority Debt

Learning Objective

2.2.4   Understand the main issuers and characteristics of supranational and public authority debt

1.5.1   Supranationals

Supranational bonds are issued by supranational organisations, such as the World Bank, the European Investment Bank and the Asian Development Bank. The World Bank has raised money through issuing bonds and, in 2009, following discussion among the G20 nations, the board of directors of the International Monetary Fund (IMF) decided to approve the issuance of bonds to the lender's 186 members for the first time.

The funds were needed for additional sources to lend during the global recession. According to a report from Bloomberg:

> *The IMF board made the decision* (to issue the bonds) *on 1 July 2009, in a vote, and did not place a limit on the note sales. The bonds are part of a wider effort to seek $500 billion in new funding as the lender helps countries from Iceland to Pakistan combat the global financial crisis.*

> *The securities, the culmination of months of talks between the fund and its members, will offer the largest emerging-market nations a new way of making IMF contributions, while they seek greater say at the fund. China, Brazil and Russia have favoured the bonds, instead of regular contributions, as they wrangle with other members over redistributing the IMF's voting power.*

ECB and IMF Assistance

In response to the euro crisis, several EU member states, including Ireland, Greece and Portugal, have found themselves in a position where they have needed to secure multi-billion euro funding from the ECB and the IMF. Governments in these countries have been forced to enter into austerity programmes in exchange for these massive cash injections.

In June 2011, the GRY on ten-year Greek government bonds climbed to almost 30%, indicating that the markets believed there was a very high likelihood that the Greek government would eventually have to restructure its debt or possibly experience an outright default. By the summer of 2015, Greece's national debt was €320 billion and the country had an S&P credit rating of CCC–. As of June 2021, it stands at BB– with a positive outlook.

1.5.2   Government-Sponsored Enterprises (GSEs) or Agencies

Government-sponsored enterprises (GSEs) or agencies issue bonds, known as agency bonds, for particular purposes. These are common in the US, where examples include the Federal Home Loan Banks (FHLB), the Federal National Mortgage Association (Fannie Mae) and the Federal Home Loan Mortgage Corporation (FHLMC) – also known as Freddie Mac – which was created in 1970. Along with other GSEs, the rationale for Fannie Mae and Freddie Mac as set up by the US Congress, was to buy mortgages in the secondary market, pool them, and sell them as mortgage-backed securities to investors on the open market.

The nature of the government guarantee for the obligations of GSEs was put in the spotlight during the global banking crisis of 2008. Whereas GSE obligations had previously been issued with an implied federal guarantee, this became explicit as GSEs have, since 2008, come under the direct conservatorship of the US Treasury. The public underwriting of the entire liabilities of the GSEs is now measured in hundreds of billions of dollars.

1.5.3   Local Government and Municipalities

In the UK, local government accounts for about 25% of UK public spending. A large proportion of this is funded through the central government block grant, allocated on the basis of a complex formula which determines each authority's grant-related expenditure (GRE) level.

Local authority bonds in the UK were once used to build the civic infrastructure and utilities, and they were a common source of public finance until the 1980s, when the central government began the era of constraining local financial independence and increasing centralised economic control.

Recently, there have been some developments suggesting that local authorities may be seeking to issue further bonds in the future. An important precedent was set in 2006 whereby the Treasury authorised Transport for London (itself a local authority in legal terms) to issue, eventually, £600 million of bonds, as part of its borrowings to improve transport infrastructure. There was a good reaction from investors to the issue.

Many sub-sovereign, provincial, state and local authorities issue bonds. In the US, state and local government bonds are known as municipal bonds, and municipalities in the US issue these bonds to finance local borrowing. These bonds are often tax-efficient, particularly for investors who reside in that municipality.

US municipal bonds are usually guaranteed by a third party, known in the market as a monoline insurer, and the bonds' credit quality may be enhanced by this guarantee, enabling the municipality to secure funds on more advantageous terms. This relies on the monoline insurers having a strong credit rating and some of the well-known monoline insurers in the US extended their activities to provide a range of far riskier guarantees for asset-backed securities, which has resulted in them losing their own investment grade ratings.

2. Corporate Debt

Learning Objective

2.3.1 Understand the main investment characteristics, behaviours and risks of corporate debt: financial institutions and special purpose vehicles; fixed and floating charges; debentures; types of asset-backed securities; mortgage-backed securities; securitisation process; roles of participants

2.1 Secured Debt

Corporate debt is simply money that is borrowed by a company that has to be repaid. Generally, corporate debt also requires servicing by making regular interest payments. Corporate debt can be subdivided into money borrowed from banks via loans and overdrafts, and directly from investors in the form of IOU instruments, typically debentures or, as they are more commonly known, bonds.

Debt finance can be less expensive than equity finance, ie, issuing shares, because investing in debt finance is less risky than investing in the equity of the same company. The interest on debt has to be paid before dividends, so there is more certainty to the investor in corporate debt rather than corporate equity. Additionally, if the firm were to go into liquidation, the holders of debt finance are paid back before the shareholders receive anything.

However, raising money via debt finance does present dangers to the issuing company. The lenders are often able to claim some or all of the assets of the firm in the event of non-compliance with the terms of the loan. For instance, a bank providing mortgage finance is technically able to seize property assets of a firm if there is any default, and not necessarily an outright bankruptcy of the company. For a corporation the power to borrow needs to be laid out in the Articles of Association, and the decision about taking on new debts is taken by the board of directors and may have to be agreed at an **annual general meeting (AGM)** of the company's shareholders.

2.1.1 Financial Institutions and Special Purpose Vehicles (SPVs)

Like other companies or corporates, financial institutions issue bonds to finance borrowing. These financial institutions also arrange borrowing for themselves and others by creating **special purpose vehicles (SPVs)** to enable money to be raised that does not appear within the accounts of that entity. This type of finance is often described as off-balance sheet finance, because it does not appear in the statement of financial position/balance sheet that forms part of a company's accounts.

2.1.2 Fixed and Floating Charges

When a company is seeking to raise new funds by way of a bond issue, it will often have to offer security to provide the investor with some guarantee for the repayment of the bond. In this context, security usually means some form of charge over the issuer's assets (eg, its property or trade assets) so that if the issuer defaults, the bondholders have a claim on those assets before other creditors (and so can regard their borrowings as safer than if there were no security).

In some cases, the security takes the form of a third-party guarantee – for example, a guarantee by a bank that, if the issuer defaults, the bank will repay the bondholders. The greater the security offered, the lower the cost of borrowing should be.

Domestic corporate bonds are usually secured on the company's assets by way of a fixed or a floating charge. A fixed charge is a legal charge, or mortgage, specifically placed upon one or a number of the company's fixed, or permanent, assets. A floating charge, however, places a more general charge on those assets that continually flow through the business and whose composition is constantly changing, such as the issuing company's stock-in-trade.

It is important to note that, unlike with a fixed charge, a company may not be inhibited from disposing of any specific assets if its borrowing is only subject to a floating charge. The floating charge may simply cover whatever the company has in its possession at any time and, unless itemised in an addendum to a floating charge, no sale or disposition is excluded.

In liquidations, fixed charges have priority over floating charges.

Fixed and floating charges need to be registered, and this is usually done through a debenture trustee.

2.1.3   Debentures

In relation to UK securities, a debenture is a long-term debt instrument issued by a corporation, which is backed by specific collateral or assets of the borrower. This collateral may be in the form of a fixed charge over a particular asset, such as machinery, or based on a floating charge, where the assets are not individually specified but cover the other assets which are not subject to a fixed charge. Somewhat surprisingly, the convention in the US is more or less the converse, as a debenture is not secured but traditionally backed by those assets which have not been pledged otherwise. While it may be considered in a certain sense as unsecured debt, it does come with the non-specific backing of the creditworthiness and reputation of the debenture issuer.

In both the US and the UK, debentures are usually issued by large, financially strong companies with excellent bond ratings. The debenture is documented by an agreement called an indenture.

The holder of a debenture issue in the UK has an advantage in the case of liquidation because particular assets of the company have been identified as collateral for the debt instrument. Debentures are thus a debt instrument which provide greater security to the lender than holding an unsecured bond or loan.

2.1.4   Asset-Backed Securities (ABSs)

ABSs are bonds that are backed by a particular pool of assets. These assets can take several forms, such as mortgage loans, credit card receivables or car loans. ABSs have been used in the financing of entertainment properties, such as on the future royalties from music-publishing interests.

The assets provide the bondholders' security, since the cash generated from them is used to service the bonds (pay the interest), and to repay the principal sum at maturity. Such arrangements are often referred to as the securitisation of assets.

Securitisation reflects the fact that the resulting financial instruments used to obtain funds from the investors are considered, from a legal and trading point of view, as securities.

Diagrammatically:

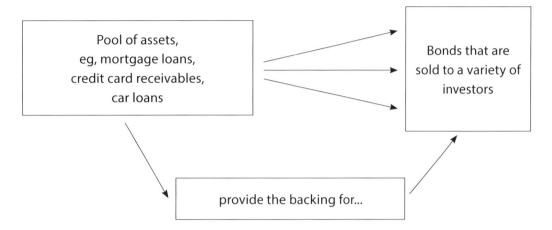

Mortgage-backed securities (MBSs) are one example of ABSs. They are created from mortgage loans made by financial institutions like banks and building societies. MBSs are bonds that are created when a group of mortgage loans are packaged (or pooled) for sale to investors. As the underlying mortgage loans are paid off by the homeowners, the investors receive payments of interest and principal.

The MBS market began in the US, where the majority of issues are made by (or guaranteed by) an agency of the US government. The Government National Mortgage Association (commonly referred to as Ginnie Mae), the Federal National Mortgage Association (Fannie Mae) and the Federal Home Loan Mortgage Corporation (Freddie Mac) are the major issuers. These agencies buy qualifying mortgage loans, or guarantee pools of such loans originated by financial institutions, securitise the loans and issue bonds. Some private institutions, such as financial institutions and house builders, issue their own mortgage-backed securities.

MBS issues are often sub-divided into a variety of classes (or tranches), each tranche having a particular priority in relation to interest and principal payments. Typically, as the underlying payments on the mortgage loans are collected, the interest on all tranches of the bonds is paid first. As loans are repaid, the principal is paid back to the first tranche of bondholders, then the second tranche, third tranche and so on. Such arrangements will create different risk profiles and repayment schedules for each tranche, enabling the appropriate securities to be held according to the needs of the investor. Traditionally, the investors in such securities have been institutional investors, such as insurance companies and pension funds, although some now attract the more sophisticated individual investor.

Investors in ABSs have recourse to the pool of assets, although there may be an order of priority between investors in different tranches of the issue. The precise payment dates for interest and principal will be dependent on the anticipated and actual payment stream generated by the underlying assets and the needs of investors. ABSs based on a pool of mortgage loans are likely to be longer-dated than those based on a pool of credit card receivables. Within these constraints, the issuers of ABSs do create a variety of tranches to appeal to the differing maturity and risk appetites of investors.

Many ABSs utilise an SPV in order to lessen the default risk investors face when investing in the securities. This SPV is often a trust; the originator of the assets, such as the bank granting the mortgage loans, sells the loans to the SPV and the SPV issues the asset-backed bonds. This serves two purposes:

1. The SPV is a separate entity from the originator of the assets, so the assets leave the originator's financial statements, to be replaced by the cash from the SPV. As already mentioned, this is often described as an off-balance-sheet arrangement, because the assets have left the originator's balance sheet.
2. The SPV is a stand-alone entity, so if the originator of the assets suffers bankruptcy the SPV remains intact, with the pool of assets available to service the bonds. This is often described as bankruptcy remote and enhances the creditworthiness of ABSs, potentially giving them a higher rating than the originator of the assets.

Diagrammatically:

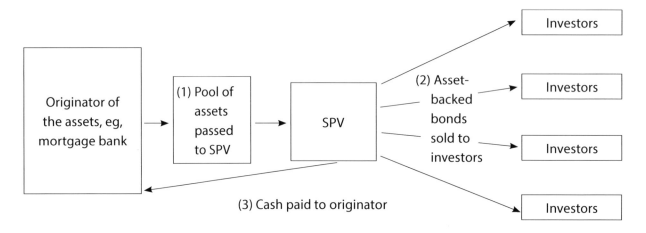

The Securitisation Process

A significant advantage of ABSs is that they bring together a pool of financial assets that otherwise could not easily be traded in their existing form. By pooling together a large portfolio of these illiquid assets, they can be converted into instruments that may be offered and sold freely in the capital markets.

For securitisation issues, the complex nature of the instruments means that the credit rating agencies consider the following:

*   The credit quality of the securitised assets, focusing on the effect of worst case stress scenarios.
*   Legal and regulatory issues and, in particular, whether the securitised assets have been appropriately isolated from the bankruptcy or insolvency risk of any entities that participate in the transaction.
*   Payment structures and how cash flows from the securitised assets are dealt with.
*   Operational and administrative risks associated with the company responsible for managing the securitised assets.
*   Counterparty risk arising from the ability of third parties to meet obligations, such as financial guarantees, bank liquidity or credit support facilities, letters of credit, and interest rate and currency swaps.

2.1.5 Roles of Participants

The principal participants with regard to corporate debt are the issuer, the underwriter who is responsible for issuing bonds into the primary market, the debenture trustee and brokers/dealers who are involved in maintaining and making a secondary market for the bonds issued. Bonds can trade on traditional exchanges, such as the LSE, but also on numerous decentralised electronic networks of dealers and bond-trading platforms, a number of which are global in their coverage.

2.2 Unsecured Debt

Learning Objective

2.3.2   Understand the main investment characteristics, behaviours and risks of the main types of unsecured debt: income bonds; subordinated; high yield; convertible bonds; contingent convertible bonds

2.2.1 Income Bonds

Income bonds are the most junior of all bonds. Their payments are made only after the issuer earns a certain amount of income. The issuer is not bound to make interest payments on a timely or regular basis if the minimum income amount is not earned. The investor is aware of the risks involved and may be willing to invest in these bonds if there is an attractive coupon rate or high GRY.

2.2.2 Subordinated Debt

Subordinated debt is not secured and the lenders have agreed that, if the company fails, they will only be reimbursed when other creditors have been paid back, and then only if there is enough money left over. Interest payments on subordinated borrowings will be higher than those on equivalent unsecured borrowings that are not subordinated, because of the additional default risk faced by subordinated lenders.

It should be noted that all three of the main categories of debt – senior, subordinated and junior – can themselves contain sub-categories, such as senior secured, senior unsecured, senior subordinated and junior subordinated. In practice, the credit rating agencies (CRAs) look at debt structures in these narrower terms. Seniority can be contractual as the result of the terms of the issue, or based on the corporate structure of the issuer.

2.2.3 Subordinated Loan Stock

This is a loan stock issued by a company that ranks above its **preference shares** but below its unsecured creditors in the event of the company's liquidation.

2.2.4 Permanent Interest-Bearing Securities (PIBSs)

- PIBSs are irredeemable fixed-interest securities issued by mutual building societies.
- PIBSs pay relatively high semi-annual coupons and potentially offer attractive returns. Interest is paid gross, which means that PIBSs are attractive to zero-rate taxpayers and those who have some means of sheltering the gross payment. However, this income is non-cumulative and PIBS holders rank behind all other creditors in the event of liquidation.
- When the building society has demutualised, its PIBSs are reclassified as perpetual subordinated bonds (PSBs). Both PIBSs and PSBs can be traded on the LSE.
- The liquidity of PIBS is generally not considered to be high and they tend to have a wide bid-offer spread.

2.2.5 High-Yield Bonds

Customarily participants in the markets regard all debt that does not have an investment grade, according to the above table, as speculative, and sometimes refer to this as junk debt. Bonds with a grade below BBB–, using S&P's rating system, are also typically known as high-yield bonds, as they will require issuers to provide a high coupon to the bond in order to compensate investors for the higher credit risk associated with the inferior credit rating.

In the 1980s, Michael Milken was a pioneer of the use of junk bonds as a way of financing new companies or companies which had a track record of credit problems. Although his demise from the world of finance was linked to an abusive mode of operation with high-yielding debt, which also added some stigma to the term junk, there is no inherent obstacle to capital markets issuing and raising money by using high-yielding debt instruments. The market should know how to price in the additional risk of the issue including the amount of the coupon.

Bonds known as 'fallen angels' have seen their former investment-grade rating reduced to junk bond status. Following this, they may issue high-yield debt which may become appealing if the long-term outlook of the business is strong or if the net assets of the business or cash flow easily outweigh the debt servicing cost or borrowings outstanding.

2.2.6 Convertible Bonds

Typically, a **convertible bond** will pay a lower coupon, as this is compensated for by an option to convert into the equity of the issuer at the conversion date. Convertibles are often subordinated, meaning that all senior creditors must be settled in full before any payment can be made to holders in the event of insolvency.

Convertible bonds are often deployed as a form of deferred share. Issuers expect them to be converted into equity at the conversion date. Convertibles have some of the characteristics of bonds, responding to changes in interest rates, and some of the characteristics of shares, responding to share price movements of the company issuing the convertible.

By convention, the right is normally to convert the debt into the ordinary shares of the company in a given conversion ratio – for example, £100 nominal is converted into 30 shares (a conversion ratio of 30). The conversion right may exist for a period of time during the bond's life (the conversion window), or may only be available on maturity.

2.2.7 Contingent Convertible Bonds (CoCos)

Contingent convertible bonds (also known as CoCos) are very similar to traditional convertible bonds. The key difference is that a price is set, which the underlying equity share price must reach before conversion can take place (ie, conversion is contingent on the ordinary shares attaining a certain market price over a specified period of time).

They are also quite useful to the banking industry, where CoCos can be issued whereby conversion happens when an uplift in the percentage of capital is required in order for the bank to remain solvent. Thus, conversion into shares is automatic if the specified capital ratio is likely to be breached.

3. Eurobonds

Learning Objective

2.4.1 Understand the main investment characteristics, behaviours and risks of eurobonds: types of issuer: sovereign, supranational and corporate; types of eurobond: straight, FRN/VRN, subordinated, asset-backed, convertible; international bank syndicate issuance; immobilisation in depositories; continuous pure bearer instrument: implications for interest and capital repayment; accrued interest, ex-interest date

Essentially, **eurobonds** are international bond issues. They are a way for an organisation to issue debt without being restricted to its own domestic market. They are usually issued by a syndicate of international banks.

Generally, eurobonds are in bearer form. The bearer has all the rights attached to ownership.

Eurobonds are issued internationally, outside any particular jurisdiction, and as such they are largely free of national regulation. For example, a US dollar eurobond can be issued anywhere in the world, outside the US. Eurobonds are usually administered by a custodian who is responsible for arranging interest payments and the repayment of principal at the bond's maturity. Eurobond interest is usually paid gross of withholding tax.

3.1 Types of Eurobonds

Most eurobonds are bought by major institutions looking for a sound long-term investment delivering a fixed rate of return. Eurobond prices in the secondary market tend to be less sensitive than a company's shares to changes in its commercial performance or business prospects. Instead, eurobond prices are more sensitive to wider economic shifts, such as changes in interest rates and currency fluctuations.

A London listing of a eurobond consists of admission to listing by the FCA – and admission to trading on a recognised investment exchange (RIE) such as the LSE.

Typically, eurobonds pay coupons gross and usually annually.

The **investment banks** that originate eurobond issues have been innovative in their structure to accommodate the needs of issuers and investors. Accordingly, there are many different flavours for eurobonds. The basic forms are:

- straight or bullet bonds
- floating rate notes/variable rate notes
- subordinated
- asset-backed, and
- convertible.

Straight, fixed-coupon eurobonds or bullet bonds normally pay the coupons once a year. Additionally, there are some straight zero coupon eurobonds.

Floating rate eurobonds (variable rate) are bonds where the coupon rate varies. The rate is adjusted in line with published market interest rates. The published interest rates that are normally used are based on LIBOR or Euribor. The LIBOR is the average rate at which banks in London offer loans to other banks. The Euribor is the average interest rate at which a panel of more than 50 European banks borrow funds from one another. Both LIBOR and Euribor rates are published for various maturities of up to one year.

Typically for an FRN, a margin is added to the reference rate, measured in basis points, each basis point representing one hundredth of 1%. A eurobond issuer may offer floating rate bonds to investors at three-month sterling LIBOR plus 75 basis points. If LIBOR is at 4%, then the coupon paid will be 4.75%, with the additional 75 basis points compensating the investor for the higher risk of payment default.

- **Subordinated eurobonds** – have a junior or inferior status within the capital structure hierarchy and have greater risk than a senior or secured note.
- **Asset-backed eurobonds** – where a specific asset or item of collateral has been pledged by the issuer as security for the bond.
- **Convertible eurobond issues** – where the issuer has granted certain rights to the holder to convert the bond into equity of the issuer according to the terms of the offering prospectus.

As far as the FCA is concerned, issuers of convertible bonds and bonds with equity warrants must also include more detailed disclosures in order to gain admission to trading on the LSE. The additional disclosures include the following:

- Profit and loss accounts, statements of financial position and cash flow statements for the last three years and, where appropriate, an interim statement.
- Information on the shares into which the bonds are convertible.
- Information on the issuer's directors, including their aggregate remuneration and their total interest in the issuer's shares.

3.2   Immobilisation

As bearer documents, it is important that eurobonds are kept safe. This is often achieved by holding the bonds in depositories, particularly those maintained by Euroclear and Clearstream. Eurobonds which are deposited at the clearing house are described as being immobilised. Immobilised means that the bonds are safely held with a reputable depository and a buyer is likely to retain the bonds in their immobilised form. As the eurobond market has grown, a self-regulatory organisation was been formed to oversee the market and its participants – the International Capital Market Association (ICMA).

Settlement and accrued interest conventions have been established for the secondary market. Settlement is on a **T+2** basis and, historically, accrued interest has been calculated on the basis of 30 days per month and 360 days per year (30/360 basis). However, more recently issued eurobonds that are in currencies other than the US dollar tend to use the actual/actual day count convention.

3.3   Dealing and Settlement

There is no formal marketplace for eurobond trading, although several exchanges can provide a **listing** for major issues. The market is electronic, with telephone contact between the main investment houses primarily based in London. The market is regulated by ICMA, which operates rules regulating the conduct of these dealers.

Settlement is carried out by two independent clearing houses, Euroclear and Clearstream. Remember that the important feature about the registers maintained by these two clearing houses is that they are not normally available to any governmental authority, thereby preserving the bearer nature of the documents. The methods of eurobond issuance are similar to those of corporate bond issues in the domestic markets. A disposal of a eurobond is usually assessed for capital gains tax (CGT) in the same way as other CGT-eligible financial instruments.

3.4   Interest Payments on Eurobonds

Eurobonds usually pay interest gross. The buyer is responsible for paying any tax due.

3.5   Accrued Interest on Eurobonds

Accrued interest is the portion of coupon interest applicable to a bond, should it be traded between two coupon dates. Accrued interest is either cum interest or ex-interest. The terms ex-dividend and ex-coupon are often used and have the same meaning in respect of bonds.

'Cum interest' means 'with interest' and is the portion of accrued interest between settlement date and the last coupon date. It is payable by an investor to the previous investor as the new investor is obviously not entitled to the full coupon, as they have not held it for the full period. 'Ex-interest' means 'without interest' and is the portion of coupon interest between settlement date and the next coupon date. It is payable by the previous investor to the new investor when bonds transacted are settled after the book closing date, but before coupon date. In this circumstance it is assumed that the new investor will have insufficient time to register the bond and therefore the previous investor receives the full coupon and pays the portion of interest due to the new owner of the bond.

4. Issuing Fixed-Income Securities

Learning Objective

2.5.1 Understand the responsibilities and processes of the UK Debt Management Office in relation to the management and issue of UK government debt: gilts; Treasury bills; primary market makers: gilt-edged market makers (GEMMs); intermediaries: inter-dealer brokers (IDBs)

4.1 The UK Debt Management Office (DMO)

4.1.1 Participants in the Government Bond Markets

In addition to the government's issuing agency, the **Debt Management Office (DMO)** itself, there are three major groups of participants that facilitate deals in the government bond markets:

- Primary dealers – such as gilt-edged market makers (GEMMs).
- **Broker-dealers.**
- Inter-dealer brokers.

4.1.2 The Issuing Agency – the Role of the DMO

The DMO is the issuing agency for the UK government. It is an executive agency of the Treasury, making new issues of UK government securities (gilt-edged securities or gilts). Once issued, the secondary market for dealing in gilts is overseen by two bodies, the DMO and the LSE. The main responsibility of the DMO is to ensure that the government is able to borrow the money it requires to fund the public sector net cash requirement (PSNCR). Issues by the DMO may be for a new gilt with a coupon/maturity dissimilar to any existing issues.

Currently, the DMO believes that the range of issues in the market is, if anything, too large and may lead to excessive fragmentation of supply and demand. In order to avoid this problem, the DMO may issue a tranche of an existing stock. This entails issuing a given amount of nominal value on exactly similar terms to an existing gilt.

The DMO refers to this as opening up an existing gilt. The advantages of tranches are that they avoid adding further complexity to the gilts market and increase the liquidity of current issues. When a tranche is issued, it may be identified by the letter A in order to indicate that, when the tranche is issued, a full coupon may not be paid on the next payment date, to reflect the fact that the gilt has only been an issue for part of the coupon period. A small tranche may be referred to as a tranchette.

The DMO is the body that enables certain LSE member firms to act as primary dealers, known as GEMMs. It then leaves it to the LSE to prescribe rules that apply when dealing takes place.

4.1.3   Primary Issuance: Auctions and Tenders

The DMO can use a variety of methods for gilt issuance. The most commonly used is the auction method, when the DMO announces the auction, receives bids and allocates the gilts to those that bid highest, at the price they bid. GEMMs are expected to bid for gilts when the DMO makes a new issue, and the DMO reserves the right to take the gilts onto its own books if the auction is not fully taken up.

A tender is an alternative method to an auction and is best explained using the following examples.

Example: Auction

The DMO auctions the proposed issuance on the basis of the bids received. The GEMMs place bids for the gilt and the successful bidders pay the price at which they bid.

Let us suppose the auction is for £1 million nominal. The bids from the GEMMs are as follows:

- A offers to buy £0.5 million nominal and is willing to pay £101.50 for every £100 nominal.
- B offers to buy £0.5 million nominal and is willing to pay £100.75 for every £100 nominal.
- C offers to buy £0.5 million nominal and is willing to pay £100.50 for every £100 nominal.

The auction results in A and B being awarded the gilts for the prices that they bid and, since the whole issuance has been bought by A and B, there is nothing left for C.

Example: Tender

Let us suppose the DMO tender process is for £1 million nominal and the DMO has set a minimum price of £100 for each £100 nominal. The bids from the GEMMs are exactly as before:

- A offers to buy £0.5 million nominal and is willing to pay £101.50 for every £100 nominal.
- B offers to buy £0.5 million nominal and is willing to pay £100.75 for every £100 nominal.
- C offers to buy £0.5 million nominal and is willing to pay £100.50 for every £100 nominal.

In this instance, A and B are awarded the gilts, but both pay the lower price of £100.75, which is effectively the highest price at which all the gilts can be sold. The C bid, as before, fails to get any fill as the price offered is below the price at which £1 million can be cleared.

One of the metrics which is used to judge the success of a government auction is the bid-to-cover ratio, which is used to express the demand for a particular security during offerings and auctions. It is computed in two ways: either the number of bids received is divided by the number of bids accepted; or the total amount of the bids is used instead. It is a metric which is especially followed by financial analysts in the sale of US Treasury bonds and is becoming more of a focus in the DMO's auctions as well.

In general terms, the simple point that needs to be made is that the higher the bid-to-cover ratio in an auction, the higher the demand. A ratio above 2.0 indicates a successful auction comprised of aggressive bids. A low ratio is an indication of a disappointing auction, often marked by a wide spread in the yields bid.

Example

Consider the following scenario where the DMO is seeking to raise £10 billion in ten-year notes with a 4.125% coupon. In order to keep the example simple, the aggregate number of bids received (which would have been expressed in price terms) will have equated to the following yields shown below:

· £4.00 billion at 4.115%.
· £4.50 billion at 4.120%.
· £3.50 billion at 4.125%.
· £3.75 billion at 4.135%.
· £3.75 billion at 4.140%.

The total of all bids is £19.5 billion and the number of bids placed, where the prices provided by bidders will have equated to a yield at least equivalent to the required coupon value, is in excess of the £10 billion on offer. In such a scenario, the bid-to-cover ratio can be stated as 1.95 which is a satisfactory auction result.

Either new issues or tranches of existing stock can be sold by way of an auction. Running alongside each competitive auction are non-competitive bids, when investors can apply for up to £500,000 of nominal value. Applicants through non-competitive bids will receive the gilts they applied for, at a weighted average of accepted prices in the auction. This enables smaller investors to participate in the primary market for gilts, while avoiding the necessity of determining an appropriate price.

4.1.4 Treasury Bill Issuance

Alongside gilts, sterling **Treasury bills** form an important constituent in the DMO's exchequer cash management operations and an intrinsic component in the UK government's stock of marketable debt instruments. Treasury bills are zero coupon eligible debt securities and the DMO financing remit from the government includes a target end-year Treasury bill total.

Treasury bills are routinely issued at weekly tenders, held by the DMO on the last business day of each week (ie, usually on Fridays), for settlement on the following business day. Treasury bills can be issued with maturities of one month (approximately 28 days), three months (approximately 91 days), six months (approximately 182 days) or 12 months (up to 364 days), although to date no 12-month tenders have been held. Members of the public wishing to purchase Treasury bills at the tenders will have to do so through one of the Treasury bill primary participants and purchase a minimum of £500,000 nominal of bills.

As of June 2021, the following banks act as Treasury bill primary participants:

· Banco Santander SA, London Branch.
· Bank of America Merrill Lynch International.
· Barclays Bank plc.
· BNP Paribas.
· Citigroup Global Markets ltd.
· Credit Agricole Corporate & Investment Bank.
· Credit Suisse Securities (Europe) ltd.
· Danske Bank A/S, London Branch.

- Deutsche Bank, London Branch.
- Goldman Sachs International.
- HSBC Bank London.
- Investec Bank plc.
- Jefferies International ltd.
- JP Morgan Securities plc.
- King and Shaxson ltd.
- Lloyds Bank Corporate Markets plc.
- Mitsubishi UFJ Securities International plc.
- Morgan Stanley & Co International ltd London.
- NatWest Markets plc.
- Nomura International.
- Royal Bank of Canada.
- Scotiabank.
- The Toronto Dominion Bank (London Branch).
- UBS AG (London Branch).

Source: UK Debt Management Office

In addition to primary participants, direct bidding by telephone in Treasury bill tenders is open to the following other eligible participants:

- DMO cash management counterparties – who can bid on existing direct dealing lines.
- A limited range of wholesale market participants who have established a relationship with the DMO.

The operational format of Treasury bill tenders is as follows:

- All bids must be received by 11.00am (London time) on the day of the tender.
- All bids must be made (on a money market yield basis) to three decimal places.
- Bids at tenders must be for a minimum of £500,000 nominal of bills.
- The minimum issuance denomination of Treasury bills will be £25,000.

TreasuryDirect, an internet-based platform, is also available through which individuals can buy and hold all of Treasury's marketable issues available to the general public, as well as savings bonds. TreasuryDirect does not offer savings bonds or the four-week bill, seven-year note, 30-year Treasury inflation-protected securities (TIPS) or 30-year bond.

4.1.5 Interim Funding or Taps

The government's current principal method of funding is through regular competitive auctions. However, the government may still wish to issue smaller quantities of stock to improve liquidity or improve market efficiency. In such situations, the DMO will sell smaller quantities of stock to investors via the GEMMs.

When tapping stock into secondary markets in this way, it will often be a tranche of existing stock, or a tranchette if a relatively small amount. Alternatively, it could be as a result of a failed auction when the DMO has not received sufficient applications to account for the nominal value on offer. In such a situation, the remaining stock will be available 'on tap' from the DMO.

4.1.6 Gilt-Edged Market Makers (GEMMs)

The GEMM, once vetted by the DMO and registered as a GEMM with the LSE, becomes a primary dealer and is required to provide two-way quotes to customers (clients known directly to them) and other member firms of the LSE throughout the normal trading day. There is no requirement to use a particular system like those run by the LSE for making those quotes available to clients, and GEMMs are free to choose how to disseminate their prices.

The obligations of a GEMM can be summarised as follows:

- To make effective **two-way prices** to customers on demand, up to a size agreed with the DMO, thereby providing liquidity for customers wishing to trade.
- To participate actively in the DMO's gilt issuance programme, broadly by bidding competitively in all auctions and achieving allocations commensurate with their secondary market share – effectively informally agreeing to underwrite gilt auctions.
- To provide information to the DMO on closing prices, market conditions and the GEMM's positions and turnover.

The privileges of GEMM status include:

- exclusive rights to competitive telephone bidding at gilt auctions and other DMO operations, either for the GEMM's own account or on behalf of clients
- an exclusive facility to trade as a counterparty of the DMO in any of its secondary market operations, and
- exclusive access to gilt inter-dealer broker (IDB) screens.

A firm can register as a GEMM to provide quotes in either:

- all gilt-edged securities, or
- gilt-edged securities excluding index-linked gilts, or
- index-linked gilts only.

There are exceptions to the requirement to provide quotes to customers, including the members of the LSE. The obligation does not include quoting to other GEMMs, fixed-interest market makers or gilt inter-dealer brokers.

As of June 2021, the following are registered as GEMMs:

- Banco Santander SA, London Branch.
- Barclays Bank plc†.
- BNP Paribas (London Branch).
- Citigroup Global Markets ltd.
- Deutsche Bank AG (London Branch).
- Goldman Sachs International.
- HSBC Bank PLC†.
- Jefferies International ltd*.
- JP Morgan Securities plc.
- Lloyds Bank Corporate Markets plc.
- Merrill Lynch International.

- Morgan Stanley & Co. International plc.
- NatWest Markets plc†.
- Nomura International plc.
- Royal Bank of Canada Europe ltd.
- The Toronto-Dominion Bank (London Branch)*.
- UBS AG (London Branch).
- Winterflood Securities ltd†*.

† STRIPS market participant

* Retail GEMM

Source: UK Debt Management Office

4.1.7 Broker-Dealers

These are non-GEMM LSE member firms that are able to buy or sell gilts as principal (dealer) or as agent (broker). When acting as a broker, the broker-dealer will be bound by the LSE's best execution rule, ie, to get the best available price at the time.

When seeking a quote from a GEMM, the broker-dealer must identify at the outset if the deal is a small one, defined as less than £1 million nominal.

4.1.8 Gilt Inter-Dealer Brokers

Gilt inter-dealer brokers arrange deals between gilt-edged market makers anonymously. They are not allowed to take principal positions, and the identity of the market makers using the service remains anonymous at all times. The IDB will act as agent, but settle the transaction as if it were the principal. The IDB is only allowed to act as a broker between GEMMs, and has to be a separate company and not a division of a broker-dealer.

4.1.9 Standing Repo Facility

The smooth running of the gilts market is further assisted by the DMO's standing repo facility. This enables any GEMM, or other DMO counterparty, to enter into a reverse repo arrangement with the DMO, perhaps to cover a short position in gilts. This facility is for next-day settlement, and the facility can be rolled forward for up to two weeks. The DMO does charge a slightly higher than normal repo rate for firms accessing the standing repo facility.

4.2 Bond Pricing Benchmarks

Learning Objective

2.5.2 Understand the main bond pricing benchmarks and how they are applied to new bond issues: spread over government bond benchmark; spread over/under inter-bank benchmarks; spread over/under swap

---

4.2.1 Spreads

Financial analysts and investment professionals pay close attention to spreads in the bond markets. A spread is simply the difference between the yield available on one instrument and the yield available elsewhere. It is usually expressed in basis points.

A basis point is equal to 0.01%, which means that a 100 basis point uplift or premium is equal to 1%.

Spreads are commonly expressed as spreads over government bonds. For example, if a ten-year corporate bond is yielding 6% and the equivalent ten-year gilt is yielding 4.2%, the spread over the government bond is 6% – 4.2% = 1.8% or 180 basis points. This spread will vary, mainly as a result of the relative risk of the corporate bond compared to the gilt, so for a riskier corporate issuer the spread will be greater.

4.2.2 Benchmarks

At times of financial stress, such as during the banking crisis in the autumn of 2008, the spread between LIBOR and the applicable base rates can widen dramatically, which in this instance reflected the incapacity or unwillingness of banks to engage in normal money market activities.

Spreads are tracked by many market data vendors including Bloomberg and Markit. Indeed, the latter company has played a pioneering role in creating numerous benchmarks and indices for the credit markets which enable all kinds of spreads to be calculated and compared.

The use of a particular pricing benchmark is generally determined by the type of debt asset class. Also, specific features of a bond can mean that pricing off a benchmark security/rate becomes more difficult. For example, a ten-year corporate bond with a put/call feature is unlikely to price off the ten-year gilt but rather a benchmark curve, as the estimate of the maturity of the corporate bond is unlikely to coincide with the specific maturity of the given gilt because of the put/call feature. (Pricing off simply means the price/value of one thing – here a bond – being determined from the price/value of something else – here another bond.)

4.2.3 Spread Over/Under Swap Rates

There is a very active market in exchanging floating rates for fixed rates in the so-called swaps market. Credit default swaps (CDSs), which are a form of insurance against the risk of borrowers defaulting on their debt, are some of the most actively traded instruments in the capital markets. The rates available on various swaps – both for corporate credits and also sovereign credits – are also used as benchmarks against which to benchmark the yield available on any specific security.

The swap spread is the difference between the ten-year Treasury and the swap rate, which is the fixed rate on a LIBOR-based interest rate swap. Under normal market conditions, the ten-year Treasury yield will be lower than the swap rate, reflecting the credit quality of the US government versus that of the participants in the interbank credit markets.

In general terms, the swap spread is defined as the difference between the swap rate and yield of (on-the-run) government bonds of equal maturity. On-the-run means the most recent issuance of a US Treasury bond or UK gilt.

4.2.4   Swap Spread Inversion

In the spring of 2010, a rare occurrence took place in the US markets, when the ten-year swap spread inverted. It was also reported by the *Financial Times* that, in the UK, the spread to gilts inverted in December of that year.

One explanation provided for this unusual inversion focuses on the concern over the magnitude of government borrowing. The reasoning provided is that pension funds, for example, are matching assets and liabilities synthetically – ie, receiving a fixed rate through a swap contract rather than by purchasing bonds. This could plausibly reflect concern over the supply deluge in government bonds and the effect this will have on yields.

4.3   Issuance of Fixed-Income Securities

Learning Objective

2.5.3   Understand the purpose, structure and process of the main methods of origination and issuance and their implications for issuers and investors: scheduled funding programmes and opportunistic issuance (eg, MTN); auction/tender; reverse inquiry (under MTN)

4.3.1   Scheduled Funding and Opportunistic Issuance

Traditionally, borrowing money via a bond issue was sensible only when large sums of money were being raised in a single capital-raising transaction. The sums had to be large enough to make the costs involved in issuance worthwhile. The details of the bond would be established, including its coupon and maturity, and the bonds would be marketed to potential investors. The investors would either be invited to bid for the bonds in an auction-type process, or a tender method was adopted (see section 4.1.3).

The rather rigorous requirements that were traditional in bond issuance, for example in the US, meant that it was awkward and expensive to regularly raise bond finance, because each bond issue had to be separately registered with the financial regulator – in the US, the Securities and Exchange Commission (SEC). Because many issuers, particularly companies, needed to borrow money regularly in line with the developments of their business, they tended to prefer to set up scheduled funding programmes with their banks under which they looked to borrow money, instead of issuing bonds.

However, a US innovation was introduced that has been subsequently adopted in many other jurisdictions which enables bond financing to be much more flexible. A process known as 'shelf registration' was introduced that enabled a single registration to be used for a number of bond issues over a period of up to two years. As detailed below, shelf registration has been heavily used in the medium-term note (MTN) market, for bonds with generally two to ten years between issue and maturity. Shelf registration introduced flexibility to the bond market, allowing companies to issue smaller batches of bonds with the coupons and maturity varying according to market demand at the time.

4.3.2   Medium-Term Notes (MTNs)

MTNs are a form of corporate debt financing. They originated in the 1970s in the US when auto finance companies, and especially General Motors Acceptance Corporation (GMAC), started issuing debt securities with maturities falling between those of commercial paper and corporate bonds. The goal was to achieve better asset-liability management (ALM) for their auto loan books. The debt securities required registration with the SEC just like corporate bonds. However, such registrations are expensive and time-consuming. As the auto finance companies wanted to make frequent small issuances to satisfy their evolving ALM needs, they needed a streamlined issuance process.

In 1982, the SEC adopted Rule 415, which launched today's MTN market. This allows issuers to continually offer MTNs to investors. The MTNs must be registered, but registration is required only once every two years. During those two years, the issuer is free to modify the MTNs' nominal yield or term, as the issuer's needs or market demand require. The process is called shelf registration, and it makes MTNs resemble commercial paper. Differences are that MTNs have longer terms, are registered with the SEC and are usually coupon-bearing instruments, as opposed to discount instruments.

4.3.3   Shelf Registration in the UK

The shelf registration system also exists in the UK. It allows an issuer listed on the Official List of the FCA to produce, on an annual basis, a document (shelf document) which contains most of the information required in listing particulars. The FCA publishes the shelf document on its website. If, during the next 12 months, the issuer wishes to issue and list further shares or debt securities, all that is necessary is the publication and circulation of a short document (issue note) containing the information required to complete the listing particulars and update the shelf document in respect of the issue in question. Similar systems operate in many other countries, for example the US, Canada, Japan, France, Spain and Belgium.

A shelf document can be produced at any time during the year, although there are likely to be considerable cost savings if an issuer does it in conjunction with the production of its annual report and accounts. The shelf document will remain current until the earliest of:

- the publication of the issuer's next audited annual report and accounts
- 12 months from the date the shelf document is published on the website (being the maximum period under European law)
- the date the shelf document is removed from the website at the written request of the issuer.

4.3.4   Characteristics of the MTN Market

An issuer will generally engage two or more dealers to offer the MTNs on a best efforts basis. Through those dealers, the issuer advertises a rate schedule indicating nominal yields available for various terms up to ten years. The issuer changes its rates depending on market conditions and its immediate need for funds. At times, it may temporarily suspend issuing notes. If an investor is interested in purchasing notes at the offered rates, it contacts one of the dealers, who arranges the transaction. Should an investor want to buy notes for a term or nominal yield not offered, it may place a request through one of the dealers. If the issuer finds the request appealing, it may accept the proposed terms. This process is called a reverse inquiry, and it accounts for a considerable fraction of MTN issuances.

Because MTNs entail credit risk, they are rated just like corporate bonds. The vast majority of issues are rated BBB– or better.

There is a secondary market for MTNs supported by issuing dealers. If a dealer buys notes held by an investor, the dealer may try to resell the notes or hold them in their own inventory.

Traditionally, MTNs were issued as senior unsecured debt securities paying a fixed coupon for terms of between 270 days and ten years. Today, MTNs are structured in many ways. Even the name 'medium-term note' has become a bit of a misnomer. The market is not defined by the instruments' terms so much as it is by shelf registration. Shelf-registered securities have been issued with terms of as much as 30 years, and they are called MTNs. There are floating rate MTNs. Some structures have coupons linked to equity or **commodity** indexes. Securitisations are also issued as MTNs. One appeal of the market is the flexibility it affords.

5. Fixed-Income Markets and Trade Execution

5.1 Government Bond Markets

Learning Objective

2.6.1   Understand the role, structure and characteristics of government bond markets in the developed markets of the USA, Germany, Japan and the UK, including: market environment: relative importance of exchange versus OTC trading versus organised trading facilities (OTFs); participants – primary dealers, broker dealers and inter-dealer brokers; access considerations; regulatory/supervisory environment

A government bond is one issued by a national government denominated in the country's own currency. As an example, in the US, Treasury securities are denominated in US dollars. The first-ever government bond was issued by the English government in 1693 to raise money to fund a war against France. Germany's federal government issues bonds known as *Bunds*. The word *Bund* in German is short for *Bundesanleihe*, meaning federal bond. The Government of Japan issues bonds commonly known as Japanese Government bonds (JGBs).

Government bonds are usually referred to as risk-free bonds because the government can raise taxes to redeem the bond at maturity. Some counter examples do exist when a government has defaulted on its domestic currency debt, such as Russia in 1998 (the rouble crisis), though this is relatively rare. In this instance, the term risk-free means free of credit risk. However, other risks still exist, such as currency risk for foreign investors. Secondly, there is inflation risk, in that the principal repaid at maturity will have less purchasing power than anticipated, if inflation turns out to be higher than expected. Many governments issue inflation-indexed bonds, which should protect investors against inflation risk.

The most common process of issuing corporate bonds is through underwriting. In underwriting, one or more securities firms or banks, forming a syndicate, buy an entire issue of bonds from an issuer and re-sell them to investors. The security firm takes the risk of being unable to sell on the issue to end investors. However, government bonds are instead typically auctioned. The way in which auctions are conducted by the UK's DMO was covered in section 4.1.3.

Most government bond trades take place between firms in the OTC market (off-exchange). With the introduction of the second Markets in Financial Instruments Directive (MiFID II) in January 2018, a new type of trading venue, known as an **organised trading facility (OTF)**, was introduced. An OTF is a multilateral system that is not a regulated market or a **multilateral trading facility (MTF)**. It allows multiple third-party buying and selling interests in bonds, structured finance products, emission allowances or derivatives to be traded; equities cannot be traded through an OTF. An OTF is an investment service of an authorised investment firm and, therefore, the operation of an OTF is a regulated activity that requires **authorisation**.

The Sovereign Debt Crisis

The financial crisis saw a widening of bond yield spreads and extreme sovereign bond price volatility, particularly in those countries who have received ECB/IMF bail outs. Also resulting from the crisis, was an unprecedented increase in gilt issuance levels by the UK's DMO. Programmes of quantitative easing (QE) have been introduced by many global central banks to attempt to stimulate national economies. This involves the central bank buying large amounts of financial assets from commercial banks and other private institutions in an attempt to improve money supply.

5.1.1   Conduct of US Treasury Auctions

To finance the public debt of the US, the US Treasury sells bills, notes, bonds, and Treasury Inflation Protected Securities (TIPS) to institutional and individual investors through public auctions. Treasury auctions occur regularly and have a set schedule; the current pattern involves more than 250 auctions taking place each year.

There are three steps to an auction: announcement of the auction; bidding (which is conducted through the Treasury's designated primary dealer network); and issuance of the purchased securities.

Auction Announcements

The auction announcement details are as follows:

- Amount of the security being offered.
- Auction date.
- Issue date.
- Maturity date.
- Terms and conditions of the offering.
- Non-competitive and competitive bidding close times.

Bidding in Auctions and the Role of Primary Dealers

The bidding process for auctions of US Treasury securities is dominated by the primary dealer network. As of June 2021, there were 24 large financial institutions, such as banks and several foreign investment banks, designated as primary dealers by the US Treasury. Primary dealers not only participate actively in the auction of US Treasury securities but are required to make bids or offers when the Fed conducts open market operations (see chapter 1, section 1.2). Between them, these primary dealers purchase the vast majority of the US Treasury securities sold at auction and resell them to other institutions, such as pension funds and the public.

When participating in an auction there are two bidding options – competitive and non-competitive.

- **Competitive bidding** – limited to 35% of the offering amount for each bidder, and a bidder specifies the rate or yield that is acceptable.
- **Non-competitive bidding** – limited to purchases of $5 million per auction. With a non-competitive bid, a bidder agrees to accept the rate or yield determined at auction. Bidding limits apply cumulatively to all methods that are used for bidding in a single auction.

At the close of an auction, the Treasury accepts all non-competitive bids that comply with the auction rules and then accepts competitive bids in ascending order in terms of their rate or yield until the quantity of accepted bids reaches the offering amount.

On issue day, the Treasury delivers securities to bidders who were successfully awarded them in a particular auction. In exchange, the Treasury charges the accounts of those bidders for payment of the securities.

5.1.2   The Regulatory Environment

The issuance of government bonds, the procedures and protocols for their auction and the conducting of trade in the secondary market are subject to the full force of regulators, as government bond markets must be seen to be transparent and not open to abuse.

There have been well-known cases when dealers have been suspended and fined with substantial penalties for engaging in abusive actions during the auction of government bonds. In the US in 1991, a trader with Salomon Brothers was caught submitting false bids to the US Treasury, in an attempt to purchase more Treasury bonds than permitted by one buyer, between December 1990 and May 1991. Salomon was fined $290 million, the largest fine ever levied on an investment bank at the time, weakening it and eventually leading to its acquisition by Travelers Group.

Other malpractices have occurred in other markets, and the actions taken by regulators are often harsh to discourage others from violating the strict procedures that need to be followed with the issue and trading of government bonds. China has moved to regulate bond market makers who have long provided unregulated critical services. Dealers can now apply for promotion to formal market-making status. By the end of 2014, it was reported that China's interbank market had outstanding bonds worth nearly 30 trillion yuan ($4.8 trillion). The move will see the exchange monitor and supervise quotations by market makers.

In June 2017, it was reported that the Chinese corporate bond market issuance had hit a low, with many bonds maturing. In addition, market circumstances had dissuaded new issuance. In 2018–19, more than $1 trillion of local bonds matured and it became increasingly expensive for companies to roll over their borrowings. In addition, yields on AAA-rated bonds have doubled and companies defaulted on 39.2 billion yuan ($5.8 billion) of domestic bonds in the first four months of 2019 which was 3.4 times the total for the same period in 2018.

Over the first four months of 2021, Chinese bond defaults rose by over 70% to USD 18 billion, mainly in the areas of real estate, aviation and electronics. 37% of these defaults were linked to the Chinese conglomerate – the HNA Group.

Despite this, Chinese corporate bond issuance increased in Q1 2021, with the trend continuing in April, indicating an improving investor sentiment.

5.1.3   Emerging Bond Markets

Learning Objective

2.6.2   Understand the differences between the developed markets and the emerging economies

Emerging market countries often have economies that are less diverse and mature than developed economies. Bonds in emerging markets are issued by the governments or corporations of the world's less-developed nations. Bonds from such countries are generally regarded as much higher risk. Some of the reasons for this are:

- greater likelihood of economic swings
- common political upheaval
- government interference
- taxation on foreign investment
- less liquidity
- less stable political systems, and
- greater market volatility.

On top of this, trading markets can be less efficient and emerging market bonds are often lower-rated and not as financially secure as those with higher credit ratings from more developed nations. These bonds tend to have higher yields in order to attract investment and are often regarded as highly speculative and considered a longer-term investment that is not suitable for those with an investment aim to preserve capital.

However, since the 1990s, emerging market debt has evolved from being a very volatile asset class to a much more mature segment of global markets.

Many emerging countries have enjoyed greater political stability and manageable levels of government debt. While many emerging market investors and **fund managers** will invest in such bonds, ETFs can also provide exposure to the emerging bond markets, both corporate and government.

Bonds of emerging markets can help to make a portfolio more diverse as price movements in bond markets in developed countries do not necessarily correlate to moves in emerging markets. Holdings in both sectors can produce very different investment returns.

A large number of emerging nations now issue debt. Of the countries issuing debt, among the most prominent are the following:

- **Europe** – Bulgaria, Hungary, Russia, Serbia and Ukraine.
- **Asia** – China, India, Indonesia, Malaysia, Philippines and Vietnam.
- **Latin America** – Argentina, Brazil, Chile, Colombia, Dominican Republic, El Salvador, Mexico, Panama, Peru, Uruguay and Venezuela.
- **Middle East/Africa** – Egypt, Ghana, Iraq, Ivory Coast, Lebanon, Morocco, South Africa and Turkey.

Historical Events

The emerging country bond market throughout modern day history has generally been a very small part of the overall global debt market. Primary issuance was quite a rare occurrence and generally small in size.

Despite the emergence of less developed bond markets as a key part of global financial markets, the fact is that they have been more prone to crises than developed markets. Examples of such crises are:

- **1994 economic crisis in Mexico** – caused by an unexpected and sudden devaluation of Mexico's currency, the Mexican peso.
- **1997 Asian financial crisis** – compounded by global fears of contagion across the world.
- **1998–2002 Argentine depression** – the economy shrank by 28%, the government fell and defaulted on its debt.
- **1998 Russian financial crisis** – caused by declining productivity and a high artificial exchange rate.
- **2011 euro sovereign debt crisis** – particularly affecting Portugal, Ireland, Greece and Spain and three Icelandic banks who defaulted. Greece was subsequently downgraded to an emerging market in 2013.

5.2   The Global Strips Market

Learning Objective

2.6.3   Understand the purpose and key features of the global strip market: result of stripping a bond; zero coupon securities; access considerations

5.2.1   Overview of Bond Stripping

Stripping a bond involves the separation of each of the cash flows arising from ownership of a bond during its lifetime. A bond will generate a coupon payment, most frequently on a semi-annual basis throughout its lifetime, and will also pay out the redemption amount of the bond on the final maturity date. The deconstruction of these individual payments can be considered as providing several new securities, each of which can be held and traded by investors.

The term 'stripping' arises from separate trading of registered interest and principal of securities (STRIPS). In effect, as suggested in the previous paragraph, stripping a bond involves trading the interest (each individual coupon) and the principal (the nominal value) separately. Each strip forms the equivalent of a ZCB. It will trade at a discount to its face value, with the size of the discount being determined by prevailing interest rates and time.

A STRIPS market has been developed in the UK within the gilts market. Only those gilts that have been designated by the DMO as strippable are eligible for the STRIPS market, not all gilts. Those gilts that are stripped have separate registered entries for each of the individual cash flows that enable different owners to hold each individual strip, and this facilitates the trading of the individual strips. Only GEMMs, the BoE and the Treasury are able to strip gilts.

The US Treasury market also has a well-developed STRIPS market, with a wide variety of bonds of different maturities with different coupons available for stripping. The secondary market for the zero coupon instruments resulting from the stripping process is very active.

As an example, a ten-year gilt can be stripped to make 21 separate securities: 20 strips based on the semi-annual coupons, which are entitled to one of the half-yearly interest payments; and one strip entitled to the redemption payment at the end of the ten years. This process of stripping enables different owners to hold each individual strip, with a view to achieving more precisely an investment objective than available by holding the original bond with all of the cash flows associated with it during its lifetime.

Let us consider a simpler example of a stripped bond and, as illustrated in the diagram, we shall consider a two-year gilt with a nominal or face value of £10 million and a coupon of 6%.

There will be four separate payments of £300,000 paid in coupons, and after two years, the £10 million will be redeemed. The cash flows can be considered independently as laid out in the following diagram.

80

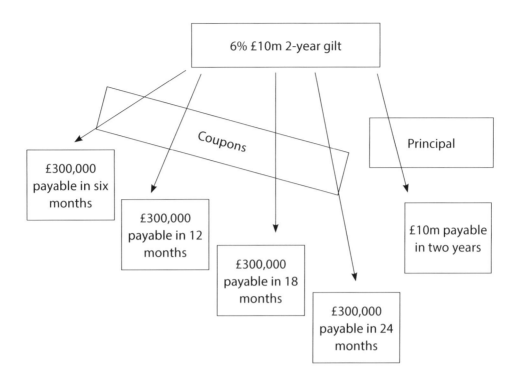

Assuming that the gilt shown above has been designated by the DMO as strippable, each of the individual cash flows generated can be registered separately with the DMO and traded independently of the other strips that result from the bond's decomposition. As in the US, the secondary STRIPS market also facilitates the trading of the individual strips.

5.2.2 Benefit of a Stripped Bond to Investors

The key benefit of STRIPS is that investors can precisely match their liabilities, removing any reinvestment risk that is normally faced when covering liabilities with coupon-paying bonds. The nature of the reinvestment risk arises because, in a volatile interest rate environment, the returns available at the time of receiving a coupon payment may not have the desired long-term yield-to-maturity characteristics required by an investor, such as a pension fund. Furthermore, investors in government bond STRIPS from countries like the US and the UK need not worry about the risk that the issuer of the bonds will default.

Example

An investor wants to fund the repayment of the principal on a £5 million mortgage, due to be paid in five years' time. Using gilts, there are three major choices:

1. The investor could buy a £5 million nominal coupon-paying gilt, but the coupons on this would mean that it would generate more than £5 million.

2. The investor could buy less than £5 million nominal, attempting to arrive at £5 million in five years. However, they will have to estimate how the coupons over the life of the bond could be reinvested and what rate of return they will provide. The investor's estimate could well be wrong.

3. The investor could buy a £5 million strip. This will precisely meet their needs.

5.2.3   Pricing a Zero Coupon Bond (ZCB)

As indicated, a stripped bond effectively can be considered as a series of separate zero coupon bonds (ZCBs). The table below shows how to value the final redemption payment for a five-year strip which pays out no coupons, as these have been stripped and sold separately. The required yield-to-maturity (YTM) in this case is 10% and this will require that the final ZCB consisting of the redemption amount will have to be discounted as shown in the table, using the semi-annual convention in the gilt market of discounting at 5% twice annually. The ZCB with a five-year term priced to realise a YTM of 10% will have to trade at £61.39.

Estimating Current Bond Price	Annual Coupon	0.00%	Desired Yield	10.00%
Semi-Annual Cash Flows	Cash Flow in £	Discount Factor	Discount Factor at Desired Yield	Present Value
0	£0.00	$[1/0.05] \times [1-(1/1.050^0)] = 20$	0.00	£0.00
10	£100.00	$[1/1.050^{10}] = 0.61$	0.61	£61.39
			Bond Price	£61.39

5.2.4   Minimum Units for Stripping and Reconstitution in the UK Gilts Market

For each strippable stock there will be a minimum amount below which the system will not accept a strip request. The need for this arises because nominal holdings of a gilt, whether of an unstripped bond or a strip, must be in multiples of one penny. This implies that, for example, at least £4 of a bond will need to be stripped if the annual interest payable is, say, 7½%, because each six-month coupon will be denominated in ¼ percentage points (in this case a coupon of 3¾%). In the same way, the minimum strippable amount of a 7¼% stock will need to be £8, and of a 7⅛% stock £16.

The system also needs minimum units for the strippability of stock in amounts above the minimum and for a minimum re-constitutable amount. For example, for a 7¼% gilt it will not be possible to reconstitute to, say, an amount of £500, as the necessary coupon strips will be £18.125p and, thus, not in whole pence.

Unless otherwise stated at the time of issue, the minimum strippable amount for a gilt is £10,000 nominal, which will be increased in multiples of £10,000 (ie, gilts will be strippable in amounts of £10,000, £20,000, £30,000 and so on). Similarly, the minimum reconstitutable amount of a strippable gilt will be £10,000 of the gilt being reconstituted, again unless otherwise stated at the time of issue.

5.3   Global Corporate Bond Markets

Learning Objective

2.6.4   Understand the role, structure and characteristics of global corporate bond markets: decentralised dealer markets and dealer provision of liquidity; relationship between bond and equity markets; bond pools of liquidity (including OTFs) versus centralised exchanges; access considerations; regulatory/supervisory environment

5.3.1   The Impact of Default Risk on Bond Prices

In the corporate bond market, unlike the government bond markets where it is assumed that most sovereign borrowers will not default, the determination of the likelihood that a corporate borrower may default is a vital part in the pricing mechanism for corporate bonds.

The price of a corporate bond will be influenced by the prices (and inversely the yields) on an equivalent government bond. However, the corporate bond's price will be subject to a discount to represent the risk that the corporate may default compared to the default risk-free nature of the government bond. Credit-rating agencies provide a rating system for corporate bonds. See sections 6.1 and 6.2.

5.3.2   The Relationship between Bond and Equity Markets

The primary difference between the corporate bond market and the equity market relates to the nature of the security being traded. A corporate bond usually has a specified income stream in the form of coupon payments, which will be paid to the holder of the bond, and a bondholder has a more senior claim against the assets of the issuer in the case of a bankruptcy or restructuring.

Investors in **equities** may receive a **dividend** payment from the corporation, but this is less certain and can fluctuate. Indeed, less mature companies may not even pay a dividend. The equity holder also has a greater risk that, if the corporation which has issued the shares becomes insolvent or undergoes a restructuring, there may be insufficient assets to be liquidated or reorganised and then distributed to shareholders. In such instances, shareholders may find that their equity stakes in a corporation have little or no residual value.

5.3.3   The Equity Risk Premium

The reason behind this premium stems from the risk-return trade-off, in which a higher rate of return is required to entice investors to take on riskier investments. As already explained, the risk-free rate in the market is often quoted as the rate on longer-term government bonds, which are considered risk free because of the low chance that the government will default on its loans. Investment grade bonds, ie, those rated BBB− and above by S&P and Fitch, and Baa3 for Moody's, are considered to be relatively low in risk and are of greater appeal to a conservative investor. On the other hand, an investment in stocks is far less guaranteed, as companies regularly suffer downturns or go out of business. If the return on a stock is 15% and the risk-free rate over the same period is 7%, the equity risk premium will be 8% for this stock over that period of time.

5.3.4 The Decentralised Dealer Market for Bonds

The primary function and role of market makers in corporate bonds is to provide liquidity to the marketplace and to act as a facilitator or agent in trades between the principals. Dealers are those that have been appointed by the corporate issuer to act as distributors on their behalf in the issuance and underwriting of bond issues. There is often a combination of such roles by large financial institutions.

Unlike the traditional centralised stock exchanges for dealing in equities, a decentralised dealer market structure is one that enables investors to buy and sell without a centralised location. In a decentralised market, the technical infrastructure provides traders and investors with access to various bid/ask prices and allows them to deal directly with other traders/dealers rather than through a central exchange.

The FX market is an example of a decentralised market because there is no single exchange or physical location where traders/investors have to conduct their buying and selling activities. Trades can be conducted via an interbank/dealer network that is geographically distributed. The trading in corporate bonds is also conducted through a decentralised dealer network that can provide pools of liquidity for the conduct of trade between buyers and sellers without the requirement of all trades to be cleared through an exchange.

As mentioned in section 5.1, MiFID II introduced OTFs. These allow multiple third-party buying and selling interests in non-equity instruments, including bonds, as a service of an already authorised investment firm. OTFs are subject to the same transparency requirements that apply to regulated markets and MTFs.

5.3.5 The Regulatory/Supervisory Environment

FCA Regulations

All authorised dealer firms, and all of the individuals employed within them in the UK, are subject to all of the rules and regulations of the FCA.

The supervisory approach of the UK regulator has changed dramatically as a result of the banking crisis of 2007–08. The risks of discipline and criminal prosecution resulting from violation of FCA regulations by somebody who is FCA-authorised, or is an approved person at an FCA-authorised firm, are greater now than previously.

The FCA now has a credible deterrence policy, which includes enforcing search warrants and carrying out arrests as appropriate, seeking custodial sentences and imposing larger fines. In 2019, the FCA imposed fines totalling over £392 million and over £192 million in 2020.

Furthermore, while the FCA (as the FSA) previously focused on firms, it is now concentrating on disciplinary action against individuals who are approved persons at authorised firms, and individuals who are fulfilling a role which requires FCA-approved person status. Approved persons include directors, senior management, compliance officers and those in customer-facing roles at an FCA-authorised firm. The regime has recently been extended to any person who exercises significant influence over the regulated firm whether in the UK or overseas, including those at a parent company who have decision-making power over the actions of the authorised firm.

It has also been extended to include proprietary traders who are likely to exert significant influence, on the basis that they can commit the regulated firm. Approved persons have a contract with the FCA, which has its own code of conduct and principles to follow. They can be disciplined by the FCA for breaches of these, with penalties including a public reprimand (which has associated reputation issues) and/or a fine, or a prohibition order, which prevents the individual from acting in the financial services sector.

LSE Regulations

In addition to the decentralised dealer network model, there is trading of bonds on the LSE. This trading is subject to the rules and regulations of the exchange.

The complete rules and conditions for listing securities in London are set out in the Listing Rules and in the Admission and Disclosure Standards. The Listing Rules are maintained by the FCA, whereas the Admission and Disclosure Standards are maintained by the LSE.

The FCA and the LSE have a statutory obligation to protect all investors on an ongoing basis and to maintain a fair and orderly market. To fulfil this obligation, the FCA requires all issuers of eurobonds listed in London to meet a number of continuing obligations.

Issuers of London-listed securities have the ongoing obligation to disclose to the investor community any information deemed to be price-sensitive, which must be disseminated to the market via a regulatory information service such as the LSE's Regulatory News Services (RNS).

International Capital Market Association (ICMA)

Most new eurobond issues are placed by an international securities house, appointed by the issuer to act as the lead manager to the issue. This lead manager will then form a syndicate of other securities houses through which the bonds will be marketed and sold to their respective clients.

Once issued, trading takes place OTC between ICMA dealers, rather than being conducted on a physical exchange. ICMA dealers will, upon request, quote a two-way price for a specific transaction in a particular issue, although, as most issues tend to be held until maturity, the secondary market is relatively illiquid.

5.4   Bond Pricing and Yield Quotations

Learning Objective

2.6.5   Understand the different quotation methods and the circumstances in which they are used: yield; spread; price

There are two major elements of a quote for a bond: the price and, as a result of the price, the yield. Most investment managers will be looking for bonds with particular yields and maturity dates, and by using the relatively simple mathematics which underlies bond pricing (at least for relatively simple bond issues) it is possible to determine with precision how much a bond which meets their requirement should be priced at and at what price it should be trading in the secondary market.

5.4.1 Spreads

When dealing in corporate bonds, or across different bond markets (such as different countries' government bonds), traders and researchers will also be looking at the yield spreads that are available and anticipating changes in those spreads.

Many different factors, including global credit market liquidity, macroeconomic factors within the world economy and their influence on capital markets as well as issuer-specific considerations, will be taken into account in the pricing of bonds. The use of spreads to other issues will play a major part in such pricing (see section 4.2), along with judgements about credit quality and the future course of inflation, as well as monetary policy and the direction of interest rates. Also relevant is the term structure of interest rates, which is often called the **yield curve**, and which reveals the different yields across a spectrum of different maturities, ranging from the yield available on three-month Treasury bills all the way out to the yield on 30-year bonds (or even longer in the case of some government issues).

5.4.2 Spreads in the Government Bond Market

At present, with so many governments having to issue very large quantities of bonds to finance public deficits there is a competition for capital, and investors will allocate funds according to the relative yields available from different governments and by assessing the appeal of the bonds of different issuers in relation to yields being offered by benchmark issuers.

To cite one example which has become very widely quoted in regard to the difficulties faced by several member states within the eurozone, the spread between the bonds of the troubled states, such as Greece, Portugal and Spain, with German bunds of similar maturity (typically the ten-year maturity) are quoted in the financial media. The bund is considered to be the safest government bond issued by any EU member state, and Germany has an AAA rating from the credit rating agencies.

In the summer of 2011, both S&P and Fitch cut their credit rating for Greece to CCC, which was the lowest grade possible prior to default; Moody's had the rating at Ca, which was its second lowest.

The spreads between a ten-year bund and a similar maturity issue from the Greek government had surpassed 2,500 basis points. With the ten-year bund yielding below 2% pa (June 2012), the equivalent Greek bond was effectively yielding more than 27% pa.

The excessive size of the spread reflected the fact that private sector banks and other financial institutions had no appetite or demand for the bonds issued by the Greek government, while many market participants believed that they would default.

5.4.3 Key Bond Quotation Characteristics

Quoted Price

The quoted price shows the current market value of the bond. Both the bid price and the ask price should be included to provide the spread between the two. The price that the buyer is willing to pay is the **bid price**. The ask price is the amount a seller is willing to let go of the bond for. The size of the spread will reflect the liquidity of the bond.

The price quotation will, with one important exception, be expressed in 1/100th of a point or basis point. The price can be thought of as referencing a nominal or principal amount of £100 (or other unit of currency). A quote, for example, of 105 shows that the bond has a current price which is five points or 5% above its principal nominal value, or the par value which will be paid at redemption.

US Treasury issues follow a few quirky conventions. Prices are given as percentages of face value, with fractions like 1/32 as the last digits, not decimals. For example, a bond quote for the US ten-year note may show that the price has risen by 8/32 to sell for 108 22/32. The quote can easily be converted to the more standard system of pricing in 1/100 of a unit (effectively a basis point). The rise of 8/32 is equivalent to 25 basis points or ¼ of a point, and the price of the bond at 108 22/32 can be simply expressed as 108.6875.

Coupon

This tells you the percentage of the principal amount or par that will be paid annually. A coupon of 5% means that, for a bond with a £1,000 par value, £50 will be paid annually. The quote should indicate the frequency of coupon payment. Semi-annual coupon payments are standard for most global government issues, including the US and UK, but annual payments are to be found with German bunds and are also standard in the eurobond market.

Maturity

This is the date when the principal amount will be repaid. A ten-year bond will be redeemed ten years from the issue date and will include a last coupon payment as well as the repayment of the principal.

Current Yield

The current yield or flat yield is the coupon rate divided by the bond's current price (see section 6.4.1). It does not include the timing of the payments of coupons and does not reflect the internal rate of return of all of the payments to be made during the lifetime of the bond.

Yield and price are inversely proportional to each other. As a simple rule of thumb, if the current price of the bond is higher than the par value, the yield is lower than the coupon, and, if the current price of the bond is lower than the par value, the required yield is higher than the coupon value.

Gross Redemption Yield (GRY)/Yield to Maturity (YTM)

The convention in the US bond market is to quote the GRY as the key characteristic of a bond's current market value. The YTM is also known as the gross redemption yield (GRY) and, in essence, it represents the rate of return, expressed in the form of an annualised percentage rate, if one were to hold on to the bond until maturity and receive all of the coupons and the redemption of principal. See section 6.4.2.

One key assumption of the GRY calculation, which in fact makes it unrealistic, is that one is able to continually reinvest all the interest payments received at the same yield throughout. It also takes into account any profit or loss incurred due to the current price of the bond being over or under par. A discounted cash flow (DCF) procedure is the appropriate method for determining the appropriate price to pay for a bond which has a known maturity date and fixed regular coupon payments. See sections 1.3.1 and 1.3.2.

The pricing of bonds or notes is more complex when they have floating rate coupons, or embedded options, such as the ability of the issuer to call the bond before it reaches maturity, or when they have been issued with step-up coupons, ie, the amount of the coupon steps up by a specified amount during the lifetime of the bond. This is found in bonds issued by the government of India, for example. However, all approaches use the underlying principle of DCF, which is to determine the net present value of future income streams by reference to a required yield in annual percentage terms, and then use this percentage as the rate of discounting the cash flows.

Yield to worst (YTW) is another factor, often considered when trading in the bond market. YTW represents the overall return on investment if all market factors perform in the most negative manner possible, ie, the worst case scenario. In calculating YTW, it is assumed that the current prevailing interest rate will remain unchanged. Put simply, it is the lowest potential yield that can be received on a bond without the issuer actually defaulting.

Miscellaneous

More specifics about individual bonds are identified in shorthand. 'M' means matured bonds and 'cld' means called. Some bond quotations will include the credit rating of the company selling the bond as well as indicating whether the bond is callable or not. Callable bonds can be redeemed earlier than the maturity date.

6. Present Value, Yield and Conversion Calculations

6.1 Credit Ratings and Debt Seniority

Learning Objective

2.7.1 Understand the purpose, influence and limitations of global credit rating agencies, debt seniority and ranking in cases of default/ bankruptcy: senior; subordinated; mezzanine; payment in kind (PIK); tiers of bank debt

6.1.1 Credit Ratings

A credit rating estimates the creditworthiness of an individual, corporation or even a country. Leaving aside the case of credit ratings for individuals, in the world of corporate and sovereign credits (ie, the creditworthiness of governments), a rating is an evaluation made by credit-rating agencies of a borrower's overall credit history. It provides a classification system, enabling a lender or investor to estimate the probability of the issuer of a credit, such as a bond, being able to make repayment in accordance with the terms of the borrowing, or more specifically the offering prospectus for a bond issuance. An inferior credit rating indicates a higher risk of defaulting on a loan, and investors will want to be compensated for this additional risk by higher interest rates and other provisions, or they may simply be unwilling to purchase the bonds being offered by the issuer.

Although the three major rating agencies – Standard & Poor's (shortened to S&P) Moody's Investors Service (known simply as Moody's) and Fitch Ratings inc (known as Fitch) – use similar methods to rate issuers and individual bond issues, essentially by assessing whether the cash flow likely to be generated by the borrower will comfortably service and ultimately repay its debts, the rating each gives often differs, though not usually significantly so.

As a reminder, bond issues subject to credit ratings can be divided into two distinct categories: those accorded an investment grade rating and those categorised as non-investment grade or speculative. Further detail on credit ratings available from the three agencies is provided in section 6.2.

Issues such as ABSs are credit enhanced in some way to gain a higher credit rating. The simplest method of achieving this is through some form of insurance scheme that will pay out should the pool of assets be insufficient to service or repay the debt.

6.1.2   The Seniority Structure of Debt

Debt issued by companies can come in a variety of forms including bonds and bank borrowing. When there are multiple forms (or tiers) of debt, the issuer will have to establish an order as to which debt will be serviced and the so-called seniority within the entity's capital structure in the event of financial difficulties leading to a restructuring or liquidation.

In broad terms, the seniority of debt falls into three main headings: senior; subordinated; and mezzanine and payment in kind (PIK).

Senior

Senior debt is a class of corporate debt that has priority with respect to interest and principal over other classes of debt and over all classes of equity by the same issuer.

Senior debt is often secured by collateral on which the lender has put in place a first lien or charge. Usually this covers all the assets of a corporation and is often used for revolving credit lines. Senior debt has priority for repayment in a debt restructuring or the winding-up of a company.

However, in various jurisdictions and under exceptional circumstances, notwithstanding the nominal label given to senior debt, there can be special dispensations which might subordinate the claims of holders of senior debt. Holders of particular tranches of debt which may have been designated and sold as senior debt may find that other claimants have super-senior claims.

As an example, in 2008, the Washington Mutual Bank was seized by the Federal Deposit Insurance Corporation (FDIC) in the US, and, under an agreement between the FDIC and JPMorgan Chase, all of the assets and most of the Washington Mutual Bank's liabilities (including deposits, covered bonds and other secured debt) were assumed by J.P. Morgan. However, other debt claims, including unsecured senior debt, were not. By doing this, the FDIC effectively subordinated the unsecured senior debt to them, thereby fully protecting depositors while also eliminating any potential deposit insurance liability to the FDIC itself. In this and similar cases, specific regulatory and oversight powers can lead to senior lenders being subordinated in potentially unexpected ways.

Furthermore, in US Chapter 11 bankruptcies, new lenders can come in to fund the continuing operation of companies and be granted status as super-senior to other (even senior-secured) lenders. This so-called debtor-in-possession status also applies in other jurisdictions, including France.

Subordinated

Subordinated debt or bond-holders have accepted that their claim to the issuer's assets ranks below that of the senior debt in the event of a liquidation. As a result of accepting a greater risk than the senior debt, the subordinated borrowing will be entitled to a higher rate of interest than that available on the senior debt.

Tiers of Bank Capital

Capital in banks is vital as it provides the safety net for depositors when things go wrong. As a result, international standards for capital at banks have been issued via the Bank for International Settlements (BIS) in Basel for some time. The requirements are referred to as Basel Accords, since they are reached by committee under the auspices of the BIS.

The different levels of capital defined by the Basel Accords are commonly referred to as tiers 1 and 2, with tier 2 subdivided into upper tier 2 and lower tier 2. It is within tier 2 that debt instruments can appear.

Tier 1 is the bank's core capital and includes capital that has no contractual obligations to pay dividends or interest. This is typically the ordinary shares/common stock and the retained earnings that have been accumulated. It also includes any preferred stock/preference shares that are perpetual and are not cumulative. Upper tier 2 includes cumulative preferred stock/preference shares and any perpetual subordinated debt that is either able to be deferred or able to be converted into equity if required. The recent description for such instruments is contingent convertibles or CoCos, because they may be treated as equity in the event of the bank facing serious problems.

Lower tier 2 capital includes other subordinated debt that stands below other debt holders, in particular the bank's depositors, in the event of the bank being closed down and wound up.

Mezzanine and PIK

The mezzanine level of debt, if it exists at all, will be even riskier than the subordinated debt. It will rank below other forms of debt, but above the equity in a liquidation. As the most risky debt, the mezzanine debt will offer a higher rate of interest than the subordinated and senior levels of debt. Interest on mezzanine debt is not always paid fully in cash. Interest can be split into a portion that is paid in cash and a portion that is instead added to the amount owed. This latter portion is known as a payment in kind (PIK). Some mezzanine debt pays no cash interest at all and instead all of the interest is rolled up to become an increased amount owed. These notes are often referred to as PIK notes. PIK notes are a little like ZCBs in that they free the issuer from the need to service the borrowing with cash until the notes/bonds reach maturity.

It should be noted that each of the three main categories can themselves contain sub-categories such as senior secured, senior unsecured, senior subordinated and junior subordinated. In practice, the various rating agencies look at debt structures in these narrower terms. Seniority can be contractual as the result of the terms of the issue, or based on the corporate structure of the issuer.

6.2   Credit Ratings

Learning Objective

2.7.2   Be able to analyse sovereign, government and corporate credit ratings from an investment perspective: main rating agencies; country rating factors; debt instrument rating factors; investment and sub-investment grades; use of credit enhancements; impact of grading changes; considerations when using credit rating agencies

6.2.1   Credit Risk

We have already noted in various contexts that the credit risk for bonds – the probability of an issuer defaulting on their payment obligations and the extent of the resulting loss – can be assessed by reference to the independent credit ratings given to most bond issues.

6.2.2   Global Credit Rating Agencies

The three most prominent global credit-rating agencies that provide credit ratings (Standard & Poor's, Moody's and Fitch) carry on business across the world and all have major operations in New York, London and Tokyo. The credit rating agencies are paid by the debt issuer and offer different types of rating services: public ratings; private ratings for internal or regulatory purposes; shadow ratings – again for private consumption – and model-based ratings. Each kind involves differing degrees of evaluation.

In the case of Standard & Poor's, the agency is a division of the US publishing company McGraw-Hill, which trades on the NYSE under the symbol MHP. Moody's is also an NYSE-listed company, trading under the symbol MCO, and among its major shareholders is the renowned investor Warren Buffett. Fitch Ratings inc is headquartered in New York and London and is part of the Fitch Group.

The best known and largest of the three agencies, S&P, states that its mission is, *'to provide investors who want to make better informed investment decisions with market intelligence in the form of credit ratings, indices, investment research and risk evaluations and solutions'*. Standard & Poor's is also widely known for maintaining one of the most widely followed indices of large-cap American stocks: the S&P 500.

The rating agencies, which have been the subject of much criticism and scrutiny in the wake of the collapse of the mortgage-backed securities market in 2007–08, have an unusual relationship with the principal participants in bond markets. On the one hand, their ratings are used by buyers of bonds, such as pension funds and other asset management companies, and are regarded as independent and objectively determined; on the other hand, their instruction and appointment come from the seller of the bonds.

As was seen in cases which have been the focus of testimony before the US Congress, there are grounds for believing that the manner in which the agencies are commissioned by and paid by bond issuers provides a reasonable question as to the reliability and independence of the assessments made. In the corporate debt market, this is far more of an issue than in the case of the credit ratings provided for sovereign and government bonds, when the agencies are acting as free agents.

The following table provides a complete listing of the ratings grades used by the three main credit-rating agencies, and a brief description of each category and the implications for investors who are seeking knowledge regarding risk and as a way of assisting in determining the appropriate prices at which bonds of each category should trade in the secondary markets for such issues.

Bond Credit Ratings			
Description	Moody's	Standard & Poor's	Fitch Ratings
Investment Grade			
Prime	Aaa	AAA	AAA
High grade	Aa1, Aa2, Aa3	AA+, AA, AA−	AA+, AA, AA−
Upper medium grade	A1, A2, A3	A+, A, A−	A+, A, A−
Lower medium grade	Baa1, Baa2, Baa3	BBB+, BBB, BBB−	BBB+, BBB, BBB−
Non-Investment Grade			
Speculative	Ba1, Ba2, Ba3	BB+, BB, BB−	BB+, BB, BB−
Highly speculative	B1, B2, B3	B+, B, B−	B+, B, B−
Substantial risks	Caa1	CCC+	CCC
Extremely speculative	Caa2	CCC	C
In default with little prospect for recovery	Caa3, Ca	CCC−, CC, C	CCC
In default	C	D	D

The highest-grade corporate bonds are known as AAA or Aaa, and these are bonds that the three agencies have deemed the least likely to fail. Lower-grade corporate bonds are perceived as more likely to default, when the borrower will have to entice lenders with a higher coupon payment and higher yield to maturity. Indeed, bonds with a rating below BBB− (in the case of Standard and Poor's and Fitch Ratings), or Baa3 (in the case of Moody's) are often referred to as junk bonds or speculative bonds which are non-investment grade.

Since the financial crisis, the effectiveness of credit-rating agencies has come under scrutiny. Flaws in the system were apparent during the sub-prime mortgage crisis in 2007 where many credit ratings of highly rated securities were questioned because of insufficient collateral tied to the underlying loans, which many claim should have been factored into the overall ratings.

Other considerations when using a ratings agency are as follows:

- Of the 150 or so worldwide credit rating agencies, only a few are considered to be major. Thus, there is often a market view that there is a lack of competition with the three dominant players possessing the lion's share of influence.
- There may be perceived conflicts of interest as the rating agencies receive fees from the companies whose structures they rate, putting pressure on the agency not to upset the company. Critics would assert that this perceived conflict could lead to overly high ratings.

6.2.3   Country-Rating Factors

The cutting of a credit rating makes it more expensive for governments to raise money with their sovereign bond issues, as they require higher coupon payments to attract investors who perceive more risk, for example, in an Irish government bond than a US Treasury one.

The list below shows the kinds of factors or indicators which credit-rating agencies employ to determine a country's credit rating. By scoring these factors and calculating an overall score, each country's sovereign debt can be graded.

- Debt profile (foreign exchange reserves, debt-service ratio and absolute level of debt).
- Banking/financial stability.
- Balance of payments/current account.
- Government fiscal policy.
- GDP growth.
- Governance (regulatory regime, rule of law, corruption, transparency).
- Political system.
- National security (external threats, internal strife, terrorism).
- Export profile (growth, diversity).

The increasingly important derivatives markets, which are constantly pricing sovereign credit default swap rates, are also becoming a major influence on the way in which markets trade government debt.

Country	Currency volatility vs Euro	Currency change vs euro in 1 year	GDP growth	Sovereign credit rating	Ten-year sovereign bond yields	World Bank DB score	Euler Hermes rating	GDP $ per person
	Lower better	Higher better	Higher better	Higher better	Lower better	Higher better	AA best, D worst	Higher better
Albania	8.3%	-1.2%	-10.3%	35	NA	67.7	D	5,352
Armenia	13.0%	-7.8%	-13.7%	16	NA	74.5	D	4,622
Austria			-10.4%	96	-0.4%	78.7	AA	50,277
Belarus	41.5%	-26.2%	-0.2%	28	N/A	74.3	D	6,663
Bosnia & Herzegovina	2.4%	0.0%	2.1%	27	N/A	65.4	D	6,073
Botswana	17.8%	-11.0%	-24.8%	70	4.5%	66.2	B	7,961
Bulgaria	1.8%	0.0%	-10.0%	60	0.4%	72	B	9,738
Colombia	26.9%	-16.4%	-14.9%	57	5.1%	70.1	A	6,432
Czech Republic	12.0%	-5.4%	-8.7%	83	0.8%	76.3	A	23,101
Denmark	1.4%	0.3%	-6.8%	100	-0.4%	85.3	AA	59,822
Estonia			-5.6%	83	N/A	80.6	AA	23,660
France			-13.8%	92	-0.3%	76.8	AA	40,494
Finland			-6.4%	96	-0.4%	80.2	AA	48,685
Georgia	29.9%	-17.0%	-12.3%	45	N/A	83.7	D	4,789
Germany			-11.3%	100	-0.6%	79.7	AA	46,259
Indonesia	21.3%	-11.1%	-4.2%	60	6.9%	69.6	B	4,136
Ireland			-3.0%	78	-0.18%	79.6	A	78,661
Italy			-17.7%	61	0.9%	72.9	A	33,189
Kazakhstan	25.2%	-15.1%	-1.8%	56	N/A	79.6	D	9,731
Kenya	18.8%	-10.5%	1.1%	33	11.7%	73.2	C	1,816
Kosovo			-9.3%	N/A	N/A	73.2	N/A	4,417

Country	Currency volatility vs Euro	Currency change vs euro in 1 year	GDP growth	Sovereign credit rating	Ten-year sovereign bond yields	World Bank DB score	Euler Hermes rating	GDP $ per person
	Lower better	Higher better	Higher better	Higher better	Lower better	Higher better	AA best, D worst	Higher better
Latvia			-8.9%	73	0.6%	80.3	BB	17,836
Lithuania			-4.2%	75	0.3%	81.6	BB	19,455
Mexico	36.1%	-18.4%	-18.7%	60	5.8%	72.4	BB	10,118
Moldova	6.0%	-2.3%	-14.0%	25	NA	74.4	D	4,498
Namibia	33.3%	-16.5%	-11.1%	45	10.7%	61.4	C	4,957
Netherlands			-9.4%	100	-0.43%	76.1	AA	52,448
Nigeria	18.4%	-11.3%	-6.1%	30	7.74%	56.9	D	2,230
North Macedonia	2.3%	0.0%	-12.7%	45	N/A	80.7	C	6,093
Phillipines	7.2%	-0.1%	-16.5%	61	3.0%	62.8	B	3,485
Poland	9.4%	-4.7%	-8.2%	71	1.3%	76.4	BB	15,595
Romania	3.0%	-2.4%	-10.5%	55	3.5%	73.3	B	12,919
Russian Federation	36.7%	-23.4%	-8.0%	55	6.3%	78.2	C	11,585
Slovakia			-12.1%	76	-0.25%	75.6	A	19,329
South Africa	32.8%	-16.7%	-17.1%	46	9.5%	67	C	6,001
Spain			-21.5%	71	0.3%	77.9	A	29,613
Turkey	46.3%	-31.7%	-9.9%	36	12.9%	76.8	C	9,042
Ukraine	29.9%	-18.4%	-11.4%	26	14.1%	70.2	D	3,592
UK	13.6%	-2.4%	-21.5%	91	0.2%	83.5	AA	42,300
Vietnam	10.8%	-6.0%	0.4%	43	2.7%	69.8	C	2,715
Zambia	65.0%	-38.4%	-2.1%	30	34.0%	66.9	D	1,291

6.2.4 Debt Instrument-Rating Factors

The financial obligation to which a rating refers is usually a bond or similar debt instrument. The company wishing to raise money by issuing a bond relies on an independently verified credit rating to inform potential investors regarding the relative ability of the company to meet its financial commitments. The agencies themselves make it clear that they are not in the business of recommending the purchase or sale of any security, but address only credit risk.

There are two types of issue credit ratings, dependent upon the length of time for which the financial obligation is issued. There are long-term-issue credit ratings and short-term-issue credit ratings, each with their own set of standards. The latter relate to obligations which are originally established with a maturity of less than 365 days (and to short-term features of longer-term bonds). Ratings may be public or private. They provide opinions, not recommendations, and are derived from both audited and unaudited information.

It is important to appreciate that credit ratings are tailored to particular sectors. Ratings should be comparable across different sectors, but a rating may serve a very specific purpose in, say, the banking or insurance sectors; for example, assessing the likelihood of a bank running into serious financial difficulty requiring support, and whether it will get external support in such an event. Obviously, this has no equivalent outside the financial sector.

The credit rating for a particular instrument is not meant to be a recommendation to an investor to buy, sell or hold onto the instrument. That is a decision for individual investors based on their appetite for risk. The debt instruments with the lowest credit ratings will carry the highest levels of potential reward but also the highest level of risk of default by the borrower, so the investor will have to balance risk against potential reward.

6.2.5 The Use of Credit Enhancements

Credit enhancement is often a key part of the securitisation transaction when issuing securities that are backed by assets, such as loans. However, the credit crisis of 2007–2008 discredited the process of credit enhancement of structured securities as a financial practice as the risk was not assessed correctly and defaults began to rise. If the credit rating had been properly assessed and higher interest rates assigned to structured securities, the crisis might have been averted. Credit enhancements include excess spreads, over-collateralisation and the use of reserve accounts as well as other external credit enhancement techniques detailed below.

Excess Spread

The excess spread is the difference between the interest rate received on the underlying collateral and the coupon on the issued security. It is, typically, one of the first defences against loss. Even if some of the underlying loan payments are late or default, the coupon payment can still be made.

Over-Collateralisation (OC)

Over-collateralisation (OC) is a commonly used form of credit enhancement. With this support structure, the face value of the underlying loan portfolio is larger than the security it backs. Thus, the issued security is over-collateralised.

In this manner, even if some of the payments from the underlying loans are late or default, principal and interest payments on the ABS can still be made. In the mortgage market the over-collateralised loans might not work well when the value of the collateral kept as part of the loan that is the real estate itself starts depreciating in value.

Reserve Account

A reserve account is created to reimburse the issuing trust for losses up to the amount allocated for the reserve. To increase credit support, the reserve account will often be non-declining throughout the life of the security, meaning that the account will increase proportionally up to some specified level as the outstanding debt is paid off.

6.2.6   External Credit Enhancement

Surety Bonds

Surety bonds are insurance policies that reimburse the ABS for any losses. They are external forms of credit enhancement. ABSs paired with surety bonds have ratings that are the same as that of the surety bond's issuer. By law, surety companies cannot provide a bond as a form of a credit enhancement guarantee.

Letter of Credit (LOC)

With a LOC, a financial institution – usually a bank – is paid a fee to provide a specified cash amount to reimburse the ABS-issuing trust for any cash shortfalls from the collateral, up to the required credit support amount.

LOCs are becoming less common forms of credit enhancement, as much of their appeal was lost when the rating agencies downgraded the long-term debt of several LOC-provider banks in the early 1990s.

Wrapped Securities

A wrapped security is insured or guaranteed by a third party. A third party or, in some cases, the parent company of the ABS issuer may provide a promise to reimburse the trust for losses up to a specified amount. Deals can also include agreements to advance principal and interest or to buy back any defaulted loans. The third-party guarantees are typically provided by AAA-rated financial guarantors or monoline insurance companies.

6.3 Factors Influencing Bond Prices

Learning Objective

2.7.3   Be able to analyse the factors that influence bond pricing: credit rating; default risk; impact of interest rates; market liquidity; inflation

6.3.1   Credit Rating

Bondholders face the risk that the issuer of the bond might default on their obligation to pay interest and the principal amount at redemption. As seen, this so-called credit risk – the probability of an issuer defaulting on their payment obligations and the extent of the resulting loss – can be assessed by reference to the independent credit ratings given to most bond issues.

6.3.2 Interest Rate Risk

Probably the most important risk to a bondholder is the impact of changing interest rates, because of the method of discounting future cash flows at the prevailing rate of interest to calculate the net present value of the bond's cash flow and thereby arrive at the current bond price. In simple terms, it can be said that as the interest rate or discount rate increases in determining the present value of the bond's cash flows so the current price of the bond will decrease. There is an inverse relationship between the price of a bond with a fixed coupon and the prevailing rate of interest.

For example, a bond issued with a 5% coupon will be less desirable as interest rates increase and further bonds are issued with higher coupon rates – for example, issued with 6% coupons. In simple terms, the price of the bond obtainable in the secondary market will have to decline so that the YTM for the 5% bond becomes equal to the YTM for the 6% bond: the manner in which the lower coupon bond remains competitive in YTM is by having a lower current price. Duration and modified duration (volatility) are the means of measuring this risk more precisely. Convexity is a measure that is used to explain the sensitivity of a bond's price to changes in the discount rate.

6.3.3 Inflation Risk

Inflation risk is linked to interest rate risk, as interest rates have to rise to compensate bondholders for declines in the purchasing power of money.

6.3.4 Market Liquidity Risk

The ease with which an issue can be sold in the market will affect the investor's perception of the risk of holding a bond. Smaller issues especially are subject to this risk. In certain markets, the volume of trading tends to concentrate into the benchmark stocks, or the on-the-run stocks, especially in the government bonds market, thereby rendering most other issues illiquid. Other bonds become subject to seasoning as the initial liquidity dries up and the bonds are purchased by investors who wish to hold them to maturity.

The difficulties that can arise in the liquidity and trading conditions of bonds were especially acute during the 1998 crisis, which began with the default by Russia on its bonds and led to the collapse of Long-Term Capital Management (LTCM) – a major fund that specialised in the trading of fixed-income instruments and various arbitrage strategies.

One of the difficulties that arose during this crisis was the mispricing in the US Treasury market where the most recently issued long-term bond, which is known as the on-the-run bond, trades at a premium to those bonds which had been issued previously and which are known as off-the-run. If investors have a preference, during a crisis, for the most liquid instruments, they may hoard the on-the-run bonds and force their price to be out of normal alignment with similar bonds which have a slightly different maturity date. This can result in a breakdown in complex strategies designed to exploit the spreads or price differences across the yield spectrum.

6.3.5   Issue-Specific Risk

This may arise from factors specific to the bond issue which tend to either increase or decrease the risk, eg, issuer options such as the right to call for early redemption or possibly, holder options.

6.3.6   Fiscal Risk

This represents risk that withholding taxes will be increased. For foreign bonds, there is also the risk of the imposition of capital controls locking an investor's money into the market. For an investor purchasing overseas or international bonds denominated in a currency other than that of the borrower's domestic currency or currency of account, there is obviously also a currency risk.

6.3.7   Macroeconomic Factors Affecting Bond Prices and Yields

A major driver of bond prices is the prevailing interest rate and expectations of interest rates to come. Yields required by bond investors are a reflection of their interest rate expectations. For example, if interest rates are expected to rise, bond prices will fall to bring the yields up to appropriate levels to reflect the interest rate increases. To remain competitive, equities prices will also suffer.

The interest rate itself is heavily impacted by inflationary expectations. Simplistically, if inflation is expected to be 4% pa, the interest rate will have to be greater than this in order to provide the investor with any real return. The interest rate might stand at 7% pa. If economic news suggests that inflation is likely to increase further, to, say, 6%, then the interest rate will increase too, perhaps up to 9%. The reverse will be true if inflation is expected to fall.

Technically, the interest rate referred to in the preceding paragraphs is the nominal interest rate. The nominal rate is the interest rate including inflation. The interest rate excluding inflation is generally referred to as the real interest rate.

6.3.8   Summary of Factors Influencing Bond Prices

The factors that influence the prices of bonds can be sub-divided into two:

*   Specific issuer factors.
*   Macroeconomic or market factors.

The characteristics of a particular issue and the quality of the issuer encompass the following:

*   Issuer's current credit rating (which itself will reflect the issuer's specific prospects) that highlights the issuer's default risk.
*   The structure and seniority of the particular issue – for example, the bonds may be of high or low priority in the event of default by the issuer and may be structured in a way that gives the bonds particular priority in relation to particular assets (such as mortgage-backed bonds).

- The above aspects, combined with prevailing yields available on other benchmark bonds (such as government issues in the same currency, with similar redemption dates), will determine the required YTM and, therefore, the appropriate price.
- Liquidity – the more liquid bonds tend to be more expensive, encompassing a liquidity premium and having lower bid/offer spreads.

6.4 Valuation of Fixed-Income Securities

Learning Objective

2.7.4 Be able to analyse fixed-income securities using the following valuation measures and understand the benefits and limitations of using them: flat yield; yield to maturity; nominal and real return; gross redemption yield (using internal rate of return); net redemption yield; modified duration

In bond markets, the single most important measure of return is the bond yield. There are, however, several different yield measures which can be calculated, each having its own uses and limitations. For each of these measures, we need to know the following:

- How is the measure calculated?
- How useful is this measure?
- What are the limitations of this measure?

6.4.1 Flat Yield

The simplest measure of the return used in the market is the flat (interest or running) yield. This measure looks at the annual cash return (coupon) generated by an investment as a percentage of the cash price. In simple terms, it provides the regular annual return that is generated on the money invested.

The calculation of the flat or running yield is provided by this formula.

$$\text{Flat yield} = \frac{\text{Annual coupon rate}}{\text{Market price}} \times 100$$

For example, the flat yield on a 5% gilt, redeeming in six years and priced at £104.40, will be (5/104.40) x 100 = 4.79%.

The flat yield only considers the coupon and ignores the existence of any capital gain (or loss) through to redemption. As such, it is best suited to short-term investors in the bond, rather than those investors that might hold the bond through to its maturity and benefit from the gain (or suffer from the loss) at maturity. Using the flat yield, it is simple to see how a change in interest rates will impact bond prices. If interest rates increase, investors will want an equivalent increase in the yield on their bonds. However, because the coupon is fixed for most bonds, the only way that the yield can increase is for the price to fall. This is the inverse relationship between interest rates and bond prices.

When interest rates rise, bond prices fall and vice versa.

The flat yield for an 8% annual coupon bond redeemable at par in four years can be calculated as follows if the current price is £98.60:

$$\text{Flat yield} = \frac{8.00}{98.6} = 0.081136 \text{ or } 8.11\%$$

Uses

This measure assesses the annual income return only and is the most appropriate measure when the bond under consideration is an irredeemable, which pays a perpetual coupon but no redemption amount. Alternatively, the flat or running yield can be useful if the focus is on the short-term cash returns that the investment will generate.

Limitations

There are three key drawbacks for using flat yield as a robust measure in assessing bond returns.

Since it only measures the coupon flows and ignores the redemption flows, when applicable, it is giving an incomplete perspective on the actual returns from the bond. A bond which has been purchased at a price away from redemption will be significantly undervalued when the par value is excluded from the calculation. The calculation completely ignores the timing of any cash flows and, because there is no discounted cash flow analysis, the time value of money is completely overlooked.

Negative Yields

In May 2020, gilts were sold by the UK government for the first time with a negative yield. This meant that investors were effectively paying for the privilege of lending money to the UK Government. The three-year bond, maturing in 2023, raised $3.75 billion with a yield of -0.003%. The bond's coupon is 0.75% annually, but the premium over par means that investors will receive back less than they paid.

Negative interest rates have been a key feature in many parts of the world for some time. Investors that purchase bonds with negative yields typically include insurance companies, pension funds and fund managers whose asset allocation rules necessitate them having to invest certain percentages of funds into bonds.

With floating rate notes, the return in any one period will vary with interest rates. If the coupon is not a constant, then using a flat yield basis for measuring returns becomes an arbitrary matter of selecting which coupon amount, among many possible values, to use for the calculation. For these reasons, the flat yield is not a very useful measure.

6.4.2   Gross Redemption Yield (GRY)/Yield to Maturity (YTM)

The gross redemption yield (GRY) for a bond is also known as the yield to maturity (YTM). The GRY for a bond is the internal rate of return (IRR) of the bond. The IRR is simply the discount rate that, when applied to the future cash flows of the bond, produces the current price of that bond. Expressed in its simplest form, the GRY is the IRR of:

- the dirty price paid to buy the bond
- the gross coupons received to redemption
- the final redemption proceeds.

The mathematical formulation is:

$$GRY = r = \sum \frac{Coupon_t}{(1+r)^t} + \frac{Redemption}{(1+r)^n}$$

where:

r = the yield to maturity, expressed as a decimal

t = the time period after which the cash flow arises

n = the time period at redemption

The GRY is a much fuller measure of yield because it takes both the coupons and any gain (or loss) through to maturity into account. As such, it is more appropriate for long-term investors than the flat yield. In particular, because it ignores the impact of any taxation (hence gross redemption yield), this measure of return is useful for non-taxpaying, long-term investors such as pension funds and charities. The GRY is the IRR of the bond. The IRR is simply the discount rate that, when applied to the future cash flows of the bond, produces the current price of that bond.

Mathematical Formulations

$$\text{Price of bond where the GRY is } r = \sum \frac{Coupon_t}{(1+r)^t} + \frac{Redemption}{(1+r)^n}$$

$$\text{Price of bond where the GRY is } r = \frac{Coupon_1}{(1+r)} + \frac{Coupon_2}{(1+r)^2} + \frac{Coupon_3}{(1+r)^3} + \ldots + \frac{C_n+R}{(1+r)^n}$$

where:

r = the redemption amount

n = the number of years to maturity

t = the time period after which the cash flow arises

Unfortunately neither of these formulae can be solved algebraically (except in very rare circumstances) and therefore the process of interpolation represents the only practical method.

Interpolation Approach

The interpolation approach is based on the fact that there is an inverse relationship between yields and bond prices, ie, as yields rise, bond prices fall, and vice versa. In order to calculate the GRY, we select two interest rates and calculate the net present value of the bond cash flows at each of these two rates. These calculations establish two reference points in terms of values and rates, which can be used to determine a linear relationship between changes in the bond price and changes in interest rates. The following two tables show how we can establish two reference points with regard to homing in on the actual IRR by using the simple annual discounted cash flow approach for the bond considered earlier (8% annual coupon, four years to maturity, priced at 98.60). Let us first determine the net present value (NPV) of all the cash flow with an assumed GRY of 7% and deduct the current market price in the cash flow calculation.

	Annual Coupon	8.00%	Assumed GRY	7.00%
Annual Cash Flows	Cash Flow in £	Discount Factor	Discount Factor at Desired Yield	Present Value
Current Bond Price				−98.6
1	£8.00	$[1/1.07]^1$	0.93	£7.48
2	£8.00	$[1/1.07]^2$	0.87	£6.99
3	£8.00	$[1/1.07]^3$	0.82	£6.53
4	£108.00	$[1/1.07]^4$	0.76	£82.39
			Difference from Bond Price	£4.79

This provides us with a reference point at 7%, so let us also get a reference point in terms of the NPV of the cash flows with an assumed GRY of 11%.

	Annual Coupon	8.00%	Assumed GRY	11.00%
Annual Cash Flows	Cash Flow in £	Discount Factor	Discount Factor at Desired Yield	Present Value
Current Bond Price				−98.6
1	£8.00	$[1/1.11]^1$	0.90	£7.21
2	£8.00	$[1/1.11]^2$	0.81	£6.49
3	£8.00	$[1/1.11]^3$	0.73	£5.85
4	£108.00	$[1/1.11]^4$	0.66	£71.14
			Difference from Bond Price	−£7.91

With this approach we are in the first instance assuming that there is a linear relationship between the NPVs and the GRY, so, having established two reference points, we are able to draw a line through both the points. This can be seen from the diagram below.

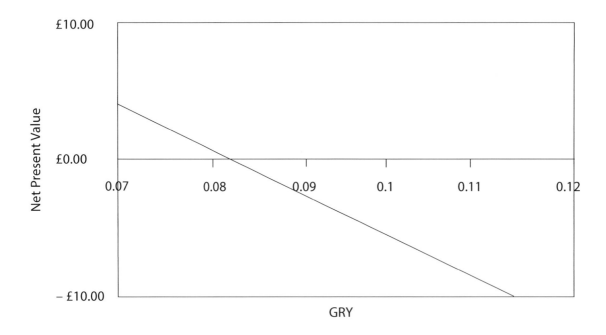

Even though the true relationship between bond prices and interest rates is not linear, using this approach provides us with a much greater sense of where the approximate range is to refine our exploration of the intervals and continue with the process of interpolation. From the graph above, it would seem that the more approximate interval is close to 8.5%.

The following table shows the annuity formula for discounting cash flows, and here we have selected the two much closer reference points, which are an assumed GRY of 25 basis points below the 8.5% level that the previous reasoning brought us towards, and 25 basis points above that level.

	Annual Coupon	8.00%	Assumed GRY	8.25%
Timing of Cash Flows	Cash Flow in £	Discount Factor	Discount Factor at Desired Yield	Present Value
Current Bond Price				−98.6
4	£8.00	$\dfrac{1}{0.0825}\left[1-\dfrac{1}{1.0825^4}\right] = 3.2938$	3.2938	£26.35
Redemption in Year 4	£100.00	$\dfrac{1}{1.0825^4} = 0.7283$	0.7283	£72.83
			Difference from Bond Price	£0.58

			Assumed GRY	8.75%
Timing of Cash Flows	Cash Flow in £	Discount Factor	Discount Factor at Desired Yield	Present Value
Current Bond Price				−98.6
4	£8.00	$\dfrac{1}{0.0875}\left[1-\dfrac{1}{1.0875^4}\right] = 3.2576$	3.2576	£26.06
Redemption in Year 4	£100.00	$\dfrac{1}{1.0875^4} = 0.7150$	0.7150	£71.50
			Difference from Bond Price	−£1.04

Conclusion

We have found that the rate of 8.25% is too low and 8.75% is too high, hence the GRY must lie between these two points. The total range of values covered as a result of this 0.5% (8.75% − 8.25%) yield difference is a value of £1.62 (£0.58 + £1.04). In other words, we need to move so far from 8.25% towards 8.75% that we eradicate £0.58 of this £1.62.

The GRY is, therefore, 8.25% + (58p/162p x 0.5%) = 8.25 + 0.179 = 8.429%.

The actual GRY is 8.428%. Hence this calculation has proved to be accurate to about one hundredth of a basis point.

6.4.3 Net Redemption Yield (NRY)

The net redemption yield (NRY) is very similar to the GRY, in that it takes both the annual coupons and the profit (or loss) made through to maturity into account. The NRY, however, considers after-tax cash flows rather than the gross cash flows. As a result, it is a useful measure for tax-paying, long-term investors.

The coupon received from gilts is generally taxable, but any gain made on redemption (or subsequent sale) is not taxable. This makes gilts with a low coupon attractive to higher-rate taxpayers, as the price will be lower than par, resulting in a substantial part of the return coming in the form of a tax-free capital gain.

The net redemption yield for individual investors can be formulated as follows in two different formulae.

$$\text{Price} = \sum \frac{C_t(1 - T_p)}{(1+r)^t} + \frac{R}{(1+r)^n}$$

where: Tp = personal tax rate

The formula cannot be solved algebraically, and to calculate the IRR for NRY, an interpolation approach represents the only practical method.

As each individual has a different tax position, the NRY will obviously be different for different individuals. The market convention is to compute the NRY at assumed levels of personal tax such as 40%.

The net redemption yield can, therefore, be calculated as the IRR of the:

- dirty price paid to buy the bond
- net coupons received to redemption (net of the appropriate rate of tax)
- final redemption proceeds which are paid gross.

It will be useful to continue with the bond example which we have analysed throughout this section, which is an 8% annual coupon bond with a price of £98.60, and four years to maturity, assuming a 40% level of tax.

Previously when considering the GRY we used the interpolation method with two reference points determined by homing in on the likely interval for the GRY, which would produce an NPV of zero for the cash flows. Let us simplify matters and look at two reference points for this analysis – the first at 5%, which is approximately 60% of 8.25% (our lower reference point from before) and an upper reference yield of 5.5% – since we do not know more exactly what interval may be covered and a 0.5% interpolation interval should still deliver quite satisfactory results, as was seen when calculating the GRY.

The table below again uses the annuity discount factor, and the two assumed GRY rates have been entered for the two scenarios. The important modification that has been made to the cash flows is that the 8% coupon has been netted to a 4.8% coupon, although the redemption amount of the bond – which is not subject to tax – has been left at its gross value – also its par value of £100.

	Annual Coupon	8.00%	Assumed GRY	5.00%
Timing of Cash Flows	Cash Flow in £	Discount Factor	Discount Factor at Desired Yield	Present Value
Current Bond Price				−98.6
4	£4.80	$\dfrac{1}{0.05}\left[1-\dfrac{1}{1.05^4}\right] = 3.5460$	3.5460	£17.02
Redemption in Year 4	£100.00	$\dfrac{1}{1.05^4} = 0.8227$	0.8227	£82.27
			Difference from Bond Price	£0.69

			Assumed GRY	5.50%
Timing of Cash Flows	Cash Flow in £	Discount Factor	Discount Factor at Desired Yield	Present Value
Current Bond Price				−98.6
4	£4.80	$\dfrac{1}{0.055}\left[1-\dfrac{1}{1.055^4}\right] = 3.5052$	3.5052	£16.82
Redemption in Year 4	£100.00	$\dfrac{1}{1.055^4} = 0.8072$	0.8072	£80.72
			Difference from Bond Price	−£1.05

As can be seen from the above analysis of the cash flows, the GRY rate of 5% is too low and 5.5% is too high, hence the GRY must lie between these two points.

The total range of values covered as a result of this 0.5% (5.5% − 5%) yield difference is a value of £1.74 (£0.69 + £1.05). To follow the method of interpolation we need to move so far from 5% towards 5.5% that we extinguish £0.69 of this £1.74 interval.

The GRY is, therefore, 5% + (69p/174p x 0.5%) = 5.00 + 0.19828 = 5.198%.

The actual GRY (which will deliver a zero NPV) is 5.197%, hence this calculation has proved to be accurate to within a single basis point. Since the beginning of the 1996–97 tax year, the tax treatment of the income and gain elements of the return on a bond have been harmonised for corporate investors, ie, both are taxed as income.

As a result, ignoring the time delay on the payment of the tax, the NRY for a corporate investor can be calculated according to the following simple formula:

$$NRY = GRY \times (1 - T_C)$$

where: T_C is the corporate tax rate

Uses of NRY

Since it is based on discounted cash flow techniques, the NRY measure overcomes the major deficiencies highlighted in relation to the flat yield and the GRY. It considers all cash returns and their tax implications for the investor.

Limitations of NRY

The limitations of NRY are as for GRY. Specifically, it only represents the net return that will be achieved if interest rates to maturity remain constant throughout the holding period.

6.4.4   Macaulay Duration

For bonds, cash flows at different points in time have different sensitivities to rate movements (different risks). A bond may be thought of as an amalgamation of differently timed cash flows, each with their own sensitivity. Hence, the sensitivity of a bond to changes in rates must be a weighted average of the sensitivities of the individual cash flows. This is a bond's duration. Duration is an estimate of the weighted average length of time to the receipt of a bond's benefits (coupon and redemption value), the weightings being the present value of the benefits involved.

This concept can be illustrated diagrammatically.

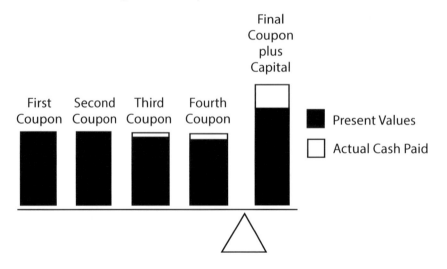

The fulcrum or point of balance in the diagram represents the duration of the bond.

In terms of a mathematical formula this can be expressed as follows:

$$\text{Macaulay Duration (D)} = \sum \frac{(t \times PV_t)}{\text{Price}}$$

$$\text{Macaulay Duration (D)} = \frac{(1 \times PV_1) + (2 \times PV_2) + (3 \times PV_3) + ... + (n \times PV_n)}{\text{Price}}$$

where:

PV_t = present value of cash flow in period t (discounted using the redemption yield)

n = number of periods to maturity

The table below shows the calculation for a five-year bond with a 7% coupon and a required yield to maturity or GRY of 8%.

Calculation of Macaulay Duration			
Bond Price	£96.01	Gross Redemption Yield (GRY)	8.00%
Face Value	£100.00	Coupon Frequency	1
Coupon Rate	7.00%		
Life in Years	5		
Period	Cash Flow	PV Cash Flow	Duration Calculation
		Cash Flow/[(1+GRY/Coupon Frequency)^Period]	PV Cash Flow x Period
1	£7.00	£6.48	£6.48
2	£7.00	£6.00	£12.00
3	£7.00	£5.56	£16.67
4	£7.00	£5.15	£20.58
5	£107.00	£72.82	£364.11
	Totals	£96.01	£419.85
	Macaulay Duration	£419.85/£96.01	4.373

Duration is one of the most useful ways of assessing the risk of holding a bond, as the higher the duration of the bond, the higher its risk or sensitivity to interest rates.

As a measure of relative risk for a bond, it is just as valuable as knowing the **beta** for a share.

Duration needs to be determined for a portfolio of bonds in order to establish a bond fund-management strategy called immunisation. See chapter 7, sections 5.4 and 7.7. The basic features of sensitivity to interest rate risk are all mirrored in the duration calculation.

- Longer-dated bonds will have longer durations.
- Lower-coupon bonds will have longer durations. The ultimate low-coupon bond is a zero coupon bond where the duration will be the maturity.
- Lower yields will give higher durations. In this case, the present value of flows in the future will fall if the yield increases, moving the point of balance towards the present day, therefore shortening the duration.

The duration of a bond will shorten as the lifespan of the bond decays. However, the rate of their decay will not be the same.

As was seen in the previous example, a five-year bond with a 7% annual coupon and a GRY or YTM of 8% has a Macaulay Duration of 4.373 years. Let us now examine what will happen for that same bond after another year has elapsed, and when the bond will only have a remaining life of four years. As can be seen in the table below, assuming again the same expectation with respect to the GRY or yield to maturity, the result of the new calculation for duration is now the equivalent of 3.617 years.

Calculation of Macaulay Duration			
Bond Price	£96.69	Gross Redemption Yield (GRY)	8.00%
Face Value	£100.00	Coupon Frequency	1
Coupon Rate	7.00%		
Life in Years	5		
Period	Cash Flow	PV Cash Flow	Duration Calculation
		Cash Flow/[(1+GRY/Coupon Frequency)^Period]	PV Cash Flow* Period
1	£7.00	£6.48	£6.48
2	£7.00	£6.00	£12.00
3	£7.00	£5.56	£16.67
4	£107.00	£78.65	£314.59
5	£0.00	£0.00	£0.00
	Totals	£96.69	£349.75
	Macaulay Duration (Years)	£349.75/£96.69	3.617

The lifespan of the bond will have decayed by a full year, but the duration by only 0.756 of a year.

Modified Duration

At the same time as the Macaulay Duration was being promoted as a means of expressing the sensitivity of a bond to movements in the interest rate, J. R. Hicks, an economist at Cambridge in the 1930s, developed a formula to explain the impact of yield changes on price. Not surprisingly, the two measures are linked.

Hicks' basic proposition was that the change in yield multiplied by this sensitivity measure will give the resultant percentage change in the bond's price, ie, the volatility gives the percentage change in price per unit change in yield.

Modified duration is the percentage change in the price of a bond arising from a 1% change in yields. The formula may be derived through the use of calculus, specifically differentiation of the price equation with respect to yields.

Fortunately, there is an easier definition, specifically:

$$\text{Modified Duration/Volatility} = \frac{-\text{Macaulay Duration}}{1 + \text{GRY}}$$

The use of modified duration is to provide a first estimate of the change in the price of a bond that will result from a given change in yields. Returning to the earlier example of a five-year bond with a 7% annual coupon, a GRY/YTM of 8% and a Macaulay Duration of 4.373 years, if the required yield were to increase by 1% the price of the bond would fall by 4.0491%, from the modified duration formula:

$$\text{Modified Duration} = -4.373/(1.08) = -4.0491$$

6.5 Investment Perspective of Bonds

Learning Objective

2.7.5   Be able to analyse the specific features of bonds from an investment perspective: coupon and payment date; maturity date; embedded put or call options; convertible bonds; exchangeable bonds

The term 'fixed income' is given to securities that pay a pre-specified or fixed return, in the form of capital and income. Following the more widely adopted usage, such securities are also collectively called bonds.

Bonds can be considered to be a contractual asset with claims on a series of cash flows which are committed by the issuer to the purchaser. Another way of expressing this same idea is to call them negotiable instruments. Such instruments, or, more simply stated, paper can be bought and sold, traded in a marketplace where there can be differences of opinion about their risk and reward characteristics. Bonds issued by large governments – sovereign issuance – tend to be highly liquid, ie, very easy to buy or sell, whereas certain corporate bonds can be far less liquid and may have to be held to maturity by the initial buyer.

6.5.1　The History of Bonds

Historically, bonds began as very simple negotiable debt instruments, paying a fixed coupon for a specified period, then being redeemed at face value. The term 'straight bond' was, and still is, used to describe the plain vanilla version of bonds with the simplest characteristics. Traditionally, bonds were seen as being investment vehicles for very cautious investors, and the term widows and orphans has sometimes been applied to the kinds of individuals for which fixed-interest securities were deemed to be most suitable.

The 1970s was a period during which there were several momentous changes in the world's financial system, which included the abandonment of convertibility of dollars into gold, the end of the era of fixed exchange rates, the emergence of serious inflation which required continuing adjustments of interest rates, the development of the euro currency markets (ie, the market in dollar and other currency assets not based in their home jurisdiction) and the beginnings of innovations in financial markets including financial futures, swaps and other derivatives. The volatility in interest rates and currencies enabled global bond markets to emerge from the shadows during the mid-1970s and since then they have become, over the past few decades, more complex investments with many variations on the basic straight bond theme.

6.5.2　Maturity Date

The maturity date is the point at which the nominal value of the bond is repaid. For example, an issue may have a maturity date of 15 February 2022, which is the date on which the redemption of the principal will take place or the bond has reached its maturity. There is a secondary market for many bonds which means that they can be sold prior to that date, but the true redemption will only take place on the date of maturity. However, as bonds have become more complex, there are now a number of variations which need to be considered. These can be classified as follows:

Irredeemable/Perpetual Bonds

With irredeemable/perpetual or undated bonds, there is no maturity date. The issuer is under no obligation to redeem the principal sum, but they may have the right to do so if desired. With these bonds, the coupon will be paid into perpetuity.

Redeemable Bonds

The majority of bond issues are redeemable with a single date at which the nominal value is repaid.

Occasionally, the issuer may be given the right to repay the bond at an earlier date, or a range of earlier dates. Such bonds are known as callable bonds, because the issuer has the right to call the bond back and redeem it early. Simplistically, the bond issuer is likely to call the bond back when the cost of replacement finance is cheaper than the interest rate being paid on the callable bond. The UK government has issued a particular type of callable bond known as a double-dated gilt. These gilts are issued with two maturity dates and the government (via the DMO) can give notice and choose to redeem these gilts on any day between the first and final maturity dates.

In contrast to callable bonds, some issuers give the holders of their bonds the right to sell their bonds back to the issuer, prior to maturity. These are referred to as putable bonds.

6.5.3 Coupons

While there is a variety of bond known as zero coupon bonds which are issued at a discount to their face value and do not pay out coupons, the vast majority of bonds are issued with a periodic payment obligation embedded in the instrument. These periodic payments are known as coupon payments.

The basis for the determination of the bond coupon is set before issue, although this does not mean that the value is known at that date. While the vast majority of bonds issued are straights (ie, a fixed coupon), there are a number of variants on this theme. Some bonds have coupons which vary with economic factors, some are index-linked to protect the bondholder from inflation, and some have more esoteric features which can alter the amount of the coupon payment based upon other factors. In essence, the majority of bonds are issued with a predetermined value for the coupon, but many are subject to variability in the amount of the coupon payment to be made.

One example of coupons that are subject to some variability is the floating rate bond, when the coupons are typically linked to a reference interest rate at the time, such as LIBOR. Clearly if LIBOR increases, the coupons will increase and vice versa for falls in LIBOR.

Another example is an index-linked bond when the coupons and usually the principal are increased by reference to an index of inflation, such as the RPI.

However the amount is calculated, the full coupon for the period will be paid to the holder of the bond on the ex-coupon date. The category of pre-determined coupons includes the vast majority of bonds. On these bonds, the gross annual coupon (ie, the amount due to be paid in a one-year period, irrespective of the frequency of payment) is specified as a percentage of the nominal value of the bond.

How often the coupon is paid is determined at issue. The frequency is typically every six months or once each year. Occasionally, coupons are paid quarterly, rather than annually or semi-annually. The frequency tends to be consistent in certain sectors of the bond market. For example, the UK, US, Japanese and Italian government bonds tend to pay coupons semi-annually. The government bonds issued by Germany and France and most other eurobonds tend to pay coupons annually.

6.5.4 Redemption at Maturity

Most bonds are redeemed, but there are a few variations to be aware of. The vast majority of bonds are redeemed in cash at maturity. This redemption may be either:

*   **At par value** – redeemed at the nominal value of the bond at the redemption date.
*   **At a premium** – redeemed at a specified premium above the nominal value of the bond at the redemption date.

Other variations exist when, instead of obliging the issuer to repay cash at the maturity date, the bond may offer the holder the choice between normal cash redemption proceeds and some other asset, such as an alternative bond of a later maturity or shares issued by a corporation.

6.5.5 Embedded Options

Embedded options are sometimes a part of a bond's characteristics. An embedded option is a part of the formal structure of the bond that gives either the bondholder or the issuer the right to take some action against the other party.

There are several types of options that can be embedded. Some common types of bonds with embedded options include callable bonds, putable bonds, convertible bonds and exchangeable bonds.

Callable Bond

A callable bond, which is also known as a redeemable bond, allows the issuer to retain the privilege of redeeming the bond at some point before the bond reaches the date of maturity. If the bond contains such an option, on the call date(s), the issuer has the right, but not the obligation, to buy back the bonds from the bondholders at a defined call price.

The call price will usually exceed the par or issue price. In certain cases, mainly in the high-yield debt market, there can be a substantial call premium.

Thus, the issuer has an option, for which it pays in the form of a higher coupon rate. If interest rates in the market have gone down by the time of the call date, the issuer will be able to refinance its debt at a cheaper level and so will be incentivised to call the bonds it originally issued.

The largest market for callable bonds is that of issues from the GSEs in the US, such as Fannie Mae and Freddie Mac, which own mortgages and issue mortgage-backed securities (see sections 1.5.2 and 2.1.4 of this chapter). In the US, mortgages are usually fixed-rate, and can be prepaid early without cost, which has given rise to a highly developed mortgage refinancing market. If adjustable rates on mortgages go down, a lot of home-owners will refinance at a lower rate, which will result in the GSEs seeing a loss in assets. By issuing a large number of callable bonds, they have a natural hedge, as they can then call their own issues and refinance at a lower rate.

The price behaviour of a callable bond is the opposite of that of putable bond. Since call options and put options are not mutually exclusive, a bond may have both options embedded.

$$\text{Price of callable bond} = \text{Price of straight bond} - \text{Price of call option}$$

- The price of a callable bond is always lower than the price of a straight bond because the call option adds value to an issuer.
- The yield on a callable bond is higher than the yield on a straight bond.

Putable Bond

The putable bond or put bond is a combination of a straight bond and embedded put option. The holder of the putable bond has the right, but not the obligation, to demand early repayment of the principal. The put option is usually exercisable on specified dates.

This type of bond protects investors: if interest rates rise after bond purchase, the future value of coupon payments will become less valuable. Therefore, investors sell their bonds back to the issuer and may lend the proceeds elsewhere at a higher rate. Bondholders are ready to pay for such protection by accepting a lower yield relative to that of a straight bond.

Of course, if an issuer has a severe liquidity crisis, it may be incapable of paying for the bonds when the investors wish. The investors also cannot sell back the bond at any time, rather on specified dates. However, they will still be ahead of holders of non-putable bonds, who may have no more right than timely payment of interest and principal (which could perhaps be many years to get all their money back).

The price behaviour of putable bonds is the opposite of that of a callable bond.

$$\text{Price of putable bond} = \text{Price of straight bond} + \text{Price of put option}$$

- The price of a putable bond is always higher than the price of a straight bond because the put option adds value to an investor.
- The yield on a putable bond is lower than the yield on a straight bond.

Convertible Bonds

A convertible note (or, if it has a maturity of greater than ten years, a convertible debenture) is a type of bond that the holder can convert into shares of common stock in the issuing company or cash of equal value, at an agreed-upon price. It is a hybrid security with debt- and equity-like features. Although it typically has a low coupon rate, the instrument carries additional value through the option to convert the bond to stock, and thereby participate in further growth in the company's equity value. The investor receives the potential upside of conversion into equity while protecting the downside with cash flow from the coupon payments.

From the issuer's perspective, the key benefit of raising money by selling convertible bonds is a reduced cash interest payment. However, in exchange for the benefit of reduced interest payments, the value of shareholders' equity is reduced due to the stock dilution expected when bondholders convert their bonds into new shares.

Exchangeable Bonds (XBs)

An exchangeable bond (or XB) is a straight bond with an embedded option to exchange the bond for the stock of a company other than the issuer (usually a subsidiary or company in which the issuer owns a stake) at some future date and under prescribed conditions. An exchangeable bond is different from a convertible bond as the convertible only gives the holder the option to convert bonds directly into shares of the issuer.

The pricing of an exchangeable bond is similar to that of a convertible bond, splitting it into a straight debt part and an embedded option part and valuing the two separately.

$$\text{Price of exchangeable bond} = \text{Price of straight bond} + \text{Price of option to exchange}$$

- The price of an exchangeable bond is always higher than the price of a straight bond because the option to exchange adds value to an investor.
- The yield on an exchangeable bond is lower than the yield on a straight bond.

6.6 Present Value, Yield and Conversion Calculations

Learning Objective

2.7.6   Be able to calculate and interpret: simple interest income on corporate debt; conversion premiums on convertible bonds; flat yield; accrued interest (given details of the day count conventions)

6.6.1   Simple Interest Income on Corporate Debt

The simplest measure of the return on a corporate bond used is the flat (interest or running) yield. This measure looks at the annual cash return (coupon) generated by an investment as a percentage of the cash price. See section 6.4.1 for the formula for its calculation and a discussion of its limitations.

6.6.2   Conversion Premiums on Convertible Bonds

A convertible bond gives the holder the right, but not the obligation, to convert into a predetermined number of ordinary shares of the issuer. Given this choice, the holder will choose to convert into shares if, at maturity, the value of the shares they can convert into exceeds the redemption value of the bond. Because there is this upside potential to the value of a convertible bond if the share price rises, and the downside protection of the redemption value if the shares do not perform well, convertible bonds generally trade at a premium to their share value.

Example

A convertible bond issued by XYZ plc is trading at £114. It offers the holder the option of converting £100 nominal into 25 ordinary shares of the company. These shares are currently trading at £3.90. We need to calculate the share value of the conversion choice which is, for £100 nominal, equal to 25 times £3.90 or £97.50. The bond is currently trading at £114 so the premium at present is £114–£97.50 = £16.50. It is common to express the premium as a percentage of the conversion value so this convertible has a premium of £16.50/£97.50 or 16.9%.

Convertible bonds enable the holder to exploit the growth potential in the equity while retaining the safety net of the bond. Therefore, convertible bonds trade at a premium to the value of the shares they can convert into. If there were no premium, there would be an arbitrage opportunity for investors to buy the shares more cheaply via the convertible than in the equity market. Usually, convertible bonds are issued where the price of each share is set at the outset and that price will be adjusted to take into account any subsequent bonus or **rights issues**. Given the share price, it is simple to calculate the conversion ratio – the number of shares that each £100 of nominal value of the bonds can convert into.

$$\text{Conversion ratio} = \frac{\text{Nominal value}}{\text{Conversion price of shares}}$$

If the issuing company has a 1-for-1 **bonus issue**, then the conversion price will halve and the conversion ratio will double.

6.6.3 Flat Yield and Accrued Interest

Accrued interest is the interest that has been earned, but not paid, and is calculated by the following formula:

$$\text{Accrued interest} = \text{Interest payment} \times \frac{\text{Number of days since last payment}}{\text{Number of days between payments}}$$

Calculating the Purchase Price for a Bond with Accrued Interest

You purchase a corporate bond with a settlement date on 15 September with a face value of £1,000 and a nominal yield of 8%, that has a listed price of 100 $^{8}/_{32}$ and that pays interest semi-annually on 15 February and 15 August. How much must you pay assuming an actual/actual convention?

The semi-annual interest payment is £40 and there were 31 days since the last interest payment on 15 August. If the settlement date fell on an interest payment date, the bond price will equal the listed price: 100.25% x £1,000.00 = £1,002.50 (8/32 = 1/4 = 0.25, so 100 $^{8}/_{32}$ = 100.25% of par value). Since the settlement date was 31 days after the last payment date, accrued interest must be added. Using the above formula, with 184 days between coupon payments, we find that:

$$\text{Accrued interest} = 40 \times 31/184 = £6.74$$

Therefore, the actual purchase price for the bond will be £1,002.50 + £6.74 = £1,009.24.

Day Count Conventions

Common day count conventions that affect the accrued interest calculation are:

- **Actual/360 (days per month, days per year)** – the period 1 February to 1 April is considered to be 59 days (28 days for February, plus 31 days for March) divided by 360.
- **30/360** – each month is treated as having 30 days, so a period from 1 February to 1 April is considered to be 60 days. The year is considered to have 360 days. This convention is frequently chosen for ease of calculation: the payments tend to be regular and at predictable amounts.
- **Actual/365** – each month is treated normally, and the year is assumed to have 365 days, regardless of leap year status. For example, a period from 1 February to 1 April is considered to be 59 days. This convention results in periods having slightly different lengths.
- **Actual/Actual (ACT/ACT) (1)** – each month is treated normally, and the year has the usual number of days. For example, a period from 1 February to 1 April is considered to be 59 days. In this convention, leap years do affect the final result.
- **Actual/Actual (ACT/ACT) (2)** – each month is treated normally, and the year is the number of days in the current coupon period multiplied by the number of coupons in a year, eg, if the coupon is payable 1 February and 1 August then on 1 April the number of days in the year is 362, ie, 181 (the number of days between 1 February and 1 August) x 2 (semi-annual).

End of Chapter Questions

Think of an answer to each question and refer to the appropriate section for confirmation.

1. What is the defining characteristic of a dual-dated gilt?
    Answer reference: Section 1.1.1

2. How does the clean price of a bond differ from the dirty price?
    Answer reference: Section 1.3.2

3. If the prevailing rates of interest are rising, what will be the effect on bond prices?
    Explain your answer.
    Answer reference: Section 1.3.4

4. How does the calculation of the retail prices index and the consumer prices index differ?
    Answer reference: Section 1.4.1

5. Explain the difference between a fixed and floating charge in relation to a corporate bond or
    debenture and indicate which will have priority in a liquidation.
    Answer reference: Sections 2.1.2 and 2.1.3

6. What are PIBSs and why might they be attractive to investors?
    Answer reference: Section 2.2.4

7. Name three of the five basic forms of eurobond issues?
    Answer reference: Section 3.1

8. If a ten-year corporate bond is yielding 5% and the equivalent ten-year gilt is yielding 3.3%, what is
    the spread expressed in basis points?
    Answer reference: Section 4.2.1

9. What is the key benefit of STRIPS?
    Answer reference: Section 5.2.2

10. For the three main credit ratings agencies, there are two classifications which represent the lowest
    form of investment grade debt. What are those classifications, and which agencies issue them?
    Answer reference: Section 6.2.2

Chapter Three
Equities

This syllabus area will provide approximately 20 of the 80 examination questions

1. Characteristics of Equities

1.1 Equity and Share Capital

Learning Objective

3.1.1   Understand the main investment characteristics, behaviours and risks of different classes of equity: ordinary, cumulative, participating, redeemable and convertible preference shares; voting rights, voting and non-voting shares; ranking for dividends; ranking in liquidation

An equity or stock represents a unit of ownership in a company. Shares are issued by stock corporations or associations limited by shares and traded on the stock exchange where, on a continuous basis, prices are calculated by matching demand and supply.

The bearer or owner of a share (the shareholder) owns part of the company's capital stock, indicated either as a percentage of the total **share capital** or as a par value that is printed on the share certificate.

Basic shareholder rights include the right to:

*   attend annual general meetings (AGMs) and extraordinary general meetings (EGMs)
*   vote at the AGM
*   receive a share of the company's profits, and
*   subscribe to new shares.

Shares are classified according to various criteria, such as the way in which the capital stock is divided up and the rights attached to the shares.

*   **Par value shares versus no-par-value shares** – a par value share states a fixed amount of the capital stock; no-par-value shares place a value in the share based on (perhaps just a percentage of) the capital stock of a company.
*   **Bearer shares versus registered shares** – the owner of a registered share is named in a company's shareholder record. Registered shares with restricted transferability are a particular type of equity because the transfer of ownership is subject to approval by the stock corporation. As far as bearer shares (see section 1.1.5) are concerned, the shareholder right is merely bound to the ownership of the share.
*   **Ordinary shares versus preferred shares** – unlike ordinary shares, preferred shares do not carry voting rights. Instead, preferred shares usually take precedence over ordinary shares when it comes to the distribution of profits and liquidation proceeds of a stock corporation.

1.1.1   Ordinary Shares

Ordinary shares are by far the most common security representing ownership in a company. Holders of ordinary shares exercise control by electing a board of directors and voting on company policy. Ordinary shareholders occupy the lowest tier of the capital structure of a company: in the event of liquidation, ordinary shareholders have rights to a company's assets only after bondholders, preference shareholders and other debt holders have been paid in full. The ordinary shareholders of a company, therefore, take the greatest risk.

If the company is sufficiently profitable, the ordinary shareholders may receive dividends. Dividends for ordinary shareholders are proposed by the directors and generally ratified by the shareholders at the AGM. However, the ordinary shareholders will only receive a dividend after any preference dividends have been paid.

Each ordinary share is typically given the right to vote at AGMs and general meetings, although sometimes voting rights are restricted to certain classes of ordinary shares. Such different classes of shares (often called A ordinary and B ordinary shares) are created to separate ownership and control.

Each shareholder has the right to vote at both an AGM and general meetings but may, if they so wish, appoint a third party, or **proxy**, to vote on their behalf. A proxy may be an individual or group of individuals appointed by the board of directors of the company to formally represent the shareholders who send in proxy requests and to vote the represented shares in accordance with the shareholders' instructions.

Each ordinary share has a nominal value which represents the minimum amount that the company must receive from subscribers on the issue of the shares. Occasionally, the company may not demand all of the nominal value at issue; the shares are then referred to as being partly paid. At a later date, the company will call on the shareholders to pay the remaining nominal value.

Non-Voting Ordinary Shares

When companies wish to raise finance from people other than the existing shareholders without diluting the control of the existing shareholders, they may issue non-voting shares.

These shares are identical in all respects to ordinary shares except that they carry no voting rights (called NV or A shares) or restricted voting rights (RV shares).

Such shares offer no greater return (they receive the same ordinary dividend), though the shareholder faces a much higher risk since they cannot influence the operations of the company. As a result, it is becoming increasingly difficult for companies to raise new capital by issuing non-voting shares.

Redeemable Ordinary Shares

Since the Companies Act 1985, companies have been allowed to issue redeemable ordinary shares, providing that they also have shares in issue that are not redeemable. See section 1.1.3 for a definition of redeemable. The company may now also purchase its own shares subject to satisfying a number of conditions.

1.1.2   Deferred Shares

Deferred shares are shares that do not rank for a dividend until a particular circumstance is satisfied, typically either until:

- the ordinary dividends have reached a predetermined level, or
- a specified period after the issue.

1.1.3   Types of Preference Shares

Preference, or preferred, shares can come in a variety of forms.

Cumulative Preference Shares

A cumulative preference shareholder will not only be paid this year's dividend before any ordinary shareholders' dividends, but will also receive any unpaid dividends from previous years. If the dividend on a cumulative preference share is not paid in any one year, it must be accumulated and paid later; that is, it should be accrued in the accounts even if the company cannot afford to pay it this year. This accumulated liability must be paid off in full in later years before any ordinary dividend can be paid.

Redeemable Preference Shares

Redeemable preference shares are preference shares that enable the company to buy back the shares from the shareholder at an agreed price in the future. The money provided by the preference shareholders can be repaid, removing any obligation the firm has to them.

Redeemable preference shares are repayable either at a predetermined price, which is normally quoted as being at a premium above their nominal value, or on the occurrence of a predetermined event or date. As such, the shares represent a temporary source of financing for the company that will rank for dividends for a short period of time and then be repaid. The shares, from the company's perspective, are similar to debt.

Participating Preference Shares

One drawback of preference shares, when compared with ordinary shares, is that if the company starts to generate large profits the ordinary shareholders will often see their dividends rise, whereas the preference shareholders still get a fixed level of dividend. To counter this, some preference shares offer the opportunity to participate in higher distributions.

As noted above, preference shares usually carry a fixed dividend, representing their full annual return entitlement. Participating preference shares will receive this fixed dividend plus an additional dividend, which is usually a proportion of any ordinary dividend declared. As such, they participate more in the risks and rewards of ownership of the company.

Convertible Preference Shares

Up to the date of conversion, a convertible preference share offers the shareholder all the normal risks and returns associated with preference shares, ie, fixed dividend returns and preferential rights to any capital repayment. On reaching the date of conversion, the shareholders will have the option of converting the preference shares into ordinary shares or taking a predetermined cash alternative.

Convertible preference shares will have a specified conversion ratio which sets out how many convertible shares can be converted into one ordinary share. As a result, a conversion premium or discount can be calculated.

If it is at a discount, the convertible is a less expensive way of buying into the ordinary shares than buying these shares directly. This happens when the price of the convertible has lagged behind the rise in the ordinary share price or offers a relatively less attractive rate of dividend. The opposite is true if the convertible stands at a premium.

The conversion premium/discount is calculated as follows:

[(Conversion Ratio x Market Price of Convertible Shares / Market Price of Ordinary Shares) – 1] x 100

The conversion ratio in the formula refers to the number of convertible preference shares that have to be converted into one ordinary share. The calculation and its use can be seen by the following example.

Example

A company has issued 7% cumulative redeemable preference shares at 110p. They are currently priced at 125p per share and can be converted into the company's ordinary shares at the rate of five preference shares for one ordinary share.

If the ordinary shares are priced at 600p, the conversion premium or discount is calculated as follows:

[(5 x 125 / 600) – 1] x 100 = 4.2%

The result shows that the convertible shares are at a premium to the ordinary shares and so buying the convertible preference shares is a more expensive route than buying the ordinary shares directly. However, the fixed rate of dividend currently being paid on the preference shares may be sufficiently attractive when compared to that being paid on the ordinary shares to justify the premium.

The fact that the shares are at a premium also indicates that it will not be worth exercising the option to convert into ordinary shares. This can be seen by simply comparing the respective values of the shares as follows:

Shares	Number of Shares	Price	Market Value
Convertible Preference Shares	5	1.25	6.25
Ordinary Shares	1	6.00	6.00

1.1.4 Rankings for Dividends and Liquidation

Preference shares are less risky than ordinary shares, but also potentially less profitable. Holders generally do not have the right to vote on company affairs, but they are entitled to receive a fixed dividend each year (as long as the company feels they have sufficient profits). These dividends must be paid before any dividends to ordinary shareholders, hence the term preference. Although preference shares tend to be non-voting, it is common for preference shareholders to become entitled to vote in the event of no dividend being paid for a substantial period of time.

Preferred shares are the first class of equity to participate in any liquidation proceeds. For that reason, preferred shares are usually the security of choice for many venture capital investors. Essentially, they adopt a last in, first out philosophy respecting repayment of capital at liquidation.

Venture capital investors may also be provided with different classes of preference shares which command a liquidation preference of two or three times their initial capital before other share classes can participate in any liquidation proceeds. The ordinary shareholders rank last in the event of a company liquidation.

1.1.5 Bearer and Registered Shares

In general, a bearer instrument is a document that indicates that the bearer of the document has title to property, such as shares or bonds. Bearer instruments differ from normal registered instruments, in that no records are kept of who owns the underlying property or of the transactions involving transfer of ownership. Whoever physically holds bearer shares is the owner of the claims that are entailed even though the name of that owner does not have to be registered. This means that not only can the ownership of a company be hidden, it can be transferred at will without this being known, without stamp duty or capital gains being paid, and without any organisation dealing with the company being any the wiser. Money laundering regulation becomes virtually impossible in such circumstances.

Bearer shares are accordingly useful for investors and corporate officers who wish to retain anonymity, although ownership is extremely difficult to recover in event of loss or theft.

Usually, the legal shareholders of a limited company are those persons whose names appear on the corporation's official shareholders' list, or register. These shareholders may or may not be issued a tangible stock certificate which they may possess. A common stock certificate will bear the name of the shareholder, and how many shares of stock the certificate represents. It will contain other information such as the name of the company, any par value the shares have and, most importantly, whether there are restrictions on the transfer of the shares.

Although, traditionally, there were not many UK companies that issued bearer shares, they were abolished in February 2016 in order to improve the transparency of company ownership.

1.2 Depository Receipts

Learning Objective

3.1.2 Understand the purpose, main investment characteristics, behaviours and risks of depositary receipts: American depositary receipts; global depositary receipts; beneficial ownership rights; structure; unsponsored and sponsored programmes; transferability

1.2.1 American Depositary Receipts (ADRs)

American depositary receipts (ADRs) were introduced in 1927 and were originally designed to enable US investors to hold overseas shares without the high dealing costs and settlement delays associated with overseas equity transactions.

An ADR is dollar-denominated and issued in bearer form, with a depository bank as the registered shareholder. ADRs confer the same shareholder rights as if the shares had been purchased directly. The depository bank makes arrangements for issues such as the payment of dividends, also denominated in US dollars, and voting via a proxy at shareholder meetings. The beneficial owner of the underlying shares may cancel the ADR at any time and become the registered owner of the shares.

The US is a huge pool of potential investment and so ADRs enable non-US companies to attract US investors to raise funds. ADRs are listed and freely traded on the NYSE and **NASDAQ**. An ADR market also exists on the LSE.

Each ADR has a particular number of underlying shares or is represented by a fraction of an underlying share. For example, Sanofi (the French Pharmaceutical and Biotech company) is listed in France and New York. There are separate ADRs in existence for the ordinary shares. Each ADR represents two individual Ord shares. ADRs give investors a simple, reliable and cost-efficient way to invest in other markets and avoid high dealing and settlement costs. Other well-known companies, such as BP, Nokia, and Vodafone have issued ADRs.

1.2.2 Global Depositary Receipts (GDRs)

Depositary receipts (DRs) issued outside the US are termed global depositary receipts (GDRs). These have been issued since 1990 and are traded on many exchanges. Increasingly, depositary receipts are issued by Asian and emerging market issuers.

For example, over 400 GDRs from over 44 countries are quoted and traded on a section of the LSE and are settled in US dollars through Euroclear or the DTCC Depository Bank. Both Euroclear and DTCC will collect the dividend on the underlying share and then convert this into payments that can be paid out to the GDR holders. Any voting rights are exercised through the Depository Bank, but GDR holders are not able to take up rights issues; instead these are sold and the cash distributed.

Both ADRs and GDRs are negotiable certificates evidencing ownership of shares in a corporation from a country outside the US. Each DR has a particular number of underlying shares, or is represented by a fraction of an underlying share.

1.2.3 Creation and Structure of Depositary Receipts

DRs are typically created (or sponsored) by the foreign corporation (Sanofi in the above example). They will liaise with an investment bank regarding the precise structure of the DR, such as the number or fraction of shares represented by each DR. A depository bank will then accept a certain number of underlying shares from the issuer, create the DRs to represent the shares and make these DRs available to the US, and potentially other investors, probably via local brokers.

This creation process for an ADR is illustrated by the following diagram:

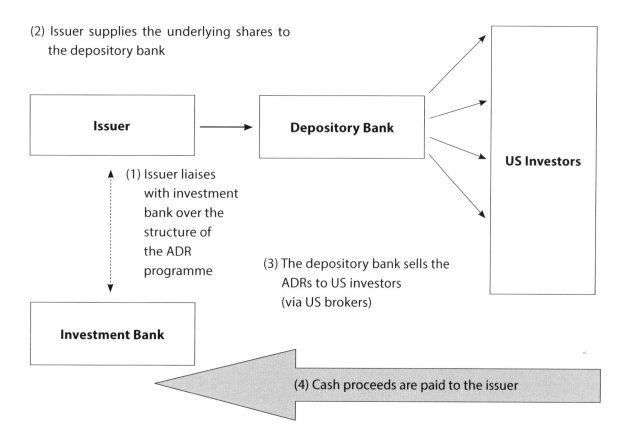

(2) Issuer supplies the underlying shares to the depository bank

(1) Issuer liaises with investment bank over the structure of the ADR programme

(3) The depository bank sells the ADRs to US investors (via US brokers)

(4) Cash proceeds are paid to the issuer

One characteristic of DRs that must also be considered is pre-release trading (or grey market trading). When a DR is being created, the depository bank receives notification that, in the future, the shares will be placed on deposit. As long as the depository bank holds cash collateral, even though the shares are not yet on deposit, the depository bank can create and sell the receipt (the DR) at this time. Effectively, investors are buying a receipt that entitles them to all the benefits of a share that will, in the future, be held on deposit for them. The DR can be treated in this way for up to three months before the actual purchase of the underlying shares.

The shares underlying the DR are registered in the name of the depository bank, with the DRs themselves transferable as bearer securities. The DRs are typically quoted and traded in US dollars and are governed by the trading and settlement procedures of the market on which they are traded.

The depository bank acts as a go-between for the investor and the company. When the company pays a dividend, it is paid in the company's domestic currency to the bank, which then converts the dividend into dollars and passes it on to the DR holders. US investors, therefore, need not concern themselves with currency movements. Furthermore, when a DR holder decides to sell, the DRs will be sold on in dollars.

This removal of the need for any currency transactions for the US investor is a key attraction of the DR. DR holders are entitled to vote, just like ordinary shareholders, except that the votes will be exercised via the depository bank.

If the DR represents a UK company's shares, there are tax ramifications in the form of stamp duty. The UK tax authority, Her Majesty's Revenue & Customs (HMRC) levies this tax on share purchases, at 0.5% of the price paid to purchase shares. However, because DRs may trade outside the UK, in the US, there is no stamp duty charged on the purchase of a DR. Instead, HMRC charges a one-off fee for stamp duty of 1.5% when the DR is created.

If an investor wants to sell their DRs, they can do so either by selling them to another investor as a DR, or by selling the underlying shares in the home market of the company concerned. The latter route will involve cancelling the DR by delivering the certificates to the depository bank. The depository bank will then release the appropriate number of shares in accordance with the instructions received.

The logistics of settling transactions and then arranging for custody of the securities purchased can be fraught with difficulty. In addition, property rights are not as well defined as in developed nations. However, these problems can be mitigated by using GDRs.

Unsponsored ADRs are issued by a depository bank with no involvement by the issuer. Certain shareholder benefits may not apply to these instruments, which are largely traded OTC.

2. Issuing Equity Securities

2.1 Overview of Security Issuance

Learning Objective

3.2.1 Understand the purpose and key features of the following: primary issues; secondary issues; issuing, listing and quotation; dual listings; cross listings; delisting (cancelling)

Recognised stock exchanges, such as the London Stock Exchange (LSE) in the UK and the New York Stock Exchange (NYSE) in the US, are marketplaces for issuing securities and then facilitating the trading of those securities via the trading and market-making activities of their member firms. All stock exchanges provide both a primary and a secondary market.

2.1.1 Primary Issues

The primary market, or the new issues market, is where securities are issued for the first time. The primary markets exist to enable issuers of securities, such as companies, to raise capital, and enable the surplus funds held by potential investors to be matched with the investment opportunities the issuers offer. It is a crucial source of funding.

The terminology often used is that companies float on the stock exchange when they first access the primary market. The process that the companies go through when they float is often called the **initial public offering (IPO)**. Companies can use a variety of ways to achieve flotation, such as offers for investors to subscribe for their shares (offers for subscription). Offers can be underwritten by an investment bank or else the shares sold in an offering may be sold on a best efforts basis by the manager of the IPO. There are no guarantees that an IPO will succeed in selling all of the shares being offered, and, if markets are going through periods of adversity and turmoil, it is common for an IPO to be withdrawn.

A large IPO is usually underwritten by a syndicate of investment banks led by one or more major investment banks (known as lead underwriter or lead manager). Upon selling the shares, the underwriters keep a commission based on a percentage of the value of the shares sold (called the gross spread). Usually, the lead underwriters, ie, the underwriters selling the largest proportions of the IPO, take the highest commissions – up to 8% in some cases.

The secondary market, not to be confused with secondary issuance, is where existing securities are traded between investors, and the stock exchanges provide a variety of systems to assist in this, such as the LSE's SETS system that is used to trade the largest companies' shares. These systems provide investors with liquidity, giving them the ability to sell their securities if they wish. The secondary market activity also results in the ongoing provision of liquidity to investors via the exchange's member firms. Each jurisdiction has its own rules and regulations for companies seeking a listing plus continuing obligations for those already listed. In the UK, there is the FCA and in the US, the Securities and Exchange Commission (SEC). For further details, see section 2.2.2.

A special purpose acquisitions company (SPAC) is a company with no commercial buying or selling operations. The company is set up by investors solely to raise capital through an IPO, which it eventually uses to acquire another existing company. SPACs have become increasingly popular in recent years, as seen in 2020 when SPACs raised $82 billion in the US.

2.1.2 Secondary Issues

Secondary issuances or secondary public offerings of shares are often referred to as a follow-on offering as they refer to an issuance of stock subsequent to the company's IPO. A follow-on offering can be either of two types (or a mixture of both): dilutive and non-dilutive (as rights issue). Furthermore, it could be a cash issue or a capital increase in return for stock. A secondary offering is an offering of securities by a shareholder of the company (as opposed to the company itself, which is a primary offering).

In the case of some offerings, there can be a hybrid offering amalgamating both primary and secondary issuance. For example, Google's IPO included both a primary offering (issuance of Google stock by Google) and a secondary offering (sale of Google stock held by shareholders, including the founders).

In the case of the dilutive offering, a company's board of directors agrees to increase the share float for the purpose of selling more equity in the company. The proceeds from the secondary offering might be used to pay off some debt or used for needed company expansion. When new shares are created and then sold by the company, the number of shares outstanding increases and this causes dilution of earnings on a per share basis. Usually, the gain of cash inflow from the sale is strategic and is considered positive for the longer-term goals of the company and its shareholders.

The non-dilutive type of follow-on offering is when privately held shares are offered for sale by company directors or other insiders (such as venture capitalists) who may be looking to diversify their holdings. Because no new shares are created, the offering is not dilutive to existing shareholders, but the proceeds from the sale do not benefit the company in any way. As with an IPO, the investment banks who are serving as underwriters of the follow-on offering will often be offered the use of a greenshoe or over-allotment option by the selling company.

2.1.3 Issuing, Listing and Quotation

To offer shares for sale to the public via an IPO, a UK company must be a public limited company (plc). The kinds of IPOs that can be conducted and the listing requirements of the exchanges vary, and in the case of a large corporation, the most likely route for a UK company is to seek a full listing on the Main Market of the LSE. If the company is smaller or has less of a trading track record, it may join the LSE's less closely regulated **alternative investment market (AIM)** (see section 2.3.5).

Companies seeking a full listing on the LSE have to meet stringent entry criteria, known as the Listing Rules, administered by the FCA. The requirements are detailed in section 2.3.4.

The advantages to a company of obtaining a full listing include:

- raising its public profile
- increasing the liquidity and marketability of its shares so that they can be more easily traded, and
- gaining easier and less expensive access to new capital.

The disadvantages, however, include:

- the costs and increased accountability associated with obtaining and maintaining a full listing as a result of greater disclosure and compliance requirements
- relinquishing an element of control, and
- becoming a potential **takeover** target.

Once a company has undertaken a listed offering, its share prices will be quoted in the normal fashion for all listed companies, ie, with a bid and ask quotation, and the shares can be traded on a variety of platforms.

Delisting (Cancelling)

Delisting is really the opposite of listing and means that the listed security is removed from the exchange's official list. Delisting can be voluntary or involuntary and can be for a variety of reasons. Such reasons are:

- failure to meet the listing regulations or requirements of the exchange. Listing requirements include minimum share prices, certain financial ratios and minimum sales levels
- the company goes out of business
- the company declares bankruptcy
- the company has become a private company (eg, resulting from a management buy out) after a merger or acquisition
- the company wishes to reduce or remove an element of its regular reporting requirements, or
- the company no longer seeks a listing because of factors such as low volumes on the exchange on which it is listed or for financial reasons, eg, to save on listing fees.

It is not always the case that companies who are delisted are bankrupt. Some delisted shares continue trading OTC.

2.1.4 Dual Listing

Dual listing refers to the fact that many securities are listed on more than one exchange. This can be the case when a company's shares are listed and traded internationally both on the LSE and the NYSE, such as in the case of BP, Vodafone and HSBC. Dual listing can also refer to stocks trading on more than one exchange within the same jurisdiction. Many stocks are traded on the NYSE and on one or more of the regional exchanges – for example, the common stock of General Motors. Although dual listing theoretically should improve the liquidity of a stock, thereby benefiting investors, most dual-listed securities trade chiefly on one exchange.

One consequence of a dual listing for multinational corporations is in reference to the Sarbanes-Oxley Act (often referred to as SOX). Passed in 2002 by the US Congress, the Act's objective is *'to protect investors by improving the accuracy and reliability of corporate disclosures made pursuant to the securities laws, and for other purposes'*. It applies to US public companies and their global subsidiaries, and to foreign companies that have shares listed on US stock exchanges. As a result of their dual listing, SOX, therefore, applies to some of the UK's largest companies by **market capitalisation**, such as BP, HSBC, Prudential, Royal Dutch Shell and Vodafone, as well as many other international companies.

With dual listing, there are two legal companies acting as one, and their shares list and trade as those legal companies.

2.1.5 Cross Listing

The practice of cross listing involves an issuer listing its shares in more than one market and in addition to being listed on its own domestic exchange, ie, it is where the same shares are listed in more than one country.

Many cross-listed securities have their prices quoted in different currencies, eg, GBP in London and EUR in Paris. Prices, therefore, are subject to exchange rate fluctuation, as well as local market price formation from natural supply and demand. Sometimes, small differences can exist between the prices of both markets (taking into account the exchange rate), but this is usually very small, momentary and quickly arbitraged away.

Some high frequency traders employ trading algorithms that look to profit from such differences by buying in one market and selling in another. For some securities, however, there may be delays in settlement due to re-registration of the bought security to settle the sale and thus settlement risk arises, even though both securities are technically identical and fungible.

There are some advantages for a company to cross list, including a lower cost of finance in capital raising, improved liquidity and the local labour market advantage of creating improved visibility and perception of the company/brand. Additionally, companies may perhaps introduce share option schemes for the benefit of employees in these local markets.

The main disadvantage, of course, is cost to the issuer as each listing will have its own reporting and disclosure obligations, as well as additional fees for listing.

2.2 The Regulatory Framework

Learning Objective

3.2.2 Understand the main regulatory, supervisory and trade body framework supporting UK financial markets: Companies Acts; the Financial Conduct Authority (FCA); HM Treasury; Payment Systems Regulator; the Panel on Takeovers and Mergers (POTAM); exchange membership and rules; relevant trade associations and professional bodies

The regulatory framework that underlies the way that the financial markets operate, in general in the UK, and the LSE in particular, includes oversight and compliance with the following fundamental principles:

- Company law – in particular, the various Companies Acts and especially the Companies Act 2006.
- Regulations and requirements of the Financial Conduct Authority (FCA).
- Supervision and vigilance by HM Treasury.
- The Panel on Takeovers and Mergers (POTAM).
- Rules of membership laid down by exchanges such as the LSE rule book.

The Companies Acts detail requirements for companies generally, such as the requirement to prepare annual accounts, the need to have accounts audited and for AGMs. Of particular significance to the LSE are the Companies Act requirements necessary to enable a company to be a plc, since one of the requirements for a company to be listed and traded on the exchange is that the company is a plc. There have been many versions of the Companies Act over the years, but the one which received royal assent in November 2006 provided, at the time, a complete overhaul of the previously enacted legislation.

The 2006 Act contains 1,300 sections, 16 schedules and covers many of the key areas including:

- company names
- Memorandum of Association
- Articles of Association
- share capital and maintenance of capital
- meetings
- communication with shareholders
- directors' duties
- company secretary and company records, and
- annual reports and accounts.

2.2.1 The Financial Conduct Authority (FCA)

The FCA has to give its recognition before an exchange is allowed to operate in the UK. It has granted recognition to the LSE and, by virtue of this recognition, the exchange is described as a recognised investment exchange (RIE). In granting recognition, the FCA assesses whether the exchange has sufficient systems and controls to run a market. Furthermore, the FCA lays down the detailed rules that have to be met before companies are admitted to the official list that enables their shares to be traded on the exchange.

2.2.2   Listing in the UK

The FCA is responsible for setting and administering the listing requirements and continuing obligations for plcs seeking and obtaining a full listing on the LSE. The FCA, when the FSA, was appointed as the listing authority in May 2000.

Each jurisdiction has its own rules and regulations for companies seeking a listing, plus continuing obligations for those already listed. The FCA is the 'competent authority for listing' – making the decisions as to which companies' shares and bonds (including gilts) can be admitted to be traded on the LSE. It is the FCA that sets the rules relating to becoming listed on the LSE, including the implementation of any relevant EU directives. The LSE is responsible for the operation of the exchange, including the trading of the securities on the secondary market, although the FCA can suspend the listing of particular securities and, therefore, remove their secondary market trading activity on the exchange.

In a similar way in the US, the SEC requires companies seeking a listing on the US exchanges (such as Euronext and Nasdaq) to register certain details with the SEC first. Once listed, companies are then required to file regular reports with the SEC, particularly in relation to their trading performance and financial situation.

2.2.3   HM Treasury

Her Majesty's Treasury (commonly known as HM Treasury) is the economics and finance ministry, with overall responsibility for fiscal policy, as well as providing a supervisory role for the entire financial framework in the UK. The department of government is headed by the Chancellor of the Exchequer.

2.2.4   The Chancellor of the Exchequer

The Chancellor of the Exchequer is the title held by the British Cabinet minister who is responsible for all economic and financial matters, controls HM Treasury and plays a role akin to the posts of Minister of Finance or Secretary of the Treasury in other nations. The position is considered one of the four Great Offices of State in the UK, and in recent times, has come to be the most powerful office in British politics after the Prime Minister.

HM Treasury administers the sanctions regime in the UK. In 2011, sanctions were applied against the government of Libya and, in addition to sanctions being applied against Al-Qaeda and the Taliban regimes, there are sanctions which have also been applied against, among others, persons associated with Burma, the Democratic Republic of the Congo, Iraq, Ivory Coast, Lebanon, Russia, Sudan, Zimbabwe and, more recently, North Korea. The main instrument for administering financial sanctions is the publication of a consolidated list of financial sanctions targets which is used by banks and other financial institutions to scan their customer databases and discover financial assets controlled by those who are the targets of the sanctions and, typically, freeze any funds.

2.2.5   The Panel on Takeovers and Mergers (POTAM)

The UK supervisory authority that carries out the regulatory functions required under the EU Takeover Directive is the Panel on Takeovers and Mergers (the Panel or POTAM).

The Panel's requirements are set out in a code that consists of six general principles and a number of detailed rules. The Code is designed principally to ensure that shareholders are treated fairly and are not denied an opportunity to decide on the merits of a takeover. Furthermore, the Code ensures that shareholders of the same class are afforded equivalent treatment by an offeror. In short, the Code provides an orderly framework within which takeovers are conducted and is designed to assist in promoting the integrity of the financial markets.

The Code is not concerned with the financial or commercial advantages or disadvantages of a takeover. These are matters for the company and its shareholders. Nor is the Code concerned with competition policy, which is the responsibility of government and other bodies. Each of the six general principles is reproduced below, and it is useful to be able to review the principles to appreciate fully the spirit of the Code. At its broadest, the Code simply requires fair play between all interested parties.

1. All holders of the securities of an offeree company of the same class must be afforded equivalent treatment; moreover, if a person acquires control of a company, the other holders must be protected.
2. The holders of the securities of an offeree company must have sufficient time and information to enable them to reach a properly informed decision on the bid; where it advises the holders of securities, the board of the offeree company must give its views on the implementation of the bid on employment, conditions of employment and the locations of the company's places of business.
3. The board of an offeree company must act in the best interests of the company as a whole and must not deny the holders of securities the opportunity to decide on the merits of the bid.
4. False markets must not be created in the securities of the offeree company, or the offeror company or of any other company concerned by the bid in such a way that the rise or fall of the prices of the securities becomes artificial and the normal functioning of the markets is distorted.
5. An offeror must announce a bid only after ensuring that they can fulfil in full any cash consideration, if such is offered, and after taking all reasonable measures to secure the implementation of any other type of consideration.
6. An offeree company must not be hindered in the conduct of its affairs for longer than is reasonable by a bid for its securities.

2.2.6   Trade Associations and Professional Bodies

The British Bankers' Association (BBA)

The BBA is the leading association for the UK banking and financial services sector, speaking for over 200 banking members from 50 countries on the full range of UK or international banking issues.

The BBA website states:

'We have the largest and most comprehensive policy resources for banks in the UK and represent our members domestically, in Europe and on the global stage. Our network also includes over 80 of the world's leading financial and professional services organisations. Our members manage more than £7 trillion in UK banking assets, employ nearly half a million individuals nationally, contribute over £60 billion to the UK economy each year and lend over £150 billion to UK businesses'.

The Investment Association (IA)

The IA is the trade body for the UK's £7.7 trillion asset management industry. Its stated purpose, according to its website, is: '*to support and promote a commercially successful and growing UK investment management industry as we seek to improve the financial outcomes for customers – savers and investors*'.

The Chartered Institute for Securities & Investment (CISI)

The CISI website states: '*The Chartered Institute for Securities & Investment is the largest and most widely respected professional body for those who work in the securities and investment industry in the UK and in a growing number of major financial centres round the world*'.

Evolved from the LSE, the CISI has more than 45,000 members and sets over 40,000 examinations covering a range of vocational qualifications.

The CISI's charitable objectives are to:

- promote, for the public benefit, the advancement and dissemination of knowledge in the field of securities and investments
- develop high ethical standards for practitioners in securities and investments and to promote such standards in the UK and overseas, and
- act as an authoritative body for the purpose of consultation and research in matters of education and public interest concerning investment in securities.

The Personal Investment Management & Financial Advice Association (PIMFA)

On 1 June 2017, the Association of Professional Financial Advisers (APFA) merged with the Wealth Management Association (WMA) to form the Personal Investment Management & Financial Advice Association (PIMFA).

The mission of PIMFA is to '*create an optimal operating environment so that member firms can focus on delivering the best service to clients and providing responsible stewardship for their long-term savings and investments*'.

2.2.7 The Payment Systems Regulator (PSR)

The Payment Systems Regulator (PSR) is an independent economic regulator that came into force on 1 April 2015. The PSR is a subsidiary of the FCA but has its own statutory objectives, managing director and board. It is funded by the payments industry and is accountable to the UK Parliament. Payment systems are a key component of the financial system in the UK and they handle £75 trillion payments annually.

The PSR's statutory objectives are summarised as follows:

- to ensure that payment systems are operated and developed in a way that considers and promotes the interests of all the businesses and consumers that use them
- to promote effective competition in the markets for payment systems and services (between operators, PSPs and infrastructure providers), and
- to promote the development of, and innovation in, payment systems, in particular the infrastructure used to operate those systems.

The PSR will liaise with payment system operators (cards and interbank), payment service providers, including banks and building societies, infrastructure providers and businesses that rely on these systems. It also works with industry bodies and consumer groups. One of its key purposes is to use its powers where it feels that the payment systems industry is failing to provide adequate competition and provide greater benefits for businesses or consumers. Among other powers are giving directions to take action and requiring operators to provide direct access to payment systems.

2.3 The London Stock Exchange (LSE)

Learning Objective

3.2.3 Understand the structure of the UK exchanges, the types of securities traded on their markets, and the criteria and processes for companies seeking admission: London Stock Exchange Main Market; high-growth segment; AIM; Aquis; market participants; implications for investors

The LSE began life in 1773 when traders who regularly met to buy and sell the shares of joint stock companies in Jonathan's Coffee House voted to change the name of the coffee house to that of the LSE. The LSE is Europe's largest stock exchange, accounting for over 35% of European stock market capitalisation, about 10% of world stock market value and over 50% of foreign equity trading on world stock exchanges. In the rapidly changing financial markets, the LSE has to continue evolving to adapt to the new platforms and technologies of a very competitive global marketplace.

The LSE is a recognised investment exchange (RIE) and, as such, is responsible for:

- providing a primary and secondary market for equities and fixed-interest securities
- supervising its member firms
- regulating the markets it operates
- recording all transactions, or bargains, executed on the exchange, and
- disseminating price-sensitive company information received by its regulatory news service (RNS) and distributed through commercial quote vendors, also known as secondary information providers (SIPs).

The LSE operates both a primary and secondary market. In its guise as a primary market, the LSE will provide facilities for new issuance of securities by existing listed companies and new companies which have satisfied the listing criteria detailed in section 2.3.4.

In its capacity as a secondary market, the role which comprises the majority of its day-to-day activities, the LSE provides a marketplace, nowadays exclusively an electronic market, for the dealing (trading) of a variety of securities.

The LSE provides real-time market information to various organisations around the world which subscribe to the data feeds and trading facilities of the firm. The LSE's website outlines the following three key considerations regarding membership of the exchange.

2.3.1 Eligibility for Membership

Membership is available to investment firms and credit institutions authorised in the European Economic Area (EEA). Other non-EEA-regulated companies/institutions may be eligible. Members may also be eligible for stamp duty reserve tax (SDRT) exemption and may apply for this as part of their application.

2.3.2 Connectivity

Member firms can connect directly to the exchange's markets. The exchange offers several types of connectivity options with varying levels of management and performance. These range from full host-to-host solutions to vendor access network (VAN) connections. Each firm will have different requirements and the LSE can help them choose the right form of access for their firm.

2.3.3 Clearing and Settlement

Firms that choose to connect directly to the exchange need to have in place appropriate clearing and settlement arrangements. Members of the LSE benefit from an efficient and competitive clearing and settlement infrastructure across its domestic and international markets.

The major securities which are traded daily on the LSE are:

- shares of domestic plcs which are of two main varieties:
  - companies with a full listing, and
  - usually, smaller UK plcs are admitted to AIM.
- exchange-traded funds (ETFs) and other new investment products
- international equities
- domestic corporate bonds
- UK Treasury issuance including gilts
- local authority fixed-interest securities, and
- international bonds including eurobonds.

2.3.4 Full Listing

Companies seeking a full listing on the LSE have to meet stringent entry criteria. These criteria are known as the Listing Rules and are administered by the FCA.

The Listing Rules include the following requirements:

- The market value of the company's issued share capital, or market capitalisation, must be at least £700,000, of which no less than 25% must be made freely available to the investing public to ensure an active market in the shares. This 25% is known as the free float.
- The market value of any company bond issues must be at least £200,000. Should a company bring both debt and equity to the market, the total value must therefore be at least £900,000.
- All securities issued by the company must be freely transferable, that is, third-party approval to deal in these securities must not be required.
- Any subsequent issue of ordinary shares or of securities that can be converted into the company's ordinary shares must be made to existing shareholders first unless the shareholders pass a **special resolution** to forgo their pre-emption right.

- No one shareholder can hold 30% or more of the company's ordinary voting shares.
- The company must have at least three years of audited accounts.
- The company must publish a statement showing that it believes it has sufficient working capital to last at least the next 12 months.
- The company's directors must have appropriate expertise and experience for managing the business.

UK and European high-growth companies that do not meet all of the eligibility criteria to join the premium segment of the main market can seek admission to the high-growth segment (HGS) of the main market. HGS provides medium- and large-sized high-growth companies with an additional route to the main market, to raise capital and to use the public market as a platform to build their business. Companies applying for a listing on the HGS must demonstrate growth in revenues of at least 20% over a three-year period prior to admission and must have at least 10% of the number of securities admitted in public hands with a value of at least £30 million (the majority of which must be raised at admission).

2.3.5   AIM

Gaining admission to AIM is far less demanding than obtaining a full listing, as a minimum market capitalisation, free float and past trading record are not required.

Most AIM companies tend to be those in the early stages of development, typically operating in growth industries or in niche sectors, with a view to applying for a full listing once they become more established.

The criteria to be satisfied to gain admission to AIM include:

- The company will have to appoint a nominated adviser (NOMAD) to advise the directors of their responsibilities in complying with AIM rules. The NOMAD will also have to advise the firm on how to prepare a prospectus that accompanies the company's application for admission to AIM.
- The company will also have to appoint a nominated broker to make a market and facilitate trading in the company's shares, as well as provide ongoing information about the company to interested parties.

2.3.6   Continuing Obligations

Once companies have obtained a listing, they are subject to a strict set of rules and regulations set by the FCA known as continuing obligations.

Among other things, these require a company to promptly make all price-sensitive information public and issue the annual and interim reports and accounts to shareholders within a set time frame. AIM companies must publish accounts in accordance with the UK Generally Accepted Accounting Principles (GAAP) – audited annual accounts within six months of the financial year-end, and half-yearly reports within three months of the period to which they relate.

The Brexit transition period ended at 11pm on 31 December 2020 and the UK's onshored EU legislation now applies. 'Onshoring' was the process of amending EU legislation and regulatory requirements so that they work in a UK-only context, including directly applicable EU legislation such as the EU Regulations and Decisions that form part of UK law by virtue of the European Union (Withdrawal) Act 2018, now that the Brexit transition period has ended.

Price-sensitive information is information which would be expected to move the company's share price in a material way once in the public domain. This includes releasing details of any significant change to a company's current or forecasted trading prospects, dividend announcements, directors' dealings and any notifiable interests in the company's shares.

A notifiable interest is when a shareholder or any parties connected to the shareholder has at least a 3% interest in the nominal value of the company's voting share capital. When that is the case, they must inform the company of their interest within two business days. From July 2016, the EU's Market Abuse Regulation (MAR) restricted all employees and directors from using inside information when dealing in the company's shares. MAR also imposed additional restrictions on directors and persons discharging managerial responsibilities (PDMRs).

2.3.7　Market Participants

LSE membership consists of all major multinational banks as well as smaller boutique private client banks, brokers, dealers, market makers, clearing firms and other financial intermediaries.

Historically, the main buyers and sellers responsible for the bulk of trading activities on the LSE were high net worth individual investors and corporate investors who were investing in the shares and bonds of other companies. In more recent times, participation in the daily activities of the LSE, in common with all financial markets, is overwhelmingly conducted by institutional investors such as pension funds, index funds, exchange-traded funds, hedge funds, investor groups, banks and other miscellaneous financial institutions.

2.3.8　Aquis Exchange

Aquis Exchange is authorised and regulated by the FCA in the UK and AMF (Autorité des Marchés Financiers) in France. It operates as a multilateral trading facility (MTF) in the UK under the name Aquis Exchange UK and in the EU as Aquis Exchange Europe.

In March 2020, the FCA approved Aquis Exchange's acquisition of the NEX exchange from CME. Aquis operates order books and offers pan-European equities trading. It does not permit aggressive non-client proprietary trading. Aquis offers a subscription-based pricing model and charges according to usage, which Aquis cites as having the potential to significantly reduce the cost of trading.

2.4 Listing Securities without a Prospectus

Learning Objective

3.2.4 Understand the process of issuing securities in the UK with or without a prospectus: Prospectus Directive (PD) or equivalent where applicable; eligibility and registration criteria for natural persons and small and medium-sized enterprises (SMEs)

For most public offerings of securities, a vital prerequisite is a prospectus or offering document which the issuer has to make available to all prospective investors and the exchanges upon which it intends to list its securities. Such a prospectus has to fully disclose all of the pertinent details regarding the offering including a detailed business plan, an explanation of how the proceeds from the offering will be used, details of all owners/directors of the entity, and, most importantly, a comprehensive disclosure of all of the risks associated with the investment.

There are, however, offerings of securities which are made, not to the general public, but to a subset of so-called sophisticated investors, where the rigorous kinds of disclosures that have to be made in an IPO prospectus can be avoided.

2.4.1 Prospectus Directive (PD)

Under the Market in Financial Instruments Directive (MiFID), which were coordinated among members of the EU, provisions have been allowed for offerings which can be made to a restricted class of investors in Europe when a formal prospectus is not statutorily required.

The Prospectus Regulations 2005, implementing the EU Prospectus Directive 2003/71/EC, were made on 26 May 2005. The Statutory Instrument (No. 1433) was laid before Parliament on 27 May 2005. The Prospectus Directive (PD) sets out the initial disclosure obligations for issuers of securities that are offered to the public or admitted to trading on a regulated market in the EU. It provides a passport for issuers, which in turn enables them to raise capital across the EU on the basis of a single prospectus.

The rules apply to prospectuses for public offers of securities and admission of securities to trading on a regulated market. The following are the key provisions:

- **Prospectus requirements** – prescribing the contents and format of prospectuses; allowing issuers to incorporate by reference; allowing the use of three-part prospectuses; setting out the exemptions from the requirement to produce prospectuses.
- **Approval and publication of prospectus** – setting out procedures for the approval of prospectuses and how and where they must be published.
- **Passport rights** – introducing administrative measures to facilitate the passporting of prospectuses on a pan-European basis, making it easier for companies to raise capital across Europe.
- **Third country issuers** – prospectuses drawn up under a third country's law can be treated as equivalent to directive requirements. This will be determined on a case-by-case basis.
- **Other provisions** – requiring issuers to produce annual information updates and the establishment of a qualified investor register.

One very significant provision of the PD, as implemented in the UK, is that issuers/offerors are exempt from the obligation to produce a prospectus where offers of securities are made only to qualified investors (QIs).

The PD was repealed on 21 July 2019 by the Prospectus Regulation ((EU) 2017/1129). The review of the PD was a key strategic priority for the European Commission (EC). With effect from January 2021, the UK has its own prospectus regime which largely retains the requirements of the EU Prospectus Regulation, but with some changes to reflect the UK's EU departure.

The main requirements of the revised Regulation include:

- **Simplified Disclosure Regime** – a new regime to assist small growth companies plus a simplified disclosure regime for companies seeking to raise further capital.
- **Universal Registration Document (URD)** – a new form of shelf registration mechanism for regular issuers of securities.
- **Wholesale Disclosure Regime** – permits a reduced standard of disclosure for prospectuses prepared by issuers for admissions to trading of non-equity securities.
- **Risk Factors** – issuers will need to limit the risk factors in a prospectus to 15.
- **Requirements for Prospectus Summaries** – requirements for summaries to be included.

2.4.2 Qualified Investors (QIs)

A QI, in relation to an offer of transferable securities, would usually have to be deemed, under MiFID, to be a professional client, have agreed to be treated as a professional client or be an eligible counterparty. QIs include investment institutions, certain small and medium-sized entities (SMEs) and natural persons meeting prescribed criteria.

Taxation Issues for a Qualified Investor Scheme (QIS)

A qualified investor scheme (QIS) is a type of authorised investment fund (AIF) which is subject to regulation by the FCA. The general treatment of investors in an AIF is designed to recognise that they have bought units in a pooled investment scheme where the investors have no control over the decisions of the fund manager about when and what investments to buy and sell. Instead of being charged a tax on their share of the income and gains of the scheme, they are liable to tax (income tax or corporation tax) on the distributions they receive and to CGT (or to corporation tax on chargeable gains) on the gains made when they sell their units. This treats their holding of units in a fund (that is, units in an AIF or shares in an **open-ended investment company (OEIC)**) in a similar way to a holding of shares in a normal company.

2.5   Initial Public Offering (IPO)

Learning Objective

3.2.5   Understand the purpose, structure and stages of an initial public offering (IPO) and the role of the origination team: structure – base deal plus greenshoe; stages of an IPO; underwritten versus best efforts; principles and process of price stabilisation

3.2.6   Understand the benefits for the issuer and investors of the different processes used in an IPO

For the issuer the key benefits of an IPO over other capital-raising methods are that IPOs can raise substantial sums of capital and create a great deal of publicity for the issuing companies. The money raised in the form of an IPO is known as risk capital and the company assets are not encumbered or hypothecated in the same manner as they would be if the capital were raised from a debt offering.

For investors, the benefit of buying shares in a new issue is that, providing that they have conducted adequate due diligence (ie, fully researched the business plans and risk disclosures in the offering document), they can diversify their existing holdings with the shares of a new company which may, over time, become very successful.

The early stage investors who purchased shares in the IPOs of companies such as Microsoft, Intel, Apple and Google could have amassed fortunes if they had retained their shares. The extraordinary capital gains seen in the shares of such companies represents one of the most exciting opportunities for returns in the financial markets.

Of course, not all IPOs will be such success stories. A company may only perform in a mediocre fashion following an IPO, and, as was seen during the dot com mania of the late 1990s, many internet ventures, with little or no revenues, were taken to market in a bubble-like mania of IPOs and many of these companies have subsequently disappeared. Others were absorbed by acquiring companies, and, in many cases, the purchasers of shares in an IPO were eventually issued shares in the company which acquired the original issuers. In some cases, the returns from these acquisitions have also produced extraordinary returns.

However, the May 2012 IPO for Facebook saw the market price of the shares lose over a quarter of its IPO value in under a month and, by three months, the price was less than half of its IPO value. However, there was a subsequent improvement in the trading price during the second half of 2012, throughout 2013, and in the first half of 2014, where it often significantly outperformed a rising market. At the time of writing (June 2021), the share price was around $330, over eight times the IPO price of $38.

2.5.1   The Origination Team

Deciding to list (or float) securities on a stock exchange is a significant decision for a company to take. Flotations have both pros and cons. The fact that the company can gain access to capital and enable its shares to be readily marketable are often-quoted positives. The most often-quoted negatives are that the original owners may well lose control of the company, and that the ongoing disclosure requirements, and attention paid to the company after listing are much greater than previously.

Once the decision has been made to list, the company will need to find and appoint a sponsor. The sponsor is likely to be an investment bank, a stockbroking firm or a professional services firm such as an accountancy practice. The role of the sponsor includes assessing the company's suitability for listing and the best method of bringing the company to the market, and coordinating the production of the prospectus. This is a detailed document about the company, including financial information, enabling prospective investors to decide on the merits of the company's shares.

The sponsor is only part of the origination team helping the company in the flotation. In addition to the sponsor, the issuing company will appoint a variety of other advisers, such as reporting accountants, legal advisers, public relations (PR) consultants and a corporate broker. The reporting accountants will attest to the validity of the financial information provided in the prospectus and the legal advisers will make sure that all relevant matters are covered in the prospectus and the statements made are justified. The combination of the reporting accountants and the legal advisers is said to be providing due diligence for the prospectus – making sure the document is accurate and complies with the regulations.

A PR consultant is generally appointed to optimise the positive public perception of the company and its products and services in the run-up to listing.

Finally, the origination team may require a corporate broker to ensure that there is a market in the company's shares, to facilitate trading in those shares and to provide ongoing information about the company to interested parties. This role will most likely be provided by the sponsor if the sponsor is an investment bank or stockbroking firm.

2.5.2 Structure of the Offering

Let us take as an illustration of how the IPO is structured in the case of a relatively new technology company which intends to sell one million shares of its stock in a public offering through an investment banking firm (or group of firms, known as a syndicate) whom the company has chosen to be the offering's underwriter(s).

The underwriters function as the broker of these shares and find willing buyers among their clients. A price for the shares is determined by agreement between the sellers (the company's owners and directors) and the buyers (the underwriters and their clients). A part of the responsibility of the lead underwriter in running a successful offering is to help ensure that, once the shares begin to trade publicly, they do not trade below the offering price. When a public offering trades below its offering price, it is said that the offering broke issue or broke syndicate bid. This creates the perception of an unstable or undesirable offering, which can lead to further selling and hesitant buying of the shares. To manage this possible situation, the underwriter initially oversells (shorts) to their clients the offering by an additional 15% of the offering size. In our example, then, the underwriter will sell 1.15 million shares of stock to their clients.

Now, when the offering is priced and those 1.15 million shares are effective (become eligible for public trading), the underwriter is able to support and stabilise the offering price bid (which is also known as the syndicate bid) by buying back the extra 15% of shares (150,000 shares in this example) in the market at or below the offer price. They are able to do this without having to assume the market risk of being long this extra 15% of shares in their own account, as they are simply covering (closing out) their 15% oversell short.

An IPO is usually structured with a base number of shares that the company is planning to issue. However, the issuing company may also reserve the right to increase the number of shares that it issues if significant levels of demand would remain unsatisfied if only the base number of shares were issued. The option to increase the number of shares is referred to as a greenshoe option. A greenshoe option is a clause contained in the underwriting agreement of an IPO. The greenshoe option, also often referred to as an over-allotment provision, allows the underwriting syndicate to buy up to an additional 15% of the shares at the offering price if public demand for the shares exceeds expectations and the stock trades above its offering price.

The mechanism by which the greenshoe option works to provide stability and liquidity to a public offering can be illustrated by continuing with the example outlined above, but assuming in this case that the offering has such strong demand (as was the case for a number of the dot com IPOs of the 1990s) that the price of the stock immediately goes up and stays above the offering price.

Under this scenario, the underwriter is left having oversold the offering by 15% and is now technically short those shares. If they were to buy back that 15% of shares, they would be buying back those shares at a higher price than they sold them at, and would incur a loss on the transaction.

This is when the over-allotment (greenshoe) option comes into play: the company grants the underwriters the option to take from the company up to 15% of shares additional to the original offering size at the offering price. A reverse greenshoe allows underwriters to sell shares back to the issuer in order to support the secondary market price following the IPO, if the price falls. The underwriter can purchase shares in the secondary market and sell them back to the issuer, thus helping to stabilise the price.

If the underwriters were able to buy back all of their oversold shares at the offering price in support of the deal, they would not need to exercise any of the greenshoe. But if they were only able to buy back some of the shares before the stock went higher, then they would exercise a partial greenshoe for the rest of the shares. If they were not able to buy back any of the oversold 15% of shares at the offering price (syndicate bid) because the stock immediately went and stayed up, then they would be able to completely cover their 15% short position by exercising the full greenshoe.

2.5.3   The Stages of an IPO

There are three broad stages to an IPO:

- **The decision** – the issuing company (in conjunction with its advisers, particularly the investment bank) makes a decision to raise capital via an IPO. This will involve careful consideration of the pros and cons of a public offer.
- **The preparation of the prospectus** – this is the necessary document that must accompany an IPO, involving the whole team of advisers, including the investment bank, reporting accountants and legal advisers. In the US, a prospectus has to be filed with the SEC and must strictly follow prescribed procedures and full risk disclosures in accordance with regulations covering new issues. In the UK, similar policies are in place and regulated by the FCA.
- **The sale of securities** – the investment bank will lead-manage the sale and may well establish a syndicate of co-managers to assist in selling the securities to their clients.

2.5.4 Underwritten Versus Best Efforts

Underwriting an offer is generally the responsibility of the investment bank(s) and they typically arrange firm underwriting where there are guarantees in place to buy the securities. An IPO is said to be underwritten when there is a firm undertaking by the investment bank(s) that are conducting the offering that all of the offering will be fully subscribed. In other words, the underwriting bank(s) will guarantee that any shortfall by subscribers will be purchased by the bank(s) for their own account.

Investment banks may not provide a firm undertaking to place all of the securities on behalf of their clients. Instead, the lead underwriter along with the co-managers of the offer may provide a best efforts underwriting, in which they will do their best to sell the shares involved in the offering but where there is no formal guarantee that this will be achieved. In practice, this means that the managers of the underwriting are not committing to purchase any unplaced securities for their own account in an unconditional manner. However, by an underwriter and the co-managers inserting the best efforts conditionality, should there be a failure to fully complete a sale of the offering, there is a risk to the underwriter of reputational damage and not being invited to participate in future IPOs.

2.5.5 Price Stabilisation

Stabilisation is the process whereby, to prevent a substantial fall in the value of securities when a large number of new securities are issued, the lead manager of the issue agrees to support the price by buying back the newly issued securities in the market if the market price falls below a certain predefined level. This is done in an attempt to give the market a reasonable chance to adjust to the increased number of securities that have become available, by stabilising the price at which they are traded.

By increasing the demand for the securities in the market at the same time as more securities become available, the price should remain more stable. This will mean the issuing company's securities appear less volatile, and existing investors will be less likely to begin panic selling and creating a downward spiral in the security's price. The securities that are bought back by the lead manager of the issue will then be sold back into the market over time.

Due to the need to maintain an orderly market, and to protect it from market abuse, there are strict rules laid down by regulators regarding stabilisation practices. For example, the FCA restricts the stabilisation period and requires disclosure to the market that stabilisation is happening, and that the market price may not be representative because of the stabilisation activities.

3. Equity Markets and Trade Execution

3.1 Trade Execution and Reporting

Learning Objective

3.3.1 Apply fundamental UK regulatory requirements with regard to trade execution and reporting: best execution; aggregation and allocation; management of conflicts of interest and prohibition of front running

3.1.1 Best Execution

The best execution provisions are contained in the section of the FCA Handbook which is known as the Conduct of Business Sourcebook (COBS). The provisions apply to firms executing client orders, to portfolio managers and to firms who receive and transmit client orders.

The initial provisions for implementation of best execution by the FCA followed in the wake of the Markets in Financial Instruments Directive (MiFID) which, among other provisions, introduced unified European requirements for the best execution of client orders in all MiFID financial instruments. The MiFID draft implementing measures (published by the EC on 6 February 2006) imposed requirements on investment firms providing the service of portfolio management or the reception and transmission of orders for execution.

In 2006, under FSA (now FCA) rules then prevailing, a firm that executed transactions could agree with its intermediate customers (including expert private customers classified as intermediate customers) that it did not have to provide best execution. Exclusions from best execution were provided for certain spread betting, venture capital and stock lending activities. In contrast, MiFID did not provide a mechanism for member states to exempt particular products or activities from best execution requirements. The FCA (while known as the FSA) subsequently amended the best execution provisions applicable in the UK to reflect the comprehensive requirements stipulated by MiFID.

The overarching best execution principle requires firms to take all reasonable steps to obtain the best possible result for their clients, taking into account a range of execution factors, when executing client orders or placing orders with (or transmitting orders to) other entities to execute. Firms are now required to comply with more detailed rules relating to arrangements and policies, disclosure, consent, demonstrating compliance and monitoring and review.

In a press release available from the FCA website released at around the time of the publication of the MiFID in 2006, the FCA Director for Conduct of Business Standards commented as follows:

'Our policy on best execution is designed to ensure that customers get a good deal. Standards are set in relation to price and other aspects of an order to ensure that firms execute dealing instructions as well as they are able. This is an important consumer protection measure, particularly for retail customers who do not have access to the same information as market professionals and who therefore find it difficult to judge the quality of price that a firm has obtained.

We recognise that markets are developing in ways that are making the existing rules increasingly difficult to interpret, not least the development of new electronic trading venues that offer a wider choice of execution options and possibly lower costs of trading. We are taking a fresh look at our policy and seeking the views of a wide range of firms, consumers and other interested parties'.

The FCA (as the FSA) then published a discussion paper in connection with the review of its guidelines on best execution which set out a number of issues for debate. These issues on which it sought feedback from the financial services sector can be summarised as follows:

Referencing a Benchmark

The FCA (as the FSA) raised questions about the use of a price benchmark as the best way of encouraging firms to achieve the best price. In the UK equity market, for example, a price benchmark (the SETS price on the LSE) is used as a reference against which best execution can be assessed.

Greater Disclosure of Execution Policies

The FCA (as the FSA) considered the merit of greater disclosure to customers of a firm's execution policy (that is, how firms execute orders and which execution venues are used). This helps consumers make more informed choices when selecting firms and may also facilitate competition between firms. It also enables journalists and other commentators to publish analyses comparing the execution capability between firms.

Trade Venue Execution Quality

The FCA (as the FSA) raised the possibility of requiring execution venues to publish data on execution quality in order to provide information to enable firms to select appropriate places for order execution. Data on volumes, prices, spreads and other relevant information, published in a standard format, could facilitate comparisons of execution performance.

Minimum Venue Access

The FCA (as the FSA) considered whether it should require firms to have access to a minimum number of execution venues in order to ensure that firms obtain an acceptable price.

Trade-off Between Price and Timeliness of Execution

The FCA (as the FSA) considered to what extent there should be a trade-off between price and other elements of an order, such as timely execution or settlement constraints. Should, for example, the researching of the best price be sacrificed in the interests of speedy execution?

Execution in OTC Markets

The FCA (as the FSA) also considered the application of best execution in markets other than equities, especially OTC markets such as derivative markets.

Current Position for Best Execution

Following a detailed examination of the issues discussed above, the FCA (as the FSA) developed its current policy approach to this area and introduced amendments to Section 11.2 of COBS during 2011.

Some relevant details include the following:

- In order to comply with the obligation to act in accordance with the best interests of its clients when it places an order with, or transmits an order to, another entity for execution, a firm must take all reasonable steps to obtain the best possible result for its clients, taking into account the execution factors. The relative importance of these factors must be determined by reference to the execution criteria and, for retail clients, to the requirement to determine the best possible result in terms of the total consideration.
- A firm satisfies its obligation to act in accordance with the best interests of its clients, and is not required to take the steps mentioned above, to the extent that it follows specific instructions from its client when placing an order with, or transmitting an order to, another entity for execution.
- A firm must monitor the effectiveness of its order execution arrangements and execution policy in order to identify and, when appropriate, correct any deficiencies. In particular, it must assess on a regular basis whether the execution venues included in the order execution policy provide the best possible result for the client or whether it needs to make changes to its execution arrangements. The firm must notify clients of any material changes to its order execution arrangements or execution policy.
- A firm must, when providing the service of portfolio management or, for a management company, collective portfolio management, comply with the obligation to act in accordance with the best interests of its clients when placing orders with other entities for execution that result from decisions by the firm to deal in financial instruments on behalf of its client.

3.1.2 Aggregation and Allocation

The FCA guidance is that orders for customers may only be aggregated when this is in the overall best interests of those customers. In addition, the FCA imposes the requirement that customers must be made aware that the aggregation may operate on some occasions to their disadvantage. Firms must also consider the provisions of rules on best execution and timely allocation when aggregating orders, together with any further requirements laid down by the LSE.

The FCA's General Principles require regulated firms to implement procedures and arrangements which provide for the prompt, fair and expeditious execution of customers' orders relative to the trading interests of the firm.

As an example of the implementation of this guidance, one well-known brokerage firm states that it does not undertake to carry out (a customer's) order or a transaction for its own account in aggregation with another client order, unless it has satisfied the following conditions:

- It is unlikely that the aggregation of orders and transactions will work overall to the disadvantage of any client whose order is to be aggregated.
- It has been disclosed to each client whose order is to be aggregated that the effect of aggregation may work to its disadvantage in relation to a particular order.
- It has established and effectively implemented an order allocation policy. This policy should provide in sufficiently precise terms for the fair allocation of aggregated orders and transactions, including how the volume and price of orders determines allocations and the treatment of partial executions.

When a firm aggregates a client order with one or more other orders and the aggregated order is partially executed, it will further allocate the related trades according to this order allocation policy.

3.1.3 Front Running and Conflicts of Interest

Front running is a practice in which a trader takes a position to capitalise on advance knowledge of a sale that is expected to influence the price of stocks or commodities.

Large-scale criticisms of the manner in which financial securities firms on both side of the Atlantic are allowed to act as both a principal and agent in trading securities focus on the inherent conflict of interest which this dual role creates. This more serious criticism suggests that it is not just individual traders who may front-run on the basis of prior knowledge, but investment banks as a whole.

If an investment bank acts both as an agent/broker for customers who are engaging in trading/investment decisions and placing orders with the investment bank, while at the same conducting trading for its own account through its proprietary trading desk, the allegation is that there is a great temptation for the prop trading desk to front-run the customer's order.

Let us consider an example to illustrate how this might happen.

Example

An investment bank has, as a client, a large pension fund which makes periodic adjustments to its holdings. The pension fund will tend to trade in large-sized orders known as block trades.

The pension fund decides to purchase a large block of several million shares in ABC Telcom plc and places instructions with the customer execution desk of the investment bank.

Meanwhile, the bank's proprietary trading desk, which is operating with the bank's own capital and running a P&L for its own trading activities, could become aware of this instruction to a separate department, and will then have the possibility of acting on this prior knowledge that a large buy order for Vodafone shares is about to enter the market. The bank's own proprietary trading desk could then get ahead of, or front-run, this large buy order and take a position in the stock itself before the large trade is made public.

As there will be a tendency for a large buy order to move the price up, even by a couple of pennies, the bank could realise a quick profit from acting ahead of the order being entered into the marketplace.

The traditional rejoinder to this suggestion is that large institutions operate with Chinese walls, which separate the different functions within the institutions, and that the confidentiality and observance of secrecy by different divisions of the firm will ensure that this does not create a conflict of interest for the institutions.

Under Section 118 of the UK Financial Services and Markets Act 2000, money managers are barred from trading on the kind of information just presented in the above illustration.

Front running can also be considered as a form of insider trading and/or market abuse.

The following broad guidelines have been considered by the FCA (as the FSA) to address the general issue of potential conflicts of interest, insider trading and the more specific example of front running in conjunction with the execution of specific trades. The FCA has guidelines covering what is called PA Dealing – which covers dealing for the personal accounts of individual traders/money managers.

The following guidelines are suggested for good practice:

- Trading should not be allowed by analysts until seven to ten days after research is published by a registered firm.
- Staff should be required to hold stock for a minimum of one month.
- Staff should be required to sign a form confirming that they do not have any inside information.
- Funds needed for stock for staff have to be provided up front.
- No short selling is allowed.
- Written permission from the CEO or compliance manager is required when trading in-house stocks and dealing is not allowed when the firm holds principal positions.
- A blanket ban for corporate finance staff on trading in-house stocks.
- PA trading conducted in batch sessions (three times a day), therefore reducing the risk of front running.

3.2 The Main Trading Venues

Learning Objective

3.3.2 Understand the key features of the main trading venues: regulated and designated investment exchanges; recognised overseas investment exchanges; whether quote- or order- driven; main types of order – limit, market, fill or kill, execute and eliminate, iceberg, named; liquidity and transparency

3.2.1 Recognised Investment Exchanges (RIEs)

The FCA recognises and supervises a number of recognised investment exchanges (RIEs) and recognised clearing houses (RCHs) under the Financial Services and Markets Act 2000 (FSMA).

Recognition gives an exemption from the need to be authorised to carry on regulated activities in the UK. To be recognised, RIEs and RCHs must comply with the recognition requirements laid down in the Financial Services and Markets Act 2000 (Recognition Requirement for Investment Exchanges and Clearing Houses) Regulations 2001.

RIEs, in their capacity as market operators, may operate regulated markets and multilateral trading facilities (see section 3.3).

The following is a list of regulated markets operated by RIEs:

- Cboe Europe Equities Regulated Market
- Euronext – Euronext London
- **ICE Futures Europe**
- NEX Exchange

- London Stock Exchange (LSE)
- London Metal Exchange, and
- International Property Securities Exchange (IPSX).

3.2.2 Recognised Overseas Investment Exchanges (ROIEs)

The FCA has recognised and supervises a number of recognised overseas investment exchanges (ROIEs):

- Australian Securities Exchange ltd
- Borsa Italiana SpA
- Börse Frankfurt Zertifikate AG
- Cboe Europe BV
- Chicago Board of Trade (CBOT)
- The Chicago Mercantile Exchange (CME)
- Commodity Exchange inc (COMEX)
- Deutsche Börse AG
- EUREX Frankfurt AG
- Euronext Amsterdam NV
- Euronext Paris SA
- European Energy Exchange AG
- ICE Endex Markets BV
- ICE Futures US, inc
- MTS SpA
- NASDAQ OMX Oslo ASA
- The Nasdaq Stock Market llc
- New York Mercantile Exchange inc. (NYMEX inc)
- Singapore Exchange Derivatives Trading ltd
- Singapore Exchange Securities Trading ltd
- SIX Swiss Exchange AG

3.2.3 Designated Investment Exchanges (DIEs)

An investment exchange which does not carry on a regulated activity in the UK and is not a regulated market may apply to the FCA to be included on its list of designated investment exchanges. Before adding an investment exchange to the list of designated investment exchanges, the FCA will look at whether the investment exchange provides an appropriate degree of protection for consumers. The FCA will also undertake a public consultation prior to adding the investment exchange to the list of designated investment exchanges.

Designation allows firms to treat transactions effected on a designated investment exchange in the same way as they would treat transactions effected on a RIE.

Current DIEs recognised by the FCA are:

- American Stock Exchange
- Australian Stock Exchange
- Bermuda Stock Exchange
- Bolsa Mexicana de Valores

- Bourse de Montreal inc
- Channel Islands Stock Exchange
- Chicago Board of Trade
- Chicago Board Options Exchange
- Chicago Stock Exchange
- Coffee, Sugar and Cocoa Exchange, inc
- Euronext Amsterdam Commodities Market
- Hong Kong Exchanges and Clearing ltd
- International Securities Market Association
- Johannesburg Stock Exchange
- Kansas City Board of Trade
- Korea Stock Exchange
- MidAmerica Commodity Exchange
- Minneapolis Grain Exchange
- New York Cotton Exchange
- New York Futures Exchange
- New York Stock Exchange (NYSE)
- New Zealand Stock Exchange (NZX)
- Osaka Securities Exchange
- Pacific Exchange
- Philadelphia Stock Exchange
- Singapore Exchange
- South African Futures Exchange
- Tokyo International Financial Futures Exchange
- Tokyo Stock Exchange
- Toronto Stock Exchange.

3.2.4   Trading Systems

Trading systems provided by exchanges around the world can be classified on the basis of the type of trading they offer. Broadly, trading systems are either **quote-driven** or order-driven. The difference in the manner of operation is described below.

Quote-Driven Systems

Quote-driven trading systems employ market makers to provide continuous two-way, or bid and offer, prices during the trading day in particular securities regardless of market conditions. The buying price is the bid and the selling price is the offer. Market makers make a profit, or turn, through this price spread. Although this practice is outdated in many respects, many practitioners argue that quote-driven systems provide liquidity to the market when trading would otherwise dry up. Nasdaq and the LSE's SEAQ trading systems are two of the last remaining examples of quote-driven equity trading systems, although market makers can display both quotes and orders in Nasdaq.

Order-Driven Systems

On order-driven systems, the investors (or agents acting on their behalf) indicate how many securities they want to buy or sell, and at what price. The system then simply brings together the buyers and sellers. Order-driven systems are very common in the equity markets, where the NYSE, the Tokyo Stock Exchange (TSE) and the LSE's Stock Exchange Electronic Trading Service (SETS) are all examples of order-driven equity markets.

Hybrid Market

From 2007, most NYSE-listed securities could be traded via a hybrid system. Orders can be sent for immediate electronic execution or directed to the market floor for auction. Market makers can also display both quotes and orders in Nasdaq.

3.2.5 Liquidity and Transparency

The traditional classifications between quote-driven and order-driven systems are beginning to lose their sharp focus with the advent of several innovative approaches to the kinds of software platforms which are now being employed to host trading activities. There are initiatives and technologies provided by systems such as the LSE's Turquoise system and by the NYSE/Arca systems which actively reward member firms for liquidity provisioning. The following press release from NYSE Euronext summarises the key issues for innovative forms of market making which are, in turn, creating a new breed of electronic market-making firms known for their (sometimes controversial) use of what are known as high frequency trading (HFT) algorithms.

> 'The New York Stock Exchange (NYSE) and NYSE Arca, units of NYSE Euronext (NYX), today announced new transaction pricing, effective March 1, 2009, pending SEC filing. The NYSE fee change will include customer rebates for adding liquidity while continuing to offer the lowest transaction fees for taking liquidity in NYSE-listed securities among the major market centers. The fee change is expected to be rolled out in conjunction with significant NYSE execution speed improvements. The NYSE Arca fee change raises the rebate for active traders in Tape A (NYSE-listed) and Tape C (Nasdaq-listed) securities, as well as a higher rebate on Mid-Point Passive Liquidity (MPL) orders for all customers in all securities. Together, the dual-exchange model of the NYSE and NYSE Arca deliver the best rate combination among major exchanges and superior liquidity when trading NYSE-listed securities, in addition to the lowest take fee on NYSE and highest rebate on NYSE Arca.
>
> In addition, NYSE Euronext's Global Multi-Platform Incentive Program offers additional savings to active global customers trading on the NYSE, NYSE Arca and Euronext markets. The program provides rebates for customers with a specified average daily volume'.

Other developments, which are also features of the Turquoise system, have encouraged the development of dark pools of liquidity in which there is, by design, little or no transparency provided to the general investment community for large-scale trading activities (see section 3.3.4).

3.2.6 Order Book and Order Types

Outside the realm of dark pools, and still transparent to market participants, is the constantly updated flow of orders that await matching and which constitute the so-called order book. The buy side of the order book lists orders to buy, and the sell side of the order book lists orders to sell. New sell orders entered into the system potentially match existing orders on the buy side. New buy orders potentially match existing sell side orders in the order book. Increasingly trading systems are run electronically, allowing participants to trade via computer screens. However, there are notable exceptions – for example, the NYSE still retains a physical trading floor where buyers and sellers gather to trade.

Examples of Common Order Types

- **Limit orders** have a price limit and a time limit. For example, a limit order may state 'sell 1,000 shares at 360p by next Tuesday'. Any time limit up to a maximum of 90 days can be put on these orders. If no time limit is placed on the order, it will expire at the end of the day that it is entered. Limit orders can be partially filled, and it is only limit orders that are displayed on the SETS order book.

- **Iceberg orders** are a particular type of limit order. They enable a market participant with a particularly large order to partially hide the size of their order from the market and reduce the market impact that the large order might otherwise have. The term iceberg comes from the fact that just the top part of the order is on view (the peak of the iceberg), and the rest is hidden (the bulk of the iceberg is below the water). Once the top part of the order is executed, the system automatically brings the next tranche of the iceberg order onto the order book. This process continues until the whole of the iceberg order has been executed, or the time limit for the order expires.

- **At market** (also known as at best) orders can only be input during automatic execution and have no specified price. The order will fill as much as possible at any available price and the remainder will be cancelled; it does not wait on the order book to match against later orders.

- **Execute and eliminate** orders can only be entered during automatic execution. As with the at best order, this type will execute as much of the trade as possible and cancel the rest. However, unlike an at best order, this order type has a specified price and will not execute at a price worse than that specified.

- **Fill or kill** orders can only be entered during automatic execution. They normally have a specified price (although they can be entered without one) and either the entire order will be immediately filled at a price at least as good as that specified, or the entire order will be cancelled (ie, if there are not enough orders at the price specified or better).

- A **market order** is a buy or sell order that is to be executed immediately at prevailing market price. Providing that there are available buyers and sellers, market orders are executed. The purpose of these order types is to achieve execution rather than specifying a price, which means the order giver cedes any real control over the price that will be achieved. The order can be executed with a number of different 'fills' being split across more than one order book counterparty. There may also be different prices for each fill.

Named Order

The International Order Book (IOB) is an order-driven trading service primarily for depositary receipts of international securities. It operates in a similar way to SETS, and has the facility for inputting orders that are not anonymous. Such orders are commonly referred to as named orders and are placed by LSE member firms dealing in a principal capacity and wanting to display their willingness to deal on the order book. The acronym that identifies the firm appears next to their order on the IOB.

3.2.7 The Role of Market Makers

Some of an exchange's member firms have chosen to take on the special responsibilities of a market maker. When a firm acts as a market maker it stands ready to provide a source of liquidity to certain sections of the market such as the LSE's SETSqx system. By being prepared to provide a bid for shares that third parties want to sell and an ask for parties that want to buy shares, at any time, the market maker smoothes out the more erratic price movements that can occur without this additional source of market liquidity.

To become a market maker a member firm must apply to the stock exchange, giving details of the securities in which it has chosen to deal. It must provide prices at which it is willing to buy and sell a minimum number of its chosen shares throughout the course of the trading day.

Because some of the exchange systems rely on market makers to honour their commitments, the exchange closely vets firms before allowing them to quote prices to investors. In return for agreeing to take on these extra responsibilities, market makers hope to enjoy the benefits of a steady stream of business, from broker-dealers and from other investors.

3.2.8   Stock Borrowing and Lending Intermediaries (SBLIs)

Another key contributing factor to the liquidity and transparency of exchanges is the role taken by stock borrowing and lending intermediaries (SBLIs). These are firms that arrange for one party (perhaps a market making member firm) to borrow shares from another party (perhaps a long-term holder of shares, like a pension fund). This may arise because the market maker has sold shares it does not own – known as selling short.

By borrowing shares, the market maker can satisfy the need to deliver the shares. After an agreed period, the borrower will return an equivalent number of the same shares to the lender. The borrower is charged a fee for arranging the transaction (paid to the SBLI), and for borrowing the shares (paid to the lender). During the period of the loan, the lender retains all the benefits of owning the shares (such as dividends) except the voting rights. Transparency requirements are now in force which require the full disclosure of stock borrowing and lending.

3.3   Alternative Trading Venues

Learning Objective

3.3.3   Understand the key features of alternative trading venues: multilateral trading facilities (MTFs); organised trading facilities (OTFs); systematic internalisers; dark pools

Keeping abreast of developments in the various trading platforms in use in today's financial markets is a daunting challenge. There is a constant drive towards new IT architectures and new software technologies, which means that the pace of innovation and the changes in the actual systems in effect will have a tendency to make textbooks such as this outdated in relatively short timeframes.

In understanding the evolution of trading platforms from the more conventional systems which were in place up until the mid-1990s, and which many non-professionals today still envisage as the model for workflow in markets, it is important to take a brief historical perspective.

In 1998, the SEC in the US authorised the introduction of electronic communication networks (ECNs). In essence, an ECN is a computerised trading platform which allows trading of various financial assets, primarily equities and currencies, to take place away from a specific venue such as a stock exchange. The primary motivation for the SEC to authorise the introduction of ECNs was to increase competition among trading firms by lowering transaction costs, giving clients full access to their order books, and offering order-matching outside of traditional exchange hours.

Since an ECN exists as a large number of networked computers/workstations, it effectively has no centre or physical location but rather is decentralised and virtual. ECNs are sometimes also referred to as alternative trading networks or venues. The term venue has to be understood in a metaphorical sense, since a network is accessible from anywhere through an IT infrastructure and there is no specific place where trades are executed.

Alternative trading systems (ATSs) have come to play a dominant role in public markets for accessing liquidity. The most popular among varieties of ATSs are ECNs and crossing networks.

An example of an ECN is Bloomberg's TradeBook which, according to its website, describes its mission as follows:

> '...(we) believe that traders equipped with advanced algorithms to manage complexity and supported by analytics to provide the right market insights can achieve superior executions. We partner with our clients to develop technology and services that give them better control of their transactions and keep them more informed of market opportunities'.

Examples of crossing networks are Liquidnet and Posit. Liquidnet, which has a presence in Europe and in Asian markets, provides not only a crossing network, but is also a major provider, among others, of dark pools of liquidity. In essence, the idea with dark pools is that automated platforms offer the opportunity to match off exchange with other buyers and sellers, without showing the available liquidity to the market. This innovation in market technology has significant consequences with respect to the transparency of trading in publicly-listed securities (see section 3.3.4).

As a way of demonstrating the manner in which innovations in alternative trading systems have transformed the *modus operandi* of today's financial markets it is worth considering Better Alternative Trading System (BATS), a Kansas-based company that was founded only in June 2005, and which has become the third-largest exchange in the world by volume behind the NYSE and Nasdaq. The founder and CEO of BATS provided testimony, in June 2010, to the SEC Commission on market structure, which looked into the highly unusual trading activity that took place in US markets on 9 May 2010. During a ten-minute interval, the **Dow Jones Industrial Average (DJIA)** index dropped by 1,000 points and the S&P 500 dropped by almost 100 points. Although the markets quickly recovered a substantial portion of these abrupt losses, the incident has become known as the Flash Crash. Some market observers have interpreted the incident as a warning signal that highly automated markets with high-frequency algorithmic trading are potentially hazardous. The following excerpt from the testimony conveys the essential characteristics of modern electronic markets:

> 'Nearly all equity trading in the US today is automated in some fashion and can exhibit characteristics that fall under the umbrella label of high-frequency trading. These characteristics include direct access to a market, the sending of a large number of orders into the market, orders generated by computer algorithms, trading through a co-located broker, or subscribing to an exchange's direct data feed. Future regulations targeted in this area should take into account that the phrase high frequency more broadly describes the state of our market than it does any particular segment of trading participants'.

It should be expected that the implementation of similar technologies to those prevalent in the US today will become widespread within Europe – indeed, BATS has already developed a substantial presence in the UK equity markets.

In addition to the absorption of new trading technologies, European markets and exchanges are still in the process of implementing all of the changes associated with MiFID initiatives. MiFID expressed the goal of improving pre-trade and post-trade transparency. With regard to pre-trade transparency the requirement was that operators of continuous order-matching systems must make aggregated order information on liquid shares available at the five best price levels on the buy and sell side; for quote-driven markets, the best bids and offers of market makers must be made available. In regard to post-trade transparency the requirement was that firms must publish the price, volume and time of all trades in listed shares, even if executed outside of a regulated market, unless certain requirements are met to allow for deferred publication.

Although MiFID was intended to increase transparency for prices, in fact the fragmentation of trading venues has had an unanticipated effect. Where once a financial institution was able to see information from just one or two exchanges, it now has the possibility (and in some cases the obligation) to collect information from a multitude of multilateral trading facilities, systematic internalisers and other exchanges from around the EEA. The overall result of all of these developments is a need for ever-faster and more efficient technologies to process the amount of information that is available from so many diverse trading venues in order for investors to benefit from the transparency that MiFID wished to introduce.

3.3.1 Multilateral Trading Facilities (MTFs)

An MTF is a system that brings together multiple parties (eg, retail investors or other investment firms) that are interested in buying and selling financial instruments and enables them to do so. These systems can be crossing networks, or matching engines that are operated by an investment firm or a market operator. Instruments may include shares, bonds and derivatives. This is done within the MTF operator's system.

An example of an equities-trading platform which captures the key characteristics of an MTF is Turquoise, which has been adopted by the LSE as pivotal to its new trade execution platform. Turquoise was originally created by a consortium of nine major investment banks and is a hybrid system that allows trading both on and off traditional exchanges. Turquoise has been majority-owned by the LSE Group since February 2010. Turquoise gives customers access to pan-European and US equity trading in more than 4,300 securities. Unique functionality in Turquoise's integrated book combines visible and non-displayed orders to deliver increased likelihood of execution and price improvement.

One of the aims of MiFID was to promote competition between traditional exchanges and other trading systems. Regulated market status is still viewed by many as the gold standard trading venue. However, the distinction between regulated markets and MTFs is nowadays arguably rather blurred to the extent that this view ceases to make a great deal of commercial sense. Regulatory standards for MTFs and regulated markets are broadly the same in areas such as transparency and market abuse. Banks and large institutions have backed the MTFs both through their custom and increasingly, as seen in the example of Turquoise, through involvement in actually establishing them. Many banks and large institutions see MTFs as an opportunity for forcing recognised exchanges to lower their fees. The trend towards increasing market fragmentation is unlikely to be halted unless there is a change of policy on the part of financial regulators.

MTF Documentation

Usually an MTF will have a members' agreement which incorporates all of the rules to which the member signs up to with the MTF. Usually there is no flexibility to negotiate these rules, so it is necessary to be pretty clear on what is being signed up for. Normally the agreement gives the MTF discretion to cancel trades, suspend trading and amend the rules, as well as giving it a broad indemnity.

Best Execution

The ability to access sources of liquidity other than merely a single exchange is of particular significance to achieving the MiFID obligation for best execution. While the requirement to obtain the best result for clients on a consistent basis does not necessarily mandate access to all venues, it is likely to mean that trading houses will require access to at least the larger MTFs in addition to the exchanges themselves.

3.3.2 Organised Trading Facilities (OTFs)

With the implementation of MiFID II in January 2018, a new type of trading venue was introduced – the organised trading facility (OTF). As mentioned earlier, an OTF is a multilateral system that is not a regulated market, nor an MTF. It allows multiple third-party buying and selling interests in bonds, structured finance products, emission allowances or derivatives to be traded. Equities cannot be traded through an OTF. An OTF is a service of an authorised investment firm, and the operator of an OTF is not permitted to trade against its own proprietary capital.

3.3.3 Systematic Internalisers (SIs)

A systematic internaliser (SI) is, in broad terms, an investment firm making markets outside a regulated market or an MTF. The firm executes orders from its clients against its own book or against orders from other clients. MiFID treats systematic internalisers as mini-exchanges. For example, they are subject to the same pre-trade and post-trade transparency requirements.

3.3.4 Dark Pools of Liquidity

Dark pools refer to the non-displayed or hidden nature of the buy and sell orders that reside in a crossing platform. The term 'dark liquidity' can also be applied to all forms of non-displayed liquidity such as the order blotters of buy-side dealing desks.

One investment manager has described the appeals of dark liquidity pools as follows:

'A dark pool is a very simple way you can hopefully capture lots of liquidity and achieve a large proportion of your order being executed without displaying anything to the market'.

In the US, the influx of crossing networks and alternative venues, and the rapid adoption of electronic trading technologies, has been driving the growth of dark pools for several years. Dark pools are primarily a US phenomenon, with more than 50 estimated to exist in the US and only a small number operating in Europe. However, the fragmentation of the market, which has been largely encouraged by the MiFID directives as well as the technological 'arms race' is responsible for the emergence of dark pools in Europe.

According to UBS *'there are only two crossing networks outside of the exchanges in Europe – ITG and Liquidnet'.* But there is dark liquidity. One area is through the exchanges having iceberg orders, where people may have a lot more to trade than is displayed on the screen at any time. The biggest sources of dark liquidity are within the investment banks and major brokers.

3.3.5 Summary of MTFs and Dark Pools

By making use of certain waivers for pre-trade transparency under MiFID, dark pools and MTFs are allowing institutions to execute large volume trades away from the visible order book. As there is no pre-trade transparency, there is no visible price formation. This is essentially what makes them dark.

The large transaction size waiver on which the majority of trades in dark pools will rely is, in relative terms, not actually that large. The effect of the waiver therefore means that large institutions are increasingly able to conduct the majority of their trades in the dark through the new MTFs. There are a number of different models on which dark pool MTFs are based. While certain models offer a basic dark matching facility, certain systems provide a pass-through function that allows a user to send an order through to a light venue. For instance, the order can be passed through to a standard MTF or exchange if it cannot be filled in the dark pool. Brokers are now allowing combined access to liquidity in light and dark pools. This method of combined access ties in with the best execution obligations of both buy and sell side market participants.

Looking at the benefits that a dark pool may offer, users are likely to cite key advantages such as reducing the market impact of large orders, securing more favourable security pricing (by crossing orders at the mid-price) and lower execution costs.

3.4 High Frequency Trading (HFT)

Learning Objective

3.3.4 Understand algorithmic trading: reasons; high frequency trading (HFT); potential consequences for the market (eg, flash crashes, increased liquidity, increased volume, illusion of volume)

High frequency trading (HFT) is the use of technologically advanced tools and algorithms to trade financial instruments. The key differences between HFT and traditional forms of trading are:

- in HFT, trading takes place solely through computer algorithms, and
- orders are processed by HFT firms and positions are opened and closed within seconds and fractions of seconds (eg, microseconds/one millionth of a second).

3.4.1 How can High Frequency Traders make Profits?

Many HFT firms try to catch momentary moves in everything from stocks to currencies between different trading platforms. This has essentially similar characteristics to traditional arbitraging when firms take advantage of short-term market gyrations. Their algorithms will seek temporary inefficiencies in the market and trade so that they can make money before the brief distortions go away, ie, they will buy at a lower price in one market and sell at a higher price in another in identical or similar instruments.

Market making and liquidity provision also form part of HFT strategies that involve placing a limit order to sell (or offer) or a buy limit order (or bid) in order to collect the bid-offer spread. By doing so, market makers become counterparty to incoming market orders. This role has been traditionally fulfilled by specialist firms, once known as stock jobbers.

3.4.2 The Effect of HFT on the Markets

Some institutional investors and market participants have voiced concerns that HFT increases the cost of investing and damages the markets. Others suggest that HFT creates more accurate and faster securities pricing, narrows bid-offer spreads, lowers volatility and adds liquidity to markets, and thus benefits investors. The matter has been the subject of great debate. It is possible for HFTs to trade a single stock hundreds of times in less than a minute. Concerns have been raised that this creates the illusion of liquidity in a particular stock without there actually being any demand or settlement. It has been suggested that this, in turn, could attract interest and investment from traditional investors.

Regulators claim that HFT may have caused volatility during the 'flash crash' on 6 May 2010, when the Dow Jones Industrial Average (DJIA) fell by about 1000 points (about 9%) and then recovered much of that fall within a few minutes. It was the highest ever one-day fall intraday in DJIA history. In July 2011, a report was issued by the International Organisation of Securities Commissions (IOSCO). The report commented that while 'algorithms and HFT technology have been used by market participants to manage their trading and risk, their usage was also clearly a contributing factor in the flash crash event of 6 May 2010'.

Algorithmic behaviour is becoming increasingly faster and more complex. This makes it often extremely difficult to make sense of trading patterns. Media reports have cited flash spoofs that last a fraction of a second and are designed to seek a reaction from other algos. These have been termed 'predatory algos'.

Other causes that have been cited include a large E-mini S&P 500 seller that set off a chain of events triggering the flash crash, and a large purchase of S&P 500 Index put options by a hedge fund shortly before the crash. Whatever the reason, the HFT debate continues.

Several European regulators have proposed curtailing or banning HFT due to concerns about it causing volatility. It is estimated that in 2015 in the US, HFT trading accounted for around 50% of all equity trading volumes, down from as high as 73% in 2009, although it is now thought to be much lower than 50%. Among some of the largest HFT firms in the US are Virtu Financial, Jump Trading and Citadel llc.

3.5   Characteristics of Dividend Payments

Learning Objective

3.3.5   Understand the concepts of trading cum, ex, special cum and special ex: the meaning of books closed, ex-div and cum div, cum, special ex, special cum, and ex rights; effect of late registration

Dividends have many dates associated with them, and some of them have multiple names. For example, the books closed date is also known as the date of record or record date.

3.5.1   Declaration Date

The declaration date is the date the company's board of directors announces the company will pay a dividend to its shareholders. This is the day on which the dividend goes on the company's financial statements as a liability that must be paid. It is also when the board announces the book closing date.

3.5.2   Ex-Dividend Date

The ex-dividend date is the day by which you must have purchased the stock to receive the dividend. The ex-dividend date is different from the books closed date because it takes two to three days to be officially recognised as a shareholder. After this date, anyone who purchases the stock is not entitled to receive the dividend. Typically, the stock's price will be decreased by the amount of the dividend after this date because a new investor will not receive the payment.

3.5.3   Books Closed Date/Record Date

The books closed or record date for a dividend is the day by which you must be registered as an owner of the stock to receive the dividend. On this day, a record is taken of all the owners of the company and how many shares they own so the company knows whom to pay the dividend to on the payment date. It typically takes two days to become registered as a shareholder of a company, so this is not the last day to buy the stock; that is the ex-dividend date.

3.5.4   Payment Date

The payment date is the day on which you receive your dividend. The payment date is usually about three weeks after the books closed date. Dividends are typically paid in cash, but they also can be paid in stock or property.

Normally, a company's shares are quoted **cum-dividend (cd)**. This means that buyers of the shares have the right to the next dividend paid by the company. However, there are brief periods when the share becomes ex-dividend, meaning that it is sold without the right to receive the next dividend payment. The ex-dividend period occurs around the time of a dividend payment.

The sequence of events, based upon the dates described above, which leads up to the dividend payment is as follows.

- **Dividend declared** – on this date, the company announces its intention to pay a specified dividend on a specified future date. The declaration must occur at least three clear business days before the ex-dividend date.
- **Ex-dividend date** – the ex-dividend date is invariably the first Thursday that falls at least three clear business days after the day that the dividend was declared.
- **Record or books closed date** – the record, or books closed date is the date on which a copy of the shareholders' register is taken. The people on the share register at the end of this day will be paid the next dividend. The books closed date is the business day after the ex-dividend date. Because the ex-dividend date is a Thursday, the books closed date is usually a Friday, except when the Friday is a public holiday, in which case the books closed date is the next available business day.

- **Dividend paid** – the dividend is paid to those shareholders who were on the register on the record/books closed date.

3.5.5 Ex-Dividend Period

The period from the ex-dividend date up to the dividend payment date is known as the **ex-dividend** period. Throughout this period the shares trade without entitlement to the next dividend.

The relationship between the ex-dividend date and the books closed date is explained as follows. Since the equity settlement process takes two business days, for a new shareholder to appear on the register on the Friday they would have to buy the shares by Wednesday at the latest. Wednesday is the last day when the shares trade cum-dividend, because new shareholders will be reflected in the register before the end of the books closed date. A new shareholder buying their shares on the Thursday will not be entered into the register until the following week – too late for the books closed date and therefore ex-dividend.

On the Thursday, when the shares first trade without the dividend (ex-dividend), the share price will fall to reflect the fact that if an investor buys the share they will not be entitled to the impending dividend.

At all times other than during ex-dividend periods, shares trade cum dividend – ie, if an investor purchases shares at this time, they will be entitled to all the future dividends paid by the company for as long as they keep the share.

During the ex-dividend period, it is possible to arrange a special cum trade. That is where, by special arrangement, the buyer of the share during the ex-dividend period does receive the next dividend. These trades can be done up to and including the day before the dividend payment date, but not on or after the dividend payment date.

In a similar manner to a special cum trade, an investor can also arrange a special ex trade. This is only possible in the ten business days before the ex-date. If an investor buys a share during the cum-dividend period, but buys it special-ex, they will not receive the next dividend.

Using special cum or special ex transactions enables the sellers or buyers to avoid the receipt of a dividend – essentially deciding whether or not they want to collect their right to the dividend. During the period when the LSE allows such trading, it effectively allows the right to the dividend to be traded. The motivation for investors buying or selling with or without the dividend entitlement tends to be related to tax: dividend income is normally subject to income tax, so selling the right to the dividend may avoid some income tax.

3.5.6 Late Registration

The inherent disadvantage of special cum trades and special ex trades is that they may potentially result in dividends from the company being paid to the wrong person.

If a trade settles later than the schedule prescribed, this could result in late registration and would mean that the correct owner is not reflected in the shareholders' register on the books closed date. As such, the dividend paid out will not be to the actual owner of the shares. In such situations, it is the broker acting for the buyers (or seller, as appropriate) that will need to make a claim for the dividend.

3.6 Developed and Emerging Markets

Learning Objective

3.3.6 Apply knowledge of the key differences between international markets; regulatory and supervisory environment; corporate governance; liquidity and transparency; access and relative cost of trading

3.6.1 Overview

The emergence of vitally important new markets and dynamic emerging economies has been very much a feature of the investment landscape of the last 20 years or so. Many investors nowadays are focused on opportunities provided by the non-traditional markets of the developed world and are looking increasingly at investing substantial portions of an investment portfolio in emerging market assets.

The classification and categorisation schemes for investment markets are made by several of the main financial information providers including the FTSE Group, Dow Jones and Standard & Poor's.

The FTSE Group, an independent company which originated as a joint venture between the *Financial Times* and the LSE, has, in addition to maintaining the **FTSE 100** Index, also developed a system for classifying the world's markets according to certain categories.

Developed Countries

The following countries are classified by the FTSE as developed countries: Australia, Austria, Belgium, Canada, Denmark, Finland, France, Germany, Hong Kong, Luxembourg, Ireland, Israel, Italy, Japan, the Netherlands, New Zealand, Norway, Poland, Portugal, Singapore, South Korea, Spain, Sweden, Switzerland, the UK and the US.

Developed countries have all met criteria adopted by the FTSE under the following categories:

- They are high-income economies (as measured by the World Bank gross national income (GNI) per capita rating.
- Market and regulatory environment:
  - formal stock market regulatory authorities actively monitor market (eg, SEC, FCA, SFC)
  - fair and non-prejudicial treatment of minority shareholders
  - no or selective incidence of foreign ownership restrictions
  - no objections or significant restrictions or penalties applied on the repatriation of capital
  - free and well-developed equity market
  - free and well-developed foreign exchange market
  - no or simple registration process for foreign investors.
- Custody and settlement:
  - settlement – rare incidence of failed trades
  - custody – sufficient competition to ensure high-quality custodian services
  - clearing and settlement – T+2, T+3 or shorter, T+7 or shorter for frontier markets (see below)
  - stock lending is permitted
  - settlement – free delivery available
  - custody – omnibus account facilities available to international investors.

- Dealing landscape:
  - brokerage – sufficient competition to ensure high quality broker services
  - liquidity – sufficient broad market liquidity to support sizeable global investment
  - transaction costs – implicit and explicit costs to be reasonable and competitive
  - short sales permitted
  - off-exchange transactions permitted
  - efficient trading mechanism
  - transparency – market depth information/visibility and timely trade reporting process.
- Derivatives:
  - developed derivatives markets.
- Size of market:
  - market capitalisation
  - total number of listed companies.

Advanced Emerging Countries

The following countries are classified by the FTSE as advanced emerging countries: Brazil, Czech Republic, Greece, Hungary, Malaysia, Mexico, South Africa, Taiwan, Thailand and Turkey.

Secondary Emerging Countries

The following countries are classified by the FTSE as secondary emerging countries: Chile, China, Columbia, Egypt, India, Indonesia, Kuwait, Pakistan, Peru, the Philippines, Qatar, Russia, Saudi Arabia and the UAE.

Frontier Markets

The term 'frontier markets' is commonly used to describe the equity markets of the smaller and less accessible, but still investable, countries of the developing world. The frontier or pre-emerging equity markets are typically pursued by investors seeking high long-run return potential as well as low correlations with other markets. The implication of a country being labelled as frontier, or pre-emerging, is that the market is less liquid and significantly less correlated with developed and even traditional emerging markets.

MSCI World Index

The MSCI World Index is a stock market index of over 1,650 world stocks. It is maintained by MSCI inc., formerly Morgan Stanley Capital International, and is often used as a common benchmark for world or global stock funds.

The index includes a collection of stocks of all the developed markets in the world, as defined by MSCI. The index includes securities from over 20 countries but excludes stocks from emerging economies, making it less worldwide than the name suggests. A related index, the MSCI All Country World Index (ACWI), incorporated both developed and emerging countries.

3.6.2   UK

The Global Financial Centres Index (GFCI) is an annual survey of the leading financial centres in the world. The GFCI makes the point that *'London and New York are still leading the field in 1st and 2nd place respectively. They remain the only two truly global centres'.*

London Stock Exchange (LSE)

Normal continuous trading sessions are from 8.00am to 4.30pm every day of the week except Saturdays, Sundays and holidays declared by the exchange in advance.

The LSE operates in the following primary areas:

- **Equity markets and primary issuance** – the LSE enables companies from around the world to raise capital. There are four primary markets: the Main Market, the Alternative Investment Market (AIM), the Professional Securities Market (PSM) and the Specialist Fund Market (SFM).
- **Trading services** – the LSE provides an active and liquid secondary highly active market for trading in a range of securities, including UK and international equities, debt, covered warrants, exchange-traded funds (ETFs), exchange-traded commodities (ETCs), **real estate investment trusts (REITs)**, fixed interest, and depositary receipts.

Regulatory Structure of the UK Market

The main regulatory, supervisory and trade body frameworks supporting the UK financial markets are:

- **Companies Acts** – the Companies Acts detail the requirements for companies generally, such as the requirement to prepare annual accounts, have accounts audited and for annual general meetings. Of particular significance to the LSE are the Companies Acts requirements to enable a company to be a plc, since one of the requirements for a company to be listed and traded on the LSE is that the company is a plc.
- **Financial Conduct Authority (FCA)** – the FCA has to give its recognition before an exchange is allowed to operate in the UK. It has granted recognition to the LSE and, by virtue of this recognition, the exchange is described as a recognised investment exchange (RIE). In granting recognition, the FCA assesses whether the exchange has sufficient systems and controls to run a market. Furthermore, the FCA lays down the detailed rules that have to be met before companies are admitted to the official list that enables their shares to be traded on the exchange. In April 2013, banking supervisory functions that were performed by the FSA were taken over by the Prudential Regulation Authority.
- The FCA is responsible for setting and administering the listing requirements and continuing obligations for plcs seeking and obtaining a full list on the LSE. The FSA (now the FCA) was appointed as the listing authority in May 2000 and is the 'competent authority for listing' – making the decisions as to which companies' shares and bonds (including gilts) can be admitted to be traded on the LSE. It is the FCA that sets the rules relating to becoming listed on the LSE, including the implementation of any relevant EU directives. The rules are contained in a rulebook called the Listing Rules. The LSE is responsible for the operation of the exchange, including the trading of the securities on the secondary market, although the FCA can suspend the listing of particular securities and therefore remove their secondary market trading activity on the exchange.

- **Her Majesty's Treasury** – Her Majesty's Treasury (HM Treasury) is the UK's economics and finance ministry, with overall responsibility for fiscal policy as well as providing a supervisory role for the entire financial framework in the UK. The department of government is headed by the Chancellor of the Exchequer.
- **Panel on Takeovers and Mergers (POTAM)** – the UK supervisory authority that carries out the regulatory functions required under the EU Takeover Directive is the Panel on Takeovers and Mergers (the Panel or POTAM). The Panel's requirements are set out in a Code that consists of six general principles, and a number of detailed rules. The Code is designed principally to ensure that shareholders are treated fairly and are not denied an opportunity to decide on the merits of a takeover. Furthermore, the Code ensures that shareholders of the same class are afforded equivalent treatment by an offeror. In short, the Code provides an orderly framework within which takeovers are conducted, and is designed to assist in promoting the integrity of the financial markets.

Corporate Governance in the UK

In addition to the regulatory framework outlined in the previous paragraphs, there have been several initiatives in the UK in recent years to improve corporate governance in relation to financial services.

In general terms, the term 'corporate governance' describes the processes, customs, policies, laws and institutions affecting the way a corporation (or company) is directed, administered or controlled. Corporate governance also includes the relationships between the many stakeholders involved and the goals at which the corporation is aiming.

An important theme of corporate governance is the nature and extent of accountability of particular individuals in the organisation, and mechanisms that try to reduce or eliminate conflicts of interest between the different stakeholders within a corporation (especially where stakeholders may have conflicts of a principal/agent nature). For example, the chief executive of a company has a duty to shareholders to maximise the returns available to the owners of the corporation, but also has a stake in securing the best possible remuneration for themselves.

An example of how this type of conflict can be addressed through corporate governance regulation is the requirement that all large corporations must have a remuneration committee which should consist of, at least, some independent directors who can monitor those circumstances in which the executives of a company may decide to put their own interests ahead of the interests of the shareholders or other stakeholders.

The FCA requires companies to disclose in their annual reports both how they have applied principles of good governance and whether they have complied with the provisions of its code of best practice.

Numerous committees have reported, and from their recommendations a Corporate Governance Code (the 'Code') has been drawn up by the FCA. The Code is derived from the recommendations of the Greenbury, Cadbury and Higgs committee reports and, in particular, was much influenced by the final report of the Hampel Committee in 1998. After the financial crisis of 2007–08, the Walker Review published a report on the banking industry that also made recommendations for other industries. Paul Myners also completed two major reviews of the roles of institutional investors for the Treasury. An updated version of the Code was issued in 2010.

The Code was updated again in 2018 for the purpose of placing greater emphasis on relationships between companies, shareholders and stakeholders. It also promotes the importance of establishing a corporate culture that is aligned with the company purpose and business strategy, while promoting integrity and valuing diversity.

The key issues of the Corporate Governance Code are:

- Every listed company should be headed by an effective board, which should lead and control the company.
- The board should meet regularly.
- Directors should bring independent judgement to bear on issues of strategy.
- No one individual should have unfettered powers of decision.
- A decision to combine the posts of chairman and chief executive officer in one person should be publicly explained.
- There should be a strong and independent non-executive element on the board.
- The board should have a balance of executive and non-executive directors so that no small group of individuals can dominate the board's decision-taking.
- There should be a formal and transparent procedure for the appointment of new directors.
- All directors should submit themselves for re-election at least every three years.

There are also provisions concerning directors' remuneration:

- Levels of remuneration should be sufficient to attract and retain directors needed to run the company successfully.
- Remuneration should be structured to link rewards to corporate and individual performance.
- Remuneration committees should be responsible for this and should only include non-executive directors.
- There should be an objective of having service contracts with notice periods of a maximum of one year.
- The annual report should contain a statement of remuneration policy and details of the remuneration of each director.

3.6.3   US

Since nearly 16% (after adjusting for purchasing power parity) of global GDP is accounted for by the US, it is no surprise that two of its many exchanges, the NYSE and Nasdaq, comprise almost half of the world's total stock exchange activity. As well as trading domestic US stocks, these exchanges are also involved in the trading of shares in major international companies.

The NYSE is the largest and most liquid stock exchange in the world as measured by domestic market capitalisation, and is significantly larger than any other exchange worldwide. Although it trails Nasdaq for the number of companies quoted on it, it is still larger in terms of the value of shares traded. The NYSE trades in a continuous auction format. Member firms act as auctioneers in an open outcry auction market environment, in order to bring buyers and sellers together and to manage the actual auction. This makes it highly unusual in world stock markets but, as more than 50% of its order flow is now delivered to the floor electronically, there are proposals to adopt a hybrid structure combining elements of open outcry and electronic markets.

Nasdaq is an electronic stock exchange with over 3,000 companies listed on it. It is the third-largest stock exchange by market capitalisation and has the second-largest trading volume. There are a variety of companies traded on the exchange, but it is well known for being a high-tech exchange. Many of the companies listed on it are telecoms, media or technology companies; it is typically home to many new, high-growth and volatile stocks. Although it is an electronic exchange, trades are still undertaken through market makers who make a book in specific stocks, so that when a broker wants to purchase shares they do so directly from the market maker.

The main depository in the US is the Depository Trust Company (DTC), which is responsible for corporate stocks and bonds, municipal bonds and money market instruments. The Federal Reserve Bank is still the depository for most US government bonds and securities. Transfer of securities held by DTC is by book entry, although shareholders have the right to request a physical certificate in many cases. However, about 85% of all shares are immobilised at DTC, and efforts are under way in the US to eliminate the requirement to issue physical certificates at the state level.

US equities settle at T+2, while US government fixed-income stocks settle at T+1. Corporate, municipal and other fixed-income trades settle at T+2.

There are three levels of circuit breaker that can result in trading halts in the US. These are enacted if the S&P500 falls by 7%, 13% or 20%. These circuit breakers are a key control put in place to limit sharp sell-offs and halt trading for a set period of time.

Regulatory Environment in the US

The principal financial regulators and policy makers in the US market are as follows, with a brief description of each:

- **Securities and Exchange Commission (SEC)** – the SEC has a role analogous to the FCA in the UK. The SEC requires companies seeking a listing on the US exchanges to register with the SEC first. Once listed, companies are then required to file regular reports with the SEC, particularly in relation to their trading performance and financial situation.
- **Commodity Futures Trade Commission (CFTC)** – the role of the CFTC, which is an independent agency, is to protect market users and the public from fraud, manipulation and abusive practices related to the sale of commodity and financial futures and options, and to foster open, competitive and financially sound futures and option markets.
- **Federal Reserve System ('The Fed')** – similar to the Bank of England it is the central bank of the US and has very broad powers with relation to monetary policy.
- **Federal Deposit Insurance Corporation (FDIC)** – the FDIC is a government agency which is responsible for administering the underwriting of customer deposits in the banking system and the winding up or resolution of failed banks.
- **Office of the Comptroller of the Currency (OCC)** – established by the National Currency Act of 1863, the OCC serves to charter, regulate, and supervise all national banks and the federal branches and agencies of foreign banks in the US.

3.6.4   Japan

The Tokyo Stock Exchange (TSE) is one of five exchanges in Japan and is one of the more important world exchanges.

The TSE uses an electronic, continuous auction system of trading. This means that brokers place orders online and, when a buy and sell price match, the trade is automatically executed. Deals are made directly between buyer and seller, rather than through a market maker. The TSE uses price controls so that the price of a stock cannot rise above or fall below a certain point throughout the day. These controls are used to prevent dramatic swings in prices that may lead to market uncertainty or stock crashes. If a major swing in price occurs, the exchange can stop trading on that stock for a specified period of time. In 2013, the TSE became the world's third-largest exchange by listed companies after it and the Osaka Securities Exchange merged their cash-equity trading platforms.

The Japan Securities Depository Centre (JASDEC) acts as the central securities depository (CSD) for equities. The Bank of Japan (BOJ) provides the central clearing system and depository for Japanese government bonds (JGBs) and Treasury bills.

Settlement within JASDEC is by book entry transfer, but without the simultaneous transfer of cash. However, these movements are coordinated through the TSE.

The settlement cycle of Japanese government bonds (JGBs) shortened to T+1 from T+2 in 2018; and for both equities and other fixed-income trades to T+2 from T+3 in 2019.

Regulation

The Financial Services Agency (FSA) is a Japanese government organisation responsible for overseeing banking, securities and exchange, and insurance in order to ensure the stability of the financial system of Japan. The agency operates with a commissioner and reports to the Minister of Finance (Japan). It oversees the Securities and Exchange Surveillance Commission and the Certified Public Accountants and Auditing Oversight Board.

3.6.5   Germany

Deutsche Börse is the main German exchange and provides services that include securities and derivatives trading, transaction settlement, the provision of market information, as well as the development and operation of electronic trading systems.

The cash market comprises both floor trading and a fully electronic trading system. Both platforms provide efficient trading and optimum liquidity.

Xetra is Deutsche Börse's electronic trading system for the cash market and matches buy and sell orders from licensed traders in a central, fully electronic order book. In May 2011, floor trading at the Frankfurt Stock Exchange migrated to Xetra technology. The new Xetra Specialist trading model combines the advantages of fully electronic trading – especially in the speed of order execution – with the benefits of trading through specialists who ensure that equities remain liquid and continually tradeable. The machine fixes the price, the specialists supervise it; investors benefit from faster order processing.

Deutsche Börse also owns the international central securities depository Clearstream, which provides integrated banking, custody and settlement services for the trading of fixed-interest securities and shares. Clearstream Banking Frankfurt (CBF) performs clearing and settlement for the German market. At the end of March 2003, Eurex Clearing AG (part of the Deutsche Börse group) took on the role of CCP for German stocks traded on Xetra and held in collective safe custody.

Both equities and bonds have a T+2 settlement cycle. Transfer is by book entry via one of two settlement processes, the Cascade system for domestic business, and through Clearstream for international users.

Regulation

The Federal Financial Supervisory Authority, better known by its abbreviation BaFin, is the financial regulatory authority for Germany. It is an independent federal institution with headquarters in Bonn and Frankfurt and falls under the supervision of the Federal Ministry of Finance. BaFin supervises about 2,700 banks, 800 financial services institutions and over 700 insurance undertakings.

3.6.6 Developing Markets

Although most overseas investment held by UK investors is in developed equity markets, emerging markets represent a rapidly increasingly proportion of UK overseas investment. The term 'emerging market' can be defined in various ways:

- markets in countries classified by the World Bank as low or middle income, and
- markets with a stock market capitalisation of less than 2% of the total world market capitalisation.

The attractions of investing in emerging markets comprise:

- **Rapid economic growth** – developing nations tend to grow at faster rates of economic growth than developed nations, as they attempt to catch up with rich country living standards by developing their infrastructure and financial systems. This process is assisted by domestic saving rates being generally higher than in developed nations and the embracing of world trade and foreign direct investment. Rapid economic growth tends to translate into rapid profits-growth.
- **Low correlation of returns** – emerging markets offer significant **diversification** benefits when held with developed market investments, owing to the historically low correlation of returns between emerging and developed markets. There is a notion that the BRIC economies have de-coupled with the developed markets, but this is highly debatable as it still appears to be the case that, as a result of financial contagion, adverse developments in the US market especially, or even the plight of the euro currency, will cause disruptions to the BRIC markets (see section 3.6.7) as well as those in the developed economies.
- **Access to exchange-traded funds (ETFs)** – many of the emerging markets, including the BRIC markets, are now easily accessible to investors through a variety of ETFs which either track the MSCI indices for the major geographical regions or provide more specialised baskets of assets for certain regions.
- **Inefficient pricing** – traditionally, emerging markets were not as well researched as their developed counterparts, and pricing anomalies and inefficiencies were to be found. The increased interest in the BRIC economies suggests that much of this alleged benefit may be disappearing.

However, there can be significant drawbacks to investing in emerging markets:

- **Lack of transparency** – the quality and transparency of information is generally lower than for developed nations, while accounting and other standards are generally not as comprehensive or as rigorously applied.
- **Lax regulation** – regulation is generally more lax in emerging than in developed markets, and incidents of insider trading and fraud by local investors more prevalent. Corporate governance also tends to be lacking.
- **Volatility** – emerging market performances have been more volatile than those of developed markets, owing to factors such as developing nations being less politically stable and more susceptible to banking and other financial crises (although it should be noted the 2007-08 crisis was primarily a crisis in the developed world).
- **Settlement and custodial problems** – the logistics of settling transactions and then arranging for custody of the securities purchased can be fraught with difficulty. In addition, property rights are not as well defined as in developed nations. However, these problems can be mitigated by using global depositary receipts (GDRs) (see section 1.2.2).
- **Liquidity** – as emerging markets are less liquid, or more concentrated, than their developed counterparts, investments in these markets tend not to be as readily marketable and, therefore, tend to trade on wider spreads. In times of financial stress, it may be very difficult to exit certain assets where there is no active market.
- **Currencies** – emerging market currencies tend to be less stable than those of developed nations and periodically succumb to crises resulting from sudden significant outflows of overseas investor capital.
- **Controls on foreign ownership** – some developing nations impose restrictions on foreign ownership of particular industries.
- **Taxation** – emerging market returns may be subject to local taxes that may not be reclaimable under double taxation treaties.
- **Repatriation** – there may be severe problems in repatriating capital and/or income from investments made in some emerging markets.

3.6.7   BRIC Markets

BRIC is an acronym that refers to the economies of Brazil, Russia, India and China. The four countries combined currently account for more than a quarter of the world's land area and more than 40% of the world's population. The acronym has been prominently used by the investment bank Goldman Sachs since 2001. Goldman Sachs argued that, since the BRICs are developing rapidly, by 2050 their combined economies could eclipse the combined economies of the current richest countries of the world. The way momentum for growth in the world economy is shifting is also reflected in the political structures that are emerging. Previously, the semi-annual G8 summits and meetings of the respective finance ministers were the pivotal meetings for global policy coordination. However, the G20 summits, which include all of the BRIC economies as well as those of the existing G8 and nations such as Mexico and South Korea, are now becoming as important as, if not more so than, the G8 gatherings.

On 16 June 2009, the leaders of the BRIC countries held their first summit in Yekaterinburg, and issued a declaration calling for the establishment of a multi-polar world order. Part of the discussions among the BRIC nations have included calls for less reliance on the US dollar as the global reserve currency, and there have been discussions about creating a new global unit of account similar to the special drawing rights (SDRs) of the IMF. The BRIC nations are becoming increasingly significant contributors to the IMF and are demanding a stronger representation in the formation of international monetary policy (to the extent that there is such a policy).

Investing in the BRIC Economies

Certain collective investment vehicles are available to investors who wish to have investment exposure to the BRIC economies, including specialised unit trusts and ETFs. For example, some ETFs that allow exposure to the BRIC markets are available on the NYSE/Arca platform. One fund, BKF, holds assets from all of the BRIC countries, and another, EWZ, reflects the MSCI Brazilian index. A third fund, iPath, provides exposure to a broad selection of Indian equities by tracking the MSCI India index.

3.7 Fluctuations in Equity Market Prices

Learning Objective

3.3.7 Be able to assess how the following factors influence equity markets and equity valuation: trading volume and liquidity of domestic and international securities markets; relationship between cash and derivatives markets and the effect of timed events; market consensus and analyst opinion; changes to the economic outlook; implications of foreign exchange

The prices of equities, in common with most asset classes, move continually during trading hours.

3.7.1 Liquidity

The liquidity of an asset is determined by how easily it can be bought and sold, and how quick it can be converted into cash. This factor is extremely relevant when portfolio planning and selecting investments with a view to selling them at a point in the future to realise cash. There are two sources of risk connected with asset values. There is market risk (of asset value) and liquidity risk which is the uncertainty of the ability to liquidate the asset when required.

Investors will differ as to their valuations of security prices based on different time horizons, different economic outlooks and different vested interests, and their differing demand and supply criteria affect the price. For markets to work properly there need to be disagreements, different time horizons among the participants and different agendas and priorities. While some investors and traders think that an asset is worth buying at a specified price, there must be others who, for various reasons, think that it is worth selling at that same price.

The two most common frameworks for financial markets are the open outcry model and the electronic order book; in both cases, for sustained trading to take place, there needs to be a fragmentation of opinions. Assuming that there are a dedicated group of traders that want to trade a particular asset, the more evenly divided opinions are, regarding the suitability of the current price, the more liquid the market will be.

In very liquid markets, buying and selling preferences will show a high degree of non-alignment. Trading stances will be dispersed and there will be no obvious internal coherence to them. But, when the fragmentation is replaced by a near-consensus view among traders, the liquidity evaporates and markets are prone to behaving in erratic ways: sometimes dramatic price swings and crashes can result.

3.7.2   The Relationship Between Cash and Derivatives Markets

Some of the most actively traded derivative instruments are stock index futures. The contract for the S&P 500, which has two versions – a fully blown contract and what is called the E-mini version (see below) – are probably the most traded index future in the world. The cash index which underlies this derivative – the Standard & Poor's 500 Index – consists of many of the largest **capitalisation issues** which trade on the US exchanges NYSE and Nasdaq. Fund managers and traders desire exposure to this index for numerous purposes, both as an indirect investment through the purchase of an index proxy such as the popular exchange-traded fund SPY, or through a position in futures contracts.

The motivation could be to gain long exposure to this broad-based index of multinational equities and/or as a hedging instrument for a portfolio of direct holdings in equities. In the UK, there is a futures contract which tracks the FTSE 100, and there are also similar instruments that trade globally on the CME Globex electronic trading platform, and which track among others, the **Nikkei 225** Index in Japan and the Xetra Dax Index in Germany.

Stock index futures, including the S&P futures, are popular because they trade 24 hours a day and allow traders and brokers to gauge the futures level before the actual stock markets open for trading. This gives a sense of where the market is likely to head at the start of trading.

The common characteristic of stock index futures contracts is that they have quarterly expirations. For example, if one wants to purchase the Mini S&P 500 contract (ie, take a long position) one could purchase the September 2010 futures contract. This contract has the following specification. The larger full version of the S&P 500 contract is five times the size of the E-mini contract described below.

Mini S&P 500 Futures

Mini S&P 500 futures are legally binding agreements to buy or sell the cash value of the S&P 500 Index at a specific future date. The contracts are valued at $50 x the futures price. For example, if the Mini S&P 500 futures price is at 920.00, the value of the contract is $46,000 ($50 x 920.00).

The minimum price movement of the futures or options contracts is called a tick. The tick value is 0.25 index points, or $12.50 per contract. This means that if the futures contract moves by the minimum price increment (one tick), say, from 920.00 to 920.25, a long (buying) position will be credited $12.50; a short (selling) position will be debited $12.50.

All futures positions (and all short option positions) require posting of a performance bond (or margin). Positions are marked-to-market daily. Additional deposits into the margin account may be required beyond the initial amount if the position moves against the investor.

Mini S&P 500 contracts are cash-settled, just like the standard S&P 500 futures; there is no delivery of the individual stocks. Mini S&P 500 daily settlements and quarterly expirations use the exact same price as the S&P 500. The same daily settlement prices allow E-mini contracts to benefit from the liquidity of the S&P 500 futures.

Like the S&P 500, which is settled using a special opening quotation (SOQ), all Mini S&P 500 positions are settled in cash to the same SOQ on the third Friday of the quarterly contract month.

Interaction Between Futures and Cash

Arbitrage opportunities arise if misalignments or discrepancies between the futures prices and the cash prices on the S&P 500 arise. Indeed, programme trading is an arbitrage strategy which exists to exploit these opportunities, which tend to be fairly small discrepancies and which therefore require very fast executions to deliver profits.

The possibility of arbitrage and the fact that the futures contracts are very convenient for many speculative purposes means that there is a real sense in which the action in the futures market can tend to drive the price behaviour of the cash market. While this may seem like an aberration, in the very complex and algorithmic nature of most cash market transactions today, the notion of the tail (derivative) wagging the dog (underlying) is not so hard to contemplate.

The expirations of futures contracts can sometimes provide short-term volatility in the cash markets as many large speculators and commercials (ie, investment banks) which are rolling over futures positions will sometimes create whipsaw and turbulent market conditions. This situation is described by some in the market as 'witching' and when contracts on futures, options on individual stocks, and options on stock index futures occur (once each quarter) this phenomenon is referred to as 'triple witching'.

For long-term investors, these kinds of activities might be considered as examples of 'noise' in the equity markets, however, the impact of the derivatives markets upon the cash market is often not as uni-directional as some commentators and textbooks imply. Rather than the derivative deriving its value from the behaviour of the underlying cash instrument, the situation can often be better understood from the converse perspective.

3.7.3 Market Consensus

Because it is unquantifiable and generally misunderstood by most traders and investors, psychology is the often overlooked intangible aspect of trading.

In relation to trading and investing, we can consider two very different approaches to psychology in the markets: individual psychology and group psychology. Attempting to draw conclusions based on the actions of crowd psychology (sometimes disparagingly referred to as 'herd behaviour') is done by examining how the behaviour of investors en masse exerts an effect on stock prices.

The foundations of how crowd behaviour relates to investing have a long history. Speculative investors will often buy particular shares, or even shares in general, in the hope of taking advantage of a rising trend in prices. As more investors buy, prices are driven higher still and this may encourage still further buying. The process cannot continue indefinitely and eventually the bubble will burst when prices fall back and there is a sudden change in sentiment. The fall in prices can then be as steep as the original rise and those who bought at the highest prices will suffer losses. Famous historical examples of bubbles include the South Sea Bubble, the Dutch tulip mania and the dot com mania of the 1990s. When most investors are in consensus and are driving the market in a particular direction, one naturally thinks that the consensus will continue *ad infinitum* and that the best trading decision is to follow the crowd.

However, it has been suggested that historical examples prove this to be a paradox. When driven strongly by consensus, crowd behaviour is actually a contrary indicator. When the consensus of the majority of investors or traders is strongest, the individual trader should do exactly the opposite of what the crowd is doing. When the market is strongly bullish, according to the contrarian view it is more prudent to short the market. When the consensus is bearish, it is time to get ready to buy.

Mass psychology may continue to drive the trend for a longer period of time. The question that is asked by investors who subscribe to the notion that the consensus is wrong at important market turning points is: how can one expect to identify the moment when the consensus indicator is strongest and what is the best moment to make a contrary investment decision? The answer is, of course, that there is no way of determining the timing or, for that matter, of empirically verifying that treating consensus as a contrarian indicator actually results in profitable investment. Market consensus can be used only as one clue that a trading/investment opportunity may be available. It may simply indicate that it is a good time to apply more detailed analyses to particular stocks or currencies.

The second question is: how does one establish the market consensus? Several tools are used to help investors roughly identify the consensus of the market. Most of these tools tabulate a numerical consensus indicator on the basis of advisory opinions, signals from the press or even polling that is done among investment managers.

- The **Commitments of Traders (COT) Report** was first published by the Commodity Futures Trading Commission (CFTC) in 1962 for 13 agricultural commodities to inform the public about the current conditions in futures market operations. The data was originally released just once a month, but moved to once every week by the year 2000. Along with reporting more often, the COT report has become more extensive and has expanded to include information on most futures contracts. Among the information published is the positions of so-called 'commercials'. These are entities involved in the production, processing, or merchandising of a commodity, using futures contracts primarily for hedging. 'Non-commercials' are traders, such as individual traders and large institutions, who use the futures market for speculative purposes and meet the reportable requirements set forth by the CFTC.
- **Advisory opinion** – advisers can often take the form of newsletter writers or bloggers and web commentators who provide opinions on the future direction of markets or individual stocks. Sources such as *Investor's Intelligence* and *Market Vane*, both active in the US, poll these newsletters to track the bullishness or bearishness of market commentators and advisers. These polling opinion research services have developed special numerical figures to analyse these newsletters/blogs and will assign either a bullish or bearish value to each of the opinion letters. These services then tabulate the overall bullishness or bearishness of their entire universe of advisers. When this numerical value crosses a certain threshold, either a buy or a sell signal is issued. The signal is issued contrary to the balance of advisory opinion.

Share prices can change as a result of information becoming available to investors about various matters, including:

- the earnings prospects and asset values of individual companies
- the membership of the board
- adverse factors affecting companies, such as legal action against it, or action by a bank to call in loans
- industry and economy surveys, for example, about levels of retail sales, or productivity

- macroeconomic developments, for example, the expected level of interest rates, or where an economy appears to be located in the business cycle
- changes in government policy, for example fiscal and monetary policy
- movements in other stock markets around the world, such as the US, China and Japan
- geopolitical developments including wars, and threats from terrorist groups.

Many companies aim to present a stable and steadily rising pattern of dividend payments from year to year. Sharp changes from the usual pattern may be taken by investors as a signal of a change in the company's fortunes, which may cause a shift in the share price. One of the consequences of the global banking crisis of 2008 and the ensuing economic downturn has been that many large organisations, especially in the financial services sector, have either cut their dividends or suspended them entirely. One further consequence of this development is that many institutional investors, such as pension funds, will then sell the shares of companies which suspend dividends, creating a downward cycle in share prices.

The large US bank Citigroup is an example of a company which has suspended payment of a dividend and seen its share price move into low single digits with a corresponding 90% fall in its market capitalisation. 'Market capitalisation' refers to the value that is placed on a company by multiplying the outstanding equity of a company by its current share price. In some ways it is a flawed notion, since it places a value on the entire company from the value of the marginal shares traded during a particular session, which may have been particularly troubled by the overall market. This gives rise to the rather perverse way in which the market capitalisation of equity markets has moved up and down during the 2008–09 banking crisis and subsequent market recovery by many trillions of dollars or pounds.

Investors will look for evidence of the quality of a company's management, although such evidence can be difficult to obtain in practice. Changes in board membership can affect investors' assessment of a company's prospects and the share price may move as a result. If a director resigns, investors will be interested in the reason for the resignation. If new directors are appointed, their experience and past track record will be of interest.

The prices of some companies' shares are affected more by the state of the economy than others. For example, because house purchase decisions are influenced by mortgage rates, housebuilding companies will be particularly sensitive to interest-rate changes. If people are moving house less as a result of interest rate increases, businesses such as DIY and carpeting firms may also face a downturn in demand and, therefore, earnings.

Given the increasing interdependence of national economies through globalisation of trade and capital flows, share prices will be heavily affected by economic conditions around the world, particularly the state of the economy in the world's largest debtor nation, the US. Some studies have suggested that the inter-linkage between global stock markets is becoming much more pronounced than it used to be. Correlation analysis shows that there is a much greater degree of co-movement between indices in the US, UK, Western Europe and Japan. Emerging markets are less correlated with the more mature market economies and this has given rise to the de-coupling thesis, which suggests that the fortunes of the newly emerging dynamic economies – sometimes called the BRIC countries (ie, Brazil, Russia, India and China) – are less coupled with the fortunes of, say, the US economy than in previous eras. The evidence on this hypothesis is far from convincing, however, as evidenced by the dramatic declines seen in all global stock markets in late 2008 and early 2009.

On a related theme, there is a strong influence between the state of the world economy and final demand and the price levels of major commodities such as oil, copper, and other industrial metals. The emerging markets are greatly influenced by the prices of commodities both as major consumers (in the case of China) and as producers (in the case of Russia and Brazil).

In 2010, there was a notable change in the manner in which the credit ratings for sovereign debt had a very large impact on the behaviour of asset markets and investor sentiment. The downgrading of the debt of Greece to junk status – which was finally confirmed by the major agencies in June 2010, although anticipated by money market participants well before that – had a major impact on the European credit markets, the value of the euro currency and also, for a time, brought a sharp correction in equity markets.

3.7.4 Impact of Exchange Rates

The impact that foreign exchange rate fluctuations can have on share prices and indices is regularly seen with the FTSE 100 index. Many of the component companies of the index have large international operations where profits are realised in US dollars. If the foreign exchange markets see a fall in the value of sterling, the dollar revenues of these companies will be worth more. As a consequence, the FTSE 100 index can rise, even if all other factors are unchanged.

A good example of this concerns Brexit and the aftermath of the UK's announcement in June 2016 of its intention to leave the EU. Companies like GlaxoSmithKline saw their prospective overseas profits rise significantly, when converted back to sterling. The anticipated increases in the companies' revenues caused their share prices to rise. In the month following the Brexit referendum, GlaxoSmithKline's share price saw a 23% rise.

In fact, in the three months following the referendum, the FTSE 100 rose by 10.4%, while in the same period sterling fell 12.8% against the US dollar.

Another example of a currency influencing shares prices was seen following the US election in 2016. During the month after Donald Trump's election to president in November, the S&P 500 rose 10% to new highs and the key reasons were the strength of the US dollar, as well as expectations of tax cuts for corporates. Trump's election policies raised expectations of inflation rate and interest rate rises. With higher interest rates can come higher rates of return and a more attractive currency. If the US dollar is likely to become stronger, then so can the earnings of US companies.

3.8   Stock Market Indices

Learning Objective

3.3.8   Understand the purpose, construction, application and influence of indices on equity markets: market regional and country sectors; market capitalisation sub-sectors; free float and full market capitalisation indices; fair value-adjusted indices

A stock market index is a method of measuring a section of the stock market. Many indices are cited by news or financial services firms and are used as benchmarks, to measure the performance of portfolios and to provide the general public with an easy overview of the state of equity investments. Their methods of construction vary according to whether they are capitalisation-weighted or not.

There are various organisations which have become specialists in constructing equity indices and managing their composition, making periodic adjustments and publishing the index data in real time and on a historical basis. Standard & Poor's is the manager of the S&P 500 Index and selects the constituents of the index from the largest capitalisation issues which trade on US exchanges. It consists of stocks from the NYSE and Nasdaq and there is an overlap with the constituents of the better-known Dow Jones Industrial Average, which is maintained by the Dow Jones company, former owners of the *Wall Street Journal*. In addition, the Russell Investment Group in the US is well known for maintaining several indices of US stocks including the Russell 2000, which represents the smallest-capitalisation issues trading in US markets and is often used as a benchmark for what are called micro-cap stocks.

In the UK, the best known index is the FTSE 100 Index, which consists straightforwardly of the one hundred largest companies traded on the LSE as measured by market capitalisation. The index is maintained by the FTSE Group, a UK provider of stock market indices and market data services, wholly owned by the LSE, which originated as a joint venture between the *Financial Times* and the LSE. It is calculated in real time and published every 15 seconds.

Index Name	Composition	Scope
FTSE 100	Largest 100 UK companies listed on the LSE and measured by market capitalisation.	UK and multinationals.
Dow Jones Industrial Average (DJIA)	30 large US companies selected by the editors of the Wall Street Journal.	US-domiciled multinationals.
Nikkei Stock 225	225 large and regularly traded Japanese companies traded.	Japanese corporations.
Hang Seng	50 companies listed on the Hong Stock Exchange selected on the basis of market value, turnover and financial performance.	Hong Kong/China.
DJ Stoxx	A family of indices, based around the DJ Stoxx Global 1800 Index that consists of the 600 largest-capitalisation companies from each of the three regions – Europe, Americas and Asia/Pacific.	Global developed markets.

MSCI World	A market capitalisation-based index, including companies from over 20 countries, totalling over 1,650 companies. See section 3.6.1.	Global developed markets.
FTSE Eurofirst 300	300 largest listed companies by market capitalisation from across Europe.	European-domiciled corporations.
CAC 40	A capitalisation-weighted measure of the 40 most significant values among the 100 highest market caps on Euronext Paris.	French-domiciled companies; about 45% of its listed shares are owned by foreign investors, more than any other main European index.
Deutscher Aktien IndeX (DAX)	DAX is the capitalisation-weighted blue chip index for the Frankfurt Stock Exchange. The DAX includes the 30 major German companies trading on the Frankfurt Stock Exchange.	German stocks.
S&P 500	Standard & Poor's manages the composition of the index. The 500 constituents are selected by S&P from the largest-cap stocks traded in the US.	US-traded stocks which are multi-national companies operating in global markets.
FTSE All-Share	The FTSE All-Share Index, originally known as the FTSE Actuaries All-Share Index, is a capitalisation-weighted index, comprising around 600 of more than 2,000 companies traded on the LSE.	To qualify, companies must have a full listing on the LSE with a sterling- or euro-dominated price on SETS.
Nasdaq Composite	The Nasdaq Composite covers issues listed on the Nasdaq stock market with over 3,000 components. It is an indicator of the performance of stocks of technology companies and growth companies.	Since both US and non-US companies are listed on the Nasdaq stock market, the index is not exclusively a US index.
Nasdaq-100	The Nasdaq-100 Index consists of the largest non-financial companies listed on Nasdaq. It is a modified market value-weighted index.	Does not contain financial companies incorporated outside the US.

FTSE 100 companies represent about 81% of the market capitalisation of the whole LSE. Trading lasts from 8.00am to 4.29pm (when the closing auction starts), and closing values are taken at 4.35pm.

The previous table provides information on the composition and geographical scope of many of the largest and best known global equity indices.

As previously outlined, the FTSE Group, which is the principal provider of index information for the UK as well as many other regions of the world, uses a classification system for segmenting different markets according to their state of development. See section 3.6.1. Other companies, such as Dow Jones, use similar criteria for their classification systems.

3.8.1   National and Sector Indices

A national index represents the performance of the stock market of a given nation and reflects investor sentiment on the state of its economy. The most regularly quoted market indices are national indices composed of the stocks of large companies listed on a nation's largest stock exchanges. The concept may be extended well beyond an exchange.

The Wilshire 5000 Index, the original total market index, represents the stocks of nearly every publicly traded company in the US, including all US stocks traded on the NYSE (but not ADRs or limited partnerships) and the Nasdaq Biotechnology Index, which consists of over 150 securities of Nasdaq-listed companies in the biotechnology or pharmaceuticals industries. The Russell Investment Group, as previously mentioned, also maintains dozens of indices covering different sectors within the US market.

More specialised indices exist tracking the performance of specific sectors of the market. Some examples include the Wilshire US REIT which tracks more than 100 American real estate investment trusts (REITs) and the Morgan Stanley Biotech Index, which consists of 36 American firms in the biotechnology industry.

Some indices, such as the S&P 500, have multiple versions. These versions can differ based on how the index components are weighted and on how dividends are accounted for. For example, there are three versions of the S&P 500 Index: price return, which only considers the price of the components; total return, which accounts for dividend reinvestment; and net total return, which accounts for dividend reinvestment after the deduction of a withholding tax. As another example, the Wilshire 4500 and Wilshire 5000 indices have five versions each: full capitalisation total return; full capitalisation price; float-adjusted total return; float-adjusted price and equal weight. The difference between the full capitalisation, float-adjusted, and equal weight versions is in how index components are weighted.

3.8.2   The Construction of Indices and Weighting

Construction of an index usually involves the total market capitalisation of the companies weighted by their effect on the index, so the larger stocks will make more of a difference to the index as compared to a smaller market cap company.

Price-Weighted

However, there is one major exception to this method of construction and calculation which is the Dow Jones Industrial Average (DJIA). Since it is such a widely quoted index, and since it is not capitalisation-weighted, it is worth considering the method of calculation.

The sum of the prices of all 30 DJIA stocks is divided by the Dow divisor. The divisor is adjusted in case of stock splits, spinoffs or similar structural changes, to ensure that such events do not in themselves alter the numerical value of the DJIA. Early on, the initial divisor was composed of the original number of component companies. This made the DJIA at first a simple arithmetic average. The present divisor, after many adjustments, is less than one (meaning the index is larger than the sum of the prices of the components).

That is:

$$DJIA = \frac{\Sigma p}{d}$$

where:

Σ = sum

p = the prices of the component stocks

d = the Dow divisor

Events like stock splits or changes in the list of the companies composing the index alter the sum of the component prices. In these cases, in order to avoid discontinuity in the index, the Dow divisor is updated so that the quotations right before and after the event coincide:

$$DJLA = \frac{\Sigma p_{old}}{d_{old}} = \frac{\Sigma p_{new}}{d_{new}}$$

The Dow Divisor was 0.1519 in June 2021. Every \$1 change in price in a particular stock within the average equates to a 6.5839 (or $1 \div 0.1519$) point movement.

The DJIA is often criticised for being a price-weighted average, which gives higher-priced stocks more influence over the average than their lower-priced counterparts but takes no account of the relative industry size or market capitalisation of the components. For example, a \$1 increase in a lower-priced stock can be negated by a \$1 decrease in a much higher-priced stock, even though the lower-priced stock experienced a larger percentage change. In addition, a \$1 move in the smallest component of the DJIA has the same effect as a \$1 move in the largest component of the average. Many critics of the DJIA recommend the float-adjusted market-value-weighted S&P 500 or the Wilshire 5000 as better indicators of the US stock market.

Float-Adjusted Market Capitalisation Method

This is also called the free-float method. The basic formula for any index is (be it capitalisation-weighted or any other stock index) is:

Index level= Σ(price of stock x number of shares) x free-float factor/index divisor

The free-float adjustment factor represents the proportion of shares that is floated as a percentage of issued shares and then is rounded up to the nearest multiple of 5% for calculation purposes. To find the free-float capitalisation of a company, first find its market cap (number of outstanding shares x share price) then multiply its free-float factor.

The free-float method, therefore, does not include restricted stocks, such as those held by company insiders. Traditionally, capitalisation- or share-weighted indices all had a full weighting, ie, all outstanding shares were included.

Many of them have changed to a float-adjusted weighting, which has some variations as explained as follows:

- **Actual free float** – the number of freely tradable shares available, expressed in percentage terms after deducting the portion classified as restricted holdings from the shares in issue.
- **Investible market capitalisation** – the company's market capitalisation is used to calculate the index value. It may differ from the full market capitalisation, due to the application of free-float restrictions, capping weight, style weight or basket weight.

All FTSE equity index constituents are fully free-float-adjusted in accordance with FTSE's index rules, to reflect the actual availability of stock in the market for public investment. Each FTSE constituent weighting is adjusted to reflect restricted shareholdings and foreign ownership to ensure an accurate representation of investable market capitalisation.

Total Return Index

An index that calculates the performance of a group of stocks assuming that dividends are re-invested into the index constituents. For the purposes of index calculation, the value of the dividends is re-invested in the index on the ex-dividend date. Total return index data is not available at the stock level.

Fair Value-Adjusted Index

In the futures market, fair value is the equilibrium price for a futures contract. This is equal to the spot price after taking into account compounded interest (and dividends lost because the investor owns the futures contract rather than the physical stocks) over a certain period of time. In relation to an index, fair value is the forward value (at the time of a futures contract expiration) of an index spot price, where compounding takes into account time to expiration and dividends lost due to holding index futures rather than underlying stocks. If the fair value before the open is lower than the futures contract price, you may expect that a market index will go higher after the opening bell.

Calculation of fair value for futures contracts on equity indices is a feature of arbitrage strategies.

3.9 Accounting for Corporate Actions

Learning Objective

3.4.1 Understand the purpose and structure of corporate actions and their implications for investors: stock capitalisation or consolidation; stock and cash dividends; rights issues; open offers, offers for subscription and offers for sale; placings

There are more than 150 different types of corporate action, but for present purposes it will only be necessary to consider some of the principal ones that are often encountered by investors.

3.9.1 Dividend Payments

The payment of dividends represents a share in the profits made by a company that are paid to a shareholder as a return for providing its risk capital.

Dividends are usually paid twice a year and are expressed in pence per share. Interim dividends are paid in the second half of a company's accounting period, while final dividends, usually the larger of the two payments, are paid after the end of the company's accounting year.

It is up to the company's directors to determine the amount of any dividend to be paid, if any, and their decision needs to be ratified by the shareholders at the AGM. Although shareholders can vote for the final dividend to be paid at or below its proposed rate, they cannot vote for it to be increased above this level.

Once a dividend has been declared, the company's shares are traded on an **ex-dividend (xd)** basis until the dividend is paid, typically six weeks after the announcement. Shares purchased during this ex-dividend period do not entitle the new shareholder to this next dividend payment.

At the election of the board of directors, a company may decide to pay a dividend by issuing new shares to the current shareholders of record, known as a scrip dividend. This will be dilutive for the company and may be done to conserve cash. In the summer of 2010, when BP was facing mounting pressure from the US government to suspend payments of a cash dividend until the full costs of the oil spillage in the Gulf of Mexico were known, one of the options considered by the company was to pay a dividend in newly issued shares of BP.

3.9.2   Final Redemption

A final redemption involves the repayment in full of a debt security at the maturity date stated in the terms and conditions of an issue.

3.9.3   Warrant Exercise

Warrants give a holder the right to buy a prespecified number of a company's ordinary shares, at a preset price, on or before a pre-determined date. Warrant exercise relates to the act of exercising, or buying, the shares over which the warrant confers a right.

3.9.4   Bonus (Capitalisation/Scrip) Issue

A bonus issue, also referred to as a capitalisation issue or **scrip issue**, is when a company issues further units of a security to existing holders based on the holdings of each member on record date. A company quite simply converts its reserves, which may have arisen from issuing new shares in the past at a premium to their nominal value or from the accumulation of undistributed past profits, into new ordinary shares. These shares rank *pari passu* with those already in issue and are distributed to the company's ordinary shareholders in proportion to their existing shareholdings free of charge.

Rationale for Bonus Issues

Occasionally, a company may issue new shares to its shareholders without raising further capital, often as a public relations exercise to accompany news of a recent success or as a means to make its shares more marketable.

Once a UK company's share price starts trading well into double figures, its marketability starts to suffer as investors shy away from the shares. Therefore, a reduction in a company's share price as a result of a bonus issue usually has the effect of increasing the marketability of its shares and often raises expectations of higher future dividends. This, in turn, usually results in the share price settling above its new theoretical level and the company's market capitalisation increasing slightly.

3.9.5 Subdivision (Stock Split)

A subdivision, also referred to as a stock split, covers the case when a company increases the number of issued securities, for example by dividing every one share currently existing into four shares of a quarter of the old nominal amount.

3.9.6 Consolidation (Reverse Split)

This covers the case when a company decides to decrease the number of issued securities, for example, by consolidating every four shares currently existing into one share of four times the nominal amount. This is often undertaken by a company if its listed share price falls below a certain threshold amount. A reverse split was undertaken by AIG following its share price collapse and the takeover of 80% of its equity by the US federal government. The reverse split, which took effect on 1 July 2009, was a 1:20 split and applies to the public float which is still traded on the NYSE.

3.9.7 Rights Issue

When a company wishes to raise further equity capital, whether to finance expansion, develop a new product or replace existing borrowings, it can make a rights issue to its existing ordinary shareholders.

The rights issue is accompanied by a prospectus, which outlines the purpose of the capital-raising exercise, but it does not require an advertisement of the issue to be placed in the national press.

New shares are offered in proportion to each shareholder's existing shareholding, usually at a price deeply discounted to that prevailing in the market to ensure that the issue will be fully subscribed and often to avoid the cost of underwriting the shares. The number of new shares issued and the price of these shares will be determined by the amount of capital to be raised. This price, however, must be above the nominal value of the shares already in issue.

The choices open to shareholders under a rights issue are:

- take up the rights in full by purchasing all of the shares offered
- sell the rights
- sell a sufficient proportion of the rights to take up the balance, or
- take no action and allow the rights to lapse.

With regard to lapsed rights, the following circumstances then apply. Rights issues are usually underwritten by a third party and, in the case that shareholders do not take up their total entitlements, the third party will take up, or underwrite, the remaining rights and then sell all the new ordinary shares received. Any premium (positive difference) over the sale price of the ordinary shares and the take-up price will then be distributed to those shareholders who did not either sell or take up their rights.

If no premium was attained during the sale of new ordinary shares sold by the underwriters, no lapsed rights proceeds will be distributed and nil-paid shares will be removed from the client's accounts with no associated value.

3.9.8   Open Offer, Offer for Subscription and Offer for Sale

An open offer is similar to a rights issue, in that shareholders are entitled to buy newly-issued shares in proportion to their existing holdings. Unlike a rights issue, however, an open offer does not allow shareholders to sell the right to subscribe to shares. Under an open offer the shareholders have an entitlement rather than a tradeable right to subscribe to new shares. For this reason, an open offer is sometimes called an entitlement issue.

Any entitlement that is not taken up is simply allowed to lapse, or the shares are sold to another party with no compensation to the original shareholder for the loss in value of their holding that results from the dilution that comes from the new issue.

As with a rights issue, the price of the offer is likely to be at a discount to the current share price and the effect of the open offer on the price is calculated in essentially the same way.

An offer for sale is a public invitation by a sponsoring intermediary, such as an investment bank acting as an underwriter or issue manager.

An offer for subscription, or direct offer, is a public invitation by the issuing company itself. The offer can be made at a price that is fixed in advance or it can be by tender where investors state the price they are prepared to pay. After all bids are received, a strike price is set which all investors must pay.

3.9.9   Placing

In placing its shares, a company simply markets the issue directly to a broker, an issuing house or other financial institution, which in turn places the shares to selected clients. A placing is also known as selective placing.

A company may undertake a placing to raise additional finance by placing new shares in the market rather than by making a rights issue, and this requires the shareholders to firstly pass a special resolution to forgo their **pre-emption rights**.

A placing is the least expensive IPO method, as the prospectus accompanying the issue is less detailed than that required for the other two methods and no underwriting or advertising is required. If the company is seeking a full listing, the issue must still be advertised in the national press.

A placing is the preferred new issue route for most AIM companies.

3.9.10 Placing with Clawback

If a company makes a placing with clawback, new shares are placed with institutions only after they have been offered to existing shareholders. Depending on the take up of these new shares by existing shareholders, the allocation to these institutions may be clawed back, or made on a pro rata basis.

4. Mandatory and Optional Corporate Actions

Learning Objective

3.4.2 Be able to calculate the theoretical effect on the issuer's share price of the following mandatory and optional corporate actions: bonus/scrip; consolidation; rights issues

4.1 The Effect of Corporate Actions on Share Price

A corporate action can be simply defined as any event that brings material change to a company and affects its stakeholders. This includes shareholders, both common and preferred, as well as bondholders. These events are generally approved by the company's board of directors, and in certain circumstances, the shareholders are permitted to vote on proposed corporate actions.

Splits, dividends, mergers, acquisitions and spin-offs are all examples of corporate actions. Bondholders are also subject to the effects of corporate actions. For example, if interest rates fall sharply, a company may call in bonds and pay off existing bondholders, then issue new debt at lower interest rates.

Certain kinds of corporate action will bring direct change to a company's capitalisation structure and impact its stock price. Some examples are bonus issues, stock splits, reverse splits, acquisitions, rights issues and spin-offs. Some of these types of actions will be considered in this section.

4.2 Bonus, Scrip or Capitalisation Issue

A scrip issue is also known as a bonus or capitalisation issue. One factor which can lead to a scrip or bonus issue is when a company transfers profits to a fund called its capital redemption reserve and uses it to issue bonus shares to the members in proportion to their existing holdings.

A scrip or bonus issue can reduce the amount of money available for paying dividends, so the term 'bonus' is not always appropriate. That is why the term 'capitalisation of reserves' is sometimes used. A company can also use a capitalisation issue to credit partly paid shares with further amounts to make them paid up. This is explained in the table below.

The following table shows the impact of a one for three scrip issue on a company. The company started with 750,000 £1 ordinary shares in issue and net assets valued at £2.25 million, so the market capitalisation of the company is £2.25 million. A transfer of £0.25 million from retained profits to the share capital account is required to cover the scrip issue.

When the market capitalisation of £2.25 million is divided by this enlarged number of one million shares, the resultant share price is £2.25 per share. Therefore, the impact of the scrip issue has been to reduce the share price from £3.00 to £2.25.

Bonus, Scrip or Capitalisation			
Impact on the Accounts (all amounts in £'000s)			
	Before	Issue	After
Net assets	2,250		2,250
Issued share capital			
750,000 £1 ordinary shares	750		1,000
250,000 ordinary shares		250	
Share premium	1,000		1,000
Retained profit	500	(250)	250
Totals	2,250	0	2,250
Impact on the Share Price			
	Shares ('000s)	Price £	Value (£'000s)
Before	750	3.00	2,250
Scrip issue	250		
After	1,000		2,250

4.3   Share Split

The reduction in the share price as a result of a bonus issue may have its advantages, but it also has disadvantages. If share prices are falling, it may result in the price dropping below the nominal value, which under corporate law will prevent a company from raising finance by issuing more shares. An alternative way of lowering the price per share but avoiding this problem is to undertake a split. A **share split** is achieved by dividing the existing share capital into a larger number of shares with a lower nominal value per share, even though the overall nominal value of all the shares will remain the same.

Example

Consider the case of a company which has issued one million ordinary shares at £1 nominal value but wishes now to reduce the price of its shares by replacing that issue with a new issue of 2.5 million shares at a nominal value of 40p. The results can be seen on the simplified section of the statement of financial position as follows. In effect, the company is engaging in a 5:2 stock split. Before the new issue the shares are trading at £3 each. The example below illustrates the changes in the capital structure and the impact on the share price of a split issue along the lines just described.

Share Split			
Impact on the Accounts (all amounts in £'000s)			
	Before	**Issue**	**After**
Net assets	2,000		2,000
Share capital			
1m £1 ordinary shares	1,000	(1,000)	
2.5m 40p ordinary shares		1,000	1,000
Share premium	500		500
Profit and loss	500		500
Totals	2,000	0	2,000
Impact on the Share Price			
	Shares ('000s)	**Price £**	**Value (£'000s)**
Before	1,000	3.00	3,000
Split issue	1,500		
After	2,500		3,000
Market price for shares		£1.20	

In terms of market capitalisation, it can be seen that the price per share will drop to 120p per share. The prior market capitalisation was £3 million based on one million shares, but there are now 2.5 million shares issued and the market price for the shares is therefore £3 million/2.5 million shares. The new share price of 120p is considerably above the new nominal value of 40p per share. Hence, this will not cause any problems in issuing new shares.

Although both a capitalisation and a share split appear to be the same in many ways, it is important to note the difference in terms. For example, a three-for-one capitalisation will result in shareholders having three additional shares for each share held, whereas a three-for-one stock split will result in each share becoming three shares.

To summarise, the results of each are as follows:

- **Three-for-one capitalistion** – the holder of one share now has four shares.
- **Three-for-one stock split** – the holder of one share now has three shares.

Capitalisation is more associated with the UK market, and the stock split more so with the US market.

4.4 Consolidation (Reverse Split)

A reverse stock split, or consolidation, reduces the number of shares and increases the share price proportionately. For example, if you own 10,000 shares of a company and it declares a one-for-ten reverse split, you will own a total of 1,000 shares after the split. A reverse stock split has no effect on the value of what shareholders own. Companies often split their stock when they believe the price of their stock is too low to attract investors to buy their stock. Some reverse stock splits cause small shareholders to be 'cashed out' so that they no longer own the company's shares.

Example

A company has decided to issue half a million new shares with a nominal value of £2 each to replace its one million existing shares with a nominal value of £1 each. The reverse split is in effect a one-for-two split. The company's share capital remains the same at £1 million, but the stock price has effectively doubled as there are now only half the shares outstanding compared to those before the reverse split.

Reverse Split			
Impact on the Accounts (all amounts in £'000s)			
	Before	**Issue**	**After**
Net assets	2,000		2,000
Share capital			
1m £1 ordinary shares	1,000	(1,000)	
0.5m £2.00 ordinary shares		1,000	1,000
Share premium	500		500
Profit and loss	500		500
Totals	2,000	0	2,000
Impact on the Share Price			
	Shares ('000s)	**Price £**	**Value (£'000s)**
Before	1,000	3.00	3,000
Consolidation or reverse split	(500)		
After	500		3,000
Market price for shares		£6.00	

4.5   Rights Issue

A rights issue is an issue of new shares whereby a company wishes to raise additional cash from existing shareholders by offering new shares at a discount to the current market price. With a rights issue of shares, existing shareholders are given the right, or strictly speaking the first refusal, to buy new shares that the company is issuing.

Example

To illustrate the impact on the share price for a company which undertakes a rights issue, the following are the key variables.

- Prior to the rights issue, the company has issued one million shares with a nominal value of £1 each. The par value is the nominal value which has been determined by an issuing company as a minimum price.
- The share premium account shows a balance of £0.5 million. The share premium account of a company is the capital that a company raises upon issuing shares that is in excess of the nominal value of the shares.
- The company wishes to raise new capital for expansion and undertakes a one-for-four rights issue at a price of 160p in order to raise £400,000.
- The company's accounts before the rights issue show that net assets are £2 million and retained profits are £0.5 million.
- The market price of the shares prior to the rights offering is 300p per share.

What is the impact on the accounts and the theoretical market price per share of this issue?

A one-for-four rights issue means that for every four shares previously in existence, one new share will be issued. In our example, one million shares were previously in issue, and 250,000 new shares will be issued at a price of 160p in order to raise the £400,000 cash required.

In terms of the accounts, the 250,000 new share issue will increase the share capital to 1.25 million shares, the profit and loss will remain unchanged but the share premium account will need to be adjusted. The reason for this adjustment is that for the £400,000 raised, each of the 250,000 new shares can be issued at the nominal value of £1 but the additional £150,000 raised in excess of the nominal or face value of the shares is allocated to the share premium account as indicated in the simple statement of financial position perspective in the table below.

The total capitalisation of the company will have increased to £2.4 million and can be broken down according to the upper part of the table which reflects the rights issue from an accounting perspective.

The impact on the share price can be seen from the calculation of the theoretical market price in the lower part of the table. The price for the shares should have fallen from 300p per share before the rights issue to 272p after the issue to reflect the new capitalisation divided by the greater number of shares now outstanding.

Rights Issue			
Impact on the Accounts (all amounts in £'000s)			
Before	**Issue**	**After**	
Net assets	2,000	400	2,400
Share capital			
1m £1 ordinary shares	1,000	250	1,250
Share premium	500	150	650
Profit and loss	500		500
Totals	2,000	400	2,400
Impact on the Share Price			
Shares ('000s)	**Price £**	**Value (£'000s)**	
Before	1,000	3.00	3,000
Rights issue	250	1.60	400
After	1,250		3,400
Market price for shares		£2.72	

Another perspective on this can be seen simply by looking at the following formula, which only requires knowledge of the share price before the rights issue and the actual terms of the rights issue. The formula for the theoretical ex-rights price is as follows:

$$\left[\frac{\begin{array}{c} \text{No. of Shares Held Cum-Rights} \quad + \quad \text{No. of Rights Allocated} \\ \times \qquad\qquad\qquad\qquad \times \\ \text{Cum-Rights Share Price} \qquad\quad \text{Rights Issue Price} \end{array}}{\text{Total No. of Shares Held Assuming Rights Exercised}} \right]$$

This is easily demonstrated in the following table based on the example above, which leads to the same theoretical ex-rights price of 272p per share.

Description	Number of Shares	Price per Share (pence)	Total Value of Holdings (pence)
Shares held cum-rights	4	300	1,200
Rights allocated – new share entitlement	1	160	160
Post rights issue assuming rights taken up	5		1,360
Theoretical ex-rights price = 1,360/5		272	

5.   Corporate Actions and Share Dilution

Learning Objective

3.4.3   Be able to analyse the following in respect of corporate actions: rationale offered by the company; the dilution effect on profitability and reported financials; the effect of share buybacks

5.1   Overview

Corporate actions are multi-faceted, but those which are of most relevance to financial analysts and investors are those which will impact the capital structure of the corporation.

One of the most important metrics for any company is the determination of the company's earnings per share or EPS. In arriving at the EPS, most concern will be in respect to the denominator or divisor of the equation, ie, the number of ordinary shares which are outstanding. If there have been no changes in the capital structure during the course of a year there should be no problems in simply stating the number of shares outstanding as of the year-end and using this as the denominator. However, if there have been modifications to the capital outstanding during the course of the year as a result of a corporate action, then pro rata adjustments to the number to reflect the changes in capitalisation will be required. The purpose of the adjustments will be:

- To ensure the EPS ratio for the current year is valid by comparing the full year's earnings to the representative number of shares in issue during the year, not simply the number of shares in issue at the year-end. For example, the value for the number of shares outstanding will be distorted by an issuance of new shares close to the preparation of year-end statements.
- In order to provide a consistent historical view of a company's accounts and profitability trends, it is important to ensure that the previous year's earnings per share figures have been calculated on a similar basis. In order for this to take place, it will often be necessary to re-state a previous year's EPS figures.

The following are the principal kinds of corporate actions, the rationale behind them, and their impact on capitalisation are also outlined.

5.2   Rights Issue

A rights issue is a corporate action designed to raise additional capital under a secondary market offering of shares. With the issued rights, existing shareholders have the privilege to buy a specified number of new shares from the firm at a specified price within a specified time. A rights issue is in contrast to an initial public offering (primary market offering), when shares are issued to the general public for the first time.

A rights issue is directly offered to all shareholders of record, or through broker dealers of record and may be exercised in full or partially. Subscription rights may either be transferable, allowing the subscription right-holder to sell them privately, on the open market or not at all. The company receives shareholders' money in exchange for shares, meaning a rights issue is a source of capital.

There are various reasons why companies may elect to undertake a rights issue. They may have problems raising capital through borrowing or issuance of debentures, or they may prefer to avoid high interest charges on loans or high coupons in conjunction with a bond issuance.

Several leading banks had to undertake rights issues both in the UK and elsewhere to rebuild their Tier 1 capital following the drastic fall in property prices in 2007–08 and the write-down of many of their assets. Tier 1 capital is a key measure of a bank's reserves as defined first in Basel 1.

In May 2010, Prudential Insurance announced plans for the biggest rights issue in UK history to raise £14.5 billion to buy AIA Group – the Asian arm of US insurer AIG. Under the proposal, every shareholder was entitled to buy 11 new shares for every two existing ones, at an issue price of 104p, which was an 80% discount to the price of the shares at the time of the announcement. The terms of the offer meant that an existing shareholder could either buy the full entitlement of shares, sell part of the entitlement and use the resulting money to pay for the balance or sell the entitlement. Shareholders who did anything other than take up their full entitlement would see their existing shareholding diluted, or reduced in value. The rights issue met such opposition from institutional shareholders in the UK that it was subsequently withdrawn and the company decided to abandon the acquisition.

5.2.1   New Share Issue to Acquire a Subsidiary

If shares are issued as part of the consideration to acquire a subsidiary, the treatment is exactly the same as a full price issue.

From the date when the subsidiary is acquired it will be necessary to consolidate into the group accounts the profit of the subsidiary. In other words, from the date of acquisition the enlarged group's earnings will rise by the earnings generated by the subsidiary.

It will be necessary to apply a weighted average number to the shares as and when they were issued and, therefore, outstanding.

5.3   Bonus Issues and Share Splits

A bonus share is a free share of stock given to current/existing shareholders in a company, based upon the number of shares that the shareholder already owns at the time of the announcement of the bonus. While the issue of bonus shares increases the total number of shares issued and owned, it does not increase the value of the company. Although the total number of issued shares increases, the ratio of the number of shares held by each shareholder remains constant.

A bonus issue does not raise any new cash and therefore will not generate any new earnings.

From a statement of financial position perspective a bonus issue has the effect of increasing share capital and reducing reserves, ie, restructuring shareholders' funds. It does not change the total shareholders' funds or total net assets.

From an operational viewpoint, these bonus shares may as well have been issued at the same time as the underlying shares on which they are now being paid.

In terms of accounting procedure, the best way to think about a bonus issue is to backdate the bonus issue and in effect imagine that those shares had always been in issue. Similar considerations apply in the case of a share split – for example, all existing shareholders are given another share in a two-for-one split – so following such an event there are a greater number of shares outstanding, but, since the split was on a *pro bono* basis, no new finance has been raised. The main reason for a bonus issuance or share split is that the price of the existing share has become unwieldy.

During the 1990s internet and technology boom, many Nasdaq companies such as Intel, Apple and Amazon saw their share prices increase by several orders of magnitude and the companies decided that the share prices had become too high for the average retail investor. A company would undertake, for example, a three-for-one split which would mean that, after the bonus issue (or split), all the existing investors would have three shares for every one share before the split. So if the share price had risen to $150 before the split, after the split or bonus issue the share price would have dropped to $50 per share.

A pure bonus issue will require an adjustment to be made to the number of shares previously in issue by use of the bonus or split fraction as follows.

$$\frac{\text{Number of shares after the issue}}{\text{Number of shares before the issue}}$$

The alternative to the splits discussed above is the corporate action of a reverse split. In this case, a company will announce that it will be reducing the number of shares outstanding but that the reduction will be applied across the board to all current shareholders so that the number of shares outstanding is adjusted for each individual shareholder. Following a reverse split, while the earnings per share (EPS) will have risen, all things being equal, the entitlement or claim to a specific portion of the company's earnings by any shareholder will remain the same.

In essence, a split or reverse split in the number of a company's shares outstanding will affect the EPS for the individual shares. However, it will not affect the market capitalisation of the company. Moreover, it will not affect the claims to participate in a different portion of the earnings of the company for the current shareholders, since their revised holding will only entitle them to the same portion of the earnings prior to the split or reverse split. If they have more shares as in the case of a split, the individual shares will have a lower EPS, but when added together, and with the earnings as the same numerator as before, their holding will entitle them to the same share of the company's earning before the split. If an investor has fewer shares, as in the case of a reverse split, the individual shares held will now have a higher EPS, but the investor's new holding, given that total earnings have remained the same, means that their entitlement will still be to the same share or portion of the company's earnings as before.

The reasons for undertaking a reverse split are usually the converse of those for a split. The company may consider that the price of its shares is too low and, therefore, wants to boost the price by withdrawing a large number of outstanding shares.

This can also be undertaken for listing purposes where, for example, the NYSE does not allow stocks below a trading price of one dollar to be listed. Also, for institutional investors many are not allowed to purchase stocks that are priced below a minimum amount. This is more typically the case in the US, where share prices tend to have higher nominal amounts. The typical price for a US share is approximately $40 and it is not permitted for many investment managers to buy shares that are priced below $5, or sometimes even higher thresholds.

Example

In the aftermath of the collapse of Lehman Brothers and the CDO market in 2008, AIG's board of directors decided that the company should undertake a reverse split in July 2009. The split was a 1:20 split which meant that each shareholder exchanged 20 of the old shares for one new share.

Before the split, the shares had traded below $2 for much of the year, weighed down by the company's nearly $100 billion in losses in the previous year and a taxpayer bailout that left the US government owning almost an 80% stake in the company. In August 2012, the shares of AIG were trading at approximately $34.

5.4 Share Buybacks

A share repurchase, or **share buyback**, is usually a positive event for shareholders. It usually involves a company buying back its own shares through the stock market or by way of a tender offer to shareholders. The repurchased shares are often absorbed into the company which has the effect of reducing the number of outstanding shares or market capitalisation. As this happens, shareholders have a relatively larger stake in the company as there are fewer shares in issue on which the company returns profits in the form of dividends.

From the issuer's perspective, a buyback is often regarded as a good use of its capital and, indeed, can create a positive opinion of the company by the markets as it is seen to be heavily investing in itself.

Buybacks have the effect of reducing the size of the assets on the statement of financial position so, naturally, return on assets increases because the return is compared to a lower capital base. Another effect is that return on equity increases for a similar reason – because there is less equity outstanding. This also means that the price/earnings ratio will increase – there are fewer shares in issue with the same earnings.

Issuers who operate employee share schemes can use buybacks to reduce or eliminate the diluting effect that these options have over time. Employee share schemes increase the amount of shares in issue and would have the opposite effect on key metrics as a buyback. Therefore, buybacks can negate the effect of the employee share scheme and retain equilibrium.

5.5 Post-Statement of Financial Position Events

The basic EPS is required to be altered to incorporate the effect of certain share issues on the number of ordinary shares when the issue occurs between the statement of financial position date and the date on which the accounts are approved.

When the company undertakes a bonus issue, share split or consolidation, or when there is a bonus element to another issue (eg, rights issue), the number of shares must include the extra shares now in issue after the event.

In the case of an issue that impacts on earnings, such as a rights issue, only those shares that have no earnings impact should be included in the EPS calculation. For a rights issue, this would be just the bonus element.

5.6   Diluted Earnings Per Share (EPS)

The purpose of publishing a diluted EPS figure is to warn shareholders of potential future changes in the EPS figure as a result of events that hypothetically may have taken place. The reason why the term 'hypothetically' is used in this context is because there is only a possibility – legally certain rights have been granted which could be exercised and require further issues of shares – and the prudent method of accounting is to assume, from the point of view of share dilution, the worst-case scenario.

There are two possible factors that could cause share dilution and which need to be covered in the method of conservatively calculating a true and accurate picture of the EPS. A company may have either or both of the following kinds of securities outstanding:

*   convertible loan stock or convertible preference shares
*   options or warrants.

Each of these circumstances may potentially result in more shares being issued and thereby qualifying for a dividend in future years, which will have the material effect of diluting the current EPS. The diluted EPS figure is a theoretical calculation based on assumptions about the future (which may or may not actually take place) and it is considered of such importance to the reader of the accounts and a potential investor that its calculation and disclosure is required by IAS 33 – earnings per share (FRS 22 in the UK). IAS 33 requires the disclosure of basic and diluted EPS on the face of the statement of profit and loss, both for net profit or loss for the period and profit or loss for continuing operations. Any additional information, such as alternative methods of calculating the EPS, can only be disclosed by way of a note to the accounts. A note needs to be included in the accounts detailing the basis upon which the calculations are done, specifically the earnings figure used and the number of shares figure used within the calculation, both for the year in question and the comparative year.

6.   Warrants and Contracts for Difference (CFDs)

6.1   Warrants

Learning Objective

3.5.1   Be able to analyse the main purposes, characteristics, behaviours and relative risk and return of warrants and covered warrants: benefit to the issuing company; right to subscribe for capital; effect on price of maturity and the underlying security; exercise and expiry; calculation of the conversion premium on a warrant

A warrant gives the right to the holder to buy shares from the company that issued the warrant at a specified price on or before a specified date. Essentially, a warrant is very similar to a call option, which gives the right to buy a share. Warrants have all the characteristics of call options, such as volatility, risk and valuation factors. The major difference is that warrants are issued by and exercisable on the company, which will issue new shares on **exercise**. Traded and traditional options are issued by investors and relate to shares already in issue; their exercise does not result in new shares being issued.

6.1.1 Company

Advantages to a Company of Issuing Warrants

- Raising immediate cash without the need to finance dividend payments to new shares.
- Increasing the attraction of a debt issue. Many warrants are attached to a debt issue, giving debt investors the added attraction of an equity kicker. This will translate into lower required yields on the debt, meaning that the initial financial burden on the company is lower.
- After the debt is issued, the warrants are usually detached from the debt and traded separately in the marketplace. There is a secondary market for some of the more attractive and liquid warrants.
- If the company believes that its own share price will fall, then any warrants issued are unlikely to be exercised. This means that the company will receive the money on issue of the warrants, but anticipates that it will not have to issue any new shares.

Disadvantages to the Company of Issuing Warrants

If and when the warrant is exercised:

- New shares must be issued by the company, potentially at a significant discount to the then share price.
- The required dividend payments in total may increase dramatically if the share price is not to be adversely affected.

6.1.2 Investors

Advantages to Investors

- A geared investment in a company's shares, being a cheaper alternative to buying the share itself, much in the same way as for a call option.
- The buyer of a warrant does not suffer from the decay of time premium in the same manner as the buyer of a call option.
- A way of securing an income yield while keeping open the possibility of high equity performance, through buying debt plus warrants from the company. This is similar to the principle of buying a convertible debt issue.

Disadvantages to Investors

- As a geared investment, percentage losses can be extreme if the share underperforms.
- The risk of a takeover. If a company is taken over, it is often the case that the exercise date of the warrants will be accelerated to the takeover date. This will destroy any time value in the warrant, meaning that an investor could suffer a serious loss. If the warrant is out-of-the-money, having just been issued for example, then it may become worthless.

6.1.3 Additional Factors when Considering an Investment in Warrants

Warrants are frequently attached to bonds or preferred stock as a sweetener, allowing the issuer to pay lower interest rates or dividends. They can be used to enhance the yield of the bond, and make it more attractive to potential buyers. Warrants can also be used in private equity deals. Frequently these warrants are detachable, and can be sold independently of the bond or stock.

Note that a warrant-holder will not be affected by bonus issues or rights issues because the terms of the warrant will adjust in the same way as the terms of options contracts.

Warrants have similar characteristics to those of other equity derivatives, such as options – for instance:

- **Exercising** – a warrant is exercised when the holder informs the issuer of their intention to purchase the shares underlying the warrant.
- **Premium** – a warrant's premium represents how much extra has to be paid for shares when buying them through the warrant as compared to buying them in the regular way.
- **Gearing (leverage)** – a warrant's gearing is the way to ascertain how much more exposure the investor has to the underlying shares using the warrant as compared to the exposure if they were buying shares through the market.
- **Expiration date** – this is the date the warrant expires. If the investor plans on exercising the warrant, they must do so before the expiration date. The more time remaining until expiry, the more time for the underlying security to appreciate, which in turn will increase the price of the warrant (unless it depreciates). Therefore, the expiration date is the date on which the right to exercise no longer exists.

6.1.4 Secondary Market

Sometimes, the issuer will try to establish a market for the warrant and register it with a listed exchange. In this case, the price can be obtained from a broker. But often, warrants are privately held or not registered, which makes their prices less obvious. Unregistered warrant transactions can still be facilitated between accredited parties, and in fact several secondary markets have been formed to provide **liquidity** for these investments.

6.1.5 Comparison with Call Options

Warrants are much like call options, will often confer the same rights as an equity option, and can even be traded in secondary markets. However, warrants have several key differences:

- Warrants are issued by private parties, typically the corporation on which a warrant is based, rather than a public options exchange.
- Warrants issued by the company itself are dilutive. When the warrant issued by the company is exercised, the company issues new shares of stock, so the number of outstanding shares increases. When a call option is exercised, the owner of the call option receives an existing share from an assigned call writer (except in the case of employee stock options, when new shares are created and issued by the company upon exercise).
- Unlike common stock shares outstanding, warrants do not have voting rights.
- A warrant's lifetime is measured in years (as long as 15 years), while options are typically measured in months. Even long-term equity anticipation securities (LEAPS), the longest stock options available, tend to expire in two or three years. Upon expiration, the warrants are worthless if not exercised, unless the price of the common stock is greater than the exercised price.
- Warrants are not standardised like exchange-listed options. They are considered over-the-counter instruments, and thus are usually only traded by financial institutions with the capacity to settle and clear these types of transactions.

Example

Warrants are available in a (fictional) investment company, Carmerside Investment Trust. Carmerside Investment Trust shares are currently trading at 77p each, and warrants are available giving the investor the right to buy shares at £1 each, up until 2028. The warrants are trading at 4p each.

In the above example, the warrant's expiry date is in 2028 and its exercise price is 100p.

What are the advantages to Carmerside Investment Trust that persuade it to issue warrants? Clearly, the sale of warrants for cash will raise money for the company, and if the warrants are exercised then further capital will be raised by the company. Similarly to call options, holding the warrant does not entitle the investor to receive dividends or to vote at company meetings, so the capital raised until the warrant is exercised could be considered as free. Obviously warrants offer a highly geared investment opportunity for the investor, and warrants are often issued alongside other investments, rather than sold in their own right.

Example

ABC plc is attempting to raise finance by issuing bonds. Its advisers inform the company that it could issue bonds paying a coupon of 6% pa, or lower this to 5% pa if it were to give away a single warrant with each £100 nominal of the bonds. The warrants are detachable from the bonds. In other words, the investors could decide to sell their warrants or keep them, regardless of whether they retain the bonds.

Traditional warrants are issued in conjunction with a bond (known as a warrant-linked bond), and represent the right to acquire shares in the entity issuing the bond. In other words, the writer of a traditional warrant is also the issuer of the underlying instrument. Warrants issued in this way make the bond issue more attractive and can reduce the interest rate that must be offered in order to sell the bond issue.

6.1.6   Warrant Price Behaviour

Warrants (including covered warrants, see section 6.1.8) are highly-geared investments. A modest outlay can result in a large gain, but the investor can lose everything. Their value is driven by the length of time for which they are valid (their maturity or period until expiry) and the value of the underlying security.

Comparison of Warrants

There is a relatively simple method of looking at the price of one warrant relative to other warrants – using a conversion premium. The conversion premium is the price of the warrant plus the **exercise price** required to buy the underlying share, less the prevailing share price. For example, calculating the conversion premium for the Carmerside Investment Trust encountered above:

Warrant price	=	4p
Plus exercise price	=	100p
Less share price	=	77p
Conversion premium	=	27p

Note that if the resulting figure were a negative, the warrant would be trading at a conversion discount.

Valuation of Warrants

Since a warrant has the same commercial effect for the investor as an option, its valuation can be achieved in the same way, eg, through use of the binomial model or the Black-Scholes model.

In undertaking this, however, we need to consider the differences between an option and a warrant: specifically that, when a warrant is exercised, new shares are issued by the company, diluting the value of the shares in existence.

The value of a warrant can therefore be established as follows:

$$\text{Warrant value} = \frac{A}{1+q} \times \text{Number of shares}$$

where:

A = value of an equivalent option derived from a suitable option pricing model

q = percentage increase in the number of shares in issue once the warrant is exercised (expressed as a decimal)

6.1.7 Warrant Premium and Gearing

The warrant premium is the amount by which the warrant price plus the exercise price exceeds the share price. This is also the time value of the warrant expressed as a percentage of the share price.

Warrant Premium =

[(Warrant Price + Exercise Price – Current Share Price)/Current Share Price] x 100

Options are highly geared investments. The same is true for warrants. The warrant gearing ratio indicates how highly geared the warrant is, and it is calculated as follows:

$$\text{Gearing Ratio} = \frac{\text{Share Price}}{\text{Warrant Price}} \times 100\%$$

	Warrant A	Warrant B
Issuer	XYZ plc	XYZ plc
Share Price	180	180
Exercise Price	100	300
Expiry Date	2029	2029
Price of Warrant	160	30
Gearing Ratio	112.50%	600.00%

Warrant A is considered to be deeply in-the-money (ie, the exercise price is lower than the share price), and Warrant B is deeply out-of-the-money. The price of Warrant A is consequently much higher and will almost certainly be exercised and has in effect become like a share. If the share price moves to 181p, then the warrant price will probably move to 161p. It is not a highly geared investment, and investing in the warrant will give around the same percentage returns as investing in the share itself.

The situation with Warrant B is very different. A change in the share price from 180p to 181p is unlikely to affect the value of the warrant significantly. If the share price rises significantly, however, then the price of the warrant could also rise significantly, giving a very high percentage return on the initial investment. Warrant B is much more highly geared than Warrant A.

6.1.8 Covered Warrants

Covered warrants are warrants based on an underlying share or index which are issued by a financial institution, such as an investment bank, rather than by a corporate issuer. The warrant is called 'covered' because the issuing institution will hold the underlying asset, to cover its exposure. From an investor's perspective the purchase of covered warrants is a speculative and risky investment, although significant profits can be earned due to the gearing or leverage effect of warrants.

Covered warrants are priced according to a calculation of their fair value rather than on the basis of supply and demand. The cost of the warrants is called the premium (which represents the maximum potential loss to the holder). They are exercised at the exercise price, and expire at the expiry or expiration date.

Call warrants give a right to buy at a specified price within a specified time period, while put warrants give a right to sell at a specified price within a specified time period. A call warrant may be purchased as a bet on the price of the underlying asset rising, while a put warrant may be bought as a bet on the price falling. Covered warrants typically have a life of six to twelve months at issue, although this may be up to five years.

Example

The ordinary shares of X plc trade at 120p currently (at 15 June). An investor who believes the price will rise may be able to buy a call warrant to buy at 150p by, say, 30 September. This warrant might be priced at, say, 5p for each share. If the X plc share price rises to 160p, the warrant can be excised for a profit since 160p–150p = 10p proceeds, compared with the cost of 5p. If the share price does not reach 150p by 30 September, the warrant will be worthless on expiry.

A put warrant to sell X plc at 100p by 30 September could be exercised if the share price of X plc falls below 100p. The profit on exercise will depend on how far below 100p the price falls, less the initial warrant cost.

Covered warrants can be sold on in the market before being exercised, in which case part of their value will be the time value attributable to the hope that the warrant can eventually be exercised at a profit. Covered warrants are available on the LSE, covering a range of blue chip and mid-cap shares and indices. Covered warrants have also even been available for house price indices.

6.1.9 Warrant Pricing

A puzzle for investors might be how a warrant price is actually arrived at, because the forces of supply and demand take a back seat. Ordinarily, for equities and for traditional listed warrants, the price is purely a function of the demand from buyers and the supply from sellers.

For covered warrants, it is different. The issuer will usually be the sole market maker (or committed principal), who is obliged to make a two-way price in the warrant throughout the trading day. And supply and demand are, most of the time, only tangential factors in setting the price. Instead, computers use algorithms to move the price automatically in relation to the changes in the underlying asset. There are too many warrants to price manually, and because covered warrants are a synthetic creation there is no need to balance supply and demand because the quantity in the market is more fluid.

Some potential issues relating to conflicts of interest can arise. What is to stop the issuer from fixing the price to the detriment of investors? What is to stop the issuer from widening the dealing spread to prevent sensible dealing during times of financial stress? And how are the prices really determined?

The single market-maker model, where only the issuer makes a price in its warrants, is a tried and tested approach in overseas warrants markets, and it works well without abuse. Competition occurs across warrants rather than within each individual security.

It is also reputational. On a popular security, warrants may be issued by several issuers, all competing for business. If one has a price which is less favourable than the others, it will very quickly become apparent in the market – good sources of electronic information make the process of comparison quick and efficient – and that issuer will lose out on trade.

The twin forces of inter-warrant competition and reputation work to ensure an orderly and fairly priced market for investors.

6.2 Contracts For Difference (CFDs)

Learning Objective

3.5.2 Be able to analyse the main characteristics of contracts for difference (CFDs); types and availability of CFDs; CFD providers – market maker versus direct market access; margin; market, liquidation and counterparty risks; size of CFD market and impact on total market activity; differences in pricing, valuing and trading CFDs compared to direct investment; differences in pricing, valuing and trading CFDs compared to spread bets

Contracts for difference (CFDs) were originally developed in the early 1990s in London and were based on a similar structure to an equity swap. Essentially, a swap is a general term for a contractual asset when payments on one or both sides to the agreement – called counterparties – are linked to the performance of an underlying asset such as an equity index.

The motivation for developing equity swaps and, in turn, CFDs has been guided by several different factors including the desire to avoid stamp duty and, in some instances, withholding taxes and also to obtain leverage and enjoy the returns from ownership without actually owning equity.

Equity swaps and customised CFDs are used by hedge funds and institutional investors to hedge their exposure to equities in a cost-effective way. Along with futures and options, contracts for difference come under the FCA's definition of derivatives.

CFDs are different from traditional cash-traded instruments (such as equities, bonds, commodities and currencies) in that they do not confer ownership of the underlying asset. Investors can take positions on the price of a great number of different instruments. The price of the CFD tracks the price of the underlying asset, and so the holder of a CFD benefits from, or loses because of, the price movement in the stock, bond, currency, commodity or index. But the CFD holder does not take ownership of the underlying asset.

CFDs are margin-traded, meaning that the investor does not have to deposit the full value of the underlying asset with the CFD provider.

CFDs allow the investor to benefit from downward movements in a share or other price if they choose. This has the effect of adopting a position of 'short selling' the stock. This flexibility, and the possibility of margin trading, means that CFDs can be used either for hedging or speculation.

To understand how CFDs work, it is helpful to consider how the company offering the CFD is able to pay an investor whose CFD has resulted in a price movement that is favourable for the investor. A broker offering CFDs may seek to hedge its own liability to pay out for price movements in the stock concerned, by buying a matching quantity of the stock in the market. The broker is likely to have customers adopting long and short positions so these can be netted out, and the degree to which the company has to hedge will be reduced.

The costs of CFDs comprise a cost built into the spread of the CFD price, together with a funding charge. CFDs have the advantage that there is no stamp duty or stamp duty reserve tax (SDRT) to pay, although the holder will be liable to capital gains tax (CGT).

CFD contracts are subject to a daily financing charge, usually applied at a previously agreed rate linked to LIBOR. The parties to a CFD pay to finance long positions and may receive funding on short positions in lieu of deferring sale proceeds. The contracts are settled for the cash differential between the price of the opening and closing trades.

CFDs are subject to a commission charge on equities that is a percentage of the size of the position for each trade. Alternatively, an investor can opt to trade with a market maker, forgoing commissions at the expense of a larger bid/offer spread on the instrument.

Investors in CFDs are required to maintain a certain amount of margin as defined by the brokerage – usually ranging from 1% to 30%. One advantage to investors of not having to put up as collateral the full notional value of the CFD is that a given quantity of capital can control a larger position, amplifying the potential for profit or loss, ie, the investment is geared. On the other hand, a leveraged position in a volatile CFD can expose the buyer to a margin call in a downturn, which often leads to losing a substantial part of the assets (or having the CFD position automatically closed out). As with many leveraged products, maximum exposure is not limited to the initial investment, and it is possible to lose more than one put in. These risks are typically mitigated through use of stop loss orders and other risk-reduction strategies.

Example

Suppose you wish to buy 1,000 shares of XYZ at £12 each. In a normal non-margin broker account you would need to have an initial cash deposit or balance of £12,000. Using CFDs, trading on a 5% margin, you will only need an initial deposit of £600.

An example is the easiest way to show the use of leverage.

If you had £600 to invest, and wished to purchase XYZ shares at £12 and sell them at £13, a standard trade would look as follows:

BUY: 50 x £12 = £600

SELL: 50 x £13 = £650

PROFIT = £50 or £50/£600 = 8.33%

Using leverage, the above transaction with CFDs is possible:

BUY: 1,000 x £12 = £600 (5% deposit) + £11,400 (95% borrowed funds)

SELL: 1,000 x £13 = £13,000

PROFIT = £1,000 or £1,000/600 = 167%

The profit received after using leverage was far greater – in fact, 20 times greater – than without using leverage, ie, the borrowing of 95% of the contract amount. Clearly, though, the losses are also magnified to the same extent when using leverage.

CFDs allow a trader to go short or long on any position using a margin. There are always two types of margin with a CFD trade:

- **Initial margin** – the initial margin for shares of individual companies is normally between 5% and 30%. For exchange-traded funds, stock indices and foreign exchange, where relatively less risk of volatility is perceived by CFD brokers, the initial margin can be as low as 1% and more typically at 5%. In the case of the example above, we saw that this would be 5% of the contract price.
- **Variable margin** – the CFD will be marked-to-market at currently prevailing prices and if the position has moved beyond the amount taken as initial margin – eg, the position has moved adversely – the additional margin required to support the borrowing (in the example, at 95% for XYZ) will have to be deposited or available in the current balance of the customer's cash account.

Regulatory Restrictions

In 2019, following consultation feedback, the FCA confirmed new rules restricting the sale, marketing and distribution of CFDs and CFD-like options to retail customers.

6.2.1 Market and Risk

The CFD market in the UK is operated by numerous large brokerages including such firms as IG Markets, City Index and MF Global. As brokers, these are the companies which create and package the CFD arrangements and which effectively become the counterparties to the trades with principal customers.

It is incumbent on the broker offering the CFD to assure itself that the customer has sufficient collateral, and is sufficiently aware of the risks of trading CFDs that offer a high degree of leverage. Risk warnings are prominently displayed on all advertising and web pages. The FCA stipulates that CFD providers must assess the suitability and appropriateness of CFDs for each new client, based on their experience; CFD providers must also provide a risk warning document to all new CFD clients.

There have been some publicised cases in which a CFD customer has been unable to meet a margin call for substantial losses resulting from a trade which turned out to be ill-conceived, and this raises the possibility that the CFD broker that took the other side of the trade could potentially have liquidity/solvency problems. If a CFD broker suffers difficulties in honouring its contracts with customers it will also suffer immediate reputational damage and, while the customers may have collateral at risk their losses will be confined to the marginal sums involved in CFD trading rather than the nominal sums (ie, the total size of the trade as opposed to the amount of margin required to control that position size).

6.2.2   The Size of the CFD Market

CFDs have proven to be a very successful innovation in financial markets and their development was spearheaded in the UK. CFDs have become ubiquitous in most European markets. Surprisingly, even at present, there is no comparable product sold domestically in the US, which has been attributed to a lack of clarity as to which US regulatory agency should provide supervision for these instruments.

It has been estimated that CFD trading in the UK has accounted for approximately 50% of all London equity trading. This percentage is, if anything, likely to increase, as both professional and retail investors have demonstrated a strong interest in the features of the products which have been described above.

6.2.3   CFDs and Spread Bets

CFDs and spread bets allow investors to do similar things; however, CFDs differ from spread bets in one crucial respect – tax. While a spread bet offers tax-free gains, a CFD does not. CGT applies to profits on CFDs – and investors can use capital losses on CFDs to reduce future CGT bills.

Furthermore, spread bets are essentially bets made with a bookmaker such as IG Index, and the bookmaker will try to make its money on the spread between bid and offer prices, just like a market maker in the equity markets. In contrast, CFDs can be matching trades on what is essentially an order-driven system that may make them more cost-effective.

CFDs may also attract a financing charge if they are held over time, which does not apply to spread bets.

As a general rule, CFDs are more appropriate for more experienced participants taking larger positions, such as day traders and institutions like hedge funds, while spread bets tend to be more appropriate for trades undertaken by less sophisticated individuals.

End of Chapter Questions

Think of an answer to each question and refer to the appropriate section for confirmation.

1. What does the term 'cumulative' entail when applied to the preference shares of a company?
    Answer reference: Section 1.1.3

2. If shares issued as part of a public offering include a certain block of shares from company directors or venture capitalists, are those shares dilutive or non-dilutive?
    Answer reference: Section 2.1.2

3. What is the minimum market capitalisation requirement (ie, shares held by the public) for a company to be admitted for a listing on the London Stock Exchange's high-growth segment?
    Answer reference: Section 2.3.4

4. With respect to a London Stock Exchange-listed company, what is a notifiable interest?
    Answer reference: Section 2.3.6

5. Which provision of MiFID enables the issuance of securities to qualified investors without the rigorous disclosure requirements of a full-blown public offering?
    Answer reference: Section 2.4.1

6. What is meant by the term 'greenshoe option' in regard to a public offering of securities?
    Answer reference: Section 2.5.2

7. What does the term 'front running' mean in regard to the activities of brokers and other financial intermediaries?
    Answer reference: Section 3.1.3

8. What is an iceberg order?
    Answer reference: Section 3.2.6

9. What strategies do high-frequency traders use to generate profits?
    Answer reference: Section 3.4.1

10. Which organisation in the UK makes decisions as to which companies' shares and bonds (including gilts) can be admitted to be traded on the London Stock Exchange?
    Answer reference: Section 3.6.2

Chapter Four
Collective Investments

This syllabus area will provide approximately 8 of the 80 examination questions

1.   Collective Investment Funds and Companies

1.1   Unit Trusts

Learning Objective

4.1.2   Be able to analyse the key features, accessibility, risks, charges, valuation and yield
characteristics of unit trusts

A unit trust is a professionally managed collective investment fund. Unit trusts have been available in the
UK since the 1930s.

*   Investors can buy units, each of which represents a specified fraction of the trust.
*   The trust holds a portfolio of securities.
*   The assets of the trust are held by trustees and are invested by managers.
*   The investor incurs annual management charges and possibly also an initial charge.

An authorised unit trust (AUT) must be constituted by a trust deed made between the manager and the
trustee.

The basic principle with AUTs is that there is a single type of undivided unit. This is modified where
there are both income units (paying a distribution to unitholders) and accumulation units (rolling up
income into the capital value of the units). As with an open-ended investment company (OEIC), if the
fund manager wishes to market the unit trust in other member states of the EU, the manager may apply
for certification under the Undertakings for Collective Investment in Transferable Securities (UCITS)
Directive.

1.1.1   Trustees and Trust Deed

1.   Trustees of a unit trust must be authorised by the FCA and fully independent of the trust manager.
2.   The primary duty of the trustees is to protect the interests of the unitholders.
3.   The investor in a unit trust owns the underlying value of shares based on the proportion of the units
     held. They are effectively the beneficiary of the trust.
4.   The trust deed of each unit trust must clearly state its investment strategy and objectives, so that
     investors can determine the suitability of each trust.
5.   The limits and allowable investment areas for a unit trust fund are also laid out in the trust deed
     together with the investment objectives.

1.1.2   The Role of the Manager

The manager must also be authorised by the FCA and the role covers:

*   marketing the unit trust
*   managing the assets in accordance with the trust deed
*   maintaining a record of units for inspection by the trustees
*   supplying other information relating to the investments under the unit trust as requested
*   informing the FCA of any breaches of regulations.

1.1.3 Buying and Selling Units

Units in unit trusts can be purchased in a number of ways: for example, via a newspaper advertisement, over the phone or over the internet. These methods will generally require payment with the order, or some form of guarantee of payment. A contract note will be produced and sent to the investor as evidence of the purchase.

Investors can sell their units through the same source that they purchased them, or can contact the fund managers directly, for example by telephone.

Liquidity Risk

Liquidity risk is a financial risk concerning how easily a security or financial asset (including investment funds) can be traded quickly, especially when selling an asset to realise cash. It also refers to the ability to sell an asset without impacting the market price.

For investment funds, liquidity is generally seen as the ability for the fund to fulfil redemption orders as requested. Authorised funds and those that are less complex would generally carry less liquidity risk – ie, if an asset has a lack of liquidity depth, there is a risk that the price will move significantly, eg, a sale is attempted.

1.1.4 Unit Trust Pricing

The calculation of buying and selling prices take place at the valuation point, which is at a particular time each day. The fund is valued on the basis of the net value of the constituent assets. Most unit trusts use dual pricing, and a typical spread between buying and selling prices in the market will be in the range of 5–7%. Some fund managers, however, use single pricing, in which case there is the same price quoted for buying and selling units, with any charges being separately disclosed.

Offer Basis and Bid Basis

If the market is moving upwards, it is likely that investors will be buying. In these circumstances, managers can move the spread to the top of the range. This effectively means that the offer price being paid by investors will be at the highest level allowed by the FCA's rules and increases the price for buyers. However, it also increases the price for sellers of units, who get a price of 5–7% below the offer price. When this happens, prices are said to be on an offer basis.

If the market is moving downwards, it is likely that investors will be selling. In these circumstances, managers can move the spread to the bottom of the range. This effectively means that the buying price being paid will be the lowest bid price allowed under the FCA's rules (the cancellation price) and reduces the price for sellers. However, it also reduces the price for buyers of units, who get a price of 5–7% above the cancellation price. When this happens, prices are said to be on a bid basis.

Historic Pricing and Forward Pricing

Prices can be set on a historic or forward pricing basis. If the price the investor pays is based on the previous valuation point, the pricing is described as historic. All units purchased up to the valuation point on the following day will be at the same, previous price. If the investor pays a price based on the next valuation point, it is called forward pricing. All units purchased up to the next valuation point will be at that price.

Each system has merits. With historic pricing the investor knows the price they will pay for units, but the value of the underlying securities may not be reflected in the price paid. This is good if prices have moved up, but bad if they have moved down. Investors find future pricing confusing, as it is not possible to determine in advance the price they will pay, but the price will be more reflective of the underlying value of the securities.

On a historic pricing basis, the manager creates units at the valuation point, according to the amount of sales expected up to the next valuation point. If sales exceed expected levels, the manager must either move to forward pricing or risk loss of money for the fund, if there is an unfavourable price movement.

On a forward pricing basis, the manager must create units at the valuation point sufficient to cover transactions since the last valuation point.

A manager using the historic pricing basis must move to a forward pricing basis if the value of the fund is believed to have changed by 2% or more since the last valuation and if the investor requests forward pricing.

1.1.5 Charges

Generally speaking, the charges on a unit trust can be taken in three ways: an initial charge which is made up front, an annual management charge made periodically and an exit charge levied when the investor sells. Whatever charges are made must be explicitly detailed in the trust deed and documentation. The documents should provide details of both the current charges and the extent to which the manager can change them.

The upfront initial charge is added to the buying price incurred by the investor. Initial charges tend to be higher on actively managed funds, often in the range of 3.0% to 6.5%. Lower initial charges are typically levied on index trackers. Some managers will discount their initial charges for direct sales including those made over the internet. It is not unusual for those managers that charge low or zero initial charges to make exit charges when the investor sells units. Over time, an increasing number of UK fund managers are abolishing initial charges in their aim to become more cost competitive against tracker funds and exchange-traded funds (ETFs).

If they apply, exit charges are generally only made when the investor sells within a set period of time, such as the first three or five years. Furthermore, these exit charges tend to be made on a sliding scale with a more substantial charge made for those exiting earlier than those exiting later. Both the set period and the sliding scale reflect the fact that, if the investor holds the unit for longer, the manager will benefit from the regular annual management charges that effectively reduces the need for the exit charge.

The annual management charge is generally levied at a rate of 0.5–1.5% of the underlying fund. Like the initial charge, the annual management charge will typically be lower for trusts that are cheaper to run, such as index trackers, and higher for more labour-intensive actively-managed funds.

The FCA's rules permit performance-related charges. These may be based on growth of the fund or outperformance of the fund's standard benchmark. The basis of the charges must be disclosed in the fund prospectus and key features document.

On 31 December 2012, the Retail Distribution Review (RDR), which is designed to give consumers greater confidence and trust in the retail financial services market, including greater transparency of fees and commissions, came into force. Following this, the market has seen fee margins being compressed across the industry with some fund managers innovating lower cost products.

1.1.6 Unauthorised Unit Trusts

In order to be marketed to the public, a unit trust must be authorised by the FCA. This has a direct impact on the taxation of the fund, in that authorisation is a requirement for the trust to be treated as exempt from CGT.

Unauthorised unit trusts are used for specific applications such as enterprise zone property holdings (see section 1.4.3), where they are not marketed directly to the public, and these are subject to income tax and CGT within the fund. Investors are liable to any additional income tax and CGT on disposal.

There is a further exempt type of unauthorised unit trust that may be used as investments for pensions and registered charities. Exempt unit trusts are free of CGT on disposals within the fund and are subject to income tax rather than corporation tax.

1.2 Investment Companies

Learning Objective

4.1.1 Be able to analyse the key features, accessibility, risks, charges, valuation and yield characteristics of open-ended investment companies (OEICs)/investment companies with variable capital (ICVCs)/SICAVS

1.2.1 Open-Ended Investment Companies (OEICs)

Open-ended investment companies (OEICs) are a type of open-ended collective investment formed as a corporation under the Open-Ended Investment Companies Regulations of the UK. They are pronounced 'oiks' and are also known as investment companies with variable capital (ICVCs). The terms ICVC and OEIC are used interchangeably, with different investment managers favouring one over the other. A variant of the name is also SICAV, which is an acronym for *société d'investissement à capital variable*. Translated to English, it becomes **investment company with variable capital (ICVC)**.

An open-ended fund, such as an OEIC or unit trust, is one where the company or trust can create new shares or units when new investors subscribe and can cancel shares or units when investors cash in their holdings. In the case of a **closed-ended** fund, such as an **investment trust**, the number of shares in issue is fixed and new investors buy shares from existing holders of the shares who wish to sell.

In 1997, new regulations provided for the incorporation in the UK of OEICs that fall within the scope of the UCITS Directive. This means they can invest only in transferable securities (eg, listed securities, other collective investment schemes, certificates of deposit). UCITS schemes must be open-ended. UCITS certification allows the fund to be marketed throughout the European Economic Area (EEA).

With the implementation of FSMA 2000, the range of UK-authorised OEICs was extended to be similar to that of unit trusts (see section 1.1), including money market funds and property funds.

Unit trusts and OEICs are authorised investment funds (AIFs) – often collectively referred to simply as funds. The FCA's Collective Investment Schemes Sourcebook (COLL) rules apply to OEICs as well as unit trusts. OEICs can be set up as UCITS retail schemes or non-UCITS retail schemes, or set up for qualified investors (QIs).

As stated above, OEICs and unit trusts are similar in that they are both types of open-ended collective investments. However, with a unit trust, the units held provide beneficial ownership of the underlying trust assets, whereas a share in an OEIC entitles the holder to a share in the profits of the OEIC. The value of the share will be determined by the net asset value (NAV) of the underlying investments. For example, if the underlying investments are valued at £125,000,000 and there are 100,000,000 shares in issue, the NAV of each share is £1.25. The open-ended nature of an OEIC means that it cannot trade at a discount to NAV, as an investment trust can (see section 1.3) .

The holder of a share in an OEIC can sell back the share to the company in any period specified in the prospectus.

An OEIC may take the form of an umbrella fund, with a number of separately priced sub-funds adopting different investment strategies or denominated in different currencies. Each sub-fund will have a separate client register and asset pool.

Classes of shares within an OEIC may include income shares, which pay a dividend, and accumulation shares, in which income is not paid out and all income received is instead added to net assets.

The Structure of OEICs

OEICs are similar to investment trusts (see section 1.3) and different from unit trusts in that both have corporate structures. The objective of the company in each case is to make a profit for shareholders by investing in the shares of other companies. They differ in that an investment trust is a closed-ended investment and an OEIC is open-ended.

An OEIC has an **authorised corporate director (ACD)**, who may be the only director. The responsibilities of the ACD include the day-to-day management of the fund. It must also have a depository. This a firm (usually a bank) authorised by the FCA, independent of the OEIC or ICVC and of its directors. The depository has legal title to the OEIC investments and is responsible for their safe custody.

The depository can appoint sub-custodians to take custody of the assets but will remain ultimately responsible. The depository also has responsibility for ensuring compliance with the key regulatory requirements.

The ACD and the depository must be regulated by the FCA, and approved as authorised persons. FCA rules cover the sales and marketing of OEICs and there are cancellation rules.

Pricing, Buying and Selling

The shares in the OEIC express the entitlement of the shareholders to a share in the profits of the underlying fund which, like a unit trust, is valued on a net asset value basis. Unlike most companies, where there are a limited number of shares available in each company and a shareholder must sell their share before another can buy, an OEIC is open-ended, so the number of shares in issue can be increased or reduced to satisfy the demands of the investors.

OEICs are single-priced instruments, which means that there is no bid/offer spread. The buying price reflects the value of the underlying shares, with any initial charge reflecting dealing costs and management expenses being disclosed separately. Costs of creation of the fund may be met by the fund.

When the investor wishes to sell OEIC shares, the ACD will buy them. The money value on sale will be based on the single price less a deduction for the dealing charges. The ACD may choose to run a box. Shares sold back to the ACD will be kept and reissued to investors, reducing the need for creation and cancellation of shares.

Advantages of OEICs for the Investor

- As for unit trusts, the general advantages of collective investment vehicles apply to OEICs.
- Like unit trusts, there is a wide range of types of fund available.
- The introduction of OEICs was expected to lead to a reduction in costs for the investor and transparency of charges. At the same time, there is no dilution in investor protection.
- The charges with OEICs may be lower than for unit trusts, particularly in respect of cost of entry (setting up) and exit (encashing the investment) due to single pricing.
- Annual management costs are not set out as a separate charge as with unit trusts.

1.3   Investment Trusts

Learning Objective

4.1.3   Be able to analyse the key features, accessibility, risks, tax treatment, charges, valuation and yield characteristics of investment trusts

Investment trusts have a long history in the UK. The F&C Investment Trust (formerly The Foreign and Colonial Investment Trust) was the first to be founded in 1868 with the aim of *'giving the investor of moderate means the same advantage as the large capitalist'*. Today it invests in more than 450 different companies in several different countries.

The company's stated aim is as follows:

'The objective of the trust is to secure long-term growth in capital and income through a policy of investing primarily in an internationally diversified portfolio of publicly listed equities, as well as unlisted securities and private equity, with the use of gearing'.

The trust is benchmarked against a composite index of 40% **FTSE All-Share Index**/60% FTSE All World ex-UK. In general, investment trusts provide a way for the small investor to have some exposure to investments in overseas stocks that it would be impractical for the investor to buy individually.

1.3.1   What is an Investment Trust?

An investment trust is a form of collective investment, pooling the funds of many investors and spreading their investments across a diversified range of securities. Despite its name, it is a company, not a trust in the legal sense of the term. Investment trusts are plcs listed on the LSE. Whereas other companies may make their profit from providing goods and services, an investment trust makes its profit solely from investments. The investor who buys shares in the investment trust hopes for dividends and capital growth in the value of the shares.

Investment trusts are managed by professional fund managers who select and manage the stocks in the trust's portfolio. Investment trusts are generally accessible to the individual investor, although shares in investment trusts are also widely held by institutional investors such as pension funds.

1.3.2   Comparison with Unit Trusts and OEICs

Investment trusts have wider investment freedom than unit trusts and OEICs/ICVCs. They can:

- invest in unquoted private companies as well as quoted companies, and
- provide venture capital to new companies or companies requiring new funds for expansion.

The corporate structure of an investment trust gives it a further advantage over unit trusts and OEICs, because it can raise money more freely to help it to achieve its objectives. Unit trusts' and OEICs' powers to borrow are more limited. The ability to borrow allows an investment trust to leverage returns for the investor. Such gearing will also increase the volatility of returns.

Unlike unit trusts and OEICs, investment trusts are closed-ended investments. This means that the number of shares in issue is not affected by the day-to-day purchases and sales by investors, which allows the managers to take a long-term view of the investments of the trust. With an open-ended scheme such as a unit trust or an OEIC, if there are more sales of units or shares by investors than purchases, the number of units reduces and the fund must pay out cash. As a result, the managers may need to sell investments even though it may not be the best time to do so from a strategic and long-term viewpoint.

The price of shares of the investment trust rises and falls according to demand and supply, and not directly in line with the values of the underlying investments. In this way, investment trust prices can have greater volatility than unit trusts and OEICs, whose unit prices are directly related to the market values of the underlying investments.

Because prices are dependent on supply and demand, the price of the shares can be lower than the net asset value (NAV) of the share. When the prices of the trust's share are below the NAV, investors can buy investment trusts at a discount, while the income produced by the portfolio is based on the market value of the underlying investments. The income yield is, therefore, enhanced.

Charges incurred on investment trust holdings can be compared with the alternatives. Some unit trusts and OEICs have initial charges of around 5%. Initial charges may be much lower than this (at around 0.25%) for some investment trust savings schemes. However, there may be charges imposed when selling investment trust holdings.

1.3.3   Management

As a company, an investment trust has a board of directors. The objective of a company is to invest the money of the shareholders according to an investment strategy. Such a strategy and the decision making which flows from it may be formulated by the directors (in a self-managed trust), or it may be delegated to an external fund management company.

1.3.4   Regulatory Aspects

An investment trust is a listed company, governed by the Companies Act and Stock Exchange regulations. As with other companies, it is bound by the rules set out in its Memorandum and Articles of Association, which are set up when the company is formed.

An investment trust is also subject to the rules of the FCA, the overall regulator of the financial services sector in the UK.

The following principles set down by the FCA apply to a company that seeks to apply for a listing as an investment trust:

- The investment managers must have adequate experience.
- An adequate spread of investment risk must be maintained.
- The investment trust must not control, seek to control or actively manage companies in which it invests.
- The board of the investment trust must be free to act independently of its management.
- The investment trust must seek approval by HMRC (under s.842, Income and Corporation Taxes Act 1988 (ICTA 1988)).
- The trust itself does not have direct dealings with the public. If the management company offers the shares of the trust for sale to the public through a savings scheme, then the company must be authorised by the FCA to carry on investment business under the Financial Services and Markets Act 2000.

1.3.5   Buying and Selling Shares in Investment Trusts

Shares in investment trusts can be bought through a stockbroker, who is likely to charge the same level of commission as for other equities. When a broker is not providing any advice and is providing an execution-only service, then commission may be as low as 0.5%, or £10 per deal. Stamp duty is payable at 0.5% of the purchase consideration.

If the broker is providing an advisory service, then commission will be higher, eg, 1.5% or 2% of the purchase consideration. Some brokers provide discretionary investment trust management services for individuals with larger sums to invest. The broker will select trusts that meet the investor's investment objectives and will charge an annual management fee in addition to dealing charges.

An investor can usually deal through the investment trust managers instead of through a broker, and may incur lower charges by doing so.

Small investors who do not have an account with a broker may prefer to deal through the managers. However, the managers may only deal on a daily basis, while a broker will be able to quote an up-to-the-minute price and a deal can be made instantly by telephone.

1.3.6   Investment Trust Share Pricing

The quotation of the price of investment trust shares is similar to that for equities generally, and a dealer will give two prices:

- The higher price is the offer price, at which an investor can buy the shares.
- The lower price is the bid price, at which a holder of the shares can sell.

In a price quote in the financial media a single price may be given: this will typically be the mid-market price, between the offer and bid prices. The difference between the offer price and the bid price is the spread.

1.3.7   Savings and Investment Schemes

The major trust management groups also operate regular savings schemes, through which an investor can make monthly investments.

- Drip-feeding an investment through such a scheme takes advantage of pound cost averaging with regular fixed investments. Fewer units are bought when the units are relatively expensive. More units are bought when unit prices are lower.
- Typically, such schemes will have a minimum investment of £25 or £50 per month.
- Charges are typically in the range of 0.25% to 1% of the initial investment. Dealing may be at no extra charge.
- Dividend reinvestment may be available as an option for investors who do not require income, in which case their dividends are converted into new shares.
- A low-cost share exchange service is offered by some investment trust groups, enabling investors to realise their existing equity investments and to be given investment trust shares in return.

1.4   Real Estate Investment Trusts (REITs)

Learning Objective

4.1.4   Be able to compare and contrast the key features, accessibility, risks, tax treatment, charges, valuation and yield characteristics of real estate investment trusts (REITs) with property authorised investment funds (PAIFs)

1.4.1   Key Features of REITs

Real estate investment trusts (REITs) were first formed in the US, where the name originated. Other countries, including Japan, the Netherlands and France, now have their own versions of REITs. The UK introduced its version in January 2007.

Tax-transparent property investment vehicles, such as REITs, distribute nearly all of their taxable income to investors. Provided they do this, the vehicles are granted exemption from capital gains tax and from corporate taxes. Investors pay tax on the dividends and capital growth at their own marginal tax rates, thus avoiding the double taxation that would otherwise affect investors in UK property companies.

In order to qualify as a REIT, a company must meet certain conditions:

- The company must be a UK-resident, closed-ended company and have its shares listed or admitted to trading on a qualifying stock exchange (which includes the London Stock Exchange (LSE), Tokyo Stock Exchange (TSE) and the AIM).The shares in the company must not be 'closely held', which means that no one person (individual or corporate) should hold more than 10% of the shares.
- The property-letting business, which will be tax-exempt, must be effectively ring-fenced from any other activities and should comprise at least 75% of the overall company, with regard to both its assets and its total income.
- A minimum of 90% of the REIT's profits from the ring-fenced letting business must be distributed to investors.
- The REIT is required to withhold basic rate tax on the distribution of profits paid to investors.
- The distributions are taxed as property income at the holder's marginal rate.
- The company will be subject to an interest-cover test on the ring-fenced part of its business, a measure of the affordability of any loans.
- Other distributions will be taxed in the same way as normal dividends.
- The ratio of interest on loans to fund the tax-exempt property business to rental income must be less than 1.25:1.

It is possible to hold REITs within ISAs, child trust funds (CTFs) and Junior ISAs (JISAs). UK property companies are able to choose to convert to become REITs. The conversion charge for companies wishing to become REITs in the UK is 2% of the market value of the properties concerned. The charge can be spread on a graduating basis over four years.

A property company converting to REIT status will benefit from the tax exemption and should be better able to raise funds through the stock market. This is because many property companies currently trade at discount to net asset value, partly as a result of double taxation suppressing the value of the shares. A more tax-efficient vehicle should help to correct this anomaly.

1.4.2   Property Authorised Investment Funds (PAIFs)

A property authorised investment fund (PAIF) is a tax-efficient investment vehicle. The funds are able to pay dividends free of income and corporation tax if the monies derive from rental income. PAIFs were introduced by HMRC in 2008 and have been relatively slow to become a popular alternative to existing differing fund structures but offer a means of accessing returns from real estate portfolios that are professionally managed.

PAIFs invest in property directly or by buying shareholdings in property companies.

Before PAIFs were introduced, property funds were established as unit trusts, whereby 20% of income from rental payments had to be withheld. PAIFs taxation is more akin to how an individual would be taxed as a holder of an underlying asset. Some of the benefactors of this new taxation regime include tax-exempt UK investors, charities and pension schemes.

The key features of a PAIF are:

- The taxation obligation is of the investor rather than the fund itself.
- Distribution income is classed as either income from property, interest from cash or dividend income and are applied according to the type of distribution.
- Property income and capital gains (within the fund) are corporation tax exempt.
- Individuals who do not invest through an ISA or SIPP will receive all distributions free of income tax.
- Effectively, investors have the same tax treatment with PAIFs as they have with an ordinary dividend.
- PAIFs must be established as an OEIC as well as being authorised by the FCA.

There are also HMRC rules regarding the diversity of ownership and also some corporate ownership restrictions. At least 60% annual fund profits and at least 60% total fund asset value must relate to direct property investments or shares in REITs.

1.4.3   Enterprise Zone Property

In the UK, enterprise zones were introduced by the Thatcher government in 1979. They were urban areas, usually suffering from widespread job losses and capital flight, which were granted freedom from normal planning controls with a ten-year relief from local rates. 11 enterprise zones were established in 1980 and a further 13 in 1982. They varied from inner cities to areas of post-industrial dereliction.

Expenditure on industrial and commercial buildings in an enterprise zone qualifies as a 100% deduction against the investor's income. The investor can make a direct investment or via a unit trust. The advantage of the unit trust is a lower initial investment and a spread of properties. Nevertheless, there is typically a high risk within the fund.

An individual who invests in such a unit trust is treated as if they have incurred a proportion of the trust's expenditure on enterprise zone property and they will qualify for industrial buildings allowances. These allowances can be set against other income for tax purposes.

1.5   Exchange-Traded Products (ETPs)

Learning Objective

4.1.5   Be able to analyse the key features, accessibility, risks, charges, valuation and yield characteristics of the main types of exchange-traded products (ETPs)

An exchange-traded product (ETP) is an investment fund with specified objectives which is traded on many global stock exchanges in the same manner as a typical stock for a corporation. An ETP holds assets such as stocks or bonds and trades at approximately the same price as the net asset value (NAV) of its underlying assets over the course of the trading day.

Among the different kinds of ETP, the best known are ETFs, which will often track an index, such as the S&P 500 or the FTSE 100.

In general, ETPs can be attractive as investment vehicles because of their low costs, tax-efficiency, and stock-like features.

1.5.1   Different Kinds of ETPs

Exchange-Traded Funds (ETFs)

Only authorised participants (typically, large institutional investors) actually buy or sell shares of an ETF directly from/to the fund manager, and then only in creation units (large blocks of tens of thousands of ETF shares), which are usually exchanged in-kind with baskets of the underlying securities. Authorised participants may wish to invest in the ETF's shares long term, but usually act as market makers on the open market, using their ability to exchange creation units with their underlying securities to provide liquidity of the ETF shares and help ensure that their intra-day market price approximates to the net asset value of the underlying assets. Other investors, such as individuals using a retail broker, trade ETF shares via a secondary market, such as the NYSE/Arca Exchange in the US.

Closed-ended funds are not usually considered to be ETFs, even though they are funds and are traded on an exchange. ETFs have been available in the US since 1993 and in Europe since 1999. ETFs traditionally have been index funds, but in 2008 the US Securities and Exchange Commission (SEC) began to authorise the creation of actively managed ETFs.

A popular ETF innovation in recent years has been the leveraged ETF which makes use of derivatives to further leverage the returns of a basket or index. Leveraged ETFs are available for most major indices and aim to create two or four times the return of its underlying index. However, there is some controversy surrounding the products as they carry higher risk, borrowing issues and often index tracking error.

Synthetic ETFs also come with considerable risk. They attempt to replicate the performance of key indices by using derivatives to track the index rather than owning the component shares. They are also known as swaps-based exchange-traded funds.

220

Exchange-Traded Notes (ETNs)

An exchange-traded note (ETN) is a senior, unsecured, unsubordinated debt security issued by an underwriting bank. Similar to other debt securities, ETNs have a maturity date and are backed only by the credit of the issuer. When an investor buys an ETN, the underwriting bank promises to pay the amount reflected in the index, minus fees upon maturity. Thus, an ETN has an additional risk compared to an ETF – upon any reduction of credit ratings or if the underwriting bank goes bankrupt, the value of the ETN will be eroded.

Though linked to the performance of a market benchmark, ETNs are not equities or index funds, but they do share several characteristics of the latter. Similar to equities, they are traded on an exchange and can be shorted. Similar to index funds, they are linked to the return of a benchmark index but, like debt securities, ETNs do not actually own anything they are tracking.

The first ETN, marketed as the iPath Exchange-Traded Notes, was issued by Barclays Bank plc on 12 June 2006. ETNs may be liquidated before their maturity by trading them on an exchange or by redeeming a large block of securities directly to the issuing bank. The redemption is typically on a weekly basis and a redemption charge may apply, subject to the procedures described in the relevant prospectus.

Since ETNs are unsecured, unsubordinated debts, they are not rated, but are backed by the credit of underwriting banks. Like other debt securities, ETNs do not have voting rights but, unlike other debt securities, interest is not paid during the term of most ETNs.

Exchange-Traded Commodities (ETCs)

Exchange-traded commodities (ETCs) are investment vehicles that track the performance of an underlying commodity index, including total return indices based on a single commodity. Similar to ETFs and traded and settled exactly like normal shares on their own dedicated segment, ETCs have market maker support with guaranteed liquidity, enabling investors to gain exposure to commodities, on-exchange, during market hours.

Most ETCs implement a futures trading strategy, which may produce results quite different from owning the commodity. In the case of many commodity funds, they simply roll so-called 'front-month' futures contracts from month to month. This gives exposure to the commodity, but subjects the investor to risks involved in different prices along the term structure of futures contracts, which may include additional costs as the expiring contracts have to be rolled forward.

In addition to investment vehicles that track commodities, there are also ETPs that provide exposure to FX spot rate changes and local institutional interest rates.

Leveraged ETFs

Leveraged exchange-traded funds are a specialised type of ETF that attempt to achieve returns that are more sensitive to market movements than non-leveraged ETFs. Leveraged index ETFs are often marketed as bull or bear funds. A leveraged bull ETF fund might, for example, attempt to achieve daily returns that are 2x or 3x more pronounced than an index such as the FTSE 100 or the S&P 500. A leveraged inverse (bear) ETF fund will attempt to achieve returns that are –2x or –3x the daily index return, meaning that it will gain double or triple the loss of the market. Leveraged ETFs require the use of financial engineering techniques, including the use of equity swaps, derivatives and rebalancing, to achieve the desired return.

1.5.2   Trading Features of an ETP

The range of ETPs available to investors is now very diverse and provides investors with a real alternative to more traditional funds.

One of the key features of an ETP is that, since they are listed securities and trade in the same manner as shares, the pricing takes place in real time and the funds can be bought or sold at all times when the markets are open. This is unlike the position with many types of collective investment vehicles, such as unit trusts and other investment funds, where the pricing of the fund based on the NAV of the constituents is computed at the end of each day and where the ability to transact is also limited to certain prescribed times. For investors and traders who want to be able to react quickly to market movements, and have immediate pricing and settlement for their positions (subject only to the normal settlement period for any listed share), ETP products are preferable to the more traditional structured investment products.

Another feature of ETPs is that investors and traders can use limit orders and stop loss orders in a similar fashion to the way in which equities are traded, and which, again, are not features available in the trading of shares of traditional unit trusts or mutual funds.

One can purchase an ETP which has been designed and constructed to track a general stock index, such as the S&P 500 (SPY) or the Nasdaq 100 Index (QQQ), or indices for market sectors (eg, industrials, financials), geographical regions, currencies, commodities such as gold, silver, copper and oil, and even certain managed funds with objectives and management criteria laid out in an offering prospectus.

Another reason which has led to the increasing popularity of ETPs is that many of them are offered as inverse funds, which means that they are constructed in a manner so that the ETF has either outright short positions in the underlying instruments for the sector or derivatives that provide a synthetic short position for that sector. Accordingly, an investor who buys or takes a long position in such an inverse fund is effectively short the sector or index-designated and will benefit from a downward movement in that particular sector or index. This feature makes it easier for many investors to take a short position rather than having to borrow stock from a brokerage.

For example, if one has a bearish view on the direction of the S&P 500 Index, it is possible to purchase an ETF which trades on the NYSE/Arca Exchange under the symbol SDS, which is known as UltraShort S&P500 ProShares fund, and this fund will return twice the inverse return of a long position in the S&P 500 Index. In essence, the mechanics for many kinds of inverse ETFs are that one buys (or goes long) the ETF and this will profit as the sector or index goes down.

ETPs are also available to track the performance of various fixed-income instruments such as US Treasury bonds, and of indices that track high-yield bonds and other corporate bonds. Again these can be used to take a long position on higher yields, in effect to be short the bond on a price basis. One well-known ETF, traded in the US under the symbol TBT, tracks the yield on US Treasury bonds of 20 years plus maturity. The fund moves in line with the real-time yields of the long end of the US Treasury curve and therefore the fund moves inversely to the price of such US Treasury bonds.

1.5.3 Charges and Taxation

Many ETP products are managed by large financial intermediaries (including Barclays and JPMorgan Chase) and the fees and charges are very competitive and often considerably lower than those applied to more traditionally managed funds. Also, no stamp duty is applied to purchases of ETPs available from UK exchanges as they are domiciled outside the UK in such centres as Dublin or Jersey.

1.5.4 Tracking Methods

While the operation, marketing and construction of an ETP requires skills on the part of the ETP management company, many funds are in effect tracker funds and therefore have to reflect the composition of a reference index or commodity. There are different ways to achieve this, some of which are discussed more fully in chapter 7, section 7.5, but in summary the main methods are:

- **Full replication** – this is an approach whereby the fund attempts to mirror the index by holding shares in exactly the same proportions as in the index itself.
- **Stratified sampling** – this involves choosing investments that are representative of the index in similar manner to the manner in which statisticians conduct surveys on a sampling which reflects the stratification of an entire population. For example, if a sector makes up 16% of the index, then 16% of shares in that sector will be held, even though the proportions of individual companies in the index may not be matched. The expectation is that, with stratified sampling, overall the tracking error or departure from the index will be relatively low. The amount of trading of shares required should be lower than with full replication, since the fund will not need to track every single constituent of an index. This should reduce transaction costs and, therefore, will help to avoid such costs eroding overall performance.
- **Optimisation** – this is a computer-based modelling technique which aims to approximate to the index through a complex statistical analysis based on past performance. The constituent companies in indices such as the FTSE 100 Index are reviewed from time to time, and some companies will usually drop out while others will join.

The large amounts of funds invested in tracker funds can have a distorting effect on the market for example, if many tracker funds buy a particular share at the point when it is included in the index. Undoubtedly, inclusion in an index can be beneficial to the price of a share, while exclusion may be a factor causing a share to receive less attention from investors and to fall out of favour.

1.6 Non-Mainstream Pooled Investments (NMPIs)

Learning Objective

4.1.6 Be able to analyse the key features, accessibility, charges, valuation and yield characteristics of the main types of non-mainstream pooled investments (NMPI)

1.6.1 Overview

In June 2013, the FCA published its statement on 'restrictions on the retail distribution of unregulated collective investment schemes and close substitutes'.

The FCA identified a number of issues concerning the distribution of high-risk, complex investments. From 1 January 2014, they ordered the cessation of the promotion of unregulated collective investment schemes (UCISs) and similar or equivalent pooled vehicles to ordinary retail investors. The FCA introduced new rules which introduced the instrument type non-mainstream pooled investments (NMPIs).

1.6.2   Types of NMPIs

Any of the following can be an NMPI:

- a unit in an unregulated CIS
- a unit in a qualified investor scheme (a type of UK-authorised CIS)
- a security issued by a special purpose vehicle
- a traded life policy investment, and
- rights to, or interests in, these types of investments.

1.6.3   Risks and Suitability

The FCA has publicly stated that it does not believe that NMPIs are likely to be suitable for retail investors of ordinary wealth or sophistication and has suggested that they should be excluded from the relevant market when a firm is dealing with such clients. NMPIs are collective investment schemes (CISs) that are not authorised or regulated in the UK. The feature of these schemes is that they have few regulatory rules and constraints on the types of instruments they invest in, and so can invest in highly speculative, complex or non-traditional assets and be highly geared. They may also be dependent on just a single asset.

Other risks are:

- the fund's assets may be speculative, illiquid and difficult to value
- the fund's terms and conditions may be very complex
- their structures can often carry governance risks because they are potentially less regulated.

1.6.4   Charges and Tax

Many NMPIs will not be subject to the rules governing the disclosure of fees and charges. The taxation rules in respect of these products are not likely to be of concern to most individuals as firms are not allowed to market them to retail clients. For other investors, the taxation requirements are likely to vary from product to product and according to the type of non-retail investor.

1.7   Money Market Funds

1.7.1   Overview

A money market fund is a form of collective investment vehicle which specialises in investing in short-term, low-risk credit securities. The funds offered can be tailored for both the institutional market and the retail market, are often structured in the form of an OEIC, and their aim is to achieve maximum returns while minimising credit, market and liquidity risks. They typically invest in assets such as government securities, short-term bonds, commercial paper, repurchase agreements or even other money market funds.

The rates paid should reflect wholesale money market rates represented by LIBOR – established daily as a summary of actual rates offered in the money market between banks.

1.7.2   Cash and Near-Cash Instruments

Cash deposits can be categorised as follows:

- short-term tactical cash
- longer-term strategic cash and near-cash instruments, or
- enhanced cash.

Cash balances can be held on a high-interest-bearing overnight deposit facility with a leading highly rated bank. They can also include overnight money market instruments such as very short-term Treasury bills.

Investments are made in cash and near-cash facilities or in funds which hold high-quality short-term bonds and money market instruments. Generally there is no requirement to commit capital for any set period. The money market fund may stipulate whether its holding are in short-term government securities only, such as 30- and 90-day Treasury bills, which are assumed to be risk-free, or whether it has exposure to non-government issues. The latter class could be in holdings of AAA corporate paper but in uncertain times this may be deemed to have more risk than government securities only. In the US, money market funds may also be marketed as having holdings in municipal bonds which offer exemption from federal income tax.

Enhanced cash funds will typically invest some of their portfolio in the same assets as money market funds, but others in riskier, higher-yielding, less liquid assets such as:

- lower-rated bonds
- longer maturity bonds
- foreign currency-denominated debt
- asset-backed commercial paper (ABCP)
- mortgage-backed securities (MBSs), and
- structured investment vehicles (SIVs).

As can be seen from the list above, the enhanced cash instruments which reach out for higher yield by investing in much riskier and less liquid securities have been responsible for some significant problems for certain of the more aggressive money market funds. In fact several funds offering exposure to enhanced cash should not properly be considered as money market funds at all, and some have gone out of business.

1.7.3   Institutional Money Market Funds

Money market funds have been available in the US since they were approved under the Investment Company Act of 1940, and they are important providers of liquidity to financial intermediaries.

Institutional money market funds are high-minimum-investment, low-expense share classes which are marketed to corporations, governments or fiduciaries. They are often set up so that money is swept to them overnight from a company's main operating accounts.

In the US, the largest institutional money fund is the JPMorgan Prime Money Market Fund, with over US$100 billion in assets.

1.7.4   Retail Money Market Funds

Retail money market funds are offered primarily to individuals. In the UK, there are many providers of money market funds for retail clients, and one such offering from HSBC is outlined in the details given below:

- The term of a deposit can be tailored to a client's individual needs and a specific rate of return can be customised for each client.
- The minimum required deposit is £50,000.
- Deposits can be accepted on a fixed-term or notice basis.
- Monthly interest option available for all call/notice accounts, and for fixed-term accounts of six months and above.
- Deposits can be viewed through personal internet banking, which includes transfer functionality for all call/notice accounts.

	Fixed-term		Call/Notice
Minimum Balance	£50,000	£250,000	£50,000
Term	Seven days to five years	Overnight to six days	Immediate (Call), seven or 14 days, one, three, or six months.
Maximum Balance	No limit		No limit
Minimum Additions	Not allowed		£1,000
Withdrawals	Not permitted before expiry of term		Minimum £1,000 (provided minimum balance is maintained)
Interest Rate	Fixed for term		Variable

1.7.5   Risks in Money Market Funds

Reserve Primary Fund

In September 2008, at the height of the banking crisis, the oldest money-market fund in the US, the $60 billion Reserve Primary Fund, 'broke the buck'. The term meant that it would return less than investors had put in (97 cents in the dollar, in this case). Reserve Primary was holding $785 million of Lehman Brothers debt, which had to be written down to zero after the bank went into bankruptcy.

Threadneedle UK Money Securities Fund

In October 2009, Threadneedle UK Money Securities Fund began closure proceedings following approval from the FSA and shareholders. It cited the fact that:

'The main reason for the closure is because the fund continued to suffer redemptions while no improvement in its performance was expected. We thought it was fairer to remaining shareholders to liquidate the fund in an orderly way. The market for mortgage-backed securities (MBSs) and asset-backed securities (ABSs) became illiquid and we were unable to buy securities which were once an integral part of the investment strategy of the fund. All clients have been advised of the closure'.

According to Trustnet data, over one year to 2 October 2009 the fund made total returns of –20%, in contrast to the sector average return of 0.7%. Over three and five years the fund returned –21.8% and –16.2% in contrast to the sector averages of 8% and 14.7%.

The fund had 40% of its investments in floating rate notes – issued by companies to raise money on the financial markets – and included investments in derivatives of these instruments such as collateralised loan obligations.

Threadneedle added:

'The fund's underperformance is attributable to some degree to its holdings in floating rate notes (FRNs) which have been marked down during the credit crunch. In September 2007, FRNs constituted just over 40% of the fund's total holding. The whole range of the FRN market has been affected by the credit crunch'.

1.7.6 Money Market Fund Dealing

Although money market funds can have different underlying structures, the method of dealing is similar to the purchase of shares in a unit trust or other collective investment fund. Before making a subscription, a potential investor must open a shareholder account with the company operating the money market fund.

The managers of the fund will require an original complete share purchase agreement form and documentation required to discharge the manager's duties in respect of any anti-money laundering laws and/or other regulations applicable.

Shareholders will normally be able to redeem all or some of their shares on any business day at the last calculated NAV per share.

2. Retail-Structured Products

Learning Objective

4.2.1 Be able to analyse the key features, accessibility, risks, valuation and yield characteristics of the main types of retail structured products and investment notes (capital protected, autocall, buffer zone): structure; income and capital growth; investment risk and return; counterparty risk; expenses; capital protection.

A retail structured product, often known as a market-linked product, is an embodiment or 'packaging' of an investment strategy based on derivatives, such as a single security, a basket of securities, options, indices, commodities, debt issuances and/or foreign currencies and swaps. The heterogeneous nature of structured products available illustrates the fact that there is no single uniform definition of a structured product.

Structured products were created to meet specific needs that cannot be met from the standardised financial instruments available in the markets. They can be used as an alternative to a direct investment, as part of the **asset allocation** process to reduce risk exposure of a portfolio or to utilise the current market trend.

In the US, the Securities and Exchange Commission (SEC), Rule 434, defines structured securities as:

'Securities whose cash flow characteristics depend upon one or more indices or that have embedded forwards or options or securities where an investor's investment return and the issuer's payment obligations are contingent on, or highly sensitive to, changes in the value of underlying assets, indices, interest rates or cash flows'.

2.1 Retail-Structured Products in the UK

Until recently, the UK structured retail product market was quite small relative to UK markets for other retail investment products. However, following the tumultuous conditions in traditional markets during 2007–08, UK consumers have begun to look to products that offer the potential for capital growth, including products with the significant added feature of capital protection.

2.2 Capital or Principal Guarantee

A feature of some structured products is a principal guarantee function (often referred to as capital protected), which offers protection of principal if held to maturity. However, the nature of the guarantee has to be clearly understood as it almost certainly will not be analogous to the FSCS guarantee, of up to £85,000, on a deposit at an authorised deposit-taker in the UK. The following illustration will help to properly qualify the nature of the guarantee.

228

Example

Let us consider an example of how this might work and the risk/reward to the retail investor.

An investor pays £1,000 for an equity-linked note or structured product, perhaps on the advice of an IFA, which is structured or financially engineered by and issued by an investment bank and marketed by a consumer-facing financial services firm.

The product provides the investor with the following:

- A guarantee that the £1,000 will be repaid after five years. This can be called the principal guarantee or capital protection.
- The investor will benefit from one half of the returns from the FTSE 100 Index during the five-year period. This can be called the equity index linkage.

The engineering could be relatively simple and work as follows. Part of the purchase value is used to buy a zero coupon bond or strip with a redemption value of £1,000 in five years. If the zero coupon bond is priced to yield 5% to maturity, the amount required will be £783.53 and this can be straightforwardly calculated as £1,000/(1.05^5).

With the net balance of the purchase amount – and the fees earned can be quite considerable for these products – the bank's structuring team could purchase options, warrants or even agree an equity swap with a counterparty, in order to deliver the 50% returns on the FTSE 100 Index which will deliver the required equity index linkage.

Theoretically, an investor could package such a simple product themselves, but the market access, knowledge, costs and transaction volume requirements of many options and swaps are beyond many individual investors. The package is sold as a capital-guaranteed product but, even though the ZCB or STRIP is a risk-free government bond, the retail purchaser will not take physical possession of that, but rather have it as a component in the packaging performed by the product structuring agent. If the packager were to default, as did Lehman Brothers, which packaged several products like this, the purchaser's guarantee may not be nearly as risk-free as was portrayed in the offering document.

2.3 Autocalls and Buffer Zone Features

Most structured investments fall into one of three categories, each with its own risk/return profile:

- principal-protected
- buffer-zone, and
- return-enhanced.

As shown in the previous section, principal-protected investments offer the full downside protection of a bond while having the upside potential of a typical equity investment. Investors, typically, give up a portion of the equity appreciation in exchange for principal protection.

These are often of interest to clients wishing to participate in some of the more volatile asset classes or emerging markets, but who are unwilling to risk their principal or who may have long-term financial obligations.

Generally, investors will receive 100% of the principal amount of their notes if they are held to maturity, regardless of the performance of the underlying investment. Maturities generally range from five to seven years, and investors should be willing to hold the investments to maturity. Buffer-zone investments, in exchange for risking principal, offer investors greater upside potential relative to a fully principal-protected investment. In general, buffer-zone investments can be structured to have a shorter maturity than principal-protected investments, often in a two- to four-year span.

These investments may be of interest to clients with a range-bound view – those who are comfortable taking some downside risk but would like a 'buffer' to mitigate potential losses. Buffer-zone investments do not guarantee return of principal. These investments will be fully exposed to any decline in the underlying investment below the buffer zone.

In exchange for accepting full downside exposure in the underlying investment, a return-enhanced investment offers leveraged equity returns, up to a pre-specified maximum. These products are often of interest to clients with an appetite for risk. If an investor believes that near-term market returns are likely to be flat or slightly up, a return-enhanced investment may be an investment vehicle to consider. A key example is a structured product which includes an 'autocall' feature.

Autocalls, also known as 'kick-out plans', have captured a large part of the structured product market in recent years. Product-providers use them to offer higher payoffs than other structured products that automatically run to a full term. Autocalls pay out a defined return providing that a predefined event takes place. A simple FTSE-based product may offer 10% per annum if the index rises by a set amount from its initial starting point. If the trigger event occurs, the plan terminates early and returns investor cash plus the offered coupon. Should the trigger not occur, the plan keeps going to subsequent trigger anniversaries until kick-out conditions are met, rolling up coupons as it goes. If the plan reaches maturity, it pays out the cumulative coupons and returns the initial investment.

Many current products are based on single index structures that kick out if the market is flat or higher than its strike rate on each anniversary. Even if plans do not kick out on an anniversary, investors should remember they have not necessarily lost an annual coupon, merely rolled it up.

Some of these products have capital-at-risk structures, typically losing money if the FTSE index has fallen 50% or further from its strike level.

2.4 Investment Risk and Return

The main type of investment risk associated with retail structured products is that they can involve a loss of principal due to market movements which have not been anticipated or hedged adequately by the person(s) responsible for structuring the product. For example, in the case of a structured product which has a component that is linked to the performance of an index or other instrument, the price paid within the structured product could, under certain circumstances, suffer a similar fate to that of an option element which, if it fails to reach its strike price (or target), can effectively become worthless upon expiration.

The failure of a component within a structured product to perform in accordance with the manner prescribed in the structuring could lead to a partial or complete loss of that portion of the investment, plus whatever expenses might have been incurred in the implementation of that failed component.

It is not always easy to determine exactly how much potential for loss of capital may be entailed. The returns from some structured products can be substantial, as they may depend on unlikely outcomes for which the assessment of the risk/reward trade-off is inefficient. However, the general rule is that the more uncertain the outcome in relation to returns, the more risk that is taken by the investor.

A second kind of risk involves the possibility of default by the issuer of the product or any counterparty which is contractually obligated to perform in a specified manner. For UK retail investors, there was a significant impact, involving complete or partial failure of capital protection, of a number of structured products where that capital protection wholly or partially comprised debt assets issued by Lehman Brothers' European or offshore subsidiaries. In the case of a principal-protected product, these products are not always insured by a statutory body such as the FDIC in the US or the Financial Services Compensation Scheme (FSCS) in the UK. To spell this out clearly, one should consider the following warning from the FCA with regard to structured investment products. They *'carry a greater risk of capital loss than deposits. Most structured investment products do not have FSCS coverage, and, while the probability of counterparty failure may be low, this means the impact of a default could be catastrophic for a customer (up to 100% loss of capital)'.* Some structured products of a once-solvent company have been known to trade in a secondary market for as low as pence in the pound.

Another risky instrument is known as a precipice bond, which is marketed as a high-income investment, advertising double-digit returns. What is often less clear in promotional literature is the propensity for capital loss as the products offer no, or little, capital protection. This can mean that while the income is high for maybe three to five years, the initial capital is eroded.

2.4.1   Suitability

Of course, structured products can offer tax efficiency and other benefits but there is an obligation to ensure that they are suitable for a client. Under the FCA's suitability rules, a firm must obtain information concerning the client in order to adequately assess their investment objectives, financial situation and knowledge and experience. They must ask the client to provide information about their knowledge and experience in potential investments so the firm can determine whether a product or service is appropriate for the client. The danger is that a client may invest in a structured product without an understanding of the structure or possibly the actual risks. The product may not be consistent with the risk profile or investment objectives of the client.

Things to consider when assessing suitability of a structured product are as follows:

- As described in section 2.4, capital risk and the ability of the product provider to repay at the end of the fixed term.
- How much of the capital is protected or guaranteed.
- Whether the risk behind the structured product is akin to a similar risk which is already a part of the client's existing investments. The instrument may look different but the market risk may be very similar.
- Taxation would need to be planned for carefully, as some products have an early repayment mechanism built in that could mean the client unexpectedly breaching tax allowance thresholds in the year.

2.5   Accessibility

Interest in structured investment products has been growing in recent years and high net worth investors now use structured products as way of portfolio diversification. Structured products are also available at the mass retail level, particularly in Europe, where national post offices, and even supermarkets, sell investments in these to their customers.

Structured products are by nature heterogeneous – as a large number of derivatives can be used – but can broadly be classified under the following categories:

*   Interest rate-linked notes and deposits.
*   Equity-linked notes and deposits.
*   FX and commodity-linked notes and deposits.
*   Hybrid-linked notes and deposits.
*   Credit-linked notes and deposits.
*   Market-linked notes and deposits.

The fees payable for these products will be higher than for many simpler and direct holdings of assets, reflecting the fact that some high-margin packaging skills are required. The fee structure should be transparent and laid out clearly in the offering documentation. In addition, an IFA may be rewarded with a significant commission arrangement for introducing a client to a structured investment product.

2.6   Summary of Benefits and Disadvantages

The benefits of structured products may include:

*   Principal protection from the issuer, but caution is advised as outlined above, as they are not covered under the FSCS scheme.
*   They can provide a tax-efficient access to fully taxable investments. Structured products are normally created so as to ensure the proceeds returned at maturity are categorised as capital gains rather than income.
*   Enhanced returns within an investment. The ingenuity that is used to create structured products can sometimes be very rewarding. In addition, the returns available may provide diversification within a portfolio consisting primarily of more mainstream assets. In other words, the correlation with other market instruments may be low.
*   Reduced volatility (or risk) within an investment. Some of the ingenuity that is involved in crafting and structuring the products can be used to smooth returns, which may make them more appealing to retail investors who do not like the drawdowns and volatility associated with direct holdings in equities, for example.
*   Some structured funds may be located offshore, in other words, not within the jurisdiction of the UK.

Disadvantages of structured products may include:

*   **Credit risk** – structured products are unsecured debt from investment banks and, as the case of Lehman Brothers shows, the possibility exists of a complete loss of capital either permanently or until the administration process is completed, which may take years to work out.
*   **Lack of liquidity** – structured products rarely trade after issuance and someone who wants or needs to sell a structured product before maturity should expect to sell it at a significant discount.

- **No daily pricing** – structured products are priced on a matrix, not at NAV. Matrix pricing is essentially a best-guess approach, and the lack of pricing transparency can make it very hard for present valuation purposes.
- **Highly complex** – the complexity of the return calculations means few truly understand how the structured product will perform relative to simply owning the underlying asset.

3. Analysis of Collective Investments

Learning Objective

4.3.1 Be able to analyse the factors to take into account when selecting collective investments: quality of firm, management team and administration; investment mandate – scope, controls, restrictions and review process; investment strategy; exposure, allocation, valuation and quality of holdings; prospects for capital growth and income; asset cover and redemption yield; track record compared with appropriate peer universe and market indices; tax treatment; key person risk and how this is managed by a firm; shareholder base; measures to prevent price exploitation by dominant investors; liquidity, trading access and price stability; suitability

A collective investment vehicle is a way of investing money with other people to participate in a wider range of investments than those feasible for most individual investors, and to share the costs of doing so. Terminology varies with country, but collective investment schemes (CISs) are often referred to as investment funds, managed funds, unit trusts (in the US these are commonly called mutual funds) or simply funds. Large markets have developed around collective investment, and these account for a substantial portion of all trading on major stock exchanges.

Collective investments are marketed with a wide range of investment aims, either targeting specific geographical regions (eg, emerging markets) or specified sectors (eg, biotechnology). There is often a bias towards the domestic market to reflect national self-interest and the lack of currency risk. Funds are often selected on the basis of these specified investment aims, their past investment performance and other factors such as fees.

The type of investors in collective investments vary considerably according to the type of fund. Types of collective investment vehicles include:

- unit trusts
- open-ended investment companies (OEICs)
- offshore funds
- exchange-traded funds (ETFs)
- hedge funds
- investment trusts, including split capital investment trusts
- venture capital trusts, and
- structured investment funds.

With so many products on offer, there are many factors to be taken into account when selecting a collective investment, some of which are covered in the following sections.

3.1 Quality of Firm and Management Team

For funds that fall under the jurisdiction of the UK authorities, the manager(s) must be authorised by the FCA. They are responsible for the operation of the funds.

A fund manager with a good past performance record may be able to repeat the performance in the future. It should be noted that past performance is not an indicator of future performance. There is also no assurance that a fund with a successful manager will be able to retain the services of the manager over extended periods.

3.1.1 Key Person Risk (KPR)

One important risk for investors in certain high-profile funds relates to the possible loss of a key manager. The manager may be lured away by higher compensation from a competitor, may go out on their own to start a new fund, or may be required to leave a firm for violation of FCA rules.

Firms which rely heavily on the input of a star manager can find themselves subject to large-scale redemptions if the manager leaves. This can lead to loss of capital, the possible recall of any borrowed funds and reputational damage. Fund management companies have devoted considerable resources to reduce the impact of senior figures. Paying the key managers more, insuring against executives' departure and inventing quant systems to do away with manager decisions altogether are just some of the tactics that have been used.

From the short-term perspective, the loss of a key manager may cause a lot of disruption to a firm, although the more diversified the team of professionals within the fund as well as the more diversified the investment strategy, the less likely that reputational damage will be lasting. Perhaps the biggest risk is in hiring a top manager, paying them too much and then finding that the manager fails to consistently deliver above-average returns.

3.2 Administration

The back-office functions of collective investment vehicles, which refer to the administration and reporting to clients, are sometimes a major source of differentiation from the client's perspective. With many funds to choose from, and often very little in terms of performance differentiation, the funds which have the best methods of communicating with clients and following the best procedures with respect to administration will have a competitive edge.

3.3 Investment Mandate

The mandate of a collective investment vehicle is a statement of its aims, the limits within which it is supposed to invest, and the investment policy it should follow. A fund mandate will typically define:

- the aim of the fund (eg, to generate dividend income or long-term growth)
- the type of strategy it will follow (which will tend to follow from the above)
- what regions it will invest in (UK, Europe, emerging markets)
- what sectors it will invest in
- what types of securities it will invest in (equities, bonds, or derivatives)

- whether the fund will short sell and whether it will be hedged
- whether it will be geared and to what extent
- a benchmark index that the fund aims to beat (or match if it is a tracker fund)
- the maximum error in tracking the benchmark.

Fund mandates are set by the fund management company, but publicised so that investors can choose a fund that suits their requirements.

There are also legal limits on how some types of investment vehicle can invest.

3.4 Investment Strategy

The Investment Association (IA), the body that represents the UK investment management industry, has published a classification system for the investment strategies. These are broadly followed by the major collective investment vehicles – unit trusts and OEICs. The following diagram shows the groupings of funds in the IA classifications.

The groups correspond to broadly different investment objectives.

- Some income funds principally target immediate income, while others aim to achieve growing income.
- Growth funds which mainly target capital growth or total return are distinguished from those that are designed for capital protection.
- Specialist funds cover other, more niche areas of investment.

The IA classifications above are based on broad criteria. Within particular categories such as UK All Companies, there will be some funds focusing on mainstream blue chip stocks, some funds investing in recovery stocks and some funds concentrating on special situations such as companies that are rich in cash relative to their share price.

IA Sector Classification Schematic

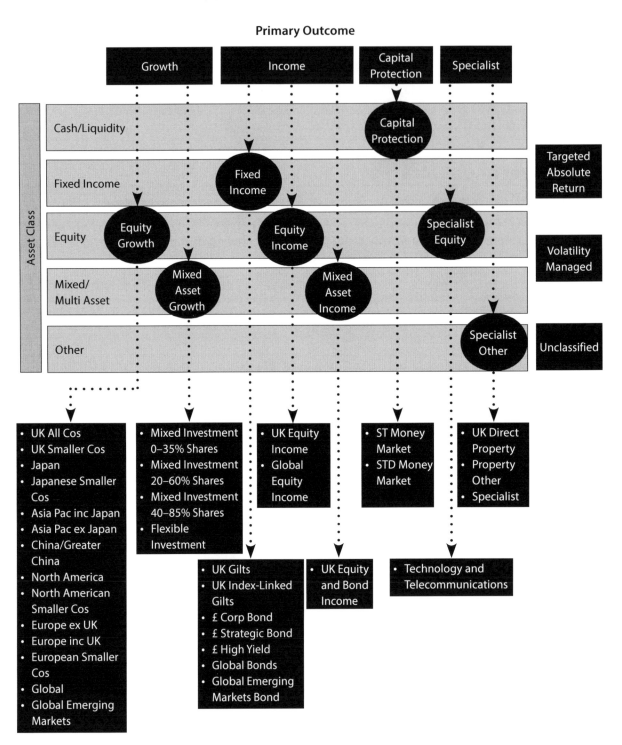

Source: The Investment Association

Within the specified IA categories of funds are the following types of fund for which there is not a separate classification:

- **Index-tracking funds** which track a share index such as the FTSE 100 Index rather than being actively managed by fund managers.
- **Ethical funds** which aim to satisfy the criteria of some investors who only wish to invest in companies whom they consider to be ethical. For example, there are some investors who do not wish to invest in tobacco companies or companies that have dealings with certain foreign jurisdictions or who may employ labour in developing world countries under relatively poor working conditions.

3.5   Asset Allocation

The asset allocation of the fund will be decided by the management team and there is scope for a fair degree of discretion. However, if the mandate or trust deed for the fund is very specific then there will be fewer degrees of freedom for the class of assets and individual securities that the manager can select for the fund. The assessment of the fund by the trustees and the reporting of the list of assets to fund participants will provide a means of ascertaining whether the fund is being managed in accordance with its stated strategy and the domain of permissible assets.

3.6   Valuation and Quality of Holdings

The NAV of a collective investment scheme is calculated by reference to the total value of the fund's portfolio (its assets) less its accrued liabilities (money owed to lending banks, fees owed to investment managers and service providers and other liabilities).

The portfolio's assets are generally valued by objective criteria established at the outset of the fund. When assets are traded on a securities exchange or cleared through a clearing firm, the most common method of valuation is to use the market value of the assets in the portfolio (using, for example, the closing bid price or last traded price). The value of **over-the-counter (OTC) derivatives** may be provided by the counterparty to the derivative, who may be trading similar derivatives with other parties. Where there is no objective method of calculating the value of an asset, the fund manager's own valuation methods subject to a fund's directors or trustees is usually used.

The last issue raised in the valuation techniques is very relevant to the quality of the assets under management. Some funds have made investments in assets for which there may be illiquid markets, for example complex asset-backed securities, which not only hinders the mark-to-market valuation methodology but can also prove to be a major problem if the fund has to liquidate holdings following client redemptions in adverse market conditions. It is certainly not fair to conclude that assets which do not trade in liquid markets suffer from inferior quality. However, the percentage of such assets should be relatively small in a fund where the shareholders or participants can exit the fund at short notice. This is less of a problem for some hedge funds, which have 'gating' provisions that allow the fund manager to suspend redemptions in adverse market conditions.

3.7 Prospects for Capital Growth and Income

The table of fund classification in section 3.4 illustrates that investors have the choice between funds that are primarily focused on capital growth and those which are mainly focused on income. There are also funds of a hybrid nature which attempt to provide both.

Certain objectives will be more suited to different kinds of investor profiles and will not only include the investor's needs for income on a current basis but also will depend on their appetite for risk and their investment horizons. As a simple rule of thumb, for those investors who have a low propensity to liquidate their holdings in a short time-frame and who do not require a steady stream of income, the focus on more adventurous asset classes such as emerging markets and equity investments in technology funds may offer the highest long-term prospects for capital gains. For an investor that is looking for current yield or income, the most appropriate kinds of collective investment vehicles are those focused on fixed-income securities and high dividend stocks such as utility companies.

3.8 Asset Cover and Redemption Yield

A split capital investment trust (split) is a type of investment trust which issues different classes of share to give the investor a choice of shares to match their needs. Most splits have a limited life determined at launch, known as the wind-up date. Typically, the life of a split capital trust is five to ten years.

Split capital trusts will have at least two classes of share, and other varieties include:

- **Zero dividend preference shares** – no dividends, only capital growth at a pre-established redemption price (assuming sufficient assets).
- **Income shares** – entitled to most (or all) of the income generated from the assets of a trust until the wind-up date, with some capital protection.
- **Annuity income shares** – very high and rising yield, but virtually no capital protection.
- **Ordinary income shares** (income and residual capital shares) – a high income and a share of the remaining assets of the trust after prior-ranking shares.
- **Capital shares** – entitled to most (or all) of the remaining assets after prior-ranking share classes have been paid; very high risk.

Capital shares, if issued by a split capital trust, are the most risky, whereas zero dividend preference shares have conventionally been the most popular, although in recent years their popularity has been declining relative to newer CISs.

Zeros are the lowest risk class of share issued by split capital trusts because, as preference shares, they have a higher priority over the assets of the underlying trust than other types of shareholder. Zeros have no right to receive a dividend but instead are paid a predetermined maturity price at a specified redemption date, providing that the trust has sufficient assets to fund this.

Providing that a trust has sufficient assets to meet the redemption price payable to zero shareholders, the return is predictable, as is the timing of when an investor will realise their gain. As all the return comes in the form of capital, zeros are also very tax-efficient for those investors who are unlikely to exceed their annual capital gains tax allowance. For these reasons, zeros were once a popular tool for school fees and retirement planning.

The question that should be first and foremost in any investor's mind is: what is the potential for this zero not to pay out its stated redemption price? There are a number of financial ratios that can be used to analyse zeros but essentially each stock should be assessed on three criteria: hurdle rate/asset cover; portfolio quality; and gearing.

- Firstly, a trust which already has sufficient assets to fully fund the redemption price to the zero shareholders is lower-risk than one which still needs to appreciate in the remaining time before maturity.
- Secondly, gearing is an important factor to consider since financial institutions who have loaned money to the trust have a higher priority over the assets in the event of a wind-up than all types of shareholder.
- Thirdly, the quality of the underlying portfolio is important. A trust may have sufficient asset cover to meet the full redemption price of the zero shareholders, but if the underlying portfolio is volatile or comprises specialist types of investments this undoubtedly puts the zeros more at risk than a trust invested in a portfolio of mainstream shares that will be easy to sell in the event of a wind-up.

There can be potential to make relatively high returns at the more speculative end of the zero market, where trusts may not yet have sufficient asset cover to meet their zero redemption prices. Returns from the higher-quality zeros which have sufficient asset care are still sufficiently attractive for much less risk. Gross redemption yields on quality zero funds are currently higher than prevailing gilt yields, and also attractive compared to yields on UK equities which are riskier.

3.9   Benchmark Comparisons

Funds usually choose an index to be their performance benchmark. The index will match the region or sector in which the fund invests. A British technology fund might choose one of the Techmark indices, whereas an emerging markets fund may choose one of the MSCI indices.

The use of indices as benchmarks is one of the reasons why so many different indices exist: they need to match the variety of funds. Even so, some funds and portfolios are better served by using a composite of several indices.

One danger this brings is that it tempts managers to track their benchmark index (and thus avoid the risk of underperforming) rather than genuinely trying to beat it: supposedly actively managed funds thus become closet trackers.

Indices are not perfect benchmarks for performance measurement. Limitations include the range available (although this can be overcome by using synthetic indices specially calculated for a specific portfolio). Another problem is that changes in composition introduce a form of survivorship bias. This is the tendency for failed companies to be excluded from performance studies because they no longer exist. It often causes the results of studies to skew higher because only companies which were successful enough to survive until the end of the period are included. For example, a fund company's roster of funds today will include only those that are successful now. Many losing funds are closed and merged into other funds to hide poor performance.

3.10 Undertakings for Collective Investment in Transferable Securities (UCITS)

UCITS are not a separate type of investment, but a classification for existing investments such as unit trusts that can be marketed throughout the EEA.

UCITS were created as a result of the UCITS Directive introduced by the Council for the European Communities on 20 December 1985. The idea of the directive was that it would introduce a framework under which a fund management group could market a fund domiciled within one member state to investors resident in another member state. Under the framework, a manager of a mutual fund certified as a UCITS in its country of domicile may not be refused permission to market the fund in another member state providing that it complies with local marketing requirements. Note that when the UK finalises its withdrawal agreement with the EU, UK-domiciled UCITS funds will likely no longer be able to be passported. For a fund to continue to be marketed in this way, it may have to re-domicile to an EU member state, such as Ireland.

The directive does not cover closed-ended funds (such as UK investment trusts), and UCITS funds cannot hold commodities or property.

A fund is authorised by the regulatory authority of its domicile and it is granted a UCITS certificate. Application is then made to the regulatory authority of other member states in which the provider wishes to market the fund. After two months the fund may be marketed.

3.11 Uses of Offshore Funds

Offshore-pooled investments may be useful for those who require a wider choice of funds than is available onshore. Offshore funds are particularly attractive to investors who wish to use currency funds or hedge funds. A fixed-interest fund with distributor status may be useful for a non-taxpayer. Earnings from the offshore fund will be invested in a fixed-interest fund which is rolling up tax-free and can pay out a gross dividend.

Within a non-distributor fund, the taxpayer will pay no tax while the income is rolling up. If a currently higher-rate taxpayer can take encashment when they will be a basic rate taxpayer later, this would be advantageous. A non-distributor fund may also be useful for a UK resident who is anticipating retiring abroad. Earnings can be rolled up and encashed when the taxpayer is no longer a UK resident and subject to UK tax.

3.12 Passporting

EEA financial services firms established in any EEA member state can use the EU's passporting regime to establish a branch or provide services in another EU state (before Brexit this regime also included the UK). The passporting regime also allowed EEA-based investment funds to be marketed in the UK. As part of the UK's preparations for Brexit, the UK Government established the temporary marketing permissions regime (TMPR) for EEA-based investment funds to continue to be marketed in the UK in the same manner as they were before the end of 2020, subject to having notified the FCA before the end of 2020. They can do this for a limited period while seeking UK recognition to continue to market in the UK.

3.13   Tax Treatment

In the UK, unit trusts and OEICs can be held in the tax-advantaged wrapper of an individual savings account (ISA) or an existing personal equity plan (PEP). On 6 April 2008, PEP accounts automatically became stocks and shares ISAs.

Most collective investment vehicles can also be a constituent of a self-invested pension plan (SIPP), which provides shelter from current taxation within a self-managed pension scheme.

3.14   Liquidity, Trading Access and Price Stability

Units in unit trusts and OEICs are priced by the manager based on net asset value. The valuation point will be at a particular time each day and the pricing could be on a forward or historical basis. Furthermore, pricing could be provided on a single price basis (especially for OEICs) or a dual-priced basis, when units may be priced at a bid or offer basis. Dealing is with the manager of the scheme.

In contrast, closed-ended vehicles like investment trusts are priced based on supply and demand factors and are purchased or sold through stockbrokers on stock exchanges just like other listed equities. As a result, the traded price could be different to net asset value, exhibiting either a discount or a premium.

Exchange-traded funds are effectively hybrids. They are exchange-traded and **open-ended**, so the possibility of creating more shares, or exchanging shares for the underlying constituents should mean that the price is at, or close to the NAV.

3.15   Suitability

An investment firm always has an obligation to ensure that it makes an assessment of suitability when selecting investments on behalf of a client. A firm is required to assess the client's:

*   investment objectives
*   financial situation, and
*   knowledge and experience.

It is also incumbent on the firm to assess the nature of the investment, its risks and benefits, and whether the provider is an organisation to which it believes it is appropriate to entrust its client's assets.

End of Chapter Questions

Think of an answer to each question and refer to the appropriate section for confirmation.

1. How and when are the units within a unit trust valued and priced?
   Answer reference: Section 1.1.4

2. What is an alternative and more commonly used name for an investment company with variable capital (ICVC)?
   Answer reference: Section 1.2.1

3. Describe the main characteristics of an investment trust and how they are accessible to the single investor.
   Answer reference: Section 1.3.1

4. What is the difference between an open-ended fund and a closed-ended fund?
   Answer reference: Section 1.3.2

5. At what times of the day can one purchase an exchange-traded product (ETP)?
   Answer reference: Section 1.5.2

6. What is an inverse exchange-traded fund (ETF) and why would one decide to invest in such an instrument?
   Answer reference: Section 1.5.2

7. What risk feature of retail-structured products was exemplified by the collapse of Lehman Brothers in 2008?
   Answer reference: Section 2.2

8. What is meant by the term 'survivorship bias'?
   Answer reference: Section 3.9

9. What are passporting rights with respect to the operation of multi-national collective investment vehicles?
   Answer reference: Section 3.12

10. When selecting investments on behalf of a client, what is an investment firm required to assess?
    Answer reference: Section 3.15

Chapter Five
Settlement, Safe Custody and Prime Brokerage

5

This syllabus area will provide approximately 7 of the 80 examination questions

1. Clearing, Settlement and Safe Custody

1.1 Settlement of Trades

Learning Objective

5.1.1 Understand how fixed income, equity, money market and foreign exchange transactions are cleared and settled in the UK, Germany, US and Japan: principles of delivery versus payment (DvP) and free delivery; trade confirmation process; settlement periods; international central securities depositories (ICSDs) – Euroclear and Clearstream; international exchanges

Settlement occurs after a deal has been executed. At its simplest, settlement refers to the transfer of ownership from the seller of the investment to the buyer, combined with the transfer of the cash consideration from the buyer to the seller.

The settlement process consists of several key stages, collectively described as clearing and settlement:

- **Confirmation** of the terms of the deal or trade by the participants.
- **Clearance** – the calculation of the obligations of the deal participants, the money to be paid and the securities to be transferred.
- **Settlement** – the final transfer of the securities (delivery, which is almost exclusively electronic delivery rather than transfer of physical documents, although the latter can still be stipulated) in exchange for the final transfer of funds (payment – also made electronically).

1.1.1 Traditional versus Electronic Settlement

Traditionally, securities settlement involved the physical movement of paper instruments, or certificates and transfer forms. Payment was usually made by cheque, which introduced an element of risk and delay into the process of fully resolving and settling a transaction. It was also risky, inasmuch as paper instruments, certificates and transfer forms were relatively easy to lose, steal, and forge.

The electronic settlement system came about largely as a result of *Clearance and Settlement Systems in the World's Securities Markets*, a major report in 1989 by the Washington-based think tank, the Group of Thirty (G30). This report made nine recommendations with a view to achieving more efficient settlement. This was followed up in 2003 with a second report, called *Clearing and Settlement: A Plan of Action*.

Electronic settlement takes place between participants to the system. If a non-participant wishes to settle its interests, it must do so through a participant acting as a custodian. The interests of participants are recorded by credit entries in securities accounts, maintained in their names by the operator of the system. This permits both quick and efficient settlement by removing the need for paperwork, and the synchronisation of the delivery of securities with the payment of a corresponding cash sum, called delivery versus payment (DvP).

In any situation, the seller of a security is unlikely to be willing to hand over legal title to that security unless they are sure that the cash is flowing in the opposite direction. Similarly, the buyer is unlikely to be willing to hand over the cash without being sure that the legal ownership is passing in the other direction, known as cash against delivery (CAD).

There are two basic elements to the settlement of trades that can differ across different instruments and/or markets: timing and the settlement system that is used.

- **Timing of settlement** – this is normally based on a set number of business days after the trade is executed, known as rolling settlement.
- **Settlement system used** – there are a variety of settlement systems that are used in particular markets. For example, the majority of transactions in UK and Irish equities are settled via an electronic settlement facility called **CREST**. CREST is a computer system that settles transactions in shares, gilts and corporate bonds, primarily on behalf of the London Stock Exchange (LSE). It is owned and operated by a company that is part of the Euroclear group of companies, called Euroclear UK & Ireland (EUI). EUI has the status of a recognised clearing house (RCH) and, as such, it is regulated by the PRA.

Dematerialisation involves dispensing of paper instruments and certificates altogether. **Dematerialised** securities exist only in the form of electronic records. The legal impact of dematerialisation differs in relation to bearer and registered securities respectively. The financial instruments settled by CREST are dematerialised.

1.1.2   Summary of the UK Settlement System

The CREST system clears a deal or trade by matching the settlement details provided by the buyer and the seller. The transaction is then settled when CREST updates the register of the relevant company, instructing it to transfer the shares to the buyer, and at the same time instructing the buyer's bank to transfer the appropriate amount of money to the seller's bank account.

To complete the settlement of a trade, CREST simultaneously:

- **Updates the register of shareholders** – CREST maintains the so-called operator register for UK companies' dematerialised shareholdings.
- **Issues a payment obligation** – CREST sends an instruction to the buyer's payment bank to pay for the shares.
- **Issues a receipt notification** – CREST notifies the seller's payment bank to expect payment.

If a trading system provides a central counterparty (CCP) to the trades (such as LCH ltd for trades on SETS), it is the CCP that assumes responsibility for settling the transaction with each counterparty. The buyer and seller remain anonymous to each other.

CCP services are available in a range of markets in order to mitigate risks, such as credit risk. The European Market Infrastructure Regulation (EMIR) establishes a set of common organisational, conduct of business and prudential standards for CCPs with activities in EU member states.

For SETS trades, CREST gives the option to LSE member firms to settle with LCH ltd or SIX x-clear AG as counterparty on a gross basis or on a net basis. If a firm has 20 orders executed in the same security through SETS, they can either settle 20 trades with LCH ltd or SIX x-clear AG (settling gross), or choose to have all 20 trades netted so that the firm just settles a single transaction with LCH ltd or SIX x-clear AG. SIX x-clear is the clearing subsidiary of Swiss group SIX Securities Services.

Brexit

A consequence of Brexit is that CREST, as a central securities depository (CSD), is no longer authorised in Ireland. As a result, Ireland's listed securities have migrated to Euroclear Bank, the international CSD, which will provide a replacement holding and settlement system for securities of Irish companies listed or quoted on Euronext Dublin and/or the LSE. The transition took place in March 2021.

1.1.3 Settlement Period

The settlement period (the time between the trade and the transfer of money and registration) for UK equities moved from a T+3 basis to a T+2 basis on 6 October 2014. 'T' is the trade date and '2' is the number of business days after the trade date that the cash changes hands and the shares' registered title changes.

In other words, if a trade is executed on a Wednesday, the cash and registered title will change two business days later, on the Friday. Alternatively, should the trade be executed on a Thursday, it will be the following Monday that settlement will occur. This is referred to by the LSE as standard settlement. Standard settlement applies to all deals automatically executed on an LSE trading system, such as SETS.

The move to T+2 was in advance of the deadline of 1 January 2015 in the proposed EU Central Securities Depositories Regulation (CSDR), which aimed to harmonise the settlement period for all European securities settlement. The legislation required full alignment of settlement periods across EEA countries (plus Switzerland) to T+2.

Among the key advantages of a shorter settlement cycle are:

*   a reduction in risk
*   a shorter period of providing margin for CCP clearing positions
*   for investors, transactions will be concluded within a shorter period of time meaning that investors will receive securities (buyers) and cash (sellers) a day earlier.

1.1.4 Global Settlement Systems and Periods

The following table provides an overview of the settlement systems in the UK, EU, the US and Japan.

Country/Region	Instruments Settled	Settlement Period	System Name
UK	Listed equities and corporate bonds	T+2	CREST
UK	Government bonds (gilts)	T+1 (cash settlement)	CREST
EU	Listed equities	T+2	Clearstream
EU	International bonds	T+2	Clearstream/ Euroclear
US	Listed equities	T+2	Depository Trust Company and National Services Clearing Corporation, both subsidiaries of DTCC
US	Government bonds	T+1	Fixed Income Clearing Corporation (FICC), a subsidiary of Depository Trust & Clearing Corporation
Japan	Listed equities and convertible bonds	T+2*	Japan Securities Depository Center (JASDEC)

* Japan changed to T+2 from T+3 for both equities and fixed-income trades in July 2019. Japan also recently shortened the settlement cycle of Japanese government bonds (JGBs) to T+1 from T+2.

1.1.5 Central Securities Depositories (CSDs)

Functions of a CSD

- **Safekeeping** – securities may be in dematerialised form, book-entry only form (with one or more global certificates) or in physical form immobilised within the CSD.
- **Deposit and withdrawal** – supporting deposits and withdrawals involves the relationship between the transfer agent and/or issuers and the CSD. It also covers the CSD's role within the underwriting process or listing of new issues in a market.
- **Dividend, interest and principal processing**, as well as **corporate actions** including proxy voting.
- **Paying and transfer agents**, as well as issuers are involved in these processes, depending on the level of services provided by the CSD and its relationship with these entities.
- **Other services** – CSDs offer additional services aside from those considered core services. These include securities lending and borrowing, matching, and repo settlement.

The Depository Trust & Clearing Corporation (DTCC)

The Depository Trust & Clearing Corporation (DTCC), based in New York, is the world's largest post-trade financial services company. The DTCC was established in 1999 to provide an efficient and safe way for buyers and sellers of securities to make their exchange, and thus clear and settle transactions. It also provides custody of securities.

Through its subsidiaries, the DTCC provides clearance, settlement and information services for equities, corporate and municipal bonds, unit investment trusts, government and mortgage-backed securities, money market instruments and over-the-counter (OTC) derivatives.

Japan Securities Depository Center (JASDEC)

The Japan Securities Depository Center (JASDEC), the central depository for Japan's stock market, has been a leading advocate in educating Japanese investors about the benefits of dematerialisation and ensuring a seamless transition to a paperless environment.

1.1.6   International Central Securities Depositories (ICSDs)

An ICSD's role is to settle international transactions. There are two ICSDs globally, Clearstream International (previously known as Cedel) and Euroclear. Both were established in the early 1970s to provide an efficient settlement environment for the then nascent eurobond market. Both have a joint arrangement with so-called 'common depositories' in multiple countries to allow them to move securities between clients in both organisations on a book-based basis. In addition to the ICSD functionality, both organisations also provide international custody and settlement services in international securities and in various domestic securities, usually through direct or indirect (through local agents) links to local central securities depositories (CSDs).

In this activity, they are joined by two other CSDs, SIX SIS (a subsidiary of SIX Securities Services) and the DTCC.

1.2   Settlement Risk

Learning Objective

5.1.2   Understand how settlement risk arises, its impact on trading and the investment process and how it can be mitigated: underlying risks: default, credit and liquidity; relative likelihood of settlement-based risks in developed and emerging markets; effect of DvP and straight-through processing (STP) automated systems; risk mitigation within markets and firms; continuous linked settlement

Settlement risk is the risk that a settlement in a transfer system does not take place as expected. Generally, this happens because one party defaults on its clearing obligations to one or more counterparties. As such, settlement risk comprises both credit and liquidity risks.

- **Credit risk** arises when a counterparty cannot meet an obligation for the full value on the due date or thereafter because it is insolvent.

- **Liquidity risk** refers to the risk that a counterparty will not settle for the full value at the due date but could do so at some unspecified time thereafter, causing the party which did not receive its expected payment to finance the shortfall at short notice.

Sometimes, a counterparty may withhold payment even if it is not insolvent (causing the original party to scramble around for funds), so liquidity risk can be present without being accompanied by credit risk. Unsurprisingly, such settlement-based risks are considerably more likely to be an issue in emerging markets than in the developed markets where sophisticated systems are utilised.

Example: Herstatt Risk

The best known example of settlement risk is the failure of a small German bank, Bankhaus Herstatt in 1974. The firm's banking licence was withdrawn, and it was ordered into liquidation during the banking day, but after the close of the German interbank payments system. Some of Herstatt Bank's counterparties had irrevocably paid Deutschmarks to the bank during the day but before the banking licence was withdrawn. They had done so in good faith, believing they would receive US dollars later the same day in New York. Following the loss of its banking licence, Herstatt's New York correspondent bank suspended all outgoing US dollar payments from Herstatt's account.

In addition, banks had entered into forward trades that were not yet due for settlement, and some lost money replacing the contracts. In short, there were serious repercussions in the foreign exchange market after the Bankhaus Herstatt default, and the intra-day settlement risk highlighted has subsequently been termed Herstatt risk.

Herstatt risk has arisen in similar circumstances, and not just in the settlement of foreign exchange transaction. The collapse of US investment bank Drexel Burnham Lambert in 1990, Bank of Credit and Commerce International (BCCI) in 1991, Barings in 1995, Long-Term Capital Management (LTCM) in 1998 and Lehman Brothers and AIG in 2008, have all provided similar ingredients to that found for Herstatt risk. The common thread to such settlement failures arises when parties are relying on the simultaneity in processing of payments and, for reasons of default, illiquidity or even criminality, one side of the settlement does not perform.

Examples: LTCM and Lehman Brothers

LTCM was bailed out by a consortium of 14 banks, under the supervision of the Federal Reserve Bank of New York, in 1998 after being caught in a cash flow crisis when economic shocks resulted in excessive mark-to-market losses and margin calls. The fund was engaged in complex arbitrage strategies in the fixed-income market and, partly precipitated by a default in Russian bonds in August of 1998, many of its positions became extremely illiquid and it was not able to fund its positions. Without the intervention of the US central bank, obligations involving billions of dollars owed to counterparties would have failed, raising the prospect of financial systemic risk.

The story of LTCM's collapse, which incidentally had two Nobel laureates as part of its advisory team, can be found in an excellent book on the subject, *When Genius Failed* by Roger Lowenstein.

In September 2008, Lehman Brothers, one of the five largest investment banks at the time, collapsed after the US Treasury and Federal Reserve decided not to rescue the firm, following a collapse in confidence by the clients of the firm. The firm was unable to meet margin calls, could not find funding in the repo market and the share price collapsed. Despite efforts at the eleventh hour to find some means of rescue, the firm declared Chapter 11 in the US and was subsequently liquidated.

The failure of the firm resulted in many trades, swaps and obligations of the firm failing to be honoured and many disputes about whether trades had been settled or not. The lawsuits and damage from the firm's collapse was a far more dramatic example than the LTCM episode of the systemic risk posed by the failure of a major hub in a highly interconnected global system. Counterparty risk is deemed to pose such a threat to the financial system that financial regulators are considering the replacement of the traditional methods of OTC settlement – which was the nature of many of the transactions of both LTCM and Lehman Brothers – by central counterparty mechanisms such as the clearing house systems used at futures exchanges.

1.2.1 The Committee on Payment and Settlement Systems (CPSS)

The Committee on Payment and Settlement Systems (CPSS) is part of the BIS and is a standard-setting body for payment and securities settlement systems. It also serves as a forum for central banks to monitor and analyse developments in domestic payment, settlement and clearing systems as well as in cross-border and multicurrency settlement schemes.

From a historical perspective, following the Herstatt incident, a report prepared by the CPSS recognised the gravity of settlement risk in the foreign exchange markets. It made the point that without adequate safeguards, and since a bank's maximum foreign exchange settlement exposure could equal or even surpass the amount receivable for three days' worth of trades at any point in time, the amount at risk to even a single counterparty could exceed a bank's capital.

The stock market crashes of 1987 (when the Dow Jones Industrial Average fell by 22% in a single day on 19 October) prompted regulators to review securities settlement procedures with a view to reducing or eliminating principal risk. The CPSS concluded that the best way of eliminating principal risk was the creation of DvP systems.

1.2.2 The Effect of Delivery versus Payment (DvP) and Straight-Through Processing (STP) Automated Systems

DvP is a sale transaction of negotiable securities (in exchange for cash payment) that can be instructed to a settlement agent using SWIFT Message Type MT 543. Use of such standard message types is intended to reduce risk in the settlement of a financial transaction, and enable automatic processing. Ideally, title to an asset and payment are exchanged simultaneously. Such simultaneity is often the case when a central depository system is available such as Euroclear or the US Depository Trust & Clearing Corporation.

Three main types of DvP systems are in use:

- Systems that settle transfer instructions for both securities and funds on a trade-by-trade (gross) basis, with final (unconditional) transfer of securities from the seller to the buyer (delivery) occurring at the same time as final transfer of funds from the buyer to the seller (payment).
- Systems that settle securities transfer instructions on a gross basis with final transfer of securities from the seller to the buyer (delivery) occurring throughout the processing cycle, but settle funds transfer instructions on a net basis, with final transfer of funds from the buyer to the seller (payment) occurring at the end of the processing cycle.

- Systems that settle transfer instructions for both securities and funds on a net basis, with final transfers of both securities and funds occurring at the end of the processing cycle.

Straight-Through Processing (STP)

STP has been deemed as best practice for settlement but has not been implemented comprehensively in trade settlement. The goal is that the entire trade process for capital markets and payment transactions be conducted electronically without the need for re-keying or manual intervention, subject to legal and regulatory restrictions.

Currently, the entire trade life cycle, from initiation to settlement is commonly referred to as T+2 processing. Industry practitioners viewed STP as meaning at least same-day settlement or faster, ideally minutes or even seconds. The goal was to minimise settlement risk for the execution of a trade and its settlement and clearing to occur simultaneously. However, for this to be achieved, multiple market participants must realise high levels of STP. In particular, transaction data needs to be made available on a just-in-time basis, which is a considerably harder goal to achieve for the financial services community than the application of STP alone.

Some industry analysts believe that STP is not an achievable goal, in the sense that firms are unlikely to find the cost/benefit justification for reaching 100% automation. Instead they promote the idea of improving levels of internal STP within a firm, while encouraging groups of firms to work together to improve the quality of the automation of transaction information between themselves, either bilaterally or as a community of users (external STP). Other analysts, however, believe that STP will be achieved with the emergence of business process interoperability.

1.2.3 Continuous Linked Settlement (CLS)

CLS is a process by which most of the world's largest banks manage settlement of foreign exchange among themselves (and their customers and other third parties). The process is managed by CLS Group Holdings and regulated by the Federal Reserve Board of New York. Since it began operations, CLS has rapidly become the market standard for foreign exchange settlement between major banks.

Eighteen currencies are currently eligible for CLS settlement. They are: US dollar, euro, UK pound, Japanese yen, Swiss franc, Canadian dollar, Australian dollar, Swedish krona, Danish krone, Norwegian krone, Hungarian forint, the Singapore dollar, the Hong Kong dollar, the New Zealand dollar, the Korean won, the South African rand, the Israeli shekel and the Mexican peso.

CLS settles transactions on a payment versus payment (PvP) basis which means that the two parties to a foreign exchange transaction will buy and sell the respective currencies exchanged and the payments made will occur simultaneously. The CLS settlement process is focused on a five-hour window each business day from 7.00am to 12.00 midday in Central European Time (CET). This window was created to provide an overlap across the business days in all parts of the world and facilitate global trading.

By 6.30am CET the settlement members must submit their settlement instructions for transactions to settle that day. At 6.30am each settlement member receives a schedule of what monies need to be paid in that day. From 7.00am the settlement members pay in the net funds that are due to settle in each currency to their central banks, and CLS will then begin to attempt to settle deals. In the event that CLS Bank's strict settlement criteria are not met for each side of a trade, then no funds are exchanged. This achieves the payment versus payment system that removes the Herstatt risk. Those trades that can be settled are settled and money is paid out via the central banks.

As outlined above, the payments made to CLS Bank are made via the central banks. In the UK, both sterling and euro payments are made via the Clearing House Automated Payment System (CHAPS). CHAPS is the electronic transfer system for sending payments between banks that operates in partnership with the Bank of England.

1.3 Financial Transaction Taxes (Stamp Duty and Stamp Duty Reserve Tax (SDRT))

Learning Objective

5.1.3 Understand which transactions may be subject to or exempt from financial transaction taxes

Stamp duty is a transaction tax payable on documents that transfer certain kinds of property by the purchaser of that property. If property can be handed over – for example, an item of furniture – there is no charge to stamp duty, because there is no document executed on which to charge the duty.

Some properties, such as houses, land and shares in a company, can only be transferred in a prescribed legal form. Legislation requires that documents transferring ownership or title to a property which is liable to stamp duty may not be registered or used unless they have been duly stamped. Since owners need to be able to demonstrate their title to property, they are effectively required to have their document stamped if they want it to be recognised as their own.

There are different rates of transaction tax for shares and for other property. Stamp duty on share transfers is charged to the purchaser at 0.5% of the price (excluding any commissions payable to the stockbroker), with no threshold. Normally there is no charge on the issue, as distinct from the transfer, of shares. Stamp duty is rounded up to the next £5. However, there is a charge of 1.5% made on the creation of a bearer share, and on the transfer of shares into a depositary receipt such as an ADR, because subsequent transfers will not attract stamp duty.

Stamp duty depends upon there being a document to stamp. It cannot be used for paperless transactions or when ownership is in dematerialised form. Another transaction tax, stamp duty reserve tax (SDRT), was, therefore, introduced to cater for the paperless transfer of shares through settlement systems such as CREST. SDRT applies in place of stamp duty when the agreement is not completed by an instrument of transfer (ie, a document, the stock transfer form). The SDRT regulations impose an obligation on the operator of CREST (Euroclear UK & Ireland) to collect SDRT on transfers going through the system.

Ultimate liability for paying SDRT falls upon the purchaser or transferee. However, unlike stamp duty, there is an overlying concept of accountable person (which arises under the SDRT Regulations 1986). In general terms, the accountable person rules are designed to place the primary reporting and payment obligations upon an involved financial intermediary, such as a broker. In many cases, typically those involving on-market sales of listed shares, such an intermediary will be accountable (although the accountable person will recover from the liable person any SDRT paid on that person's behalf).

The tax is charged at 0.5% on the consideration given for the transfer, payable by the purchaser. Unlike stamp duty, there is no rounding to the next £5, and it is charged to the penny.

1.3.1 Securities Exempt from Financial Transaction Taxes

Gilts and bonds are not liable to transaction tax unless they are equity-related, for example, convertible into equity. Gifts are not liable to transaction tax, since there is no consideration paid on the transactions. Non-convertible bonds, are also exempt and there is an exemption for stamp duty on certificated shares up to and including trades of £1,000. Certain shares traded on AIM and ISDX markets are also exempt from transaction tax.

According to Schedule 15 of the Finance Act of 1999, which relates to the application of the duty for bearer instruments, the following are relevant exemptions from stamp duty:

- renounceable letters of allotment, and
- letters of rights or other similar instruments when the rights under the letter or other instrument are renounceable not later than six months after its issue.

Also exempt are certain specified instruments relating to non-sterling stock.

Stamp duty is also not chargeable under Schedule 15 on the issue of an instrument which relates to stock expressed:

- in a currency other than sterling
- in units of account defined by reference to more than one currency (whether or not including sterling), or
- on the transfer of the stock constituted by or transferable by means of any such instrument.

The following table illustrates the differences between the application of transaction taxes.

	Stamp Duty	**Stamp Duty Reserve Tax**
Payable by the buyer or transferee	Shares with paper certification	Non-certificated shares in dematerialised form
		Shares bought and sold on same day. No entry required in register
		New issues in renounceable form such as allotment letters under a rights offering
		Share options
		Convertible loan stock
Rate	0.5% rounded up to the next £5	0.5% rounded to nearest penny
Persons exempt from either tax	Intermediaries, such as LSE member firms	
	Registered charities	
	CISs	
	Those receiving shares as gifts	
Instruments exempt from either tax	Gilts	
	Non-convertible bonds (loan stock) denominated in sterling	
	Bearer stocks	
	Foreign registered stocks	
	New issues of securities (via rights offering) to existing owners	
	CFDs and some derivatives	
	Exchange-traded funds available through UK exchanges	

Holdings in CISs are exempt only if the scheme is a bond or gilt fund (of the sort previously falling within Section 101 of the Finance Act 1980). This includes funds which invest in foreign bonds as well as those investing in UK bonds, but is restricted to authorised funds. Direct investments are exempt if they are neither:

- investments the transfers of which would be liable to *ad valorem* stamp duty, nor
- chargeable securities for the purposes of SDRT.

For example, gilts, commercial paper and other exempt loan capital are exempt, whereas UK shares or interests in UK land are not.

A unit under a unit trust scheme or a share in a foreign mutual fund is treated as capital stock of a company formed or established in the territory by the law of which the scheme or fund is governed, and as such is not subject to SDRT. A 'foreign mutual fund' means a fund administered under arrangements governed by the law of a territory outside the UK under which subscribers to the fund are entitled to participate in, or receive payments by reference to, profits or income arising to the fund from the acquisition, holding, management or disposal of investments.

Derivatives are exempt investments only if they relate wholly to exempt investments. So, for example, an index-tracking derivative will only be exempt if the index or indices concerned do not include any non-exempt investments.

Contracts for difference (CFDs), which are becoming widely used by investors as a way of participating in markets through a derivative rather than through the direct ownership of an underlying security, are exempt from SDRT. For example, if one purchases a CFD to support a particular view on the future direction of an individual equity or the FTSE 100 Index product, that CFD instrument is exempt from SDRT.

Cash or other funds held for day-to-day management do not count as investments.

1.3.2 Purchasers Exempt from Transaction Taxes

There are also exemptions from transaction taxes for purchases by registered charities, on-exchange stock lending transactions, gifts and purchases by LSE member firms (who are granted intermediary status) and the clearing house.

1.4 Safe Custody

Learning Objective

5.1.4   Understand the principles of safe custody, the roles of the different types of custodian and how client assets are protected: global; regional; local; subcustodians; clearing and settlement agents

1.4.1 Services Provided by Custodians

When an institutional investor invests in securities, it will commonly employ the services of a custodian to administer these securities by:

- providing safekeeping of the investor's assets in the local market
- making appropriate arrangements for delivery and receipt of cash and securities to support settlement of the investor's trading activities in that market
- providing market information to the investor on developments and reforms within that market
- collecting dividend income, interest paid on debt securities and other income payments in the local market
- managing the client's cash flows
- monitoring and managing entitlements through corporate actions and voting rights held by the investor in the local market
- managing tax reclaims and other tax services in the local market
- ensuring that securities are registered and that transfer of legal title on securities transactions proceeds effectively, and
- ensuring that reporting obligations to the regulatory authorities, and to other relevant bodies, are discharged effectively.

1.4.2   The Role and Responsibility of a Custodian

The primary responsibility of the custodian is to ensure that the client's assets are fully protected at all times. Hence, it must provide robust safekeeping facilities for all valuables and documentation, ensuring that investments are only released from the custodian's care in accordance with authorised instructions from the client.

Importantly, the client's assets must be properly segregated from those of the custodian, and appropriate legal arrangements must be in place to ensure that financial or external shock to the custodian does not expose the client's assets to claims from creditors or any other party.

1.4.3   Global, Local or Regional Custody

An investor faces choices in selecting custody arrangements in regard to a portfolio of global assets. The possible paths can be summarised as follows:

*   Appointing a local custodian in each market in which they invest (often referred to as direct custody arrangements).
*   Appointing a global custodian to manage custody arrangements across the full range of foreign markets in which they have invested assets.
*   Making arrangements to settle trades and hold securities and cash with a CSD within each market, or use an ICSD.

Global Custodian

A global custodian provides investment administration for investor clients, including processing cross-border securities trades and keeping financial assets secure (ie, providing safe custody) outside of the country where the investor is located.

The term 'global custody' came into common usage in the financial services world in the mid-1970s, when the Employee Retirement Income Security Act (ERISA) was passed in the US. This legislation was designed to increase the protection given to US pension fund investors. The Act specified that US pension funds could not act as custodians of the assets held in their own funds; instead, these assets had to be held in the safekeeping of another bank. ERISA went further, to specify that only a US bank could provide custody services for a US pension fund.

Subsequently, the use of the term 'global custody' has evolved to refer a broader set of responsibilities, encompassing settlement, safekeeping, cash management, record-keeping and asset-servicing (for example, collecting dividend payments on shares and interest on bonds, reclaiming withholding tax, advising investor clients on their electing on corporate actions entitlements) and providing market information. Some investors may also use their global custodians to provide a wider suite of services, including investment accounting, treasury and FX, securities lending and borrowing, collateral management, and performance- and risk-analysis on the investor's portfolio.

Some global custodians maintain an extensive network of branches globally and can meet the local custody needs of their investor clients by employing their own branches as local custody providers. Citi Transaction Services (part of Citigroup), for example, is the trusted custodian of over $21 trillion in assets under custody, and has a network which spans 106 markets, of which 60 are proprietary endpoints.

In locations where a global custodian does not have its own branch, or in situations when it may find advantage by looking outside of its proprietary branch network, a global custodian may appoint an external agent bank to provide local custody services. For example, in a number of markets, Citi does not feel that there is a sound economic rationale for maintaining its own branches, and it employs external agents to act as its subcustodian in these markets. Similarly, investment banks and global broker-dealers (eg, Morgan Stanley, Goldman Sachs and UBS) will also typically employ a network of agent banks to meet their needs for clearing, settlement, asset-servicing and cash management in markets around the world where they have investment activities.

A subcustodian is, therefore, employed by a global custodian as its local agent to provide settlement and custody services for assets that it holds on behalf of investor clients in a foreign market. A subcustodian effectively serves as the eyes and ears of the global custodian in the local market, providing a range of clearing, settlement and asset servicing duties. It will also typically provide market information relating to developments in the local market, and will lobby the market authorities for reforms that will make the market more appealing and an efficient target for foreign investment.

In summary, when selecting a subcustodian, a global custodian may appoint:

- one of its own branches, when this option is available
- a local agent bank that specialises in providing subcustody in the market concerned, or
- a regional provider that can offer subcustody across a range of markets in a region.

Local Custodian

Agent banks that specialise in providing subcustody in their home market are sometimes known as single-market providers. Stiff competition from larger regional or global competitors has meant that these are becoming a dying breed. However, some continue to win business in their local markets, often combining this service with offering global custody or master custody for institutional investors in their home markets. Examples include MUFG Bank, Mizuho Bank and Sumitomo Mitsui Banking Corporation in Japan, Maybank in Malaysia, and United Overseas Bank in Singapore.

A principal selling point is that they are local market specialists. They remain focused on their local business without spreading their attentions broadly across a wide range of markets. A local specialist bank may be attractive in a market in which local practices tend to differ markedly from global standards, or where a provider's long-standing relationship with the local regulatory authorities and/or political elite leaves it particularly well placed to lobby for reforms on behalf of its cross-border clients.

Reciprocal arrangements may be influential in shaping the appointment of a local provider in some instances. Under such an arrangement, a global custodian (A) may appoint the local provider (B) to deliver subcustody in its local market (market B). In return, the custodian (A) may offer subcustody in its own home market (market A) for pension and insurance funds in market B that use provider B as their global custodian.

In summary, the strengths of a local custodian may include that they:

- are country specialists
- can be the 'eyes and ears' of a global custodian or broker-dealer in the local market
- will have regular dealings with financial authorities and local politicians, and may be well placed to lobby for reforms that will improve the efficiency of the local market

- have expert knowledge of local market practice, language and culture, and
- may offer opportunities for reciprocal business.

A local custody bank may have the following disadvantages when compared with a regional custodian:

- Their credit rating may not match up to requirements laid down by some global custodians or global broker-dealers.
- They cannot leverage developments in technology and client service across multiple markets (unlike a regional custodian). Hence product and technology development may lag behind the regional custodians with which it competes.
- They may not be able to offer the price discounts that can be extended by regional custodians offering custody services across multiple markets.

Regional Custodian

A regional custodian is able to provide agent bank services across multiple markets in a region. For example, Standard Chartered Bank and HSBC have both been offering regional custody and clearing in the Asia-Pacific and South Asian region for many years, competing with Citi and some strong single-market providers for business in this region. In Central and Eastern Europe, Bank Austria Creditanstalt/Unicredit Group, Deutsche Bank, ING Group, Raiffeisen Zentralbank Österreich and Citi each offer a regional clearing and custody service. In Central and South America, Citi and Itaú Unibanco (the Brazilian bank that purchased Bank Boston's established regional custody service) offer regional custody, in competition in selected markets with HSBC, Santander and Deutsche Bank.

Employing a regional custodian may offer a range of advantages to global custodian or global broker-dealer clients:

- Its credit rating may be higher than that of a single-market custodian.
- It can cross-fertilise good practice across multiple markets. Lessons learned in one market may be applied, when appropriate, across other markets in its regional offering.
- It can leverage innovation in technology, product development and client service across multiple markets, delivering economies of scale.
- It can offer standardised reporting, management information systems and market information across multiple markets in its regional offering.
- Economies of scale may support delivery of some or all product lines from a regional processing centre, offering potential cost savings and efficiency benefits.
- Its size and regional importance, plus the strength of its global client base, may allow a regional custodian to exert considerable leverage on local regulators, political authorities and infrastructure providers. This may be important in lobbying for reforms that support greater efficiency and security for foreign investors in that market.
- A global client may be able to secure price discounts by using a regional custodian across multiple markets.

In some situations, a regional provider may have certain disadvantages when compared with a local custody bank:

- A regional custodian's product offering may be less well attuned to local market practice, service culture and investor needs than a well-established local provider.

- A regional custodian may spread its focus across a wider range of clients and a wider range of markets than a single-market provider. Hence, a cross-border client may not receive the same level of attention, or the same degree of individualised service, as may be extended by a local custodian.
- Some regional custodians may lack the long track record, customer base and goodwill held by some local custodians in their own market.

1.4.4 Custody Agreements

Standard Custody Agreement

In order to formalise the custody arrangements outlined above, it is standard for the institutional investor and the global custodian to sign a custody agreement that details:

- the legal conditions under which the investor's assets are held by the global custodian, and are protected and segregated from the assets of the global custodian
- the responsibilities and obligations required of the global custodian under the custody relationship, and
- authority for the custodian to accept instructions from fund managers, when an institutional investor employs investment managers to manage assets on its behalf.

The global custodian will negotiate a separate custody agreement with each institutional investor that it conducts business with. Given that these institutions may have markedly different investment strategies, allocating their assets across a different range of markets and investment instruments, the structure and content of the legal agreement may differ significantly from client to client.

A custody agreement is likely to address the following issues:

- The method through which the client's assets are received and held by the global custodian.
- Reporting obligations and deadlines.
- Guidelines for use of CSDs and other relevant use of financial infrastructure.
- Business contingency plans to cope with systemic malfunction or disaster.
- Liability in contract and claims for damages.
- Standards of service and care required under the custody relationship.
- A list of persons authorised to give instructions.
- Actions to be taken in response to instructions and actions to be taken without instructions.

Institutional investors and global custodians are required to adhere to the legal framework prevailing in the countries in which assets are invested.

The custody agreement will typically include provision on the part of the investor to conduct periodic reviews of the custodian's internal control environment, in order to ensure that it has effective procedures in place to monitor and manage risk. These controls should ensure that the investor's assets are held securely and that procedures for accepting, and acting on, authorised instructions are in place.

The custody agreement will commonly detail the level of indemnity that the global custodian will provide to the client in instances of error or negligence on its own part or on the part of subcustodians that it employs. It will also define the level of indemnity, if at all, that it will provide to clients against catastrophic events, default by a CSD or clearing house, theft or fraud, and a wide range of other contingencies.

Subcustody Agreement

When the global custodian employs a subcustodian to provide custody on its behalf in a foreign market, it will sign a legal agreement with the subcustody provider that will detail:

- the legal conditions under which client assets are held by the sub-custodian, and are protected and segregated from the assets of the subcustodian
- the responsibilities and obligations required of the subcustodian by the global custodian under the custody relationship.

Subcustodians, global custodians and their foreign investor clients are bound by the legal regulations prevailing in the overseas market. Hence, while many provisions of the subcustodian agreement will resemble those appearing in the investor-global custodian agreement outlined above, these provisions will be amended in certain instances to comply with local regulatory requirements and legal practice.

Service Level Agreement (SLA)

Detailed specifications pertaining to the standards of service required by an investor from its custodian are spelt out in a service level agreement. This lays down required standards for service areas including:

- Record-keeping and maintenance of accurate and up-to-date documentation.
- Settlement on both recognised exchanges and in OTC markets.
- Communication and reporting.
- Processing of corporate actions – eg, rights issues and other capitalisation matters.
- Income-processing, for example from dividends and coupon payments.
- Tax services.
- Cash management.
- Management information systems.
- Stock lending and borrowing.
- Market information and market knowledge.
- Standards of service expected from account officers and relationship managers that represent primary points of contact with the investor.

1.4.5   Selecting a Custodian

When selecting a global custodian, an institutional investor will typically invite statements of interest from suitable candidates. The investor may ask for further detail of services offered by applicants via a request for information (RFI). Eligible candidates will typically then be asked to complete a detailed request for proposal (RFP) submission as a preliminary stage in the appointment process. An RFP is a tendering process for buyers of global financial services.

Although the size and scope of the RFP will vary slightly from client to client, it will generally be a lengthy questionnaire, requesting background information on the custodian's staffing and IT capacity, its track record and experience in the custody area, the strength of its existing client base and assets under custody, its creditworthiness and its record of recent losses.

The RFP should be viewed as an early stage in the selection process, rather than a selection process in its own right. Typically, it will be used to screen out candidates that do not meet the client's selection criteria, and then to provide a springboard for further investigation at a subsequent site visit and/or interview stage.

1.4.6 Regulation and Legislation Affecting Custodians

Legislation governing the responsibilities held by pension fund trustees and other fiduciaries can be important in shaping the procedures through which custodians are appointed and standards of service monitored. For example, standards of fiducial conduct laid down in the US in Section 404 of the Employment Retirement Income Security Act of 1974 (ERISA) or the 1995 UK Pensions Act require pension fund trustees to be directly responsible for the appointment of custodians. This makes trustees liable for civil penalties if they rely on the skill or judgement of any person who is appointed (other than by the trustees) to exercise a prescribed function. To put it simply, this requires that pension fund trustees should have a direct legal relationship with their custodian, not an indirect one via the investment manager or any other appointed intermediary. Trustees must take full responsibility for appointing and monitoring the actions of custodians acting on behalf of their fund.

In their capacity as fiduciaries, pension fund trustees are generally required to uphold the following prudential standards:

- They must demonstrate that they have the necessary familiarity with the structure and aims of their pension scheme and have an appropriate level of training and skill to carry out their responsibilities to scheme members effectively.
- Fiduciaries have a responsibility to monitor and review the tasks that they delegate to third parties (including custodians and investment management companies) in order to ensure that these tasks are discharged effectively.
- The duty of loyalty demands that trustees administer their pension scheme solely in the best interests of the scheme members.
- Trustees must avoid undue risk in the way that they manage scheme assets and appoint intermediaries to manage or administer scheme assets on the scheme's behalf.

Also, legislation guiding safekeeping of client assets typically requires that a firm that holds safe custody investments with a custodian must have effective and transparent procedures in place for custodian selection and for monitoring performance. The frequency of these risk reviews should be dependent on the nature of the market and the type of services that the custodian delivers to the client.

1.5 Registered Title

Learning Objective

5.1.5 Understand the implications of registered title for certificated and uncertificated holdings: registered title versus unregistered (bearer); legal title; beneficial interest; right to participate in corporate actions

1.5.1 Registered Title

In regard to a trade involving UK shares, settlement must involve communicating the change in ownership to the company **registrar**. This is because the issuing company maintains a register listing all of its shareholders. Whenever shares are bought or sold, a mechanism is required to make the company registrar aware of the change required to the register.

So, 'registered title' simply means ownership that is backed by registration. In terms of share ownership, registered title gives shareholders the right to vote on important company matters, to claim dividends on their shares, and to participate in other corporate actions such as rights issues. Registered title can apply equally to holdings which are certificated, ie, where there is a paper instrument which underlies the holding, or, as is increasingly the case, to uncertificated holdings which are often commonly known as paperless. When shares are bought and sold, it is the company registrar who is responsible for updating the register of members and giving the new owner registered title.

1.5.2 Bearer Shares or Unregistered Title

A bearer share or security is an ownership certificate which is not registered in any name. As with other bearer securities, bearer stock is a negotiable certificate that can be transferred between owners without endorsement. Bearer stock is popular in Europe but not in the US. Eurobonds and ADRs have traditionally been issued as bearer securities and, in most cases, a register of the owners of these instruments is not maintained by the issuers.

If an issuer of securities does not maintain a register, all of the securities issues are described as unregistered or bearer securities. Proof of ownership and the right to transfer the security will depend on physically handing over the shares and executing any other documentation to affect the validity of a transfer of ownership. However, no formal registration with the issuer of the security is required. Many short-term instruments which are issued in the money markets, such as commercial paper and bills of exchange, will tend to be issued in bearer form. Bunds, which are long-term fixed-income debt instruments issued by the German government, are also bearer instruments.

Owners of bearer instruments will usually place these for safekeeping with a custodian or nominee, who will also take on the responsibility of collecting dividends or coupon income as appropriate. The obligation for disclosure of the formal ownership of bearer securities can become an issue if there are grounds to suspect that there has been any criminal wrongdoing or tax evasion on the part of the actual owner of a bearer security. The default position is that the information regarding the actual owner should be treated as a matter of confidentiality, unless the actual owner consents to declaration of this information.

The key characteristics of bearer securities are:

- Bearer securities are easier to transfer since there is no register.
- Transfer of ownership is normally as simple as the physical transfer of certificates of ownership.

However, this does raise a few problems:

- It is difficult for the authorities to monitor ownership, making them attractive investments for money launderers.
- The issuing company has difficulty knowing to whom dividend or interest payments should be sent.
- The actual physical security of the certificates is of greater importance and can increase the cost of holding the investment.

1.5.3 Legal Title

To have legal title means having clear and enforceable ownership of an asset or property.

The term 'title' can be defined more specifically as having the legal rights of ownership, possession and custody, evidenced by a legal document (instrument) such as a bill of sale, certificate of title or title deed. Legal title empowers its holder to control and dispose of the property, and serves as a link between the title holder and the property itself.

In law, to prove the ownership of an asset or property requires the ability to be able to show legal title to that asset, and this is usually provided by a legal document, which establishes unequivocally that the rights of ownership have been conveyed or transferred to the person who claims ownership. This also provides the simple answer that legal title is a valid and enforceable claim to ownership. To provide an example, from a legal perspective, of how title is transferred, it is worth considering the transfer of ownership into a trust. Under a bare trust arrangement, as with any trust, assets are transferred into trust by the settlor. At this point the settlor gives up the legal title to the assets. They cease to be their property, and instead become the property of the trust.

1.5.4 Beneficial Ownership or Interest

The case of transfer to a trust was cited above but the case of a nominee or custodian having legal title to an asset which is held on behalf of the actual owner serves to highlight the difference between legal title and beneficial ownership.

Large institutions as a matter of course, as well as smaller investors by choice, will often want to avoid the administrative tasks connected with registered title of shares and other investments. If an investor wishes to retain the right to participate in all corporate actions but, for whatever reason, does not want to be the registered owner of a security, the appropriate vehicle and legal form to use is for the investor to appoint a nominee to hold the securities.

The nominee – often a stockbroker or custodian – takes the registered title to the shares and all the responsibilities that go with it but the nominee's client retains the benefits of ownership, mainly the dividends and capital growth. It is the client that ultimately receives all of the income generated by the shares. The nominee is referred to as the legal owner of the shares and the client is known as the beneficial owner.

The beneficial owner who has appointed a nominee or custodian to hold the registered title of a security will, as a result of the 'pass-through' arrangements incorporated in the custodian or nominee agreement, be entitled to receive dividends arising for that security, coupon payments or entitlements under rights issues and other capitalisation issues and, in general, have all of the benefits and obligations of the corporate actions undertaken by the issuer of the security.

1.6 Nominees

Learning Objective

5.1.6 Understand the characteristics of nominees: designated nominee accounts; pooled nominee accounts; corporate nominees; details in share register; legal and beneficial ownership

1.6.1 Background

UK company law prevents registrars and companies from recognising anyone other than the name on register or, in the case of a corporation, its duly appointed attorney. Institutional investors employing professional investment management firms to manage their assets are highly unlikely to hold these securities in their own name ('name on register'). The reason for this is simple. The person whose name appears on the share register receives every piece of documentation sent out by the company and is obliged to sign all share transfers and other relevant forms such as instructions for rights issues and other corporate events.

To ensure safe custody of assets and remove this administrative burden from the investor, thus allowing the speedy processing of transfers, institutional (and, increasingly, private client) shareholdings are held in the names of nominee companies.

Nominee arrangements have long been established as the mechanism by which asset managers and custodians can process transactions on behalf of their clients. Given that many investment management firms outsource some or all of their investment administration activities to specialist custodians, the vast majority of institutional shareholdings in fact now reside in nominee accounts overseen by these specialist custodians.

As far as the company is concerned, the nominee name appearing on its share register is the legal owner of the shares for the purposes of benefits and for voting. However, as explained in section 1.5, beneficial ownership continues to reside with the underlying client.

It is this separation of ownership which allows the custodians, under proper client authorities, to transfer shares to meet market transactions and to conduct other functions without the registrar requiring sight of the signature or seal of the underlying client.

Registrars cannot recognise a trust as the beneficial owner of shares, so, in order to look beyond the legal ownership of any holding, the registrar can issue at any time a notice under Section 793 of the Companies Acts. This will require the nominee company to disclose the name of the beneficial owner of the shares, so that at least the company may be aware for whom the nominee is acting.

A notice issued under Section 793 of the Companies Acts (which came into force on 20 January 2007 and replaced the Section 212 notice under the Companies Act 1985) allows a public company to issue a notice requiring a person it knows, or has reasonable cause to believe, has an interest in its shares (or to have had an interest in the previous three years) to confirm or deny the fact, and, if the former, to disclose certain information about the interest, including information about any other person with an interest in the shares.

1.6.2   Types of Nominee Companies

Nominees can be classified into three types:

- **Pooled** (or **omnibus**) – whereby individual clients are grouped together within a single nominee registration
- **Designated** – where the nominee name includes unique identifiers for each individual client, eg, XYZ Nominees Account 1, Account 2, Account 3, and so on
- **Sole** – where a single nominee name is used for a specific client, eg, ABC Pension Fund Nominees ltd.

It is now generally accepted that there are no real advantages from a security point of view as to which type of nominee arrangement is used to register the shares. However, how the shareholdings are registered is of vital importance when it comes to voting. Clients brought together with others in a pooled nominee have no visibility to the company; it is the single nominee name, covering multiple clients, which the company recognises. Importantly, from a voting perspective, it is therefore only the single bulk nominee who is entitled to vote. No separate entitlement accrues from the registrar's standpoint to each individual client making up the total holding.

Another disadvantage of the use of a nominee is that some companies offer their shareholders certain perks, such as discounts on their products. By using a nominee (either a designated or a pooled structure), the shareholder perks may not be available to the individual investor. This is simply because the stockbrokers may be unwilling to undertake the necessary administration to facilitate the provision of these perks.

One reason for registering shares in a designated or sole nominee name would be if the underlying investor required dividends to be mandated to a particular bank account, rather than being collected by the custodian, in which case registration in an omnibus account would not be practical. Both designation and individual registration, as opposed to a pooled account, can help with some aspects of auditing, and either affords a good control mechanism when identical trades may have been executed for different clients (for example on the same date, for the same number of shares and for the same settlement consideration).

One reason frequently cited by custodians for insisting on pooled nominee arrangements is the vexed question of costs. However, operating a designated nominee account should give rise to few additional costs from the custodian's point of view, as the existing nominee name can easily be used with the addition of a unique designation. While there may be a slight increase in the receipt of Section 793 requests and a small amount of extra work involved, for example in the receipt of separate income payments, the actual procedures are identical and should be capable of being easily absorbed into the existing administration and processing routines.

If the client insists on using a sole nominee name to register the shareholdings, this might involve some costs for the custodian connected with the establishment of a nameplate nominee company, the requisite appointment of directors and the completion of annual returns. The custodian may seek to pass these comparatively meagre costs on to the client, but more usually they will be absorbed within the standard custody tariff.

Neither of these two nominee approaches are likely to give rise to additional transaction charges imposed on the custodian by CREST, the UK's electronic share settlement system, as individual sales and purchases are relayed across the system regardless of how the assets are registered. One area where additional transactions may occur, giving rise to additional costs, is in respect of securities lending.

However, the CREST charges for such transactions are reasonably low and a client would need to undertake a lot of loans and recalls for these transaction charges to become a significant amount. Such small additional amounts need to be seen against the typical custody tariff for UK securities of around one basis point (0.01%) of the value of assets under custody and a further charge of approximately £20 for each trade settled. Also, in the case of securities lending, the custodian usually retains a share of the extra income generated. This is often around 30%, again drawing any additional transaction costs in respect of loan movements created by a separately registered or designated nominee account.

1.6.3 Corporate Nominee

A corporate nominee (alternatively referred to as a corporate sponsored nominee) is when the issuing company itself provides a facility for its smaller shareholders to hold their shares within a single corporate nominee.

The corporate nominee is a halfway house between the pooled and the designated nominee structures offered by stockbrokers. It will result in a single entry for all the shareholders together in the company's register (like the pooled nominee) but beneath this the issuing company (or its registrar) will be aware of the individual holdings that make up the nominee. In a similar way to the designated nominee structure, the company will be able to forward separate dividend payments to each of the individual shareholders, as well as voting rights and other potential shareholder perks.

Shares held within a corporate nominee in dematerialised form enable quick and easy transfer through CREST.

1.6.4 The Share Register

Shares in the UK are held in registered form. This means that the certificate is simply evidence of ownership. The proof that counts is the name and address held on the company's share register. There is a statutory requirement for a minimum of one shareholder and for the details of shareholders to be put on public record.

Upon incorporating a company (be it a new or ready-made shelf company or a tailor-made company), one can either act as a shareholder in one's own name, or a financial services firm equipped to handle incorporations or a custodian can provide a nominee shareholder, with a view to securing corporate privacy.

In other words, for the purpose of privacy, some clients do not wish to be identified as shareholders of the companies that they have set up and will therefore wish to appoint nominee shareholders. These nominee shareholders will hold the shares on trust for the beneficial owners and only they will be identified on the register of shareholders.

Each nominee shareholder appointed will sign a declaration of trust to the beneficial owner that they are holding the shares on behalf of the beneficial owner and will return the shares into the name of the beneficial owner or will transfer them to another party as requested. A nominee shareholder is normally a company created for the purpose of holding shares and other securities on behalf of investors.

1.6.5 Summary

Custodians and their nominees now control the majority of share registrations for institutional investors, even for clients who may not have directly appointed custodians, but whose asset management firms have outsourced their investment administration to these providers.

Custodians uniquely identify their clients' holdings by segregating these in their computer systems, as it is largely these systems that drive the calculation and application of dividends and other entitlements. However, this segregation is not the same as having an individually identifiable holding for a particular client on company share registers.

It is largely impractical for an institutional investor to achieve 'name on register', so the recognised practice is to use nominee names whereby the custodian, or other duly authorised agent, is legally entitled to perform the transfer and administration of the assets on behalf of, and under the authority of, the underlying beneficial owner.

Many custodians prefer to pool all their clients into one single nominee registration but this does remove the visibility of the underlying investor and makes individual client voting much more cumbersome. Clients can request their custodian to adopt an individual registration solely for their particular shareholdings. Typically this takes the form of a standard nominee name with a unique designation for each client. The costs of such separate registration and its ongoing maintenance are minimal relative to overall custody and securities lending charges and are often absorbed by the custodians.

2. Prime Brokerage and Equity Finance

2.1 Stock Lending

Learning Objective

5.2.1 Understand the purpose, requirements and implications of securities lending: benefits and risks for borrowers and lenders; function of market makers, intermediaries and custodians; effect on the lender's rights; effect on corporate action activity; collateral; potential risks of lack of consolidated disclosure by funds

Stock lending is the temporary transfer of securities by a lender to a borrower with agreement by the borrower to return equivalent securities to the lender at a pre-agreed time.

There are two main motivations for stock lending: securities-driven, and cash-driven. In securities-driven transactions, borrowing firms seek specific securities (equities or bonds), perhaps to facilitate their trading operations. In cash-driven trades, the lender is able to increase the returns on an underlying portfolio by receiving a fee for making its investments available to the borrower. Such transactions may boost overall income returns, enhancing, for example, returns on a pension fund.

The terms of the securities loan will be governed by a securities lending agreement, which requires that the borrower provide the lender with collateral in the form of cash, government securities, or a letter of credit of value equal to or greater than the loaned securities. As payment for the loan, the parties negotiate a fee, quoted as an annualised percentage of the value of the loaned securities. If the agreed form of collateral is cash, then the fee may be quoted as a rebate, meaning that the lender will earn all of the interest which accrues on the cash collateral, and will 'rebate' an agreed rate of interest to the borrower.

Securities lending covers all sorts of securities including equities, government bonds and corporate debt obligations. Securities lenders, often simply called 'sec lenders', are institutions which have access to lendable securities. This can be asset managers, who have many securities under management, custodian banks holding securities for third parties, or third-party lenders who access securities automatically via the asset-holder's custodian.

2.1.1 Benefits of Stock Lending

The initial driver for the securities lending business was to cover settlement failure. If one party failed to deliver stock to you, it could mean that you were unable to deliver stock that you have already sold to another party. In order to avoid the costs and penalties that can arise from settlement failure, stock could be borrowed at a fee and delivered to the second party. When your initial stock finally arrived (or was obtained from another source) the lender would receive back the same number of shares in the security they lent.

More recently, the principal reason for borrowing a security is to cover a short position. As you are obliged to deliver the security, you will have to borrow it. At the end of the agreement, you will have to return an equivalent security to the lender. Equivalent in this context means fungible, ie, the securities have to be completely interchangeable. Compare this with lending a ten-euro note: you do not expect exactly the same note back, as any ten-euro note will do.

Securities lending and borrowing is often required, by matter of law, in order to engage in short selling. In fact, regulations enacted in 2008 in the US, Australia and the UK, among other jurisdictions, required that, before short sales were executed for specific stocks, the sellers first pre-borrow shares in those issues. There is an ongoing debate among global policy makers and regulators about how to impose new restrictions on short selling, and Germany took a unilateral step in banning the naked short selling of CDSs (ie, where the short seller had no interest in the underlying security for the credit default swap) in June 2010, during a period of turbulence for the eurozone. The Short Selling Regulation (SSR) provides EU regulators and the FCA with the power to apply short- or long-term bans on short sales in shares, and certain other financial instruments and this was utilised in various jurisdictions during the COVID-19 pandemic.

The FCA lists the following positive aspects of stock lending in its guidance to the investment community:

- It can increase the liquidity of the securities market by allowing securities to be borrowed temporarily, thus reducing the potential for failed settlements and the penalties this may incur.
- It can provide extra security to lenders through the collateralisation of a loan.
- It can support many trading and investment strategies that otherwise would be extremely difficult to execute.
- It allows investors to earn income by lending their securities on to third parties.
- It facilitates the hedging and arbitraging of price differentials.

2.1.2   Risks of Stock Lending

Many feel that securities lending could aid market manipulation through short selling, which can potentially influence market prices. Short selling as such is not wrong (although market manipulation certainly is) and stock lending can assist those that have sold stock short, thus adding liquidity to the market.

As already noted, the debate about the merits and validity of short selling is sometimes emotionally charged and often features in the rhetoric of politicians in populist attacks on the financial services sector. It probably is fair to say that for most investment professionals who actually work in the financial markets the notion that short selling in itself is an abusive practice is not palatable. There may be times when the activity can be disruptive, but markets have a tendency to overreact in either direction, and the periodic focus given to short selling when a market is moving down should be counterbalanced by the tendency for markets to become too frothy and for long investors to become exuberant when markets are rising.

Another alleged potential abuse is that of tax evasion. However, the act of stock lending itself does not lead to tax evasion.

In the UK, those involved in securities lending will generally be supervised by the FCA. They will be subject to the FCA's Handbook, including the inter-professional conduct chapter of the Market Conduct Sourcebook, and also subject to the provisions of the Financial Services and Markets Act on, among other things, market abuse. They will also have regard to the provisions of the Stock Borrowing and Lending Code, produced by the Stock Lending and Borrowing Committee, a committee of market participants, chaired by the Bank of England and including a representative of the FCA.

Archegos Capital Management, on 26 March 2021, defaulted on margin calls from several global investment banks. The firm had large, concentrated positions in ViacomCBS, Baidu, Vipshop, Farfetch, and other companies, and used swaps rather than common stock to stealthily amass huge positions. Like derivatives, short sales are also largely excluded from the need to disclose large holdings, while if it had transacted in regular stocks it would have had to. The fund was also heavily leveraged and transacted business with several banks which were thought to be unaware of Archegos' large positions.

The SEC requires certain institutional investment managers to file a Form 13F, disclosing the names, shares, and fair market value of certain securities over which the managers exercise control, but total return swaps are not on the list of securities required to be disclosed. However, some reports have suggested that Archegos-owned equities were in sufficient amounts that meant they should have indeed filed a 13F.

As a result of exposure to Archegos, in April 2021, Credit Suisse reported losses of $5.5 billion, Morgan Stanley nearly $1 billion, Japan's Nomura Holdings $2 billion (later revised to $2.85billion) and UBS Group AG $774 million – all in connection with Archegos' failure.

As a result of this event, SEC officials are exploring how to increase transparency for the types of activity that caused Archegos to default.

2.1.3   Legalities

Securities lending is legal and clearly regulated in most of the world's major securities markets. Most markets mandate that the borrowing of securities be conducted only for specifically permitted purposes, which generally include to:

*   facilitate settlement of a trade
*   facilitate delivery of a short sale
*   finance the security, or
*   facilitate a loan to another borrower who is motivated by one of these permitted purposes.

Parties to a stock-lending transaction generally operate under a legal agreement, such as the **Global Master Securities Lending Agreement (GMSLA)**, which sets out the obligations of the borrower and lender. The GMSLA was developed as a market standard for securities lending, drafted with a view to compliance with English law and covers the matters which a legal agreement ought to cover for securities lending transactions. The agreement is kept under review and amendments are periodically made, although parties to an existing agreement need to agree that those amendments do apply.

2.1.4   Effect on a Lender's Rights and Corporate Actions

When a security is loaned, the title of the security transfers to the borrower. This means that the borrower has the advantages of holding the security, just as though they owned it – they can even lend the securities on to another party. Specifically, the borrower will receive all coupon and/or dividend payments, and any other rights such as voting rights. In most cases, these dividends or coupons must be passed back to the lender in the form of what is referred to as a manufactured dividend. If the lender wants to exercise its right to vote it should recall the stock in good time so that a proxy voting form can be completed and returned to the registrar by the required deadline.

Similar issues are involved in other corporate actions such as a capitalisation issue. Technically the consequences arising from any corporate action, such as a capitalisation matter or rights issue, by the issuer of a security that has been lent to another would *prima facie* be to the benefit/cost of the borrower. It is customary that these costs/benefits should flow back to the lender, and the exact manner in which this will be implemented should be reflected in the securities lending agreement.

The term 'securities lending' is sometimes used erroneously as a synonym of 'stock loan'. The latter term is used in private hedged portfolio stock collateralised loan arrangements, where the underlying securities are hedged so as to convert the variable asset to a relatively stable asset against which a usually non-recourse or limited recourse loan can be placed.

2.1.5   Tax Consequences of Stock Lending

The tax position in relation to stock lending is complex and varies from country to country. If in doubt those involved in stock lending should obtain professional advice from their tax specialist.

2.1.6   Collateral – Stock Lending versus Repo

While stock lending and sale/repurchase agreements (repos) are similar, the difference is that a stock lender charges a fee to the borrower, whereas a repo counterparty pays (or receives) a rate of interest.

Example _____

A large pension fund manager with a position in a particular stock agrees that the security can be borrowed by a securities lender. The securities lender, a prime broker or investment bank, will then allow a hedge fund client to borrow the stock and sell it short. The short seller would like to buy the stock back at a lower price and realise a profit when returning the security to the broker from whom it has been borrowed.

Once the shares are borrowed and sold, cash is generated from selling the stock. That cash would become collateral for the borrower. The cash value of the collateral is marked-to-market on a daily basis so that it exceeds the value of the loan by at least 2%. The pension fund manager has access to the cash for overnight investment and this enables the pension fund to maintain a long position in the stock. The pension fund manager is able to earn additional income from lending the stock, and the hedge fund manager is able, providing that their call that the price of the security is going to decline is correct, to profit from the short sale. In addition, the prime broker earns a spread from facilitating the transaction and also by providing this prime brokerage service to the hedge fund client.

2.1.7   Money Markets Committee

The Money Markets Committee (MMC) is a senior-level forum for market participants and the relevant UK public authorities to discuss issues concerning the UK unsecured deposits and funding market, the securities lending market and the repo market.

The MMC is chaired by the Bank of England (BoE). The Committee meets quarterly and also has two permanent sub-committees: the UK Money Markets Code Sub-Committee and the Securities Lending Committee

The objectives of the Money Markets Committee are:

1. to discuss important domestic and global market or structural developments affecting the UK money-, repo- and securities-lending markets
2. where appropriate, to propose responses to any issues identified
3. to aid understanding and enhance monitoring of the functioning of the UK money markets
4. to endorse and facilitate continuing market-wide adoption of the UK Money Markets Code, a voluntary code of good practice for the money and securities financing markets
5. to identify and address any high-level issues concerning contingency planning in the UK money markets and payment systems, having regard to international developments.

International Securities Lending Association (ISLA)

The international trade organisation for the securities lending industry is the International Securities Lending Association (ISLA).

2.2   Prime Broker Services

Learning Objective

5.2.2   Understand the purpose and main types of prime broker equity finance services and their impact on securities markets: securities lending and borrowing; leveraged trade execution; cash management; core settlement; custody; rehypothecation; repurchase agreements; collateralised borrowing; tri-party repos; synthetic financing

---

Prime brokerage is the term given to a collection of services provided by investment banks to their hedge fund clients and other asset management boutique firms.

Hedge funds are investment funds that are typically only open to a limited range of investors. They tend to follow complex investment strategies, often involving derivatives. However, among the more straightforward strategies adopted is the equity long/short strategy. This involves taking both long positions in equities (in other words buying shares) and, at the same time, committing to sell equities that are not held by the fund (described as selling short).

The hope is that the gain in one half of the strategy (the long or the short) will more than cover the loss (or 'hedge') on the other half of the strategy (the short or the long). Selling short inevitably means that the fund will need to borrow the securities it has sold until the position is unwound.

Whereas the managers of a hedge fund or alternative asset management vehicle are primarily concerned with formulating and executing investment strategies, the actual execution and administration of the fund's account is usually left to the prime broker, which has the expertise and organisational systems to offer more specialised and supportive services, and can also assist in providing additional credit and financing facilities to the client funds.

The typical services that are provided by a prime broker include the following.

2.2.1   Securities Lending and Borrowing

Prime brokers can arrange for the appropriate shares to be borrowed to cover the hedge fund's short positions, and also use the fund's long positions to lend to others and provide additional returns to the fund as a result.

2.2.2   Leveraged Trade Execution

Many hedge funds will wish to use leverage in executing certain strategies, and in order to do so they will often use the margin facilities provided by a prime broker. The broker will operate the margin account in accordance with an underlying security arrangement in which the fund pledges collateral, which may be financed via a repo, or where the margin account is subject to the constraints of mark-to-market on a regular basis.

With the latter, if the fund's marks fall below a certain stipulated threshold, the fund will be required to provide more collateral to the prime broker or the broker is entitled to start liquidating investment positions held by the fund in order to restore the margin account to an acceptable level of leverage as agreed in the security agreement.

2.2.3   Cash Management

Prime brokers will also use opportunities that they have available to maximise the return that is generated from any unfettered cash which is held by the fund and which has not been used as collateral for a repo or in a margin account.

2.2.4   Core Settlement

The prime broker will take the necessary steps to make sure that any securities purchased become the property of the fund and the appropriate cash is received in a timely manner for any sales made of the fund's securities.

2.2.5   Custody

The prime broker may provide the services of a custodian, ie, registering and keeping safe the securities held by the fund, and processing any corporate actions promptly and in accordance with the fund's wishes. Sometimes this role will be handled by a separate custodian.

2.2.6   Rehypothecation

In addition to holding collateral and having a charge over the fund's portfolio, the prime broker might also require a right to re-charge, dispose of or otherwise use the customer's assets which are subject to the security, including disposing of them to a third party. This is commonly described as a right of rehypothecation. When assets have been rehypothecated, they become the property of the prime broker as and when the prime broker uses them in this way, for instance by depositing rehypothecated securities with a third-party financier to obtain cheaper funding, or by lending the securities to another client.

2.2.7   Repurchase Agreements

Repurchase agreements (or repos) are essentially when the prime broker arranges the sale of securities owned by the fund for cash, while agreeing to buy back the equivalent securities later for a slightly inflated price. The increase in price is effectively the borrowing cost of the cash, and is often referred to as the repo rate.

In the case of a tri-party repo, a custodian bank or clearing organisation acts as an intermediary between the two parties to the repurchase or repo agreement outlined above. The tri-party agent is responsible for the administration of the transaction including collateral allocation, the marking-to-market, and, when required, the substitution of collateral. The lender and the borrower of cash both enter into tri-party transactions in order to avoid the administrative burden of the simpler form of bilateral repos. Moreover, there is an added element of security in a tri-party repo because the collateral is being held by an agent and the counterparty risk is reduced.

2.2.8 Collateralised Borrowing

Prime brokers advance cash to the customer against the security of a first fixed charge over the customer's portfolio. In the event of the customer's default, this gives the prime broker a right of recourse against the charged assets for the amounts owing to it. The availability of the portfolio as collateral in this way should enable the bank to provide loans at more competitive rates than is the case with an unsecured loan.

2.2.9 Synthetic Financing

This is when the prime broker will create exposure to particular securities by using derivatives, such as swaps, rather than directly buying and holding the securities themselves. This route is generally substantially cheaper than outright purchases.

End of Chapter Questions

Think of an answer to each question and refer to the appropriate section for confirmation.

1. What is the settlement period for exchange-listed equities in Germany?
   Answer reference: Section 1.1.4

2. What body does the acronym JASDEC refer to and what is its function?
   Answer reference: Section 1.1.5

3. In relation to settlement of securities transactions, what is liquidity risk?
   Answer reference: Section 1.2

4. What is the function of the Committee on Payment and Settlement Systems?
   Answer reference: Section 1.2.1

5. What is the goal of straight-through processing (STP) in trade settlements?
   Answer reference: Section 1.2.2

6. What is the principal reason behind the difference between stamp duty and stamp duty reserve tax?
   Answer reference: Section 1.3

7. Are trades using contracts for difference (CFDs) subject to stamp duty or stamp duty reserve tax?
   Answer reference: Section 1.3.1

8. Provide at least one reason why a local custodian may be preferred by a client to a regional custodian.
   Answer reference: Section 1.4.3

9. When investors elect to have a nominee or custodian hold the registered title to securities that they own, how does it affect their right to the benefits of dividends and other corporate actions?
   Answer reference: Section 1.5.4

10. What is the difference between a repo and a tri-party repo?
    Answer reference: Section 2.2.7

Chapter Six
Securities Analysis

This syllabus area will provide approximately 6 of the 80 examination questions

6

1. Statements of Financial Position

1.1 Balance Sheets

Learning Objective

6.1.1 Understand the purpose, structure and relevance to investors of statements of financial position

1.1.1 Statement of Financial Position

A company's statement of financial position (balance sheet) is a snapshot of its overall financial position at a particular moment in time. The construction of the statement of financial position is underpinned by the accounting equation assets equals liabilities plus equity and its presentation is split into two halves that must always balance each other exactly. The key information that it provides to shareholders, customers and other interested parties is what the company owns (its assets), what the company owes to others (its liabilities or creditors) and the extent to which shareholders are providing finance to the company (the equity).

Note that the Revised Accounting Standards of the International Accounting Standards Board (IAS 1: The Presentation of Financial Statements) provide new terminology for the term balance sheet which is now the statement of financial position.

The statement of financial position should reflect all of the reporting company's assets and liabilities but, over the years, companies and their advisers often developed creative structures to enable items to remain off-balance sheet rather than on-balance sheet. The International Accounting Standards Board (IASB) and the adoption of its accounting standards should ensure that everything that should appear on the statement of financial position is categorised as such, and those items that are legitimately not assets or liabilities of the company should remain off-balance sheet (off the statement of financial position).

The typical format of a statement of financial position, with example figures, is provided on the next page for a fictitious company called XYZ plc. There will be further discussion of the actual performance of this company in this chapter and we shall look at separate entries on the statement of financial position, statement of profit and loss and statement of cash flows for XYZ plc. In sections 1.4, 1.5 and 1.6, we will examine certain financial ratios, using key information available in a company's financial statements, to facilitate financial ratio analysis which, in turn, provides useful guidance to investors when they are deciding where to allocate investment funds.

The statement of financial position of XYZ plc is drawn up as of 31 December 2018, which is in accordance with its **fiscal year**, ie, the annual period selected for its accounts. In the case of XYZ plc, the fiscal year also coincides with the calendar year, but this is not a necessary requirement as companies may elect a different annual period from the calendar year to use as their fiscal year.

XYZ plc Statement of Financial Position as at 31 December 2020		
All amounts are in £000s		
Assets		
Non-current assets		
Property, plant and equipment		8,900
Intangible assets		2,100
Investments		300
Total non-current assets		11,300
Current assets		
Inventories	3,600	
Accounts receivable	2,600	
Short-term investments	120	
Cash	860	
Total current assets		7,180
Total assets		18,480
Non-current liabilities		
Bank loans	1,780	
Finance leases	1,120	
Provisions for re-organisation	145	
Total non-current liabilities		−3,045
Current liabilities		
Accounts payable	5,140	
Finance lease current obligation	130	
Bank overdraft	1,080	
Tax	1,110	
Total current liabilities		−7,460
Net assets		7,975
Capital		
Share capital – 5 million £1 ordinary shares		5,000
Share capital – preference shares		890
Share premium account		330
Revaluation reserve		380
Retained earnings		1,375
Shareholders' funds		7,975

The statement of financial position is shown in a format prescribed by the Companies Acts for the statement of financial positions of plcs. Although not seen in the example, the format requires the previous year's comparative statement of financial position numbers to be set out alongside those of the current year, and for a numerical reference to be inserted in the notes column to support explanatory notes to the various statement of financial position items.

1.1.2 The Structure of a Statement of Financial Position

Assets

An asset is anything that is owned and controlled by the company and confers the right to future economic benefits. Statement of financial position assets are categorised as either non-current assets or current assets.

Non-current assets are those in long-term, continuing use by the company. They represent the major investments from which the company hopes to make money. Non-current assets are categorised as:

- tangible, or
- intangible.

A company's tangible non-current assets are those that have physical substance, such as land and buildings and plant and machinery. Tangible non-current assets are initially recorded in the statement of financial position at their actual cost or book value. However, in order to reflect the fact that the asset will generate benefits for the company over several accounting periods, not just in the accounting period in which it is purchased, all tangible non-current assets with a limited economic life are required to be depreciated. The concept of depreciation will be covered in more detail later in this section.

IAS 16 allows a choice of accounting. Under the cost model, the asset continues to be carried at cost. Under the alternative revaluation model the asset can be carried at a revalued amount, with revaluation required to be carried out at regular intervals.

Intangible non-current assets are those assets that, although without physical substance, can be separately identified and are capable of being sold. Ownership of an intangible non-current asset confers rights known as intellectual property. These rights give a company a competitive advantage over its peers and commonly include brand names, patents, trademarks, capitalised development costs and purchased goodwill.

Purchased goodwill arises when the consideration, or price, paid by an acquiring company for a target company exceeds the fair value of the target company's separable, or individually identifiable, net assets. This is not necessarily the same as the book, or statement of financial position, value of these net assets:

Purchased Goodwill =
(Price Paid for Company – Fair Value of Separable Net Tangible and Intangible Assets)

Purchased goodwill is capitalised and included in the statement of financial position. Once capitalised, it cannot be revalued.

Fixed-asset investments are typically long-term investments held in other companies. They are initially recorded in the statement of financial position at cost, and then subsequently revalued (or marked-to-market) at their fair value at each period end. Any gains or losses are reflected directly in the equity section of the statement of financial position and disclosed in the statement of changes in equity. However, if they suffer an impairment in value, then such a fall is charged to the statement of profit and loss.

If the shareholding represents at least 20% of the issued share capital of the company in which the investment is held, or if the investing company exercises significant influence over the management policies of the other, then the investing company is subject to additional reporting requirements.

Current assets are those assets purchased with the intention of resale or conversion into cash, usually within a 12-month period. They include stocks (or inventories) of finished goods and work in progress, the debtor balances that arise from the company providing its customers with credit (trade receivables) and any short-term investments held. Current assets also include cash balances held by the company and prepayments. Prepayments are simply when the company has prepaid an expense, as illustrated by the following example:

Example

ABC plc draws up its statement of financial position on 31 December each year. Just prior to the year end ABC pays £25,000 to its landlord for the next three months' rental on its offices (to the end of March in the next calendar year).

This £25,000 is not an expense for the current year – it represents a prepayment towards the following year's expenses and is, therefore, shown as a prepayment within current assets in ABC's statement of financial position.

Current assets are listed in the statement of financial position in ascending order of liquidity, and appear in the statement of financial position at the lower of cost or net realisable value (NRV).

Net Realisable Value (NRV)

NRV is defined as the estimated selling price of each stock item, less any further costs to be incurred in both bringing the stock, work in progress or raw materials into a saleable condition, including any associated selling and marketing costs.

Therefore, if for reasons such as obsolescence the NRV of the stock has fallen below cost, the item must be written down to this NRV for statement of financial position purposes.

Determining what constitutes cost should be relatively straightforward, unless the company purchases vast quantities of stock in different batches throughout its accounting period, making the identification of individual items or lines of stock particularly difficult when attempting to match sales against purchases.

In such instances, cost can be determined by making an assumption about the way stock flows through the business. Companies can account for their stock on one of three bases:

- **First in first out (FIFO)** – FIFO assumes that the stock first purchased by the business is the first to be sold. Therefore, the value of the closing stock at the end of the accounting period is given by the cost of the most recent stock purchased. This produces a closing stock figure in the statement of financial position that closely resembles the current market value of the stock. It also results in the highest reported profit figure of the three bases in times of rising prices.
- **Last in first out (LIFO)** – LIFO assumes that the most recent stock purchased by the company is the first to be sold. IAS 2 does not permit the use of LIFO since, in times of rising prices, the statement of financial position value of closing stock will be that of the stock first purchased and will therefore not resemble current prices. It also produces the lowest reported profit figure of the three bases.
- **Weighted average cost (WAC)** – WAC values closing stock at the weighted average cost of stock purchased throughout the accounting period. This method produces a closing stock figure and a reported profit between that of the FIFO and LIFO methods.

Depreciation and Amortisation

Depreciation is applied to tangible non-current assets, such as plant and machinery. An annual depreciation charge is made in the year's statement of profit and loss. The depreciation charge allocates the fall in the book value of the asset over its useful economic life. This requirement does not, however, apply to freehold land and non-current asset investments which, by not having a limited economic life, are not usually depreciated.

By reducing the book value of tangible non-current assets over their useful economic lives, depreciation matches the cost of the asset against the periods from which the company benefits from its use.

On occasion, tangible assets such as land are not depreciated but periodically revalued. This is done on the basis of providing the user of the accounts with a truer and fairer view of the assets, or capital, employed by the company. To preserve the accounting equation (total assets = equity + liabilities), the increase in the asset's value arising on revaluation is transferred to a revaluation reserve, which forms part of the equity.

Closely linked to the idea of depreciating the value of a tangible asset over its useful economic life is the potential need for intangible assets to be amortised over their useful economic lives. **Amortisation**, like depreciation, is simply a book entry whose impact is felt in the company's reported income and financial position but which does not impact its cash position.

Liabilities

A liability is an obligation to transfer future economic benefits as a result of past transactions or events; more simply, it could be described as money owed to someone else. Liabilities are categorised according to whether they are to be paid within, or after more than, one year.

Non-current liabilities comprise the company's borrowing not repayable within the next 12 months. This could include bond issues as well as longer-term bank borrowing. In addition, there is a separate sub-heading for those liabilities that have resulted from past events or transactions and for which there is an obligation to make a payment, but the exact amount or timing of the expenditure has yet to be established. These are commonly referred to as provisions. Provisions may arise as a result of the company undergoing a restructuring, for example.

Given the uncertainty surrounding the extent of such liabilities, companies are required to create a realistic and prudent estimate of the monetary amount of the obligation, once they are committed to taking a certain course of action. Current liabilities include the amount the company owes to its suppliers, or trade payables, as a result of buying goods and/or services on credit, any bank overdraft, and any other payables such as tax, that are due within 12 months of the statement of financial position.

Equity

Equity is referred to in a number of ways, such as shareholders' funds, owners' equity or capital. Equity usually consists of three sub-elements: share capital, capital reserves and revenue reserves. Additionally, when group accounts are presented, there may be minority interests within the group equity figure.

- **Authorised and issued share capital** – as a company is created, the share capital with which the company proposes to be registered, and the division of that share capital into shares of a fixed amount, is decided upon. This capital amount is known as the authorised share capital and acts as a ceiling on the amount of shares that can be issued, although it can subsequently be increased by the passing of an ordinary resolution at a company meeting. The issued share capital is the actual number of shares that are in issue at any point in time.
- **Share capital** – this is the nominal value of equity and preference share capital the company has in issue and has called up. This may differ from the amount of share capital the company is authorised to issue as contained in its constitutional documents. The company may have only called up some of its share capital and may not have issued all of the share capital that is authorised. Under the Companies Act 2006, the requirement to have an authorised share capital has been removed. Instead, directors can be authorised by the Articles or by a **resolution** to allot shares up to a maximum amount and for a limited period.
- **Capital reserves** – capital reserves include the revaluation reserve, share premium reserve and capital redemption reserve.
  - The **revaluation reserve** arises from the upward revaluation of tangible and intangible assets.
  - The **share premium reserve** arises from issuing shares at a price above their nominal value.
  - The **capital redemption reserve** is created when a company redeems, or buys back, its shares and makes a transfer from its revenue reserves to its capital reserves, equal to the nominal value of the shares redeemed.

  Capital reserves are not distributable to the company's shareholders as apart from forming part of the company's capital base, they represent unrealised profits, though they can be converted into a bonus issue of ordinary shares.
- **Retained earnings** – retained earnings is a revenue reserve and represents the accumulation of the company's distributable profits that have not been distributed to the company's shareholders as dividends, or transferred to a capital reserve, but have been retained in the business. Retained earnings should not be confused with the amount of cash the company holds, which is sometimes simply referred to as the notion that 'profit is not cash'.
- **Minority interests** – these arise when a parent company controls one or more subsidiary companies, but does not own all of the share capital. The equity attributable to the remaining shareholders is the minority interests and this is reflected in the statement of financial position.

In total, equity is the sum of the called-up share capital, all the capital reserves and the revenue reserves:

Equity = Share Capital + Reserves

1.1.3 The Relevance of the Statement of Financial Position to Investors

Prospective investors will make use of all of a company's accounts and financial statements to assess the viability of investing in a business. In addition, financial institutions such as commercial banks, credit ratings agencies and investment banks will also pay particular attention to a company's statement of financial position, in order to decide whether to provide working capital in the form of a revolving credit facility or overdraft, or when evaluating whether to facilitate the issuance of debt instruments such as debentures to finance expansion and other significant expenditures.

As part of the exercise of due diligence by any potential investor in a solicitation for loan stock or bonds by a company, the statement of financial position will be one of the key documents to assess the overall financial soundness of a potential purchase of such securities.

In addition to the specific information made available by a company's statement of financial position, IAS 1 requires companies to present a separate Statement of Changes in Equity (SOCE) as one of the components of financial statements. Companies are obliged to provide details of transactions with owners, showing separately contributions by and distributions to owners and changes in ownership interests in subsidiaries that do not result in a loss of control. For small- and medium-size enterprises (SMEs), the SOCE should show all changes in equity including:

- total comprehensive income
- owners' investments
- dividends
- owners' withdrawals of capital, and
- treasury share transactions.

A vital consideration for any investor or lender is the relative size of shareholders' equity compared to debt, as this provides insight about how a company is financing its operations. Large short-term liabilities, for example, increase a company's sensitivity to interest rate changes and also influence the credit rating which is granted to a company by a credit-rating agency. Credit-rating agencies will in fact be one of the principal users of corporate statement of financial position information, and the ratings which are provided to the investment community will have a major impact on to what extent the company is perceived as a credit risk and consequently the terms that need to be provided by the company (ie, the amount of the coupon payment) in a bond offering.

The assets portion of the statement of financial position can contain large amounts of intangible assets. Assets such as goodwill are also worth close examination by investors since, if they become disproportionate when compared to other current and long-term assets, this could be a warning that there are other issues which require closer attention.

The notes (or footnotes) to the statement of financial position and to the other financial statements are part of the financial statements. The notes inform the readers about such things as significant accounting policies, commitments made by the company, and potential liabilities and potential losses. The notes contain information that is critical to properly understanding and analysing a company's financial statements.

Some of the more pertinent details that an investor would want to examine in the notes to the financial statements are the following:

- Companies are required to disclose the accounting policies that have been used to present the company's financial condition and results. Disclosure of any items which are extraordinary will take on special significance. The comments will also provide insight into the quality of judgements of the key management team, including any specific comments from the managing director/chief executive officer as well as the chairman of the board.
- Footnotes will provide detailed information about the company's current and deferred income taxes.
- Footnotes need to disclose the company's pension plans and other retirement or post-employment benefit programmes. The notes contain specific information about the assets and costs of these programmes, and indicate whether the plans are adequately funded.
- The notes also contain information about stock options granted to officers and employees, including the method of accounting for stock-based compensation and the effect of the method on reported results.

All of these items, as well as the statement from the chairman of the board will be scrutinised carefully by the investment community to determine how willing they are to purchase securities from the issuer, and on what terms such securities should be offered.

Additionally, investors will want to examine the external auditor's report and any comments or qualifications to the financial statements, as these could, if they are not routine, be a warning that there may be deeper issues that require further investigation.

1.1.4 Trend Analysis

Financial ratios are examined in section 1.4 of this chapter. Ratios which measure liquidity, asset turnover and dividend cover are based upon quantitative information about a company which is found in its financial statements, including the statement of financial position.

Over and beyond ratio analysis, there is considerable benefit to be gained from what can be called trend analysis. In this case the current statement of financial position, for example, is compared to those for the preceding years, often five, with a view to establishing the trends of the data and to provide early indicators for investors to changes which might be a cause for concern.

One technique for examining trends is known as common-size analysis. Common-size analysis (also called vertical analysis) expresses each line item on a single year's statement of financial position as a percentage of one line item, which is referred to as a base amount. The base amount for the statement of financial position is usually total assets (which is the same number as total liabilities plus stockholders' equity) and for the statement of profit and loss it is usually net sales or revenues.

By comparing two or more years of common-size statements, changes in the mixture of assets, liabilities and equity become evident. On the statement of profit and loss (see section 1.2), changes in the mix of revenues and in the spending for different types of expenses can be identified.

The common-size statement is a valuable tool for identifying changes in the way in which assets employed are financed and the breakdown of the assets employed.

Statement of Financial Position Summary for XYZ plc					
	2016	2017	2018	2019	2020
	£000s	£000s	£000s	£000s	£000s
Assets					
Non-current assets	400	500	520	600	550
Current assets	420	460	530	660	650
Total	820	960	1,050	1,260	1,200
Financing					
Share capital	200	200	210	300	400
Capital reserves	120	130	160	200	220
Retained earnings	216	340	300	310	330
Loans	50	150	150	150	50
Current liabilities	234	140	230	300	200
Total	820	960	1,050	1,260	1,200

Figures used are for illustrative purposes only.

The table above shows a summary statement of financial position for XYZ plc as of five year-ends. It provides a high-level overview of the financial state of the company but the interpretation of the numbers in each column is facilitated by a comparison of each row of the table to the two base amounts of the total for each year of the assets and the total for each year of the liabilities. In this manner the breakdown or composition of the assets and liabilities and financing becomes more readily apparent.

For example, we can see that, in 2017, XYZ plc took an additional £100,000 loan, and that in 2020, the loan was paid back, essentially through the issue of new share capital. It can also be more clearly seen, in the common-size statement which is calculated from the previous table, and which follows, that the company is experiencing a steady decline in the ratio of non-current assets to the total assets throughout the period.

Common-Size Statement of Financial Position Summary for XYZ plc					
	2016	2017	2018	2019	2020
	Percentages				
Assets					
Non-current assets	49%	52%	50%	48%	46%
Current assets	51%	48%	50%	52%	54%
Total	100%	100%	100%	100%	100%
Financing					
Share capital	24%	21%	20%	24%	33%
Capital reserves	15%	14%	15%	16%	18%
Retained earnings	26%	35%	29%	25%	28%
Loans	6%	16%	14%	12%	4%
Current liabilities	29%	15%	22%	24%	17%
Total	100%	100%	100%	100%	100%

In 2016, the company's loan amount of £50,000 represented just 6% of its liabilities/financing, whereas after taking the loan of £100,000 in 2017, this ratio jumped to 16% of the company's liabilities. When the £100,000 of new shares were issued, and added to the share capital of the company in 2020, the proceeds were used to pay back the loan and the ratio of loans to total financings dropped back to 4%, indicating that the coverage has less leverage or gearing on its statement of financial position.

In summary, the trends that are discernible using the above approach will reveal what is happening beneath the surface of the day-to-day operations of a company. By performing such an analysis, it is possible to have much greater insight into a company's financial position than is accessible from consideration of just one year's statement of profit and loss, useful as that is.

1.2 Statement of Profit and Loss

Learning Objective

6.1.2 Understand the purpose, structure and relevance to investors of statements of profit and loss

1.2.1 The Purpose of a Statement of Profit and Loss

The statement of profit and loss (income statement) summarises the amount of income earned by a company, and the expenditure incurred by that company, over the accounting period. The purpose of the statement of profit and loss is to detail how much profit (or loss) has been earned as a result of the company's ongoing operations. As a result, the statement of profit and loss is often referred to as the profit and loss account. However, since the statement of profit and loss is constructed on an accruals basis, rather than a cash basis, profit must not be confused with the company's cash position.

In accordance with the statement of financial position, the format of the statement of profit and loss is governed by the Companies Acts and its construction is underpinned by accounting standards and industry best practice.

Additionally, IAS 1 has brought about changes to the statement of profit and loss. The amendment requires companies to present other comprehensive income items such as revaluation gains and losses, and actuarial gains and losses, as well as the usual statement of profit and loss items, on the face of the primary financial statements. IAS 1 allows this information to be presented either in one statement of comprehensive income or in two separate statements: a statement of profit and loss and a statement of comprehensive income.

The amount of profit earned over an accounting period has an impact on the company's ability to pay dividends and how much can be retained to finance the growth of the business from internal resources.

There are different ways of presenting a statement of profit and loss and there is no uniform agreement as to which is the preferred method. In essence the two-column approach, which is shown in the example statement of profit and loss for XYZ plc on the next page, is the most common format, although there are variations as to exactly the format followed.

In the following example, the statement shows the most recent set of results for fiscal year 2018 and alongside, for comparative purposes and to make the data more useful for investors who are looking at the underlying trends of the business (as discussed later in this section), the comparable figures for the year ending 2017 are shown. Also presented in this format are, for each line item, the percentage of the amount shown in relation to the total revenue or turnover of the business, which enables the reader to discern any notable shifts or changes in the broad categories of expenditures and other variables displayed.

Statement of Profit and Loss for XYZ plc as at 31 December 2020				
All figures are in £000s except per share earnings				
	2019	% of revenue	2020	% of revenue
Revenue	65,690		66,478	
Cost of sales	(46,310)		(47,375)	
Gross profit	19,380	30%	19,103	29%
Distribution costs	(8,090)	12%		13%
Administration	(7,800)	12%	(8,333)	12%
Loss on disposal of plant	(1,309)	2%	(7,956)	0%
Operating costs	(17,199)	26%	(16,289)	25%
Operating profit	2,181	3%	2,814	4%
Financial Income				
Income from affiliate	206		200	
Interest receivable	350		123	
Interest payable	(1,530)		(1,561)	
Profit before taxation	1,207	2%	1,577	2%
Taxation	(422)	35%	(522)	35%
Profit after taxation	785	1%	1,025	2%
Preference share dividends	(124)		(126)	
Profit attributable to the group	661		898	
Dividends				
Ordinary	349		356	
Earnings per share	13.21		17.97	
Dividend per share	6.98		7.12	

1.2.2 The Structure of a Statement of Profit and Loss

Revenue

The statement of profit and loss starts with one of the most important things in any company's accounts: its sales revenues. In accounts, sales revenues are generally referred to as revenue, or sometimes turnover. It is simply everything that the company has sold during the year, regardless of whether it has received the cash or not. For a manufacturer, revenue is the sales of the products that it has made. For a company in the service industry, it is the consulting fees earned or perhaps commissions earned on financial transactions.

Revenue is calculated on an accruals basis and represents sales generated over the accounting period regardless of whether cash has been received. However, since there are no prescriptive rules as to when revenue should be recognised in the profit and loss account, this leaves scope for subjective judgement.

IAS 18 prescribes the accounting treatment for revenue arising from certain types of transactions and events, essentially only allowing recognition of revenues when appropriate. Revenue is recognised in the statement of profit and loss when it meets the following criteria:

- It is probable that any future economic benefit associated with the item of revenue will flow to the company.
- The amount of revenue can be measured with reliability.

The IASB has published guidance on when revenue from the sale of goods, rendering of services and interest, royalties and dividends should be recognised.

Revenue arising from the sale of goods should be recognised when all of the following criteria have been satisfied:

- The seller has transferred to the buyer the significant risks and rewards of ownership.
- The seller retains neither continuing managerial involvement to the degree usually associated with ownership nor effective control over the goods sold.
- The amount of revenue can be measured reliably.
- It is probable that the economic benefits associated with the transaction will flow to the seller.
- The costs incurred or to be incurred in respect of the transaction can be measured reliably.

For revenue arising from the rendering of services, revenue should be recognised based on the stage of completion of the transaction, providing that all of the following criteria are met:

- The amount of revenue can be measured reliably.
- It is probable that the economic benefits will flow to the seller.
- The stage of completion at the statement of financial position date can be measured reliably.
- The costs incurred, or to be incurred, in respect of the transaction can be measured reliably.

When the criteria are not met, revenue should be recognised only to the extent of the expenses that are recoverable.

For interest, royalties and dividends, revenue should be recognised as follows:

- **Interest** – on a time proportion basis that takes into account the effective yield.
- **Royalties** – on an accruals basis.
- **Dividends** – when the shareholder's right to receive payment is established.

Cost of Sales

Cost of sales = [Opening stock (if any) + Purchases – Closing stock]

The cost of sales is arrived at by adding purchases of stock made during the accounting period, again by applying accruals rather than cash accounting, to the opening stock for the period, and deducting from this the value of the stock that remains in the business at the end of the accounting period.

The opening stock figure used in this calculation will necessarily be the same as the closing stock figure that appears in the current assets section of the statement of financial position from the previous accounting period.

Gross Profit

The gross profit figure is simply the revenue less the cost of sales.

Operating Profit

Operating profit is also referred to as profit on operating activities. It is the gross profit, less other operating expenses, that the company has incurred. These other operating expenses might include costs incurred distributing products (distribution costs) and administrative expenses such as management salaries, auditors' fees and legal fees. Administrative expenses also include depreciation and amortisation charges. Additional items may be separately disclosed before arriving at operating profit, such as the profit or loss made on selling a non-current asset. When a non-current asset, such as an item of machinery, is disposed of at a price significantly different from its statement of financial position value, the profit or loss when compared to this net book value (NBV) should be separately disclosed if material to the information conveyed by the accounts.

Operating profit is the profit before considering finance costs (interest) and any tax payable. It can be described as profit before interest and tax (PBIT).

Finance Costs/Finance Income

Finance costs are generally the interest that the company has incurred on its borrowings. That may be in the form of bonds or may be bank loans and overdrafts. Finance income is typically the interest earned on surplus funds, such as from deposit accounts.

Profit Before Tax

This is the profit made by the company in the period, before considering any tax that may be payable on that profit.

Corporation Tax Payable

This is simply the corporation tax charge that the company has incurred for the period.

Net Income

Net income is the company's total earnings or profit. In the UK it is also referred to as profit after tax.

It is calculated by taking the total revenues adjusted for the cost of business, interest, taxes, depreciation and other expenses. The net income is the profit that is attributable to the shareholders of the company and is stated before the deduction of any dividends because dividends are an appropriation of profit and are at the discretion of the company directors.

The net income is added to the retained earnings in the statement of financial position and disclosed within the statement of changes in equity. It is also within this statement that the dividends paid during the year are deducted from the retained earnings. As will be seen in section 1.3, dividends paid are also disclosed in the statement of cash flows.

Earnings Per Share (EPS)

EPS is one of the most important figures for investors and financial analysts and is reflected at the bottom of the statement of profit and loss, in pence. EPS is the amount of profit after tax that has been earned per ordinary share. EPS is calculated as follows:

$$\text{EPS} = \frac{\text{Net Income for the Financial Year}}{\text{Number of Ordinary Shares in Issue}}$$

Dividends

Some, or all, of the profit for the financial year can be distributed as dividends. Dividends to any preference shareholders are paid out first, followed by dividends to ordinary shareholders at an amount set by the board and expressed as a number of pence per share. The dividends for most listed companies are paid in two instalments: an interim dividend paid after the half-year stage and a final proposed dividend paid after the accounts have been approved. The dividends are shown in the accounts in a note that reconciles the movement in equity from one statement of financial position to another.

Provisions and Exceptional Items

IAS 37 details how provisions should be recognised and measured and requires that sufficient information is disclosed in the notes to the financial statements to enable users to understand their nature, timing and amount. The key principle is that a provision should be recognised only when there is a liability resulting from past events where payment is probable, and the amount can be estimated reliably.

IAS 1 does not actually use the term 'exceptional item'. However, the term is widely used in accounting. Essentially, the idea behind classifying an item as exceptional is to remove the distorting influence of any large one-off items on reported profit so that users of the accounts may establish trends in profitability between successive accounting periods and derive a true and fair view of the company's results.

IAS 1 acknowledges that, due to the effects of a company's various activities, transactions and other events that differ in frequency, potential for gain or loss and predictability, disclosing the components of financial performance assists in understanding that performance and making future projections. In other words, if an item is exceptional, it should be separately disclosed.

An exceptional item could be the profit made on selling a significant fixed asset or the loss on selling an unprofitable operation. These profits and losses only represent book profits and losses rather than actual cash profits and losses. We will return to this point when considering statements of cash flows in section 1.3.

Exceptional profits are added to, and exceptional losses deducted from, operating profit in arriving at the company's profit before taxation.

Capital Versus Revenue Expenditure

Money spent by a company will usually fall into one of two possible forms: capital expenditure or revenue expenditure.

Capital expenditure is money spent to buy non-current assets, such as plant, property and equipment. It is reflected on the statement of financial position. Revenue expenditure is money spent that immediately impacts the statement of profit and loss. Examples of revenue expenditure include wages paid to staff, rent paid on property, and professional fees, such as audit fees.

1.2.3   The Relevance of the Statement of Profit and Loss to Investors

For obvious reasons, a company's statement of profit and loss will be a main focus of attention to the investment community, as it directly reflects the performance level of the company from current operations. Moreover, analysis of the items in the statement of profit and loss reveals not only the size of a company's profit or losses, but also considerable details on the quality of its income and expenditures.

Investors will want to look closely at the breakdown of expenditures to see if there are signs that the company's management is overspending, especially in relation to previously released targets or forecasts from previous financial statements.

The gross profit margin, ie, the percentage of gross profit to turnover or total revenues, may provide further insights. A change that sees gross profit margin increase might be due to the company becoming dominant, enabling it to increase the sales price and/or decrease the prices it is paying its suppliers. A decrease in gross profit margin might arise because the company is facing increased competition and has been forced to lower its sales prices and/or pay more to its suppliers. Alternatively, it may be a strategic decision by the company to pursue market share.

The key figure which will be examined by investors and analysts is the EPS figure, as this will provide guidance to the marketplace as to the company's valuation. Analysts will want to see whether the company's EPS shows it to be performing in line with the applicable price/earnings (P/E) multiples for the sector in which the company operates, and, if not, one would want to understand the reasons for outperformance or underperformance. Detailed examination and analysis of the statement of profit and loss may reveal whether there are unusual or exceptional circumstances that would explain a higher or lower multiple than that which was expected from the company.

There are no absolute rules of reference for deciding how to evaluate a company's EPS. Rather the figure should be seen in the context of previous performance by the company. Companies have very different business models. Some companies are suppliers of merchandise to mass markets, while others occupy more specialised niches.

Some companies are keen to have a very large share of the available market in the product/service which they supply, and work on the principle of low margins and high volume. Other companies may prefer the converse model of having a high margin and relatively low volume. All of this needs to be taken into consideration when assessing a company's performance as revealed in its statement of profit and loss.

Different sectors of the marketplace will have different P/E multiples and it is not easy to compare company performances across different sectors. Also to be factored into the assessment is the fact that to a large extent all companies will have earnings and costs which will fluctuate depending on economic factors such as whether GDP is growing or contracting, on exchange rates, and in most general terms on the state of the economy.

1.2.4 Statement of Profit and Loss – Trend Analysis

In similar fashion to the approach used in consideration of the common-size technique for trend analysis of a company's statement of financial position, seen in section 1.1.4, a similar approach can be taken with respect to the statement of profit and loss. Key performance metrics are not considered in annual isolation but within the context of a broader time frame – perhaps five years, which is a widely used frame of reference in the investment world.

The table below provides some highlights from the statement of profit and loss of a company over a five-year period. The top line of the table reflects the gross revenues and shows that, in the period under consideration, the revenues doubled to the point where, for year-end 2020, the company had annual revenues of £1.6 million.

	2016	2017	2018	2019	2020
	£000s	£000s	£000s	£000s	£000s
Gross revenue	800	880	1040	1280	1600
Gross profit	140	170	200	210	240
Gross margin	18%	19%	19%	16%	15%
Profit before tax	130	160	180	200	220
Profit margin	16%	18%	17%	16%	14%
Dividends	4	5	6	7	10

The second line of the table indicates the monetary amount of gross profit being made in each year. Below that there is a percentage figure showing the gross margin achieved in each of the five years and, as can be seen, the company is in the somewhat concerning condition where, despite the impressive growth in top-line revenue, the amount of gross profit as a percentage of revenue is declining. From 2018 to 2020, for example, the gross margin has dropped from 19% to 15%.

A somewhat similar decline in an important ratio is seen in the line for the profit margin for the company (ie, profit before tax divided by revenues). The final line shows that the company has decided, not through any logic of necessity but circumstance, to boost its annual dividend to shareholders by 150% during the same period that its sales have doubled.

	2016	2017	2018	2019	2020
	£000s	£000s	£000s	£000s	£000s
Gross revenue	100	110	130	160	200
Gross profit	100	121	143	150	171
Gross margin	100	110	110	94	86
Profit before tax	100	123	138	154	169
Profit margin	100	112	107	96	85
Dividends	100	125	150	175	250

The table above provides a trend analysis for the previous set of data and makes it even easier to conduct a proper comparison of key parameters and track down areas of concern or merit. The 2016 levels for each of the six variables are used as the base amounts and an index value has been created for each of the subsequent years, with 2016 values set at an index value of 100.

It can be seen that the revenues have doubled and that the profit before tax has expanded by 69% (ie, from 100 to 169). It is also clear that the increase in the index level of gross profit has failed to match that seen on the top-line revenue.

One useful feature of the above way of presenting the data is that ratio values or percentages can themselves be expressed in terms of index values. The gross margin has in fact declined from 110 in 2017 to 86 in 2020, and the net profit margin has declined to 85% of what it was in 2016. Clearly the company is in a position where its expanding share of a market is leading to higher turnover but the underlying profitability is deteriorating, which would call for a detailed analysis of its cost structure and, in particular, its marginal costs. One final point is well demonstrated by the fact that the dividends have increased by 150%, which is above the rate of growth of turnover and considerably beyond the rate of growth in profitability.

Gross Revenue Growth	2016	2017	2018	2019	2020
A	100	110	130	160	200
B	100	140	200	220	250
Company		2017	2018	2019	2020
A		10.0%	18.2%	23.1%	25.0%
B		40.0%	42.9%	10.0%	13.6%

The table above focuses just on the revenue growth of two companies and uses a combination of the index-based approach discussed previously with a simple expression of the percentage change for each company.

Company A is the same company which was examined in more detail previously and the gross revenue index levels have been included from 2016 to 2020. Company B is another company where similar index values are available but we are not given access to the underlying data, so it may well be that the two firms are of quite different orders of magnitude. But for the purposes of trend analysis this can be overlooked by simply tracking the year-over-year percentage changes of each company.

The bottom two rows of the table above indicate the rates of growth of companies A and B from 2017 onwards. The 2016 figures are set aside since we are considering a progression from a starting year. What can be clearly seen from the percentage changes is that the rates of growth are very different. Company A is growing at an expanding rate, whereas company B is more erratic, and after two years of strong growth its rate of growth in the most recent two-year period is substantially slower.

1.3   Statement of Cash Flows

Learning Objective

6.1.3   Understand the purpose, structure and relevance to investors of statements of cash flows

1.3.1   The Purpose of the Statement of Cash Flows

A statement of cash flows (as it is now known in accordance with the IAS 1 Revised) is required by accounting standard IAS 7. The statement of cash flows is basically a summary of all the payments and receipts that have occurred over the course of the year, the total reflecting the inflow (or outflow) of cash over the year.

The principal features of a statement of cash flows, and the purposes behind it, are as follows:

- Removal of accruals, or amounts payable and receivable, from the income statement so that these amounts may be accounted for on a cash paid and received basis. The removal of accruals allows the actual cash available to a company at any point in time to be more precisely determined.
- Adjustment for statement of financial position items such as an increase in the value of a company's stock or accounts receivable (also often referred to as debtors) or a decrease in accounts payable (also often referred to a creditors), all of which increase reported profit but do not impact cash.
- Adding back non-cash items, such as depreciation charges, amortisation and book losses from the sale of fixed assets, while deducting book profits from fixed-asset disposals recorded in the statement of profit and loss, which impact recorded profit but not the company's cash position.
- Bringing in changes in statement of financial position items that impact the company's cash position, such as finance raised and repaid over the accounting period and fixed assets bought and sold. While these items are not readily accessible from an examination of a company's profit and loss accounts, the financial statement of cash flows may also contribute significantly to the company's current cash holdings.

Analysis of the statement of cash flows shows that it is important that a company generate positive cash flow at the operating level, otherwise it will become reliant upon fixed-asset sales and borrowing facilities to finance its day-to-day operations.

A company's survival and future prosperity is also dependent upon it replacing its fixed assets to remain competitive. However, these assets must be financed with capital of a similar duration to the economic life and payback pattern of the asset; otherwise the company will have insufficient funds to finance its operating activities. The statement of cash flows will also identify this.

1.3.2   The Structure of Statements of Cash Flows

IAS 7 regarding statement of cash flows requires a company's cash flows to be broken down into three particular headings:

1. **Operating cash flow** – operating activities is the cash that has been generated from the trading activities of the company, excluding financing cost (interest).

2. **Investment or enterprise cash flow** – investing activities details the investment income (dividends and interest) that has been received in the form of cash during the year and the cash paid to purchase new non-current assets less the cash received from the sale of non-current assets during the year.

3. **Financing cash flow** – financing activities includes the cash spent during the year on paying dividends to shareholders and the cash raised from issuing shares or borrowing on a long-term basis, less the cash spent repaying debt or buying back shares.

When all three sections of the statement of cash flows are consolidated, the resultant total should explain the changes in cash (and cash equivalents) between the statement of financial position.

In order to establish the cash generated from the operating activities figure in the statement of cash flows – essentially the company's operating cash flow – IAS 7 allows one of two alternative presentations on the face of the cash flow statement.

Of the two methods, the first is the direct method, where the cash received from customers and paid to suppliers and employees is shown. Alternatively, the indirect method is where reconciliation is shown between the company's other financial disclosures, primarily those found in the statement of financial position and the cash generated from operations in the statement of cash flows. This reconciliation requires the following adjustments to be made to the operating profit figure:

• Non-cash charges such as the depreciation of tangible fixed assets and the amortisation of intangible assets must be added back, as these do not represent an outflow of cash.
• Any increase in debtors or stock or decrease in short-term creditors over the accounting period must be subtracted, as these all increase reported profit but do not increase cash.
• Any decrease in debtors or stock or increase in short-term creditors over the accounting period must be added, as these all decrease reported profit but do not decrease cash.

Operating Statement of Cash Flows for XYZ plc for Year Ending 31 December 2020		
All figures are in £ sterling		
Net income after tax		240,000
Other additions to cash		
Depreciation and amortisation	35,000	
Decrease in accounts receivable	17,000	
Decrease in inventory		
Decrease in other current assets	19,000	
Increase in accounts payable	26,000	
Increase in accrued expenses		
Increase in other current liabilities		
Total additions to cash from operations		97,000
Subtractions from cash		
Increase in accounts receivable		
Increase in inventory	(33,000)	
Increase in other current assets		
Decrease in accounts payable		
Decrease in accrued expenses	(19,000)	
Decrease in other current liabilities	(23,000)	
Total subtractions from cash from operations	(75,000)	(75,000)
Total operating cash flow		262,000

Figures used are for illustrative purposes only.

The Structure of the Operating Statements of Cash Flows

The statement provided above shows an example of using the indirect method for preparing the operating statement of cash flows and each item will be explained briefly:

Additions to Cash

- **Depreciation and amortisation** – depreciation is not a cash expense; it is added back into net income for calculating cash flow.
- **Decrease in accounts receivable** – if accounts receivable decrease, more cash has entered the company from customers paying off their accounts – the amount by which accounts receivable has decreased is an addition to cash.
- **Decrease in inventory** – a decrease in inventory signals that a company has spent less money to purchase more raw materials. The decrease in the value of inventory is an addition to cash.
- **Decrease in other current assets** – similar reasoning to above for other current assets.

- **Increase in accounts payable** – if accounts payable increases it suggests more cash has been retained by the company through not paying some bills. The amount by which accounts payable has increased is an addition to cash.
- **Increase in accrued expenses** – for example deferring payment of some salaries will add to cash.
- **Increase in other current liabilities** – similar reasoning to above for increase in taxes payable.

Subtractions from Cash

- **Increase in accounts receivable** – if accounts receivable increases less cash has entered the company from customers paying their accounts. The amount by which accounts receivable has increased is a subtraction of cash.
- **Increase in inventory** – an increase in inventory signals that a company has spent more money to purchase more raw materials. If the inventory was paid with cash, the increase in the value of inventory is a subtraction of cash.
- **Increase in other current assets** – similar reasoning to above for other current assets.
- **Decrease in accounts payable** – if accounts payable decreases it suggests more cash has been used by the company to pay its bills. The amount by which accounts payable decreased is a subtraction from cash.
- **Decrease in accrued expense** – for example an increase in prepaid expenses results in a subtraction of cash.
- **Decrease in other current liabilities** – similar reasoning to above for decrease in taxes payable.

The simple formula to arrive at the total operating cash flow is:

Net income after tax

+ Total additions to cash from operations

– Total subtractions from cash from operations

The following table shows the additional items that are required in addition to the operating statement of cash flows and includes both the activities of investments, sometimes called the enterprise statement of cash flows, and the financing statement of cash flows.

Statement of Cash Flows for XYZ plc for Year Ending 31 December 2020		
All figures are in £ sterling		
Total Operating Cash Flow		262,000
Investment/Capital Expenditures		
Additions to cash from investments		
Decrease in fixed assets	150,000	
Decrease in notes receivable	12,000	
Decrease in securities investments		
Decrease in intangible non-current assets		
Total additions to cash from investments		162,000
Subtractions from cash for investments		
Increase in fixed assets		
Increase in notes receivable		
Increase in securities investments	−64,000	
Increase in intangible non-current assets	−250,000	
Total subtractions from cash for investments		(314,000)
Total enterprise cash flow		110,000
Financing Activities		
Additions to cash from financing		
Increase in borrowings		50,000
Increase capital stock		–
Total additions to cash from financing		50,000
Subtractions from cash for financing		
Decrease in borrowings		
Decrease in capital stock		–
Total subtractions from cash for financing		–
Total equity cash flow		160,000
Subtractions from Cash for Dividends		
Dividends paid		(100,000)
Total free cash flow		60,000
Cash at beginning of period		450,000
Cash at end of period		510,000

Figures used are for illustrative purposes only.

The Structure of the Investment or Enterprise Statement of Cash Flows

Here is a brief description of the net result to the cash position of a company from its investment and capital expenditures, or, as is it is sometimes referred to, especially in the US, the enterprise cash flow statement. The statement can be compiled by reference to the changes from year to year in the company's statement of financial position.

Additions to Cash from Investments

- **Decrease in fixed assets** – sale of a building will lead to an addition to cash.
- **Decrease in notes receivable** – a reduction in notes receivable indicates that cash will have been received.
- **Decrease in securities, investments** – securities will have been sold thereby raising cash.
- **Decrease in intangible, non-current assets** – sale of a patent or copyright will lead to an addition of cash.

Subtractions from Cash from Investments

- **Increase in fixed assets** – purchase of a building will lead to a subtraction from cash.
- **Increase in notes receivable** – an increase in notes receivable indicates that cash has not been received.
- **Increase in securities investments** – securities will have been purchased thereby reducing cash.
- **Increase in intangible non-current assets** – purchase of a copyright will lead to a reduction of cash.

The Structure of the Financing Activities Statement of Cash Flows

Additions to Cash from Financing

- **Increase in borrowings** – additional net borrowing will lead to an addition of cash.
- **Increase capital stock** – additional net equity capital paid in will lead to an addition of cash.

Subtractions from Cash for Financing

- **Decrease in borrowings** – net reduction in borrowing will lead to a subtraction of cash.
- **Decrease capital stock** – retirement of net equity capital paid in will lead to a subtraction of cash.
- **Subtractions from cash for dividends** – dividends paid out will lead to a subtraction of cash.

The final line of the table shows the total free cash flow for the company:

Total Free Cash Flow = Total Equity Cash Flow – Dividends Paid Out

1.3.3 The Relevance of the Statement of Cash Flows to Investors

As listed companies typically use accrual accounting, the statements of profit and loss released each quarter by a company will not necessarily reflect changes in their cash positions. If one has invested in a company, or is contemplating an investment, one of the crucial considerations will be whether the company has sufficient cash on hand to meet its obligations or whether it is likely to face a cash crunch in which it could be forced to sell assets under duress or have to seek emergency funding under disadvantageous conditions.

While a company may be earning a profit from an accounting perspective, it may, during the quarter, actually end up with less cash than when it started the quarter. Even profitable companies can fail to adequately manage their cash flow, which is why the statement of cash flows is vitally important; it helps investors see if a company is having trouble with its cash position.

Investors will use the statement of cash flows in a variety of ways:

- Cash from operating activities is compared to the company's net income. If the cash from operating activities is consistently greater than the net income, the company's net income or earnings are said to be of a high quality. If the cash from operating activities is less than net income, a warning to investors should be raised as to why the reported net income is not turning into cash.
- Many investors have the view that cash is king. If a company is consistently generating more cash than it is using, the company could increase its dividend, buy back some of its stock, reduce its debt or acquire another company. All of these are perceived to be good for shareholder value. On the contrary, if a company is lacking cash and faces momentary bouts of illiquidity, then there may eventually be questions raised as to its ability to survive and its solvency.
- The methods of common sizing discussed in the previous two sections can also be applied to a company's statement of cash flows. For example, the financing activities revealed in the financing statement of cash flows can throw further light on the gearing position of the company, as all of the financing debits and credits to the cash account will be viewable in one place.

In summary, the casualties of a recession, such as that seen during 2020, are not always easy to identify ahead of time and may not be readily discernible from financial statements. Many economists and analysts have suggested that in the last quarter of 2008 it was as if the world economy fell off a cliff. The track record for investment analysts in anticipating the demise of institutions such as major banks, insurance companies and large manufacturers, even from a detailed perusal of financial statements has historically not been very good.

The most common malaise for business failures, both during a recession and in more normal economic circumstances, is the inability of firms to realise cash from operations to meet their unavoidable obligations. Liquidity in the capital markets, in the most general and systemic sense of the term and not just in the more literal sense of immediate access to raise cash, is at its lowest when it is most needed.

1.4 Financial Ratios

Learning Objective

6.1.4 Be able to analyse securities using the following financial ratios: liquidity; asset turnover; gearing

1.4.1 Liquidity Ratios

Financial analysts often distinguish between solvency and liquidity. In essence, the solvency of a company relates to its long-term position with respect to its assets and liabilities, and its commitments to finance its statement of financial position. Liquidity issues are more concerned with the short-term operating issues of a business and concern its ability to meet its ongoing cash requirements.

Liquidity ratios aim to establish the following:

- Does a company have the resources to meet its operating requirements from its working capital on a timely basis?
- Can a company actually realise those resources quickly enough? In other words, does it have sufficient ability to raise cash when required, to pay off the liabilities as they fall due?

Liquidity ratios are relatively simple tools and arguably lack real sophistication, but they are useful for showing trends and are frequently used in loan agreements.

Working Capital Ratio or Current Ratio

The purpose of the working capital ratio or current ratio is to determine if the current assets recoverable within one year are sufficient to cover the liabilities that fall due within one year.

Current assets normally refers to those assets that are recoverable within one year. However, it could be the case that some receivables are recoverable after more than one year. This fact would then have to be noted in the company's accounts.

$$\text{Current ratio} = \frac{\text{Current assets}}{\text{Current liabilities}}$$

This ratio indicates whether a company has enough short-term assets to cover its short-term debt. Anything below 1.0 indicates negative working capital. Anything over 2.0 means that the company is not investing excess assets in the most productive and yield-generating fashion. Most analysts believe that a ratio between 1.2 and 2.0 is desirable. However, the circumstances of every business vary and one should consider how different businesses operate before making a judgement about what should be an appropriate benchmark ratio.

A stronger ratio indicates a better ability to meet ongoing and unexpected bills, thereby taking the pressure off cash flow. Being in a liquid position can also have advantages such as being able to negotiate cash discounts with suppliers.

A weaker ratio may indicate that the business is having greater difficulties meeting its short-term commitments and that additional working capital support is required. Having to pay bills before payments are received may be the issue, in which case an overdraft could assist. Alternatively, building up a reserve of cash investments may create a sound working capital buffer. Some practical problems arise when calculating or using the current ratio:

- Overdrafts will be included within current liabilities but in practice are frequently payable after more than one year. Banks often allow companies to extend overdrafts for several years.
- Although inventory is contained within current assets on the statement of financial position of a company and is therefore assumed to be convertible into cash within one year this may not necessarily be the case. In periods of recession there may be no easy way to obtain liquidity from inventory other than through a sale at very distressed prices.
- The ratio fails to take into account the timing of cash flows within the period. It might be the case that all the liabilities are payable in very short order, whereas many of the assets are only recoverable in 12 months' time.

- The ratio is static in that it reflects values at a point in time, ie, when the statement of financial position was drawn up. It is possible for a company to 'window dress' its accounts on that date so that its ability to meet its obligations is seen in the most favourable light.

In order to alleviate the criticism that the current ratio is static a modified form of the ratio is often advised. The working capital turnover ratio is also referred to as the net sales to working capital. It indicates a company's effectiveness in using its working capital.

Working capital turnover ratio is calculated as follows:

$$\text{Working capital turnover ratio} = \frac{\text{Net annual sales}}{\text{Average amount of working capital during the same 12-month period}}$$

For example, if a company's net sales for the year 2019 were £2,400,000, and its average amount of working capital during 2020 was £400,000, its working capital turnover ratio was:

$$\frac{£2,400,000}{£400,000} = 6.0$$

Note that working capital itself is defined as the total amount of current assets minus the total amount of current liabilities. As indicated above, you should use the average amount of working capital for the year of the net sales. As with most financial ratios, you should compare the working capital turnover ratio to other companies in the same industry and to the same company's past and planned working capital turnover ratio.

1.4.2 Quick Ratio or Acid Test Ratio

The quick ratio is an adaptation of the current ratio designed to remove the problem of inventory and is alternatively called the acid test ratio or liquid ratio. The term 'acid test' comes from the way gold miners would test whether their findings were real gold nuggets. Unlike other metals, gold does not corrode in acid; if the nugget did not dissolve when submerged in acid, it was said to have 'passed the acid test'. If a company's financial statements pass the figurative acid test, this is indicative of its financial well-being.

$$\text{Acid Test Ratio} = \frac{\text{Current Assets} - \text{Inventory}}{\text{Current Liabilities}}$$

The acid test measures the ability of a company to use its near-cash or 'quick' assets to immediately extinguish or retire its current liabilities. Quick assets include those current assets that can be quickly converted to cash at close to their book values.

An alternative formulation for the ratio can be expressed more specifically as follows:

$$\text{Acid Test Ratio} = \frac{\text{Cash} + \text{Marketable Securities} + \text{Accounts Receivable}}{\text{Current Liabilities}}$$

The acid test ratio, since it excludes the value of inventory, is therefore a more stringent test than the working capital ratio. It indicates whether a firm has enough short-term assets to cover its immediate liabilities without selling inventory.

Generally, the acid test ratio should be 1:1 or better; however, this varies widely by industry. If a company has a ratio of less than 1, this does not necessarily mean that it is insolvent and unable to pay off its liabilities. Depending on the type of business, however, it may be a sign of liquidity problems.

One useful metric to look for is to see if the acid test ratio is much lower than the working capital ratio. If this is the case it means that current assets are highly dependent on inventory. Retail stores are examples of this type of business, which also helps to explain why many retailers fall victim to recessions.

1.4.3 Gearing Ratios

Financial analysts are keen to examine the gearing ratios for businesses as they consider the capital structure of a company and the relationship between its borrowings and shareholders' funds, which are not an immediate obligation of a company.

The use of gearing or financial leverage is found in many businesses and, in particular, the financial services sector. For obvious reasons, a very high level of gearing can bring with it much greater levels of financial risk.

The simplest and most direct way to think about gearing and leverage is in relation to the position of a house purchaser, who makes a down-payment to purchase a home from their own savings and then borrows (or finances) the rest of the purchase from a mortgage lender.

Example

An individual buys a £100,000 house with a £75,000 mortgage and £25,000 of their own cash. Let us examine the impact of the change in home prices under two different possible scenarios:

- The house price has doubled – a 100% increase. The individual has made a money gain of £175,000 on what was effectively a £25,000 investment. Even though the purchaser will have been responsible for other cash outlays, to keep matters simple the return would be £175,000/£25,000, ie, a 700% return.
- The house price has halved – a 50% decrease. With the house now only worth £50,000 the individual has lost £50,000 on their £25,000 investment which equates to a 200% loss.

The scale of the gains and losses for the purchaser of property with a standard mortgage which involves relatively modest gearing can be substantial. It is not difficult to see how much more drastic the amplification of gains and losses will be with much smaller down-payments and much larger mortgages, which of course leads to much greater gearing.

Operational Gearing

Operational gearing is a measure of operational risk, ie, risk to the operating profit figure. It assesses the levels of variable and fixed operating costs in the business.

- **Variable costs** are costs whose level varies directly with the level of output, eg, raw material costs. Hence if sales increase or decrease then variable costs increase/decrease.
- **Fixed costs** are costs whose level remains constant regardless of output levels, eg, rent, rates, depreciation.

The greater the level of fixed costs in the business, the greater the variation in the profit figure as a result of revenue changes.

In the table below, there are two companies which have very similar characteristics, except that Company A has fixed costs of £30,000 and Company B has fixed costs of £50,000. Both companies are operating at a level of 10,000 units of output per year and both have the same sales revenue per unit, ie, price of their product, and both have variable costs of £11 per unit.

Gearing		Company A	Company B
Output (units)		10,000	10,000
Sales revenue (per unit)	£20	£200,000	£200,000
Variable costs (per unit)	£11	−£110,000	−£110,000
Contribution	£9	£90,000	£90,000
Fixed costs		−£30,000	−£50,000
Profit before tax		£60,000	£40,000
Operational gearing ratio		1.50	2.25

The difference between the unit revenue and the unit variable cost is £9 and is known as the contribution. This is the amount that the company has to pay towards or contribute to paying for its fixed costs before it is able to determine its profit before tax.

Company A with a lower fixed cost is able to have a profit of £60,000 whereas B, which has higher fixed costs, is able to have a profit before tax of £40,000. The operational gearing ratio is determined for Company A from the formula provided above as (£200,000 − £110,000)/£60,000 = 1.5, whereas for Company B the values are (£200,000 − £110,000)/£40,000 = 2.25.

Company B, with relatively higher fixed costs compared to Company A, is said to have high operational gearing. In general terms, a company where the fixed costs are higher as a percentage of total costs will experience a higher operational gearing ratio. One of the consequences of the gearing ratio is that a company with a higher gearing ratio will see greater sensitivity in its profit ratio to sales in the case of changes in the level of output and overall revenue.

Adjusting Output for Company A		75%	100%	125%
Output (units)		7,500	10,000	12,500
Sales revenue (per unit)	£20	£150,000	£200,000	£250,000
Variable costs (per unit)	£11	−£82,500	−£110,000	−£137,500
Contribution	£9	£67,500	£90,000	£112,500
Fixed costs	−£30,000	−£30,000	−£30,000	−£30,000
Profit before tax		£37,500	£60,000	£82,500
Operational gearing ratio	1.50			
Ratio of profit to normal output		0.625	1.000	1.375

In the table above, it can be seen that the output level for Company A has been decreased by 25% (ie, the 75% level from the previous normal output level of 10,000 units remains at the previous level and then is increased by 25%).

The effect of the operational gearing ratio can be translated into the effect on the profit before tax, as shown by the fact that, for the 7,500 units of output, the profit is reduced by the percentage reduction in output multiplied by the gearing ratio, ie, −25% x 1.5 = −37.5%, and for an increase in output of 25% the profit is increased by +25% x 1.5 = +37.5%.

Adjusting Output for Company B		75%	100%	125%
Output (units)		7,500	10 000	12,500
Sales revenue (per unit)	£20	£150,000	£200,000	£250,000
Variable costs (per unit)	£11	−£82,500	−£110,000	−£137,500
Contribution	£9	£67,500	£90,000	£112,500
Fixed costs	−£50,000	−£50,000	−£50,000	−£50,000
Profit before tax		£17,500	£40,000	£62,500
Operational gearing ratio	2.25			
Ratio of profit to normal output		0.438	1.000	1.563

As can be seen in the table above, for Company B, with the higher gearing ratio, the changes to profit resulting from scaling the output up and down are more severe, with a ±56.3% change to the normal profit level from the scaling.

In order to apply this technique, one will be required to have a detailed knowledge of the company's cost structure and to be able to correctly delineate fixed and variable costs. This information is not usually included in the published company accounts. It may be possible to break these down from a more detailed examination of the statement of profit and loss.

Operational gearing is a key factor to consider in evaluating a business and its sensitivity to changes in demand for its products. Businesses with high contribution levels will generally be more robust in being able to withstand declines in their demand and output, and capital-intensive businesses will also have relatively high fixed costs due to the depreciation of their non-current assets.

1.5 Profitability Ratios

Learning Objective

6.1.5 Be able to analyse securities using the following profitability ratios: net profit margin; operating profit margin; equity multiplier; return on capital employed

1.5.1 Gross, Net and Operating Profit Margins

Profitability ratios look at the percentage return that the company generates relative to its revenues.

The gross profit looks at the percentage of revenues that the company earns after considering just the costs of sales. In accounting terminology, cost of sales is sometimes referred to as cost of goods sold.

The operating profit margin and net profit margin look at the percentage of revenues that the company earns after considering cost of sales and other operating costs (such as distribution costs and administrative expenses). Clearly, all other things being equal, a greater profit margin is preferable to a lesser profit margin. Operating margin will take into account a wider range of variable costs, such as wages, and while it does not include interest charges, net profit margin does.

The figures for the profitability ratios are drawn from the statement of profit and loss. The formulae for the profitability ratios are:

Gross profit margin (%) = (Gross profit/revenues) x 100

Operating profit margin (%) = (Operating profit/revenues) x 100

Net profit margin (%) = (Net profit less interest/revenues) x 100

1.5.2 Equity Multiplier

The equity multiplier is a measure of financial gearing or leverage for a business; indeed, it is sometimes known as the financial leverage ratio.

The method of calculating the ratio is simply equal to:

$$\frac{\text{Total assets}}{\text{Total equity (ie, shareholders' funds)}}$$

The numerator of the above ratio is the sum of the total assets of an enterprise and will be equivalent to the addition of all of the debt on the statement of financial position plus the total equity. The denominator will be equivalent to the total equity – in other words, the shareholders' funds. The denominator of the ratio is thus confined to equity, and it is the numerator which will capture any debt financing.

The higher the ratio, the more the enterprise is relying on debt instruments such as bonds and/or loans in order to finance and run the day-to-day operations of the business. The lower the ratio, the less the enterprise is relying on such debt to finance its operations. In the limiting case when the enterprise has no debt financing, the ratio would be equal to 1.0. When there is debt financing within a business, the ratio will be greater than 1.0 and will provide an indication of leverage, with higher values suggesting that the company is more highly geared or leveraged.

To the extent that the ratio is higher than would be customarily found for similar companies within specific market sectors, this will indicate increased risk that the company might encounter difficulties in servicing the obligations to its debt holders.

1.5.3   Return on Capital Employed (ROCE)

This is widely seen as the best ratio for measuring overall management performance, in relation to the capital that has been paid into the business.

The amount of capital employed is the equity plus the long-term debt. This is the money that the company holds from shareholders and debt providers, and it is from this money that the management should be able to generate profits. Effectively, the ROCE gives a yield for the entire company. It compares the money invested in the company with the generated return. This annual return can then be compared to other companies, or to less risky investments.

In summary, the key features of ROCE are:

- It looks at what returns have been generated from the total capital employed in a company including debt as well as equity.
- It expresses the income generated by the company's activities as a percentage of its total capital.
- This percentage result can then be used to compare the returns generated to the cost of borrowing, establish trends across accounting periods and make comparisons with other companies.

The simple formula for ROCE is as follows:

$$ROCE = \frac{\text{Profit before Interest and Tax}}{\text{Capital Employed}} \times 100 = x\%$$

The component parts of capital employed are shown below in an expanded version of the formula:

$$ROCE = \frac{\text{Profit Before Interest and Tax}}{\text{Equity + Long-term liabilities + Short-term interest bearing liabilities}} \times 100 = x\%$$

The capital employed should include the short-term interest bearing borrowings that the company has in its statement of financial position, as well as the long-term liabilities. This is because borrowing, for example, in the form of a bond issue, will eventually become payable in less than one year, and will be classified as a current liability before it is repaid. If this borrowing was not included in capital employed when it became short term, this would fail to reflect the reality of the company's debts. The short-term nature of the liability is simply a temporary phenomenon; after all, to repay the short-term borrowing, the company will probably need to issue a new bond that will be classified as a long-term liability in the statement of financial position.

It should be noted that the result can be distorted in the following circumstances:

- **The raising of new finance at the end of the accounting period**, as this will increase the capital employed but will not affect the profit figure used in the equation.
- **The revaluation of fixed assets during the accounting period**, as this will increase the amount of capital employed, while also reducing the reported profit by increasing the depreciation charge.
- **The acquisition of a subsidiary at the end of the accounting period**, as the capital employed will increase but there will not be any post-acquisition profits from the subsidiary to bring into the consolidated profit and loss account.

1.5.4   Net Asset Turnover and Profitability

Net asset turnover looks at the relationship between sales and the capital employed in a business describing how efficiently a company generates sales by looking at how hard the assets are working.

The relationship between ROCE and net asset turnover is shown in the following example.

Example

XYZ plc has annual sales of £5 million, a trading profit of £1.5 million and the following items on its statement of financial position:

Share Capital:	£1.0m
Reserves:	£5.0m
Loans:	£1.0m
Overdraft:	£0.5m

The ROCE and net asset turnover can be calculated as follows:

$$\text{ROCE} = \frac{\text{Profit Before Interest and Tax}}{\text{Capital Employed}} = \frac{£1.5m}{£1m + £5m + £1m + £0.5m} \text{ X } 100 = 20\%$$

$$\text{Net Asset Turnover} = \frac{\text{Turnover (Sales)}}{\text{Capital Employed}} = \frac{£5m}{£7.5m} = 0.66 \text{ times}$$

1.6 Investor Ratios

Learning Objective

6.1.6   Be able to analyse securities using the following investor ratios: earnings per share; price/ earnings (both historic and prospective); dividend yield; dividend cover; interest cover

1.6.1 Earnings Per Share (EPS)

The earnings per share (EPS) ratio is one of the most useful and often-cited ratios used in the investment world. It is used universally and more or less has the same meaning in most jurisdictions but is one ratio for which there are prescribed rules in the UK regarding its calculation. These are laid out in IAS 33, which basically defines the EPS as follows:

$$EPS = \frac{\text{Net Profit or Loss Attributable to Ordinary Shareholders}}{\text{Average Weighted Number of Ordinary Shares Outstanding in Period}}$$

Example

Let us suppose that we can determine from the financial statements of XYZ plc that the net profit attributable to the group (which is after the deduction of preference share dividends) was £898,000 in 2020, and the number of ordinary shares outstanding during the period was five million.
It is straightforward to calculate that the EPS for 2020 is equal to 18p.

The EPS ratio is expressed in pence and reveals how much profit was made during the year that is available to be paid out to each shareholder.

As such a useful figure for investors, earnings are often divided into the current share price to assess how many times the EPS must be paid to buy a share – in effect, how expensive (or cheap) those shares are. This is called the price/earnings (P/E) ratio, and it measures how highly investors value a company as a multiple of its profits. While this ratio is very widely used, and is discussed in the next section, there are alternative measures which some analysts prefer and consider as more satisfactory for making comparisons with regard to profitability and in the process of corporate valuation.

One such ratio is known as the EV/EBITDA ratio, for which the numerator, EV, represents the enterprise value or the market value of a company's debt plus the market value of its equity. The denominator of the ratio represents a value known as EBITDA, which is an acronym for earnings before interest, tax, depreciation and amortisation.

Some would argue that EBITDA is a preferable metric for a company's earnings than simply earnings before interest and tax (EBIT), which is used in the more straightforward calculation of the P/E ratio. However, others would contend that EBITDA is a non-GAAP measure which allows too much discretion in what is included and excluded in the calculation.

As with all financial analysis, it is important to know what basis has been used for determining profitability or valuation for two companies when drawing any comparative conclusions. There are several variations on the basic theme of the earnings per share ratio, for example to include expected growth multiples, but the plain vanilla version from which they derive is EPS.

The metric is so widely followed that market analysts will use, for example, the EPS of the FTSE 100 or the Standard & Poor's 500 Index in the US (S&P 500) as a critical variable in determining whether stock markets are fairly priced, overpriced or underpriced in comparison to historical norms.

1.6.2 Price/Earnings Ratio

There are various P/E ratios: historic, sometimes referred to as 'trailing', and also prospective or forward P/Es. The simple general purpose formula, as mentioned above, is:

$$\text{P/E Ratio} = \frac{\text{Price per share}}{\text{Annual earnings per share}}$$

In the equation above, the price per share in the numerator is the market price of a single share of the stock. The earnings per share, shown in the denominator of the formula, depends on the type of P/E under consideration – whether historic or forward-looking.

- **Trailing P/E (also referred to as P/E)** – earnings per share is the net income of the company for the most recent 12-month period, divided by number of shares outstanding. This is the most common meaning of 'P/E' if no other qualifier is specified. Four quarterly earnings reports are used and earnings per share is updated quarterly. Note, companies individually choose their financial year so the schedule of updates will vary.
- **Trailing P/E from continued operations** – instead of net income, this version of the P/E ratio uses operating earnings, which exclude earnings from discontinued operations, extraordinary items (eg, one-off windfalls and write-downs) or accounting changes.
- **Forward P/E or estimated P/E** – instead of net income from historic earnings (ie, those already achieved), this version of the P/E ratio uses estimated net earnings over the next 12 months. Estimates are typically derived as the mean of a select group of analysts. In times of rapid economic dislocation, such estimates become less relevant as new economic data is published and/or the basis of the analysts' forecasts becomes obsolete, and they may quickly adjust their forecasts.

The P/E ratio can alternatively be calculated by dividing the company's market capitalisation by its total annual earnings. For example, if the stock of XYZ plc is trading at £2.50 and the earnings per share for the most recent 12-month period is 18p, then XYZ's stock has a P/E ratio of 13.9.

Expressed in different terms, a purchaser of XYZ's stock is paying almost £14 for every pound of earnings. Companies with losses (negative earnings) or no profit have an undefined P/E ratio (usually shown as not applicable or N/A); sometimes, however, a negative P/E ratio may be shown.

By comparing price and earnings per share for a company, one can analyse the market's stock valuation of a company and its shares relative to the income the company is actually generating. Stocks with higher (and/or more certain) forecast earnings growth will usually have a higher P/E, and those expected to have lower (and/or riskier) earnings growth will in most cases have a lower P/E. Investors can, therefore, use the P/E ratio to compare the value of stocks.

If one stock has a P/E twice that of another stock, all things being equal (especially the earnings growth rate), it is a less attractive investment. Companies are rarely equal, however, and comparisons between industries, companies and time periods may be misleading. See section 1.7.

According to research conducted by Professor Robert Shiller, who is the Arthur M. Okun Professor of Economics Yale University, the average P/E ratio, since 1900, for the S&P 500 Index has ranged from 4.78 in December 1920 to 44.20 in December 1999, with an arithmetic mean of 16.36 and a median of 15.73.

The average P/E of the market varies in relation with, among other factors, expected growth of earnings, expected stability of earnings, expected inflation and yields of competing investments. Another important benchmark for comparing P/E ratios historically for the broad market is in comparison to the risk-free rate of return, ie, the return from three-month Treasury bills. The argument is often made by financial analysts that the lower the risk-free rate of return, the higher the P/E multiple should be, which given the unusually low interest rates prevailing globally in 2020 might suggest that there is actually no overvaluation of the S&P 500. But this is debatable, and the problem with all such valuation benchmarks is that they cannot anticipate the manner in which market prices will develop in response to uncertain future events.

1.6.3 Dividend Yield

The **dividend yield** of an ordinary share is calculated as follows:

$$\text{Dividend Yield} = \frac{\text{Dividend per Share}}{\text{Current Market Price per Share}}$$

In the case of XYZ plc, let us suppose that the dividend paid for each ordinary share in 2020 was 7p. Assuming the share price, as before, to be £2.50, the dividend yield is £0.07/£2.50 = 2.8%.

Long-term investors in equities will be much influenced by the dividends paid out by a company, as this is a vital part of the total return from holding equities. The income stream from ordinary shares via the payment of dividends, however, cannot be relied upon in the way in which the dividend income from either a bond or preferred stock can be. Alternatively, a higher dividend yield could be indicative of a company with strong cash flows and/or low capital expenditure, whereby excess cash is paid out to investors.

An issuer of a bond or preferred share is obliged to pay the dividend or coupon payment specified in the offering prospectus, whereas the decision as to whether to pay a dividend, and, if so, how much, is entirely at the discretion of the board of directors of the company. As an ordinary shareholder one is not guaranteed that there will be a dividend at all, nor is there a specific amount that can be relied upon for companies that have historically paid dividends. During the economic downturn of 2007–08, many companies abandoned the payment of dividends completely or reduced the amounts paid substantially.

It is also worth mentioning that many new companies and companies that are still at the stage of rapid growth may decide not to pay a dividend, as their shareholders might feel that the funds paid out in dividends could be better invested in further growth of the business through retained earnings.

There is not an obvious relationship between the dividend yield and the perception of the company in the marketplace. A high dividend yield could arise because a company has elected to pay a high dividend amount per share or it could also arise, as is often the case, because the shares are currently valued by the market at a low multiple to earnings and dividends. This could be because investors are risk-averse or believe that the market prospects in general are unfavourable.

In more general terms, the case could be made that, if investors believe a company has good growth prospects and is attractive this will tend to increase the share price and reduce the yield. From this perspective, there is also some value in the observation that companies with high P/E ratios tend to have low dividend yields and vice versa.

1.6.4 Dividend/Interest Cover

Dividend cover attempts to assess the likelihood of the existing dividend being maintained.

$$\text{Dividend cover} = \frac{\text{Earnings per share}}{\text{Dividend per share}}$$

From the statement of profit and loss of XYZ plc in 2020, it can be seen that the earnings per share were 18p and the dividend per share was 7p, which means that the dividend cover was: £0.18 ÷ £0.07 = 2.6 times. An unusually high dividend cover implies that the company is retaining the majority of its earnings, presumably with the intention of reinvesting to generate growth. As suggested, this is often true for companies which are still in a high growth phase, rather than more mature companies, which are sometimes referred to as cash cows.

Generally speaking, a ratio of two times or higher is considered safe – in the sense that the company can well afford the dividend – and for a ratio lower than 1.5 there has to be some question as to how sustainable the current dividend may be. If the ratio is lower than 1, the company is using its retained earnings from a previous year to pay this year's dividend and this is a cause for investor concern. The company is then said to be paying an uncovered dividend.

In a similar way to dividend cover, the interest coverage ratio is used to calculate how likely it is that a company can pay interest on its outstanding debt.

The interest coverage ratio is calculated by dividing the company's Earnings Before Interest and Taxes (EBIT) by the due interest.

$$\text{Interest Coverage Ratio} = \frac{\text{EBIT}}{\text{Interest Expense}}$$

If the ratio is 1.5 or less, the company's ability to meet interest expenses may be in doubt.

1.7 Performing Financial Analysis

Learning Objective

6.1.7 Understand the main advantages and challenges of performing financial analysis: comparing companies in different countries and sectors; comparing different companies within the same sector; over-reliance on historical information; benefits and limitations of relying on third-party research; comparing companies that use different accounting standards

1.7.1 The Benefits and Limitations of Financial Analysis

Financial analysis of a company's accounting statements and the use of a wide array of financial ratios bring to light useful and insightful ways to understand how a business works, whether it is working well and how it compares it with its peers and competitors. The kind of analysis that has been examined is the daily preoccupation of many analysts employed in the financial services whose role it is to advise companies and investors, potential or current, on the manner in which a company is operating.

Company owners and managers can benefit greatly from using these techniques to understand better their performance and how it might be improved. As most companies will be keen to show their performance to the financial community in the best possible light, there is often considerable effort employed to ensure that the ratios and metrics displayed will not disappoint investors.

The principal ratios used in financial analysis are concerned with liquidity, gearing and profitability, but there are other, more esoteric ones as well. It should be said that there is often a rather loose definition attached to some of the components that should be included in the calculation of the ratios and they can also vary from one jurisdiction to another.

The mechanics for calculating dividend cover, for example, and dilution for EPS, can vary from one side of the Atlantic to the other. Hardly any financial ratios have exact definitions, and are therefore susceptible to different methods of calculation and interpretation. For example, analysts will have quite different opinions on what ROCE exactly measures. To some extent it depends on how the analyst calculated the value and, for example, whether or not it was decided to include bank overdrafts.

Notwithstanding the methodological inexactitude, financial ratios are a very valuable tool. In particular, if they are compiled consistently for the same company on a regular basis they are very useful when looking for trends or discontinuities from one year to the next. Changes in the financial ratios will help to draw attention to where problems of efficiency or liquidity issues may be about to manifest themselves. Once a problem or point of concern is identified, one needs to look behind the ratio to find out what might be emerging problems in the underlying business fundamentals. In other words, in order to properly evaluate the trends and ratios described above, it is necessary to go on to consider the particular circumstances of the business.

316

Comparing Companies in Different Sectors

Companies have very different business models. A business model describes the key strategic direction of a company – its business philosophy – and there can be many different paths that lead to success. Some companies are suppliers of merchandise to mass markets, while others occupy more specialised niches. Some companies are keen to have a very large share of the available market in the product/ service which they supply, and work on the principle of low margins and high volume. Other companies may prefer the converse model of having a high margin and relatively low volume.

In making comparison between companies in general, it is vital to consider the most appropriate criteria to use in terms of financial ratio analysis, and not simply to take any ratio indiscriminately for comparative purposes and draw what will almost certainly be misleading conclusions.

Accounting Policies

The accounting policies adopted by a company can significantly impact its ratios and also can introduce a range of problems for comparison between different firms operating in different sectors of the economy and even more for international comparisons. For example, if non-current assets are revalued, then depreciation charges will be higher. Hence, profits will be lower but, on the statement of financial position, more non-current assets mean a higher capital employed figure. In consequence, the return on capital employed will be reduced (lower profits divided by higher capital employed). Thus, ratios can be significantly different if they are drawn from financial statements prepared under different sets of accounting standards, such as globally accepted International Financial Reporting Standards (IFRSs) versus US Standards.

In comparing two companies where one does revalue non-current assets and one does not, or in comparing one company to another where non-current assets have been revalued in between, it has to be expected that there will be a distortion between the ratios as a result of this accounting policy.

Comparing P/E Multiples

By comparing price and EPS for a company, one can analyse the market's stock valuation of a company and its shares relative to the income the company is actually generating. Stocks with higher (and/or more certain) forecast earnings growth will usually have a higher P/E and those expected to have lower (and/or riskier) earnings growth will, in most cases, have a lower P/E.

Investors can use the P/E ratio to compare the relative valuations of stocks. As stated in section 1.6.2, too simplistically, one might claim that, if one stock has a P/E twice that of another stock, all things being equal, it is a less attractive investment. Companies are rarely equal, however, and comparisons between industries, companies and time periods can be very misleading.

In general terms, companies which are in sectors of the economy where relatively high growth levels are expected – such as high technology – will have higher P/E ratios than those in sectors such as utilities or car manufacturing. Companies in different sectors of the economy will also tend to exhibit generically contrasting P/E ratios. This will itself be largely based upon the market's expectations as to future earnings growth in different sectors. For example, a relatively young technology company which has bright prospects will often be rewarded by investors with a relatively high P/E ratio as the earnings are expected to grow dynamically.

On the other hand, a mature utility company which has fairly predictable future earnings potential will tend to have a relatively lower P/E ratio based on more conservative growth estimations. Only if one were to compare two companies from the same high growth sector – such as biotechnology – and one had a P/E ratio of 20 and the other a P/E of 12 might it be reasonable to conclude that the former was more attractive, as the market's expectations for it were higher.

Comparing P/E ratios for companies in very different sectors of the economy is therefore not advisable, and even comparing the P/E ratios for companies across borders can be very misleading, owing to the different GAAP regimes. One factor which can influence any cross-border comparison between companies is the interest rate environment as well as the annual rate of inflation in the respective national economy. If short-term interest rates are relatively low, and inflation is considered to be benign, a larger P/E ratio is supportable as there is less competition for equities coming from the income obtainable from fixed-income securities and vice versa. Also relevant to such comparisons are local cost structures for companies in general, the role of capital markets in capital formation, the extent of the role of government and the financial regulatory environment.

Caution in general is suggested when using the P/E ratio unless it is for highly comparable businesses in the same jurisdiction.

Another useful application of the P/E ratio is to consider the relationship between the P/E ratio on an individual company's security and the P/E ratio of the stock market average or of the sector average. Some investors will be attracted to companies with a low P/E ratio as it suggests that the company may be undervalued. Once again this needs to be placed into the context of which sector a possible acquisition candidate occupies – so, for example, a company interested in taking over a technology company will almost certainly have to pay an above-average market P/E multiple but will look for one that is still attractively priced within that sector of the market.

Window-Dressing

One of the recurring comments made in the qualifications expressed regarding the interpretation of financial analysis relates to the timing of events recorded on a company's statement of financial position. If an event, eg, the issuance of new shares, takes place towards the end of a fiscal year, then the correct approach is to use a technique to weight the event appropriately so that the impact of the event is spread out over the year.

More deliberate efforts can be made by companies to portray their accounts in the best light possible and these are sometimes included under the heading of 'window-dressing'. Window-dressing transactions can be defined as transactions intended to mislead the user of the accounts. Another term which is sometimes used in this regard is the tendency to use 'cosmetic accounting techniques' to cover up the blemishes that would otherwise be apparent.

Window-dressing and cosmetic accounting can be more or less innocent and more or less dangerous for the unwary. It can also lead to a distorted view of relative performance between companies, whether in the same sector or jurisdiction, or for international comparisons. A common cause of distortion arises because several ratios are calculated with reference to a year-end statement of financial position figure only.

Ideally one should compare full year's transaction to a representative balance throughout the year. In assessing true profitability, one should compare the full year's profits to a representative amount of capital employed to get the most accurate and reliable measure of the return on capital employed.

Comparing Like with Like

When using financial ratios therefore, it is imperative to compare like with like. As previously discussed, the kind of depreciation methods used should be consistent and there is little value in comparing the inventory turnover ratios for a supermarket with those for a high-end retail boutique.

If one is considering the payables payment period, it is most useful to compare the invoiced payables to the invoiced cost of sales.

Also, when calculating profit margins, it is more reliable and accurate to compare the profit to the revenue that has generated that profit.

Overreliance on Historic Information

A common criticism that is made about financial analysis and then decision-making, and about the kinds of interpretation that can be drawn with respect to ratio analysis, is that, necessarily, all of the data that has informed the present ratios will be historic – ie, in assessing profitability, the analyst will be using revenues and costs and other pertinent data from the past.

While such data will have value with respect to future forecasts and can be used as a foundation for making comparisons across different companies, the key to the successful management of business is the ability of the management team to handle the unexpected, deal with contingencies and navigate their way through the uncertainties and risks that arise in a fast-changing business environment.

The global banking crisis revealed to the world that the issue of liquidity for the financial services sector had been vastly underrated. Banks that had operated for many years with very high gearing were suddenly exposed as having taken very large risks with respect to their liquidity. The business models of funding long-term obligations with short-term capital from previously highly liquid money markets turned out to have been a mirage.

In general terms, the liquidity of any business depends to a large extent on the macro monetary environment. In addition, it is useful to consider the benchmarks or norms which prevail among the competitors and peer group for the sector of business in which the particular firm operates.

To take one example from the field of credit rating, the analysis which was performed by rating agencies and regulators in assessing the risks of collateralised debt obligations (CDOs) and other mortgage-backed securities (MBSs) was, as subsequent case studies and testimony have revealed, based on a study of property prices over a relatively short time-frame. One could make the case both that the sample period proved to be too short and that the modelling of a coordinated decline in housing prices had not been properly undertaken because the analysts were too focused on the most recent historic data.

Similar risks can arise for a business when the expectation is that the future will largely resemble the recent past, but developments in business processes, the burnout of demand for products which easily become outmoded and the constant risk of disruptive innovations suggests that no business can become overly reliant upon the continuation of trends which have been present in the past. The area of business process re-engineering (ie, the continuing need for innovation and adaptation to new practices in the way that business is conducted) is very active, and so are the threats to existing businesses from brand new competitors with lower cost bases and better products and services.

1.7.2   The Benefits and Limitations of Relying on Third-Party Research

Many companies provide specialised research services for the macro economy and for particular sectors of the economy. For example, companies such as Ovum Research provide in-depth analysis of the global telecommunications industry and detailed knowledge of all of the major participants in this marketplace. They provide industry forecasts and can be engaged by specific businesses to undertake more detailed research on a custom basis.

In the financial services sector, there is a plethora of advisory and research organisations which examine the state of:

- public finances – eg, the Institute for Fiscal Studies (IFS)
- the state of the housing market – eg, Nationwide Building Society
- the state of the retail industry – eg, the British Retail Consortium.

The principal benefit to be derived from the work of such third-party research firms is that there is a depth of knowledge and expertise within such firms and organisations which can provide authoritative and useful information to both business managers and the investment community.

There can also be considerable limitations as to the value of such research. Firstly, the organisation which is providing the reports may have a hidden agenda or in the worst case a conflict of interest. For example, the research firm may be trying to ingratiate itself with, or already have a relationship with, a particular company, and may present information in a biased fashion. Furthermore, some research firms have a vested interest in only presenting positive information that will enhance their likelihood of being seen as supportive to a particular sector and more deserving of fees from potential clients.

The last issue raises the risk that the third parties may not be as independent as one would expect or require. The case of the credit-rating agencies comes to mind again. When the issuer of a bond or security engages a credit-rating firm to assess the credit risk of a security it is planning to issue, there is a *prima facie* concern that the agency will want to please the issuer. After all the issuer is paying the agency, rather than having proper diligence for the buyers of the securities who ultimately (and unwisely) use the ratings prepared by the agencies to determine the riskiness of the security. The fact that so many MBSs were issued with AAA ratings and turned out in some cases to be practically worthless provides a clear illustration of the possible conflict of interest issues, and also on the unreliability of some third-party research.

1.7.3 Summary

When considering financial ratios for the purposes of comparative analysis, the aim should always be to compare like with like, to apply the correct perspective on financings and changes in capital structure during the period under investigation, to take into account the different business models and P/E multiples applicable to different sectors of the economy, the rate of change in key levels of financial performance, and, in general, to have a cautious view to over-reaching with the conclusions that one reaches from that analysis.

2. Environmental, Social and Governance (ESG)

Learning Objective

6.2.1 Understand the main factors taken into account when conducting an analysis of Environmental, Social and Governance (ESG) risks and opportunities

Environmental, Social, and Governance (ESG) refers to a set of standards for companies to comply with. It enables socially conscious investors to effectively screen any intended investments before trading. ESG has become an increasingly popular approach for potential investors to consider environmental, social, and governance factors when deciding which companies they might want to invest in. ESG investing is sometimes referred to as:

- responsible investing
- impact investing
- sustainable investing, or
- socially responsible investing.

ESG criteria allows investors to examine a broad range of company behaviour that can be defined in three categories:

Environmental

Environmental standards may include how a company uses energy, how it deals with waste and pollution, consideration and treatment of animals and its approach to conservation of natural resource, as well as how it manages environmental issues. An example would be an environmental management system which can be certified under ISO 14001 (International Organization for Standardization) which sets out the criteria.

Social

Social factors look at how a company conducts its relationships with:

- Employees.
- Suppliers.
- Customers.
- Communities in which it operates.

For example, does the company donate funds to help the local community or allow and encourage its staff to engage in community related volunteer work? Social criteria looks at the company's business relationships. For employees, do the working conditions prioritise health and safety issues?

An example would be a 'sweatshop' that might have working conditions that are very poor and/or socially and legally unacceptable.

Governance

Governance looks at its leadership and running of the company and will include examination of factors such as:

- Executive remuneration.
- Shareholders' rights.
- Internal controls.
- Audits.
- Board nomination process.

Governance issues may include whether a company employs high standard accounting methods or whether shareholders are afforded the chance to vote on key issues. Potential investors may want to examine how the board handles such issues as conflict of interest.

The Increasing Focus on ESG

Many collective investment schemes (CISs), exchange-traded funds (ETFs), brokers and some robo-advisors promote products that incorporate some ESG criteria. This can assist investors in avoiding uninformed investment where the company might, because of their behaviour and practices, pose a large financial risk or engage in activities that conflict with the investor's own values and beliefs.

We are living in an environment where people are increasingly concerned about the global environment – especially younger investors. There is an increasing desire to invest in companies that employ practices that match their own standards and beliefs, and this will include individual pension investments. While factors such as yield, performance and risk are important factors when deciding upon an investment, ESG factors are increasingly affecting investment selection as a key criterion.

By definition, ESG involves investing in companies with sustainable business practices on the expectation that such companies have higher investment potential. Theoretically, the application of ESG criteria should, therefore, help to reduce risk. According to research carried out by MSCI, companies with high ESG ratings have historically demonstrated lower levels of systematic risk, less volatile earnings, and less systematic volatility, along with lower costs of capital compared with their low ESG-rated counterparts.

Greenwashing

Many companies have been criticised for simply labelling themselves as 'green' but not following through with their pledges – this is known as 'greenwashing'. This is the practice of companies making misleading environmental claims for marketing purposes with the aim of improving their reputation to attract environmentally and socially aware consumers, employees and investors, thereby increasing profits.

The origins of ESG can likely be traced back to the mid-18th century and the moral teachings of religious groups such as the Quakers, who used their influence in early UK banking to discourage investment in activities like slavery, alcohol and gambling.

ESG and Legislation

The **European Securities and Markets Authority (ESMA)** has set up a Coordination Network on Sustainability which engages with national competent authorities to develop policies for the inclusion of sustainability considerations in financial regulation and law.

In April 2019, ESMA issued a Consultation Paper which highlights proposed measures for the adoption of sustainability factors and risks that UCITS and AIF managers should adopt into the management of the organisation.

A month later, ESMA issued a paper of technical advice to the European Commission on possible initiatives to deal with sustainable factors within the investment industry, going as far as to recommend integrating new requirements into existing legislation such as:

- The Markets in Financial Instruments Directive II (MiFID II)
- Undertakings in Collective Investment in Transferable Securities (UCITS) Directive (investment funds), and
- The Alternative Investment Fund Managers Directive (AIFMD).

The recommendations will oblige fund management companies to incorporate sustainability factors and risks into areas of its business such as:

- Resourcing.
- Senior management oversight responsibility.
- Organisational structure.
- Investment due diligence.
- Conflicts of interest.
- Risk management.

In July 2019, ESMA issued another technical advice paper focussed on sustainability considerations for the credit rating industry and its disclosure requirements. ESMA has confirmed that credit rating agencies use different methods to consider ESG factors across asset types.

The Future for ESG

It is expected that ESMA will next consult on the draft implementing measures for the purpose of integrating ESG into financial services regulation across the EU, making compliance mandatory.

As compliance with new directives and regulations is achieved in the industry, investors will be able to be well informed on ESG factors for investments.

End of Chapter Questions

Think of an answer to each question and refer to the appropriate section for confirmation.

1. Previously known as the balance sheet, what is the taxonomy which has been adopted by the Revised Accounting Standards (IAS 1) and is the use of this new terminology mandatory?
   Answer reference: Section 1.1.1

2. What is meant by the term 'purchased goodwill'?
   Answer reference: Section 1.1.2

3. What is the purpose of common-size analysis with respect to a company's financial statements?
   Answer reference: Section 1.1.4

4. How is earnings per share (EPS) calculated?
   Answer reference: Section 1.2.2

5. If a company's accounts show a decrease in accounts receivable, how will this impact its statement of cash flows?
   Answer reference: Section 1.3.2

6. In relation to the gearing of a company and its cost structure and revenues, what is the value known as the contribution?
   Answer reference: Section 1.4.3

7. Explain what is meant by dividend cover and provide a simple formula for how it is calculated.
   Answer reference: Section 1.6.4

8. In contrasting the price/earnings (P/E) ratios of a long-established utility company and a relatively new technology company, which would be expected to have the higher ratio and why would you expect this to be the case?
   Answer reference: Section 1.7.1

9. What are some of the limitations of relying on third-party research?
   Answer reference: Section 1.7.2

10. What factors are considered important within ESG?
    Answer reference: Section 2

Chapter Seven
Portfolio Construction

This syllabus area will provide approximately 8 of the 80 examination questions

1. Market Information and Research

1.1 Economic and Financial Communications

Learning Objective

7.1.1   Understand the use of regulatory, economic and financial communications: primary and secondary information providers; government resources and statistics; broker research and distributor information; regulatory resources

Financial communications and reports from numerous bodies, both in the private and public sector, are a vital part of the tools required for the research and analysis functions that are crucial to decision-making about investment strategies and asset allocation. The data needed by an investment manager can be sourced from the following broad categories:

- **Primary and secondary information providers (news services)** – eg, Bloomberg, Thomson Reuters, Consumer News and Business Channel (CNBC).
- **Government resources and statistics** – the Office for National Statistics (ONS) and the Bank of England (BoE).
- **Broker research and distributor information** – eg, market commentary and analysis from major investment banks, such as Goldman Sachs and Morgan Stanley.
- **Desk research** – secondary source research and analysis by an investment fund management team.
- **Regulatory resources where relevant** – eg, communications from the Financial Conduct Authority (FCA).

1.1.1 Primary and Secondary Information Providers (News Services)

The major providers of financial news include the following companies:

Bloomberg

Bloomberg is a privately held financial software, news and data company. According to a market survey by the *New York Times* it has a one-third share of the market for financial information services. Bloomberg was founded by Michael Bloomberg in 1981 with a 30% ownership investment by Merrill Lynch. The company provides financial software tools such as analytics and equity trading platforms, data services and news to financial companies and organisations around the world through the Bloomberg Terminal, its core money-generating product. Bloomberg has grown to include a global news service, including television, radio, the internet and printed publications.

Thomson Reuters (TR)

Thomson Reuters (TR) is an information company created by the Canadian company Thomson Corporation's purchase of Reuters in April 2008. Thomson Reuters shares are listed on the Toronto Stock Exchange (TSE) and the NYSE. According to a *New York Times* survey, TR also has approximately one-third of the market for financial information services. The company has launched a television service called *Insider* and is very visible on the internet as a major source of financial and non-financial news coverage.

CNBC

CNBC is a satellite and cable television business news channel in the US, owned and operated by NBC Universal. The network and its international spin-offs cover business headlines and provide live coverage of financial markets. The combined reach of CNBC and its siblings is 390 million viewers around the world. It is headquartered in New Jersey and has a European headquarters in London.

A competitor of CNBC in rolling business news coverage is the Fox Business News Network which is part of News Corporation, owned partly by the Murdoch family, which also owns the *Wall Street Journal*.

Financial Times and *Wall Street Journal*

Two online publications are also widely followed by global investors and there are of course many other newspapers which provide detailed coverage of financial matters both in the UK and around the world.

The *Financial Times* reports business, and features share and financial product listings. The FT is usually in two sections; the first section covers national and international news, the second company and markets news.

The *Wall Street Journal* is an English-language international daily newspaper published by Dow Jones & Company, a division of News Corporation, in New York City, with Asian and European editions.

1.1.2 Official Sources

Office for National Statistics (ONS)

The principal source for economic data on the UK economy is the ONS. The ONS produces and publishes a wide range of information about Britain that can be used for social and economic policy making. Much of the data on which policy makers depend is produced by the ONS through a combination of a decennial population census, samples and surveys and analysis of data generated by businesses and organisations such as the National Health Service and the register of births, marriages and deaths.

Arguably the most important set of data which is released periodically by the ONS relates to UK gross domestic product (GDP). This measure is reported in essentially two formats showing the percentage change within the most recent quarter of reference and also the current quarter's relationship to the same period one year ago.

In addition to the GDP data, other widely followed economic data published by the ONS relate to inflation – the consumer prices index (CPI) and the different flavours of the retail prices index (RPI and RPIX), employment data, balance of trade data and other demographic data.

Bank of England (BoE)

The Financial Stability Report is published half-yearly by bank staff under the guidance of the Bank's Financial Stability Executive Board. It aims to identify the major downside risks to the UK financial system and thereby help financial firms, authorities and the wider public in managing and preparing for these risks.

The Report starts with an overview of key developments affecting the UK financial system. This is followed by four sections:

1. Global financial environment.
2. Short-term risks to financial stability.
3. Medium-term risks to financial stability.
4. Prospects for financial stability.

1.1.3   Broker Research

Securities research is a discipline within the financial services sector. Securities research professionals are known most generally as analysts, research analysts, or securities analysts. Securities analysts are commonly divided between the two basic kinds of securities: equity analysts (researching stocks and their issuers) and fixed-interest analysts (researching bond issuers). However, there are some analysts who cover all of the securities of a particular issuer, stocks and bonds alike.

Securities analysts are usually further subdivided by industry specialisation (or sectors). Among the industries with the most analyst coverage are technology, financial services, energy, software and retailing. Fixed-income analysts are also often subdivided, with specialised analyst coverage for convertible bonds, high-yield bonds, distressed securities and other financial products.

Securities analysts communicate to investors, through research reports and commentary, insights regarding the value, risk and volatility of a covered security, and thus assist investors to decide whether to buy, hold, sell, sell short or simply avoid the security in question or derivative securities. Securities analysts review periodic financial disclosures of the issuers (as required by the LSE and FCA in the UK and the SEC in the US) and other relevant companies, read industry news and use trading history and industry information databases. Their work may include interviewing managers and customers of the companies they follow.

Those analysts who are engaged by a brokerage firm are usually referred to as sell-side analysts. This differentiates them from buy-side analysts, who are engaged by asset management firms as part of their research efforts before they buy securities rather than sell them.

1.1.4   Regulatory Resources

The main source of information reflecting changes in financial regulations which need to be complied within the financial services sector in the UK are those which originate within the FCA. These can start out as consultation papers but may then become official rule changes and will appear in the FCA Handbook.

In addition, it is worth monitoring the FCA website for general regulatory developments, disciplinary actions, money laundering issues and other developments.

Other areas where potential changes in regulations may be relevant arise from changes in listing requirements from the FCA, changes affecting takeover regulation from the Panel on Takeovers and Mergers (PTM or POTAM or just the Takeover Panel) and changes in legislation affecting companies in general which will eventually be incorporated into updates of the Companies Acts.

1.2   Research and Reports

Learning Objective

7.1.2   Understand the different types and uses of research and reports: fundamental analysis; technical analysis; fund analysis; fund rating agencies and screening software; broker and distributor reports; sector-specific reports

1.2.1   Fundamental Analysis

Fundamental analysis involves the financial analysis of a company's published accounts, along with an analysis of its management, markets and competitive position. It is a technique that is used to determine the value of a security by focusing on the underlying factors that affect a company's business.

Fundamental analysis looks at both quantitative factors, such as the numerical results of the analysis of a company and the market it operates in, and qualitative factors, such as the quality of the company's management, the value of its brand, and areas such as patents and proprietary technology.

The assumption behind fundamental analysis is that the market does not always value securities correctly in the short term, and that by identifying the intrinsic value of a company, securities can be bought at a discount and that the investment will pay off over time once the market realises the fundamental value of a company.

Companies generate a significant amount of financial data, and so fundamental analysis seeks to extract meaningful data about a company.

In addition to this quantitative data, fundamental analysis also assesses a wide range of other qualitative factors such as:

- a company's business model
- its competitive position
- the quality and experience of its management team
- how the company is managed, the transparency of available financial data and its approach to corporate governance, and
- the industry in which it operates, its market share and its competitive position relative to its peers.

1.2.2   Technical Analysis

Technical analysis also seeks to evaluate the value of a company, but, instead of analysing a company's intrinsic value and prospects, it uses historical price and volume data to assess and estimate where the price of a security or market will move in the future. In essence, technical analysts use different quantitative and statistical tools to analyse time-series data of asset prices and other characteristics, with a view to discerning recurrences of similar price-development patterns or chart formations.

The assumptions underlying technical analysis are that:

- the market discounts everything
- prices move in trends, and
- history tends to repeat itself.

Technical analysis uses charts of price movements, along with technical indicators and oscillators, to identify patterns that can suggest future price movements. It is therefore unconcerned whether a security is undervalued and simply concerns itself with future price movements.

One of the most important concepts in technical analysis is trend. Trends can, however, be difficult to identify, as prices do not move in a straight line, and so technical analysis identifies series of highs or lows that take place to identify the direction of movements. These are classified as uptrend, downtrend and sideways movements.

The following diagram seeks to explain this by describing a simple uptrend.

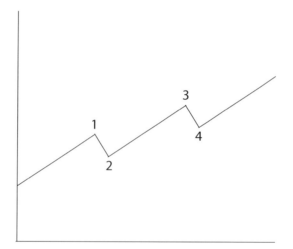

Point 1 on the chart reflects the first high and point 2 the subsequent low and so on. For it to be an uptrend, each successive low must be higher than the previous low point, otherwise it is referred to as a reversal. The same principle applies for downtrends.

Along with direction, technical analysis will also classify trends based on time. Primary movements are long-term price trends, which can last a number of years. Primary movements in the broader market are known as bull and bear markets, a **bull market** being a rising market and a **bear market** a falling market. Primary movements consist of a number of secondary movements, each of which can last for up to a couple of months, which, in turn, comprise a number of tertiary, or day-to-day movements. The results of technical analysis are displayed on charts that graphically represent price movements.

After plotting historical price movements, a trendline is added to clearly show the direction of the trend and to show reversals.

The trendline can then be analysed to provide further indicators of potential price movement. The diagram below shows an upward trend line, which is drawn at the lows of the upward trend and which represents the support line for a stock as it moves from progressive highs to lows.

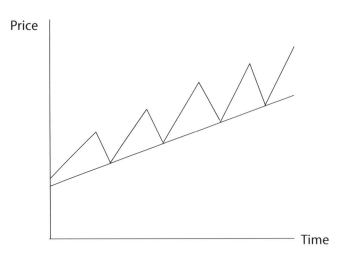

This type of trendline helps traders to anticipate the point at which a stock's price will begin moving upwards again. Similarly, a downward trendline is drawn at the highs of the downward trend. This line represents the resistance level that a stock faces every time the price moves from a low to a high.

There are a variety of different charts that can be used to depict price movements; some of the main types of chart are:

*   **Line charts** are where the price of an asset, or security, over time is simply plotted using a single line. Each point on the line represents the security's closing price. However, in order to establish an underlying trend, chartists often employ what are known as moving averages so as to smooth out extreme price movements. Rather than plot each closing price on the chart, each point on the chart instead represents the arithmetic mean of the security's price over a specific number of days. 10, 50, 100 and 200 moving day averages are commonly used.
*   **Point and figure charts** record significant price movements in vertical columns by using a series of Xs to denote significant up moves and Os to represent significant down moves, without employing a uniform timescale. Whenever there is a change in the direction of the security's price, a new column is started.
*   **Bar charts** join the highest and lowest price levels attained by a security over a specified time period by a vertical line. This time scale can range from a single day to a few months. When the chosen time period is one trading day, a horizontal line representing the closing price on the day intersects this vertical line.
*   **Candlestick charts** – closely linked to bar charts, these again link the security's highest and lowest prices by a vertical line but employ horizontal lines to mark both the opening and closing prices for each trading day. If the closing price exceeds the opening price on the day the body of the candle is left clear while, if the opposite is true, it is shaded.

Technical analysis also uses lines on charts which form a channel, which is where two trendlines are added to indicate levels of support and resistance which respectively connect the series of price lows and price highs. Users of technical analysis will expect a security to trade between these two levels until it breaks out, when it can be expected to make a sharp move in the direction of the break. If a support level is broken, this provides a sell signal, while the breaking of a resistance level, as the price of the asset gathers momentum, indicates a buying opportunity.

An example of such a breakout pattern is the one in the diagram below, where there has been an upward breakout above the price resistance line. With respect to such channels, it is often observed that price movements become progressively less volatile, and when there is a breakout, in either direction, the price movement can then be quite dramatic.

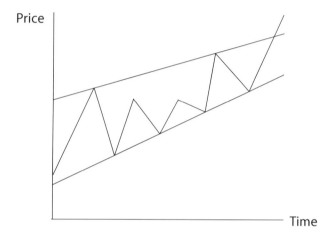

Other continuation patterns include the rectangle and the flag.

Chartists typically use what are known as relative-strength charts to confirm breakouts from continuation patterns. Relative strength charts simply depict the price performance of a security relative to the broader market. If the relative performance of the security improves against the broader market then this may confirm that a suspected breakout on the upside has or is about to occur. However, acknowledging that prices do not always move in the same direction and trends eventually cease, technical analysts also look to identify what are known as reversal patterns, or sell signals.

Probably the most famous of these is the head and shoulders reversal pattern, which is shown below.

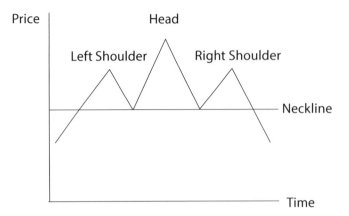

A head and shoulders reversal pattern arises when a price movement causes the right shoulder to breach the neckline – the resistance level – indicating the prospect of a sustained fall in the price of the security.

1.2.3 The Difference between Fundamental and Technical Analysis

Fundamental and technical analysis are the two main methodologies used for investment analysis and, as you can see from comparing their key characteristics, they differ widely in their approaches.

The principal differences between them can be summarised as follows:

- **Analysing financial statements versus charts**
    - ◦ At a basic level, fundamental analysis involves the analysis of the company's balance sheet, cash flow statement and income statement.
    - ◦ Technical analysis considers that there is no need to do this, as a company's fundamentals are all accounted for in the price and the information needed can be found in the company's charts.
- **Time horizon**
    - ◦ Fundamental analysis takes a relatively long-term approach to investment.
    - ◦ Technical analysis uses chart data over a much shorter time-frame of weeks, days and even minutes.
- **Investing versus trading**
    - ◦ Fundamental analysis is used to make long-term investment decisions.
    - ◦ Technical analysis is used to determine short-term trading decisions.

Although the approaches adopted by technical and fundamental analysis differ markedly, they should not be seen as being mutually exclusive techniques. Indeed, their differences make them complementary. Used collectively, they can enhance the portfolio management decision-making process.

1.2.4 Fund Analysis

The IA has published a classification system for the diverse array of funds available to UK investors including unit trusts and OEICs. The diagram in chapter 4, section 3.4, shows the IA classifications.

The groups correspond to broadly different investment objectives.

- Some **income funds** principally target immediate income, while others aim to achieve growing income.
- **Growth funds**, which mainly target capital growth or total return, are distinguished from those that are designed for capital protection.
- **Specialist funds** cover other more niche areas of investment.

Specialist fund-rating companies provide many valuable reports and surveys of the huge number of investment funds that are available globally.

In the US, and increasingly in Europe, fund-ratings providers, such as Morningstar, Fitch Ratings and Fund House, provide extensive research on mutual funds and other collective investment vehicles. Trustnet provides a similar and comprehensive service for UK-based investors.

These services allow an investor to review the performance of funds from many different perspectives, eg, total return, P/E ratios and dividend growth. It is possible to screen the databases which are accessible on the websites of these companies for a fund which matches the criteria which one specifies. For example, if one wants to invest in a fund which has exposure to Asian equities excluding Japan, where the fund manager has been running the fund for at least three years and where the standard deviation of the returns over the last five years has been below a specified amount, this can be achieved by using the Morningstar and Trustnet platforms. Similar screening facilities are supplied at no charge by companies such as Yahoo and MSN, but usually the databases are confined to single shares rather than funds.

The following screenshot shows the manner in which a user can search for funds listed by Morningstar which have a specific rating, as explained on the right-hand side of the image, and then to be more specific with the other screening criteria, including the capacity to filter out results which have failed to generate returns over (say) three years above a threshold amount supplied by the user.

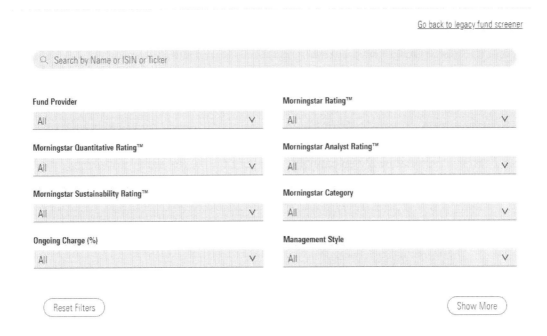

Quantitative Versus Qualitative Fund Analysis

Quantitative analysis involves metrics such as comparing the performance of specific funds with the overall market performance or the difference between a fund's performance and a given benchmark. Qualitative analysis differs in that it is more subjective and considers metrics such as fund managers' skills and expertise and the relative position of the fund compared to one's view of the market's future direction. Typically, a mixture of both quantitative and qualitative analysis will provide the optimum position.

1.2.5   Broker and Distributor Reports

All major investment banks and brokers publish research reports on numerous matters which are of interest to investors and fund managers.

These research reports may only be made available to clients of the firm, but are sometimes placed in the public domain. These reports may cover macro-analysis, eg, a broker's analyst may be showing research and evidence for the prospects for growth in the US economy over the next year, or they may be at the micro-level, examining the prospects for specific companies. The material covered by brokers can include companies which are clients of the broker and also those which are not. Indeed some brokers will publish research reports and offer ratings, ie, buy, sell or hold, on their competitors.

1.2.6   Sector-Specific Reports

In addition to the fund ratings agencies mentioned in chapter 2, section 1.1.6, there are numerous other investment research firms which provide specialised information on specific sectors of the market, as well an overview of sector performance in general.

As an example, the table below shows the performance of the eleven S&P 500 sectors.

The 2018 Sector Reclassification

As of September 2018, the S&P 500 was divided into 11 sectors, as follows, with their respective weightings by market capitalisation. The following are the weightings as of January 2021:

- Communication Services: 10.8%
- Consumer Discretionary: 12.7%
- Consumer Staples: 6.6%
- Energy: 2.38%
- Financials: 10.31%
- Health Care: 13.4%
- Industrials: 8.5%
- Information Technology: 27.65%
- Materials: 2.65%
- Real Estate: 2.48%
- Utilities: 2.7%

Here is the performance of the sectors over the past ten years:

Abbrev.	Sector Index	Annual	Best	Worst
COND	S&P 500 Consumer Discretionary Index	13.05%	43.1%	−33.5%
CONS	S&P 500 Consumer Staples Index	10.40%	27.6%	−15.4%
ENRS	S&P 500 Energy Index	0.86%	34.4%	−34.9%
FINL	S&P 500 Financials Index	3.13%	35.6%	−55.3%
HLTH	S&P 500 Healthcare Index	11.0%	41.5%	−22.8%
INDU	S&P 500 Industrials Index	8.95%	40.7%	−39.9%
INFT	S&P 500 Information Technology Index	15.21%	61.7%	−43.1%
MATR	S&P 500 Materials Index	8.49%	48.6%	−45.7%
REAL	S&P 500 Real Estate Index	5.38%	32.3%	−42.3%
TELS	S&P 500 Communication Services index	8.92%	32.7%	−30.5%
UTIL	S&P 500 Utilities Index	8.75%	29.0%	−29.0%
S&P	S&P 500 Index	9.88%	32.4%	−37.0%

Source: Annual S&P Sector Performance (Novel Investor)

2. Influencing Factors

Learning Objective

7.1.3   Be able to assess key factors that influence markets and sectors: responses to change and uncertainty; volume, liquidity and nature of trading activity in domestic and overseas markets; publication of announcements, research and ratings

2.1   Responses to Change and Uncertainty

It is an adage among investment professionals that markets hate uncertainty. Uncertainty is effectively a synonym for risk, as risk arises from the uncertainty of outcomes. As investors, each time we decide to purchase a security or invest in an opportunity, the outcome is uncertain in the same way that any future event is.

2.2   Volume and Liquidity

The presence or absence of liquidity in financial markets is one of the most important conditions for transactions to take place.

Economists have really not provided a satisfactory account of liquidity, but rather assume that it will be present in markets. The term refers to the depth of interest from both buyers and sellers for a security and if, as occurs from time to time – as in Q4 2020 – there is an absence of interest from buyers in many securities, a market will become lopsided and the desire by many to sell their shares and bonds at the same time causes disorderly market behaviour and results in rather sudden and abrupt drops in prices of securities.

In its more extreme form this can be referred to as a market crash. The classic example of such an event took place in October 1987, when global markets dropped precipitously and the NYSE fell by more than 20% in a single session on Monday 19 October of that year, with other indices such as the LSE registering similar falls. The vital role of liquidity has been touched upon and it is worth pointing to the different motives of the investor and the speculator or trader. The investor, such as a pension fund or unit trust manager, may be purchasing (or selling) securities as part of a long-term portfolio management exercise. The speculator or trader may be interested in trying to profit from short-term movements in the prices of securities without the intention of holding the securities for an extended period.

Speculators and traders help to provide liquidity to a market which would see less activity if it were just long-term investors that were conducting the activity. Trading activities create larger volumes in the markets, and thereby enhance the ability of the long-term investors and allocators of capital to buy and sell without moving the market excessively. This is a somewhat controversial topic, as there are some who would argue that the activity of speculators, rather than providing greater liquidity and acting as a way of smoothing price fluctuations, may actually lead to larger moves in prices or volatility, which has the consequence of destabilising markets.

2.3 Global Movements

There is growing evidence that, in the highly inter-connected web of markets and the macro or global investment strategies followed by large investment banks and asset managers, the degree to which major global asset classes reveal a high degree of co-movement or correlation is indicative of 'big picture' investment strategies, which are based on inter-market strategies. Although spelling out such inter-market strategies goes beyond the syllabus of this course, the inter-linked nature of alignments in foreign exchange, global equity indices, energy products and commodities in general can be fascinating to study.

There are observable relationships between the movements of, for example, the Australian dollar versus the Japanese yen, which is an example of the forex carry trade and the general appetite for riskier assets. The forex carry trade arises from the notion that, if a large hedge fund or investment bank can borrow capital in yen from Japanese sources at short-term rates that are less than 20 basis points (in general, such rates are only available to the best rated entities, eg, major investment banks) and use the proceeds to purchase Australian government securities yielding (say) 5%, there will not only be profits to be made from the simple arbitrage but consequences for the exchange rates as well. Capital flows into Australian government securities, with repo agreements then put in place, may then be associated with other strategies to invest in other products such as commodities, often with considerable leverage, and such strategies are followed by major funds and the proprietary trading desks of the large investment banks.

The consequences can be seen each day in the manner in which certain asset classes will move together depending on the degree of risk that the short-term trading desks are willing to take. For example, and to engage in simplification, following the 2007–08 banking crisis and the sovereign debt problems within the eurozone, it is possible to discern a clear pattern whereby, when markets become more anxious, there is a movement towards the US dollar and Japanese yen (which causes an 'unwinding' of the short-term carry trades) and away from the euro and the so-called commodity currencies such as the Australian and Canadian dollar. Investors/traders will also purchase US Treasury instruments and shun the emerging markets and commodities.

Example of a Carry Trade

An investor decides to invest in a 12-month euro position @ 2%: €1,000,000 against GBP @ 1.3111:

Buy €1,000,000 @ 1.3111 = £762,718. GBP is borrowed at the rate of 1%. 12 months later, sterling has dropped by 10% against the euro and the investor sells back the euro at the new rate of 1.1800.

Sell €1,000,000 @ 1.1800 = £847,457:

The loan is repaid leaving profit of £84,739 (£847,457 – £762,718).

The interest earned is 2% on €1,000,000 = €20,000 (or £16,949 @ the new rate 1.1800).

The interest payable is 1% on £762,718 = £7,627.

The total profit in the carry trade is, therefore:

Foreign exchange profit + interest earned – interest payable:

Therefore, total profit is: £84,739 + £16,949 – £7,627 = £94,061.

On the contrary, when there is more of an appetite for buying riskier assets, the converse will tend to be the case. Capital will move away from the safe harbour of the US dollar and US Treasuries, global equity indices will tend to move higher, the commodity currencies will often move up sharply against the dollar and the emerging markets will see capital inflows.

Many of these movements will be of short-term duration, but it is also possible to discern similar dynamics at work with respect to global asset allocation decision-making.

2.4   Market Abuse Regime

On 1 July 2005, the Financial Services and Markets Act 2000 (Market Abuse) Regulations 2005 came into force in order to implement the European Commission (EC) Directive on Insider Dealing and Market Manipulation (Market Abuse). The Market Abuse Directive (MAD) was a key element of the EU Financial Services Action Plan and introduced a common EU approach for preventing and detecting market abuse and ensuring a proper flow of information to the market.

The Market Abuse Regulation (MAR) took effect across the EU on 3 July 2016 and superseded the MAD. The MAR, in many ways, is similar to the former UK regime, but expands the scope of market abuse and introduces extra requirements for issuers and the way they operate. The UK has amended primary and secondary legislation to ensure it complies with, and is compatible with, the MAR.

The MAR defines market abuse as follows:

'Market abuse is a concept that encompasses unlawful behaviour in the financial markets and, for the purposes of this Regulation, it should be understood to consist of insider dealing, unlawful disclosure of inside information and market manipulation. Such behaviour prevents full and proper market transparency, which is a prerequisite for trading for all economic actors in integrated financial markets'.

Specifically, four types of behaviour are prohibited:

1. Engaging or attempting to engage in **insider dealing**.
2. Recommending that another person engage in insider dealing, or inducing another person to engage in insider dealing.
3. Unlawfully disclosing inside information.
4. Engaging, or attempting to engage, in market manipulation.

The MAR applies to financial instruments:

1. admitted to trading on a regulated market, or for which a request for admission to trading on a regulated market has been made
2. traded on a multilateral trading facility (MTF), admitted to trading on an MTF, or for which a request for admission to trading on an MTF has been made
3. traded on an organised trading facility (OTF), and
4. not covered by points (1), (2) or (3), the price or value of which depends on, or has an effect on, the price or value of a financial instrument referred to in those points, including, but not limited to, credit default swaps and contracts for difference.

The UK market abuse regime applies not only to the regulated sector, but also to the public at large, and sanctions may be imposed following a finding of severe market abuse. Offenders may face unlimited financial penalties and, if they work in the financial services sector, they could lose their livelihoods by having their authorisation/approval withdrawn or a prohibition order made against them.

The Markets in Financial Instruments Regulation (MiFIR), which has applied since January 2018, adds further requirements to the existing regime that compels firms to report transactions and plays a key role in the FCA's market abuse monitoring work. The FCA takes a serious view of firms which fail to report transactions in line with its rules or those who do not have in place adequate internal transaction reporting procedures and systems. Even in cases of market misconduct, which do not necessarily fall within the definition of civil market abuse, the FCA can still take action against a firm or individual (if they are authorised to conduct investment business) based on a breach of its principles in the FCA Handbook.

2.4.1 Insider Dealing

The first type of behaviour categorised as market abuse is insider dealing. This occurs where an insider deals or attempts to deal in a qualifying or related investment on the basis of inside information relating to the investment in question. This sits alongside the existing offence of criminal insider dealing which is an offence under Part V of the Criminal Justice Act 1993.

An insider can be defined as any person who has inside information as a result of:

- their membership of an administrative, management or supervisory body of an issuer of qualifying investments
- their holding in the capital of an issuer of qualifying investments
- having access to the information through the exercise of their employment, profession or duties
- their criminal activity, and
- other means which they know or could reasonably be expected to know.

The definition of inside information is broadly unchanged in the MAR, but is wider in scope in order to capture inside information for spot commodity contracts. In the MAR, inside information includes the following four key characteristics:

1. Information of a precise nature.
2. Information which has not been made public.
3. Information relating, directly or indirectly, to one or more issuers or to one or more financial instruments.
4. Information which, if it were made public, would be likely to have a significant effect on the prices of those financial instruments or on the price of related derivative financial instruments.

There is a separate definition of inside information for persons charged with the execution of orders (ie, traders and market makers) and a further definition for emission allowances and auction products based on these.

Front running is also classified as market abuse (ie, purchasing shares for a trader's own benefit on the basis of, and ahead of, orders from investors in order to benefit from an anticipated impact on prices).

2.4.2   Improper Disclosure

The second type of behaviour categorised as market abuse is improper disclosure. This occurs where an insider discloses inside information to another person otherwise than in the proper performance of their employment, profession or duties (this is commonly referred to as tipping off).

According to the FCA, certain factors are to be taken into account in determining whether or not disclosure is made by a person in the proper performance of their employment, profession or duties. These include whether the disclosure is:

*   permitted by FCA rules, the rules of a prescribed market, or the Takeover Code, or
*   accompanied by the imposition of confidentiality requirements upon the person to whom the disclosure is made and is reasonable, and is to enable a person to perform the proper functions of their employment, profession or duties.

2.4.3   Misuse of Information

Market abuse can also arise from the misuse of information. This occurs where behaviour is:

*   based on information which is not generally available to those using the market but which, if available to a regular user of the market, would be, or would be likely to be, regarded by them as relevant when deciding the terms on which transactions and qualifying investments should be effected, or
*   is likely to be regarded by a regular user of the market as a failure on the part of the person concerned to observe the standard of behaviour reasonably expected of the person in their position in relation to the market.

A regular user is defined, in relation to a particular market, as a reasonable person who regularly deals on that market in investments of the kind in question.

An example of this behaviour is when an employee of a company informs a friend over lunch that the company has received a takeover offer and the friend then places a spread bet with a bookmaker that the same company will be the subject of a bid within a week. Note that the person making the bet is guilty of misuse of information, but is not guilty of insider dealing as they are not dealing in qualifying investments, which is a requirement of the insider-dealing behaviour.

2.4.4   Manipulating Transactions

Market abuse can arise from manipulating transactions which occur when the behaviour consists of effecting transactions or orders to trade (other than for legitimate reasons and in conformity with accepted market practices on the relevant market) which:

*   give, or are likely to give, a false or misleading impression as to the supply of, or demand for, or as to the price of, one or more qualifying investments (for example, entering orders onto an electronic trading system at prices which are higher than the previous bid or lower than the previous offer and withdrawing them before they are executed in order to give a misleading impression that there is demand for, or supply of, the qualifying investment at that price), and

- secure the price of one or more such investments at an abnormal or artificial level (for example, trading on one market or trading platform with a view to improperly influencing the price of the same or related investments that are traded on another prescribed market).

An abusive squeeze is considered by the FCA to be a manipulating transaction. For example, a trader with a long position in bond futures buys or borrows a large amount of the cheapest-to-deliver bonds and either refuses to relend those bonds or will only lend them to parties the trader believes will not relend to the market. The purpose is to position the price at which those with short positions have to deliver to satisfy their obligations at a materially higher level, making the trader a profit from their original position.

Criminal market manipulation is an offence under Sections 89–91 of the Financial Services Act 2012.

The MAR defines and prohibits market manipulation and has been extended to capture attempted manipulation, benchmarks and, in some situations, spot commodity contracts.

2.4.5 Manipulating Devices

Manipulating devices consists of effecting transactions or orders to trade which employ fictitious devices or any other form of deception or contrivance. An example of this is taking advantage of occasional or regular access to traditional or electronic media by voicing an opinion about qualifying investments while having previously taken positions on the investments and subsequently profiting from the impact of the opinions voiced on the price of that instrument without having simultaneously disclosed that conflict of interest to the public in a proper and effective way.

'Pump and dump' (ie, taking a long position in an investment and then disseminating misleading positive information about that investment with a view to increasing its price) and trash and cash (ie, taking a short position in an investment and then disseminating misleading negative information about that investment with a view to driving down its price) are both considered by the FCA to be manipulating devices within the meaning of civil market abuse.

2.4.6 Dissemination

The sixth type of behaviour amounting to market abuse is dissemination. This consists of the dissemination of information by any means which gives, or is likely to give, a false or misleading impression, as to a qualifying investment, by a person who knew, or could reasonably be expected to have known, that the information was false or misleading.

An example of behaviour which, in the opinion of the FCA, falls within this category, is knowingly or recklessly spreading false and misleading information about a qualifying investment through the media. An example of the prohibited behaviour is the posting of information which contains false or misleading statements about a qualifying investment on an internet bulletin board or in a chat room in circumstances where the person knows that the information is false or misleading.

2.4.7   Misleading Behaviour or Distortion

The final type of behaviour amounting to market abuse is misleading behaviour or distortion, to the extent that it is not covered under the previous headings. This occurs when behaviour is likely to:

- give a regular user of the market a false and misleading impression as to the supply of, demand for or price or value of qualifying investments (misleading behaviour)
- be regarded by a regular user of the market as behaviour that will distort, or is likely to distort, the market in such an investment (distortion), or
- be regarded by a regular user of the market as a failure on the part of the person concerned to observe the standard of behaviour reasonably expected of a person in their position in relation to the market.

2.4.8   Penalties for Market Abuse

If the FCA is satisfied that a person is engaging in, or has engaged in, market abuse, or has required or encouraged another person to do so, it may:

- impose an unlimited civil fine
- make a public statement that the person has engaged in market abuse
- apply to the court for an injunction to restrain threatened or continued market abuse
- require a person to disgorge profits made or losses avoided as a result of market abuse, or
- require the payment of compensation to victims.

In some cases, the FCA may rely on individual recognised investment exchanges (RIEs) to take action and the FCA has agreed operating arrangements with such RIEs in relation to market conduct for this purpose.

2.4.9   Suspicious Transaction Reporting

The UK requirement for financial intermediaries involves the reporting of transactions giving rise to suspicions of market abuse. An FCA-authorised firm which arranges or executes a transaction with, or for, a client in a qualifying investment admitted to trading on a prescribed market, and which has reasonable grounds to suspect that the transaction may constitute market abuse, is required to notify the FCA without delay.

2.4.10 The London Stock Exchange (LSE) and Market Abuse

With the advent of the Markets in Financial Instruments Directive (MiFID), which has led to an expansion in the scope for off-exchange trading (see section 3 of this chapter), the role of the major stock exchanges to monitor the full range of MTFs has arguably diminished, which impairs the LSE's ability to monitor practices in accordance with the MAD. However, the MAR applies to financial instruments admitted to all MTFs, as well as regulated markets. Accordingly, the MAR now applies to the AIM (as an MTF) and other MTFs that admit to trading UK instruments that are also listed on the LSE.

2.5 The Panel on Takeovers and Mergers (the Takeover Panel or POTAM)

The UK supervisory authority that carries out the regulatory functions required under the EU Takeover Directive is the Panel on Takeovers and Mergers (the PTM or POTAM).

The Panel's requirements are set out in a Code that consists of six general principles and a number of detailed rules.

The Code is designed principally to ensure that shareholders are treated fairly and are not denied an opportunity to decide on the merits of a takeover. Furthermore, the Code ensures that shareholders of the same class are afforded equivalent treatment by an offeror. In short, the Code provides an orderly framework within which takeovers are conducted, and is designed to assist in promoting the integrity of the financial markets.

The European Takeovers Directive mandates that the Panel is put on a statutory footing. This was completed in the Companies Act 2006. Whenever a transaction is made on the LSE or other London-based exchange that is greater than £10,000, the details of the transaction get passed on to the panel for their evaluation, and a levy is charged of (currently) £1.00 on the transaction, which goes to the panel as payment (known as the PTM levy).

2.6 Publication of Announcements, Research and Ratings

From a short-term perspective, capital markets are highly sensitive to the publication of certain information. Among the announcements that are most likely to have an impact on market behaviour and settlement are the following.

2.6.1 Economic Data

The Office for National Statistics (ONS) in the UK publishes key economic reports regarding the labour market, inflation (CPI and RPI data) and the rate of growth or decline in GDP. All of these reports are subjected to detailed scrutiny and markets will often react to the data.

The key issue with respect to such data releases is the degree to which the published data has already been discounted by market participants. In other words, traders and investors will form opinions about the level of inflation before the actual release of the monthly CPI data and only if the numbers presented are notably out of alignment with the expectations will the market react strongly. The market is alleged to be a forward-looking discounting mechanism and as part of its pricing it will attempt to anticipate the direction of the major macroeconomic variables.

In the US, the monthly report from the Department of Labour on Non-Farm Payrolls is one of the most widely followed by market participants across the globe, as it provides one of the best indicators of the state of the US economy. Traders and investors use the data to make forward forecasts about the prospects for GDP growth and inflation and how this may affect the interest rate decisions by the Federal Reserve.

2.6.2   Central Bank Policy Announcements

Each month the Monetary Policy Committee (MPC) of the Bank of England meets to review the short-term interest rate policy – the repo rate – which is best suited to the current economic environment in the UK.

Market participants watch the announcements about rates very closely. Unexpected moves in interest rates, both upwards and downwards, have a large impact across all major asset classes. Bond prices respond well to reductions in short-term rates, sterling may suffer if the rate available for short-term sterling deposits is reduced, and the FTSE 100 will tend to move upwards on rate reductions. The opposite reactions tend to be seen on a rate increase, and more so if the rate hike was unexpected or more than had been expected.

The release of the minutes of each MPC meeting, which are usually published a few weeks after the actual meeting, are also of interest to the markets. The comments expressed by the committee members will be analysed carefully for any indications that monetary policy may be about to change.

Very similar issues arise in the case of the deliberations of the US central bank, the Federal Reserve. Since the US is the largest single economy (about 15% of world GDP) and the US dollar is the global reserve currency, the decisions about interest rates applicable on US dollar deposits/loans will have a greater impact on global capital markets than any other. However, in the current market environment, investors also pay particular attention to the activities of the Chinese government and its monetary policy, as well as the Chinese participation in the US Treasury market.

2.6.3   Credit Rating Announcements

During 2010, global capital markets became increasingly anxious about sovereign debt, and this was reflected in the enormous increase in the use of credit default swaps (CDSs) on individual sovereign borrowers. The decisions made by the major credit rating agencies to downgrade the debt of a particular sovereign issuer (such as happened to Greece, Ireland and Spain) can cause a 'flight to safety' as investors dump bonds from such issuers and seek out the safe haven of US Treasury bonds, and to some extent gilts. Even the announcement that a country is being put on credit watch by an agency will have a large impact in a market which is anxious about the levels of public debt in many nations.

2.6.4   Research Reports

The reports issued by brokerage firms and investment banks may have large macro-implications for markets in general, but will more often involve a particular sector or even a particular company's securities. The downgrade of a company's earnings outlook, which may have been triggered by the company's own announcements and forward-looking statements or even an unexpected comment on a conference call with investors, can often see a company's shares tumble.

If Goldman Sachs or J.P. Morgan tips a particular share for whatever reason, the price of that share is likely to rise. Once again this may be caused by buying or simply by the market makers pushing up the price in anticipation of likely buying.

2.6.5 Political Announcements

Some political announcements, especially relating to fiscal policy, also have the capacity to cause significant movements in markets. The recent series of announcements from governments regarding financial regulations and policies towards the banking system have introduced uncertainty into the future prospects for the banking sector. As another example of the impact of political statements on markets, in the summer of 2010, the announcements from President Obama regarding the horrendous oil spill in the Gulf of Mexico and the need for BP to be held fully accountable for the costs resulting from the damage done – both direct and indirect – saw the market capitalisation of BP fall by more than 50% since the oil spill occurred in April 2010.

3. Securities and Derivatives Markets

Learning Objective

7.1.4   Be able to assess the interactive relationship between the securities and derivatives markets, and the impact of related events on markets

7.1.5   Be able to assess the interactive relationship between different forms of fixed-interest securities and the impact of related events on markets

3.1   Derivatives and Underlying Securities

The financial markets have seen a constant stream of innovations in recent years and many of these are based on derivatives. In its simplest form a derivative is a security which is based upon or derived from another asset such as an individual equity, an equity index, a commodity or a financial instrument such as a gilt (or, in the US, a Treasury bond) or a foreign exchange rate. By its nature a derivative is a contractual asset which is traded actively, some more than others, and the valuation of the derivative is largely, if not completely, influenced by price movements in the underlying asset (often simply called the 'underlying'). In addition to price changes of the underlying, other variables, such as interest rates and price volatility (ie, variability in the price behaviour), will also be factored into the pricing and valuation of derivatives.

It is important to distinguish between those derivatives which are standardised and traded on public exchanges, and those which are customised and traded in private markets or over-the-counter (OTC). There are well known examples of both. Futures, for example, are standardised **contracts** requiring the delivery of some standard item within specific time frames and in standardised quantities. They are traded on exchanges such as the Chicago Mercantile Exchange (CME) and the London Metal Exchange (LME).

The trades are settled via clearing houses and the trading volumes and price behaviour are fully transparent and reported each day in the financial media. On the other hand, trading in credit default swaps (CDSs) is not conducted on public exchanges where clearing houses clear all of the trades, but rather they are agreements between two counterparties where the transaction takes place in an OTC marketplace, which could be facilitated by a swap dealer or broker. Such transactions are subject to counterparty risk, ie, when one or either party to such an OTC agreement could potentially default on its obligations, whereas futures contracts are cleared by a centralised clearing exchange and the risk of default is therefore transferred to a clearing house.

In this section, we shall be looking at three kinds of derivatives:

- **Options** – these are available on most asset classes, eg, equities and bonds. Options can even be written on futures.
- **Forwards** – this is a customised contract usually with a bank to buy or sell a specific item, which is often a foreign currency, for future delivery but at a rate and under terms which are agreed at the outset of entering into the contract.
- **Futures** – these are essentially standardised contracts to buy and sell a certain asset at a specified price with a delivery at some point in the future.

3.2 Options

3.2.1 Key Features

An option is a contract that confers upon the buyer the right, but not the obligation, to buy or sell an asset at a given price on or before a given date.

- The right to buy is known as a call option.
- The right to sell is known as a put option.
- The rights to buy (call) or sell (put) are held by the person buying the option, who is known as the holder.
- The person selling an option is known as a writer.
- The price at which the holder can buy or sell is the exercise price or strike price.

The following diagram shows the structure of an option agreement between the buyer or holder of an option and the seller or writer of an option.

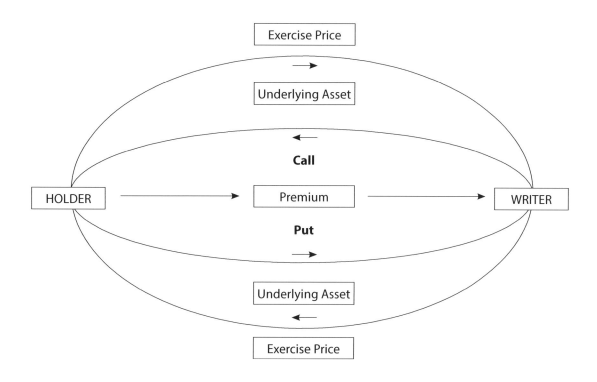

The premium is the cost of an option. It is paid by the holder and received by the writer. The holder is obliged to pay the premium, even if they do not exercise the option.

Depending on the option specification, the premium may be paid upon the purchase of the option (up front) or upon exercise of the option (on close).

In return for receiving the premium, the writer agrees to fulfil the terms of the contract, which of course are different for calls and puts.

Call writers agree to deliver the asset underlying the contract if 'called upon' to do so. When options holders wish to take up their rights under the contract, they are said to exercise the contract. For a call, this means that the writer must deliver the underlying asset for which they will receive the fixed amount of cash stipulated in the original contract.

Put writers agree that the asset can be 'put upon' them, ie, if the contract is exercised by the holder, the writer must pay the fixed amount of cash stipulated in the contract and receive delivery of the underlying asset.

The date on which an option comes to the end of its life is known as its expiry date. The expiry date is the last day on which the option may be exercised or traded. After this date the option disappears and cannot be traded or exercised.

There are four basic options trades, as follows:

- Buying a call option.
- Selling a call option.
- Buying a put option.
- Selling a put option.

Options are available in a range of different exercise styles, which are specified when the options are traded. There are four potential styles.

- **American-style options** – in which the option can be exercised by the holder at any time after the option has been purchased.
- **European-style options** – when the option can only be exercised on its expiry date.
- **Asian-style options** – when the option is exercised at the average underlying price over a set period of time. Traded average price options (TAPOs) are similar. These are fixed strike price, but are exercised against an average underlying price.
- **Bermudan option** – when the option can be exercised at a set number of dates.

A person describing an option will specify its:

- underlying asset (eg, gold, per ounce)
- expiry date (eg, May)
- exercise price (eg, $850), and
- call/put.

3.2.2 Buying an Option for Speculation

A speculator anticipating a rise in the price of gold could straightforwardly buy gold for immediate delivery and store it safely with a view to selling for a profit once the price has risen. Let us assume that the spot price of gold is $1,200 per ounce and that the speculator decides to purchase 100 ounces for a total expenditure of $120,000.

An alternative way to speculate that the price of gold is going to increase is to purchase an option – specifically, an option that gives the right, but not the obligation, for a period of three months to buy gold at a price of $1,200 per ounce. The purchaser of this option might have to pay $10 per ounce for the option at present if the spot price is at $1,200 per ounce. This would be referred to as an at-the-money option as the price for the underlying asset has the same value as the exercise price of $1,200 per ounce.

Theoretically, at-the-money options are priced on their time value premium only because at the present time the option has no intrinsic value. If the option exercise price was $1,190 per ounce, and the spot price was $1,200 per ounce, the option would have an intrinsic value of $10 per ounce in addition to the time value, so the price would, for simplicity, be equal to $20 per ounce.

The more deeply in-the-money the option is, the higher the price will be, to reflect the fact that there is substantial intrinsic value to the option. If the option were deeply out-of-the-money, for example, with an exercise price of $1,250 per ounce, there would be zero intrinsic value and the time premium would be the only value to be determined for this option which, on the surface at least, would not have a high likelihood of being exercised with a profit unless gold were to exceed $1,250 per ounce during the holding period of the option.

Remember that an option is a contract for a future delivery, so the only money to be invested at this point is the sum of $10 per ounce. A standard, exchange-cleared options contract would be for the purchase of 100 ounces, so the cost at the outset would be $1,000. It is now apparent that one of the main features of purchasing an option is that it requires substantially less outlay than purchasing the underlying asset.

If, three months later, as expected by the speculator, the price of gold has risen quite sharply from $1,200 per ounce to $1,300 per ounce, we can consider the effect on the two possible ways that the speculator could have decided to proceed:

- buying physical gold from a bullion dealer, or
- buying an option to purchase gold.

The person who bought 100 ounces of gold from the bullion dealer at $1,200 would have made a profit of $100 per ounce and therefore a total profit of 100 x 100 = $10,000.

Now, let us look at the profit for the options buyer. Three months ago, the speculator entered into a contract that gave them the right, but not the obligation, to buy gold at $1,200 per ounce and, when purchased, that right cost just $10 per ounce.

With gold now trading at $1,300, the right to buy at $1,200 must be worth at least $100 – the difference between the current price and the stated price in the contract.

The return to the option buyer is the difference between the $130,000, which the 100 ounces are currently worth in the spot market, and the $120,000 the buyer would pay to exercise the option, minus the $1,000 which was the price to purchase the option, in other words $9,000.

On an investment of $10 per ounce, a $90 profit has been achieved. In percentage terms, this profit is spectacularly greater than on the conventional purchase and sale of the physical commodity or asset. This is not even taking into account any costs of carry or storage for the buyer of physical bullion.

Options are tradeable instruments. It is not necessary for the underlying asset to be delivered or received. What more commonly occurs is that options are bought and sold. Thus, an option bought at $10 could be sold to the market at $100, realising a $90 profit, with the investor never having had any intention of buying the underlying asset. Options are used both for speculation and for hedging.

3.3   Forwards

A forward contract is very similar to that of a future (see section 3.4) in that it is an agreement to buy or sell a specific quantity of a specified asset on a fixed future date at a price agreed today. However, a forward contract is a customised OTC contract, whereas a future is standardised and exchange-traded. The differences between futures and forward contracts are summarised in the following table.

Attribute	Futures	Forward Contracts
How are they traded?	Traded on public exchanges, eg, CME, NYMEX	Over-the-counter (OTC)
Quality	Standardised, eg, the following is the specification for crude oil futures traded on the NYMEX – 1,000 barrels of West Texas Intermediate Crude Oil	Customised and the full specification is provided in the contract
Delivery dates	Standard fixed dates, eg, S&P 500 Index futures available for March, June, September and December	Bespoke (as specified in the contract)
Liquidity/ ability to close out	Most futures markets are very liquid and contracts can be traded before delivery is required	Market may lack liquidity and there can be bouts of systemic problems where trading becomes very difficult
Settlement	Most futures contracts are settled in cash or rolled forward prior to actual delivery	Bespoke (as specified in the contract)
Counterparty risk	None, owing to the workings of the clearing and settlement system	Default risk exists – if a counterparty becomes insolvent, eg, Lehman Brothers
Costs/margin	Relatively low initial costs (margin)	Costs are customised for the purpose at hand and, depending on the sophistication, may be high
Regulation	In the US, regulation is from the CFTC. In the UK, the FCA is the main regulatory authority of commodities and futures trade	Less regulated

3.4 Futures

A futures contract is an agreement to buy or sell a standard quantity of a specified asset on a fixed future date, at a price agreed today.

- **Standardised quantity** – exchange-traded futures are traded in standardised parcels known as contracts. For example, a futures contract on lead might be for 25 tonnes of the metal, or a currency future might be for €20,000. The purpose of this standardisation is so that buyers and sellers are clear about the quantity that will be delivered. If you sold one lead future, you would know that you were obliged to sell 25 tonnes of lead. Futures are only traded in whole numbers of contracts. This limitation is one of the factors which favours swaps as an attractive alternative to using futures contracts. But on the other hand, futures contracts have the benefit that they are exchange-cleared, which removes the counterparty risk element in a swap.
- **Homogeneous and specified asset** – all futures contracts are governed by their contract specifications, and legal documents set out in detail the size of each contract, when delivery is to take place, and what exactly is to be delivered. For example, in the crude oil futures market, the contract which is actively traded on the NYMEX in New York calls for delivery of oil in terms of West Texas Intermediate Crude, whereas the contracts traded in the London market call for delivery in terms of Brent Crude.

- **Fixed future date** – the delivery of futures contracts takes place on a specified date(s) known as delivery day(s). This is when buyers exchange money for goods with sellers. Futures have finite life spans so that, once the last trading day has passed, it is impossible to trade the futures for that date. At any one time, a range of delivery months may be traded and, as one delivery day passes, a new date is introduced. Contracts may be rolled over from one expiry date to another by settling the current contract and moving into a new futures contract with later expiration.
- **Price agreed today** – many people, from farmers to fund managers, use futures because they provide certainty or a reduction of risk. Futures are tradeable, so, although the contract obligates the buyer to buy and the seller to sell, these obligations can be offset by undertaking an equal and opposite trade in the market. For example, let us suppose a farmer has sold a September wheat future at £120 per tonne. If, subsequently, they decide they do not wish to sell their wheat but would prefer to use the grain to feed their cattle, they would simply buy a September future at the then prevailing price. Their original sold position is now offset by a bought position, leaving them with no outstanding delivery obligations. This offsetting is common in future markets, and very few contracts run through to delivery.

There are two parties to a futures contract – a buyer and a seller – whose respective obligations are as follows:

- The buyer of a future enters into an obligation to buy.
- The seller of a future is under an obligation to sell.

As well as futures in commodities and metals, there are also futures based on financial instruments, prices or indices. Financial futures contracts commonly used include:

- FTSE 100 Index Future.
- S&P 500 Index Future.
- Three-Month Sterling Future.
- UK Gilt Future.
- US Treasury Bond Future.
- Universal Stock Futures.

3.4.1 Tick Size and Value

With all futures contracts the tick is a fundamental concept, which needs to be clearly understood, to see how the instruments change in value and how the contractual commitment that is undertaken by both parties to the contract changes.

- The tick size is the smallest permitted quote movement on one contract.
- The tick value is the change in the value of one contract, if there is a one-tick change in the quote.

Let us begin by examining one of the most actively traded futures contracts on a daily basis, which is the S&P 500 index futures contract, traded at the Chicago Mercantile Exchange (CME).

The contract size for this index future is equal to $250 multiplied by the value of the index. So, if the index is trading at 1600, the value of the contract is $400,000. The tick size for this contract is 0.10 of the index, so a sequence of prices traded for the future might be quoted in similar fashion to the following: 1599.70, 1599.80, 1599.90, 1600.00.

The value associated with each tick will be $25. This enables us to calculate our futures dealing profit or loss by using the following formula:

$$\text{Profit} = \text{Quote change in ticks} \times \text{Tick value} \times \text{Number of contracts}$$

So if, for example, a speculator buys two contracts of the S&P 500 at 1599.1 and sells those two contracts shortly after at 1600 exactly, the profit would be:

$$\text{Profit} = 90 \text{ bps}/0.10 = 9 \text{ ticks} \times \$25 \times 2 \text{ contracts} = \$900$$

3.4.2 Hedging with Futures

Futures can be used both for speculation and for hedging. As an example, the FTSE 100 Index Future fixes the price at which the underlying index may be bought or sold at a specific future date. We may use this contract to gain exposure to, or hedge exposure against, the index, ie, the stock market in general.

Unit of Trade

$$\text{Unit of trade} = \text{Index value} \times £10$$

That is, a contract can be valued by multiplying the index value by £10. If, for example, the index stood at 6800, then one contract would have a value of $6800 \times £10 = £68,000$.

Under these circumstances we can consider the perspective of the speculator and the hedger. Either person may buy – or take a long position in – the index future, or may wish to sell – or take a short position in – the index future.

A speculator who believes that the FTSE 100 is about to move upwards could gain long exposure to the index by buying a single futures contract, which would in effect give the speculator £68,000 of exposure to the market. Another speculator who believes that the FTSE 100 is going to go down might decide to sell – or go short of – the index as a result of selling a single futures contract, which would mean that they would be short of £68,000 worth of the index and would profit if the market falls.

In contrast to the pure speculator, who is really interested in following hunches about the future direction of the index and is attempting to benefit from making the right call and going either long or short, a hedger is someone who already has a stake in the market and is looking to hedge their risk by having an offsetting position in the futures market. If by chance someone owned exactly £68,000-worth of stocks which were representative of the index and that person became nervous that the market is about to go down, then selling a single futures contract would provide an offset or hedge to the loss of value of the actual holdings of equities.

Delivery

This contract is cash-settled. That is, rather than the two parties exchanging the underlying asset and the pre-agreed price at the delivery date, they simply settle up by the payment from one to the other of the difference in value.

Quotation

The quote given is in index points.

Tick

The tick size – the smallest permitted quote movement – is 0.5 index points. The tick value is £5.00, ie, $0.5 \times £10$.

Example

We are managing a £31 million pension fund portfolio and we believe that the market is about to fall. The index and the future currently stand at 6200. The alternatives are: sell the portfolio and move into cash/bonds – this will avoid the market fall, but will clearly incur massive dealing costs; or set up a short hedge using the futures contract.

Short hedge

The future is quoted at 6200, hence each contract will hedge £62,000 (6200 x £10) of our exposure. To hedge the full portfolio, we will therefore need, quite conveniently, exactly 500 contracts (£31 million ÷ £62,000).

Let us now consider what our position is if the market (and the futures contract) falls 200 points.

Cash position

Old portfolio value £31,000,000
New portfolio value = £31,000,000 x 6000/6200 = £30,000,000
Loss = £1,000,000

Futures position

Sold index at 6200
Bought index to close position at 6000
Points gain: 200 = 400 ticks

Hence, the total profit on our 500 contracts sold short will be:

Profit = Ticks × Tick value × Number of contracts = 400 × £5.00 × 500 = £1,000,000

The profit on the short futures position exactly cancels the loss on the portfolio and hence represents a good hedging strategy.

In the case presented, there was an exact match because the size of the portfolio and the value of the index produce an integer value for the number of contracts required for hedging purposes. If a fractional value is obtained when dividing the size of the portfolio by the current size of the contract (based upon the actual FTSE 100 index value), then the number can be rounded down to the nearest integer and the hedge will not be a 100% match, but will still provide an effective way of allowing the portfolio manager to shelter the portfolio from adverse movements in the overall market.

Hedge Ratio

One assumption we have made here is that our pension fund portfolio is only as volatile as the index, ie, it has ß = 1. Beta (ß) measures the amount of fluctuation of one variable against another. If this is not the case, then we may need to sell more or fewer contracts to achieve the hedge. The important determinant is the relative volatility.

By definition, the futures contract has a ß = 1. If the portfolio has a ß = 1.3, then a 1% change in the index will cause a 1% change in the value of a future but a 1.3% change in the portfolio value. We will therefore need 1.3 times as many futures contracts to provide sufficient profit to cancel any losses suffered in the portfolio.

When we hedge with futures, we should follow the formula below for determining how many contracts will be required to ensure that the hedging reflects the relative volatilities of the portfolio and the underlying instrument upon which the futures contract is based.

$$\text{Hedging required number of contracts} = \frac{\text{Portfolio value}}{\text{Futures value}} \times h$$

where:

h is the hedge ratio, which reflects the relative volatilities of the portfolio and the hedging instrument

In the case of hedging a portfolio against the FTSE contract the value for h – the hedge ratio – is simply found by using the beta value of the portfolio.

$$h = \frac{\text{Volatility of the Portfolio}}{\text{Volatility of the Futures Contract}} = \frac{-ß_p}{ß_f} = -ß_p \text{ since } ß_f = 1$$

3.5   Credit Default Swaps (CDSs)

A CDS is a credit derivative contract between two counterparties. The buyer makes periodic payments to the seller, and in return receives a payoff if an underlying financial instrument defaults.

As an example, imagine that an investor buys a CDS from ABC investment bank where the reference entity is XYZ ltd, which is a company which has a non-investment grade rating from the major ratings agencies. The investor will make regular payments to ABC bank, and if XYZ ltd defaults on its debt the investor will receive a one-off payment from ABC bank and the CDS contract is terminated. A default could be more specifically defined but generally means that a coupon payment has been missed and the company has failed to make good on the payment during a pre-determined grace period.

The investor may or may not actually own any of XYZ ltd's debt. If the investor does, the CDS can be thought of as hedging or protection. But investors can also buy CDS contracts referencing the debt of a company without actually owning any of it. This is known as having a naked CDS position and will be done for speculative purposes, to bet against the solvency of XYZ ltd in a gamble to make money if it fails, or perhaps to hedge investments in other companies whose trading performance might be dependent on the fortunes of XYZ ltd.

If XYZ ltd defaults, one of two things can happen:

- The investor delivers a defaulted asset to the bank for a payment of the par value. This is known as physical settlement.
- The bank pays the investor the difference between the par value and the market price of a specified debt obligation, ie, there is usually some recovery value and not all value will be destroyed for a bondholder. This is known as cash settlement and is clearly the method which will be followed if the investor has a naked CDS position and does not in fact own any of the bonds which have defaulted.

The CDS is quoted in terms of a spread, and this is the annual amount the protection buyer must pay the protection seller over the length of the contract, expressed as a percentage of the notional amount. For example, if the CDS spread for XYZ ltd was 50 basis points, or 0.5%, then an investor buying $10 million-worth of protection from the bank selling the protection will have to pay the bank $50,000 per year. These payments will continue until either the CDS contract expires or XYZ ltd defaults.

If the maturity of two CDSs is the same, then a company associated with a higher CDS spread is considered by the markets to be more likely to default since a higher fee is being charged to protect against this happening. This is very similar to the notion of an insurance premium being commensurate with the likelihood of the event being insured against actually occurring. However, their factors such as liquidity and the estimated loss should a default occur will make comparison less straightforward.

Credit spread rates and credit ratings of the underlying or reference obligations are considered among money managers to be the best indicators of the likelihood of sellers of CDSs to have to perform under these contracts. In fact, in the money markets, the CDS spread rates have become some of the most widely followed of market barometers.

It is also worth mentioning the CDS market in sovereign credit risk. This market considers the possibility of a sovereign borrower – such as the UK government or the US government – defaulting on its obligations. Surprisingly, during the financial crisis of 2008–09 there had been periods when the CDS spread on US Treasuries was higher than the spread quoted on the fast food chain McDonald's.

3.5.1 Speculation

CDSs allow investors to speculate on changes in CDS spreads of single names or on changes in market indices such as the North American CDX Index or the European iTraxx Index. Or, an investor might believe that an entity's CDS spreads are either too high or too low relative to the entity's bond yields, and attempt to profit from that view by entering into a trade, known as a basis trade, which combines a CDS with a cash bond and an interest rate swap.

An investor might have reasons to speculate on an entity's credit quality, since in most circumstances a CDS spread will increase as creditworthiness declines, and diminish as creditworthiness increases. The investor might therefore buy CDS protection on a company in order to speculate that the company is about to default. Alternatively, the investor might sell protection if they think that the company's creditworthiness might improve.

Using as an example the scenario involving XYZ ltd, let us examine how a hedge fund could profit from a default by XYZ ltd on its debt. The hedge fund buys $10 million worth of CDS protection for two years from ABC Bank at a spread of 500 basis points (ie, 5%) pa.

- If XYZ ltd does indeed default after, say, one year, then the hedge fund will have paid $500,000 to the bank, but will then receive $10 million (assuming zero recovery rate, and that the bank remains solvent), thereby making a profit. The bank, *prima facie*, will incur a $9.5 million loss unless it has laid off or offset its outright exposure before the default. ABC Bank could, for example, have taken out a counterbalancing CDS with another financial institution.
- However, if XYZ ltd does not default, then the CDS contract will run for two years, and the hedge fund will have ended up paying $1 million, without any return, thereby making a loss.

Note that there is a third possibility in the above scenario; the hedge fund could decide to liquidate its position after a certain period of time in an attempt to lock in its gains or losses. For example:

- After one year, the market now considers XYZ ltd more likely to default, so its CDS spread has widened from 500 to 1,500 basis points. The hedge fund may choose to sell $10 million-worth of protection for one year to ABC Bank (or another bank) at this higher rate. Therefore, over the two years, the hedge fund will pay the bank 2 x 5% x $10 million = $1 million, but will receive 1 x 15% x $10 million = $1.5 million, giving a total profit of $500,000 (assuming XYZ ltd does not default during the second year).
- In an alternative scenario, after one year, the market now considers XYZ ltd much less likely to default, so its CDS spread has tightened from 500 to 250 basis points. Again, the hedge fund may choose to sell $10 million-worth of protection for one year to ABC Bank at this lower spread. Therefore, over the two years the hedge fund will pay the bank 2 x 5% x $10 million = $1 million, but will receive 1 x 2.5% x $10 million = $250,000, giving a total loss of $750,000 (again assuming that XYZ ltd does not default during the second year). This loss is smaller than the $1 million loss that would have occurred if the second transaction had not been entered into.

Transactions such as these do not even have to be entered into over the long term. CDS spreads can widen by a few basis points over the course of one day. The hedge fund could have entered into an offsetting contract immediately and made a small profit over the life of the two CDS contracts.

3.5.2   Hedging

CDSs are often used to manage the credit risk (ie, the risk of default) which arises from holding debt. Typically, the holder of a corporate bond, for example, may hedge their exposure by entering into a CDS contract as the buyer of protection. If the bond goes into default, the proceeds from the CDS contract will cancel out the losses on the underlying bond.

Example

A pension fund owns $10 million of a five-year bond issued by XYZ ltd. In order to manage the risk of losing money if the company defaults on its debt, the pension fund buys a CDS from Derivative Bank in a notional amount of $10 million. The CDS trades at 200 basis points (200 basis points = 2.00%). In return for this credit protection, the pension fund pays 2% of $10 million ($200,000) pa in quarterly instalments of $50,000 to Derivative Bank.

- If XYZ ltd does not default on its bond payments, the pension fund makes quarterly payments to Derivative Bank for five years and receives its $10 million back after five years from XYZ ltd. Though the protection payments totalling $1 million reduce investment returns for the pension fund, its risk of loss due to a default on the bond have been eliminated. The hedge achieved its purpose.
- If XYZ ltd defaults on its debt three years into the CDS contract, the pension fund will stop paying the quarterly premium, and Derivative Bank will ensure that the pension fund is refunded for its loss of $10 million. The pension fund still loses the $600,000 it has paid over three years, but without the CDS contract it would have lost the entire $10 million.

3.5.3   Current Issues

There is ongoing debate concerning the possibility of limiting so-called naked CDSs. A naked CDS is one when the buyer has no risk exposure to the underlying entity. Hence, naked CDSs do not hedge risk *per se*, but are mere speculative bets that actually create risk.

Some suggest that buyers be required to have a stake, or element of risk exposure, in the underlying entity that the CDS pays out on. In June 2010, the German government decided to impose a ban on the use of naked CDSs in Germany.

Others suggest that a mere partial stake in the underlying risk is insufficient, and insist that buyer protection be limited to insurable risk; that is, the actual value of the capital-at-risk in the underlying entity. This means the CDS buyer would have to own the bond or loan that triggers a payout on default.

Still others, also calling for the outright ban of naked CDSs, claim that it is poor public policy to provide financial incentive to one party which pays off only when some other party suffers a loss – the argument being that it is foolish to incentivise the first party to nefariously intervene in the affairs of the second party so as to cause, or to contribute to loss.

In 2012, the EU banned uncovered or naked positions in sovereign CDSs.

3.6   Fixed-Interest Securities and Spreads

As previously discussed, there are numerous forms of fixed-interest securities, and these cover a wide range, from sovereign issues such as the gilts issued by the UK government, the Treasury bonds issued by the US government and the *bunds* from the German government all the way across the spectrum to high-yield securities for relatively high-risk corporations which are somewhat disparagingly called junk bonds.

Fund managers will almost invariably want to have a sizeable portion of their portfolio allocated to fixed-income securities, and they could include those just mentioned as well as selections from the variety of investment grade corporate bonds, which are available from many issuers throughout global capital markets.

Much attention is placed by asset managers on the relationships which exist between the different kinds of fixed-interest securities, and much of this analysis is based upon what are commonly called spread relationships.

Spreads can exist between the same genre of fixed-interest security, for example, between different maturities of that security, the most obvious example being the relationship between government bonds of different maturities. On the other hand, there are many kinds of spreads, involving different securities from different issuers with contrasting credit qualities, and these are analysed and followed closely by asset allocators.

3.6.1 Types of Spread

The four broad kinds of spreads which are most relevant to asset managers fall into the following categories:

1. Term spreads.
2. Default spreads.
3. Credit quality spreads.
4. Sovereign spreads.

Term Spreads

The term spread is the difference between the yields of long- and short-dated bonds. The yield spread between a two-year note or gilt and a ten-year gilt is often used for the purpose of UK investors. The key value which is used for calculating the spreads is the gross redemption yield (GRY) (sometimes called, especially in the US, the yield to maturity).

The GRY of a two-year note can be expressed in basis points. For example, a two-year note which has a GRY of 1.5% can be quoted as being a yield of 150 basis points. Let us say that the GRY on a ten-year gilt is quoted at 3.5% or 350 basis points; then the 2/10 spread can be stated simply as the difference between the two yields, in this case simply as 200 basis points.

There are many reasons why following this particular spread can be advisable for investment managers. Some reasons have to do with the ability to trade the spread. For example, if one believes that the spread is going to widen to (say) 250 basis points, the asset manager could decide to have long positions in the two-year note and short positions in the ten-year gilt. Most likely the widening of the spread is based upon an increase in yield in the ten-year leg of the spread, and an increase in yield will result from a decrease in the price, which will benefit someone who has taken a short position in the ten-year leg of the spread.

All that matters is that the differential or spread moves in accordance with the anticipation of a widening of the spread and the trade can be profitable.

In general terms, the term structure of interest rates, or yield curve, is often regarded as a leading indicator of economic activity, or at least captures the market's perception of the future rate of economic activity. In the growth part of an economic cycle, 2/10 spread measure tends to be more positive, with an upward-sloping yield curve with long-bond yields exceeding short-bond yields. This spread will often exceed 200 basis points and could go much higher depending on the overall level of interest rates. At the onset of a recession, the 2/10 measure tends to flatten and can even become negative if the yield curve inverts.

The 2/10 spread can, with some allowance for other factors relating to the role of the public finances, therefore be used to predict the position in the economic cycle and what kind of interest rate environment lies ahead.

Careful analysis of the term spread can also be used to determine when a yield curve ride may be most beneficial and to undertake spread trades or engage in a form of trading activity known as 'riding the yield curve', which is covered in section 7.6.1.

Default Spreads

The default spread is the difference between the yields of investment grade corporate bonds and gilts.

In assessing the overall investment risk from a credit perspective of fixed-interest securities in general, it is customary to compare the gross redemption yield on a ten-year investment grade bond – perhaps limited to those of A– and above – with the GRY of a ten-year gilt. For a US-based investor, the comparison will be between an investment grade corporate bond and the yield to maturity on a ten-year US Treasury note.

As seen above, it is customary to quote this spread in basis points, and the prevailing level of this spread can provide a good barometer of the market's perceptions regarding the overall creditworthiness of the corporate sector.

Government bonds are assumed in most financial theory to be risk-free, and, if the spread between the yield on a ten-year government bond and the equivalent yield for a ten-year corporate bond is relatively speaking rather low or narrow, then this low spread will reflect the perception that the corporate fixed-interest sector is not considered to be at much risk.

In other words, in a buoyant economy, the default spread tends to narrow, whereas in a recession the spread tends to widen. This widening can be especially acute during times of financial crisis such as were seen in Q4 2008.

As before, the default spread can, if used judiciously, be helpful in predicting the position in the economic cycle for market timing purposes.

Credit Quality Spreads

Another variation on this theme is to consider the spread between high-yield bonds and investment grade corporate bonds, or the spread between so-called 'junk bonds' and gilts.

As an example, let us suppose that the typical GRY for a AAA corporate bond is quoted at 5% and the average GRY for a high-yield corporate is quoted at 8%; then the yield spread for investment grade to junk can be quoted as 300 basis points. As an alternative approach, the spread can be quoted between the GRY for high-yield corporates and government bonds of similar maturities.

During the financial crisis of 2008, there were two factors at work which caused the spread between high-yield and government bonds to widen rather dramatically. At the height of the banking crisis in 2008, there was considerable anxiety among asset managers about the possibility of bankruptcies and economic dislocation in general. This anxiety produced a flight to safety in which asset managers sold many assets that were perceived to be of inferior quality and invested the proceeds from such liquidations into government securities.

For example, at the end of 2008, the GRY on the US ten-year Treasury note was barely 2% or 200 basis points (similarly, extremely low yields were seen on gilts, bunds and in most government bond markets), while the typical yield on a junk bond reached up into the mid-teens. In such circumstances, the spread between government and junk widened substantially from a more typical value of 200/300 basis points to as high as 1,500 basis points.

Admittedly, there were some very extreme spreads between many kinds of fixed-interest securities during the 2008 crisis, and many astute investors and traders decided to purchase those securities which were very much out of favour as they anticipated that, given an eventual return to more normal circumstances, the spreads would revert back to their more typical levels. By purchasing out-of-favour speculative and non-investment grade corporate bonds during the early part of 2009, many fund managers were able to make huge profits when the liquidity of the corporate bond markets returned to more normal conditions.

Another feature of this spread relationship to observe is that the yields on government bonds will tend to increase when there is less anxiety about systematic (and systemic) risk and less desire to seek out the safe haven of gilts and Treasury securities.

Sovereign Spreads

There is one further type of spread which is becoming increasingly important for investment managers to follow, and this one relates to the difference between the yields available on the government bonds of different sovereigns. This has become especially significant since 2010 when there have been much-publicised difficulties for peripheral states in the eurozone countries in terms of their creditworthiness. Beginning in 2010, the government of Greece had to be assisted with borrowings in excess of €100 billion in order to stave off insolvency. This was followed shortly thereafter by the governments of Ireland and Portugal.

In the summer of 2011, the Greek government was subject to emergency funding by the IMF and the EU, as it was unable to raise any capital from private investors in the capital markets and had to rely on continual funding provided by the European Central Bank (ECB). The GRY on ten-year Greek government bonds climbed to almost 30% during June 2011, indicating that the markets believed there was a very high likelihood that the Greek government would eventually have to restructure its debt or possibly experience an outright default.

By the summer of 2015, Greece's national debt was €320 billion, and it had a credit rating of CCC– from S&P.

Historically, several governments have defaulted on their debt obligations, with Argentina and Russia being two of the most notable.

One method for determining the creditworthiness of different sovereign issues is by quoting the spread between the issues of governments which are perceived by the markets as being extremely low risk, ie, AAA-rated sovereigns, and the yields of more problematic sovereigns. During the crisis of 2010–11, among the peripheral states, the most commonly quoted spread was between the ten-year yield on (say) Greek, Irish or Portuguese debt and the yield on the ten-year *bund* from Germany, which is considered to be the safest government issue in the eurozone (and even one of the safest credits available globally).

So when the ten-year *bund* yielded 300 basis points and the yield on Irish bonds was 13% or 14%, there was a 1,100 basis point spread between these two sovereign issues.

Factors which will affect sovereign spreads are clearly related to macroeconomic circumstances in the various economies and, specifically, the differences in such factors as GDP growth rates, the level of public finance deficits and the competitiveness of the two economies for which the spread is quoted. Again looking at Greece, the debt/GDP ratio exceeds 150%. In comparison with Germany, Greece has an unattractive cost structure within its economy, too large a public sector and a failure to collect taxation revenues to assist in financing its large obligations to the public sector.

The credit-rating agencies have been very active during the crisis in the eurozone in monitoring the creditworthiness of sovereign borrowers. Many states have suffered serious downgrades as the agencies have become very focused on the high levels of public sector debt, weak tax revenues and very slow economic growth.

While Greece dropped to a CCC-, it was then upgraded to a CCC+ in July 2015 after agreeing to a series of concessions to obtain short-term financing from other European nations to assist meeting debt payments, restructuring debts and implementing austerity measures. In 2018, Greece's credit rating was upgraded by S&P in April 2021 to BB, with a positive outlook by Moody's in November 2020 to Ba3 (each with a stable outlook), and in April 2020 by Fitch to BB- with a stable outlook.

Also troubling is the fact that many other European governments have been placed on alert by the agencies with negative outlooks. As a consequence, large private sector investors – mainly the large banks, insurance companies and pension funds – have either decided not to buy the debt of those sovereigns which are seen to be at risk, or are demanding very substantial yields, ie, high interest coupons, to compensate them for the possibility of restructurings or default. This makes any new debt more expensive to service for the sovereign borrower.

In addition, the market for sovereign CDSs has been extremely active, with many fund managers deciding to either hedge or insure against default on existing exposure to sovereign credit risk, or to speculate on widening or narrowing of spreads, even if they have no actual cash positions in the underlying sovereign debt market to protect.

3.6.2 The Impact of Related Events to Spreads between Fixed-Interest Securities

For a fund manager, the impact of many kinds of events will lead to asset reallocations among different securities in general, and more specifically to the mix they hold of different fixed-interest securities. Such reallocations are often referred to as policy switching.

Some of the factors which will instigate policy switches can be summarised as follows.

Changes in Interest Rates

Intuitions about the future direction of interest rates, and market timing in general, is one of the primary factors that will encourage fund managers to switch between different bonds. Switching from low-duration to high-duration bonds if interest rates are expected to fall is an example of a policy switch which will cause spreads to change.

Changes in the Structure of the Yield Curve

Normally, the yield curve is a smooth relationship between yield and maturity. Often, however, there may be humps or dips in the curve. If the humps or dips are expected to disappear, then the prices of the bonds on the hump can be expected to rise (and their yield fall correspondingly), and the prices of the bonds in the dips can be expected to fall (and their yields correspondingly rise). A policy switch would involve the purchase of the high-yield bond and the sale of the low-yield bond.

Expectations about the Future Shape of the Yield Curve

A downward-sloping or inverted curve suggests that markets believe that rates will fall. In the inverse pattern to that when expectations are for higher rates in the future, if the expectation is for lower rates in the future, bond purchases will be keen to lock in higher coupons now as the expectation is that coupons will decline in the future.

A flat yield curve suggests that the market thinks that rates will not materially change in the future.

Changes in Bond Quality Ratings

A bond whose credit quality rating as, for example, rated by Standard & Poor's or Moody's is expected to fall will drop in price. To prevent a capital loss, it can be switched for a bond whose quality rating is expected to rise or remain unchanged. This is an uncertain process and often there are no advance warnings of the re-rating of credit by the major rating agencies.

Changes in Sector Relationships

An example of a change in sector relationships is a change in taxes between two sectors. For example, one sector may have withholding taxes on coupon payments, eg, domestic bonds, whereas another, eg, eurobonds, may not.

Anticipation of Monetary Policy

The only point on the yield curve which can be fixed is immediate short-term rates, set by intervention of the Bank of England or other central banks through operations in the money markets.

If short-term interest rates are deliberately being moved higher by the Bank, the market's expectation may well be that eventually this will lead to a downward-sloping yield curve, referred to as an 'inverted' curve. This reflects the market's expectations that the Bank may be trying to arrest inflationary pressures in the economy. If the market believes that inflation will rise in the future, then the yields on longer-dated gilts will have to rise in order to compensate investors for the fall in the real value of their money.

The expectation of inflation is more of a problem with the long end, rather than the short end, owing to the greater sensitivity to interest rates of longer-duration fixed-interest instruments. Once again, this will be reflected in the 2/10 spread referred to in section 3.6.1.

3.6.3   Summary

The financial markets have become very sophisticated in analysing the co-movements of yields and interest rates across a wide spectrum of fixed-income instruments. Many spreads are quoted in real time in the money markets, and the manner in which other sectors of capital markets respond to these changes in spreads has led to increasingly coordinated movements across multiple asset classes. Many market observers and sophisticated investors have observed that the manner in which many assets behave in reaction to changing financial spreads has introduced a new kind of risk dynamic into asset management.

As with many other kinds of relationships, the influence is best seen as a two-way feedback loop in which changed circumstances in one sector of the market – for example a ratings downgrade for a sovereign state – will lead to a widening of spreads in many other parts of the market. As governments have undertaken to protect their banking systems from critical points of failure, there has been a blurring of the distinction between the creditworthiness of sovereigns, banks and private sector corporations.

4. Portfolio Risk

Learning Objective

7.2.1   Understand the main types of portfolio risk and their implications for investors: systemic risk; market/systematic risk – asset price volatility, currency, interest rates, commodity price volatility; non-systematic risk; liquidity, credit and default risk

4.1   An Overview of Portfolio Risk

Risks and reward are important aspects of investment decisions. Risk and potential reward are generally positively correlated: investments with a higher potential return generally carry a higher risk of loss. High-risk investments generally have potential for a higher reward, plus a greater possibility of loss. Low-risk investments generally have a lower reward, with a lower possibility of loss.

Risk arises from the uncertainty of outcomes. Each time, as an investor, that we decide to purchase a security, or invest in an opportunity, the outcome is uncertain in the same manner that exists for any future event. We are concerned that we might incur a loss if we have miscalculated the opportunity or that we may not realise, fully or even partially, the expected return.

At the macro level, we may be concerned about the risks of market crashes, terrorist incidents that cause markets to plunge and other critical events. All of these contribute to the potential for profit from investment and speculation, but also to the accompanying uneasiness that we all feel about the possibility of losses or adverse consequences from our investment or speculation activities. The prevalence of uncertainty in the outlook for financial assets reflects a major part of our general notion of risk.

Another form of risk which concerns investors is the risk relating to the volatility of asset prices. While it is commonplace and to be expected for the prices of assets to fluctuate on a day-to-day basis, there are periods when markets exhibit a high degree of variability in price behaviour. Financial analysts use the statistical value known as standard deviation, as a way of quantifying this variability of prices around their mean price, which is used as a metric for volatility, and the larger the standard deviation value (ie, the higher the asset price volatility), the more investors perceive the riskiness of holding financial assets.

4.2   Systemic Risk

Systemic risk is sometimes erroneously referred to as 'systematic risk'. The latter term has quite a specific meaning in financial theory and is a cornerstone of the capital asset pricing model (CAPM), where it refers to what might better be described as market risk or more specifically non-diversifiable risk. See section 4.3. Systemic risk is the risk of collapse of the entire financial system or entire market, as opposed to risk associated with any one individual entity, group or component of the financial system.

To say that the entire financial system might collapse may have appeared fanciful – a scenario conjured up by a febrile and apocalyptic imagination – until relatively recently. But in the second half of 2008, when major financial institutions such as Lehman Brothers, AIG, Fannie Mae and Freddie Mac effectively went bankrupt or entered the conservatorship of the US government, the spectre of a financial meltdown became more credible. Central bankers, including the Governor of the Bank of England, have since gone on record since to describe how close the world's financial system came to a total collapse.

One of the characteristics and vulnerabilities of the financial system which was exposed as a result of the crisis in asset-backed finance in 2007–08 were the interdependencies in the credit markets and banking system, where the failure of a single entity or cluster of entities had the potential to cause a cascading failure, which could potentially have bankrupted or brought down the entire system, causing widespread panic and chaos in the capital markets.

Insurance is often difficult to obtain against systemic risks because of the inability of any counterparty to accept the risk or mitigate against it, because, by definition, there is likely to be no (or very few) solvent counterparties in the event of a systemic crisis. In the same way, it is difficult to obtain insurance for life or property in the event of nuclear war.

The essence of systemic risk is that it is highly dependent on the correlation of losses. Under normal market conditions, many asset classes and individual securities will show a significant degree of independence of co-movement. In other words their price action will be weakly correlated. When, however, markets become subject to financial contagion and panic, there is a tendency for most assets and securities to become much more highly correlated. In fact, the correlation can approach unity as their price behaviour will tend towards a uniform direction, ie, downwards, and, because of the interdependencies between market participants, an event triggering systemic risk is much more difficult to evaluate than specific risk.

For instance, while econometric estimates and expectation proxies in business-cycle research led to a considerable improvement in forecasting recessions, good analysis on systemic risk protection is often hard to obtain, since interdependencies and counterparty risk in financial markets play a crucial role in times of systemic stress, and the interaction between interdependent market players is extremely difficult (or impossible) to model accurately. If one bank goes bankrupt and sells all its assets, the drop in asset prices may induce liquidity problems in other banks, leading to a general banking panic.

One concern is the potential fragility of liquidity – the ability to raise cash through selling securities – in highly leveraged financial markets. If major market participants, including investment banks, hedge funds and other institutions, are trading with high degrees of leverage, in other words, at levels far in excess of their actual capital bases, then the failure of one participant to settle trades (as in the case of AIG) may deprive others of liquidity, and through a domino effect expose the whole market to systemic risk.

One of the functions of the Bank of England in the UK is to act as the lender of last resort in times of financial panic and to ensure that the money markets can still function when there is a systemic risk to the market. The Bank acted as lender of last resort to Northern Rock when it got into difficulties during 2007, and there was effectively a 'run on the bank', with depositors queuing to withdraw deposits from branches of the bank. The Bank of England has provided even more extensive support to the money markets since the financial crisis of Q4 2008 and has undertaken massive injections of liquidity and quantitative easing to facilitate the functioning of the banking system and credit market.

4.3   Market (Systematic) and Diversifiable Risk

Market or systematic risk (as opposed to systemic risk) will be primarily influenced by macroeconomic conditions but will also reflect the conditions and liquidity within the financial system at large. Unlike systemic risk, when there could be financial contagion and ultimately a failure of the whole system, the definition of market or systematic risk is that risk which cannot be avoided as the risk affects the market as a whole. For the typical investor, however, it can be reduced by using a process of asset selection guided by diversification across numerous securities.

By spreading the investments made in a portfolio over several different securities, from different asset classes (eg, stocks, bonds and commodities), it is possible to get more or less the same returns that any one of them can offer but with a much lower risk since, though one may become worthless, it is unlikely that they will all do so simultaneously. This process, of spreading asset selection over many classes of securities, is known as diversification, and when performed skilfully it can reduce risk without necessarily reducing returns.

Not all risk can be diversified away. Systematic or market risk cannot be diversified away by holding a range of investments within one particular market such as equities. If the global economy is performing poorly and share prices generally are falling and returns are declining, then a wide and diversified portfolio of shares is very likely to fall in line with the wider market. The risk of this happening affects the whole market. An investor with limited funds to invest can achieve a high degree of diversification across asset classes by investing in collective funds such as unit trusts and investment trusts, and this can reduce non-systematic, specific risk to very low levels. However, it cannot be eliminated.

The risk that can be diversified away is that relating to specific or particular investments. This kind of risk is called non-systematic or unsystematic risk as well as specific risk. In the case of an equity investment, the company concerned might, for example, lose a major customer or it might suffer a loss in its share of sales in its particular market. Such events can adversely affect the share price of that particular company.

4.4   Asset Price Volatility

As mentioned in the overview above, financial theory tends to focus on a more restrictive and quantitative notion of risk which concerns the variability of returns in a market. The standard deviation of the returns of asset prices is the principal metric used by financial analysts using modern portfolio theory (MPT) and the CAPM. The simple notion is that investors will seek out those assets and securities which deliver the highest rate of return which is commensurate with a given level of risk – and where risk is equated with the standard deviation of the returns from that asset.

4.5 Other Types of Risk

There are a number of risks faced by investors that are difficult to avoid, some of which are outlined below.

4.5.1 Inflation Risk

Inflation will erode returns or purchasing power and, even if the investor has taken account of inflation in their analysis, the actual and expected inflation may be different from that assumed in calculating expected returns.

4.5.2 Interest Rate Risk

Changes in interest rates will affect prices, therefore interest rate risk might be considered a subcategory of market risk.

In addition, there are a number of risks specific to particular companies or sectors, which can be avoided by diversification or by ignoring an investment altogether.

4.5.3 Exchange Rate Risk

Any investor who purchases securities which are denominated in a foreign currency may suffer (or benefit) from changes in the exchange rates between the home or base currency or the other currency. In addition, one has to consider the risk that one's base or home currency may fall against other currencies, thereby diminishing one's purchasing power for global assets.

4.5.4 Default Risk

An investor may find that a company from which they have purchased a security could become insolvent due to a harsh operating environment, high levels of borrowing, poor management or other financial miscalculations. Fixed-income investors, who purchase the bonds of companies, have some access to alerts of possible credit defaults through the credit rating agencies.

4.5.5 Liquidity Risk

The assumption is usually made that large capital markets such as the LSE and the NYSE provide liquidity for investors to easily sell a security with a narrow spread between the ask and the bid prices. During stressful periods this liquidity can diminish, and it can become much harder to readily sell a security. In extreme cases a market can effectively seize up or, to use a more consistent metaphor, its liquidity can evaporate. There may be an almost complete absence of bids for securities and meanwhile anxious asset managers are being forced to sell securities to raise cash for redemptions, and this can lead to a free-fall in asset prices resulting in market crashes.

5. Mitigating Portfolio Risk

Learning Objective

7.2.2 Understand the core principles used to help mitigate portfolio risk: correlation; diversification; active and passive strategies; hedging and immunisation

5.1 Correlation

From an investment perspective, the statistical notion of correlation is fundamental to portfolio theory. The very simplest idea is that, if one is seeking diversification in the holdings of a portfolio, one would like to have, say, two assets where there is a low degree of association between the movements in price and returns of each asset. The degree of association can also be expressed in terms of the extent to which directional changes in each asset's returns, or their co-movement, are related.

If assets A and B have a tendency to react to the same kinds of business conditions in a very simple and predictable manner, they could be said to be strongly correlated. Let us assume that a certain kind of regular release of economic data (eg, the monthly CPI data) is announced and company A's shares move up by 3% and company B's shares move up by 2.5% when the data is below expectations, and that the inverse pattern of price movement is seen when the data is above expectations. In such a case there is a strong correlation between the movements (or changes) in the performance returns of A and B, and this is expressed as strong positive correlation.

The following two diagrams will demonstrate how the monthly returns for two assets can be correlated either negatively or positively and also how this can be plotted on a scatter diagram to illustrate the degree to which there is a strong linear trend in place between the pairs of values recorded at each time that the returns are calculated.

Strong Positive Correlation

Month	Asset A Return	Asset B Return
1	2.0%	3.0%
2	3.0%	5.0%
3	−1.0%	−1.5%
4	12.0%	8.0%
5	7.0%	4.0%
6	−5.0%	−7.5%
Correlation Coefficient		0.92

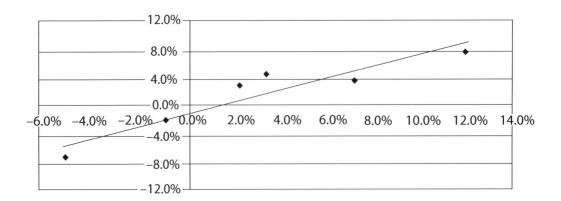

In the table above, the returns on the assets over a six-month period are shown and it will be seen that there is a strong tendency of the returns to move together in a close association. This has resulted in a coefficient of correlation between the returns for A and B of 0.92, which indicates a strongly positive correlation.

There is strong correlation because there is close degree of co-movement in the returns and the relationship is one of positive correlation because not only are the magnitudes of the changes in returns similar but the sign of the changes track each other, ie, when A is going up so is B, and when A is going down so is B. The chart plots these pairs of monthly values and a linear trend line (or linear regression) has been shown. In cases of high correlation the points on the scatter graph will tend to be close to the trendline.

Strong Negative Correlation

Month	Asset A Return	Asset B Return
1	2.0%	−3.0%
2	3.0%	−5.0%
3	−1.0%	1.5%
4	12.0%	−8.0%
5	7.0%	−4.0%
6	−5.0%	7.5%
Correlation Coefficient		−0.92

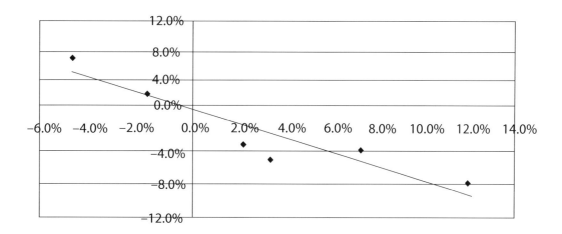

The chart above shows almost exactly the same as the previous chart except that the signs of the changes in returns have been reversed. The magnitudes of the changes have not been changed, which has also resulted in high correlation of the values, but this time there is an inverse relationship between the returns of A and B. For example when, in month 6, A has a negative return of 5%, the return for B is positive 7.5%.

The diagram below the chart reveals that the relationship is one of strong correlation in that most of the points are close to the trendline but that this line is downward-sloping and also that the coefficient of correlation is –0.92. This is an example of strong negative correlation.

Weak Positive Correlation

Month	Asset A Return	Asset B Return
1	2.0%	7.0%
2	3.0%	7.0%
3	−1.0%	−5.5%
4	12.0%	3.0%
5	7.0%	2.0%
6	−5.0%	−1.5%
Correlation Coefficient		0.13

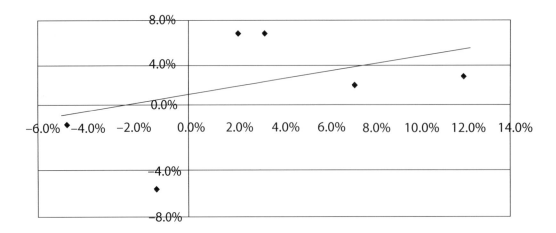

The situation in the above diagram shows that there is much weaker correlation between the returns of assets A and B, as expressed in the lower coefficient value of 0.13. The relationship is still one of positive correlation, but the strength of the association is weaker. Diagrammatically, this can be seen on the scatter graph by the fact that the distances from each point of data are much further away from the trendline than seen in the previous two diagrams.

Summary

The above results demonstrate that there are really two dimensions to the correlation coefficient. The first is the magnitude of correlation, and the second is the sign.

The limiting cases for the coefficient of correlation are –1, which would be perfect negative correlation, and +1, which would be perfect positive correlation. The closer that the actual value is to either of the limiting cases, the stronger the correlation is, so 0.92 and –0.92 are both very strong correlations, but one is positive and the other negative.

The example which provided a positive correlation coefficient of 0.13 still indicates a degree of correlation but it is clearly weaker than for the other two cases examined.

Theoretically, the limiting case of no correlation would be where the coefficient had a value of zero. In practice, it would be highly unlikely to find such a relationship between the returns for two assets, as it would suggest that they move entirely independently of each other. From a macroeconomic perspective, it can be estimated that the same types of large-scale business conditions will impact all assets in a somewhat coordinated fashion, even if it is a loose and inverse one, and the notion of two assets taking completely uncorrelated paths in their returns is not likely to be found in the actual world.

Any elementary text in statistics will make the point that high levels of correlation do not imply that there is a causal relationship between the two variables. Sales of sun protection lotion and snake bites are correlated in the US but there is no causal link – they are related via a third variable – the incidence of extremely hot weather.

Not only does previously observed correlation have no predictive capacity, but the correlation between returns from two financial assets over time can be highly unstable.

The use of correlation measurements is becoming increasingly a part of financial engineering and underlies several fairly complex strategies which are being practised in the financial markets today by so-called algorithmic trading.

The coefficient of correlation as used in finance is usually squared to form a value known as the coefficient of determination or R^2.

5.2 Diversification of Returns

The explanation of correlation given above will help to guide our intuitions with respect to the benefits of diversification and how they follow the observed correlations seen above.

In the first case, cited above, of high positive correlation, ie, 0.92, it can be stated that, to a large degree, the performance of the two assets track each other, or experience the same degree of change and movement, to an extent of about 92%. A portfolio with equal amounts of asset A and B in it will have a tendency to perform not dissimilarly from a portfolio which has either 100% A or 100% B in it.

From this can be inferred the simple notion that diversification will be better achieved when the degree of correlation is lower, subject to further refinements which will be seen below.

Consider a portfolio which had 50% of A and B but where the returns were highly negatively correlated, ie, −0.92. The issue now is that the inverse nature of the returns will tend to cancel each other out. As a position in asset A was improving and contributing profit towards the overall portfolio, this gain would be almost entirely (or about 92%) offset by a corresponding loss in asset B.

The relationship depicted in the table, where the degree of correlation is 0.13, is the more promising to investigate for the purposes of diversification, because there is a lower matching of the returns and more likelihood that gains in one will not very closely resemble (either directly or inversely) the returns in the other asset.

5.2.1 Combining Assets and Calculating Portfolio Standard Deviation

The key formula for calculating the standard deviation for a two-asset portfolio is shown below. (Portfolios involving more than two assets require a more complex version.)

$$\text{Variance of portfolio} = pa^{2*}\sigma a^2 + pb^{2*}\sigma b^2 + 2^*pa^*pb^*\sigma a^*\sigma b^*Cor(ab)$$

where:

pa	=	proportion of the portfolio allocated to security A
pb	=	proportion of the portfolio allocated to security B
σ^2	=	variance of the security
Cor	=	coefficient of correlation between the expected returns of A and B
σ	=	standard deviation of the security

The above formula can be applied to the previous assets A and B which had a correlation coefficient of 0.13.

By combining Assets A and B into a portfolio with a ratio of 50:50, the standard deviation of the portfolio has been reduced to a value below that for holding either 100% of asset A or 100% of asset B. The actual monetary returns for each of A, B and A&B are also shown with the compounded monthly returns being given as well.

| Month | Monthly Returns | | | Ratio A:B |
	Asset A	Asset B	Portfolio A&B	0.5
1	2.0%	7.0%	4.5%	
2	3.0%	7.0%	5.0%	
3	−1.0%	−5.5%	−3.3%	
4	12.0%	3.0%	7.5%	
5	7.0%	2.0%	4.5%	
6	−5.0%	−1.5%	−3.3%	
Correlation Coefficient Cor(ab)		0.13		

Variance of Portfolio = $pa^2 \times \sigma a^2 + pb^2 \times \sigma b^2 + 2 \times pa \times pb \times \sigma a \times \sigma b \times Cor(ab)$		Portfolios Showing Compounded Returns			
		Month	Portfolio A	Portfolio B	Portfolio A&B
		0	£100.00	£100.00	£100.00
Proportion of Portfolio Invested in A – pa	50%	1	£102.00	£107.00	£104.50
Proportion of Portfolio Invested in B – pb	50%	2	£105.06	£114.49	£109.73
Standard Deviation Asset A σa	5.4%	3	£104.01	£108.19	£106.10
Standard Deviation Asset B σb	4.5%	4	£116.49	£111.44	£114.06
Standard Deviation Portfolio A&B	3.7%	5	£124.64	£113.67	£119.19
		6	£118.41	£111.96	£115.26
		Compound Return	18.41%	11.96%	15.26%

From the above it can be seen that a combination of A&B provides a six-month compounded return of 15.26% and a standard deviation of 3.7%, and this illustrates the benefit of diversification when there is relatively weak correlation between the assets.

5.3 Active and Passive Management Strategies

Active fund managers are those who use discretion as to the timing of investments and asset allocation decisions and may change the composition of a portfolio on a regular basis. The underlying assumption is that the fund manager's expertise will enhance the overall return of the fund.

Active fund management rests on the notion that markets are not correctly explained by the efficient markets hypothesis (EMH) and that mispricing of securities not only exists but that it can be identified and exploited. A skilful fund manager will be able to identify such opportunities and purchase or sell the mispriced security and derive a profit when the mispricing is eliminated. A less skilful manager may suffer from not recognising such mispricing or be poor at timing the asset allocation decisions. As a matter of fact, which is somewhat awkward for active fund managers, research has shown that the average fund manager will underperform a simple index-tracking strategy.

Passive investment management aims to provide an appropriate level of return for a fund that is commensurate with a simple buy-and-hold strategy for a broad cross-section of the market. **Passive management** often takes the form of index tracking, in which the funds are simply used to replicate the constituents of a broad market index such as the FTSE 100 index or the S&P 500 index in the US. More specialised tracker funds can also be linked to the performance of securities in emerging markets, and to specific industry sectors.

Increasingly, the proliferation of ETFs allows investors to purchase shares in a fund which trades actively on a major exchange and which provides exposure to certain kinds of securities and when the minimal management fees are incorporated into the actual price of the shares of the ETF. The benefit to an investor of purchasing such ETFs is that there is usually a high degree of liquidity, the asset values of the fund constituents as well as the price of the ETF shares is updated on a real-time basis, and the costs for the packaging of the securities are minimal.

Passive fund management is consistent with the idea that markets are efficient and that no mispricing exists. If the EMH is an accurate account of the way that capital markets work, then there is no benefit to be had from active trading. Such trading will simply incur dealing and management costs for no benefit. Investors who do not believe that they can identify active fund managers whom they are confident can produce returns above the level of charges for **active management** will often elect to invest in passive funds or index trackers.

5.4   Immunisation

Passive bond strategies are employed either when the market is believed to be efficient, in which case a buy-and-hold strategy is used, or when a bond portfolio is constructed around the necessity of meeting a future liability fixed in nominal terms. Immunisation is a passive management technique employed by those bond portfolio managers with known future liability to meet. An immunised bond portfolio is one that is insulated from the effect of future interest rate changes.

Immunisation can be performed by using either of two techniques: cash-matching or duration-based immunisation.

- **Cash-matching** involves constructing a bond portfolio whose coupon and redemption payment cash flows are synchronised to match those of the liabilities to be met.
- **Duration-based** immunisation involves constructing a bond portfolio with the same initial value as the present value of the liability it is designed to meet and the same duration as this liability. A portfolio that contains bonds that are closely aligned in this way is known as a bullet portfolio.

Alternatively, a barbell strategy can be adopted. If a bullet portfolio holds bonds with durations as close as possible to ten years to match a liability with a ten-year duration, a barbell strategy may be to hold bonds with a duration of five and 15 years. Barbell portfolios necessarily require more frequent rebalancing than bullet portfolios.

5.5 Hedging

The risks that are inevitable when investing in shares, bonds and money market instruments can be mitigated, but not entirely removed by, hedging. Hedging can be difficult to implement and becomes mathematically intensive, especially when the investment portfolio contains complex instruments. Also, hedging strategies will have a cost that inevitably impacts investment performance. Hedging is usually achieved by using derivatives such as options, futures and forwards.

- Buying put options on investments held will enable the investor to remove the risk of a fall in value, but the investor will have to pay a premium to buy the options.
- Futures, such as stock index futures, as seen in section 3.4, can be used to hedge against equity prices falling – but the future will remove any upside as well as downside.
- Forwards, such as currency forwards, could be used to eliminate exchange-rate risk – but, like futures, the upside potential will be lost in order to hedge against the downside risk.

6. Key Approaches to Investment Allocation

Learning Objective

7.2.3   Understand the key approaches to investment allocation for bond, equity and multi-asset portfolios: asset class; geographical area; currency; issuer; sector; maturity

Top-down active portfolio management involves considering the big picture first (asset allocation) by assessing the prospects for each of the main asset classes within each of the world's major investment regions, against the backdrop of the world economic, political and social environment. Once the asset allocation has been decided upon, the next step is to consider the prospects for those sectors within the various asset classes, eg, equities, bonds, commodities and derivatives. Sector-selection decisions in equity markets are usually made with reference to the weighting each sector assumes within the benchmark index against which the performance in that market is to be assessed. The final stage of the process is deciding upon which specific issuers should be selected within the favoured sectors.

6.1 Asset Allocation

Within larger portfolio management organisations, asset allocation and top-down strategy are usually determined on a monthly basis by an asset allocation committee. The committee draws upon forecasts of risk and return for each asset class and correlations between these returns. It is at this stage of the top-down process that quantitative models are often used, in conjunction with more conventional fundamental analysis, to assist in determining which geographical areas and asset classes are most likely to produce the most attractive risk-adjusted returns, taking full account of the client's mandate.

Most asset allocation decisions, whether for institutional or retail portfolios, are made with reference to the peer group median asset allocation. This is known as 'asset allocation by consensus' and is undertaken to minimise the risk of underperforming the peer group. When deciding if and to what extent certain markets and asset classes should be over- or under-weighted, most portfolio managers set tracking error, or standard deviation of return, parameters against peer group median asset allocations.

Finally, a decision on whether to hedge market and/or currency risks must be taken.

Over the long term, some academic studies have concluded that the skills in decision-making with regard to asset allocation can account for over 90% of the variation in returns for pension fund managers.

6.2 Geographical Area

Many investors wish to seek out opportunities in international markets and there are many investment products now available, including a wide range of ETFs, which enable professional and retail investors to gain exposure to specific geographical regions and even specific country funds.

Diversification is a primary reason to invest in overseas markets. More specifically, it is prudent to own assets in countries whose economies have different attributes from the domestic market of the investor. A service-based economy has different attributes from a commodity-based economy; exporting surplus nations differ from importing surplus nations; economies with large public deficits (eg, the US, the UK and Japan) can be contrasted with those with large surpluses (eg, China). These different attributes can help to alleviate the coincidence of the timing of the economic cycles in these respective countries. In turn this may result in the fact that the respective stock market cycles are unlikely to be largely correlated with the business cycle in the investor's domestic market.

Whatever countries are selected for inclusion in a portfolio strategy should be blended in consistently with the required attributes. An investor who favours commodity-based economies will want exposure to such countries as Australia, Canada, Russia and South Africa. Another investor, who may want exposure to the semiconductor industry or computer hardware, may want to own a fund which specialises in South Korea or Taiwan or Asia, possibly excluding Japan. (Some ETFs are structured in such a manner that one can have exposure to most of the Asian markets but not Japan, because its economy is considered by many investors to be a special case based upon the massive decline in Japanese equities since 1990.)

6.2.1 Emerging Markets

Many enthusiasts for investing in emerging markets such as the BRIC nations (Brazil, Russia, India and China) like to point to the much greater rate of economic growth in such nations compared to the rates currently seen in the US and most of Europe. This has also given rise to the notion that the emerging markets have become decoupled from the economic cycles that manifest themselves in the developed world. While it is certainly the case that China and India, especially, have rates of GDP growth that western countries are unlikely to see in the foreseeable future, it must also be recalled that when the banking crisis occurred in 2007–8 some of the hardest-hit markets were the emerging ones.

One barometer to use for this is to consider the Hong Kong market, which is part of the emerging world but which has well-established and very liquid capital markets. From the onset of the financial crisis in the summer of 2007 the Hang Seng Index (as well as the Shanghai Index) experienced a drop of more than 60%, which was considerably in excess of the decline seen in the US and Europe. A similar situation has also been seen in 2020–21 due to the coronavirus (COVID-19) pandemic. The vaccine rollouts have been generally slower in the developing markets, while the likes of the UK, Europe and the US are leading the way in the recovery.

One other statistic is worth contemplating with regard to the notion that China in particular may be able to lead the world out of its current anaemic growth rates because of the dynamism of its economy. The IMF has estimated that the People's Republic of China is now the second-largest economy in the world (if the EU is not considered as a bloc) and has an annual GDP of about $14 trillion. However, to keep things in perspective, in 2016 this was about 40% of the total world GDP. By comparison, if one takes the US and all of the EU countries together, they account for about 50% of world GDP.

Undoubtedly, exposure to the emerging markets should be a part of most investment strategies, except for the risk-averse, and in general terms a good spread of assets across many geographical regions will provide a degree of diversification. But even this last comment needs to be qualified, as the degree of diversification appears, from some correlation studies by quant funds, to be diminishing.

6.2.2   Currency

Foreign currencies are an asset class in their own right, and not just as a medium of exchange for purchasing other assets. The volume of transactions that take place each day in the FX market makes this market by far the largest section of the capital markets.

The decision by an investor to purchase a large holding of, for example, Australian dollars, by selling US dollars, is an example of speculation perhaps, but is it any more of a speculation than the decision to purchase shares in a company or the bonds issued by a government such as Ireland or Spain? All of the examples cited have risks associated with them but all also have potentially large returns as well. As can be seen in the previous chart, the Australian dollar dropped 0% from buying US dollar-denominated assets in March 2009.

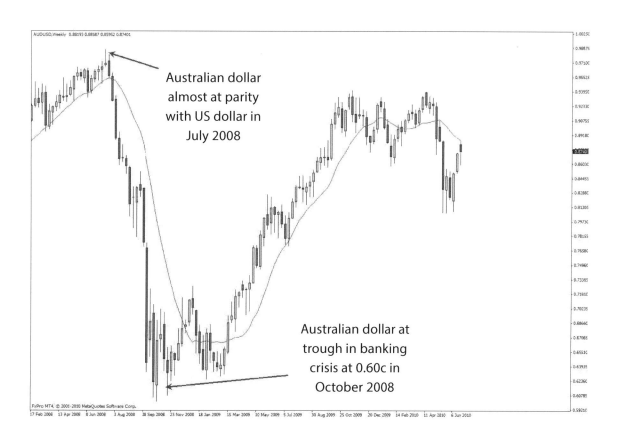

As can be seen from the chart above, the Australian dollar dropped by about 40% from having almost reached parity (ie, $1USD = $1AUD) in July 2008 to about 60 cents against the US dollar at the end of October 2008. What is also interesting about the chart is that it very closely resembles the chart for many global equity indices, including the S&P 500 and the FTSE 100. In fact, the S&P 500 lost almost exactly 40% during the comparable period to that shown on the above chart.

The question to ask is whether it was riskier to hold stocks in July 2008, or Australian dollars? Moreover, would it have been an equally good decision to have bought Australian dollars in March 2009 or to have bought stocks in the S&P 500 or FTSE 100?

The returns on both from buying at the trough of the financial crisis of 2008 would be remarkably similar. So, an investor who sold the US dollar and bought Australian dollars in March 2009 would have had a return in US dollar terms of about 30% from March 2009 until March 2010. This example also illustrates how important it is to form a frame of reference for an investor. For example, an investor based in Australia, whose currency of account for investment purposes is, let us say, the Australian dollar, would have actually lost about 30% from buying US dollar-denominated assets in March 2009.

The more traditional explanations that are given when discussing currencies relate to the importance of hedging, but in light of the previous discussion it is vital to consider what the basis is that one is using for the hedge. To finish with the example from above, the Australian investor who might have decided to purchase an ETF for an emerging market but decided to hedge that ETF against the US dollar would, if the hedge had worked effectively, have lost the same amount as if they had purchased US dollars outright.

Hedging Foreign Currency Risk

Foreign currency risk can be reduced, though not completely eliminated, by employing the hedging instruments or strategies such as:

- forward contracts
- back-to-back loans
- foreign currency options
- foreign currency futures, or
- currency swaps.

Short-Term Currency Swaps for Speculation

A currency swap is another method, along with vehicles such as futures, options and forward agreements, which will enable a speculator to speculate on the future directions of two key variables in the foreign exchange market:

- forward exchange-rate spreads
- the changes in interest rate differentials between the prevailing short-term base rates in each of the countries of the currency pair.

In terms of a swap transaction involving a currency pair, the buyer gains and a seller loses when the primary currency interest rate increases relative to the secondary currency interest rate. More specifically, it is the ratio between the two rates which is paramount – if the ratio increases from the perspective of the primary currency, the buyer of the primary currency will gain and the seller of the secondary currency will lose.

The swap structure can be demonstrated by the following scenario, in which a speculator enters a swap transaction, buying $5 million in the belief that US interest rates will increase in the near future relative to UK rates. The short-term rates applicable at the time of entering the swap are 2.5% for US dollars and 4% for sterling.

Let us assume that, for the sake of simplicity, within the next trading session US rates move up 50 basis points to 3% and UK rates are adjusted downwards by 50 basis points to 3.5%. Also, for simplicity, we shall assume that there has been no underlying change to the spot rate. The table below indicates the mechanics of this swap arrangement and demonstrates how this arrangement proves to be profitable to the speculator.

	USD	GBP		
	Initial Three-Month Interest Rates			
	2.50%	4.00%		
Current spot rate GBP/USD		1.6450		
Three-month forward GBP/USD	1.6450 x [(1+0.025/4)/(1+0.040/4)]	1.6389		
	Actual Transactions			
Spot Market Buy USD and sell sterling	$5,000,000	£3,039,514	These two notional deals will effectively cancel each other	Zero cash flow at inception
Swap Market (inception) Sell USD and buy sterling	$5,000,000	£3,039,514		
Swap Market (three-month values) Sell USD and buy sterling	$5,000,000	£3,050,841	Cash flows at maturity	

Profitable Short-Term Speculation on Direction of Interest Rates in the US and UK			
Overnight changes to interest rates	3.00%	3.50%	
Three-month forward GBP/USD	1.6450 x [(1+0.030/4)/(1+0.035/4)]	1.6430	
Swap market with three-month values	$5,000,000	£3,043,285	Cash flows at maturity
Profit for speculator	£3,050,841 – £3,043,285	£7,556	Profit

The speculator can now close out their swap position with a forward exchange contract buying $5 million in three months for £3,043,285, realising a sterling profit of £7,556 (£3,050,841 – £3,043,285) at maturity. In other words, the buyer of the primary currency – the US dollar in this transaction – has shown a profit of £7,556 in sterling terms, and this is equivalent to the loss endured by the seller of the secondary currency, ie, sterling.

However, the speculator or trader might have been incorrect in the assumption that US rates were headed upwards relative to sterling rates and in fact the short-term rates have realigned themselves as follows:

Unprofitable Short-Term Speculation on Direction of Interest Rates in the US and UK			
Overnight changes to interest rates	2.00%	4.00%	
Three-month forward GBP/USD	1.6450 x [(1.020/4)/(1.040/4)]	1.6369	
Swap market with three-month values	$5,000,000	£3,054,636	Cash flows at maturity
Loss for speculator	£3,050,841 – £3,054,636	–£3,795	Loss

In this case, the buyer of the primary currency – US dollars – has sustained a loss in sterling terms of £3,795, which is of course the gain experienced by the seller of sterling being the secondary currency to the swap arrangement.

6.3 Sector Selection

As stated in section 6.1, a top-down approach to portfolio management is one in which the major asset allocation decisions are based on first selecting asset classes which are in accordance with the objectives and constraints of the fund, as stated in the mandate or prospectus. Thereafter, sectors are selected, and then individual securities are selected to fit within this very structured approach.

When a top-down approach is adopted, investment management therefore involves the following activities in the sequence below:

- Asset allocation.
- Market timing or tactical asset allocation.
- Sector selection.
- Stock selection (see section 7.1 of this chapter).

Once the asset allocation has been decided upon, top-down managers then consider the prospects for those sectors within their favoured equity markets. Sector-selection decisions in equity markets are usually made with reference to the weighting each sector assumes within the index against which the performance in that market is to be assessed.

Given the strong interrelationship between economics and investment, however, the sector selection process is also heavily influenced by economic factors, notably where in the economic cycle the economy is currently positioned.

The investment clock below describes the interrelationship between the economic cycle and various sectors:

Recession and bear market develops

Cash; defensive equities – food retailers; utilities; pharmaceuticals;

End of the bull market

Commodities and basic resources

Growth decelerates as interest rates rise to suppress inflation

General industrial and capital-spending equities – electrical, engineering, contractors

Growth phase

Cyclical consumer equities – airlines, autos, general retailers, leisure

Start of a bull market

Bonds; interest-rate-sensitive equities – banks, house building

Growth accelerates as interest rates fall

Exchange-rate-sensitive equities – exporters, multinationals

Growth phase

Basic industry equities – chemicals, paper, steel

Growth phase

However, the clock assumes that the portfolio manager knows exactly where in the economic cycle the economy is positioned and the extent to which each market sector is operationally geared to the cycle. Moreover, the investment clock does not provide any latitude for unanticipated events that may, through a change in the risk appetite of investors, spark a sudden flight from equities to government bond markets, for example, or change the course that the economic cycle takes. Finally, each economic cycle is different and investors' behaviour may not be the same as that demonstrated in previous cycles.

6.4   Issuer Selection

The final stage of the top-down process is deciding upon which stocks should be selected within the favoured sectors. A combination of fundamental and technical analysis (see section 1.2) will typically be used in arriving at the final decision.

In order to outperform a pre-determined benchmark, usually a market index, the active portfolio manager must be prepared to assume an element of tracking error, more commonly known as active risk, relative to the benchmark index to be outperformed. Active risk arises from holding securities in the actively managed portfolio in differing proportions from that in which they are weighted within the benchmark index. The higher the level of active risk, the greater the chance of outperformance, though the probability of underperformance is also increased.

It should be noted that top-down active management, as its name suggests, is an ongoing and dynamic process. As economic, political and social factors change, so do asset allocation, sector and stock selection.

A bottom-up approach to asset allocation also focuses on the unique attractions of individual securities and the characteristics of the issuer.

The considerations in the case of an equity investment will be the P/E multiple for the issuer, the P/E multiples for competitors, the rate of earnings-growth and other financial ratios relating to profitability and gearing. All of these were examined in chapter 6, section 1. In the case of considering a bond purchase, the investor will want to examine the credit ratings reported by the major credit rating agencies, the spreads between the issuer's bonds and other benchmarks such as government issues of similar maturity.

In addition, there are opportunistic factors to consider in evaluating the attractiveness of an individual issuer of securities. Although the health and prospects for the world economy and markets in general are taken into account, these are secondary to factors such as whether a particular company is, for instance, a possible takeover target or is about to launch an innovative product.

6.5   Maturity

The ongoing fluctuation of interest rates poses a particular problem for fund managers with a portfolio of bonds because of the reinvestment risk. However, by using an approach based upon bond duration-matching or immunisation, it is possible to maintain a steady return over a specific time horizon, irrespective of any changes in the interest rate. In the frequently found case where we need to match a set of cash outflows as our liabilities, a bond portfolio with the same duration as the liabilities should be constructed.

See section 7.7.1 for an explanation of duration matching.

The process of immunisation requires the fund manager to purchase a portfolio of bonds with a duration equal to the liabilities that need to be matched. Through immunisation the fund manager can guarantee that the bond portfolio will earn the gross redemption yield, since any alteration in capital value of the bonds will be balanced by the reinvestment gain or loss.

7.   Cash, Bond and Equity Portfolio Management

Learning Objective

7.2.4   Understand the main aims and investment characteristics of the main cash, bond and equity portfolio management strategies and styles: indexing/passive management; active/market timing, including high-conviction style; passive-active combinations; smart indexing; growth versus income; market capitalisation; liability driven; immunisation; long, short and leveraged; issuer and sector-specific; contrarian; quantitative; growth versus value investing

7.1   Active Equity Selection Strategies

Stock selection, or stock picking, is important whenever the fund managers are prepared to accept the overall consensus for the market as a whole, but believe that certain individual securities are mispriced.

- An overpriced security is one that has an expected return that is less than should be expected on a risk-adjusted basis.
- An underpriced security has an expected return that is more on a risk-adjusted basis than would be expected.

Active stock selection can involve the application of various fundamental, technical or quantitative techniques.

In terms of the capital asset pricing model (CAPM), which is a methodology for valuing securities in reference to the overall market or what can be called the securities market line (SML), a security is said to be mispriced if it has a non-zero alpha value.

The objective of a stock picker is to pick portfolios of securities with positive alpha. In terms of active stock selection the manager will try to construct portfolios of securities that will have a more than proportionate weighting of the underpriced or positive alpha securities, and a correspondingly less than proportionate weighting of the overpriced securities which are exhibiting negative alpha.

7.2   Value Investing and Growth Investing

Value investing and growth investing represent two alternative approaches to investment decision-making and asset selection.

With value investment, the method is to screen the market for shares that are outstandingly cheap in relation to their chosen yardsticks. Key ratios include the relationship of the share price to assets, earnings and dividends. Value investing seeks to identify those established companies, usually cyclical in nature, that have been ignored by the market but look set for recovery. The value investor seeks to buy stocks in distressed conditions in the hope that their price will return to reflect their intrinsic value, or net worth.

A focus on recovery potential, rather than earnings growth, differentiates value investing from growth investing, as does a belief that individual securities eventually revert to a fundamental or intrinsic value. This is known as reversion to the mean.

In contrast to growth stocks, true value stocks also offer the investor a considerable safety margin against the share price falling further, because of their characteristically high dividend yield and relatively stable earnings.

Benjamin Graham, the founder of value investing, set up certain criteria for selecting 'bargain issues'. The investor sells the shares once they have reached their price target because they have no reason to continue holding them as they cease to provide good value. Warren Buffett, who has become one of the wealthiest people in the US, is a follower of Benjamin Graham and there are a number of other fund managers that follow the value investment philosophy.

The growth investment philosophy, on the other hand, aims to buy growth stocks early.

Growth investment managers are screening the universe of stocks for the following:

* Fast-growing markets, especially if there are barriers to entry for competitors.
* Sectors in which both unit sales and earnings are rising due to growth in market size/share.
* A company in which sales and earnings rise higher in each business cycle.
* Good margins and above-average earnings growth.
* Good management, strong research, valuable patents, sound finances, a good location.

7.2.1 Growth at a Reasonable Price (GARP)

Value investing and growth investing are sometimes seen as being at the opposite ends of a spectrum. Value investors may buy any shares that are priced inexpensively, even if the company's growth prospects are poor. On the other hand, growth investors may buy shares of companies that are growing rapidly without regard to how high a P/E multiple the shares might already command. At its most aggressive, growth investing simply focuses on those companies whose share price has been on a rising trend and continues to gather momentum as an ever increasing number of investors jump on the bandwagon. This is referred to as momentum investing.

Growth at a reasonable price (GARP) aims to reconcile these two approaches. It provides a framework for value investors who do not want to miss out on today's most promising growth opportunities. And it affords the growth-orientated investor a tool to help determine when a high P/E becomes too high.

True growth stocks are those that are able to differentiate their product or service from their industry peers so as to command a competitive advantage. This results in an ability to produce high-quality and above-average earnings growth, as these earnings can be insulated from the business cycle. A growth stock can also be one that has yet to gain market prominence but has the potential to do so: growth managers are always on the lookout for the next Microsoft.

The key to growth investing is to rigorously forecast future earnings growth and to avoid those companies susceptible to issuing profits warnings. A growth stock trading on a high P/E ratio will be savagely marked down by the market if it fails to meet earnings expectations.

GARP is based on the principle that any P/E ratio is reasonable if it is equal to or less than the company's annual rate of earnings growth. This is known as the PEG and can be illustrated by the simple example that one should be willing to accept a P/E multiple of up to 15 if the company's earnings are growing at an annual rate of at least 15%.

7.3 Quantitative Funds

Quantitative analysis involves using mathematical models to price and manage complex derivatives products, and statistical models to determine which shares are relatively expensive and which are relatively cheap.

Quantitative analysis aims to find market inefficiencies and exploit this using computer technology to swiftly execute trades. Exploiting mispricing may involve only tiny differences, so leverage is often used to increase returns.

Quants-based investors use specialised systems platforms to develop financial models using stochastic calculus. Quantitative models follow a precise set of rules to determine when to trade to take advantage of any mispricing opportunities. Speed of execution of each trade is also very important to investors using electronic platforms and quants-based systems.

Quants-based funds account for a significant proportion of hedge funds, and the growth of more sophisticated investment strategies has fuelled the adoption of quantitative investment analysis. The growth of quants funds has, however, meant that the models used by many funds are directing funds into the same positions. Some analysts have blamed part of the market upheaval during the credit crunch on the pack mentality of quantitative computer models used by hedge funds.

Since, in a quantitative (quant) fund, the stock selection process is driven by computer models, there is no place for a manager's judgement based on fundamental analysis. Instead, the fund manager uses predetermined or preset models to undertake this stock selection process. Such models sometimes rely on ideas such as portfolio theory, CAPM, the dividend valuation model and options pricing techniques – ie, fundamental evaluation tools – in order to determine which stocks to hold and in what proportions. Sometimes the models are more based on the identification of patterns, in conjunction with technical analysis.

Typical strategies of quant funds include:

- growth strategies
- value strategies
- statistical arbitrage strategies
- correlation strategies
- long/short equity strategies, and
- dispersion strategies.

It has been observed that quant funds tend to perform better in market downturns, whereas more fundamental funds perform better in upswings.

Quant funds, based on correlations and exploiting convergence or mean reversion strategies, assume that the historical statistical relationships between stocks will continue into the future, which clearly may not hold true.

7.3.1 Combined Approach

Many investment management houses use a combined approach, with fundamental analysis and quantitative analysis dictating the markets and stocks which they wish to buy, and technical analysis being used to determine the timing of entry into the market place. As already noted, increasing numbers of fund managers are becoming familiar with technical analysis since, if sufficient numbers do believe the technical analysts, then the markets will have a tendency to move in line with the anticipations of technically focused traders.

7.4 Buy-and-Hold

A buy-and-hold strategy involves buying a portfolio of securities and holding them for a long period of time, with only minor and infrequent adjustments to the portfolio over time. Under this strategy, investments bought now are held indefinitely, or, if they have fixed maturities, held until maturity and then replaced with similar ones.

Despite the long-term tendency of equities to outperform other assets, the following is taken from an article which appeared in the *New York Times* in February 2009 and reflects the relatively dire performance of equities during the 1998–2008 period.

> *'In the last 82 years – the history of the Standard & Poor's 500 – the stock market has been through one Great Depression and numerous recessions. It has experienced bubbles and busts, bull markets and bear markets. But it has never seen a ten-year stretch as bad as the one that ended last month.*
>
> *Over the ten years through January, an investor holding the stocks in the S&P's 500 Stock Index, and reinvesting the dividends, would have lost about 5.1% a year after adjusting for inflation, as is shown in the following chart'.*

Worst Decade Yet

Annual total return of Standard & Poor's 500 Stock Index, adjusted for inflation, over ten-year periods on date shown.

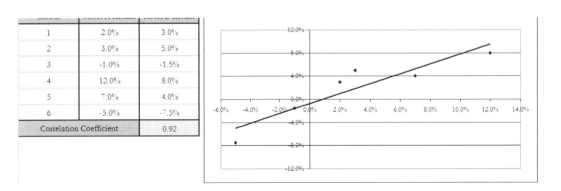

> *'Figures are based on the total return of the S&P 500, with dividends reinvested, adjusted for the change in the Consumer Prices Index (CPI). Figures are not reduced for either transaction costs or taxes, and thus overstate what the average investor would be likely to receive. Figures assume the CPI will be unchanged for January'.*

Source: Standard & Poor's, Bloomberg, Bureau of Labor Statistics via Haver Analytics

What lessons are there for investors seeking exposure to equities? One point is that spreading investment over a period can reduce some of the effects of market volatility. If, instead of a single investment of, say, £10,000 made in 1999 when the US and UK stock markets were at their peak an investor had invested perhaps £2,000 per year over the next ten years, the principle of cost averaging would have lessened the impact of poor returns for equities in recent years.

Buying and holding equities or even index-tracker products such as one based on the FTSE 100 is being questioned by more financial analysts in the light of the more recent data.

7.5   Indexation

There is a variant to the buy-and-hold strategy that eliminates the diversifiable risk and effectively replicates the performance of a market index, and this is known as index-matching or indexation.

There are several different ways of proceeding with respect to indexation, explored below, but the most fundamental one is to decide on the appropriate index for the client, as there are many different market indices available. An investor may want exposure to large-cap UK stocks, in which case the FTSE 100 is the obvious index to select. Alternatively the investor may be more interested in the large cap stocks which are primarily US-based and for this area the Standard & Poor's 500 Index would be one of the most appropriate indices. As the name suggests, the UK index consists of 100 large-cap stocks whereas its most closely matched US counterpart comprises 500 different companies.

7.5.1   Duplication or Complete Indexation

The duplication of an index by holding all of its constituents is also known as complete indexation or full replication. The requirement is to match exactly the underlying components of the relevant index and as such this can often be complex and expensive. For example, the FTSE All-Share Index contains several hundred securities weighted according to their relative market proportions. To construct a portfolio of all these securities with the same proportions as the index would involve extremely high commissions and dealing costs.

Although the large world indices are relatively stable in terms of their constituents, there is a need from time to time to make changes and modify the components. In the case of the US S&P 500, Standard & Poor's will make periodic adjustments to the constituents in light of changes in the ownership of certain companies, eg, a company may have been taken over by another. Also, the custodians of indices will periodically have to remove some stocks from an index if the market capitalisation falls below a certain threshold level, and then they will substitute another company which has grown in stature and market capitalisation to qualify for entry to the index.

If a fund manager is replicating such an index, where modifications are being made from time to time, then all of the changes and rebalancing will need to be made to the replica and this will involve dealing costs and commissions as well as dealing spreads. The manner of rebalancing is more critical in the case of an index like the S&P 500 which is market cap weighted, rather than in the case of the Dow Jones Industrial Average which is a simple average of the 30 constituent stocks and where there is not a balancing in the composition of the index based on market capitalisation.

A bond index fund will be even more complex and expensive to replicate. With the passage of time the average maturity of a bond index will decline, and to replace those bonds which are reaching redemption with suitable alternatives and preserve the duration characteristics of the bond fund is a particularly challenging undertaking.

In general terms, duplication or complete indexation is often not practical, and therefore alternative strategies designed to emulate the index's performance are used.

Smart Indexing

Smart indexing involves a different strategy, while still using an index, like the S&P 500 Index, and requires having a more balanced weighting across many different sectors. Indices, on their own, can be heavily weighted towards certain sectors. For example, the S&P 500 has a higher weighting in technology and healthcare and a lesser weighting in utilities. There are several smart ETFs that became popular after the financial crisis and bear market; these ETFs can be based on an index like the S&P 500, but not as a base index. The index components may have different weightings to create better balance. This type of strategy is regarded as active investing or management, with an objective of creating superior returns than for passively managed index trackers or funds.

7.5.2 Stratified Sampling

As in statistical theory, the use of stratified sampling involves the selection of a sample of securities from the total population comprising the index. The sample should be stratified so that it is representative of the primary characteristics of the whole population, ie, the total population of the index constituents can be divided into sectors in the case of equities and into different maturities in the case of bonds. A cross-section of securities is then selected from each sector with the intention that the sample exhibits the highest correlation to the sector's overall return and likewise that there is a strongly correlated fit between the returns from the sample and those from the entire populations of the assets in the index.

This procedure limits the initial transaction costs and subsequent rebalancing costs, but increases the risks of tracking errors, ie, the difference between the fund's return and the return on the market index.

7.5.3 Factor-Matching

Factor-matching involves the construction of an index fund using securities selected on the basis of specifically chosen factors or risk characteristics. If the first risk factor required is that the sample matches the level of systematic (market) risk, then the selected portfolio will need to be chosen to have the same level of beta as the market. Other factors may be sector breakdown, dividend pattern, firm size or financial structure, eg, gearing ratio.

The selected index fund will be a subset of the available securities within the whole index that matched the market in terms of the required factor(s) and have the highest overall correlation with the market.

7.5.4   Co-Mingling

Co-mingling involves the use of co-mingled funds, such as unit trusts or investment trusts, rather than the explicit formation of an index fund. Co-mingling may be especially suitable for clients with relatively small portfolios and may provide an acceptable compromise between the transaction costs of complete indexation and the tracking error of stratified sampling.

7.5.5   Summary and Conclusion

The desire to replicate the performance of an index with a subset or sample is prone to tracking errors. In other words, when the index is changed in some fashion, for example to remove certain securities which may have been taken over or which have fallen below the market capitalisation threshold and then to include some new entrants, the replication format used may no longer be suitable.

If the sample was based upon stratification and reflection of the sector composition of the index, the removal of one or two key securities from a sector could have quite a pronounced effect on the sample which was set up to emulate the previous composition of the index by sector. The replication may need to be quite significant in terms of changing the constituents of the sample or replica to reflect again the stratification of the whole index.

Another problem arises when the constituents of an index are changed. When the announcement of a change is made, the price of the security being deleted tends to fall, while the price of the security being added tends to rise. Fund managers are then forced to take a loss on some of their holdings as they eject them from their surrogate portfolio and to pay over the odds for the additions, where the prices will fall back over time after the index has settled down again. These effects can cause major tracking errors between index funds and the index itself.

In general terms, over the longer term there is an expectation that the fund will underperform the index, ie, suffer a tracking error.

Apart from the transaction costs involved in setting up and rebalancing, there are other problems associated with running an index fund. The most important of these concerns income payments on the securities. The total return on an index may include not only capital gains but also income in the form of dividend or coupon payments. In order to match the performance of the index in terms of income, the index fund needs to have the same pattern of income payments as the index. It will also have to make the same reinvestment assumptions. Unless complete indexation has been undertaken, it is unlikely that an index fund will exactly replicate the income pattern of the index.

In addition, the index may assume that gross income payments are reinvested without cost back into the index on the day each security becomes ex-div. In practice, however, this assumption can be violated for the following reasons:

- The dividend or coupon payment is not made until an average of six weeks after the ex-div date.
- The payment is received net of tax.
- There are dealing costs of reinvesting income payments.
- The income payments on different securities may be fairly small and it may not be worthwhile investing such small sums on the days they are received.

Indexation is, however, a popular form of fund management. It attempts to avoid, as far as possible, decisions about selection and timing of investment, yet it is not purely passive. At the very least, the choice of index and the reinvestment of income involve active intervention.

Indexation is normally used in conjunction with other active methods whereby there is an indexed core fund with actively managed peripheral funds, again with the objective of enhancing the overall return of the fund. This is called 'core-satellite management'.

7.6   Active Bond Selection Strategies

As with an equities portfolio, a bond portfolio will be actively managed whenever there are mispriced bonds available. Active bond portfolio management operates around the activities of security selection and market timing. However, there is a difference between active share selection and active bond selection. Most equity managers engage in security selection, whereas most bond managers engage in market timing.

A bond picker will construct a portfolio of bonds that, in comparison with the market portfolio, has less than proportionate weightings in the overpriced bonds and more than proportionate weightings in the underpriced bonds.

A market timer engages in active management when they do not accept the consensus market portfolio and is either more bullish or more bearish than the market. Expectations of interest rate changes are therefore a crucial input into successful market timing. A bond market timer is interested in adjusting the relative duration of their portfolio over time. Market timing with bonds is sometimes called duration switching.

High-conviction investing usually involves selecting a small amount of highly rated securities (maybe 20–30) that are considered to be blue chip, with a strong competitive position and good market share. Other characteristics might be a cash-rich business, predictable future cash flows and being run by stringent, honest and trustworthy management.

If the fund manager is expecting a bull market because they are expecting a fall in the general level of interest rates, they may want to increase the duration of their portfolio by replacing low-duration bonds with high-duration bonds. If the fund manager is expecting a bear market because they are expecting a rise in the level of interest rates, they may want to reduce the duration of their portfolio.

Active bond portfolio management is generally not as profitable as active share portfolio management. There are several reasons for this:

- There are more shares traded than bonds in the UK.
- The most liquid bonds are UK government bonds that have only certain maturities.
- The volatility of bond prices is generally much lower than that of shares, hence fewer opportunities for substantial mispricing of bonds exists.
- With only a few bonds suitable for active trading, the portfolio consisting of these bonds will be relatively undiversified.
- The cost of active bond portfolio management can be reduced using futures and options.

7.6.1   Riding the Yield Curve

'Riding the yield curve' is a valid strategy when the yield curve is upward sloping. If this is the case, then an investment manager can buy bonds with maturities in excess of their investment horizon. They proceed to hold the bonds until the end of their investment period and then sell them. If the yield curve has not shifted during that period, the investment manager will have generated higher returns than if they had bought bonds with the same maturity as their investment horizon.

This follows because, as the time to maturity declines, the yield to maturity falls and the price of the bond rises, thereby generating a capital gain (hence, the term 'yield curve ride'). These gains will be higher than those available if bonds with the same maturity as the investment horizon are used, because the maturity value of the latter bonds is fixed.

The following scenario provides an opportunity to ride the yield curve as the term structure of interest rates is upward-sloping, showing that longer-dated instruments are yielding more than shorter-dated instruments. To keep the example simple we shall assume that the two instruments are zero-coupon Treasury notes with one and two years remaining to maturity. The current yield curve reveals that a one-year note will have a yield to maturity of 8%, whereas a two-year note will have a yield to maturity of 9%. Since there are no coupons, all of this is effected in the current price of the bond.

Zero Coupon Treasury Bond	Time Left to Maturity	Yield to Maturity as per the Yield Curve	Formula	Price of Bond
A	1	8.00%	100/108^1	92.59
B	2	9.00%	100/109^2	84.17

If the fund manager buys the one-year ZCB and holds it for one year until redemption, the return will be exactly as provided for by the yield curve, ie, 8%.

$$r = \frac{100 - 92.59}{92.59} = 8\%$$

Since this is a zero-coupon held to maturity, the risk is zero.

The alternative scenario is to buy the two-year note and hold it for one year and sell it then as a zero coupon with one year remaining. The return available then is as follows:

$$r = \frac{92.59 - 84.17}{84.17} = 10.00\%$$

The return can again be determined from the holding-period return calculation, though an assumption is required regarding the selling price in one year. The risk this time is not zero, as the fund manager is exposed to movements in the yield curve. The yield curve ride is a strategy by which investors take on some risk in order to enhance returns.

During Q3 2019, the financial markets experienced a situation caused by investors having concerns over the long-term view of the global economy. This was accompanied by a change to the shape and slope of the bond yield curve.

History shows that if markets expect that the economy is going to slow down, there is an expectation that interest rates will start to fall over time which is a common response to try and stimulate growth. Consequently, longer-term investment looks to the higher interest being offered before yields start to decline, creating significant demand for longer dated bonds. As this happens, long-term bond yields fall below those of shorter-dated bonds. As a result, an inverted yield curve can present.

An inverted yield curve is accepted as a key forecaster of economic slowdown or even global recessions. It has been a reliable predictor of a coming recession. In the last seven global recessions, the spread between three-month US paper and ten-year treasuries had become inverted.

7.6.2 Bond Switching

There are valid reasons for bond portfolio adjustments involving the purchase and sale of bonds, ie, bond switching or swapping. There are two main classes of bond switches:

- anomaly switches, and
- policy switches.

Anomaly Switching

An anomaly switch is a switch between two bonds with very similar characteristics, but whose prices or yields are out of line with each other.

- **Substitution switching** – this involves switching between two bonds that are similar in terms of maturity, coupon and quality rating and every other characteristic, but which differ in terms of price and yield. Since two similar bonds should trade at the same price and yield, this circumstance results in an arbitrage between the expensive bond being sold and the cheap bond being purchased. If the coupon and maturity of the two bonds are similar, then a substitution swap involves a one-for-one exchange of bonds. However, if there are substantial differences in coupon or maturity, then the duration of the two bonds will differ. This will lead to different responses if the general level of interest rates changes during the life of the switch. It will therefore be necessary to weight the switch in such a way that it is hedged from changes in the level of interest rates.
- A **pure yield pickup switch** involves the sale of a bond that has a given yield to maturity and the purchase of a similar bond with a greater yield to maturity. With this switch, there is no expectation of any yield or price correction, so no reverse transaction will need to take place at a later date, as may be the case with a substitution switch.

Policy Switching

A policy switch is a switch between two dissimilar bonds, which is designed to take advantage of an anticipated change in:

- interest rates
- the term structure of interest rates, ie, the yield curve
- possible changes in the bond credit rating from the major rating agencies, or
- sector relationships.

Such changes can lead to a change in the relative prices and yields of the two bonds. Policy switches involve greater expected returns, but also greater potential risks, than anomaly switches.

Inter-Market Spread Switch

There is also a third kind of bond-switch. When it is believed that the difference in the yield being offered between corporate bonds and comparable gilts, for example, is excessive given the perceived risk differential between these two markets, an inter-market spread switch will be undertaken from the gilt to the corporate bond market. Conversely, if an event that lowers the risk appetite of bond investors is expected to result in a flight to quality, gilts will be purchased in favour of corporate bonds. Active management policies are also employed in which it is believed the market's view on future interest rate movements, implied by the yield curve, is incorrect or has failed to be anticipated.

Reasons for Bond Switching

- **Changes in interest rates** – intuitions about the future direction of interest rates, and market timing in general, is one of the primary factors that will encourage fund managers to switch between different bonds. Switching from low-duration to high-duration bonds if interest rates are expected to fall is an example of a policy switch.
- **Changes in the structure of the yield curve** – normally, the yield curve is a smooth relationship between yield and maturity. Occasionally, however, there may be humps or dips in the curve. If the humps or dips are expected to disappear, then the prices of the bonds on the hump can be expected to rise (and their yield fall correspondingly), and the prices of the bonds in the dips can be expected to fall (and their yields correspondingly rise). A policy switch involves the purchase of the high-yield bond and the sale of the low-yield bond. Another example of a policy switch resulting from changes in the structure of the yield curve is the bridge swap. As a result of an abnormal distortion in the yield curve, perhaps due to very high demand for bonds of a specific maturity, there may be exploitable opportunities from a form of arbitrage between different sections of the yield curve. As an example, suppose that eight- and ten-year bonds are selling at lower yields and higher prices than the nine-year bond. A bridge swap involves selling the eight and ten-year bonds and buying nine-year bonds.
- **Changes in bond quality ratings** – a bond whose quality rating is expected to fall will fall in price. To prevent a capital loss, it can be switched for a bond whose quality rating is expected to rise or remain unchanged. This is an uncertain process and often there are no advance warnings of the re-rating of credits by the major rating agencies.
- **Changes in sector relationships** – a change in sector relationships is a change in taxes between two sectors: one sector may have withholding taxes on coupon payments, eg, domestic bonds, whereas another, eg, eurobonds, may not.

7.7   Passive Bond Selection Strategies

There are three types of passive bond selection strategy suitable for the management of the bond element of the portfolios.

7.7.1   Duration Matching or Immunisation

The ongoing fluctuation of interest rates poses a particular problem for fund managers with a portfolio of bonds because of the reinvestment risk. However, by using an approach based upon bond duration, matching or immunisation, it is possible to maintain a steady return over a specific time horizon, irrespective of any changes in the interest rate. In the frequently found case where we need to match a set of cash outflows as our liabilities a bond portfolio with the same duration as the liabilities should be constructed.

Suppose that a bond is purchased with a yield of 10%. Interest rates fall to 7%. Consequently, the current price of the bond will rise. However, the overall return on the bond will fall, as it is now only possible to reinvest the coupons received at the rate of 7%. As the bond approaches maturity, this fall in the return will become greater as the reinvestment loss outweighs the gain (which will fall as the bond moves to redemption and the price pulls to redemption at its face value). Under this scenario, the overall return from the investment will fail to realise the quoted yield of 10%.

The same is true of the opposite situation when interest rates rise and bond prices fall. The downward adjustment in the bond's current price will diminish as the bond approaches maturity and the bond pulls to redemption. The coupons will have been reinvested at a higher rate, therefore generating greater returns. Under this scenario, the overall return from the investment will have outperformed the quoted yield of 10%.

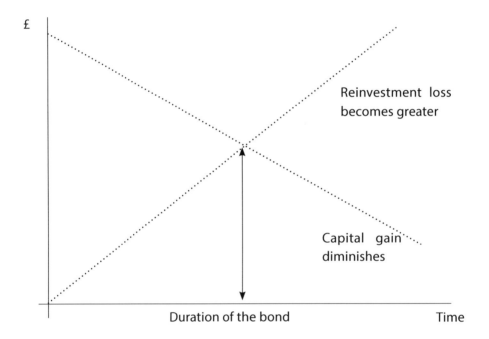

Yield is not an effective measure of the anticipated return on a bond if it is held to maturity precisely because it assumes reinvestment at the same rate as the yield.

Duration matching or immunisation relies on the fact that these two effects (price and reinvestment) are balanced at the point of duration, the weighted average life of the bond. If a bond is held to its duration and not its maturity, the return can be guaranteed.

The diagram in chapter 2, section 6.4.4, illustrates the concept behind the bond duration as it shows the pivot point where each of the cash flows from coupons have to be weighted in relationship to the larger cash flow at the time of redemption when the last coupon is also accompanied by the repayment of the principal or face value of the bond.

Liability-Driven Immunisation

The primary factor which can introduce risk into the simplified approach to immunisation outlined will be caused by non-parallel shifts in the yield curve.

The above example of immunisation showed that it works for parallel shifts in the yield curve, ie, the reinvestment rate fell equivalently on each coupon for each maturity. If this does not happen, then matching the duration of the investment to the liability horizon no longer guarantees immunisation. As is often the case, a non-parallel shift in the yield curve will lead to the income component and the capital component changing in value by differing amounts.

This risk is reduced if the durations and convexities of the individual bonds in the immunising portfolio are close to that of the liability, ie, a focused portfolio. In this case, the non-parallel yield curve shift will affect the individual bonds and the liability in similar ways.

Rebalancing

Immunisation is not a passive approach to fund management because the portfolio will require a continual rebalancing. The initial bonds are selected on the grounds of their duration values. However, duration erodes over time and, owing to immunisation risk, new bonds will have to be purchased in order to match the liability.

One possible way around this is to immunise the portfolio using zero coupon bonds. The advantage of zero coupon bonds is that their duration will change in line with time and, therefore, the portfolio will not require a constant rebalancing. However, this type of immunisation will be efficient only for institutional investors. Private investors would have to pay income tax on the notional income received. Even for institutional investors, disadvantage with using zero coupon instruments is that they are not readily available for certain categories of bonds. The strips market for government securities is active and a wide variety of zero coupon bonds are available, but this is not true of the corporate market.

7.7.2 Cash Flow-Matching (or Dedication)

Cash flow-matching is a much simpler approach to portfolio management. The approach is simply to purchase bonds whose redemption proceeds will meet a liability of the fund as it falls due.

Under the concept of matching, bonds are purchased to match the liabilities of the fund. Starting with the final liability, a bond (Bond 1) is purchased whose final coupon and redemption proceeds will extinguish the liability.

Turning next to the penultimate liability, in part this may be satisfied by the coupon flows arising from Bond 1, any remaining liability being matched against the final coupon and redemption value of a second bond (Bond 2).

This process is continued for each liability, ensuring that bonds are purchased whose final coupon and redemption values extinguish the net liabilities of the fund as and when they occur.

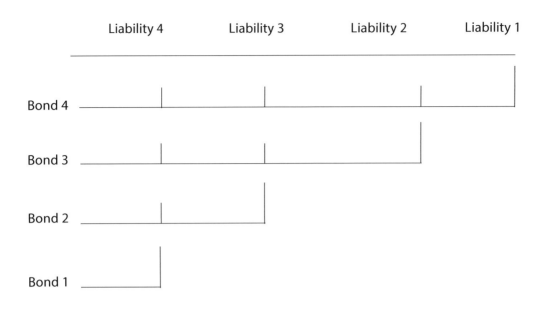

Example

Maturity Years	Coupon %	Redemption Payment
1	8.35	108.35
2	7.7	107.70
3	7.14	107.14

A fund has to meet liabilities of £1,500 arising at the end of each of the next three years. There are three bonds available and their details are revealed in the table above. The right-hand column indicates the combined final coupon payment and the redemption of the face value of the bond, assumed to be £100.

Construct a portfolio to achieve cash matching the annual £1,500 liability.

| Number of Bonds | Coupon | Principal | Maturity | Cash Flows | | |
				Year 1 £	Year 2 £	Year 3 £
14	7.14	100	3	100	100	1,500
13	7.70	100	2	100	1,400	
12	8.35	100	1	1,300		
				1,500	1,500	1,500

The approach outlined in this example is a simple buy-and-hold strategy and as such does not require a regular rebalancing. In practice, it is unlikely that bonds exist with exactly appropriate maturity dates and coupons but, intuitively, it is easier to understand.

7.7.3 Combination Matching (or Horizon Matching)

Combination matching is a mixture of the above two approaches to managed bonds. It is possible to construct a portfolio where, for example, the cash flow matches the liabilities for the next four quarters but is then immunised for the remaining investment horizon. At the end of the four quarters, the portfolio is rebalanced to cash-flow-match over the subsequent four quarters and is again immunised for the remaining period. This combination approach is also known as horizon matching, and can be reiterated at different intervals in order to meet the long-term liabilities of the fund.

8. Evaluation of Portfolio Risk and Return

Learning Objective

7.2.5   Understand how portfolio risk and return are evaluated using the following measures: holding-period return; money-weighted return; time-weighted return; total return and its components; standard deviation; value at risk; volatility; covariance and correlation; risk-adjusted returns (eg, Sharpe ratio); benchmarking; alpha; beta

Candidates will not be expected to undertake the calculation of any variables mentioned in this Learning Objective.

8.1 Holding-Period Return and Total Return

For any investment there is a basic pattern which can be thought of at its simplest in the form of a cost/benefit analysis. There will be costs for making the investment, which could be a single one-off outlay at the inception, or a continuing obligation to fund further costs through the lifetime of the investment. In return there will be a series of incoming cash flows which are the benefits side of the investment.

In its simplest form, the performance of a portfolio of investments can be measured by regarding all of the incoming cash flows in the form of dividends or coupon payments and also factor in capital growth (final market value less initial value) and express these items which could be called the total return as a percentage of the initial amount invested. This gives rise to the core concept of the holding-period return. By calculation of the percentage holding-period return for any investment it becomes possible to compare the relative performance of a variety of investments of different sizes and with different objectives and characteristics. The percentage holding-period return is the gain during the period held (money received less cost) divided by the initial cost:

$$r_p = \frac{(D + V_e - V_s)}{V_s} \times 100\%$$

where:

r_p = holding-period return

D = any returns paid out from the investment/portfolio at the end of the period

V_s = the initial cost at the start of the holding-period

V_e = the value of the investment at the end of the holding-period

Comparison of Two Investments

Investment A costs £1,000 and at the end of six months returns £50, before being sold for £1,200. How can it be compared with investment B, bought at £500, held for one year and then sold for £800 with no income paid out?

Holding-period return for Investment A:

Using this equation, the holding-period returns for Investment A can be calculated as follows.

$$r_p = \frac{(D+V_e - V_s)}{V_s} \times 100\%$$

$$r_p = \frac{(50+1,200 - 1,000)}{1,000} \times 100\%$$

$$r_p = 25\% \text{ in six months}$$

Holding-period return for Investment B:

Using this equation, the holding-period returns for Investment B can be calculated as follows.

$$r_p = \frac{(D+V_e - V_s)}{V_s} \times 100\%$$

$$r_p = \frac{(0+800 - 500)}{500} \times 100\%$$

$$r_p = 60\% \text{ in one year}$$

The holding-period returns of A and B are not yet directly comparable, since B was invested for twice as long as A. When A was sold, the proceeds could have been reinvested for another six months, but we do not know what return would have been available to the investor at that time.

To compare the returns, they must be for a standard period. This is achieved by using the equivalent period interest rate formula to annualise the returns as follows:

Investment A: $r_p = 25\%$ in six months

Annualising this return, we use the formula:

$$1+r = (1+R)^n$$

$$1+r = (1+0.25)^2 = 1.5625$$

$$r = 0.5625 \text{ or } 56.25\% \text{ pa}$$

Investment B: $r_p = 60\%$ pa

As a result of converting both returns to a common base of an annual return there is now a standardised measure of return, the annualised holding-period return.

So far so good, but this simple kind of measurement is not useful when there is a need to factor in the calculation of the return significant cash inflows or outflows from the fund during the period. This can be demonstrated by considering another simple example.

A fund has a value at inception of £5 million, and halfway through the period it has the same value and a further £5 million is deposited. At the end of the period it is worth £10 million, no dividends having been paid. What is the fund's performance?

Using our equation above, we have:

$$r_p = \frac{(D+V_e - V_s)}{V_s} \times 100\%$$

$$r_p = \frac{(0+£10m - £5m)}{£5m} \times 100\%$$

$$= +100\%$$

But this seems to be patently false, since the fund has generated no return whatsoever. The terminal value of the fund is simply the sum of what was initially held, plus the funds added. There has been no growth or positive return generated. The shortcomings of the simple holding-period return calculation can be dealt with by looking at the fund returns over each sub-period where there are no outflows or inflows and then amalgamating them. In the above simple example, the first sub-period starts at £5 million and ends at £5 million, so the return is zero. This is amalgamated with the second sub-period that starts at £10 million and ends at £10 million so is again zero. The amalgamated return is the expected value of zero per cent.

This simple approach is, therefore, insufficient. In addition to the initial outlay or the value of the fund at inception, it is necessary to account for the deposits and withdrawals that occur during the period over which the performance is being measured.

8.2   Standard Deviation

To measure the degree of variability of an investment, we can use either:

- The standard deviation, which is conventionally denoted in statistics by sigma or σ.
- The variance, which is usually denoted as sigma squared or σ^2.

In making the calculations each possible return, Ri, occurs with probability p, and the expected (arithmetic mean) return is denoted by Re.

In essence, the variance is calculated first by subtracting Re from each of the Ri values. This will lead to positive and negative percentages. Since we are concerned about the magnitude of the difference rather than the sign of the difference, each of these differences are squared.

The resulting squared amounts are then multiplied by the probability of each return, p. The sum of the squared differences weighted according to their probability is known as the variance and the square root of the variance is known as the standard deviation. The standard deviation has the advantage that it is expressed in the same units as the returns (% in the example above), whereas the variance is in the original units squared.

For some calculations in portfolio theory, it will be necessary to use the variance rather than the standard deviation, but in discussions of risk in financial theory it is more common to use the standard deviation.

There are two formulae for the standard deviation. The first is where the variability of an entire population is being calculated and, as can be seen, the denominator of the equation is equal to n – the number of items being analysed. The second formula is more conventionally used for a sample, rather than the entire population, and the denominator used is n – 1. For calculations of large sets of data the difference is minimal.

$$\text{Standard deviation of entire population} = \sigma = \frac{\Sigma p(Ri - Re)^2}{n}$$

$$\text{Standard deviation of population sample} = \sigma = \frac{\Sigma p(Ri - Re)^2}{n - 1}$$

In order to illustrate the standard deviation of returns, an example will be followed.

The table below shows the four expected (possible) outcomes from an investment requiring an initial outlay of £1,000 as surmised by an investor.

Starting Balance		£1,000	Expected Return
Probability	End Balance	Return	
20%	£1,000	0.0%	0.0%
15%	£1,100	10.0%	1.5%
35%	£1,180	18.0%	6.3%
30%	£1,200	20.0%	6.0%
100%			13.8%

Examining the matrix, it is possible to see that the expected return is simply the sum of the expected returns multiplied in each case by the likelihood (as estimated) of that outcome. The result is a weighted return where the probability is used to weight each of the expected returns. It is important that the probabilities sum to 100%, so if there is uncertainty about any outcome it is better to include it under the zero return item.

Once the expected return has been calculated, it is necessary to consider the variability of the outcomes as included in the table and these are expressed as probabilities. Determining the risk of an investment requires an assessment of the mean of the returns and the variability of the returns (or the dispersion of the outcomes). We need to determine the mean value and the standard deviation of the returns.

Value At Risk (VAR)

To measure the degree of financial or market risk being endured within a firm or an investment, we can use value at risk (VAR). It is a widely used risk measure of the risk of loss on a particular portfolio of financial instruments.

For the given portfolio, time horizon, and probability, the VAR is defined as a threshold loss value. This assumes mark-to-market pricing, normal markets and no trading within the portfolio. VAR is measured in three components:

1. The amount of potential loss.
2. The time frame.
3. The probability that amount of loss will happen.

A simple example is a fund manager who determines that on their portfolio there is a 10% probability one-day VAR of £50 million. This implies that there is a 10% probability that the fund manager or their firm could lose more than £50 million on any given day. Therefore, a £50 million loss could be expected to occur every ten days given that the portfolio has a 10% probability.

It should be noted that VAR measures just one aspect of market risk. It cannot be used on its own as a reliable measure of capital adequacy.

8.2.1   Arithmetic Mean

The most commonly used measure of expected return is the arithmetic mean, the calculation of which reflects the values and probabilities of the various possible returns. The arithmetic mean may be described mathematically as:

$$\text{Arithmetic mean} = \overline{r} = \Sigma pr$$

where:

$\overline{r}$ =   expected return

p =   probability attached to a particular outcome or return

r =   percentage return

The arithmetic mean is the most appropriate measure when assessing the expected return in any one year. However, it is less appropriate when assessing the average annual return from an accumulated total over several years. For illustration, assume that there has been a 20% return over a four-year period. It would not be appropriate to say that the mean return is 5% pa (the arithmetic mean 20%/4) since this ignores the compounding of those earlier returns. The more appropriate measure is be the geometric mean, which reflects the compounding. The geometric mean deals with compounding situations, and the formula and calculation techniques are similar to those used in the DCF techniques (see chapter 2, section 1.2).

Starting Balance		£1,000	Expected Return %	Ri – Re	(Ri – Re)^2	p*(Ri – Re)^2
Probability	End Balance	Return				
20%	£1,000	0.0%	0.0%	−13.8%	1.90%	0.380%
15%	£1,100	10.0%	1.5%	−3.8%	0.14%	0.021%
35%	£1,180	18.0%	6.3%	4.2%	0.18%	0.063%
30%	£1,200	20.0%	6.0%	6.2%	0.38%	0.114%
100%		Expected Return Re	13.8%			0.578%
		Variance = σ^2	0.578%			
		Standard Deviation = $\sqrt{σ^2}$	7.60%			

The table is a continuation of the earlier tabulation of the expected returns based on a simple probability calculation. The extension to the table shows the results in the three right-hand columns:

1. Subtracting the expected return Re from each of the returns Ri.
2. The squaring of the number determined above – so that each becomes a positive value.
3. The result from the above multiplied by each of the probabilities.

The sum of the last column is equal to the variance and the square root of the variance is the standard deviation.

8.2.2   Interpretation of the Result

It can be seen from the above that an investor contemplating whether to invest in the project has an expected return of 13.8% with a standard deviation of the returns of 7.60%. Let us also assume that the investor has a cost of capital of 10% pa. It is clear that the expected return does exceed the current cost of capital, but how should the investor take account of the variability, or the standard deviation, ie, the risk? How can the investor relate the risk and return?

One thing which can be said at this preliminary stage is that, other things being equal, the higher the standard deviation of the returns, the greater the risk. So, if an investor is faced with two projects, both of which delivered the same expected return, and one has a much greater standard deviation than the other, the investor will seek out the one with the smaller standard deviation. In very simple terms the typical (rational) investor will perform a trade-off between the expected return and the amount of risk (ie, how large is the standard deviation of the returns) and choose the one with the more favourable ratio.

To answer this question more deeply, however, it is necessary to venture into some elementary statistical theory and make references to the normal distribution. In order to make this as concrete as possible and not too theoretical, the discussion will allow us to examine the returns for an investor in the broad-based FTSE 100 Index during the year ending on 1 June 2009. We shall take the closing price of the index at the beginning of each month and calculate the percentage increase from month to month.

The following table shows the method for calculating the standard deviation of the monthly changes.

FTSE 100 Monthly Changes				
Date	Close	Percentage Change	Deviation Mean	Squared Deviation
01/05/2008	6053.5			
02/06/2008	5625.9	−7.1%	−4.7%	0.2%
01/07/2008	5411.9	−3.8%	−1.4%	0.0%
01/08/2008	5636.6	4.2%	6.5%	0.4%
01/09/2008	4902.5	−13.0%	−10.6%	1.1%
01/10/2008	4377.3	−10.7%	−8.3%	0.7%
03/11/2008	4288.0	−2.0%	0.3%	0.0%
01/12/2008	4434.2	3.4%	5.8%	0.3%
02/01/2008	4149.6	−6.4%	−4.0%	0.2%
02/02/2009	3830.1	−7.7%	−5.3%	0.3%
02/03/2009	3926.1	2.5%	4.9%	0.2%
01/04/2009	4243.7	8.1%	10.5%	1.1%
01/05/2009	4417.9	4.1%	6.5%	0.4%

Statistical Value	Greek Letter	Value
Mean Monthly Change	μ	−2.37%
Variance = Sum of Squared Deviations/12	σ^2	0.42%
Standard Deviation = $\sqrt{\text{Variance}}$	σ	6.48%

The table above actually includes 13 values, with May 2008 being inserted only in order to determine the percentage difference for the first reference value which is for June 2008.

The percentage changes are simply determined by the formula:

$$\frac{\text{Close in current month}}{\text{Close in previous month}} - 1 \times 100\%$$

In time series analysis, this value is sometimes called the first order difference and can be calculated using a logarithmic approach in which case it is known as the log difference, but for simplicity the simple percentage changes have been used in what follows. The arithmetic mean value or average monthly change is simply the sum of the monthly changes divided by the number of values – in this case 12. It is usually denoted by the Greek letter μ. As can be seen from the table the average monthly difference during the one-year period is −2.37%, which reflects the significant decline in equity prices in the UK and globally during the period.

It should be commented that this period which has been examined in the table shows some of the more extreme behaviour of financial markets from a historical perspective. For the FTSE 100 during the period examined, the standard deviation value of 6.48% for monthly returns observed is, from a historical point of view, abnormally high. However the general theoretical implications of taking the observations of mean and standard deviation and applying them to a forecast of risk and return are equally as applicable for more extreme financial periods as well as more normal circumstances.

Indeed, one could make the case that financial market analysts had underestimated the degree of systematic or market risk prior to the more extreme periods seen in the second half of 2008 and until 2009. The monthly changes have been illustrated in the column graph below and, as revealed, the back-to-back losses of 10% plus in each of September and October 2008 are quite exceptional.

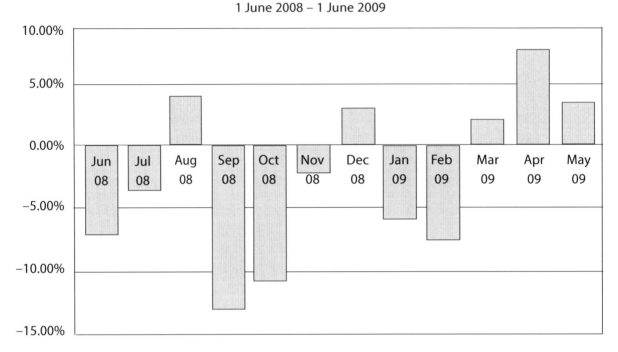

Monthly Returns for FTSE 100
1 June 2008 – 1 June 2009

The diagram above shows the considerable variability in the monthly returns of the FTSE 100 Index during a very troubled financial period. The degree of variability seen on the diagram from month to month is more in the order of magnitude of a year to year chart in more normal times and helps to address the underlying question of the riskiness of an investment. If one had taken a short-term investment view and decided to buy stocks in the FTSE 100 in August 2008, within two months the investment would have lost about 25% of its value. This is clearly a highly unusual situation which coincided with the worst financial crisis in recent history.

8.3 Volatility

There are many different opinions on what constitutes the best measurement of volatility, starting with the simplest, which is the variance in the returns of an asset, or more commonly the standard deviation in the returns. We have seen how the variability of returns in the FTSE 100 Index during 2008 would have impacted a portfolio manager with exposure to the stocks in this index.

From a macroeconomic perspective there are ways of measuring the degree of volatility across a broad range of asset classes, and one of the more useful is the Chicago Board Options Exchange's (CBOE's) Volatility Index, or VIX. It is fortunate that detailed daily records of the value of this index have been kept since 1990 so it is possible to take a good look, for a substantial period, at what has happened to the market's own perception of its likely volatility and risk.

Implied volatility has to be distinguished from the actual observed variance in the returns that we just mentioned, and which is usually referred to as historical volatility. Implied volatility is the market's perception, at the time, of the likely variation in returns as expressed in the prices of options (which incorporate a variable premium value).

The following chart shows the monthly values of the CBOE Volatility Index for the period from 1990 until 2020. As can be seen immediately, the VIX As can be seen immediately, the VIX is itself highly volatile, showing that perceptions about the future course of volatility are subject to profound and dramatic changes depending on the prevailing market conditions, contemporaneous news events and crises.

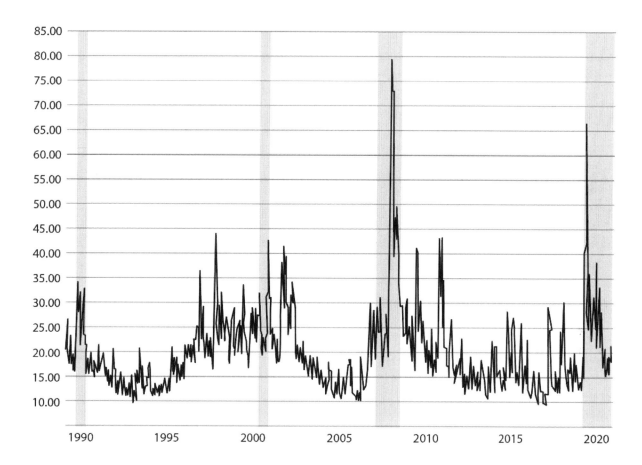

Source: https://www.macrotrends.net/2603/vix-volatility-index-historical-chart

The peak in 2008–09 shows the extreme nature of the panic surrounding the global banking crisis of 2008, when market traders were assuming an implied volatility of up to 90% at its peak and a considerable period when the readings were above 40%. The more recent spike in 2019–20 coincides with the beginning of the COVID-19 pandemic.

8.4   Beta, Covariance and Correlation

Standard deviation has been shown to be one of the key metrics in portfolio theory to measure risk but there is another important notion, which is sometimes confused with volatility, but which provides a different view of the risk of holding an asset.

The concept which plays a key role in modern portfolio theory is known as beta. Beta measures the extent to which the price movements in a particular asset are either in line with the price movements of a broad index or benchmark – such as the FTSE 100 or S&P 500 – or else exceed or are less than the benchmark.

In other words, beta is a measure of the average historic sensitivity of a fund's returns compared to the broader market. For example, a value of 1 indicates that the fund has, on average, moved in line with the general market movements.

- If the stock's beta is 1, then the stock has the same volatility as the market as a whole, ie, will be expected to move in line with the market as a whole.
- If it has a beta of greater than 1, then the stock will be expected to move more than the market as a whole.
- If a stock has a beta of 1.5, then it has 50% greater volatility than the market portfolio, ie, can be expected to move half as much again as the market. A beta of 1.5 means that the fund has moved by an average of 1.5% for every 1% market movement. A beta value of 2 for an individual UK security that has been benchmarked against the FTSE 100 means that the movements of the security should be expected to be twice that of the index. So if the index were to rise by 10% the security will be expected to rise by 20% and if the index were to fall by 5% then the security would be expected to fall by 10%.
- If it has a beta of less than 1, the stock is less volatile than the market as a whole, so a stock with a beta of 0.7 will be expected to move 30% less than the market as whole. This is sometimes referred to as acting defensively to general market moves.

Understanding the beta of a fund will, therefore, give an indication of how an asset of a fund may perform in certain market conditions. When allied with the risk tolerance of a client, its value can be seen. An asset with a high beta is potentially unsuitable for a risk-averse investor, whereas one that has acted in line with market movements or defensively may be more appropriate.

Covariance is a statistical measure of the relationship between two variables such as share prices. The covariance between two shares is calculated by multiplying the standard deviation of the first by the standard deviation of the second share and then by the correlation coefficient. A positive covariance between the returns of A and B means they have moved in the same direction, while a negative covariance means they have moved inversely. The larger the covariance, the greater the historic joint movements of the two securities in the same direction.

From this the following conclusions can be drawn:

- Although it is perfectly possible for two combinations of two different securities to have the same correlation coefficient as one another, each may have a different covariance, owing to the differences in the individual standard deviations of the constituent securities.
- A security with a high standard deviation in isolation does not necessarily have a high covariance with other shares. If it has a low correlation with the other shares in a portfolio then, despite its high standard deviation, its inclusion in the portfolio may reduce overall portfolio risk.
- Portfolios designed to minimise risk should contain securities as negatively correlated with each other as possible and with low standard deviations to minimise the covariance.

To calculate the beta of an investment we need to know the systematic risk element of the investment. Systematic risk is that part of the total risk that is related to movements in the market portfolio.

The correlation coefficient between two investment opportunities is a measure of this relationship and hence can be included in the derivation approach to beta.

$$\sigma_s = \sigma_i \, \text{Cor(im)}$$

where: σ_s = investment's systematic risk

σ_i = investment's total risk (systematic and unsystematic)

Cor(im) = correlation coefficient between the investment's returns and the market as a whole, for which one can use an appropriate benchmark such as the returns on the FTSE 100

For instance, if an investment is perfectly correlated with the market, then all of its risk will be systematic $\sigma_s = \sigma_i$. However, if an investment is uncorrelated to the market, then its systematic risk will be zero and all of its risk will be unsystematic.

$$\beta = \frac{\sigma_s}{\sigma_m} \text{ and from } \sigma_s = \text{Cor(im)} = \beta = \frac{\sigma_i \, \text{Cor(im)}}{\sigma_m} = \frac{\sigma_i \, \sigma_m \text{Cor(im)}}{\sigma_m^2}$$

If the covariance or correlation coefficient between the investment and the market can be established, the beta can be calculated. Alternatively, if we establish the systematic risk, we can establish the beta.

8.5   Risk-Adjusted Returns and Performance Ratios

Once one has calculated the returns from a portfolio, it is very useful, in assessing the amount of risk borne by the investor or fund manager, to compare the portfolio's performance against the market as a whole or against other portfolios. This requires the use of risk-adjusted performance measurements, of which there are a number of methods in use including the following:

- Sharpe ratio.
- Sortino ratio.
- Jensen measure.
- Information ratio.
- **Alpha**.

We shall consider the most widely used by portfolio managers to benchmark their performance. It is known as the Sharpe ratio and is named after William Sharpe, a Nobel laureate in economics who is Emeritus Professor of Finance at Stanford University, who devised the measure.

The simplest method to calculate the Sharpe ratio is to deduct the risk-free rate of return from the compounded annual growth rate (CAGR) and divide the result by the annualised standard deviation of the returns.

So the formula is simply:

[CAGR – RFR] / Annualised Standard Deviation of Returns

There is a slightly different approach, which is to deduct the average monthly return at the risk-free T-bill rate from the average monthly return and divide the result by the monthly standard deviation of the returns. Once that figure is obtained the result is again multiplied by the square root of 12. The alternate formula is simply:

$$\{[\text{Average Monthly Return} - \text{Average RFR}]/ \text{STD of Monthly Returns}\} \times 12^{0.5}$$

Now that we know how to calculate the ratio, we should briefly explore the significance of this value that was first proposed by Sharpe. The assumption behind the calculation and the reason why the standard deviation is used as the denominator to the equation is that, since investors prefer a smooth ride to a bumpy one, the higher the standard deviation, the lower will be the Sharpe ratio. Accordingly, high Sharpe ratios are to be preferred and positive values are obviously better than negative values, reflecting the fact that returns are positive. Obviously, the denominator of the equation will always be a positive value.

As an aside, we should note that many analysts compute the Sharpe ratio using arithmetic returns. However, the geometric mean is a more accurate measure of average performance for time series data, as the following example shows. For example, if one has returns of +50% and –50% in two periods, then the arithmetic mean is zero, which does not correctly reflect the fact that 100 became 150 and then 75. The geometric mean, which is –13.4%, is the correct measure to use. For investment returns in the 10–15% range, the arithmetic returns are about 2% above the geometric returns.

There are a few other factors that need to be noted about the simple formula for the Sharpe ratio. Since the denominator of the formula is the standard deviation of the returns, the ratio becomes numerically very unstable at extremes, or in other words when the denominator is close to zero.

The second and major problem relates to the actual sequence of returns and the different equity curves associated with them. An equity curve tracks the actual rise and fall of equity in a fund or traces out the development through time of the P&L. Dramatically different equity curves in a portfolio will not be captured by the mean and standard deviations when looked at retroactively to compute the Sharpe ratio.

Therefore, depending on the exact time frame of reference, the Sharpe ratio is the same in all three instances – the actual sequence of returns, an ascending sort of those same returns and also a descending sort of the sequence. What this illustrates is that the Sharpe ratio is essentially insensitive to the clustering of returns.

This is a serious limitation of the value, because an investor will be seriously perturbed by the extreme equity curves that could be witnessed if there were a cluster of losing months in a returns schedule. Because of the calculation mode that underlies averages and standard deviations this clustering of losing months will no longer be apparent on a retrospective basis, although at the time the volatility would have felt much worse than the Sharpe ratio suggests.

There is one further limitation of the procedure for calculating the Sharpe ratio, which is that the simple standard deviation or variability of the returns includes not only the months when returns are negative but also those when returns are positive. The presence of a number of months with superior returns in an otherwise typically positive period of performance will increase the standard deviation but for reasons that, hopefully, the investor will not find unattractive. Risk is asymmetrical, and we tend to equate negative or adverse returns as problematic, whereas the Sharpe ratio penalises the fund manager who happens to show superior performance with higher variability caused by a higher frequency of big winners. This limitation was the inspiration for the Sortino ratio – which is beyond the scope of the current syllabus.

Alpha is a risk-adjusted performance measure using the volatility of a portfolio, and compares its risk-adjusted performance to the benchmark index. The alpha is the measure of the portfolios over and above the return from the benchmark index.

8.6   Time-Weighted and Money-Weighted Returns

Time-weighted returns and money-weighted returns are a way to measure the performance/rate of return but by using different methods and criteria (the formulae for calculating these types of returns are outside the scope of this workbook due to their complexity). The main difference between the two is that time-weighted return ignores the effect of cash inflows and outflows during the calculation period.

- **Time-Weighted Return (TWR)** – a TWR is unaffected by withdrawals or contributions, but measures the compound rate of return for one investment over a set time period. When calculating a time-weighted rate of return, the effect of varying cash inflows is eliminated, so the calculation effectively compares a single investment at the start of the measured period and then measures the profit or loss at the end of the period.

  With TWR, the total measurement period is divided into several sub-periods. Each sub-period will end and be priced as an inflow or outflow occurs, or can be end of month or end of quarter, depending on the requirements of the manager. The rate of return then takes the compounded time-weighted rate for each sub-period, and calculates the average returns for the measurement period. TWR is the preferred industry standard because of the 'smoothing effect' of the calculation.

- **Money-Weighted Return (MWR)** – the MWR can be used to evaluate the performance of a single investment or an entire portfolio. Its name derives from it being based on the amount of money within an account. In calculating the MWR, the inflows and outflows are taken into account and, whatever factor is required to make the two sides equal, is the rate of return for the investment. A MWR is relative to the length of the period in which a person has invested their capital. MWRs are largely focused on the timing of inflows and outflows of cash. Unlike TWRs, MWRs measure the rate of return based on the same rate of return being earned during each sub-period.

End of Chapter Questions

Think of an answer to each question and refer to the appropriate section for confirmation.

1. What is the primary purpose of the Financial Stability Report which is published twice annually by the Bank of England?
Answer reference: Section 1.1.2

2. What is a candlestick chart and which type of market analyst would be most associated with such a chart?
Answer reference: Section 1.2.2

3. What market abuse is referred to by the term 'pump and dump'?
Answer reference: Section 2.4.5

4. What is the primary objective of the Panel on Takeovers and Mergers?
Answer reference: Section 2.5

5. What is the meaning of underlying with respect to financial derivatives?
Answer reference: Section 3.1

6. What is an American-style put option?
Answer reference: Section 3.2.1

7. A portfolio manager is holding long positions in UK equities with a current value of £10 million and largely replicates the weightings of the FTSE 100 Index. How many FTSE 100 contracts should be sold to provide a suitable hedge if the FTSE 100 Index currently has a value of 6200?
Answer reference: Section 3.4.2

8. What is meant by the term 'diversifiable' or 'non-systematic risk'?
Answer reference: Section 4.3

9. If the returns of two assets have a correlation coefficient of 0.8 and are combined in equal proportions in Portfolio A, and two other assets with returns which have a correlation coefficient of 0.3 are similarly placed in Portfolio B, which portfolio would you expect to exhibit the most diversification?
Answer reference: Sections 5.1 and 5.2

10. Explain why advocates of the efficient markets hypothesis favour a passive approach to portfolio management rather than an active one.
Answer reference: Section 5.3

Chapter Eight
Investment Selection and Administration

8

This syllabus area will provide approximately 4 of the 80 examination questions

1. Client Investment Profiles

Learning Objective

8.1.1 Apply a range of essential information and factors to form the basis of appropriate investment selection and suitability: financial needs, preferences and expectations; income and lifestyle – current and anticipated; attitude to risk/capacity for loss; level of knowledge and experience of investing; existing debts and investments

1.1 Attitude to Risk and Investment Expertise

The risk tolerance of a client will have a considerable impact on the financial planning strategy that an adviser recommends. It will exhibit itself in the importance that is given to the selection of investment products. A client needs to have a very clear understanding of their own tolerance to risk, as it is essential to choosing the right investment objectives.

Amongst the methods of assessment which can be developed by firms in order to evaluate an individual's risk profile, a questionnaire is common and useful. Questions asked to assess an individual's risk profile might include the following examples.

- How long do you expect to leave your investment in place until you sell it?
- Which outcome is most important to you from an investment portfolio? (Choose one.)
  - Preserving capital
  - Generating income
  - Long-term growth and capital gains
- Which of the following asset classes have you owned previously or do you now own?
  - Bank or building society deposit account
  - Government stocks (gilts)
  - Unit trusts or open-ended investment companies (OEICs)
  - Investment trusts
  - Individual company shares
- Which of the following best describes your main objective in investing? (Choose one.)
  - The education of my children
  - Savings
  - Capital growth and returns
  - My retirement
  - To leave money in my will
- How large is your investment plan in proportion to your total savings?
  - Less than 10%
  - Between 10% and 20%
  - Between 20% and 30%
  - Between 30% and 40%
  - Above 40%

Attitude to risk, and its definitions, are themes that financial services companies constantly revisit. The reason for this is simple: namely that they want to be able to categorise a client into a risk category and then be able to say which of their products are suitable for clients with that risk profile. Definitions of risk profiles are imprecise and there are no agreed classifications, but an overall approach could include:

- **No risk** – the client is not prepared to accept any fall in the value of their investments. Appropriate investments may be cash-type assets or short-dated government bonds priced below par.
- **Low risk** – the client is cautious and prepared to accept some value fluctuation in return for long-term growth but will invest mainly in secure investments.
- **Medium risk** – the client will have some cash and bond investments but will have a fair proportion in direct or indirect equity investments and, potentially, some in high-risk funds.
- **High risk** – the client is able to keep cash reserves to the minimum, will hold mainstream and secondary equities and be prepared to accept derivatives and other high-risk investments.

Academic research has suggested that risk tolerance can be broken down into two main areas:

- ability to take risk, or risk capacity, and
- willingness to take risk, or risk attitude.

A client's ability to take risk can be determined in an objective manner by assessing their wealth and income relative to any liabilities. By contrast, risk attitude is subjective and has more to do with an individual's psychological make-up than their financial circumstances. Some clients view market volatility as an opportunity, while for others such volatility will cause distress (see section 1.4 for more coverage of capacity for loss).

Objective Factors

There are a number of objective factors that can be established that will help define a client's ability to take risk, including:

- **Timescale** – the timescale over which a client may be able to invest will determine both what products are suitable and what risk should be adopted. For example, there would be little justification in selecting a high-risk investment for funds that are held to meet a liability that is due in 12 months' time. By contrast, someone in their 30s choosing to invest for retirement is aiming for long-term growth, and higher-risk investments would then be suitable. As a result, the acceptable level of risk is likely to vary from scenario to scenario.
- **Commitments** – family commitments are likely to have a significant impact on a client's risk profile. For example, if a client needs to support elderly relatives, or children through university, this will have a determining influence on what risk they can assume. While by nature they may be adventurous investors, they will want to meet their obligations, and this will make higher-risk investments less suitable.
- **Wealth** – wealth will clearly be an important influence on the risk that can be assumed. A client with few assets can little afford to lose them, while ones whose immediate financial priorities are covered may be able to accept greater risk.
- **Life cycle** – stage of life is equally important. A client in their 30s or 40s who is investing for retirement will want to aim for long-term growth and may be prepared to accept a higher risk in order to see their funds grow. As retirement approaches, this will change as the client seeks to lock in the growth that has been made and, once they retire, they will be looking for investments that will provide a secure income that they can live on.

- **Age** – the age of the client will often be used in conjunction with the above factors to determine acceptable levels of risk, as some of the above examples have already shown.
- **Health** – the client's health status will need to be established: that is, whether they are in good health or have any serious medical conditions that may influence their investment objectives and attitude to risk. An individual in good health, who comes from a family that traditionally lives until a very old age, will certainly want to plan for the long term, and planning for income well into retirement may well be very high on their list of priorities. This may influence the investment strategy selected, as there may be a need to generate a growing level of income for many years, implying the need for a higher exposure to equities and the growing dividend stream they provide. At the other end of the spectrum, a client may be in poor health, and this may drive an investment strategy to produce a more immediate income. This will then influence the asset allocation strategy adopted, and sway weightings away from equities to cash and fixed-income instruments. A client's health may also influence their attitude to risk.

Subjective Factors

Subjective factors enable an adviser to try and establish a client's willingness to take risks – their 'risk attitude'. A client's attitudes and experiences must play a large part in the decision-making process. A client may well be financially able to invest in higher-risk products, and these may well suit their needs, but, if they are cautious by nature, they may well find the uncertainties of holding volatile investments unsettling, and both the adviser and the client may have to accept that lower-risk investments and returns must be selected.

When attempting to determine a client's willingness to take risks, areas that can be considered include:

- **A client's level of financial knowledge** – generally speaking, investors who are more knowledgeable about financial matters are more willing to accept investment risk. This level of understanding does still need, however, to be tested against their willingness to tolerate differing levels of losses.
- **A client's comfort with a level of risk** – some individuals have a psychological make-up that enables them to take risks more freely than others, and see such risks as opportunities.
- **A client's preferred investment choice** – risk attitude can also be gauged by assessing a client's normal preferences for different types of investments, such as the relative safety of a bank account versus the potential risk of stocks and shares.
- **A client's approach to bad decisions** – this refers to how a client regrets certain investment decisions, and is the negative emotion that arises from making a decision that is, after the fact, wrong. Some clients can take the view that they assessed the opportunity fully and therefore any loss is just a cost of investing. Others regret their wrong decisions and therefore avoid similar scenarios in the future.

Attempting to fully understand a client's risk attitude requires skill and experience, but we can enhance the classifications that we have used so far as suggested below.

Classification	Characteristics
Very cautious investors	Typically have very low levels of knowledge about financial matters and very limited interest in keeping up to date with financial issues.
	Have little experience of investment beyond bank and savings accounts.
	Prefer knowing that their capital is safe rather than seeking high returns.
	Are not comfortable with investing in the stock market.
	Can take a long time to make up their mind on financial matters and can often regret decisions that turn out badly.
Cautious investors	Typically have low levels of knowledge about financial matters and limited interest in keeping up to date with financial issues.
	May have some limited experience of investment products, but will be more familiar with savings accounts than other types of investments.
	Do not like to take risks with their investments. They would prefer to keep their money in the bank, but would be willing to invest in other types of investments if they were likely to be better for the longer term.
	Prefer certain outcomes to gambles.
	Can take a relatively long time to make up their mind on financial matters and can often suffer from regret when decisions turn out badly.
Moderately cautious investors	Typically have low to moderate levels of knowledge about financial matters and limited interest in keeping up to date with financial issues.
	Have some experience of investment products but are more familiar with savings accounts.
	Are uncomfortable taking risks but willing to do so to a limited extent, realising that risky investments are likely to be better for longer-term returns.
	Prefer certain outcomes and take a long time to make up their minds.
Balanced investors	Typically have moderate levels of knowledge about financial matters but will take some time to stay up to date with financial matters.
	May have experience of investment products containing equities and bonds.
	Understand they have to take risks in order to achieve their long-term goals. Willing to take risks with at least part of their available assets.
	Usually prepared to give up a certain outcome providing that the rewards are high enough.
	Can usually make up their minds quickly enough but may still suffer from regret at bad decisions.

Classification	Characteristics
Moderately adventurous investors	Typically have moderate to high levels of financial knowledge and usually keep up to date with financial matters.
	Are usually fairly experienced investors who have used a range of investment products in the past.
	Are willing to take investment risk and understand this is crucial to generating long-term returns. Are willing to take risk with a substantial proportion of their available assets.
	Will usually make their mind up quickly and are able to accept that occasional poor outcomes are a necessary part of long-term investment.
Adventurous investors	Have high levels of financial knowledge and keep up to date.
	Will usually be experienced investors who have used a range of investment products and may have taken an active approach to managing their investments.
	Will readily take investment risk and understand this is crucial to generating long-term returns. Willing to take risks with most of their available assets.
	Will usually make their mind up quickly and are able to accept that occasional poor outcomes are a necessary part of long-term investment.
Very adventurous investors	Have high levels of financial knowledge and a keen interest in financial matters.
	Have substantial amounts of investment experience and will typically have been active in managing their investments.
	Looking for the highest possible returns on their assets and willing to take considerable amounts of risk to achieve this. Willing to take risks with all of their available assets.
	Have firm views on investment and will make up their minds on financial matters quickly. Do not suffer from regret, and accept occasional poor outcomes without much difficulty.

1.2 Financial Needs, Preferences and Expectations

Any individual is likely to have a number of objectives for which some financial provision may be required. We have seen that at the start of the financial planning process the client's general attitude to risk and objective risk tolerance should be established; however, an important refinement of this is that a client's general view of risk does not mean that the same attitude to risk should necessarily be applied to all of the individual's objectives.

An individual may have investments that they wish to use for specific purposes or objectives and for which they cannot easily afford to bear a great degree of shortfall risk. In such cases, they may wish to choose low-risk investments, so that they can be reasonably certain that their objective will be achievable by the desired date. The same individual might have other discretionary possibilities in mind for which they are prepared to tolerate a higher level of risk. The objective may be seen as less essential to the individual, and may be something that the person accepts that they will have to do without if investment returns are not sufficient.

Of course, every investor is different, and the ways in which people rank their objectives and their risk tolerance in relation to different objectives vary. For one person, having enough money to spend on a comfortable home may take a higher priority than having the funds to travel widely. Another person may treat travelling as a higher priority than spending on a home.

In general, the objectives that an individual sees as having the highest priority are those for which they will want to take the lowest risk if they are investing to achieve those objectives. Lower-priority objectives can generally be more easily forgone if investments suffer losses.

1.3   Current and Anticipated Lifestyle

1.3.1   Occupation, Earnings and Other Income Sources

Clearly, it will be necessary to establish what the client's income is, from whatever sources it arises. If generating a particular level of income is important to the client, it will obviously be essential. It will be equally relevant if the client is uninterested in income-generation, as it will be needed to establish the client's tax position.

However, the client's occupation may be a relevant factor for investment decisions in other, less obvious ways. Firstly, the client's occupation or business will give a good indication of their experience in business matters, which may be relevant when judging the suitability of a particular type of investment that carries greater risk and when the firm is required to assess the client's experience before recommending it.

Establishing the client's occupation may also lead the adviser to realise that there may be issues with dealing in certain stocks if the client holds a senior position in a company. In such a position, the client and firm face the risk of dealing on inside information. They will need to ensure that arrangements are put in place to request permission to trade, avoid closed dealing periods and ensure that any trading takes place in a manner that places neither the firm nor the client at risk.

A client may also potentially be a politician or hold a senior position which is in the public spotlight. When that is the case, they often need to distance themselves from any investment decision-making so that there can be no accusation of them exploiting their position or knowledge. In such cases, it is often common to establish a blind trust, where all investment decisions are taken on a totally discretionary basis and where the client is deliberately kept unaware of trading decisions or their rationale.

When the client is in business, the adviser will want to understand the client's plans for the business and any funds that may be forthcoming immediately or in the future that might affect the investment plans that the adviser will draw up.

420

1.3.2   Present and Anticipated Outgoings

The client's outgoings need to be understood in conjunction with their income, when it is necessary to look at budgeting, planning to meet certain liabilities or generating a specific income return.

Depending upon the client's priorities, information about both their present and anticipated future outgoings may be needed. This may be necessary, for example, if the investment plan involves generating a certain income in retirement. Any cash funding requirements, such as the need to fund school fees or university education, will particularly need to be understood so that the requirement to provide the necessary cash can be factored into the investment strategy.

1.3.3   Pension Arrangements

The pension arrangements the client has made will need to be closely linked to the investment strategy that is adopted both for retirement and other financial objectives.

The availability of tax exemptions for pension contributions may influence the choice of investments and so clearly needs to be factored in at this stage.

1.3.4   Assets and Liabilities

Full details of the client's existing assets and liabilities will need to be known. Note that as part of the anti-money laundering checks that the adviser will need to undertake, the source of the client's funds will need to be established.

As well as obtaining details of the client's assets, the adviser should also look to establish:

- the location of the assets and whether any investments are held in a nominee account
- the tax treatment of each of the assets
- whether any investments are held in a tax wrapper
- acquisition costs for any quoted investments held, including any calculations needed for assessing any liability to capital gains tax
- details of any early encashment penalties.

The information needed will vary by type of asset.

Details should be established of any liabilities that the client has, and whether these are covered by any protection products.

1.3.5   Potential Inheritances

The client should be asked to provide details of any potential inheritances they may receive and of any trusts where they are **beneficiaries**. This will be relevant if the amounts due to be inherited might influence the investment strategy adopted. For example, a client may be due to inherit a substantial sum from elderly parents and so may be able to take a view that their investments should be directed to outright growth.

1.3.6 Wealth and Investment Exposure

When considering a client's investment profile, their existing wealth is clearly an important consideration. If there is an excess of capital to invest, then clearly it is sensible for the individual to take steps to make the best use of that capital.

It is possible, although not generally advisable, for someone with little wealth to gain exposure to investment markets, for example by borrowing money to invest, or by using investments such as derivatives or spread betting to gain a greater exposure than the individual's free resources.

When investing in risky assets such as equities, a good principle is the often-stated one that someone should only invest what they can afford to lose. Someone who borrows to invest without having other capital to back it up if things go wrong has the problem that they may end up with liabilities in excess of their assets.

An investor who uses instruments such as derivatives to increase their exposure should maintain other accessible resources (eg, cash on deposit) that can be used to meet losses that may arise. Clearly, it is also important that they understand the risks they are undertaking.

There continues to be an increased regulatory focus on derivatives in recent years with extra regulations being introduced. For example, the European Market Infrastructure Regulation (EMIR) implemented a range of new measures for clearing and reporting to address the way in which the risks associated with derivative activity are managed and addressed. These measures have been amended, added to and developed over time to address new risks as they arise.

1.4 Capacity for Loss

As part of assessing a client's appetite for risk, it is necessary to be aware of the client's capacity for loss, which is considered to be part of the suitability assessment.

This can prove difficult when a client actually believes that they have unlimited capacity for loss. However, the client will not necessarily take into account everything that must be considered and, therefore, the client's opinion on potential loss is somewhat different to capacity for loss.

A firm must collect and properly account for all the information relevant to assessing the risk a customer is willing and, more importantly, is able, to take. A firm should ideally use one procedure to assess the customer's attitude to risk and a separate process to assess the capacity for loss, ensuring both are appropriately considered as part of the suitability. Even when a firm uses a risk-profiling tool, it cannot always easily determine the customer's capacity for loss.

As part of the assessment, the firm will need to know what debts the client has, and what the retirement plans of the client are, taking into account their age and any future capital needs.

2. Strategy Selection

Learning Objective

8.1.2 Be able to analyse and select strategies suitable for the client's aims and objectives in terms of: investment horizon; current and future potential for growth and yield; requirement for capital protection; protection against inflation; liquidity, trading and ongoing management; mandatory or voluntary investment restrictions; impact of fees and charges; ethical/ Environmental, Social and Governance (ESG) considerations

2.1 Capital Protection, Growth and Yield

Having collected all of the core information needed about the client, the adviser can then turn to agreeing their investment objectives.

In collecting the information above, the adviser will have started to build a picture of the client's needs. They should be able to classify these needs along the lines of the following:

* maximising future growth
* protecting the real value of capital
* generating an essential level of income, and
* protecting against future events.

The adviser will want to convert this into an understandable investment objective and will use classifications such as income, income and growth, growth, and outright growth. The purpose of this is so that there can be a common understanding of what the client is trying to achieve. Typical financial objectives include:

* **Income** – the client is seeking a higher level of current income at the expense of potential future growth of capital.
* **Income and growth** – the client needs a certain amount of current income but also wants to invest to achieve potential future growth in income and capital.
* **Growth** – the client is not seeking any particular level of income and their primary objective is capital appreciation.
* **Outright growth** – the client is seeking maximum return through a broad range of investment strategies which generally involve a high level of risk.

Once the client's investment objectives have been agreed, the adviser needs to look at developing an investment strategy that can be used to achieve these objectives. In developing an investment strategy, the adviser will need to determine the following:

* time horizons
* risk tolerance
* investment preferences (see section 1.4 of this chapter)
* liquidity requirements, and
* tax status.

2.1.1   Time Horizon

One of the most important issues to clarify within an investor's profile is their holding period or, in other words, the period for which they are committed to a particular investment programme. The phrase 'time horizon' refers to the period over which a client can consider investing their funds. Definitions of time horizons vary, but short term is usually considered to be from one to four years, while medium term refers to a period from five to ten years and long term is considered to be for a period of ten years or more.

As an investment manager, it is essential to understand the time horizons over which a client is able and willing to invest, as these will also have a clear impact on the selection and construction of an investment portfolio.

The effect of the investment timescale is particularly important for equity or equity-backed investments. Over short-term horizons, ie, less than five years, the returns from equities have often been negative but over very long-term horizons equities have usually shown a relatively high return which exceeds that of most other asset classes. Therefore, if an individual is only seeking to invest over a period of a few months, at the end of which they wish to redeem their investment, then it is inadvisable to invest the money in higher-risk investments such as equities as, given the volatility of equity returns there is an uncomfortably high probability that any investments made in equities for a short timescale may have to be liquidated at a loss. If there are known liabilities that may arise in future years, conservative standards suggest investing an appropriate amount in bonds that are due to mature near the time needed so that there is certainty of the availability of funds.

There is a wide range of available investment opportunities, and to understand which might be suitable for a client, an adviser needs to start by understanding what the client's investment or financial objectives are.

2.1.2   Liquidity Requirements

Liquidity refers to the amount of funds a client might need both in the short and long term. When constructing an investment portfolio, it is essential that an emergency cash reserve is put to one side that the client can access without having to disturb longer-term investments.

A client may have known liabilities that will arise in the future which will need to be planned for, and it will be necessary to factor in how the client will raise funds when needed. Markets can be volatile and so the investment strategy needs to take account of ensuring that funds can be readily realised without having to sell shares at depressed prices. With the need for liquidity in mind, it is wise for an investor to have sufficient funds held on deposit at any time to meet likely cash needs.

However, keeping funds liquid brings the benefit of accessibility but there is a trade-off in terms of returns: the most liquid investments, such as cash or instant access accounts, will have relatively lower returns than other assets. The lower the client's liquidity requirements and the longer their timescale, the greater will be the choice of assets appropriate to meet the client's investment objective. The need for high liquidity, allied to a short timescale, demands that the client should invest in lower-risk assets such as cash and short-dated bonds, which offer a potentially lower return than equities.

In planning terms, the adviser should agree with the client how much of a cash reserve should be held. Recognising the long-term nature of investment, this should represent their expected cash needs over, say, three to five years. This should then be supplemented by ensuring that the portfolio will contain investments that are readily realisable in the event of an emergency and which otherwise will be available to top up the cash reserve in future years.

This could be achieved, for example by using a bond ladder, which involves buying securities with a range of different maturities. Building a laddered portfolio involves buying a range of bonds that mature in, say, three, five, seven and ten years' time. As each matures, funds can become available for the investor to withdraw or can be reinvested in later maturities. See chapter 7, section 7.7.

Alternatively, structured products such as guaranteed capital growth bonds could meet the same objective, subject to establishing a spread of providers and checking the counterparty risk involved. See chapter 4, section 2.

2.1.3 Tax Status

Establishing the client's tax position is essential so that their investments can be organised in such a way that the returns attract the least tax possible. This requires the investment manager to be aware of what taxes may affect the investor, such as taxes on any income arising or on any capital gains, how these are calculated and what allowances may be available.

An adviser will also need to establish the client's residence and domicile status, as these will impact how any investments are structured. Residence is a key part of the UK tax code, and the manner in which a taxpayer qualifies as either ordinarily resident or even non-resident will substantially affect the amount of income tax and capital gains tax for which they are liable.

In the tax year 2021–22, individuals are taxed at the marginal rate of 45% on their taxable income in excess of £150,000 pa. Accordingly, such clients may have a preference for investments which can be taxed at the much lower rate for capital gains, which can vary between 10% and 28%, depending on whether the gains are on residential property or other chargeable assets, whether the individual is a basic rate or higher/additional rate taxpayer and also whether the taxpayer can qualify for entrepreneurs' relief.

Consideration also needs to be given to any tax that may be deducted on investments that may be selected for the client, for example, income tax that may have been deducted from a distribution from a collective investment scheme.

When managing tax implications for a client, it is important to appreciate the difference between tax evasion and tax avoidance. Tax evasion is a financial crime and is illegal, while tax avoidance is organising your affairs within the rules so that you pay the least tax possible. The latter is a responsibility of the adviser when they are undertaking financial planning.

The adviser will, therefore, need to establish:

- the client's residence and domicile position
- the client's income tax position

- how tax will affect any investment income
- any tax allowances which can be utilised
- how capital gains tax will affect any gains or losses made
- any capital gains tax allowances which can be utilised
- eligibility for any tax-free accounts, and
- opportunities for and the desirability of deferring any tax due.

2.2   Protection Against Inflation

Inflation can be one of the most important obstacles to successful investing because the real value of the income flow from investments such as bonds and equities, as well as the long-term value of capital, is eroded by the effects of inflation and the decline in the purchasing power of the wealth that is created.

Controlling inflation is the prime focus of economic policy in most countries, as the economic costs inflation imposes on society are far-reaching. While there are many negative consequences, the two which are most pertinent for the typical investor are:

- Inflation reduces the spending power of those dependent on fixed incomes such as pensions or fixed-coupon investments such as a typical corporate bond.
- Individuals are not rewarded for saving. This occurs when the inflation rate exceeds the nominal interest rate. That is, the real interest rate is negative. Real interest rates are calculated as follows:

Real interest rate = ([1 + nominal interest rate] / [1 + inflation rate]) − 1

So, the real return takes into account the inflation rate and in times of excessive inflation the real returns available may well become negative.

In addition to the specific impact of inflation on returns just discussed, the broader macroeconomic problems associated with periods of high inflation are well illustrated by the difficulties faced by investors during the 1970s around the world. This was a period of extremely high inflation, fuelled by surging commodity prices, especially crude oil, which in turn led to demands from organised labour for higher wages, which in turn pushed up the costs to producers of goods and services, who in turn pushed on these additional costs to end consumers in the form of higher prices. A vicious circle was created which required very drastic increases in short-term interest rates at the end of the 1970s. The base rates in the US and UK were approximately 20% as the 1980s began. This caused widespread distress for asset prices. The 1970s was one of the worst on record for global stock market returns.

Inflation will also have negative implications for holders of bonds and fixed-income instruments. A major driver of bond prices is the prevailing interest rate and expectations of interest rates to come. Yields required by bond investors are a reflection of their interest rate expectations, which in turn will be largely influenced by expectations about inflation. For example, if inflation and interest rates are expected to rise, bond prices will fall to bring the yields up to appropriate levels to reflect the interest rate increases. To remain competitive, equities prices will also suffer.

The interest rate itself is heavily impacted by inflationary expectations. Simplistically, if inflation is expected to be at 4% pa, the interest rate will have to be greater than this in order to provide the investor with any real return. The interest rate might stand at 7% pa. If economic news suggests that inflation is likely to increase further, to say 6%, then the interest rate will increase too, perhaps up to 9%. The reverse is true if inflation is expected to fall.

There are several investments that can be used if an investor is concerned to protect against the effects of inflation. For example, index-linked bonds are ones where the coupon and the redemption amount are increased by the amount of inflation over the life of the bond. The amount of inflation uplift is determined by changes in the retail prices index (RPI). As with conventional gilts, investors receive two interest payments a year and they get a redemption payment based on the nominal or face value of their gilt holding. However, these payments are adjusted to take account of inflation since the gilt was issued.

Over time, successful companies should achieve a rise in both profits and dividend payments to shareholders. This tends to be rewarded by existing shareholders and new investors placing a higher value on the price of the shares. If the annual dividend increases are in excess of the annual inflation rate over a sustained period of time, the share price and dividend receipts may well act as a healthy hedge against inflation.

One final consideration for investors during periods of inflation is to consider making gold and other commodities a part of their core portfolio holdings. Gold has traditionally been seen as not only a hedge against inflation but also a protection against the debasement of paper assets, which partly arises from inflation but might also arise from profligate government policies. Commodities such as energy products and industrial metals will also tend to have a negative correlation with more mainstream assets and should be relatively good performers during periods of inflation.

2.3   Mandatory and Voluntary Investment Restrictions

The regulatory framework adopted in the market needs to be adhered to. For collective investment schemes (CISs) in the UK, there are certain investments which some funds may not be permitted to invest in. Equally, a trust deed may exist which binds the fund manager to invest in certain securities and the manager must comply. When there is no trust deed, the provisions of the Trustee Act 2000 apply in the UK.

Some investors prefer to either exclude certain areas of the investment spectrum from their portfolios or concentrate solely on a particular investment theme or require the portfolio to be constructed in accordance with Islamic principles, ie, their religious beliefs and values about what is right and ethical versus what is wrong and unethical and this will lead to conclusions about what is acceptable and unacceptable business practice.

2.4   Trading and Ongoing Management

The issues an investment adviser faces when taking over an existing portfolio and reconstructing it are similar to those involved when constructing an entirely new portfolio. A full profiling of the client's needs will be required to determine the need for accessibility and liquidity, income needs, attitude to risk, timescale, tax position and any ethical preferences.

2.4.1 Liquidity and Accessibility

There are several meanings attributed to liquidity but specifically for many clients the key issue will be how readily the asset can be converted into cash. However, another liquidity requirement, which is particularly important for large funds that have a need to trade in large deal sizes, has to do with whether the asset can be traded in substantial quantities without the transaction causing disproportionately large changes in the price at which the trades occur.

In addition to liquidity issues, some investments are constrained in their accessibility and require long-term commitments by the investor. In some cases, the investment cannot be realised early even if the investor wishes it. Also, early redemption may be possible, but at the expense of a penalty or a significant reduction in returns.

It is sometimes possible to sell an investment before maturity on the open market, as for example with traded endowment policies. Although this should achieve a higher price than surrendering the policy to the insurance company, there is still likely to be a loss in the rate of return compared with retaining the investment until maturity. As a rule of thumb, it is prudent to avoid the premature redemption or in a worst-case scenario distressed selling of investments, and good planning should seek to alleviate the need for this.

2.4.2 Trading Frequency

From the point of view of professional ethics for fund managers it is deemed to be part of their code of conduct that they do not engage in 'churning' a client's investments. This is excessive trading or switching investments on behalf of clients often, with a view to generating fee income for the fund manager or associated brokerage firms.

There may also be tax penalties if investments are disposed of. For property, shares and collective investments not sheltered within an ISA, or other tax wrapper, there may be a capital gains tax (CGT) charge. Encashment of a life assurance investment bond may create a chargeable event, resulting in a possible higher rate tax liability.

2.4.3 Impact of Fees and Charges

The fees paid for investment management services will vary widely depending on the kinds of arrangements and vehicles which an investor selects. These could range from the fees often charged by hedge funds, which are known by the 2/20 rule (ie, 2% is paid annually to a hedge fund manager by its investors as an overall management charge and 20% of profits are paid as an incentive or bonus fee), to the very low management fees which are embedded in the purchase of an exchange-traded fund.

For many traditional funds, the annual management charges will generally range between 0.25% and 1.5% of the fund's total value.

Certain other costs, such as auditors' fees, custody fees, directors' remuneration, secretarial costs and marketing costs, may be charged in addition. They will normally be charged against the income generated. Such charges will normally be disclosed.

There are also charges that are external to the fund which the investor may incur. These can be briefly summarised as follows:

- Dealing charges, including commission and 0.5% stamp duty, are payable to the broker carrying out the transaction.
- The spread is the difference between buying and selling prices, as set by market makers.
- Product wrapper charges, usually administration charges, may be charged by the manager of a wrapper such as an ISA used to hold the investment in the collective fund.
- Charges for advice may be incurred in addition if the investor takes financial advice.
- An up front initial commission may be paid to an IFA, and there may also be a periodic trail commission payable to the adviser.
- Some advisers may agree to rebate part or all of the commission received against fees for advice.

The Financial Conduct Authority's (FCA's) *Asset Management Market Study*

In 2019, the FCA published new rules and guidance to improve the quality of the information available to consumers about the funds they invest in. The FCA's *Asset Management Market study* presented evidence of weak price competition in many areas of the asset management industry. This meant lower returns for savers, pensioners and other investors. The FCA has acted to tackle such issues.

The new rules and guidance are set out below:

- Set out how fund managers should describe fund objectives and investment policies to make them more useful to investors.
- Require fund managers to explain why or how their funds use benchmarks or, if they do not use a benchmark, how investors should assess the performance of a fund.
- Require fund managers who use benchmarks to reference them consistently across the fund's documents.
- Require fund managers who present a fund's past performance to do so against each benchmark used as a constraint on portfolio construction or as a performance target.
- Clarify that where a performance fee is specified in the prospectus, it must be calculated based on the scheme's performance after the deduction of all other fees.

Also, as a response of the *Asset Management Market Study*, in late November 2018, the Cost Transparency Initiative was launched as an independent group working to improve cost and charges transparency for institutional investors.

2.5 Clients' Preferences and Ethical/ESG Investing

An adviser will need to establish whether the client has any specific investment preferences that must be taken account of within the investment strategy. These may take the form of restrictions or a requirement to follow a particular investment theme. Some investors may wish to impose restrictions on what should be bought and sold within their portfolio. For example, they may impose a restriction that a particular holding must not be disposed of, or they may prefer to exclude certain investment sectors from their portfolios, such as armaments or tobacco.

Alternatively, a client may want to concentrate solely on a particular investment theme, such as ethical and socially responsible investment, or may require the portfolio to be constructed in accordance with religious principles.

Some investors wish to support ethical and ESG issues and they can accomplish their objectives by selecting ethical investments or following the principles of socially responsible investing (SRI). There are funds, often referred to generically as 'ethical funds', that screen investments on ethical, social or environmental criteria, and an investment adviser's task is to present the relevant information on such funds being considered to the client. Certain funds focus on a particular theme, such as renewable energy or public transport.

It may be that an investor wishes to concentrate on including positive ethical or SRI criteria, or alternatively that they wish to exclude certain investments based upon the application of exclusion or negative criteria – or, as is often the case, a mixture of both (positive and negative screening). Ethical and SRI funds are often referred to as being various shades of green: light, medium or dark green, with dark green funds applying the strictest exclusion criteria.

There are two principal SRI approaches: ethical investing and sustainability investing, both of which are considered below.

Ethical funds, occasionally referred to as dark green funds, apply strictly ethical criteria, and are constructed to avoid those areas of investment that are considered to have significant adverse effects on people, animals or the environment. This they do by screening potential investments against negative, or avoidance, criteria. In addition to those exclusions which are applied in the light green funds, exposure to oil, pharmaceuticals and banking is severely limited. Dark green funds with strict ethical screening may limit their performance by excluding whole industry sectors, for example gas and oil companies, from investment. Companies with poor management-employer relations or with evidence of excessive profits and/or tax avoidance schemes may be excluded. As a screening exercise combined with conventional portfolio management techniques, the strong ethical beliefs that underpin these funds typically result in a concentration of smaller company holdings and volatile performance, though much depends on the criteria applied by individual funds.

Sustainability funds are those that focus on the concept of sustainable development, concentrating on those companies that tackle or pre-empt environmental issues head-on. Unlike ethical investing funds, sustainability funds, sometimes known as light green funds, are flexible in their approach to selecting investments. Sustainability fund managers can implement this approach in two ways:

- **Positive sector selection** – selecting those companies that operate in sectors likely to benefit from the global shift to more socially and environmentally sustainable forms of economic activity, such as renewable energy sources. This approach is known as 'investing in industries of the future' and gives a strong bias towards growth-orientated sectors.
- **Choosing the best of sector** – companies are often selected for the environmental leadership they demonstrate in their sector, regardless of whether they fail the negative criteria applied by ethical investing funds. For instance, an oil company which is repositioning itself as an energy business focusing on renewable energy opportunities would probably be considered for inclusion in a sustainability fund but would be excluded from an ethical fund.

With the growing trend among institutional investors for encouraging companies to focus on their social responsibilities, sustainability-investing research teams enter into constructive dialogue with companies to encourage the adoption of social and environmental policies and practices so that they may be considered for inclusion in a sustainability investment portfolio. For example, engagement funds are managed with a view to positively screening investments that promote ethical and socially responsible behaviour. They might, for example, include companies which move and dispose of waste responsibly. Another criterion which is followed for this category of funds is to seek out those which follow sustainable development policies. A consequence of this may also be that the candidate companies will be more pragmatic in balancing their costs and profits, which could lead them to be more cost-efficient and avoid creating cost externalities, ie, those which are ultimately borne by society in general.

Light green funds may invest in larger companies, mainly in Western Europe and North America, thus tending to reduce risks often associated with investing in smaller companies and also in jurisdictions, where, for example, there may be an absence of legislation to protect against exploitation of child labour. Light green funds will usually permit investments in oil companies and refiners, pharmaceuticals and banks, but will usually prohibit investments in companies producing tobacco products, environmental exploitation, armaments, animal testing or companies with poor human rights records.

Medium green funds will tend to apply stricter criteria than light green, but still permit some exposure to oil exploration and refining, banking and the pharmaceuticals sector.

Integrating social and environmental analysis into the stock selection process is necessarily more research-intensive than that employed by ethical investing funds and dictates the need for a substantial research capability. Moreover, in addition to adopting this more pragmatic approach to stock selection, which results in the construction of better-diversified portfolios, sustainability funds also require each of their holdings to meet certain financial criteria, principally the ability to generate an acceptable level of investment return.

Typically, financial, environmental and social criteria are given equal prominence in company performance ratings by sustainability-investing research teams. This is known as the triple bottom line.

The following are some examples of features that an investor may wish to encourage or to avoid.

Encourage	Avoid
Animal welfare	Alcohol
Community relations	Animal testing and intensive farming
Companies with good employee records	Armaments
Disaster relief	Companies with bad employee records
Education and training	Deforestation
Energy conservation and efficiency	Food retailers with bad policies (eg, fast food, high salt, high sugar)
Environmental technology	Gambling
Equal opportunities	Genetic research
Firms with environmental aims	Human rights abuse
Food retailers with good policies (eg, organic, Fairtrade)	Land abuse
Forestry	Military
Healthcare sector	Motor industries
Healthy eating	Nuclear power
Land use	Oil companies
Plant welfare	Oppressive regimes
Pollution control	Ozone depletion
Positive products and services	Pesticides
Public transport	Political donors
Recycling	Polluters
Renewable energy projects	Pornography
Waste management	Tobacco
Water management	Water pollution

The consumer website, Vigeo Eiris (www.vigeo-eiris.com), provides a database of green and ethical funds in the UK. It also provides detailed information on ethical investment strategies as well as screening criteria. In 2001, the FTSE developed an index series, FTSE4Good, which measures the performance of companies that focus on responsible investments.

Environmental, Social and Governance (ESG)

Environmental, Social, and Governance (ESG) refers to a set of standards for companies to comply with. It enables socially conscious investors to effectively screen any intended investments before trading. ESG has become an increasingly popular approach for potential investors to consider environmental, social, and governance factors when deciding which companies they might want to invest in.

ESG investing focuses on a company's behaviours in three important areas. For example, many investors will want to make investments in companies that treat their employees positively. In addition, matters such as a company's leadership practices, remuneration to staff and shareholder rights are often important to ESG investors. The three categories are:

- **Environmental** standards may include how a company uses energy, how it deals with waste and pollution, consideration and treatment of animals and its approach to conservation of natural resource, as well as how it manages environmental issues.
- **Social** factors look at how a company conducts its relationships with employees, suppliers, customers and communities in which it operates.
- **Governance** looks at its leadership and running of the company and will include examination of factors such as staff and executive remuneration, shareholder's rights, internal controls and audits.

3. Investment Selection and Suitability

Learning Objective

8.1.3 Be able to analyse and select investments suitable for a particular portfolio strategy: direct holdings, indirect holdings and combinations, including structured products; role of derivatives, including CFDs; impact on client objectives and priorities; diversification; cash, deposits accounts and money market funds

3.1 Direct and Indirect Investments

Appreciating the need to diversify and having regard to the client's objectives and risk profile, it is unlikely that a single investment fund or one security will meet the client's requirements. Therefore, the portfolio manager needs to decide how to approach the selection of suitable investments for inclusion in the client's portfolio.

The choices can be summarised into three broad strategic approaches based upon the inclusion of the following broad kinds of asset classes:

- direct holdings
- indirect holdings, and
- combinations of direct and indirect holdings.

3.1.1 Direct Holdings

Direct holdings refer to the purchase of the fundamental kinds of financial assets and securities such as cash, equities, bonds, property, currencies and even physical commodities (although these may be held indirectly through a futures contract). These holdings are also sometimes known as forming part of the cash market, although that is a misnomer in many respects, since they are not to be considered in the same manner that a cash deposit or certificate of deposit is an asset. The use of the term 'cash' or direct holding is mainly used to distinguish this class of assets from derivatives, which are instruments that derive their value from the underlying cash market securities.

3.1.2 Indirect Holdings

Indirect holdings refer to the assets which an investor may have within a portfolio where the constituents from the first class of direct holdings may be themselves held within some form of structured instrument. A structured product is a pre-packaged strategy which can be based on a single security, a basket of securities, property, options, commodities, debt issuance or foreign currencies. It can also be a unit trust, an OEIC, an exchange-traded fund (ETF) or a more complex type of structure (possibly using derivatives). Structured products were originally designed to meet more bespoke requirements that cannot be fulfilled from more traditional and standardised instruments.

As well as holdings which are indirectly held through the intermediation of another financial entity which has packaged and managed the holdings, the most obvious other form of indirect holding is a derivative such as a futures contract, an option, a swap arrangement or a contracts for difference.

3.1.3 Combinations of Direct and Indirect Holdings

Neither of the above two categories are, of course, mutually exclusive, and many investment strategies will involve holding a combination of both.

3.2 Balance of Investments

Prudent selection and allocation between the two categories may result in a more balanced portfolio and one which may contain hedges against risk, exposure to a wider and less correlated group of assets and opportunities for returns which can consistently outperform the market.

Alpha is a term and quantitative measure which is used by fund managers to identify the extent to which a portfolio strategy outperforms a benchmark index. Successful fund managers are looking to achieve positive alpha at a minimum but are even more concerned to deliver positive absolute returns rather than simply returns which are relatively better than the overall market.

It is not very reassuring for an investor to be told, as was the case in 2008, that their portfolio outperformed the market, since general market returns for that year were spectacularly poor. A relative return of 5% specified in reference to the total return for the S&P 500 for 2008 would still have meant that an investor would have lost, by the end of 2008, approximately 32% of the capital with which they started the year.

One of the real challenges which faces an investment manager who is focused primarily on equities, when selecting the appropriate strategy, is to find ways of avoiding these large losses which occur periodically (the total return for the S&P 500 in 2002 was also strongly negative with a –22% loss) but not at the expense of forsaking the years when the overall equities market is performing well as it did in 2003, with a total return for the S&P 500 of more than 28% and, more recently in 2019, when there was a total return of 31.5% and 18.4% in 2020.

The methods used by fund managers to formulate strategies for delivering optimal returns for a given level of risk are at the cornerstone of portfolio construction methodologies. They can involve quite sophisticated financial modelling and quantitative analysis, but ultimately depend on the good judgement exercised by the fund manager in selecting the best strategy.

The different strategies employed will differ essentially according to the asset allocation strategy which is employed.

3.2.1   Asset Allocation

Asset allocation involves considering the big picture first by assessing the prospects for each of the main asset classes within each of the world's major investment regions against the backdrop of the world economic, political and social environment.

Top-Down and Bottom-Up Approaches to Asset Allocation

It is not easy to generalise about the different approaches that are taken by fund managers in terms of broad strategy. However, some funds are run on the basis of investing in the most appealing countries or asset classes. Thereafter, individual securities are selected to fit within this very structured approach. This is described as the top-down approach.

In contrast, a bottom-up approach will examine the fundamental characteristics of many individual stocks and the portfolio will be constructed from those which best satisfy the fund's objectives and constraints. This approach is appropriate when the manager is more concerned with the merits of individual securities, and the resulting combination and the broad characteristics of the portfolio will tend to emerge from the constituents rather than having been engineered or assembled from the top-down approach.

See chapter 7, section 6, for more on these strategies.

Diversification by Asset Class

This is achieved by holding a combination of different kinds of asset within a portfolio, possibly spread across cash, fixed-interest securities, equity investments, property-based investments, and other assets.

- **Cash** can be useful as an emergency fund or for instantly accessible money. At times when the future for interest rates is uncertain, it may be wise to hold some cash in variable rate deposits in the hope of a rate rise, and some in fixed-rate deposits as a hedge against a possible fall in the rate.
- **Fixed-interest securities**, such as government bonds, National Savings & Investment certificates and guaranteed income bonds give a secure income and known redemption value at a fixed future date.
- **Equities** can be used to produce a potentially increasing dividend income and capital growth. For example, a share yielding 3% income plus capital growth of 6% gives an overall return of 9% compared with a building society deposit account yielding, say, 3%.
- **Collective investments** such as unit trusts, investment trusts or unit-linked insurance products spread the risk still further. In this case, the client is participating in a pool of shares. They may choose a fund investing in a number of different economies, thereby reducing risk still further. Pooled investments may be a sensible method of obtaining exposure to some of the less sophisticated world markets where there is a high risk in holding one company's shares.
- The use of **property**, whether residential or commercial, and other types of assets such as antiques, coins or stamps, might help to spread risk further.

Diversification within Asset Classes

An investor can diversify a portfolio by holding a variety of investments within the particular asset types held. This may be achieved by holding various fixed-interest securities, by holding equities in a number of different companies, by spreading investments across different industry sectors and geographical markets, and by holding a number of different properties or property-based investments.

A portfolio that includes a collection of securities will be less exposed to any loss arising from one of the securities. Using a spread of shares across different sectors of the market can also reduce risk. In this way there is a reduced concentration of capital in any one sector.

Diversification across different markets can also be achieved within an asset class. For example, a portfolio of shares or equity-based collective investments may be spread across different national markets and regions, perhaps with holdings in Asia as well as North America, Europe and the UK. Gaining exposure to particular markets can be relatively difficult. For example, until recently there have been relatively few investment vehicles providing exposure to China, although new collective investments (such as ETFs based on the shares in an index) covering China have increasingly become available.

Sometimes a client will have a large holding in one share, perhaps because of an inheritance or as the result of a share option scheme. Such a client should be made aware of the potential risk of such a large holding.

Although different economies and stock markets influence each other, there are differences in how well different regions and national markets perform. Different economies will be at different stages of the business cycle than others at any particular time. On the same principle as that of different companies' shares, a portfolio spread across different markets or regions of the world will be less exposed to poor performance of a particular economy such as the UK.

Diversification by Manager

Diversifying risk across different funds with different managers reduces the risks from a manager performing poorly. This is one of the attractions of manager of manager and fund of fund structures.

Summary of Strategic Allocation

Strategic asset allocation, as outlined above, represents what is sometimes referred to as the core holdings that a fund should operate within over the longer term, in order to satisfy its objectives and constraints. The strategic asset allocation is based on long-run estimates of capital market conditions and is often, either explicitly or implicitly, based on the assumption of the efficient markets hypothesis (EMH) that there are no real benefits to be gained from attempting to 'time' the market and to engage in a proactive approach to asset selection.

Many clients and fund managers, as is evident from their manner of operation, also include a focus on shorter-term and tactical decision-making with respect to portfolio construction. There are a variety of techniques employed by many fund managers which reveal that, even though the fund may have a commitment to a core strategy and core holdings, there are a number of initiatives of a more opportunistic nature that supplement these core holdings. Sometimes, these activities are described as making adjustments to a satellite holding of the portfolio.

3.2.2   Market Timing

Market timing is a form of tactical asset allocation involving the short-term variation of the asset allocation of the fund in order to take advantage of market changes or fluctuations.

Market timing is, then, the variation of the asset allocation of the fund in anticipation of market movements. It involves adjusting the sensitivity of the portfolio to anticipated market changes. A fund manager engages in market timing when they do not agree with the consensus about the market, ie, they are more bullish or more bearish than the market, and may rebalance their portfolio to take advantage of this view.

If a pension fund has regular inflows from its clients, the investment manager may decide to either invest those inflows immediately or passively, or perhaps engage in a form of market timing, by holding on to the inflows and entering the market at what, in the opinion of the fund manager based upon a market outlook, is a more favourable time. If the proceeds are put to work immediately, the fund will benefit from pound cost averaging, ie, the purchases are made at both the peaks and troughs throughout the year, and the fund acquires the investments at the average cost for the year.

If the deployment of the funds is delayed and the fund manager retains these funds as cash until the most suitable time from a market timing perspective, the returns from such opportunistic deployments may be more advantageous.

Some studies have shown that the asset allocation decision (market timing) has a greater impact on performance than stock selection for most funds, especially international funds where the correlations between markets are low. This finding suggests it is not optimal to adopt a passive approach to investment management, such as a simple buy-and-hold strategy for a benchmark index (see chapter 7, section 7.4) with no attempt to second guess the timing of short-term entry and exit points.

3.3 Cash Deposits

The most tangible forms of money are banknotes and coins. Keeping money under the mattress (or in a safe) as notes and coins is one option for someone with savings. However, inflation will erode the purchasing power of the money, and no interest will be earned. There is also the risk of loss or theft. An alternative is to deposit the money with a sound financial institution such as a bank.

The key reasons for holding money as cash deposits are security, accessibility and liquidity. Accounts for holding cash deposits are generally characterised by a high level of security. Capital is very unlikely to be lost, at least in money terms. As already mentioned, there is a deposit insurance scheme in effect in the UK which protects savings up to a limit of £85,000; similar deposit insurance schemes exist in the US and the EU.

The purchasing power of capital held on deposit will, however, still be eroded by inflation. To offset this, there is the reward of any interest receivable, and the rate of interest may exceed inflation, resulting in a real rate of return for the investor.

An important advantage of cash deposits held in instant access accounts is their liquidity. Every investor may need cash at short notice, and so should plan to hold some cash on deposit to meet possible needs and emergencies. A cash deposit account can serve as a vehicle for reaching a savings target, for example, when saving for the cost of a major purchase, or for the deposit on a house.

One risk from investing in certain kinds of products, which are marketed as certificates of deposit (CD) by banks, is that the investor is locked in at a fixed rate for fixed terms, when it might be possible to obtain more attractive rates for other investment products. This is part of the interest rate risk which all investment products have to contend with when interest rates are fluctuating.

The capital on a deposit investment is secure in that the original capital is returned when the deposit is withdrawn or the account matures, subject to any penalties which will have been made explicit in the terms and conditions of the account.

3.3.1 The Risk of Cash Deposits

While it is generally assumed that there is no capital risk for the depositor up to the limits provided for under the deposit insurance arrangements which are in place in the UK, there have been historical precedents for complete losses when a deposit-taker fails and goes into liquidation. This happened with the Bank of Credit and Commerce International, which collapsed in 1991. Prior to the financial crisis in 2008, several large local authorities in the UK had placed deposits with Icelandic banks via accounts in the Isle of Man, and for some time these funds appeared to be in jeopardy. However, the vast majority of this cash has subsequently been recovered.

Under current statutes, if a UK deposit-taking institution fails, the depositor will have recourse to the Financial Services Compensation Scheme (FSCS), which is administered by the FCA. The FSCS is a statutory fund of last resort set up under the Financial Services and Markets Act 2000 to compensate customers of authorised financial services firms in the event of their insolvency. The scheme covers deposits, insurance policies, insurance brokering, investments, mortgages and mortgage arrangements. Although there are various provisions for non-cash deposits, the key provision in effect at present under this scheme for the protection of cash deposits is that 100% of the first £85,000 is guaranteed by the FSCS. For deposit claims against firms declared in default, the maximum level of compensation is also £85,000 (changed from £50,000 in April 2019).

3.3.2 Spreading Risk Across Different Deposit-Takers

The ceiling on compensation available through the FSCS leads some investors to consider spreading their capital among a number of banks and building societies in order to reduce the overall default risk. The benefit of spreading the risk in this way should be weighed against the possible disadvantage of lower rates of interest that may be earned, because of the investor missing out on higher rates offered for larger deposits.

3.3.3 Principal Deposit-Takers

Commercial Banks

Banks are listed as public limited companies and owned by their shareholders. Increasingly, governments are now becoming large shareholders in what were previously private banks. For example, the UK government holds over 70% of the equity of Royal Bank of Scotland.

Building Societies

A building society is a mutual organisation, owned by its members. The members are the holders of savings accounts – often called share accounts – and borrowers. Members of the society have voting rights.

National Savings & Investments (NS&I)

Deposits held with NS&I are guaranteed by the government and therefore can be considered to be completely secure. As a government department, NS&I is not a licensed deposit-taker as banks and building societies are.

Supervision of the prudential soundness of banks and building societies is the responsibility of the Prudential Regulation Authority (PRA).

Deposit Account Types

As the name implies, an instant access account allows the investor immediate access to funds. Most investors will want to keep some funds available on instant access, for emergency purposes. There can sometimes be certain restrictions within certain kinds of account. For example, an account might allow only two withdrawals per year.

With a notice account, the investor must give, for example, 30-, 60- or 90-days' notice of withdrawal unless they wish to lose interest. There may be a higher rate of interest available to compensate for the requirement to give notice. However, the investor should be careful to weigh the advantage of any higher-rate offered against the disadvantage of the loss of liquidity and the costs of penalties if the money needs to be withdrawn earlier than planned. Interest paid monthly will generally be slightly lower than on an instant or notice account which pays interest annually because of the increased frequency of payment of interest. When interest is credited month after month, then the interest itself will begin to earn interest as soon as it is credited.

Example

An account pays interest at an annual rate of 3.6%. Interest is credited monthly.

3.6%/12 = 0.3% will be paid monthly

The annualised rate of interest is:

$$100 \times ((1 + 0.036/12)^{12} - 1) = 100 \times ((1.003)^{12} - 1) = 100 \times (1.0366 - 1) = 3.66\%$$

This shows that the account pays the same return as an annual interest account paying 3.66%.

Time deposits or term accounts offer investors terms that involve tying up the deposit for a fixed period, often at fixed rates. The period may range from seven days to several years, and there may be a fairly high minimum for such arrangements. Time deposits may be offered as bonds. The bond offer may be open for a specified period, or the deposit-taker may reserve the right to withdraw the offer at any time. The bond could run for a fixed term: one, two, three, four or five years, with severely restricted access subject to a penalty, or no access at all. Interest may be tiered. For example, a five-year 'step-up bond' may offer a gross rate of interest of 3.0% in year one, 3.25% in year two, 3.50% in year three, rising to 4.0% in year four and a final 4.5% in year five.

3.3.4   The Tax Treatment of Cash Deposits

A UK resident is subject to tax on bank and building society deposits in the tax year in which the interest is paid at one of the following rates:

- **Basic rate taxpayers** – eligible for the £1,000 tax-free savings allowance. Those with a total income up to £46,350 a year are eligible for the £1,000 tax-free savings allowance.
- **Higher-rate/additional rate taxpayers** – eligible for a £500 tax-free savings allowance.

Since April 2016, banks and building societies have stopped automatically taking 20% in income tax from the interest earned on non-ISA savings.

The ISA Wrapper

There have been several schemes instigated by the UK government to encourage private savings, which essentially provide tax relief or a shelter from taxation for savings that fall within the limits specified in current legislation.

Cash ISAs are savings accounts where the interest is not taxed, but there is a limit to how much can be inserted into such a wrapper account. Each tax year, everyone over the age of 16 for cash ISAs, or 18 for stocks & shares ISAs has an ISA allowance which sets the maximum that can be saved within the tax-free wrapper for that tax year.

In 2021–22, the ISA limit is £20,000. New subscriptions can be split in any proportion between a cash ISA and a stocks and shares ISA.

As of April 2021, the main types of ISAs are as follows:

1. The most common is the cash ISA which includes deposits with banks and building societies and some cash-type products. Cash ISAs are the tax-free equivalent of traditional savings accounts.
2. The stocks & shares ISA can hold most fixed-interest securities and virtually all unit trusts, investment trusts and OEICs, except cash-like and limited redemption funds. They also include life assurance policies (but not pensions) which, before 2005–06, formed a separate component.
3. The Innovative Finance ISA covers peer-to-peer lending where lenders are matched with borrowers so that each enjoys better rates. Those lending through peer-to-peer platforms receive their interest tax-free.
4. The Lifetime ISA is available to those under the age of 40 and contributions of up to £4,000 can be made in each tax year. The government will add a 25% bonus on these contributions at the end of the tax year, meaning that people who save the maximum each year will receive a £1,000 bonus each year from the government.

In addition, there is also the Junior ISA (JISA), which is available to all UK-resident children (aged under 18) who do not have a child trust fund, and a Flexible ISA, whereby savers may replace money that they have withdrawn during the tax year without reducing that year's allowance. Contributions of up to £9,000 a year (for 2021–22) can be made into a JISA. Any savings or investments must be made by the end of the tax year on 5 April.

Investors are also allowed to transfer shares into a stocks & shares ISA which they have received from approved profit-sharing schemes, share incentive plans or Save As You Earn (SAYE) share options. They have to transfer such shares at market value within 90 days of receipt. The value of these transfers reduces the remaining ISA subscription balance available to the investor for that year.

Investors can transfer an existing ISA from one manager to another manager, providing that the receiving manager is prepared to accept it. Transfers of previous years' subscriptions can be in whole or just in part. Transfers of the same year's subscriptions, however, must be for the full amount.

Investors can also transfer their savings between stocks & shares ISAs and cash ISAs and vice versa. From April 2016, individuals are able to withdraw money from their cash ISA and replace it in the year without it counting towards their annual ISA subscription limit for that year.

3.3.5   Money Market Accounts

Some banks offer the facility to make money market deposits for periods ranging from overnight to five years. A bank can offer interest at a rate that is personal to the investor, based on current money market rates. Some banks offer money market deposits either for a fixed term with fixed interest, or on a notice basis with variable interest.

A call account will allow the investor to access their money by the following day. This is close to the terms of an instant access account. The principle of a fixed interest rate for a specified period is the same as for term deposits, but the use of the term 'money market deposit' usually implies that a tailored arrangement is made to meet a particular investor's needs.

Money market deposits can be appropriate for investors with a larger sum to invest – for example, proceeds from a house sale pending a later house purchase.

Money market accounts offer the depositor access to rates offered by the wholesale money market, typically through the treasury department of their clearing or merchant bank. The rates paid should reflect wholesale money market rates represented by LIBOR – established daily as a summary of actual rates offered in the money market between banks.

Money market deposits offer certain advantages:

- **Responsiveness** – they respond immediately to changes in interest rates – good when interest rates are rising.
- **Flexibility** – the length of a money market deposit – its term – can be chosen from a day up to about a year (some banks offer longer periods).
- **Higher Return** – money market rates should generally be higher than deposit account rates offered by the same bank.
- **Convenience** – once the money market account is set up, a telephone call can establish, change or end a placement.
- **Control** – rolling over your money market deposit means that the deposit can be automatically renewed each time it matures; this can include the interest accrued. This is particularly useful if you expect to need the savings at short notice, but do not know when.

There are certain disadvantages to money market deposits:

- **Commissions** – money market commissions charged by banks appear to vary significantly. The money market rate offered by one bank need not be the same as that offered by another. Daily rates are decreasingly being published on the web, so it is difficult to compare the money market rates from different banks.
- **Competitiveness** – money market rates can seem unattractive when compared with other forms of deposits, from instant access deposit accounts to savings bonds, offered by other institutions.

Minimum money market deposits can range from £25,000 to £50,000.

3.3.6   Private Banking

Private banks, as distinct from high street banks, are also able to provide a range of cash deposit services for their clients as well as wealth management, estate planning, tax planning, insurance, lending and lines of credit. Private banking can be onshore and offshore. Although both are largely the preserve of wealthy individuals, offshore banking means banking under a different financial regulatory regime to the one in place in a person's home country. Offshore banking also refers to the breadth of investment opportunities available under these different countries' regimes. The distinction between private and retail banks is gradually diminishing as private banks reduce their investment thresholds in order to compete for providing banking services to high net worth individuals.

3.4   The Use of Derivatives

The table below shows, in simplified form, how a fund manager may make short-term and tactical adjustments to a portfolio to take advantage of expectations about the near-term outlook for the overall market and specific asset classes. The bottom row of the table shows the manner in which derivatives can be used as part of a portfolio management strategy, which can be seen as part strategic asset allocation and part tactical.

Portfolio Components	Market Outlook	
	Bullish	Bearish
Equity Component	More exposure to high beta stocks	Exposure to lower beta stocks
Fixed-Income Component	More exposure to longer duration bonds	Exposure to shorter duration bonds
Tactical/Satellite Holdings	Move into higher risk assets, eg, emerging markets	Reduce/eliminate holdings of higher risk assets, eg, emerging markets
Derivatives	Purchase of stock index futures and call options	Sale of stock index futures and purchase of put options

3.4.1   Portfolio Insurance

Portfolio insurance (also referred to as hedging) is a technique for limiting the potential loss on a portfolio using derivatives, at the expense of giving up some of the potential profits. The approach is based on options theory, when the holder of a call option has unlimited exposure to any potential profits, but limited exposure to losses. As an alternative, one could consider the purchase of put options when the fund manager has the right, but not the obligation, to put a stock or instrument to the option seller at a specified price that may, in the case of a substantial fall in the value of the asset be at a much higher price than the current trading price. This acts like a form of insurance.

CFDs and futures can also be used as a useful form of portfolio insurance. Although hedging minimises risk, the cost of such insurance needs to be taken into account as it also reduces the profit potential of the portfolio. With CFDs, the margined nature of the product increases the cost daily which, over time, can erode the value of the insurance/hedge.

There are various ways in which such portfolio insurance may be implemented, although they all involve reducing the exposure to markets as they fall. To simply set the stage we can consider the following example of the purchase of a call option.

Example

In the following payoff chart, there is a stock which has a current price of £32.23 and an investor decides to purchase an out-of-the-money option with an exercise price of £35. The option has no intrinsic value because the current stock price is below that of the exercise price. The option has six months before expiration, so effectively the option buyer is paying for what is called the time premium of the option, ie, £5 in this case. This premium is based on the notion that during the six months leading up to expiration the stock will fluctuate and, if the investor's expectation is that the stock will be trading above £40 (ie, the £35 exercise price plus the cost of the option) either at or before expiration, the premium is worth paying for the right to call away the stock from the option seller or writer.

The diagram shows that the option buyer – once the premium has been factored into the calculation – will only experience a profitable payoff if the stock sells above £40. After this, the returns to the option buyer show a substantial return, owing to the inherent gearing of the option instrument.

Payoff Diagram on a Call Option		
Current Stock Price =		£32.23
Strike Price of Option =		£35.00
Price of the Option =		£5.00
Stock Price	**Payoff**	**Net Payoff**
£20.00	£0.00	–£5.00
£25.00	£0.00	–£5.00
£30.00	£0.00	–£5.00
£35.00	£0.00	–£5.00
£40.00	£5.00	£0.00
£45.00	£10.00	£5.00
£50.00	£15.00	£10.00
£55.00	£20.00	£15.00
£60.00	£25.00	£20.00

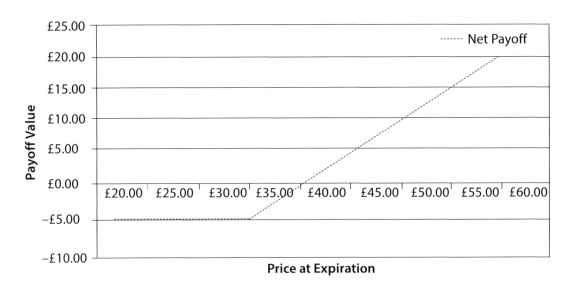

4. Managing a Client Portfolio

Learning Objective

8.2.1 Apply key elements involved in managing a client portfolio: systematic and compliant approach to client portfolio monitoring, review, reporting and management; selection of appropriate benchmarks to include: market and specialist indices; total return and maximum drawdown; arrangements for client communication

4.1 Systematic Approach to Client Portfolio Monitoring

A key requirement for an investment fund management team is the provision of current, reliable and useful reporting on the current state of a client's portfolio. Issuance of statements showing the deployment of funds and the returns currently achieved as well as historical summaries is just the basic requirement.

Given the complex nature of the investment possibilities available in the capital markets, and the fact that clients may have exposure to different currencies, derivatives, hedge instruments and diverse asset classes, then the task of presenting this information to a client becomes a major challenge for good investment managers.

The most appropriate method for client communication is for information to be made available to clients on a current, probably real-time, basis via the internet. Many fund managers will provide clients with a monitoring facility, which enables them to inspect their portfolio performance, at least in summary form, via web-based portals. Clearly the fund manager should be using state-of-the-art information technology and reporting software to generate timely information to a client.

In addition, clients may need to receive periodic hard copy documents outlining portfolio performance, as well as other material relating to compliance and taxation-related matters. Professional advisers of the client may often be the recipients of this information, so that other financial management matters can be co-ordinated with investment management. The issuance of hard copy statements is often a formality, however, as the client will require more immediate information than something which is out of date as soon as it is printed.

IT systems are a part of the systematic nature of portfolio reporting and in addition the fund manager will need to ensure that other relevant contextual information is provided to assist the client in making the best use of the information being provided. References to standard portfolio metrics should be included in the reports issued to clients. The already mentioned key ratios, such as the Sharpe ratio (see chapter 7, section 8.5), will inform the client as to the risk/reward ratio of the portfolio. The investment skills and judgments of fund managers are in fact largely determined by the manner in which their performance is calibrated by such ratios.

Meetings with clients should also be held periodically and at the specific request of the client.

4.2 Compliance and Portfolio Management

Portfolio management should address issues of compliance. The actual execution of the portfolio management strategy should be monitored regularly to ensure satisfactory progress against stated objectives, costs/charges and performance criteria.

Part of the investment management function is to regularly review the appropriateness and effectiveness of measures to manage risks.

Relevant documentation, registrations and other matters of compliance with legislation, reporting and taxation-related matters should be considered as vital to the portfolio monitoring process. In addition the portfolio manager and their team need to keep abreast of all relevant changes in legislation and rules from financial regulators in order to ensure that they are complying with the most current methods of reporting and following industry best practice.

4.3 Appraising Portfolio Performance

From portfolio construction theory, it is generally accepted that a time-weighted measure of returns is the most suitable for determining the returns achieved from an investment. The next challenge is to find a way of deciding how good a return that actually is. In other words, a benchmark should be referenced to which comparisons of the returns achieved can be referenced. For example, is a return of 15% good or poor?

Different performance appraisal criteria can be employed in answering this question and they centre on issues concerned with absolute performance and relative performance.

4.3.1 Absolute Performance

Absolute performance measures aim to establish whether the total return is at a level which is commensurate with the total risk experienced. The basis of most finance theory is that investors are rational and risk-averse; accordingly it is appropriate to determine whether they are being adequately compensated by way of absolute return for that absolute risk.

Methods available for this purpose include the following:

- Comparison of total returns to a peer group.
- Comparison of total returns to a customised benchmark index.
- Comparison of total returns to the capital market line or the securities market line.
- Excess return per unit risk measures, determining how well the excess absolute return over the risk-free rate compensates for the total risk.

4.3.2 Relative Performance

Relative performance measures may be appropriate when the investment strategy is to outperform a specific index or peer group. In this case, it will be the excess return and risk in comparison to the index that will be relevant. Almost by definition, this is best achieved by considering excess return per unit risk measure.

446

4.4 Benchmarking

4.4.1 Peer-Group or Customised Benchmarking

Portfolio performance may be measured by reference to a relevant peer group. The peer group will be portfolio or fund managers who are also responsible for the full range of management decisions (asset allocation and stock selection) for a portfolio or fund with similar objectives and constraints. With peer group benchmarking the fund management objectives may be defined as, say, 'outperform the peer group median performance'.

Peer-group benchmarking has been criticised as tending to produce asset allocation decisions based simply on what other funds are doing, rather than on the needs of the fund involved. A peer-group benchmark does not show whether a portfolio manager is performing well in absolute terms. If all of the peer group are poor managers, the portfolio manager may be top of the peer group but still be showing poor absolute performance.

An alternative to peer-group benchmarking is customised benchmarking. This is appropriate when the asset allocation decision and stock selection decisions are separated, and the asset allocation decision taken by the trustee, say, with the stock selection decisions being taken by managers.

The manager's performance can then be assessed by reference to an appropriate index or customised benchmark based on the assets under their management. Using this approach, the selection of the index is an important decision: is that index suitable for satisfying the fund's liability-matching objectives? Setting the limits for any permitted divergence from that index is also highly important. If these limits are tight, then the fund becomes a pseudo-tracker, and the investor is then paying active management fees when the true style is passive.

4.4.2 The Myners Report and Benchmarking

The Myners Report of 2001 examined these benchmarking issues, among others, especially in the context of assessing pension fund performance. As a result of the weaknesses of the peer group approach, the review concluded that this was inappropriate for managing pension funds.

The review recommended a customised benchmarking approach under which the fund should consider:

- the suitability of any index benchmarks in achieving the fund objectives, and
- each asset class whether active or passive management is most appropriate.

When fund managers believe that active management has the potential to achieve higher returns, they should:

- set divergence limits for fund managers to operate within
- set challenging targets and risk controls for outperformance against the index, allowing sufficient freedom for genuine active management to occur, and
- encourage an active management approach to be undertaken with conviction.

4.4.3 Benchmark Index

In order to assess how well a portfolio manager is performing, we can use a yardstick such as a benchmark index for comparison. Once we have determined an appropriate benchmark, we can compare whether the manager outperformed, matched or underperformed.

Some issues that would arise in selecting a benchmark are as follows:

- Appropriateness of the benchmark or index to the preferences of the fund (eg, a UK blue chip portfolio might utilise the FTSE 100 Index).
- Appropriate to the currency of the portfolio – if the portfolio is US dollar-based, then the performance of the US dollar against a range of currencies should be referenced. There is a US Dollar Index which is a weighted index of the dollar against other major currencies, and there are futures contracts based upon this index which can be used for hedging and benchmarking purposes.
- Is the benchmark itself an investable item, ie, is it composed of investments that could conceivably be held in the portfolio?
- Is the benchmark easily measurable, ie, can the return be calculated on a frequent basis as required?
- Is the benchmark representative of achievable performance, ie, is it an arithmetic weighted composition?
- Does the benchmark reflect the total return – in other words does it not only refer to the price value of an index or indices but also take into account income as well as capital growth?

4.4.4 Appraisal Using Benchmarks

Once we have established a suitable benchmark, we can appraise the portfolio manager's performance by reference to it. The benchmark performance can be calculated as the weighted average of the holding period returns on the relevant benchmark indices.

Example

Take as an illustration a situation where a pension fund manager has a portfolio with an initial value of £100 million. The company for whom the fund is run is internationally based, with 75% of its employees in the UK and 25% in the US. As such, it requires a corresponding international investment strategy concentrating on a diversified spread of shares.

The company feels that the manager should be able to at least match the following two indices on the relevant portions of the fund.

- FTSE 100 Index on the UK portion
- S&P 500 Index on the US portion.

The values on these indices at the start and end of the year were as follows:

	Portfolio £m	FTSE Index	S&P 500 Index
End of year	117	6957	1775
Start of year	100	6000	1500
Annual return	17.00%	15.95%	18.33%

The fund had a capital value of £117 million at the end of the year, there having been no cash inflows and outflows during the year.

What return has the fund manager achieved? What return has the benchmark portfolio achieved? Also, has the fund manager achieved their target of at least matching the benchmark?

Since there have been no cash inflows/outflows during the year, we can use the simple holding period return formula to assess the portfolio performance, giving:

$$r_p = \frac{(D+V_e) - V_s}{V_s} \times 100\%$$

where:

r_p = holding period return
D = any returns paid out from the investment/portfolio at the end of the period
V_s = the initial cost at the start of the holding period
V_e = the value of the investment at the end of the holding period

In the illustration, we are considering there are no outflows, so effectively D is 0.

The return for the portfolio can be simply calculated as follows:

$$r_p = \frac{(0+£117m) - £100m}{£100m} \times 100\% = +17\%$$

The benchmark performances are as follows:

FTSE 100:

$$r_p = \frac{6957 - 6000}{6000} \times 100\% = +15.95\%$$

S&P 500:

$$r_p = \frac{1775 - 1500}{1500} \times 100\% = +18.33\%$$

The initial assumption is that the pension fund manager allocates the fund between shares selected within the UK market and the US market in the same ratio as the beneficiaries of the fund, ie, 75% is allocated to UK shares and 25% is allocated to US shares.

	Portfolio £m	FTSE Index	S&P 500 Index
End of year	117	6957	1775
Start of year	100	6000	1500
Annual return	17.00%	15.95%	18.33%
Weighting between UK/US assets	75/25	75%	25%
Weighted returns of benchmarks		11.96%	4.58%
Weighted average	16.54%		
Portfolio performance compared to benchmarks		17.00% – 16.54%	0.46%

The weighted average return as shown in the table is r = (0.75 × 15.95%) + (0.25 × 18.33%) = 16.54%.

The fund has delivered a return of 17% and the weighted returns from the two appropriate benchmarks shows a return of 16.54%. From this, it can be concluded that the pension fund manager has outperformed the benchmarks by 0.46%.

It must be noted that this conclusion is only valid so long as the total return achieved was at no higher a level of risk than that of the underlying index. If the fund's return had been achieved by taking more risk (ie, higher standard deviations in the returns) than the weighted standard deviation of the applicable benchmarks the conclusion of manager outperformance would not be valid.

4.5   Total Return and Maximum Drawdown

Total return is a measure of investment performance that includes the change in price of the asset plus any other income (including dividends, interest and capital gains distributions). It is assumed that all income is reinvested over the period. The calculation of total return is expressed as a percentage of the initial asset value.

For example, long-term investors in equities will be much influenced by the dividends paid out by a company, as this is a vital part of the total return from holding equities.

Drawdown is the name given to the distance between troughs and peaks when looking at a timeline of the P&L at different periods when it is measured. A monthly sampling of returns could be depicted as an equity curve, with peaks and troughs as the curve moves up and down. The maximum drawdown will be the distance from the highest level of account equity (the 'high-water mark') to the lowest trough in the equity curve. The maximum drawdown is a key variable used by portfolio managers and is not adequately addressed by some measures of risk/return and portfolio theory.

5.   Changes that can Affect a Client Portfolio

Learning Objective

8.2.2   Understand how changes can affect the management of a client portfolio: client circumstances; financial environment; new products and services available; administrative changes or difficulties; investment-related changes (eg, credit rating, corporate actions); portfolio rebalancing; benchmark review; changing regulatory environment

5.1   Client Circumstances

Clearly, before advising any client, an adviser or fund manager must be aware of that client's various needs, preferences, expectations and financial situation.

The circumstances of the client are, however, subject to change over time. Sometimes, these changes can be anticipated and sometimes they will be almost completely unexpected.

As we saw in sections 1 and 2, the basic information about a client's circumstances that needs to be captured can be broken down into the following:

- personal and financial details
- objectives
- risk tolerance
- liquidity and time horizons
- tax status, and
- investment preferences.

Changes can take place in any one of these items.

For example, it may happen that if a client loses a regular source of income, even temporarily, there may be a need to liquidate a part of their holdings in order to raise cash. To the extent that the current portfolio has an adequate allocation of cash and short-term money market instruments available (which it should, if the financial planning has been done properly), this may not present any immediate issues. Obviously, liquidating a part of a portfolio will alter the balance of the remaining assets and will require a rebalancing exercise to be performed at some future point in time.

If the client's need for cash is in excess of the current allocation of very liquid instruments, then the need to liquidate longer-term and perhaps less liquid holdings within the portfolio may be more consequential. The redemption of certain instruments may attract penalties and charges; the need to liquidate equities at a time when the overall market is performing poorly could lead to capital losses and loss of future dividend income; and if there are derivatives in a portfolio which have been used for tactical asset allocation then the timing of the exit from derivatives contracts can be very sensitive and could trigger premature losses which would not have arisen if the instruments were held to maturity.

5.2 The Financial Environment

The changes which can take place in the overall financial environment, and which will affect the current asset allocation strategy, can be quite drastic, as was evidenced by the broad market developments that began in 2007 and which reached a climax (at least from our current perspective) in the latter part of 2008. The impact of large scale macroeconomic factors, such as the abrupt drop in GDP and employment which followed the banking crisis of 2007–8, has had an impact on many clients' individual circumstances. There will be some clients who have been faced with loss of employment income as discussed above, but the largest capacity for damage is to overall investor sentiment and the general appetite for risk. In 2020–21, we have seen reductions in returns for clients seeking an income due to global dividend cuts, while at the same time, interest rates have been persistently low.

It is fair to say that many investors are now more risk-averse than at any time in the last 25 years, and perhaps a case could be made that one would need to return to the 1930s to find a parallel era. On the one hand, this has meant that many investors will have altered their attitude towards holding assets they perceive to be too risky. On the other hand, there are many who think more opportunistically and saw the large drop in asset prices in late 2008 and early 2009 as an excellent buying opportunity. Indeed, those who bought equities and many kinds of riskier bonds such as 'junk' bonds in the spring of 2009 were very well rewarded.

Another issue to consider is that adverse market conditions can present major profit opportunities for some investors. Hedge funds which operate with net short strategies delivered some extraordinary returns during 2008, if they were correctly positioned. To cite one example, John Paulson, the owner of a US-based hedge fund which used swap agreements (a form of derivative), which benefited from the fall in mortgage-backed securities (MBSs) and their offshoots, is estimated to have personally made more than $3 billion in 2008 from correctly anticipating the collapse of the MBS market.

5.3   Availability of New Products and Services

Financial innovation over the last 20–30 years has been extraordinary. This has been especially the case in terms of the products that are now available to investors such as CFDs, ETFs, new kinds of collective investment vehicles and the proliferation of derivatives, including credit default swaps (CDSs) and other asset-backed securities.

Although derivatives are not suitable for many portfolios, their proliferation reflects the way in which the investment landscape is changing radically. Among the different kinds of services available now to investors are many kinds of hedge funds and alternative asset management companies which provide non-traditional ways of investing. The availability of such a diversified offering of products and services is transforming the whole nature of the securities industry. These changes question some of the underlying theories of investment and asset allocation and certainly require of professionals working in financial services that they constantly re-educate themselves on the conditions and products of their business.

The need for prudence and skill in investment decision-making is perhaps more than ever at a premium, and this is also leading to new attitudes towards allocation, the need for greater flexibility and pragmatism and also the possibility of fundamental changes in the regulation of the domestic and global financial environment.

5.4   Administrative Changes

The innovations just discussed, as well as the changes in the operational side of the securities industry – including new multilateral trading facilities, regulatory changes such as the dismantling of the FSA in April 2013, and the removal of the banking supervision function to the Bank of England – continues to impose a severe burden on the compliance and fund administration functions within investment management. Brexit has led to many regulatory changes since the end of the transition period and further regulatory divergence between the UK and the EU can be expected in the coming months and years.

At the same time, there are pressures on fund managers from competitors, and caused by poor performance, to cut fees and charges. The expectation is that there will need to be quite radical back office changes at many investment firms.

5.5   Credit Rating Changes

Credit ratings for corporate borrowers are regularly reviewed and are often revised in the light of changed economic conditions and/or changes in the outlook for an industry or the issuer's specific circumstances. Rating agencies will signal they are considering a rating change by placing the security on CreditWatch (S&P), Under Review (Moody's) or on Rating Watch (Fitch).

Most revisions result in credit downgrades rather than upgrades. The price change resulting from a credit downgrade is usually much greater than for an upgrade, given that the price of a bond can fall all the way to zero, whereas there is a limit to how high a bond's price can rise.

The bond issues of many large telecoms companies, as a result of taking on large amounts of additional debt to finance their acquisition of third generation (3G) telecoms licences in 2000, suffered severe credit downgrades and, as a consequence, experienced an indiscriminate marking down in the prices of their bond issues.

5.6   Corporate Actions

Corporate actions such as a rights issue will impact the pricing of securities and, in certain circumstances, the decision by a company to engage in a secondary offering or proposal to alter its capital structure may trigger a major response from the markets. Under these circumstances a decision may be made to change a portfolio holding in the wake of the proposed corporate action.

As an example, the *Financial Times* published the following report in May 2010 in reference to a proposed rights issue by the UK-based Prudential Insurance which had to be aborted:

> *'Prudential was forced to abandon the launch of its $21 billion rights issue in a deeply embarrassing move that could prove the last straw for some investors wavering over the British life assurer's $35.5 billion takeover of AIG's Asian arm. The Pru delayed its fundraising and canned its prospectus at the last minute after failing to convince UK regulators that it would have enough capital after the takeover, with up to $3 billion of AIA's capital base locked into several Asian countries.*
>
> *The company insisted that the timetable for its deal remained on track and people close to the Pru were hopeful that the Financial Services Authority's concerns could be satisfied within a couple of days. However, others said that the Pru had a much deeper problem with the regulator. The FSA was concerned that it would not have proper oversight of a company heavily biased towards Asia, they suggested. It was also worried about another complex cross-border deal going badly wrong following RBS's disastrous acquisition of the Dutch bank ABN Amro in 2007.*
>
> *The FSA wants the Pru to hold a lot more capital', said one person involved'.*

5.7   Portfolio Rebalancing

If a portfolio has to be rebalanced following a significant development either in relation to client circumstances or to changes in the financial environment, the proper approach for an investment manager is to rethink the entire asset allocation strategy. Rather than making piecemeal changes and attempting to reimplement a revised version of the previous allocation strategy, it would be preferable to devise a new strategic allocation which takes into account the new circumstances. This could even lead to a reclassification of the investor's profile and risk tolerance characteristics.

There are other circumstances, of a more routine nature, when a portfolio manager will rebalance a portfolio, and to some extent the reasons why a portfolio manager may wish to rebalance are closely related to market timing and active management strategies, such as bond switching, or bond swapping.

5.8   Benchmark Reviews

Once a portfolio has been constructed, the portfolio manager and client need to agree on a realistic benchmark against which the performance of the portfolio can be judged. The choice of benchmark will depend on the precise asset split adopted and should be compatible with the risk and expected return profile of the portfolio. When an index is used, this should represent a feasible investment alternative to the portfolio constructed. As an example, if the portfolio consists largely of small and micro-cap stocks with a US bias, the appropriate benchmark index to use would be the Russell 2000 Index.

Portfolio performance is rarely measured in absolute terms but in relative terms against a pre-determined benchmark and against the peer group (see section 4.4). In addition, indexed portfolios are also evaluated against the size of their tracking error, or how closely the portfolio has tracked the chosen index.

It is essential that the portfolio manager and client agree on the frequency with which the portfolio is reviewed, not only to monitor the portfolio's performance but also to ensure that it still meets the client's objectives and is correctly positioned given prevailing market conditions.

5.9   The Changing Regulatory Environment

The pace of change within the financial services sector is seemingly relentless, with the financial crisis of recent times serving to exacerbate the amount of new regulation and all that it brings for firms, regulators and, indeed, consumers. The financial services regulatory environment is seeing an unprecedented amount of regulatory reform across the EU and in financial centres globally. Regulated entities within financial services sectors are of course expected to keep pace with this level of change, much of which is being imposed as EU Directives and/or Regulations.

MiFID in 2007 was, in many ways, the first step to creating a more harmonised financial services environment in Europe. This has now been revised with the new rules imposed by MiFID II and the Markets in Financial Instruments Regulation (MiFIR), which is an extension of MiFID, and went live in January 2018. This affected all stages of the life cycle of transactions as well as many consumer and firm-related post-trade requirements. MiFID II and MiFIR represent an overhaul of the existing rules and also expand the scope of instruments and firms.

The new legislation not only focuses on trading venues for financial instruments but also on regulating the operation of these venues. It significantly applies to regulated entities' systems, processes and oversight/governance, and it is likely that very few firms involved in the securities industry escaped at least some impact for procedures, systems, policies, operations, oversight and reporting. The new rules again focus on greater investor protection, harmonisation of regulation across the EU, enhanced competition, greater supervisory oversight and powers for regulators and an enhanced supervisory role for the European Securities and Markets Authority (ESMA) across all European states.

The increasing cost of compliance is (and will no doubt continue to be) a much-debated subject. The continuous enhanced focus on regulatory compliance/risk (and its associated costs) can become difficult for some institutions, with firms being expected to demonstrate full compliance in an extremely complex regulatory environment. Fines for non-compliance, incomplete or poorly reported data and, of course, market abuse can pose a significant financial risk and often, more worryingly, a major reputational risk for firms.

One fact that the majority of senior industry practitioners are likely to agree upon (if asked) is the certainty of a continued flow of substantial regulatory change that is unlikely to abate significantly in the foreseeable future.

Financial Technology – Fintech

Financial technology (Fintech) is now a familiar term used when describing new technology that is constantly seeking ways to improve and automate the financial services sector.

Fintech initiatives range from the development and use of cryptocurrencies to capital market infrastructure, for example, in the execution of trades, clearing of traded positions, as well as data analytics and regulatory services.

Although the term 'Fintech' is an umbrella term, its impact covers a huge variety of services and operations.

New technologies that have already made significant inroads and are the most active areas of Fintech innovation include or are centred on the following business areas:

- predictive behavioural analytics
- risk management
- cryptocurrency and digital cash (eg, Bitcoin)
- Regtech, which assists financial service firms meet the ever demanding industry compliance rules and regulations. Areas such as Know Your Customer (KYC) and anti-money laundering (AML) have gained particular focus. Financial services are among the most heavily regulated sectors in the world
- blockchain technology which uses a distributed ledger to maintain maintain records across a network of computers without the need for a central register or database/ledger

- smart contracts, using computers programs and algorithms, automatically execute contracts between buyers and sellers
- cybersecurity in response to increasingly sophisticated cybercrime
- robo-advisers are types of automated financial advisers that provide financial advice or discretionary investment management with little need for humans. They can provide electronic financial advice based on formulae or algorithms.

Whatever sector of the financial services sector one belongs to, the use of Fintech is sure to continue to revolutionise many of the traditional human and manually-based functions.

End of Chapter Questions

Think of an answer to each question and refer to the appropriate section for confirmation.

1. What are the two main areas that risk tolerance can be broken down into?
    Answer reference: Section 1.1

2. In reviewing a client's investment profile, why is a greater exposure to assets which provide the possibility of capital gains more appropriate for a younger investor rather than an older investor?
    Answer reference: Section 2.1.1

3. What is the difference between tax evasion and tax avoidance?
    Answer reference: Section 2.1.3

4. Explain the key benefit of an index-linked gilt.
    Answer reference: Section 2.2

5. In the context of ethical/sustainable and responsible investing explain the difference between negative screening and positive screening.
    Answer reference: Section 2.5

6. What is an indirect holding as opposed to a direct holding in a portfolio?
    Answer reference: Sections 3.1.1 and 3.1.2

7. What is market timing?
    Answer reference: Section 3.2.2

8. Distinguish between absolute and relative performance.
    Answer reference: Sections 4.3.1 and 4.3.2

9. What are three issues that would arise when selecting a benchmark?
    Answer reference: Section 4.4.3

10. Explain what is meant by the maximum drawdown sustained by a portfolio.
    Answer reference: Section 4.5

Glossary

Active Management

A type of investment approach employed to generate returns in excess of an investment benchmark index. Active management is employed to exploit pricing anomalies in those securities markets that are believed to be subject to mispricing by utilising fundamental analysis and/or technical analysis to assist in the forecasting of future events and the timing of purchases and sales of securities.

Alpha

The return from a security or a portfolio in excess of a risk-adjusted benchmark return.

Alternative Investment Market (AIM)

The London Stock Exchange's (LSE's) market often used for smaller UK public limited companies. AIM has less demanding admission requirements and places less onerous continuing obligation requirements upon those companies admitted to the market than those applying for a full list on the LSE.

American Depositary Receipt (ADR)

An ADR is a security that represents securities of a non-US company that trades in the US financial markets.

Amortisation

The depreciation charge applied in company accounts against capitalised intangible assets.

Annual General Meeting (AGM)

The annual meeting of directors and ordinary shareholders of a company. All companies are obliged to hold an AGM at which the shareholders receive the company's report and accounts and have the opportunity to vote on the appointment of the company's directors and auditors and the payment of a final dividend recommended by the directors. Also referred to as an Annual General Assembly in some jurisdictions.

Arbitrage

The process of deriving a risk-free profit by simultaneously buying and selling the same asset in two related markets where a pricing anomaly exists.

Asset Allocation

The process of deciding on the division of a portfolio's assets between asset classes and geographically before deciding upon which particular securities to buy.

Auction

System used to issue securities where the successful applicants pay the price that they bid. Examples of its use include the UK Debt Management Office (DMO) when it issues gilts. Auctions are also used by the London Stock Exchange to establish prices, such as opening and closing options on SETS.

Authorisation

Required status in the UK for firms that want to provide certain financial services – examples include collective investment vehicles that want to advertise their fund to retail investors.

Authorised Corporate Director (ACD)

Fund manager for an open-ended investment company (OEIC).

Bank of England (BoE)

The UK's central bank.

Base Currency

The currency against which the value of a quoted currency is expressed. The base currency is currency X for the X/Y exchange rate.

Bear Market

A negative move in a securities market, conventionally defined as a 20%+ decline. The duration of the market move is immaterial.

Bearer Securities

Those whose ownership is evidenced by the mere possession of a certificate. Ownership can, therefore, pass from hand to hand without any formalities.

Beneficiaries

The beneficial owners of trust property.

Beta

The relationship between the returns on a stock and returns on the market. Beta is a measure of the systematic risk of a security or a portfolio in comparison to the market as a whole. In futures markets, beta measures the amount of fluctuation of one variable against another, so is used to determine the number of contracts required to hedge a portfolio.

Bid Price

Bond and share prices are quoted as bid and offer. The bid is the lower of the two prices and is the one that would be offered to the seller.

Bonus Issue (Capitalisation)

The free issue of new ordinary shares to a company's ordinary shareholders, in proportion to their existing shareholdings through the conversion, or capitalisation, of the company's reserves. By proportionately reducing the market value of each existing share, a bonus issue makes the shares more marketable. Also known as a capitalisation issue or scrip issue.

Broker-Dealer

A London Stock Exchange (LSE) member firm that can act in a dual capacity both as a broker acting on behalf of clients and as a dealer dealing in securities on their own account.

Bull Market

A rising securities market, conventionally defined as a 20%+ rise from a prior low. The duration of the market move is immaterial.

Capitalisation Issue

Another term for a bonus or scrip issue.

Central Bank

Central banks typically have responsibility for setting a country's or a region's short-term interest rate, controlling the money supply, acting as banker and lender of last resort to the banking system and managing the national debt.

Clean Price

The quoted price of a bond. The clean price excludes accrued interest to be added or to be deducted, as appropriate.

Closed-Ended

Organisations such as companies which are a fixed size as determined by their share capital. Commonly used to distinguish investment trusts (closed-ended) from unit trusts and OEICs (open-ended).

Commercial Paper (CP)

Money market instrument issued by large corporates.

Commission

Charges for acting as agent or broker.

Commodity

Items including sugar, wheat, oil and copper. Derivatives of commodities are traded on exchanges (eg, oil futures on ICE Futures).

Consumer Prices Index (CPI)

Index that measures the movement of prices faced by a typical consumer.

Contract

For derivatives, a contract is the minimum, standard unit of trading.

Convertible Bond

A bond which is convertible, usually at the investor's choice, into a certain number of the issuing company's shares.

Coupon

The regular amount of interest paid on a bond.

CREST

Electronic settlement system used to settle transactions for shares, gilts and corporate bonds, particularly on behalf of the London Stock Exchange.

Cum Dividend (cd)

The period during which the purchase of shares or bonds on which a dividend or coupon payment has been declared, entitles the new holder to this next dividend or interest. See also **Ex-Dividend (xd)**.

Debt Management Office (DMO)

Agency responsible for issuing gilts on behalf of the UK Treasury.

Dematerialised

System where securities are held electronically without certificates.

Derivatives

Instruments where the price or value is derived from another underlying asset. Examples include options, futures and swaps.

Dirty Price

The price of a bond inclusive of accrued interest or exclusive of interest to be deducted, as appropriate.

Diversification

Investment strategy that involves spreading risk by investing in a range of investments.

Dividend

Distribution of profits by a company to shareholders.

Dividend Yield

The dividend as a percentage of current share price.

Dow Jones Industrial Average (DJIA)

Major share index in the USA, based on the prices of 30 major US listed company shares.

Environmental, Social, and Governance (ESG)

A set of factors to be considered when measuring the sustainability and ethical impact of an investment in a company.

Equities

Another name for shares.

Eurobond

This is an interest-bearing security issued internationally. More strictly a eurobond is an international bond issue denominated in a currency different from that of the financial centre(s) in which it is issued. Most eurobonds are issued in bearer form through bank syndicates.

European Securities and Markets Authority (ESMA)

European Union financial regulatory institution and European Supervisory Authority located in Paris.

Exchange Rate

The rate at which one currency can be exchanged for another.

Ex-Dividend (xd)

The period during which the purchase of shares or bonds (on which a dividend or coupon payment has been declared) does not entitle the new holder to this next dividend or interest payment.

Exercise

Take up the right to buy or sell the underlying asset in an option.

Exercise Price

The price at which the right conferred by a warrant or an option can be exercised by the holder against the writer.

Financial Conduct Authority (FCA)

One of the two regulators of the financial services sector in the UK.

Fiscal Year

This is the period for reporting, alternatively referred to as a financial year. The term is particularly used by the tax authorities for a period of assessment for tax purposes.

Fixed-Interest Security

A tradeable negotiable instrument, issued by a borrower for a fixed term, during which a regular and predetermined fixed rate of interest based upon a nominal value is paid to the holder until it is redeemed and the principal is repaid.

Floating Rate Notes (FRNs)

Debt securities issued with a coupon periodically referenced to a benchmark interest rate.

Forex

Abbreviation for foreign exchange.

Forward

A derivatives contract that creates a legally binding obligation between two parties for one to buy and the other to sell a pre-specified amount of an asset at a pre-specified price on a pre-specified future date. Forward contracts are commonly entered into in the foreign exchange market. As individually negotiated contracts, forwards are not traded on a derivatives exchange.

Forward Exchange Rate

An exchange rate set today, embodied in a forward contract, that will apply to a foreign exchange transaction at a pre-specified point in the future.

FTSE 100

Main UK share index of the 100 largest listed company shares measured by market capitalisation. Also referred to as the 'Footsie'.

FTSE All Share Index

An index comprising about 98% of LSE-listed shares by market capitalisation.

Fund Manager

Firm or person that makes investment decisions on behalf of clients.

Future

An agreement to buy or sell an item at a future date, at a price agreed today. Differs from a forward in that it is a standardised contract traded on an exchange.

Global Master Securities Lending Agreement (GMSLA)

Parties to a stock lending transaction generally operate under a legal agreement, such as the GMSLA, which sets out the obligations of the borrower and lender.

Gross Domestic Product (GDP)

A measure of a country's output.

Gross Redemption Yield (GRY)

The annual compound return from holding a bond to maturity taking into account both interest payments and any capital gain or loss at maturity. Also referred to as the yield to maturity (YTM). The GRY or YTM is the internal rate of return on the bond based on its trading price.

Harmonised Index of Consumer Prices (HICP)

European equivalent of the consumer prices index (CPI) in the UK.

Hedging

A technique employed to reduce the impact of adverse price movements on financial assets held.

High Frequency Trading (HFT)

High frequency trading involves the sending of a large number of orders into the market, generated by computer algorithms.

ICE Futures Europe

The UK's principal derivatives exchange for trading financial and soft commodity derivatives products. Owned by The Intercontinental Exchange Group (ICE) inc. Was formerly known as the London International Financial Futures and Options Exchange (LIFFE).

Index-Linked Gilts

Gilts whose principal and interest payments are linked to the retail prices index (RPI).

Inflation

A persistent increase in the general level of prices. Usually established by reference to consumer prices and the CPI.

Initial Public Offering (IPO)

A new issue of ordinary shares that sees the company gain a stock market listing for the first time, whether made by an offer for sale, an offer for subscription or a placing.

Insider Dealing/Trading

Criminal offence by people in possession of unpublished price-sensitive information from an inside source who deal, advise others to deal or pass the information on.

Intercontinental Exchange (ICE)

Operates regulated global futures exchanges and over-the-counter (OTC) markets for agricultural, energy, equity index and currency contracts, as well as credit derivatives.

Investment Bank

Firms that specialise in advising companies on M&A (mergers and acquisitions), and corporate finance matters such as raising debt and equity. The larger investment banks are also heavily involved in trading financial instruments.

Investment Company with Variable Capital (ICVC)

Alternative term for an OEIC.

Investment Trust

Despite the name, an investment trust is a company, not a trust, which invests in a diversified range of investments. A type of closed-ended investment fund.

LIBOR Rates

Immediately after 31 December 2021, sterling euro, Swiss franc and Japanese yen settings, and the one-week and two-month US dollar settings will cease to be provided and will be replaced by alternative benchmark rates.

Immediately after 30 June 2023, the remaining US dollar settings will cease to be provided.

Sterling LIBOR will be replaced by SONIA, (Sterling Overnight Index Average) and US Dollar LIBOR replaced by SOFR (Secured Overnight Financing Rate).

Limit Order

An order placed on a market (such as the London Stock Exchange's SETS system) which specifies the highest price it will pay (for a buy order) or the lowest price it will accept (for a sell order).

Liquidity

Ease with which an item can be traded on the market. Liquid markets are also described as 'deep'.

Liquidity Risk

The risk that an item, such as a financial instrument, may be difficult to sell at a reasonable price.

Listing

Companies whose securities are listed are available to be traded on an exchange, such as the London Stock Exchange.

London Stock Exchange (LSE)

The main UK market for securities.

Long Position

The position following the purchase of a security or buying a derivative.

Market

All exchanges are markets – electronic or physical meeting places where assets are bought or sold.

Market Capitalisation

The total market value of a company's shares or other securities in issue. Market capitalisation is calculated by multiplying the number of shares or other securities a company has in issue by the market price of those shares or securities.

Market Maker

A stock exchange member firm registered to quote prices and trade shares throughout the trading day (such as the LSE's mandatory quote period).

Maturity

Date when the principal on a bond is repaid.

Monetary Policy Committee (MPC)

Committee run by the Bank of England that sets UK interest rates.

Multilateral Trading Facilities (MTFs)

Systems that bring together multiple parties that are interested in buying and selling financial instruments including shares, bonds and derivatives.

Nasdaq

The second-largest stock exchange in the US. Nasdaq lists certain US and international stocks and provides a screen-based quote-driven secondary market that links buyers and sellers worldwide. Nasdaq tends to specialise in the shares of technology companies.

Nikkei 225

The main Japanese share index, comprising 225 blue-chip companies that are listed on the Tokyo Stock Exchange.

Nominal Value

The amount on a bond that will be repaid on maturity. Also known as face or par value. Also applied to shares in some jurisdictions and representing the minimum that the shares are issued for.

Non-Deliverable Forward (NDF)

A short-term forward contract that does not result in the exchange of notional currencies. Instead, upon maturity, the profit/loss between parties is calculated by taking the difference between the contracted exchange rate and the spot rate.

Offer Price

Bond and share prices are quoted as bid and offer. The offer is the higher of the two prices and is the one that would be paid by a buyer.

Open-Ended

Type of investment, such as OEICs or unit trusts, which can expand without limit.

Open-Ended Investment Company (OEIC)

Collective investment vehicle similar to a unit trust. Alternatively described as an ICVC (investment company with variable capital).

Option

A derivative giving the buyer the right, but not the obligation, to buy or sell an asset in the future.

Organised Trading Facilities (OTFs)

A multilateral system that is not a regulated market or a multilateral trading facility (MTF). It allows multiple third-party buying and selling interests in bonds, structured finance products, emission allowances or derivatives to be traded. Equities cannot be traded through an OTF.

Over-the-Counter (OTC) Derivatives

Derivatives that are not traded on a derivatives exchange.

Passive Management

In contrast to active management, passive management is an investment approach that does not aspire to create a return in excess of a benchmark index. The approach often involves tracking the benchmark index.

Pre-Emption Rights

The rights accorded to ordinary shareholders to subscribe for new ordinary shares issued by the company in proportion to their current shareholding.

Preference Share

Shares which usually pay fixed dividends but do not have voting rights. Preference shares have preference over ordinary shares in relation to the payment of dividends and in default situations.

Primary Market

Also known as the new issues market, the primary market is where securities are issued for the first time, for example an IPO.

Proxy

Appointee who votes on a shareholder's behalf at company meetings.

Prudential Regulation Authority (PRA)

One of the two regulators of the financial services sector in the UK.

Quote-Driven

Dealing system driven by market makers quote buying and selling prices.

Real Estate Investment Trust (REIT)

An investment trust that specialises in investing in commercial property.

Redemption

The repayment of principal to the holder of a redeemable security.

Registrar

The official who maintains the share register on behalf of a company.

Repo

The sale and repurchase of securities between two parties: both the sale and the repurchase agreement are made at the same time, with the purchase price and date fixed in advance.

Resolution

Proposal on which shareholders vote.

Retail Prices Index (RPI)

Index that measures the movement of prices faced by retail consumers in the UK.

Rights Issue

The issue of new ordinary shares to a company's shareholders in proportion to each shareholder's existing holding. The issue is made in accordance with the shareholders' pre-emptive rights and the new shares are usually offered at a discounted price to that prevailing in the market. This means that the rights have a value, and can be traded 'nil paid'.

RPIX

UK index that shows the underlying rate of inflation, excluding the impact of mortgage payments.

Scrip Issue

Another term for a bonus or capitalisation issue.

Secondary Market

Marketplace for trading in existing securities.

Share Buyback

The purchase and typically the cancellation by a company of a proportion of its ordinary shares.

Share Capital

The nominal value of a company's equity or ordinary shares. A company's authorised share capital is the nominal value of equity the company may issue, while the issued share capital is that which the company has issued. The term share capital is often extended to include a company's preference shares.

Share Split/Stock Split

A method by which a company can reduce the market price of its shares to make them more marketable without capitalising its reserves. A share split simply entails the company reducing the nominal value of each of its shares in issue while maintaining the overall nominal value of its share capital. A share split should have the same impact on a company's share price as a bonus issue.

Short Position

The position following the sale of a security not owned or selling a derivative.

Special Purpose Vehicle (SPV)

Bankruptcy remote, off-balance sheet vehicle set up for a particular purpose such as buying assets from the originator and issuing asset-backed securities.

Special Resolution

Proposal put to shareholders requiring 75% of the votes cast in order to be accepted.

Swap

An over-the-counter (OTC) derivative whereby two parties exchange a series of periodic payments based on a notional principal amount over an agreed term. Swaps can take a number of forms including interest rate swaps, currency swaps, credit default swaps and equity swaps.

Takeover

When one company buys more than 50% of the shares of another (UK).

Treasury Bills

Short-term (often three months) borrowings of the government. Issued at a discount to the nominal value at which they will mature. Traded in the money market.

T+2

The two-day rolling settlement period over which all equity deals executed on the LSE SETS are settled. This is also a standard settlement period for many international equity markets.

Two-Way Price

Prices quoted by a market maker at which they are willing to buy (bid) and sell (offer).

Underlying

Asset from which a derivative is derived.

Unit Trust

A vehicle whereby money from investors is pooled together and invested collectively on their behalf. Unit trusts are open-ended vehicles.

Yield

Income from an investment expressed as a percentage of the current price.

Yield Curve

The depiction of the relationship between the yields and the maturity of bonds of the same type.

Multiple Choice Questions

The following questions have been compiled to reflect as closely as possible the standard that you will experience in your examination. Please note, however, that they are not actual exam questions. As part of exam security, hand-held calculators are not allowed in CISI exam venues. Candidates must use the onscreen calculator for all CISI CBT exams in all languages in the UK and internationally.

1. How does a subdivision or stock split work and how does it affect its current investors' holdings in the company?

   A. It decreases the number of shares issued, helping its price to regain a previous level. It has no immediate effect on current investors' holdings

   B. It increases the number of shares issued, reducing the price. While it has no monetary effect on current investor's holdings, they are diluted

   C. It increases the number of shares, by issuing new shares to investors at their current price, increasing their holdings

   D. It increases the number of shares issued, reducing their price. It has no effect on current investor's holdings

2. Under rules imposed by MiFID and MiFIR, how are FCA-regulated firms obliged to assist in preventing and detecting market abuse?

   A. By deterring clients from trading in financial instruments that are currently the subject of regulatory scrutiny

   B. By making transaction reports to the FCA on a timely basis

   C. By ensuring that all dealing staff and investment managers gain a relevant trading qualification covering market abuse

   D. By installing surveillance systems in order to perform routine tests against order book execution and order data

3. In a company's statement of financial position, which of the following category of asset is depreciated over time?

   A. All investments, in order to represent their current market value

   B. All tangible assets, since they have a limited life that is useful to the company

   C. All non-tangible, non-current assets, since their values change each year

   D. Tangible non-current assets with a limited life, to reflect their value over their useful life

4. In relation to the production of statements of profit and loss, under the International Accounting Standards (IAS), what two choices do firms have?

   A. Produce a statement of the amount of gross income or two separate statements showing income and expenditure separately

   B. Produce a statement of comprehensive income or in two separate statements showing income and comprehensive income

   C. Produce statements detailing the profits over the accounting period or two separate summaries of earned and unearned income

   D. Produce a statement of income and expenditure or two statements showing net income and expenditure separately

5. Which of the following retail structured investment products will be attractive to an investor who is willing to trade some potential gains for reduced capital risk. Why?

   A. A buffer zone investment, since it provides full capital protection should the market move beyond a predetermined range over the investment life span, in exchange for a slightly reduced return

   B. Auto-call investments, since they include a number of opt-out levels, which allow investors an early redemption option, with full capital protection, should specific events or triggers occur

   C. Principal-protection investments, since they provide full capital protection, for a reduced return, allowing investors to participate in more volatile assets and emerging markets

   D. Principal-protection auto-call investments, since they provide both full capital protection, as well as no counterparty risk, with pre-set exit levels, for a reduced return, that increases the longer it is held

6. Which of the following best describes how a forward exchange rate is determined and its relationship to the spot exchange rate?

   A. Managed float, keeps currencies within a specific trading range, which determines the limits of all forward rates

   B. Market expectations, most market makers include rate forecasts as part of their forward exchange rate quotes

   C. Free floating, a combination of interest rate differentials, trade policies and major economic factors determine both spot and forward quotes

   D. Interest rate parity, the simply mathematical difference between the two currencies' nominal interest rates

7. Which market practice has been cited by the FCA as providing increased liquidity for the specific securities involved, as well as proving support for a wide range of trading strategies that would be difficult to execute without it?

   A. A pooled nominee

   B. Registered title

   C. Stock lending

   D. Reverse repurchase agreements

8. In what way can contingent convertible bonds be beneficial to the banking industry?

    A. Conversion of such bonds can create an uplift in issuer's capital

    B. They are accepted as grade 1 collateral by the Bank of England

    C. They can be readily exchanged for the equivalent in deferred equity capital in order to improve the asset value

    D. Banks are able to use them as off balance sheet assets that can be brought into the main asset value calculations as required by the Bank of England

9. Which of the following is the best example of how a portfolio manager can limit potential losses on portfolios by giving up some of the potential profits?

    A. By using derivatives as insurance

    B. By implementing a programme of product diversification

    C. By intense strategic asset allocation

    D. By setting stop loss limits on all investments

10. Which of the following describes a key way to limit the risk of an open foreign exchange position?

    A. By rolling over the position's settlement date for a few days, to reduce any delivery risk

    B. By setting a stop-loss price, at which the position will be closed, if the rate moves against the position

    C. By borrowing lower interest rate currencies, when rolling over a position, to reduce any costs

    D. By setting a price at which the position will be closed, to ensure that you will not miss taking profit

11. Which of the following best describes how Her Majesty's Revenue and Customs (HMRC) collects transfer taxes in relation to the majority of UK equity trades?

    A. Through the stamping of share transfers at local stamp offices at which the submitting firm declares a stamp duty charge based on 1% of the consideration of the transaction

    B. Through the collection, by means of a stamp duty reserve tax (SDRT) charge of 1.5%, automatically applied by the CREST system on all equity purchases

    C. The stamp duty of 0.25% is collected based on consideration input by both the selling and buying counterparties within CREST

    D. SDRT of 0.5% is collected though CREST based on the input of accountable persons who act as collectors of duty on purchases

12. One of the key characteristics of an open-ended investment company (OEIC) that is attractive to most investors is:

    A. Since they are open-ended, they cannot trade at a discount to their net asset value (NAV)

    B. Their structure allows them to invest in only one fund at a time, to limit any risks, such as foreign exchange (FX) risk

    C. They are closed-ended, therefore can trade at a discount or premium to their NAV

    D. Since they do not have any dealing charges, their bid-offer spread can be wide when liquidity is limited

13. A key part of issuing medium term notes and bonds in the UK market is by using a shelf registration. This allows a borrower to issue new debt using this documentation for how long?

    A. Until the publication of the issuer's next audited annual report and accounts

    B. When the amount of debt issued reaches the document's pre-determined limit

    C. For a period of up to two years, as long as the issuer reports a profit

    D. Once the pre-determined number of issues has been reached

14. What does the Investment Association (IA) publish for investment strategies?

    A) A classification system

    B) A benchmark indexing table

    C) A list of ethical/ESG funds

    D) CGT Indexation tables

15. In relation to market abuse, which of the following best describes dissemination?

    A. Deliberately posting misleading information through the media in order to affect the market price of an instrument

    B. Giving non-public information to another individual which, if acted upon, could generate profits when made public

    C. Using member access to an electronic order book and inputting a series of fictitious orders to create an appearance of high liquidity and volume

    D. Dealing for one's personal account in advance of a large order already received from a client which is expected to move the share price in the market

16. A company is pursuing a strategy of increasing market share by reducing sales prices. The change in which of the following is most likely to reveal the change?

    A. Asset turnover

    B. Earnings per share

    C. Profit before taxes

    D. Gross profit margin

17. Why can it be difficult for analysts and researchers when undertaking financial analysis of issuers who operate in different sectors of the economy?

    A. Because they are likely to encounter differing accounting policies and standards

    B. Because most analysts develop expertise in a solitary area of the market and become known for such concentrated expertise; diversifying is often seen as diluting this focused excellence

    C. Because government and government agencies produce financial statistics and economic measures that are not compatible with cross-sector correlation

    D. Because multinationals tend to adopt the standards of their most liquid and profitable market which leads to an extremely diverse range of global economic principles

18. What is regarded as the primary objective of the Sarbanes-Oxley Act of 2002?

    A. To protect investors by improving the accuracy and reliability of corporate disclosures made pursuant to the securities laws and for other purposes

    B. To ensure the fair and orderly conduct of financial markets as protection for underlying investors, consumers and market members

    C. For investment advisers, portfolio managers and financial intermediaries to make full disclosures of risks and fees in relation to promotions, marketing and offers for sale

    D. For financial markets to ensure both pre- and post-trade transparency of listed instruments unless certain predefined waivers are necessitated by liquidity constraints

19. For investment trusts regulated by the Financial Conduct Authority (FCA), which of the following is true in relation to the underlying holdings within the fund?

    A. The investment trust must not control, seek to control or actively manage companies in which it invests

    B. It must not hold a single asset if it represents greater than 1.25% of the total fund for a period of longer than 12 months

    C. It must submit a statement of underlying holdings to the Panel on Takeovers and Mergers (POTAM) at least quarterly

    D. It must evoke best practice to avoid shareholder conflict in respect of investments which may be considered unethical

20. The type of risk that is defined as wide-spread and that can affect all markets, that cannot be completely eliminated through diversification, is known as:

    A. Global

    B. Market

    C. Default

    D. Liquidity

21. When a company issues shares that are entitled to receive a fixed annual dividend and an additional payment, which is a proportion of the ordinary share's dividend in very profitable years, these shares are known as:

    A. Deferred preference shares

    B. Cumulative preference shares

    C. Registered bearer shares

    D. Participating preference shares

22. Most convertible bonds pay a lower coupon than similar bonds. The reason for this is that investors find which of the following characteristics attractive?

    A. They are secured and therefore are backed by specific assets

    B. They have a third-party guarantee, usually by a bank or fund

    C. They include an option to convert the debt into the issuer's shares

    D. They are always senior and secured debt, with a higher credit rating

23. Which entity has published a classification system for the significant range of funds available to UK investors?

    A. The Investment Association (IA)

    B. The Bank of England

    C. Her Majesty's Revenue and Customs (HMRC)

    D. The Association of Private Client Investment Managers and Stockbrokers

24. The euro debt market crisis is a good example of investors taking positions based on which type of trading strategy spread?

    A. Credit quality spreads

    B. Default spreads

    C. Sovereign spreads

    D. Currency spreads

25. What is meant by systemic risk?

    A. The risk that an instrument's liquidity may diminish during periods of market stress

    B. The risk that a company in which an investment has been made could become insolvent due to a harsh operating environment

    C. The risk that affects overall prices of markets and indices influenced by macroeconomic conditions

    D. The risk of collapse of the entire financial system or entire market

26. Which of the following objective factors is an indication that an investor will accept higher risk investments?

    A. Those with specific commitments to meet

    B. One with limited assets and few liabilities

    C. A younger person planning for retirement

    D. One with a specific investment timescale and goal

27. In what way do shareholders gain eligibility to vote on important company matters and to receive dividends via direct communication with the company's appointed registrar?

    A. By securing beneficial ownership

    B. By placing an order to purchase an equity which is immediately executed

    C. By securing legal registered title

    D. By having physical possession of the registered certificates of legal title

28. Which of the following is deemed to be a main reason for establishing a liquidity ratio?

    A. To establish whether a company has the resources to meet its operating requirements from its working capital in a reasonable time period

    B. To evaluate the effect of bank overdrafts on the cash assets and whether any have been extended by the bank and included as current liabilities

    C. To perform an analysis of the financial viability of stated bond assets, because some accounting professionals prefer to include them as creditors, especially for lower grade corporates

    D. To compare liabilities against readily realisable assets and to determine whether a struggling company is still liquid

29. A preference shareholder can often be disadvantaged because, as a company starts to make large profits, the ordinary shareholders may see dividends rise, with the preference still paying the initial fixed rate. What class of share can mitigate this?

    A. Debentures

    B. Participating preference shares

    C. Class A consolidated loan shares

    D. Convertible preference shares

30. The Financial Conduct Authority (FCA) and most financial regulators require all large banks and brokers to establish which of the following, to ensure that none of its traders are able to benefit from front running any client orders and to avoid any conflict of interest between any of its different departments?

    A. Aggregated orders

    B. Chinese wall

    C. Allocation priority policy

    D. No proprietary trading

31. A standard service level agreement with a custodian will typically contain which one of the following?

    A. Communication and reporting

    B. Reporting obligations and deadlines

    C. The method through which the client's assets are received and held by the global custodian

    D. A list of persons authorised to give instructions

32. Why is the gross redemption yield (GRY) considered to be an ideal way of truly representing the return on a bond investment?

    A. It includes the three key factors of price paid, all of the coupon payments and the repayment of the principal

    B. As well as taking into account actual return, it includes a formula for comparing the return against benchmark rate such as the retail prices index (RPI)

    C. It includes a comparison against other benchmark bonds and thus provides a true rate of return against the overall bond markets

    D. It provides a real return compared to LIBOR, Euribor and a basket of other major global interest rates

33. Which of the following is most likely to be a non-dilutive follow-on share offering?

    A. When shares are offered by company's directors and other insiders who hold these shares and who will directly benefit by receiving the proceeds

    B. When new shares are offered by a company for specific investment goals or to finance a takeover/merger

    C. When shares are offered by the company to its directors to ensure that the company remains independent or for specific investment goals

    D. When new shares are offered by a company that will be traded on at least two different exchanges within the same regulatory jurisdiction

34. Which of the following statements describing a bond's price and yield quotations is true?

    A. Traders use the yield curve as a measure of the returns and liquidity of bonds with the same maturity of different issuers

    B. They move in opposite directions, meaning that as a bond's price falls, its yield will rise, reflecting the fact that the coupon payment does not change

    C. Every bond's coupon represents the percentage of the principal amount or par that will be paid on a quarterly basis

    D. They move in the same direction, reflecting the bond's basic credit standing, but their relative spreads usually lag behind

35. Both fundamental and technical analysis are useful in evaluating securities and potential investments. Which of the following best describes how they are used by investors?

    A. Fundamental analysis is more popular with day traders, while technical analysis is used by those who take a longer-term view

    B. Technical analysis focuses on the trends in a company's financial reports, while fundamental analysis is more concerned with market trends

    C. Both monitor the trading volume of a security and occasionally make adjustments when liquidity is considered to be limited

    D. Technical analysis uses price data that are more short-term time-frame, while fundamental analysis is more longer term

36. Which of the following best describes the liquidity risk aspect in the settlement process?

    A. It is when a counterparty is unable to meet all of its payment obligations in full on any specific due date

    B. It is when tight market conditions result in wide price spreads and limited trading amounts for an asset on any specific due date

    C. It is when a counterparty is declared insolvent after it has received several payments and it is restricted from fulfilling its payments

    D. It is when a counterparty has to finance any delivery failure by a counterparty at short notice

37. An investor holds a number of convertible bonds in a portfolio. Which of the following has the most valuable/highest conversion premium?

    I   – ABC plc trading at £107, £100 converts to 50 shares, which are trading at £1.85

    II –   EXE plc trading at £127, £100 converts to 45 shares, which are trading at £2.95

    III – XYZ plc trading at £128, £100 converts to 320 shares, which are trading at 33p

    IV – GHG plc trading at £111, £100 converts to 50 shares, which are trading at 1.80p

    A. GHG plc which has a conversion premium of 23.3%

    B. XYZ plc which has a conversion premium of £21.60

    C. ABC plc which has a conversion premium of 24.50%

    D. EXE plc which has a conversion premium of £22.25

38. In relation to tracking methods employed by exchange-traded funds (ETFs), which of the following best explains the benefits of stratified sampling?

    A. It enables the fund to reduce tracking errors and dealing costs

    B. It ensures that the fund and the indices are 100% correlated and eliminates tracking errors

    C. It enables the fund to replicate an index by using derivatives only and reduces brokers' commission

    D. It enables the fund managers to create an ETF from a sample of companies with dividend reinvestment plans (DRIPs) which allows the fund to accumulate shares, while distributing cash in lieu to holders

39. Which of the following is the best description of benchmarking?

    A. The monitoring of the overall performance of a portfolio by comparison to a peer group

    B. The setting of realistic targets for profits upon each asset purchase

    C. The financial analysis and comparative analysis of direct products sectors

    D. The plotting of prices of identical assets trading on multiple regulated markets and multilateral trading facilities (MTFs)

40. Which of the following best describes the way that pension fund trustees are expected to uphold prudential standards?

    A. The duty of governance demands that trustees execute transactions in financial instruments in the best interests of the scheme members and in accordance with markets in financial instruments directive (MiFID)

    B. Trustees must qualify targeted risk in the way that they manage members' assets or administer monies deposited with a third party

    C. They must demonstrate that they have the necessary familiarity with the structure and aims of their pension scheme and have an appropriate level of training and skill to carry out their responsibilities to scheme members effectively

    D. Senior scheme members have a responsibility to monitor and review the tasks delegated to the trustees in order to ensure that these tasks are discharged effectively, including, but not limited to, trading in financial instruments and depositing the scheme's assets with any third party

41. Securities analysts and investors use a company's liquidity ratio to establish which of the following?

    A. Whether it has access to sufficient cash to meet its ongoing liabilities

    B. The company's capital ratio measured relative to its sector

    C. How the company's profit margin measures relative to its competitors

    D. Whether it has sufficient ongoing cash to meet its long-term liabilities

42. One of the key approaches to asset selection is the bottom-up approach; which of the following best describes this method?

    A. Taking the opposite view of the current market and taking advantage of any price drop to increase holdings in specific assets

    B. Choosing individual assets whose characteristics meet the fund/investors' goals and constraints

    C. Buying specific assets at regular intervals, to avoid peaks and troughs in price throughout the investment year

    D. Selecting the types of assets and specific markets that meet the selected criteria, before buying individual securities

43. What is the main reason why central banks use repos?

    A. To control money supply

    B. To assist in collateralising banks

    C. To prop up base interest rates in times of economic slowdown

    D. To enhance revenue generation from pools of under-utilised balance sheet assets

44. Which key figure, used by financial analysts, is derived from dividing a company's net income for the financial year by the number of shares in issue?

    A. Net yield

    B. Return on capital employed

    C. Earnings per share

    D. Net revenue ratio

45. The Financial Services and Markets Act 2000 (FSMA 2000) extended the range of UK-authorised open-ended investment companies (OEICs) to include property funds and what other type of funds?

    A. Money market

    B. ETF tracker

    C. Corporate bond

    D. Leveraged

46. Which of the following is the best description of subordinated eurobonds?

    A. They have an inferior ranking within the capital structure hierarchy and have a greater risk than a senior or secured note

    B. They have a semi-superior status within the capital structure hierarchy and have greater risk than a senior note but less than a secured note

    C. The have the lowest ranking within the capital structure hierarchy and are effectively zero coupon bonds, rarely paying interest

    D. They are bonds where the coupon rate varies according to ability to pay and thus have an inferior ranking within the capital structure hierarchy but have the same market risk as a senior note

47. Which of the following best describes the purpose of a dividend cover calculation?

    A. It establishes whether an issuer of asset-backed securities has enough earned revenue to enable it to maintain its interest payments to holders

    B. It attempts to assess the likelihood of the current net dividend paid to shareholders being maintained by using the earnings per share (EPS)

    C. It measures the cash assets against dividend forecasting to predict future dividend yields

    D. It is a direct ratio of gross dividend versus EPS

48. One way that a central bank can reduce or drain liquidity from the money markets is to:

    A. Enter into a repurchase agreement as the reverse repo participant

    B. Reduce the minimum balance requirement

    C. Enter into a repurchase agreement as the repo participant

    D. Use a tri-party repurchase agreement

49. Which of the following is the best description of a SAFE?

    A. A contract which gives the right to the instrument purchaser (but not the obligation) to buy or sell a currency at a pre-agreed forex rate on a set date

    B. A contract that commits two parties to exchange pre-agreed amounts of foreign currency immediately and then re-exchange them at a given maturity date

    C. A contract where there is no exchange of principal monies at the outset or at maturity. The arrangement is a contract for difference based on notional cash sums

    D. An exchange-traded contract where a stipulated amount of a foreign currency is traded for delivery at a pre-determined future date at a price agreed at the outset

50. For what purpose were harmonised indices of consumer prices (HICPs) initially used in the EU?

    A. To assist the European Central Bank (ECB) in settling fiscal policy

    B. To establish whether prospective members of the European Monetary Union would meet the required inflation criterion

    C. To assist in the setting of the ECB base rate for the euro as the rate is strongly correlated with eurozone inflation

    D. As a benchmark rate to establish whether eurozone countries were meeting inflation targets both individually and by region

51. Which of the following financial instruments was introduced in the last 25 years and what is a key advantage of them?

    A. Exchange-traded funds – no stamp duty reserve tax (SDRT) on purchase

    B. Split unit trusts – diversify the investment

    C. Restricted for dividend equities – allow a lower entry price

    D. Dual-listed securities – improve liquidity and price stability

52. Why are a company and listed security removed from an exchange's official list involuntarily?

    A. The company's shares have fallen significantly in price beyond its banding

    B. The company's shares have experienced low volumes

    C. The company has voted at an annual general meeting (AGM) to change its capital structure

    D. The company has failed to meet the listing regulations

53. Which of the following describes how an open-ended investment company (OEIC) umbrella fund manages its client register?

    A. It has a separate register for each sub-fund

    B. All sub-funds within the umbrella are consolidated into a single register

    C. Each sub fund is split further into currencies, each with its own register

    D. A register is created for each currency, so it often has one or more sub-funds within it

54. Within a statement of profit and loss, under International Accounting Standards Board (IASB) published guidance, when is revenue from dividends recognised?

    A. When the shareholder's right to receive payment is established

    B. When confirmation is received from the bank that funds have cleared

    C. On the official pay date of the dividend

    D. On the ex-dividend date as determined by the market

55. If a CREST member trades 20 times on SETS in the same security, what are the minimum and maximum number of non-partial settlements that could take place through the central counterparty?

    A. 1 and 20

    B. 0 and 20

    C. 1 and 1

    D. 0 and 1

56. There is a statutory protection, offered to savers as high as £1,000,000 which can apply to balances in building societies, banks or credit unions if the entity fails. However, the standard protection is usually a maximum of £85,000. What is the key factor that makes the protection the higher amount?

    A. The high account balance is temporary

    B. The amount must have been constant for at least 18 months

    C. The money is held for charitable purposes

    D. The funds are held in escrow to the order of a third party

57. What key factor in relation to money market deposits and interest rates can represent a key advantage to investors?

    A. They respond immediately to interest rate changes

    B. The commission rates charged across different banks are usually consistent

    C. They offer better rates than cash deposits and savings bonds

    D. The rates are always higher than London Inter-bank Offered Rate (LIBOR)

58. Which of the following applies to commercial paper issued in the UK but not usually to commercial paper issued elsewhere?

    A. The issue must be fully backed by cash or near-cash

    B. Yields are quoted on a 365-day basis

    C. The term is restricted to 270 days

    D. They can only be marketed to professional investors

59. For mortgage-backed securities (MBSs) issued in the US, what is meant by tranches and what is their purpose?

    A. Each tranche represents a particular status with the eventual principal payment being distributed according to the priority of the tranche

    B. Each tranche represents a separate issue and fund raising and is redeemed and prioritised with the closest redemption first

    C. Each tranche has a different subscriber level with initial tranches being placed to large institutions and the final tranche, being the residue, offered generally to retail investors

    D. An MBS is generally sold in five tranches. The first is sold at a higher price, the second the next highest, etc, and this dictates the repayment priority at redemption due date

60. Open-ended investment companies (OEICs) need to appoint an authorised corporate director (ACD). Which of the following summarises the ACD's main role?

    A. To audit the accounts of the OEIC and associated funds

    B. To keep the unit holders regularly briefed on the fund's performance

    C. Day-to-day management of the fund

    D. Oversight of the investment manager and depositary

61. In what way do high frequency traders help with proper price formation and transparency in relation to securities that are cross-listed?

    A. Their arbitrage techniques generally lead to price consistency, eroding away small differences

    B. Each trader is required to make markets in any venue it has access to under market rules

    C. Traders offer plenty of liquidity and supply in otherwise illiquid securities whose trading volume would be very low

    D. A high frequency trader who trades in the same securities in different locations and currencies has to publicly quote prices and size for both

62. Which of the following investment sectors is likely to be avoided by a sustainability investing research team?

    A. Forestry
    B. Public transport
    C. Land use
    D. Pesticides

63. How does the Central Securities Depositories Regulation (CSDR) aims to improve the cost and risk for those who use central counterparty clearing houses (CCPs)?

    A. It enables non-clearing members (NCMs) to bypass general clearing members (GCMs) and settle directly with the CCP
    B. It results in a shorter time period of having to put up margin on open positions
    C. It imposes stricter credit checks on GCMs and NCMs
    D. It enables members to opt into settlement netting

64. The Payment Systems Regulator (PSR) is an independent economic regulator and has its own statutory objectives. How is it funded and who is it accountable to?

    A. It is funded by the payments industry and is accountable to the UK Parliament
    B. It is funded by government grant and reports to the Exchequer
    C. It is funded as part of the Financial Conduct Authority's (FCA's) financial accounts and also reports to it
    D. It is funded by industry donations and has no direct accountability

65. Under which circumstances would a permanent interest-bearing security become a perpetual subordinated bond?

    A. Directly following a partial default and rating downgrade
    B. When the instrument has been delisted
    C. When the issuing building society has demutualised
    D. After a merger or demerger approved at an annual general meeting (AGM)

66. Most structured products will naturally fall into one of three categories, with each having a specific risk/return profile. These are principal-protected, buffer-zone and which other?

    A. Endowment ring-fenced
    B. Capital-focused
    C. Return-enhanced
    D. Income-tax efficient

67. Fundamental analysis involves financial analysis of a company's published accounts and incorporates what two factors?

    A. Forecasted and projected

    B. Quantitative and qualitative

    C. Appreciation and depreciation

    D. Systemic and systematic

68. How does the CREST system assist in effecting the correct legal ownership status for share transactions in UK-registered equities?

    A. It ensures that actual bank-to-bank settlement follows legal registration

    B. It communicates electronically with registrars

    C. It guarantees the financial settlement of both the buyer and the seller

    D. It acts as the legal operator register

69. In respect of establishing an investor's profile, which of the following is the most accurate description of time horizon?

    A. The time between investing and an expected change in financial circumstances, eg, collecting a pension

    B. The forecasted future value of purchased investments taking into account all known factors

    C. The time period over which an investor considers investing

    D. The future value of benchmark indices given present financial condition and historical volatility

70. What specific aspect of a special purpose vehicle (SPV) makes it different from debt issued directly from the entity and, indeed, is the reason for them?

    A. It reduces the liability of the issuer in the event of insolvency

    B. It does not appear in the balance sheet of the entity

    C. SPV-issued debt is subject to a lower level of regulatory oversight

    D. SPVs can be marketed to retail investors while self-issued debt cannot be

71. The Panel on Takeovers and Mergers (POTAM) requirements for holders of the same security during a takeover offer situation specify that all shareholders:

    A. Must be treated in the same way as each other

    B. Must eventually accept an unconditional offer

    C. Must accept the offer using only electronic means

    D. Must be sent details of the offer simultaneously

72. Which of the following is a key difference between the settlement of UK equities compared to UK gilts?

    A. The equity settlement period is a day longer

    B. CREST settles equities while Euroclear settles gilts

    C. Equities require legal registration, gilts do not

    D. Equities can be central counterparty (CCP)-cleared, gilts cannot

73. What is the reason depreciation cannot be applied to freehold land?

    A. Its value can appreciate as well as depreciate

    B. Freehold land is already afforded stamp duty reliefs

    C. It does not have a limited economic life

    D. Freehold land is usually purchased to build on and improve

74. Money market funds (MMFs) should pay interest at a rate represented by London Inter-bank Offered Rate (LIBOR). Which of the following best describes how LIBOR is established?

    A. A calculation based on actual rates offered in the money market between banks

    B. The base rate plus or minus the premium on overnight deposit bank rates, averaged

    C. It is the base deposit rate, used by the Debt Management Office (DMO) and calculated across various sectors by the Bank of England

    D. It is the average two-day deposit rate announced by the seven largest lenders by loan value

75. Which aspect of a Treasury bill makes it very different from a regular gilt, certificate of deposit or other money market instrument?

    A. They are fully index-linked

    B. There is no maturity date

    C. There are no income payments

    D. They cannot be traded

76. What is depicted using a point and figure chart for price movement?

    A. Those movements that are significant

    B. A geographical comparison between countries

    C. A sectorised summary across similar businesses

    D. Those that have moved against predictions

77. What aspect of contingent convertible capital instruments (CoCos) make them a different instrument to traditional convertible bonds and which part of the industry finds them useful in uplifting capital ratios?

    A. They are convertible into a higher-yielding bond. The higher-yield bond is used by stock borrowers

    B. They are convertible only upon the expiry date and are automatically exercised if at a premium. They are used extensively by money brokers

    C. They can be exercised only when a certain price level is reached for the underlying equity and can be beneficial for banks

    D. They can be converted, when the price of the equity rises over four different subsequent quarters, into cash, usually by investment funds

78. In comparing fundamental and technical analysis, what is the distinguishing factor in relation to time horizon?

    A. Fundamental analysis uses other similar analysis for a longer-term focus while technical looks at shorter but less predictive data

    B. Technical analysis produces a more factual-based result while fundamental is a more predictive result using time factors

    C. Technical analysis focuses on the most recent data while fundamental has a more historic approach

    D. Fundamental uses a long-term approach to investment while technical uses shorter-term data

79. How can the real returns on investments in highly credit rated, fixed rate securities become negative?

    A. When the price of the investment erodes the coupon value

    B. When the inflation rate exceeds the coupon

    C. When the accrued interest is deducted upon purchase during the initial investment

    D. When the capital gain on a zero coupon bond does not bring the return to par

80. Which of the following best describes the characteristics of a certificate of deposit?

    A. Negotiable bearer instrument with fixed rate

    B. Tax-free wrapper in a single name

    C. Benchmarked to London Inter-bank Offered Rate (LIBOR) and short term

    D. Interest-bearing variable-rate investment

Answers to Multiple Choice Questions

1.   **D**   **Chapter 3, Section 3.9.5**

A subdivision, also referred to as a stock split, covers the case where a company increases the number of issued securities, for example by dividing every one share currently existing into four shares of a quarter of the old nominal amount.

2.   **B**   **Chapter 7, Section 2.4**

Both MiFID and MiFIR impose requirements on firms to report transactions. Transaction Reports play a key role in the FCA's market abuse monitoring work. The FCA takes a serious view of firms which fail to report transactions in line with its rules or which do not have in place adequate internal transaction reporting procedures and systems.

3.   **D**   **Chapter 6, Section 1.1.2**

Tangible non-current assets are initially recorded in the statement of financial position at their actual cost or book value. However, in order to reflect the fact that the asset will generate benefits for the company over several accounting periods, not just in the accounting period in which it is purchased, all tangible non-current assets with a limited economic life are required to be depreciated.

Depreciation is applied to tangible non-current assets such as plant and machinery. An annual depreciation charge is made in the year's statement of profit and loss. The depreciation charge allocates the fall in the book value of the asset over its useful economic life.

4.   **B**   **Chapter 6, Section 1.2.1**

IAS 1 has brought about changes to the statement of profit and loss. The amendment requires companies to present other comprehensive income items such as revaluation gains and losses, and actuarial gains and losses, as well as the usual statement of profit and loss items, on the face of the primary financial statements. IAS 1 allows this information to be presented either on one statement of comprehensive income or on two separate statements: a statement of profit and loss (income statement) and a statement of comprehensive income.

5.   **C**   **Chapter 4, Section 2.3**

Principal-protected investments offer the full downside protection of a bond while having the upside potential of a typical equity investment. Investors typically give up a portion of the equity appreciation in exchange for principal protection.

These are often of interest to clients wishing to participate in some of the more volatile asset classes or emerging markets, but who are unwilling to risk their principal or who may have long-term financial obligations. Generally, investors will receive 100% of the principal amount of their notes if they are held to maturity, regardless of the performance of the underlying investment. Maturities generally range from five to seven years, and investors should be willing to hold the investments to maturity.

6.   D   Chapter 1, Section 2.3.2

The relationship between the spot exchange rate and forward exchange rate for two currencies is simply given by the differential between their respective nominal interest rates over the term being considered. The relationship is purely mathematical and has nothing to do with market expectations.

7.   C   Chapter 5, Section 2.1.1

The FCA lists the following positive aspects of stock lending in its guidance to the investment community:

- It can increase the liquidity of the securities market by allowing securities to be borrowed temporarily, thus reducing the potential for failed settlements and the penalties this may incur.
- It can provide extra security to lenders through the collateralisation of a loan.
- It can support many trading and investment strategies that otherwise would be extremely difficult to execute.
- It allows investors to earn income by lending their securities on to third parties.
- It facilitates the hedging and arbitraging of price differentials.

8.   A   Chapter 2, Section 2.2.7

They are also quite useful to the banking industry, where contingent convertible bonds can be issued whereby conversion happens when an uplift in the percentage of capital is required in order for the bank to remain solvent.

9.   A   Chapter 8, Section 3.4.1

Portfolio insurance (also referred to as hedging) is a technique for limiting the potential loss on a portfolio using derivatives, at the expense of giving up some of the potential profits. The approach is based on options theory, where the holder of a call option has unlimited exposure to any potential profits, but limited exposure to losses. As an alternative, one could consider the purchase of put options where the fund manager has the right, but not the obligation, to put a stock or instrument to the option seller at a specified price that may, in the case of a substantial fall in the value of the asset, be at a much higher price than the current trading price. This acts like a form of insurance. CFDs and futures can also be used as a useful form of portfolio insurance. Although hedging minimises risk, the cost of such insurance needs to be taken into account as it also reduces the profit potential of the portfolio. With CFDs, the margined nature of the product increases the cost daily which, over time, can erode the value of the insurance/hedge.

10.   B   Chapter 1, Section 2.1.5

In trading foreign exchange, or any instrument for that matter, if one is using proper risk management techniques it is customary to establish what is called a stop loss for the position taken. This will provide a safety mechanism so that, if the trade turns adversely against the trader, then the position will be exited at a pre-determined level.

11.   D   Chapter 5, Section 1.3

The SDRT regulations impose an obligation on the operator of CREST (Euroclear UK & Ireland) to collect SDRT on transfers going through the system.

Ultimate liability for paying SDRT falls upon the purchaser or transferee. However, unlike stamp duty, there is an overlying concept of accountable persons (which arises under the SDRT Regulations 1986). In general terms, the accountable person rules are designed to place the primary reporting and payment obligations upon an involved financial intermediary, such as a broker. In many cases, typically those involving on-market sales of listed shares, such an intermediary will be accountable (although the accountable person will recover from the liable person any SDRT paid on that person's behalf).

The tax is charged at 0.5% on the consideration given for the transfer, payable by the purchaser. Unlike stamp duty, there is no rounding to the next £5, and it is charged to the penny.

12.   A   Chapter 4, Section 1.2.1

The value of an OEIC's share is determined by the net asset value (NAV) of its underlying investments. For example, if the underlying investments are valued at £125,000,000 and there are 100,000,000 shares in issue, the NAV of each share is £1.25. The open-ended nature of an OEIC means that it cannot trade at a discount to NAV, as an investment trust can.

13.   A   Chapter 2, Section 4.3.3

A shelf document can be produced at any time during the year, although there are likely to be considerable cost savings if an issuer does it in conjunction with the production of its annual report and accounts. The shelf document will remain current until the earliest of:

- the publication of the issuer's next audited annual report and accounts
- 12 months from the date the shelf document is published on the website (being the maximum period under European law)
- the date the shelf document is removed from the website at the written request of the issuer.

The shelf document must be formally approved by the UK Listing Authority before publication, and registered.

14.   A   Chapter 4, Section 3.4

The Investment Association (IA), the body that represents the UK investment management industry, has published a classification system for the investment strategies. These are broadly followed by the major collective investment vehicles – unit trusts and OEICs. The IA classifications are based on broad criteria. Within particular categories such as UK All Companies, there will be some funds focusing on mainstream blue chip stocks, some funds investing in recovery stocks and some funds concentrating on special situations such as companies that are rich in cash relative to their share price.

15.   A   Chapter 7, Section 2.4.6

The sixth type of behaviour amounting to market abuse is dissemination, which consists of the dissemination of information by any means which gives, or is likely to give, a false or misleading impression, as to a qualifying investment, by a person who knew or could reasonably be expected to have known that the information was false or misleading.

An example of behaviour which, in the opinion of the FCA falls within this category, is knowingly or recklessly spreading false and leading information about a qualifying investment through the media. An example of the prohibited behaviour is the posting of information which contains false or misleading statements about a qualifying investment on an internet bulletin board or in a chat room in circumstances where the person knows that the information is false or misleading.

16.   D   Chapter 6, Section 1.2.3

Gross profit margin, the percentage of gross profit to turnover or total revenues, will fall as the company lowers its sales prices but still faces similar costs. The impact on asset turnover, profit before taxes and earnings per share, will depend on how many more sales the company manages to achieve as a result of the strategy.

17.   A   Chapter 6, Section 1.7.1

The accounting policies adopted by a company can significantly impact its ratios and can also introduce a range of problems for comparison between different firms operating in different sectors of the economy and even more for international comparisons. For example, if non-current assets are revalued, depreciation charges will be higher. Hence, profits will be lower but, on the statement of financial position, more non-current assets mean a higher capital employed figure. In consequence, the return on capital employed will be reduced (lower profits divided by higher capital employed).

In comparing two companies where one revalues non-current assets and the other does not, or in comparing one company to another where non-current assets have been revalued in between, it has to be expected that there will be a distortion between the ratios as a result of this accounting policy.

18.   A   Chapter 3, Section 2.1.4

One consequence of a dual listing for multi-national corporations is in reference to the Sarbanes-Oxley Act (often referred to as SOX). Passed in 2002 by the US Congress, the Act's objective is *'to protect investors by improving the accuracy and reliability of corporate disclosures made pursuant to the securities laws, and for other purposes'*. It applies to US public companies and their global subsidiaries, and to foreign companies that have shares listed on US stock exchanges. As a result of their dual listing, SOX therefore applies to some of the UK's largest companies by market capitalisation, such as British Petroleum, HSBC, Prudential, Royal Dutch Shell and Vodafone, as well as many other international companies.

19.   **A**   **Chapter 4, Section 1.3.4**

The following principles, set down by the FCA, apply to a company that seeks to apply for a listing as an investment trust:

- The investment managers must have adequate experience.
- An adequate spread of investment risk must be maintained.
- The investment trust must not control, seek to control or actively manage companies in which it invests.
- The board of the investment trust must be free to act independently of its management.
- The investment trust must seek approval by HMRC (under s.842, Income and Corporation Taxes Act 1988 (ICTA 1988)).
- The trust itself does not have direct dealings with the public. If the management company offers the shares of the trust for sale to the public through a savings scheme, then the company must be authorised by the FCA to carry on investment business under the Financial Services and Markets Act 2000.

20.   **B**   **Chapter 7, Section 4.3**

Not all risk can be diversified away. Systematic or market risk cannot be diversified away by holding a range of investments within one particular market such as equities. If the global economy is performing poorly and share prices generally are falling and returns are declining, a wide and diversified portfolio of shares is very likely to fall in line with the wider market. The risk of this happening affects the whole market. An investor with limited funds to invest can achieve a high degree of diversification across asset classes by investing in collective funds such as unit trusts and investment trusts, and this can reduce non-systematic, specific risk to very low levels. However, it cannot be eliminated.

21.   **D**   **Chapter 3, Section 1.1.3**

One drawback of preference shares, when compared with ordinary shares, is that if the company starts to generate large profits the ordinary shareholders will often see their dividends rise, whereas the preference shareholders still get a fixed level of dividend. To counter this, some preference shares offer the opportunity to participate in higher distributions.

Preference shares usually carry a fixed dividend, representing their full annual return entitlement. Participating preference shares will receive this fixed dividend plus an additional dividend, which is usually a proportion of any ordinary dividend declared. As such, they participate more in the risks and rewards of ownership of the company.

22.   **C**   **Chapter 2, Section 2.2.6**

Typically, a convertible bond will pay a lower coupon, as this is compensated for by an option to convert into the equity of the issuer at the conversion date. Convertibles are often subordinated, meaning that all senior creditors must be settled in full before any payment can be made to holders in the event of insolvency.

23.   **A**   **Chapter 7, Section 1.2.4**

The Investment Association has published a classification system for the diverse array of funds available to UK investors including unit trusts and OEICs.

The groups correspond to broadly different investment objectives.

- Some income funds principally target immediate income, while others aim to achieve growing income.
- Growth funds, which mainly target capital growth or total return, are distinguished from those that are designed for capital protection.
- Specialist funds cover other more niche areas of investment.

24.   **C**   **Chapter 7, Section 3.6.1**

Sovereign spreads are one further type of spread which is becoming increasingly important for investment managers to follow, and this one relates to the difference between the yields available on the government bonds of different sovereigns. This has become especially significant since 2010 when there have been much publicised difficulties for peripheral states in the eurozone countries in terms of their creditworthiness.

Factors which will affect sovereign spreads are clearly related to macroeconomic circumstances in the various economies and, specifically, the differences in such factors as GDP growth rates, the level of public finance deficits and the competitiveness of the two economies for which the spread is quoted.

25.   **D**   **Chapter 7, Section 4.2**

Systemic risk is sometimes erroneously referred to as systematic risk. The latter term has quite a specific meaning in financial theory and is a cornerstone of the capital asset pricing model (CAPM), where it refers to what might better be described as market risk or more specifically non-diversifiable risk.

Systemic risk is the risk of collapse of the entire financial system or entire market, as opposed to risk associated with any one individual entity, group or component of the financial system.

To say that the entire financial system might collapse may have appeared fanciful until relatively recently. But in the second half of 2008, when major financial institutions such as Lehman Brothers, AIG, Fannie Mae and Freddie Mac effectively went bankrupt or entered conservatorship of the US government, the spectre of a financial meltdown became more credible. Central bankers, including the Governor of the Bank of England, have since gone on record to describe how close the world's financial system came to total collapse.

26.   **C**   **Chapter 8, Section 1.1**

The timescale over which a client may be able to invest will determine both what products are suitable and what risk should be adopted. For example, there is little justification in selecting a high-risk investment for funds that are held to meet a liability that is due in 12 months' time. By contrast, someone in their 30s choosing to invest for retirement is aiming for long-term growth, and higher-risk investments will be suitable. As a result, the acceptable level of risk is likely to vary from scenario to scenario.

27. **C** **Chapter 5, Section 1.5.1**

Registered title simply means ownership that is backed by registration. In terms of share ownership, registered title gives shareholders the right to vote on important company matters, to claim dividends on their shares, and to participate in other corporate actions such as rights issues.

28. **A** **Chapter 6, Section 1.4.1**

Financial analysts often distinguish between solvency and liquidity. In essence, the solvency of a company relates to its long-term position with respect to its assets and liabilities, and its commitments to finance its statement of financial position. Liquidity issues are more concerned with the short-term operating issues of a business and concern its ability to meet its ongoing cash requirements.

29. **B** **Chapter 3, Section 1.1.3**

One drawback of preference shares when compared with ordinary shares is that if the company starts to generate large profits, the ordinary shareholders will often see their dividends rise, whereas the preference shareholders still get a fixed level of dividend. To counter this, some preference shares offer the opportunity to participate in higher distributions.

30. **B** **Chapter 3, Section 3.1.3**

Large institutions operate with Chinese walls which separate the different functions within them and that the confidentiality and observance of secrecy by different divisions of the firm will ensure that this does not create a conflict of interest for the institution.

31. **A** **Chapter 5, Section 1.4.4**

Detailed specifications pertaining to the standards of service required by an investor from its custodian are spelt out in a service level agreement. This lays down required standards for service areas including the following:

- Record-keeping and maintenance of accurate and up-to-date documentation.
- Settlement on both recognised exchanges and in OTC markets.
- Communication and reporting.
- Processing of corporate actions, eg, rights issues and other capitalisation matters.
- Income-processing, for example from dividends and coupon payments.
- Tax services.
- Cash management.
- Management information systems.
- Stock lending and borrowing.
- Market information and market knowledge.
- Standards of service expected from account officers and relationship managers that represent primary points of contact with the investor.

A custody agreement is likely to address the following issues:

- The method through which the client's assets are received and held by the global custodian.
- Reporting obligations and deadlines.
- Guidelines for use of CSDs and other relevant use of financial infrastructure.
- Business contingency plans to cope with systemic malfunction or disaster.
- Liability in contract and claims for damages.
- Standards of service and care required under the custody relationship.
- A list of persons authorised to give instructions.
- Actions to be taken in response to instructions and actions to be taken without instructions.

32.   A   Chapter 2, Section 1.3.2

The GRY or yield to maturity of a bond represents the total return from a bond, after considering the price paid, all of the coupon payments and the repayment of the principal. Unlike flat yield, which is a rather simplistic measure, the yield to maturity is the benchmark used in the markets for measuring the so-called yield of a bond.

33.   A   Chapter 3, Section 2.1.2

The non-dilutive type of follow-on offering is when privately held shares are offered for sale by company directors or other insiders (such as venture capitalists) who may be looking to diversify their holdings. Because no new shares are created, the offering is not dilutive to existing shareholders. However, the proceeds from the sale do not flow into the company.

34.   B   Chapter 2, Section 5.4.3

Yield and price are inversely proportional to each other. As a simple rule of thumb, if the current price of the bond is higher than the par value, the yield is lower than the coupon, and, if the current price of the bond is lower than the par value, the required yield is higher than the coupon value.

35.   D   Chapter 7, Section 1.2.3

The principal differences between fundamental and technical analysis can be summarised as follows:

- Analysing financial statements versus charts – at a basic level, fundamental analysis involves the analysis of the company's balance sheet, cash flow statement and income statement. Technical analysis considers that there is no need to do this, as a company's fundamentals are all accounted for in the price and the information needed can be found in the company's charts.
- Time horizon – fundamental analysis takes a relatively long-term approach to investment. Technical analysis uses chart data over a much shorter time-frame of weeks, days and even minutes.
- Investing versus trading – fundamental analysis is used to make long-term investment decisions. Technical analysis is used to determine short-term trading decisions.

36.   D   Chapter 5, Section 1.2

Liquidity risk refers to the risk that a counterparty will not settle for the full value at the due date, but could do so at some unspecified time thereafter, causing the party which did not receive its expected payment to finance the shortfall at short notice.

37.   A   Chapter 2, Section 6.6.2

Convertible bonds enable the holder to exploit the growth potential in the equity while retaining the safety net of the bond. It is for this reason that convertible bonds trade at a premium to the value of the shares they can convert into. If there were no premium, there would be an arbitrage opportunity for investors to buy the shares more cheaply via the convertible than in the equity market.

It is common to express the premium as a percentage of the conversion value so this convertible has a premium of £16.50/£97.50 or 16.9%.

38.   A   Chapter 4, Section 1.5.4

Stratified sampling involves choosing investments that are representative of the index in similar manner to the manner in which statisticians conduct surveys on a sampling which reflects the stratification of an entire population. For example, if a sector makes up 16% of the index, 16% of shares in that sector will be held, even though the proportions of individual companies in the index may not be matched. The expectation is that, with stratified sampling, overall the tracking error or departure from the index will be relatively low. The amount of trading of shares required should be lower than with full replication, since the fund will not need to track every single constituent of an index. This should reduce transaction costs and therefore help to avoid such costs eroding overall performance.

39.   A   Chapter 8, Section 4.4.1

Portfolio performance may be measured by reference to a relevant peer group.

The peer group will be portfolio or fund managers who are also responsible for the full range of management decisions (asset allocation and stock selection) for a portfolio or fund with similar objectives and constraints. With peer group benchmarking, the fund management objectives may be defined as, for example, 'to outperform the peer group median performance'.

Peer group benchmarking has been criticised as tending to produce asset allocation decisions based simply on what other funds are doing, rather than on the needs of the fund involved.

A peer group benchmark does not show whether a portfolio manager is performing well in absolute terms. If all of the peer group are poor managers, they may be at the top of the peer group, but still be showing poor absolute performance.

40.   C   Chapter 5, Section 1.4.6

In their capacity as fiduciaries, pension fund trustees are generally required to uphold the following prudential standards:

- They must demonstrate that they have the necessary familiarity with the structure and aims of their pension scheme and have an appropriate level of training and skill to carry out their responsibilities to scheme members effectively.
- Fiduciaries have a responsibility to monitor and review the tasks that they delegate to third parties (including custodians and investment management companies) in order to ensure that these tasks are discharged effectively.

- The duty of loyalty demands that trustees administer their pension scheme solely in the best interests of the scheme members.
- Trustees must avoid undue risk in the way that they manage scheme assets and appoint intermediaries to manage or administer scheme assets on the scheme's behalf.

41.   **A**   **Chapter 6, Section 1.4.1**

Liquidity ratios aim to establish the following:

- Does a company have the resources to meet its operating requirements from its working capital on a timely basis?
- Can a company actually realise those resources quickly enough? In other words does it have sufficient ability to raise cash when required, to pay off the liabilities as they fall due?

42.   **B**   **Chapter 8, Section 3.2.1**

A bottom-up approach will examine the fundamental characteristics of many individual stocks and the portfolio will be constructed from those which best satisfy the fund's objectives and constraints. This approach is appropriate when the manager is more concerned with the merits of individual securities and the resulting combination and the broad characteristics of the portfolio will tend to emerge from the constituents rather than having been engineered or assembled from the top-down approach.

43.   **A**   **Chapter 1, Section 1.4**

The purpose of the repo market as implemented by central banks, such as the Bank of England and the European Central Bank, is to provide or remove liquidity from the money markets. If the central bank wishes to increase the money supply, it will enter into repo agreements as the reverse repo participant, with other money market institutions such as banks being the repo participant. In contrast, if the central bank wishes to drain liquidity from the money markets then it will use repo transactions. This time the central bank will be the repo participant, initially selling instruments and therefore withdrawing cash from the system.

44.   **C**   **Chapter 6, Section 1.2.2**

Earnings Per Share (EPS) is one of the most important figures for investors and financial analysts and is reflected at the bottom of the statement of profit and loss, in pence. EPS is the amount of profit after tax that has been earned per ordinary share. EPS is calculated as follows:

$$EPS = \frac{\text{Net Income for the financial year}}{\text{Number of ordinary shares in issue}}$$

45.   **A**   **Chapter 4, Section 1.2.1**

With the implementation of the Financial Services and Markets Act 2000 (FSMA 2000), the range of UK-authorised OEICs was extended to be similar to that of unit trusts, including money market funds and property funds.

46.   **A**   **Chapter 2, Section 3.1**

Subordinated eurobonds, as with subordinated notes in general, are ones which have a junior or inferior status within the capital structure hierarchy and have greater risk than a senior or secured note.

47.   **B**   **Chapter 6, Section 1.6.4**

Dividend cover attempts to assess the likelihood of the existing dividend being maintained.

$$\text{Dividend cover} = \frac{\text{Earnings per share}}{\text{Dividend per share}}$$

48.   **C**   **Chapter 1, Section 1.4**

The purpose of the repo market as implemented by central banks, such as the Bank of England and the European Central Bank, is to provide or remove liquidity from the money markets. If the central bank wishes to increase the money supply, it will enter into repo agreements with other money market institutions, such as banks, as the reverse repo participant, providing cash for the collateral provided under the repo. If the central bank wishes to drain liquidity it will use a repo mechanism with the central bank acting as the repo participant.

49.   **C**   **Chapter 1, Section 2.4.6**

A synthetic agreement for forward exchange (SAFE) is a variation on the short-term currency swap, in which there is no actual exchange of principal at inception or at maturity, the arrangement being a CFD based on notional cash sums. In this case large notional sums may be referenced in the swap agreement but the resulting cash flow may be relatively small, especially if there has been only a slight variation between the rates at the time of inception and at the time of maturity.

When the two parties agree to execute a SAFE, they agree the exchange rates at which the notional deals will be executed at inception and maturity. At maturity, one party pays to the other the difference in the value of the secondary currency between the rate originally contracted and the rate actually prevailing. In essence this is exactly how a CFD for any asset purchase works, including equity CFDs.

50.   **B**   **Chapter 2, Section 1.4.1**

HICPs were originally developed in the EU to assess whether prospective members of the European Monetary Union would pass the required inflation-convergence criterion; they then graduated to acting as the measure of inflation used by the ECB to assess price stability in the euro area.

51.   **A**   **Chapter 8, Section 5.3**

Financial innovation over the last 20 years has been extraordinary. This has been especially the case in terms of the products that are now available to investors, such as CFDs, ETFs, new kinds of collective investment vehicles and the proliferation of derivatives including CDSs and other asset-backed securities.

52.　　　**D**　　　　　**Chapter 3, Section 2.1.3**

Delisting can be voluntary or involuntary and can be for a variety of reasons. Such reasons are:

- failure to meet the listing regulations or requirements of the exchange. Listing requirements include minimum share prices, certain financial ratios and minimum sales levels
- the company goes out of business
- the company declares bankruptcy
- the company has become a private company (eg, resulting from a management buy out) after a merger or acquisition
- the company wishes to reduce or remove an element of its regular reporting requirements
- the company no longer seeks a listing because of factors such as low volumes on the exchange on which it is listed or for financial reasons, eg, to save on listing fees.

53.　　　**A**　　　　　**Chapter 4, Section 1.2.1**

An OEIC may take the form of an umbrella fund, with a number of separately priced sub-funds adopting different investment strategies or denominated in different currencies. All sub-funds will have a separate client register and asset pool.

54.　　　**A**　　　　　**Chapter 6, Section 1.2.2**

For interest, royalties and dividends, revenue should be recognised as follows:

- Interest – on a time proportion basis that takes into account the effective yield.
- Royalties – on an accruals basis.
- Dividends – when the shareholders' right to receive payment is established.

55.　　　**A**　　　　　**Chapter 5, Section 1.1.2**

For SETS trades, CREST provides the option to LSE member firms to settle with LCH ltd or SIX x-clear AG as counterparty on a gross basis or on a net basis. If a firm has 20 orders executed in the same security through SETS, they can either settle 20 trades with LCH.Clearnet or SIX x-clear AG (settling gross), or choose to have all 20 trades netted so that the firm just settles a single transaction.

56.　　　**A**　　　　　**Chapter 1, Section 1.1.9**

The FSCS will provide a £1 million protection limit for temporary high balances held with an individual's bank, building society or credit union if it fails.

57.　　　**A**　　　　　**Chapter 8, Section 3.3.5**

Money market deposits respond immediately to changes in interest rates – good when interest rates are rising.

58.　　　**B**　　　　　**Chapter 1, Section 1.3.1**

Commercial Paper (CP) yields are quoted on a discount basis. Virtually all countries use an actual/360 basis, except the UK, which uses an actual/365 basis.

59.　　**A**　　　　**Chapter 2, Section 2.1.4**

Mortgage-backed securities issues are often sub-divided into a variety of classes (or tranches), each tranche having a particular priority in relation to interest and principal payments. Typically, as the underlying payments on the mortgage loans are collected, the interest on all tranches of the bonds is paid first. As loans are repaid, the principal is paid back to the first tranche of bondholders, then the second tranche, third tranche and so on.

60.　　**C**　　　　**Chapter 4, Section 1.2.1**

An OEIC has an authorised corporate director (ACD), who may be the only director. The responsibilities of the ACD include the day-to-day management of the fund.

61.　　**A**　　　　**Chapter 3, Section 2.1.5**

Prices are subject to exchange rate fluctuation, as well as local market price formation from natural supply and demand. Sometimes, small differences can exist between the prices of both markets (taking into account the exchange rate) but this is usually very small, momentary and is usually quickly arbitraged away. Some high frequency traders (HFTs) will employ trading algorithms looking to trade across markets.

62.　　**D**　　　　**Chapter 8, Section 2.5**

Sustainability funds are those that focus on the concept of sustainable development, concentrating on those companies that tackle or pre-empt environmental issues head-on. Unlike ethical investing funds, sustainability funds, sometimes known as light green funds, are flexible in their approach to selecting investments. The following are some examples of features that an investor may wish to avoid: pesticides, land abuse, deforestation, polluters and genetic research.

63.　　**B**　　　　**Chapter 5, Section 1.1.3**

The move to T+2 was proposed by the EU Central Securities Depositories Regulation (CSDR), which requires the alignment of settlement periods within the EU and EEA countries.

Among the key advantages of a shorter settlement cycle is a shorter period of providing margin for CCP clearing positions.

64.　　**A**　　　　**Chapter 3, Section 2.2.7**

The PSR is a subsidiary of the FCA but has its own statutory objectives, managing director and board. It is funded by the payments industry and is accountable to the UK Parliament.

65.　　**C**　　　　**Chapter 2, Section 2.2.4**

When the building society has demutualised, its PIBSs are reclassified as perpetual subordinated bonds (PSBs). Both PIBSs and PSBs can be traded on the LSE.

66. **C** **Chapter 4, Section 2.3**

Most structured investments fall into one of three categories, each with its own risk/return profile:

- principal-protected
- buffer-zone
- return-enhanced.

67. **B** **Chapter 7, Section 1.2.1**

Fundamental analysis looks at both quantitative factors, such as the numerical results of the analysis of a company and the market it operates in, and qualitative factors, such as the quality of the company's management, the value of its brand, and areas such as patents and proprietary technology.

68. **D** **Chapter 5, Section: 1.1.2**

CREST updates the register of shareholders – it maintains the so-called operator register for UK companies' dematerialised shareholdings.

69. **C** **Chapter 8, Section: 2.1.1**

Time horizon refers to the period over which a client can consider investing their funds.

70. **B** **Chapter 2, Section 2.1.1**

Like other companies or corporates, financial institutions issue bonds to finance borrowing. These financial institutions also arrange borrowing for themselves and others by creating special purpose vehicles (SPVs) to enable money to be raised that does not appear within the accounts of that entity. This type of finance is often described as off-balance-sheet finance, because it does not appear in the statement of financial position/balance sheet that forms part of the company's accounts.

71. **A** **Chapter 3, Section 2.2.5**

All holders of the securities of an offeree company of the same class must be afforded equivalent treatment.

72. **A** **Chapter 5, Section 1.1.4**

The settlement period for UK equities is T+2, while for UK gilts it is T+1.

73. **C** **Chapter 6, Section 1.1.2**

Depreciation is applied to tangible non-current assets, such as plant and machinery. This requirement does not, however, apply to freehold land and non-current asset investments which, by not having a limited economic life, are not usually depreciated.

74.   **A**   **Chapter 4, Section 1.7.1**

The rates paid on MMFs should reflect wholesale money market rates represented by LIBOR – established daily as a summary of actual rates offered in the money market between banks. LIBOR is due to be replaced in 2022–23.

75.   **C**   **Chapter 1, Section 1.2**

UK Treasury bills are short-term loan instruments, guaranteed by the UK government, with a maturity date of less than one year at issue. They pay no coupon, and consequently are issued at a discount to their nominal value, the discount representing the return available to the investor.

76.   **A**   **Chapter 7, Section 1.2.2**

Point and figure charts record significant price movements in vertical columns by using a series of Xs to denote significant up moves and Os to represent significant down moves, without employing a uniform timescale. Whenever there is a change in the direction of the security's price, a new column is started.

77.   **C**   **Chapter 2, Section 2.2.7**

Contingent convertible bonds are convertible bonds where a price is set, which the underlying equity share price must reach before conversion can take place. They are also quite useful to the banking industry, where contingent convertible bonds can be issued whereby conversion happens when uplift in the percentage of capital is required in order for the bank to remain solvent. Thus, conversion into shares is automatic if the specified capital ratio is likely to be breached.

78.   **D**   **Chapter 7, Section 1.2.3**

Fundamental and technical analyses are the two main methodologies used for investment analysis. Fundamental analysis takes a relatively long-term approach to investment. Technical analysis uses chart data over a much shorter time frame of weeks, days and even minutes.

79.   **B**   **Chapter 8, Section 2.2**

The real return takes into account the inflation rate and in times of excessive inflation the real returns available may well become negative.

80.   **A**   **Chapter 1, Section 1.1.5**

Certificates of deposit (CDs) are negotiable bearer securities issued by commercial banks in exchange for fixed-term deposits, with a fixed term and a fixed rate of interest, set marginally below that for an equivalent bank time deposit.

504

Syllabus Learning Map

Syllabus Unit/ Element		Chapter/ Section
Element 1	**Cash, Money Markets and the Foreign Exchange Market**	**Chapter 1**
1.1	**Cash Instruments and Markets** On completion, the candidate should be able to:	
1.1.1	Be able to analyse the main investment characteristics, behaviours and risks of cash deposit accounts: • deposit-taking institutions and credit risk assessment • term, notice, liquidity and access • fixed and variable rates of interest • inflation • statutory protection • foreign currency deposits • structured deposits	1.1
1.1.2	Be able to analyse the main investment characteristics, behaviours and risks of Treasury bills: • purpose and method of issue • minimum denomination • normal life • zero coupon and redemption at par • market access, trading and settlement	1.2
1.1.3	Be able to analyse the main investment characteristics, behaviours and risks of commercial paper: • purpose and method of issue • maturity • discounted security • unsecured and secured • asset-backed • credit rating • market access, trading and settlement	1.3
1.1.4	Be able to analyse the main investment characteristics, behaviours and risks of repurchase agreements: • purpose • sale and repurchase at agreed price, rate and date • tri-party repos • documentation	1.4
1.2	**Foreign Exchange Instruments and Markets** On completion, the candidate should be able to:	
1.2.1	Understand the role, structure and main characteristics of the foreign exchange market: • OTC market • quotes, spreads and exchange rate information • market participants and access to markets • volume, volatility and liquidity • risk mitigation: rollovers and stop losses • regulatory/supervisory environment	2.1

Syllabus Unit/ Element		Chapter/ Section
1.2.2	Understand the determinants of spot foreign exchange prices: • currency demand – transactional and speculative • economic variables • cross-border trading of financial assets • interest rates • free, pegged and managed rates	2.2
1.2.3	Be able to calculate forward foreign exchange rates using: • adding or subtracting forward adjustments • Interest rate parity	2.3
1.2.4	Be able to analyse how foreign exchange contracts can be used to buy or sell currency relating to overseas investments or to hedge non-domestic currency exposure: • spot contracts • forward contracts • currency futures • currency options • non-deliverable forwards	2.3

Element 2	Fixed-Income Securities	Chapter 2
2.1	**Characteristics of Fixed-Income Securities** On completion, the candidate should be able to:	
2.1.1	Understand the main characteristics of fixed-income securities: • short-, medium- and long-dated • dual-dated • Floating rate • zero coupon • use of ratings • credit enhancements	1.1
2.1.2	Understand the main risks of fixed-income securities: • the impact of ratings • the concept of risk-free • currency, credit and inflation risks	1.1
2.2	**Characteristics of Sovereign and Government Bonds** On completion, the candidate should be able to:	
2.2.1	Understand the main investment characteristics, behaviours and risks government debt (for example, USA, Germany, Japan and the UK)	1.2
2.2.2	Understand the relationship between interest rates and bond prices: • yield (flat yield and yield to maturity) • interest payable • accrued interest (clean and dirty prices) • effect of changes in interest rates	1.3

Syllabus Unit/ Element		Chapter/ Section
2.2.3	Understand the main investment characteristics, behaviours and risks of index-linked debt: • retail prices and consumer prices indices as measures of inflation • consumer prices index • process of index linking • indexing effects on price, interest and redemption • return during a period of zero inflation • harmonised price index	1.4
2.2.4	Understand the main issuers and characteristics of supranational and public authority debt	1.5
2.3	**Characteristics of Corporate Debt** On completion, the candidate should be able to:	
2.3.1	Understand the main investment characteristics, behaviours and risks of corporate debt: • financial institutions and special purpose vehicles • fixed and floating charges • debentures • types of asset-backed securities • mortgage-backed securities • securitisation process • roles of participants	2
2.3.2	Understand the main investment characteristics, behaviours and risks of the main types of unsecured debt: • income bonds • subordinated • high yield • convertible bonds • contingent convertible bonds	2.2
2.4	**Characteristics of Eurobonds** On completion, the candidate should be able to:	
2.4.1	Understand the main investment characteristics, behaviours and risks of eurobonds: • types of issuer: sovereign, supranational and corporate • types of eurobond: straight, FRN/VRN, subordinated, asset-backed, convertible • international bank syndicate issuance • immobilisation in depositories • continuous pure bearer instrument: implications for interest and capital repayment • accrued interest, ex-interest date	3

Syllabus Unit/ Element		Chapter/ Section
2.5	**Issuing Fixed-Income Securities** On completion, the candidate should be able to:	
2.5.1	Understand the responsibilities and processes of the UK Debt Management Office in relation to the management and issue of UK government debt: • gilts • Treasury bills • primary market makers: gilt edged market makers (GEMMs) • intermediaries: inter-dealer brokers (IDBs)	4
2.5.2	Understand the main bond pricing benchmarks and how they are applied to new bond issues: • spread over government bond benchmark • spread over/under inter-bank benchmarks • spread over/under swap	4.2
2.5.3	Understand the purpose, structure and process of the main methods of origination and issuance and their implications for issuers and investors: • scheduled funding programmes and opportunistic issuance (eg, MTN) • auction/tender • reverse inquiry (under MTN)	4.3
2.6	**Fixed-Income Markets and Trade Execution** On completion, the candidate should be able to:	
2.6.1	Understand the role, structure and characteristics of government bond markets in the developed markets of the USA, Germany, Japan and the UK , including: • market environment: relative importance of exchange versus OTC trading versus organised trading facilities (OTFs) • participants – primary dealers, broker dealers and inter-dealer brokers • access considerations • regulatory/supervisory environment	5.1
2.6.2	Understand the differences between the developed markets and the emerging economies	5.1
2.6.3	Understand the purpose and key features of the global strip market: • result of stripping a bond • zero coupon securities • access considerations	5.2

Syllabus Unit/ Element		Chapter/ Section
2.6.4	Understand the role, structure and characteristics of global corporate bond markets: • decentralised dealer markets and dealer provision of liquidity • relationship between bond and equity markets • bond pools of liquidity (including OTFs) versus centralised exchanges • access considerations • regulatory/supervisory environment • ICMA and other relevant trade associations:	5.3
2.6.5	Understand the different quotation methods, and the circumstances in which they are used • yield • spread • price	5.4
2.7	**Valuation of Fixed-Income Securities** On completion, the candidate should be able to:	
2.7.1	Understand the purpose, influence and limitations of global credit rating agencies, debt seniority and ranking in cases of default/ bankruptcy: • senior • subordinated • mezzanine • payment in kind (PIK) • tiers of bank debt	6.1
2.7.2	Be able to analyse sovereign, government and corporate credit ratings from an investment perspective: • main rating agencies • country rating factors • debt instrument rating factors • investment and sub-investment grades • use of credit enhancements • impact of grading changes • considerations when using credit rating agencies	6.2
2.7.3	Be able to analyse the factors that influence bond pricing: • credit rating • default risk • impact of interest rates • market liquidity • inflation	6.3

Syllabus Unit/ Element		Chapter/ Section
2.7.4	Be able to analyse fixed-income securities using the following valuation measures and understand the benefits and limitations of using them: • flat yield • yield to maturity • nominal and real return • gross redemption yield (using internal rate of return) • net redemption yield • modified duration	6.4
2.7.5	Be able to analyse the specific features of bonds from an investment perspective: • coupon and payment date • maturity date • embedded put or call options • convertible bonds • exchangeable bonds	6.5
2.7.6	Be able to calculate and interpret: • simple interest income on corporate debt • conversion premiums on convertible bonds • flat yield • accrued interest (given details of the day count conventions)	6.6

Element 3	Equities	Chapter 3
3.1	**Characteristics of Equities** On completion, the candidate should be able to:	
3.1.1	Understand the main investment characteristics, behaviours and risks of different classes of equity: • ordinary, cumulative, participating, redeemable and convertible preference shares • voting rights, voting and non-voting shares • ranking for dividends • ranking in liquidation	1.1
3.1.2	Understand the purpose, main investment characteristics, behaviours and risks of depositary receipts: • American depositary receipts • global depositary receipts • beneficial ownership rights • structure • unsponsored and sponsored programmes • transferability	1.2

Syllabus Unit/ Element		Chapter/ Section
3.2	**Issuing Equity Securities** On completion, the candidate should be able to:	
3.2.1	Understand the purpose and key features of the following: • primary issues • secondary issues • issuing, listing and quotation • dual listings • cross listings • delisting (cancelling)	2.1
3.2.2	Understand the main regulatory, supervisory and trade body framework supporting UK financial markets: • Companies Acts • The Financial Conduct Authority (FCA) and UK Listing Authority (UKLA) • HM Treasury • Payment Systems Regulator • The Panel on Takeovers and Mergers (POTAM) • exchange membership and rules • relevant trade associations and professional bodies	2.2
3.2.3	Understand the structure of the UK exchanges, the types of securities traded on their markets, and the criteria and processes for companies seeking admission: • London Stock Exchange Main Market • high-growth segment • AIM • Aquis • market participants • implications for investors	2.3
3.2.4	Understand the process of issuing securities in the UK with or without a prospectus: • Prospectus Directive (PD) or equivalent where applicable • eligibility and registration criteria for natural persons and small and medium-sized enterprises (SMEs)	2.4
3.2.5	Understand the purpose, structure and stages of an initial public offering (IPO) and the role of the origination team • structure – base deal plus greenshoe • stages of an IPO • underwritten versus best efforts • principles and process of price stabilisation	2.5
3.2.6	Understand the benefits for the issuer and investors of the different processes used in an IPO	2.5

Syllabus Unit/ Element		Chapter/ Section
3.3	**Equity Markets and Trade Execution** On completion, the candidate should be able to:	
3.3.1	Apply fundamental UK regulatory requirements with regard to trade execution and reporting: • best execution • aggregation and allocation • management of conflicts of interests and prohibition of front running	3.1
3.3.2	Understand the key features of the main trading venues: • regulated and designated investment exchanges • recognised overseas investment exchanges • whether quote- or order-driven • main types of order – limit, market, fill or kill, execute and eliminate, iceberg, named • liquidity and transparency	3.2
3.3.3	Understand the key features of alternative trading venues: • multilateral trading facilities (MTFs) • organised trading facilities (OTFs) • systematic internalisers • dark pools	3.3
3.3.4	Understand algorithmic trading: • reasons • high frequency trading • potential consequences for the market (eg, flash crashes, increased liquidity, increased volume, illusion of volume)	3.4
3.3.5	Understand the concepts of trading cum, ex, special cum and special ex: • the meaning of books closed, ex-div and cum div, cum, special ex, special cum and ex rights • effect of late registration	3.5
3.3.6	Apply knowledge of the key differences between international markets: • regulatory and supervisory environment • corporate governance • liquidity and transparency • access and relative cost of trading	3.6
3.3.7	Be able to assess how the following factors influence equity markets and equity valuation: • trading volume and liquidity of domestic and international securities markets • relationship between cash and derivatives markets and the effect of timed events • market consensus and analyst opinion • changes to the economic outlook • implications of foreign exchange	3.7

Syllabus Unit/ Element		Chapter/ Section
3.3.8	Understand the purpose, construction, application and influence of indices on equity markets: • market regional and country sectors • market capitalisation sub-sectors • free float and full market capitalisation indices • fair value-adjusted indices	3.8
3.4	**Accounting for Corporate Actions** On completion, the candidate should be able to:	
3.4.1	Understand the purpose and structure of corporate actions and their implications for investors: • stock capitalisation or consolidation • stock and cash dividends • rights issues • open offers, offers for subscription and offers for sale • placings	3.9
3.4.2	Be able to calculate the theoretical effect on the issuer's share price of the following mandatory and optional corporate actions: • bonus/scrip • consolidation • rights issues	4
3.4.3	Be able to analyse the following in respect of corporate actions: • rationale offered by the company • the dilution effect on profitability and reported financials • the effect of share buybacks	5
3.5	**Warrants and Contracts for Difference** On completion, the candidate should be able to:	
3.5.1	Be able to analyse the main purposes, characteristics, behaviours and relative risk and return of warrants and covered warrants: • benefit to the issuing company • right to subscribe for capital • effect on price of maturity and the underlying security • exercise and expiry • calculation of the conversion premium on a warrant	6.1
3.5.2	Be able to analyse the main characteristics of contracts for difference (CFDs): • types and availability of CFDs • CFD providers – market maker versus direct market access • margin • market, liquidation and counterparty risks • size of CFD market and impact on total market activity • differences in pricing, valuing and trading CFDs compared to direct investment • differences in pricing, valuing and trading CFDs compared to spread bets	6.2

Syllabus Unit/ Element		Chapter/ Section
Element 4	**Collective Investments**	**Chapter 4**
4.1	**Characteristics of Collective Investment Funds and Companies** On completion, the candidate should be able to:	
4.1.1	Be able to analyse the key features, accessibility, risks, charges, valuation and yield characteristics of open-ended investment companies (OEICs)/investment companies with variable capital (ICVCs)/SICAVs	1.2
4.1.2	Be able to analyse the key features, accessibility, risks, charges, valuation and yield characteristics of unit trusts	1.1
4.1.3	Be able to analyse the key features, accessibility, risks, charges, valuation and yield characteristics of investment trusts	1.3
4.1.4	Be able to compare and contrast the key features, accessibility, risks, charges, valuation and yield characteristics of real estate investment trusts (REITs) with property authorised investment funds (PAIFs)	1.4
4.1.5	Be able to analyse the key features, accessibility, risks, charges, valuation and yield characteristics of the main types of exchange-traded products (ETPs)	1.5
4.1.6	Be able to analyse the key features, accessibility, risks, charges, valuation and yield characteristics of the main types of non-mainstream pooled investments (NMPI)	1.6
4.2	**Structured Products** On completion, the candidate should be able to:	
4.2.1	Be able to analyse the key features, accessibility, risks, valuation and yield characteristics of the main types of retail structured products and investment notes (capital protected, autocall, buffer zone): • structure • income and capital growth • investment risk and return • counterparty risk • expenses • capital protection	2

Syllabus Unit/ Element		Chapter/ Section
4.3	**Analysis of Collective Investments** On completion, the candidate should be able to:	
4.3.1	Be able to analyse the factors to take into account when selecting collective investments: • quality of firm, management team and administration • investment mandate – scope, controls, restrictions and review process • investment strategy • exposure, allocation, valuation and quality of holdings • prospects for capital growth and income • asset cover and redemption yield • track record compared with appropriate peer universe and market indices • key person risk and how this is managed by a firm • shareholder base • measures to prevent price exploitation by dominant investors • liquidity, trading access and price stability • suitability	3

Element 5	Settlement, Safe Custody and Prime Brokerage	Chapter 5
5.1	**Clearing, Settlement and Safe Custody** On completion, the candidate should be able to:	
5.1.1	Understand how fixed income, equity, money market and foreign exchange transactions are cleared and settled in the UK, Germany, US and Japan: • principles of delivery versus payment (DvP) and free delivery • trade confirmation process • settlement periods • international central securities depositories (ICSDs) – Euroclear and Clearstream • international exchanges	1
5.1.2	Understand how settlement risk arises, its impact on trading and the investment process and how it can be mitigated: • underlying risks: default, credit and liquidity • relative likelihood of settlement-based risks in developed and emerging markets • effect of DvP and straight-through processing (STP) automated systems • risk mitigation within markets and firms • continuous linked settlement	1.2
5.1.3	Understand which transactions may be subject to or exempt from financial transaction taxes	1.3

Syllabus Unit/ Element		Chapter/ Section
5.1.4	Understand the principles of safe custody, the roles of the different types of custodian and how client assets are protected: • global • regional • local • sub-custodians • clearing and settlement agents	1.4
5.1.5	Understand the implications of registered title for certificated and uncertificated holdings: • registered title versus unregistered (bearer) • legal title • beneficial interest • right to participate in corporate actions	1.5
5.1.6	Understand the characteristics of nominees: • designated nominee accounts • pooled nominee accounts • corporate nominees • details in share register • legal and beneficial ownership	1.6
5.2	**Prime Brokerage and Equity Finance** On completion, the candidate should be able to:	
5.2.1	Understand the purpose, requirements and implications of securities lending: • benefits and risks for borrowers and lenders • function of market makers, intermediaries and custodians • effect on the lender's rights • effect on corporate action activity • collateral • potential risks of lack of consolidated disclosure by funds	2.1

Syllabus Unit/ Element		Chapter/ Section
5.2.2	Understand the purpose and main types of prime broker equity finance services and their impact on securities markets: • securities lending and borrowing • leveraged trade execution • cash management • core settlement • custody • rehypothecation • repurchase agreements • collateralised borrowing • tri-party repos • synthetic financing	2.2

Element 6	Securities Analysis	Chapter 6
6.1	**Financial Statement Analysis** On completion, the candidate should be able to:	
6.1.1	Understand the purpose, structure and relevance to investors of statements of financial position	1.1
6.1.2	Understand the purpose, structure and relevance to investors of statements of profit and loss	1.2
6.1.3	Understand the purpose, structure and relevance to investors of statements of cash flows	1.3
6.1.4	Be able to analyse securities using the following financial ratios: • liquidity • asset turnover • gearing	1.4
6.1.5	Be able to analyse securities using the following profitability ratios: • net profit margin • operating profit margin • equity multiplier • return on capital employed	1.5
6.1.6	Be able to analyse securities using the following investor ratios: • earnings per share • price/earnings (both historic and prospective) • dividend yield • dividend cover • interest cover	1.6

Syllabus Unit/ Element		Chapter/ Section
6.1.7	Understand the main advantages and challenges of performing financial analysis: • comparing companies in different countries and sectors • comparing different companies within the same sector • over-reliance on historical information • benefits and limitations of relying on third-party research • comparing companies that use different accounting standards	1.7
6.2	**Environmental, Social and Governance (ESG)** On completion, the candidate should:	
6.2.1	Understand the main factors taken into account when conducting an analysis of Environmental, Social and Governance (ESG) risks and opportunities	
Element 7	**Portfolio Construction**	**Chapter 7**
7.1	**Market Information and Research** On completion, the candidate should be able to:	
7.1.1	Understand the use of regulatory, economic and financial communications: • primary and secondary information providers • government resources and statistics • broker research and distributor information • regulatory resources	1.1
7.1.2	Understand the different types and uses of research and reports: • fundamental analysis • technical analysis • fund analysis • fund rating agencies and screening software • broker and distributor reports • sector-specific reports	1.2
7.1.3	Be able to assess key factors that influence markets and sectors: • responses to change and uncertainty • volume, liquidity and nature of trading activity in domestic and overseas markets • publication of announcements, research and ratings	2
7.1.4	Be able to assess the interactive relationship between the securities and derivatives markets, and the impact of related events on markets	3
7.1.5	Be able to assess the interactive relationship between different forms of fixed-interest securities and the impact of related events on markets	3

Syllabus Unit/ Element		Chapter/ Section
7.2	**Portfolio Construction** On completion, the candidate should be able to:	
7.2.1	Understand the main types of portfolio risk and their implications for investors: • systemic risk • market/systematic risk – asset price volatility, currency, interest rates, commodity price volatility • non-systematic risk • liquidity, credit and default risk	4
7.2.2	Understand the core principles used to help mitigate portfolio risk: • correlation • diversification • active and passive strategies • hedging and immunisation	5
7.2.3	Understand the key approaches to investment allocation for bond, equity and multi-asset portfolios: • asset class • geographical area • currency • issuer • sector • maturity	6
7.2.4	Understand the main aims and investment characteristics of the main cash, bond and equity portfolio management strategies and styles: • indexing/passive management • active/market timing including High Conviction style; • passive-active combinations • smart indexing • growth versus income • market capitalisation • liability driven • immunisation • long, short and leveraged • issuer and sector-specific • contrarian • quantitative • growth versus value investing	7

Syllabus Unit/ Element		Chapter/ Section
7.2.5	Understand how portfolio risk and return are evaluated using the following measures: • holding-period return • money-weighted return • time-weighted return • total return and its components • standard deviation • value at risk • volatility • covariance and correlation • risk-adjusted returns (eg, Sharpe ratio) • benchmarking • alpha • beta Candidates will not be expected to undertake the calculation of any variables mentioned in this Learning Objective.	8

Element 8	Investment Selection and Administration	Chapter 8
8.1	**Investment Selection and Suitability** On completion, the candidate should be able to:	
8.1.1	Apply a range of essential information and factors to form the basis of appropriate investment selection and suitability: • financial needs, preferences and expectations • income and lifestyle – current and anticipated • attitude to risk/capacity for loss • level of knowledge and experience of investing • existing debts and investments	1
8.1.2	Be able to analyse and select strategies suitable for the client's aims and objectives in terms of: • investment horizon • current and future potential for growth and yield • requirement for capital protection • protection against inflation • liquidity, trading and ongoing management • mandatory or voluntary investment restrictions • impact of fees and charges • ethical/Environmental, Social and Governance (ESG) considerations	2

Syllabus Unit/ Element		Chapter/ Section
8.1.3	Be able to analyse and select investments suitable for a particular portfolio strategy: • direct holdings, indirect holdings and combinations, including structured products • role of derivatives, including CFDs • impact on client objectives and priorities • diversification • cash, deposits, accounts and money market funds	3
8.2	**Administration and Maintenance** On completion, the candidate should be able to:	
8.2.1	Apply key elements involved in managing a client portfolio: • systematic and compliant approach to client portfolio monitoring, review, reporting and management • selection of appropriate benchmarks to include: market and specialist indices; total return and maximum drawdown • arrangements for client communication	4
8.2.2	Understand how changes can affect the management of a client portfolio: • client circumstances • financial environment • new products and services available • administrative changes or difficulties • investment-related changes (eg, credit rating, corporate actions) • portfolio rebalancing • benchmark review • changing regulatory environment	5

Examination Specification

Each examination paper is constructed from a specification that determines the weightings that will be given to each element. The specification is given below.

It is important to note that the numbers quoted may vary slightly from examination to examination as there is some flexibility to ensure that each examination has a consistent level of difficulty. However, the number of questions tested in each element should not change by more than plus or minus 2.

Element Number	Element	Questions
1	Cash, Money Markets and the Foreign Exchange Market	5
2	Fixed-Income Securities	20
3	Equities	20
4	Collective Investments	8
5	Settlement, Safe Custody and Prime Brokerage	7
6	Securities Analysis	8
7	Portfolio Construction	8
8	Investment Selection and Administration	4
Total		**80**

CISI Chartered MCSI Membership can work for you...

Studying for a CISI qualification is hard work and we're sure you're putting in plenty of hours, but don't lose sight of your goal!

This is just the first step in your career; there is much more to achieve!

The securities and investments sector attracts ambitious and driven individuals. You're probably one yourself and that's great, but on the other hand you're almost certainly surrounded by lots of other people with similar ambitions.

So how can you stay one step ahead during these uncertain times?

Entry Criteria for Chartered MCSI Membership

As an ACSI and MCSI candidate, you can upgrade your membership status to Chartered MCSI. There are a number of ways of gaining the CISI Chartered MCSI membership.

A straightforward route requires candidates to have:

* a minimum of one year's ACSI or MCSI membership;
* passed a full Diploma; Certificate in Private Client Investment Advice & Management or Masters in Wealth Management award;
* passed IntegrityMatters with an A grade; and
* successfully logged and certified 12 months' CPD under the CISI's CPD Scheme.

Alternatively, experienced-based candidates are required to have:

* a minimum of one year's ACSI membership;
* passed IntegrityMatters with an A grade; and
* successfully logged and certified six years' CPD under the CISI's CPD Scheme.

Joining Fee:	Current Grade of Membership	Grade of Chartership	Upgrade Cost
	ACSI	Chartered MCSI	£85.00
	MCSI	Chartered MCSI	£30.00

By belonging to a Chartered professional body, members will benefit from enhanced status in the industry and the wider community. Members will be part of an organisation which holds the respect of government and the financial services sector, and can communicate with the public on a whole new level. There will be little doubt in consumers' minds that chartered members of the CISI are highly regarded and qualified professionals and, as a consequence, will be required to act as such.

The Chartered MCSI designation will provide you with full access to all member benefits, including Professional Refresher where there are currently over 100 modules available on subjects including Anti-Money Laundering, Information Security & Data Protection, Integrity & Ethics, and the UK Bribery Act. CISI TV is also available to members, allowing you to catch up on the latest CISI events, whilst earning valuable CPD.

Revision Express

You've bought the workbook... now test your knowledge before your exam.

Revision Express is an engaging online study tool to be used in conjunction with most CISI workbooks.

Key Features of Revision Express:
- Questions throughout to reaffirm understanding of the subject
- Special end-of-module practice exam to reflect as closely as possible the standard you will experience in your exam (please note, however, they are not the CISI exam questions themselves)
- Extensive glossary of terms
- Allows you to study whenever you like, and on any device

IMPORTANT: The questions contained in Revision Express products are designed as aids to revision, and should not be seen in any way as mock exams.

Price per Revision Express module: £35
Price when purchased with the corresponding CISI workbook: £108 (normal price: £119)

To purchase Revision Express:

call our Customer Support Centre on:
+44 20 7645 0777

or visit the CISI's online bookshop at:
cisi.org/bookshop

For more information on our elearning products, contact our Customer Support Centre on +44 20 7645 0777, or visit our website at cisi.org/elearning

Professional Refresher

Self-testing elearning modules to refresh your knowledge, meet regulatory and firm requirements, and earn CPD.

Professional Refresher is a training solution to help you remain up-to-date with industry developments, maintain regulatory compliance and demonstrate continuing learning.

This popular online learning tool allows self-administered refresher testing on a variety of topics, including the latest regulatory changes.

There are over 120 modules available which address UK and international issues. Modules are reviewed by practitioners frequently and new ones are added to the suite on a regular basis.

Benefits to firms:
- Learning and testing can form part of business T&C programme
- Learning and testing kept up-to-date and accurate by the CISI
- Relevant and useful – devised by industry practitioners
- Access to individual results available as part of management overview facility, 'Super User'
- Records of staff training can be produced for internal use and external audits
- Cost-effective – no additional charge for CISI members
- Available for non-members to purchase

Benefits to individuals:
- Comprehensive selection of topics across sectors
- Modules are regularly refreshed and updated by industry experts
- New modules added regularly
- Free for members
- Successfully passed modules are recorded in your CPD log as active learning
- Counts as structured learning for RDR purposes
- On completion of a module, a certificate can be printed out for your own records

The full suite of Professional Refresher modules is free to CISI members, or £250 for non-members. Modules are also available individually. To view a full list of Professional Refresher modules visit:

cisi.org/refresher

If you or your firm would like to find out more, contact our Client Relationship Management team:

+ 44 20 7645 0670
crm@cisi.org

For more information on our elearning products, contact our Customer Support Centre on +44 20 7645 0777, or visit our website at cisi.org/refresher

Professional Refresher

Top 5

SCORM COMPLIANT

Integrity & Ethics
- High-Level View
- Ethical Behaviour
- An Ethical Approach
- Compliance vs Ethics

Anti-Money Laundering
- Introduction to Money Laundering
- UK Legislation and Regulation
- Money Laundering Regulations 2017
- Proceeds of Crime Act 2002
- Terrorist Financing
- Suspicious Activity Reporting
- Money Laundering Reporting Officer
- Sanctions

General Data Protection Regulation (GDPR)
- Understanding the Terminology
- The Six Data Protection Principles
- Data Subject Rights
- Technical and Organisational Measures

Information Security and Data Protection
- Cyber-Security
- The Regulators

UK Bribery Act
- Background to the Act
- The Offences
- What the Offences Cover
- When Has an Offence Been Committed?
- The Defences Against Charges of Bribery
- The Penalties

Latest

Cryptocurrencies
- Bitcoin
- Altcoins
- Central Bank Digital Currency and Cryptofiat
- Trading Cryptocurrencies
- The Impact of Cryptocurrencies

Change Management
- Types of Change
- Change Theories
- The Complexities of Change
- Leading Change
- Key Skills and Competencies

Regulatory Update
- General Regulatory Changes
- Sector Changes

Common Reporting Standard (CRS)
- What is the CRS?
- Implementation and Compliance
- Practical Issues
- The Global Perspective

Cross-Border Investment Services
- The UK System
- Overseas Regulation
- Applicability
- Face-to-Face Meetings
- Distance Communications
- Brexit Implications
- Gifts and Entertainment
- Tax Evasion, Money Laundering, and Terrorist Financing

Operations

Best Execution
- What Is Best Execution?
- Achieving Best Execution
- Order Execution Policies
- Information to Clients & Client Consent
- Monitoring, the Rules, and Instructions
- Best Execution for Specific Types of Firms

Approved Persons Regime
- The Basis of the Regime
- Fitness and Propriety
- The Controlled Functions
- Principles for Approved Persons
- The Code of Practice for Approved Persons

Corporate Actions
- Corporate Structure and Finance
- Life Cycle of an Event
- Mandatory Events
- Voluntary Events

Wealth

Client Assets and Client Money
- Protecting Client Assets and Client Money
- Segregation and Holding
- Due Diligence of Custodians and Banks
- Reconciliations
- Records and Accounts
- CASS Oversight

Investment Principles and Risk
- Diversification
- Factfind and Risk Profiling
- Investment Management
- Modern Portfolio Theory and Investing Styles
- Direct and Indirect Investments
- Socially Responsible Investment
- Collective Investments
- Investment Trusts
- Dealing in Debt Securities and Equities

Banking Standards
- Introduction and Background
- Strengthening Individual Accountability
- Reforming Corporate Governance
- Securing Better Outcomes for Consumers
- Enhancing Financial Stability

Suitability of Client Investments
- Assessing Suitability
- Risk Profiling
- Establishing Risk Appetite
- Obtaining Customer Information
- Suitable Questions and Answers
- Making Suitable Investment Selections
- Guidance, Reports and Record Keeping

International

Foreign Account Tax Compliance Act (FATCA)
- Foreign Financial Institutions
- Due Diligence Requirements
- Reporting
- Compliance

MiFID II
- The Organisations Covered by MiFID II
- The Products Subject to MiFID II
- The Origins of MiFID II
- The Impact of MiFID II
- The Products Covered by MiFID II
- Cross-Border Business Under MiFID II

UCITS
- The Original UCITS Directive
- UCITS III
- UCITS IV
- Non-UCITS Funds
- Latest Developments

cisi.org/refresher

Feedback to the CISI

Have you found this workbook to be a valuable aid to your studies? We would like your views, so please email us at learningresources@cisi.org with any thoughts, ideas or comments.

Accredited Training Partners

Support for exam students studying for the Chartered Institute for Securities & Investment (CISI) qualifications is provided by several Accredited Training Partners (ATPs), including Fitch Learning and BPP. The CISI's ATPs offer a range of face-to-face training courses, distance learning programmes, their own learning resources and study packs which have been accredited by the CISI. The CISI works in close collaboration with its ATPs to ensure they are kept informed of changes to CISI exams so they can build them into their own courses and study packs.

CISI Workbook Specialists Wanted

Workbook Authors

Experienced freelance authors with finance experience, and who have published work in their area of specialism, are sought. Responsibilities include:

- Updating workbooks in line with new syllabuses and any industry developments
- Ensuring that the syllabus is fully covered

Workbook Reviewers

Individuals with a high-level knowledge of the subject area are sought. Responsibilities include:

- Highlighting any inconsistencies against the syllabus
- Assessing the author's interpretation of the workbook

Workbook Technical Reviewers

Technical reviewers to provide a detailed review of the workbook and bring the review comments to the panel. Responsibilities include:

- Cross-checking the workbook against the syllabus
- Ensuring sufficient coverage of each learning objective

Workbook Proofreaders

Proofreaders are needed to proof workbooks both grammatically and also in terms of the format and layout. Responsibilities include:

- Checking for spelling and grammar mistakes
- Checking for formatting inconsistencies

If you are interested in becoming a CISI external specialist call:
+44 20 7645 0609

or email:
externalspecialists@cisi.org

For bookings, orders, membership and general enquiries please contact our Customer Support Centre on +44 20 7645 0777, or visit our website at cisi.org